Designing
Visual Basic.NET
Applications

David Vitter

 CORIOLIS

President and CEO
Roland Elgey

Publisher
Steve Sayre

Associate Publisher
Katherine R. Hartlove

Acquisitions Editor
Jawahara Saidullah

Development Editor
Jessica Choi

Product Marketing Manager
Tracy Rooney

Project Editor
Jennifer Ashley

Technical Reviewer
Alfonso Hermida

Production Coordinator
Peggy Cantrell

Cover Designer
April E. Nielsen

Layout Designer
April E. Nielsen

The Coriolis Group, LLC
14455 North Hayden Road
Suite 220
Scottsdale, Arizona 85260

(480) 483-0192
FAX (480) 483-0193
www.coriolis.com

Library of Congress Cataloging-in-Publication Data
Vitter, David.
    Designing Visual Basic.NET applications / by David Vitter.
       p. cm.
    Includes index.
    ISBN 1-58880-128-4
    1. Microsoft Visual BASIC.   2. Applications software--Development.
3. Microsoft.net framwork.   I. Title.

QA76.73.B3 V58 2001
005.2'76--dc21

2001037171

Printed in the United States of America
10 9 8 7 6 5 4 3 2 1

CORIOLIS

The Coriolis Group, LLC • 14455 North Hayden Road, Suite 220 • Scottsdale, Arizona 85260

A Note from Coriolis

Coriolis Technology Press was founded to create a very elite group of books: the ones you keep closest to your machine. In the real world, you have to choose the books you rely on every day very carefully, and we understand that.

To win a place for our books on that coveted shelf beside your PC, we guarantee several important qualities in every book we publish. These qualities are:

- *Technical accuracy*—It's no good if it doesn't work. Every Coriolis Technology Press book is reviewed by technical experts in the topic field, and is sent through several editing and proofreading passes in order to create the piece of work you now hold in your hands.

- *Innovative editorial design*—We've put years of research and refinement into the ways we present information in our books. Our books' editorial approach is uniquely designed to reflect the way people learn new technologies and search for solutions to technology problems.

- *Practical focus*—We put only pertinent information into our books and avoid any fluff. Every fact included between these two covers must serve the mission of the book as a whole.

- *Accessibility*—The information in a book is worthless unless you can find it quickly when you need it. We put a lot of effort into our indexes, and heavily cross-reference our chapters, to make it easy for you to move right to the information you need.

Here at The Coriolis Group we have been publishing and packaging books, technical journals, and training materials since 1989. We have put a lot of thought into our books; please write to us at **ctp@coriolis.com** and let us know what you think. We hope that you're happy with the book in your hands, and that in the future, when you reach for software development and networking information, you'll turn to one of our books first.

Coriolis Technology Press
The Coriolis Group
14455 N. Hayden Road, Suite 220
Scottsdale, Arizona
85260

Email: ctp@coriolis.com
Phone: (480) 483-0192
Toll free: (800)410-0192

Look for these related books from The Coriolis Group:

Visual Basic.NET Programming for the Internet
By Lynn Torkelson, Constance Petersen, and Zac Torkelson

Visual Basic.NET Black Book
By Steven Holzner

.NET Architecture—Principles, Perspectives and Design
By Morten Strunge Nielsen

C# for Visual Basic Programmers
By Clayton Walnum

C# Black Book
By Matt Telles

C# Core Language Little Black Book
By Bill Wagner

Also published by Coriolis Technology Press:

Software Project Management: From Concept to Deployment
By Kieron Conway

C++ Black Book
By Steven Holzner

Java 2 Black Book
By Steven Holzner

Java 2 Network Protocols Black Book
by Al Williams

Microsoft Project 2000 Black Book
By Tracey J. Rosenblath

About the Author

David Vitter lives in Charlottesville, Virginia, with his wife Stephanie and their two sons, Alex and Ryan. David is a Technical Lead Developer with Computer Sciences Corporation (CSC) developing Web-based solutions for customers such as the US Army, NATO, and the DEA. Prior to joining CSC, David spent 10 years in the US Air Force where he served as both an ICBM Maintenance Technician and as an Electronic Intelligence Analyst supporting the F-16 and F-117A fighters. The Air Force helped teach him about discipline and professionalism, both of which he has put to good use in the civilian world. David is a Microsoft Certified Professional (MCP) and a Microsoft Certified Solutions Developer (MCSD) with over 7 years experience using Visual Basic and over 20 years experience in writing Basic programs. When not writing code or books, David enjoys cheering for the University of Virginia's Lacrosse team or visiting one of Virginia's many beautiful points of interest with his family.

Acknowledgments

This book represents my first experience with the publishing industry, and the great team at The Coriolis Group has made this a wonderful introduction to the world of technical writing.

The first person I must thank is my original Acquisitions Editor, Kevin Weeks. Kevin was my first contact with Coriolis, and if it wasn't for his belief and support for my book idea, this book would never have happened. The next team member I met was my Development Editor Jessica Choi, who could not have been more patient and supportive of this scared and inexperienced first-time author. She helped settle my "what have I gotten myself into" jitters, and she taught me the basics of technical writing. After all of Jessica's lessons had been learned, I was handed over to a terrific Editor, Jennifer Ashley, who has guided me and corrected me throughout the writing of this book. Jennifer has a gift for providing supportive criticism that always makes you feel good about your work, and not criticized. Bill McManus worked with Jennifer as the Copy Editor for this book. I think out of everyone on this team, Bill must have had the most work to do, having to deal with my constant grammatical errors and vague topic references page after page. Also supporting Jennifer was Alfonso Hermida, the Technical Editor, who tested all of the exercises in this book and helped provide me with another developer's insight and experience.

I'd also like to thank those behind the scenes at Coriolis who worked to put the final product together: Peggy Cantrell, the Production Coordinator, and April Nielsen, Layout Designer and Cover Designer. This has been a terrific team to work with, and I want to thank everyone for their patience and support.

I would also like to thank my home support team, my wife Stephanie and my sons Alex and Ryan, for all the quiet time they permitted me. I owe you six months of quality time, game nights, and family outings, and I love you all.

Acknowledgments

My CSC family has also been extremely supportive, and just as excited about this book as I am. Many thanks to Dave Ellis, a terrific Program Manager, who has always allowed me to run wild and free, which is how I work best. Another key player on our CSC team is Chuck Davis. Every office should have a manager like Chuck, who believes in his employees and spends every waking hour working to make things right for everyone and addressing every last concern we have. Chuck helped me to quickly get the company's approval for this project, and regularly inquired about my progress and experiences with this book.

My thanks also goes out to my brother, Craig, for sharing his technical writing experiences with me and letting me know exactly what it was I had gotten myself into.

Finally, I would like to thank my mom and dad, who have always been there to support me in both the good times and the bad. Ultimately, I have my dad to thank for my love of programming. He introduced me to my first computer, a green-screen Wang terminal, when I was 10 years old, and taught me how to program in Basic. Working together we created my first program, an unbeatable tic-tac-toe game. I've been hooked on writing code ever since.
—*David Vitter*

Contents at a Glance

Table of Contents

Introduction

Thanks for buying *Designing Visual Basic.NET Applications*. When Microsoft introduced its new development tool, Visual Studio.NET, to the world, there was a great deal of apprehension and fear in the Visual Basic community. While it is true that Visual Basic.NET introduces a great many changes to the development language you are already used to, once you are comfortable with .NET you will realize that all these changes are for the better, and learning about them was not as painful as it may first have seemed. The purpose of this book is to make your learning process as painless as possible, and to introduce you to the full range of new concepts and features that are a part of Visual Basic.NET.

> **Note**
>
> *The information in this book is based on the **Beta 2** release of Visual Studio.NET made available by Microsoft to the public June 2001. Microsoft has stated that all features available in the Beta 2 version of Visual Studio.NET are finalized, but there is no guarantee that code written in Beta 2 will work in the final released version of Visual Studio.NET, which is due out at the end of 2001. Menu items and object names are also susceptible to change between the publishing of this book and the final commercial release of .NET.*

This book was designed to introduce experienced Visual Basic developers to the new Visual Basic.NET, and quickly build upon their knowledge to help them feel comfortable and knowledgeable in a very short time. You will start by learning the basics of the .NET framework in Chapter 1, where you will gain an understanding of how .NET works and why Microsoft sees .NET as the answer to all your software development needs. Next, you will learn to design an application using the .NET principles and proven development techniques. From there you will learn to use the Visual Studio.NET environment, which provides you with a wide array of tools designed to make your job easier. Once you are comfortable with the

.NET framework and the Visual Studio.NET environment, you will start learning about the changes made to the Visual Basic language, in Chapter 4. You will also learn how to best use these new features and principles in your development projects. Entire chapters of this book are devoted to WindowsApplication development, exception handling, troubleshooting your code, and accessing data stores using ADO.NET.

Two chapters are devoted to Web development in .NET using ASP.NET and Web Services (Chapters 10 and 11). If you do not have any experience developing for the Web, these chapters will show you how easy Visual Basic.NET makes Web development, so that you won't have to learn another programming language to do it. The .NET framework was developed for the Web-enabled world, and ASP.NET and Web Services are right at the heart of the .NET framework.

I will wrap up this book with discussions on XML and SOAP and their roles in .NET (Chapter 12), .NET security (Chapter 13), a chapter on deploying your .NET applications (Chapter 14), and a chapter to help you migrate your Visual Basic 6 projects to .NET (Chapter 15). There is a lot to learn about Visual Basic.NET, and nearly every chapter could become a book of its own due to the depth of material. My hope is that this book will give you a strong understanding of Visual Basic.NET application development and provide you with the introduction you will need to start using this wonderful new tool in your latest development projects.

Is This Book for You?

Designing Visual Basic.NET Applications was written with the intermediate or advanced Visual Basic developer in mind. I do not spend any time teaching the basics of Visual Basic development, but if you are a Visual Basic developer new to organized application development or object-oriented programming concepts, you will have no problem following along with this book. I make every effort to keep my explanations simple and straightforward so that anyone who has used Visual Basic can follow along and learn to use Visual Basic.NET. Among the many topics that are covered in this book, you will find chapters on:

♦ Enhancements and changes made to the Visual Basic development language

♦ Designing .NET applications and managing your development processes

♦ Implementing data access techniques using ADO.NET

♦ Creating applications and services for the Web using ASP.NET and Web Services

♦ Migrating your Visual Basic 6 applications to Visual Basic.NET

How to Use This Book

The chapters in this book were designed to be read in order so that they can build up your .NET knowledge in stages. At first glance, certain chapters may seem specialized in nature, such as those about ASP.NET Web development. I strongly urge you to read every chapter so that you will understand all the concepts and application types available in Visual Basic.NET. There will be points in this book where you will want to jump ahead and preview some material, or jump back and review a chapter you have already read that applies to the material you are currently reading. I will provide you with references to other chapters throughout the book to let you know where you can find more information on a subject elsewhere. But be warned that if you skip over material, you will probably later encounter a reference to a new .NET feature that you will be unfamiliar with.

Exercises

I strongly believe that the best way to learn how to use a tool is the "learn by doing" approach. I make heavy use of exercises throughout this book to force the readers to put their hands on the keyboard and discover how .NET features work in the real world. Many of the key points and features of Visual Basic.NET will be learned through the exercises, so do not skip over an exercise and do not try to learn from an exercise without actually using the tools. You might miss out on some vital experience and knowledge!

Tips

The tips I provide within this book are suggestions and shortcuts you can use to master Visual Basic.NET. Often there are many ways to accomplish a task, but when I discover a method, piece of knowledge, or a development shortcut that can save a developer time, I will pass these along to your in the form of tips.

Warnings

I use warnings throughout this book to let you know about the potential pitfalls or accidents waiting to happen. Pay special attention to these items, because these warnings may save you a lot of time and frustration as you learn the ins and outs of this new development environment. It's always easier to learn from someone else's mistakes and experiences.

Best Practices

Professional software development is all about repeatable processes developed from years of experience. This experience is handed down from senior developers to junior developers in the form of best practices. All throughout this book I devote a section of each chapter to summarizing these area-specific best practices for your easy reference. (Many of these lists are presented again in Appendixes A and B.) Visual Basic.NET is a brand new development tool, and developers will continue to learn from it and create new best practices based on these experiences. Be sure to write these down and pass them along.

Checklists

Appendixes C and D contain checklists that provide an easy-to-use summary of the key pieces of information discussed throughout this book, organized so that you can copy and reuse them in your real-world development projects. Even when you are comfortable with tasks such as migrating Visual Basic 6 Projects to Visual Basic.NET, I still suggest you glance at these checklists once in a while to ensure that you are not missing any crucial steps. Feel free to add to these checklists as you become more and more experienced with developing Visual Basic.NET applications.

Contact Information

I welcome your feedback on this book. You can either email The Coriolis Group at **ctp@coriolis.com** or email me directly at **david@vitter.com**. Errata, updates, and more are available at **www.coriolis.com**.

Chapter 1

Introducing the .NET Framework

Welcome to Visual Basic .NET, I'm glad you're here. Sit down, have a latte, and put your feet up on the furniture. Comfortable? Great! Maybe I am going a bit overboard here, but my goal is to start you off in a relaxed state with an open mind. Why? Because the road ahead of you is long and sometimes steep, but it also promises to be as exciting as the first time you discovered Visual Basic. At times the .NET concepts might make you nervous, but I guarantee that you will quickly get over that queasy feeling and again feel the thrill of discovery. Maybe you've just looked at the cover of this book to double-check that you did in fact pick up a programming manual. Surprise, you did! But what I am about to cover here is not just the next installment in a fine line of Visual Basic versions. What .NET promises and delivers is a whole new way of developing applications that is bigger and better than any one programming language alone.

Prepare for your world to expand. Maybe you are a traditional Windows interface applications developer who has yet to develop for the Web. Or maybe you are a Web developer with an Active Server Pages (ASP) background who has never created a Component Object Model (COM) component. Whatever your background, it's almost certain the vast majority of you have never tried using C++ or FoxPro, let alone this new upstart language, C#, to create a piece of your project. In the past, each of these development languages had been fenced in as a specialty; you were either a Visual Basic wizard or a C++ guru. It took a lot of effort to be good at what you did, but even then you still didn't have the extra time to learn all of the development tools, right? Well, not anymore. No, no one has added hours to your day or days to your week. Instead, someone has redesigned the tools and languages smartly, allowing you not only to upgrade your current skill set but also to open the doors to other disciplines previously out of reach.

Nervous yet? Relax and help yourself to a bagel. I'm going to take a moment to go over the history of Visual Basic to help you better understand how this language evolved into the powerful tool you are here to learn about. Don't skip ahead—I promise this will be a short and painless history lesson.

The History of Visual Basic

Basic, which stands for Beginner's All-purpose Symbolic Instruction Code, was created in 1964 at Dartmouth College by John Kemeny and Professor Thomas Kurtz. Their original vision was to make a programming language that was as easy to use as possible in order to help new students learn the basic skills needed to program, and then move them onto a more advanced language taught by the school. Much of the initial Basic syntax was based on FORTRAN and ALGOL, two popular languages in the 1960s. During its first 10 years of existence, Basic was used only as a learning tool in schools. But then, in the mid 1970s, Microsoft appeared on the scene, touting something called GW-BASIC as its first product (*GW* for *Gee Whiz*). Founders Paul Allen and Bill Gates had created a version of Basic to run on the Altair, the world's first personal computer. Bill and Paul knew back then that personal computers would be a global hit, and as computers spread across the world, so did different versions of Basic. This simple and compact programming language was ported to every major operating system, from Apple to Commodore. At around this same time, the computing giant IBM created its own version of Basic known as BASICA, and an up-and-coming company called Borland distributed a version then known as Turbo Basic but now known as Power Basic. As Basic's popularity grew, Microsoft saw a need to develop its own compiler and add additional commands. Thus was born QuickBasic in the 1980s, which later evolved into QuickBasic Extended.

At the end of the 1980s, Basic was still considered a "learner's" language, and not suitable for real-world applications development. During the 1970s and 1980s, many new languages appeared, while others like ALGOL simply faded away. COBOL (Common Business-Oriented Language) was popular for business applications development in the 1970s and 1980s. FORTRAN (derived from "formula translation") was widely used by the scientific and engineering communities for its number-crunching capabilities. The C programming language was created in the mid-1970s, and in the mid-1980s evolved into C++. Widely recognized as the most powerful of all programming languages for its low-level access to system resources, C++ is at the heart of most of today's operating systems and high-performance applications. Nearly all computer games today are written in some form of C++. At the end of the 1980s, C++ was the language of choice in the industry.

Basic's big break came in May of 1991 when Microsoft released Visual Basic 1. By merging the QuickBasic language with Ruby, a drag-and-drop front-end developed by Alan Cooper, programmers could now quickly create user interfaces without hours of complicated coding. This was truly the birth of rapid application development (RAD). RAD is a very important concept in today's software development projects because, with the ever-increasing demand for software in the information age, it is critical to be able to create projects as quickly as possible. Visual Basic was created to take on the popular C++ language by offering not only easier graphical user interface (GUI) creation tools, but also a far shorter learning curve for new developers. Sadly, version 1 failed to catch on with the programming community.

In November 1992, version 2 followed and introduced open database connectivity (ODBC) data connections and multiple-document interface (MDI) parent/child forms. People started to take notice of this new language, but it had yet to gain a wide acceptance. It was not until version 3 in June 1993 that Visual Basic truly broke out and became the fastest-growing development language in the world. With the introduction of OLE automation, programmers could now access functionality from other objects and programs. OLE controls were introduced next in version 4 in October 1996. These controls later evolved into ActiveX controls in version 5, released in April 1997. Version 5 was also the first version to let Visual Basic developers create COM objects, such as ActiveX DLLs and EXEs. Finally, in October 1998, version 6 was released, touting Web classes and special GUI "designers" for making data connections and creating data reports. Looking back, you can see that six versions of Visual Basic were released over a period of seven years. Talk about rapid applications development!

At the beginning of the new millennium, Visual Basic is arguably the most widely used programming language in the world. More than 3.2 million developers currently use Visual Basic in their projects. But despite its astounding popularity and widespread usage, Visual Basic is still regarded as a lesser programming language and not a true object-oriented development tool. But that was then—and this is now.

Almost 3 years after the release of version 6 and 36 years after the birth of Basic, Visual Basic 7 (also known as Visual Basic .NET) is being released. Looking back over the previous six versions, you'll see that each version added more features and functionality to its predecessor. These versions can each be considered an "upgrade." But Visual Basic 7 is not just a simple upgrade to version 6; it is a revolution in terms of how developers will use it. Until now, each programming language in Microsoft's Visual Studio (which includes Visual C++ and FoxPro) was considered a separate and independent language. Project managers would decide which language the project would use, with little or no cross-language development happening. The reason was that in prior Visual Studio versions, the interfaces for each language were completely different, and the languages shared no common ground. A development team would require an expert in each programming skill area if it wanted to build a project cross-language. For most projects, this was not an option.

.NET to the Rescue

When you run Visual Studio .NET after installation, the first feature that you'll notice is that all of the programming languages share the same environment. In fact, you will no longer go to the Start | Programs | Visual Studio menu anymore and look for the Visual C++ or Visual Basic start icon. Instead, you just need to start Visual Studio itself. From there, you decide what type of project you want to work on. No matter which one you pick, the menus, toolbars, and windows will all be the same. If you're an adventurous Visual Basic programmer, you may have already tried to start Visual C++ in version 6 to see what it was like. But more than likely, you were quickly frustrated by the unfamiliar environment and gave up. I know I did! Well, that's not the case in Visual Studio 7. If you learn how to use the tools and windows for Visual Basic, then you know how to move around in C++, FoxPro, or C#. If you can create an interface form in one language, you can do it in any Visual Studio .NET language.

Going one step further, you can not only develop in multiple languages from a single environment, but you can now do it at the same time. Experienced Visual Basic programmers know the advantages of creating Project *Groups*. This is when you create one Project, such as a Windows form, create a second separate Project, such as an ActiveX DLL, and then run these two together in a Project Group. This is a real timesaver when it comes to troubleshooting your DLLs because you can now step through the form Project and right into the class code of the DLL Project. Now, imagine that you could add a C++ DLL to your Visual Basic Windows form. In Visual Studio 7, you can! You are now able to trace your program's execution from the Visual Basic form, into and through the C++ class, and back out to the form.

Microsoft realized that one language is not always the answer. You may be developing a project in Visual Basic for its rapid development features and find that you have a need for a high-performance component in the business tier that should be created in C++. You might also need to create dynamic Web pages as an alternative front end for your application. All of these items can be created and tested in one single environment now. Many of the walls between the Visual Basic developers and their C++ and FoxPro counterparts have been torn down in Visual Studio 7, eliminating the question of "Which tool is the best one for this project?" and leaving it up to the developers to decide instead "Which language do I want to use for this piece?" This new concept for building applications is what Microsoft refers to as its .NET Framework. Previously, you may have imagined frames or boxes around each of the different languages and development platforms with little or no overlap. The new .NET Framework was designed to be one big box that encompasses all languages, platforms, and operating systems (and not just those made by Microsoft). Hey, you can't accuse Microsoft of thinking small, can you?

The Common Language Runtime

In the .NET Framework, it's the Common Language Runtime, from here on out referred to as the CLR, that makes it all possible. The CLR manages all of your code and components at runtime and makes it easy to create multilanguage projects. With the CLR, you can implement and troubleshoot cross-language exception handling in multilanguage projects. You can also create classes in Visual C++ and derive other classes from it when coding in Visual Basic. To see how this works, you have to open the hood and dig deep into the inner workings of .NET.

Previously, each language had its own runtime libraries that had to be distributed with your project, thus increasing the size of your distributions. In Visual Basic 6, the runtime was named MSVBVM60.DLL, and C++ ran in its own runtime engine. If you used MTS or COM+ transactions in your project, the runtime called another DLL to manage these. Now with CLR, all languages share one common runtime that can handle all the different language-specific management functions. The CLR runtime is made up of the files MSCORE.DLL and MSCORLIB.DLL. Of course, with the added demand of supporting so many languages, the size of this runtime has increased dramatically. But the best part is that the CLR is a part of the operating system and will not need to be distributed with your projects. Microsoft plans to include the CLR with future operating systems and provide it in service packs for older systems.

The CLR also comes into play when you are developing your application in Visual Studio. Before, each language had its own set of libraries: Visual C++ had the Microsoft Foundation Classes (MFC), Java used the Windows Foundation Class, and Visual Basic had its own set of classes and APIs to use. In .NET, all languages share one common set of libraries, knocking down yet another barrier between the languages and making true cross-language development possible. This unified class framework ensures your code can interoperate and inherit features from Assemblies written in any other .NET language. Your programs can be written and compiled in a specific compiler—in your case, the Visual Studio Basic compiler, which is aptly named VBC.EXE. But you might also create some code in C#, which would compile with the separate C# compiler. While the .NET languages share one common runtime, they each have their own unique compiler. In order for there to be interoperability between two different languages, these compilers must share some common ground. This is the job of the Common Language Specification, or CLS. Compilers that support the CLS produce binaries that speak a common tongue. CLS seeks to standardize many things across all of the supporting languages, such as how exceptions are raised and handled within your code, and how your object's properties and methods are declared and called upon by other objects.

A big part of the CLS is the Common Type System (CTS), which creates a set of universal data types, both primitive and complex, that can now be communicated between modules written in different languages. Now when your Visual Basic component asks for a parameter of type **Long**, a calling C++ component will pass it a **Long** parameter and it will be a perfect match. Prior to now, different environments often had different definitions of what a data type was. For ASP developers, everything was a variant and they had to create their COM components to accept this limiting fact. In Chapter 3, you will learn more about how the CLS and CTS have overcome this problem and changed Visual Basic.

If your code compiles with a CLS compiler, then your code should be CLS-compliant. But there will be exceptions to this rule, such as when you create a customized feature or data type. If this feature or data type is made public, you need to ensure it meets the CLS guidelines for your code to be considered CLS-compliant. Any code that cannot be publicly seen does not need to comply with CLS, because it cannot be called by other components. Each platform's CLR contains the entire set of CLS-supportable features and rules, while each compiler created only supports a subset of these rules and uses its own special syntax. In this way, Visual Basic has a very different syntax from C++, and though they both now have common features, not all of the CLS features and rules are shared between them.

In the future, CLS-compliant compilers could be created for virtually any programming language out there, making their code accessible to any .NET application you create. Microsoft is shipping Visual Studio .NET with four compilers: Visual Basic, Visual C++, C#, and JScript (Microsoft's version of the JavaScript language, previously a runtime interpreted language that will now be compilable under .NET). Many other language compilers are in the works, including one for Java and a Perl .NET compiler. Imagine being able to call a Perl or Java function from your Visual Basic code!

.NET Source Code

The .NET Framework changes not only the way your programs run, but also the way your programs are written and organized. Previously, you created Visual Basic Projects (with a VBP file as the central managing file) that were composed of many smaller parts, such as classes (CLS files), modules (BAS files), controls (CTL files), your Windows interface forms (FRM files), and many other pieces you could add to your projects. When you thought about creating a business object, you added a class, and when you wanted to create your user interface, you added a form. If you wanted two different objects, such as a customer object and a products object, that meant two different classes named appropriately. Looking back, this was kind of limiting and forced you to think in these little sandboxes of code chunks.

In .NET, those sandboxes are now one big sandy beach to play on. Throw out all of those file names, because you only have to remember one now: the VB file, and .vb is the file extension your source code will have if you are coding in Visual Basic. For C#, it would be .vs (you'll often see the s as an abbreviation for the "sharp" in C#) and .vc for C++ source code. So, if all of your Visual Basic code has the same extension, how can you tell the difference between a form and a class? Simply put, you don't. One single VB file can contain many forms, many classes, or a combination of anything you want to create. You could easily put all of the code for your Project into one VB source file. This greatly simplifies the source code management and sharing, because you no longer have to worry about having all the right forms and classes. You can still break up your Project into multiple files, as I'm sure many of you will do in order to facilitate team-based development. You now have a Nick.vb, a Dave.vb, and a Mike.vb; compile these all together and end up with a full-blown business application.

Namespace

How can one source code file contain many different classes and constructs? .NET introduces the concept of Namespace to Visual Basic, which allows you to divide up one long source code file into smaller standalone sections that are subordinate to the overall assembly you are building. The entire .NET system is made up of Namespaces, with the highest level being appropriately named the System Namespace. From this global parent, all other constructs are born. If you want to use a Windows form in your project, it will be inherited from the **System.Windows.Forms** Type. When you put a button on a form, this comes from the **System.Windiws.Forms.Button** Class. The diagram in Figure 1.1 shows the hierarchal relationship between a Namespace, a Type, and a Class. Get used to using the word Type, because everything in .NET comes from a Type, which will be grouped by Namespaces in the Framework.

Namespaces are a way of organizing Types. A Namespace is not limited to one physical file or Assembly; you could create one DLL with a Customer's Namespace containing some Classes, and then create a second DLL also with a Customer's Namespace but with some different Classes. In the overall scheme of a client application, this would appear as one big Customer's Namespace. You could also create a DLL with many different Namespaces, each containing different Classes. Namespaces help create hierarchies, and you can even have Namespaces subordinate to other Namespaces, such as a Company.Customers Namespace. An example of this in .NET would be the System.Net Namespace that you use to access Web protocols such as HTTP requests. When we begin looking at code in later chapters, Namespaces will be everywhere.

Projects and Solutions

Beyond the source code files, Visual Studio still uses Projects to group files written in one language together, but now the file extension is called .vbproj. And the Project Group you are used to using to join different Projects into one environment has changed. This is now called a Solution in .NET, and a Solution file ending in .sln is automatically generated whenever you create a Project, even if you do not intend to join it with another Project. As you now know after learning about the CLR, a Solution can contain Projects written in different languages, enabling the developer to test and debug cross-language Solutions from one common environment.

In the following exercise, you will create a simple Visual Basic .NET Project with a Windows form in it, just like the very first Visual Basic Project you have created in every version

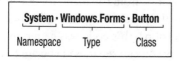

Figure 1.1
The Namespace, Type, and Class relationship.

before now. You will not do any coding in this example, but you will use this simple Project to look at the code behind a simple form and to see the Project files that are created on the hard drive.

Exercise 1.1: Examining the Project Files

1. Open Visual Studio.NET and click "Create New Project" from the Home Page.

2. From the folder, Visual Basic Projects, select the WindowsApplication Project and click on the OK button.

   You now have a form open in the main designer window. In the Solution Explorer window on the right, you will see a Form1.vb under the References folder. The Project name above it will be WindowsApplication1 (or some other integer depending on whether you have made other WindowsApplications already). Your Visual Studio interface will look something like Figure 1.2, depending on how you have your toolbars set up. Notice in the Solution Explorer, the top-level item is the Solution, below which is one Project, and that Project has a References folder under which you see your Form1.vb, your only source code file at this time.

3. Click the Save Form1.vb icon, and then open the My Documents folder on your desktop.

4. In this folder, open the Visual Studio Projects folder. This is where .NET stores all of your Projects by default. On a multilogin system, like your personal documents, this folder will be customized for your user (meaning you will not see other users' Projects here).

5. Open the folder called WindowsApplication1. Here you will see your Form1.vb file, the .vbproj file, and the .sln Solution file. If you open the Form1.vb file with Notepad, you will see that this is a plain old ASCII file that you could easily edit outside Visual Studio. This will apply to all the files in the Project directory (go ahead and try it).

6. Below this directory you will notice two other directories. The obj folder contains debugging information for testing your Project, and the bin folder is where the compiled files will be after you build your Project (this folder will empty for a new Project).

The Code behind the Form

In the WindowsApplication Project you created in Exercise 1.1, you can right-click the item Form1.vb in the Solution Explorer and select View Code from the menu to look at the source code behind the form. As you will see in Figure 1.3, there is already a lot of code behind this blank default form. In prior Visual Basic versions, this code was generated for you but was hidden from view to keep things simple. Now you can see it, and you are free to modify and change it as you wish. You will also notice in Figure 1.3 that the code segments in this window are expandable and collapsible via the + and − signs to the left. Toward the

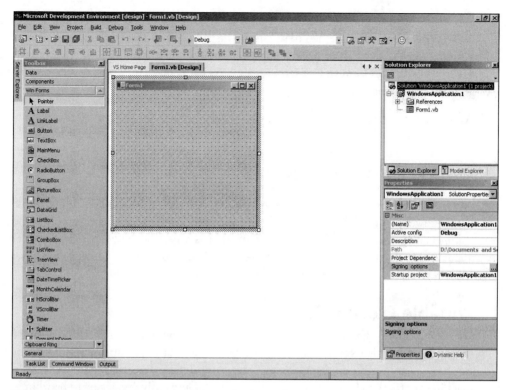

Figure 1.2
Visual Studio WindowsApplication Project.

```
Imports System.ComponentModel
Imports System.Drawing
Imports System.WinForms

Public Class Form1
    Inherits System.WinForms.Form

    Public Sub New()
        MyBase.New

        Form1 = Me

        'This call is required by the Win Form Designer.
        InitializeComponent

        'TODO: Add any initialization after the InitializeC
    End Sub

    'Form overrides dispose to clean up the component list.
    Overrides Public Sub Dispose()
        MyBase.Dispose
        components.Dispose
    End Sub

    Windows Form Designer generated code

End Class
```

Figure 1.3
Source code for an empty Windows form.

bottom you will notice the Windows Form Designer Generated Code section. This is the behind-the-scenes code needed to set all the display factors for this form and its contents, from the form's caption to the placement coordinates of the form itself. If you were to drop a textbox onto your form and set its text value to First Name, you would see the positioning and text value being set in this section of your code.

At the top of the screen, notice the Imports commands referencing the System Namespace discussed earlier. This is where your code defines what System Types it will be using later. One last thing to point out here is the Public Class Form1 area. Before, you may not have thought of your forms as classes, but they really were. Now in .NET, a Class will truly appear as a class, with no attempt to hide the code or make things simple for you. Looking at the line below the Public Class Form1 line, you will see my first example of Inheritance, the newest jewel in Visual Basic's crown. In my example, Form1 is inheriting all of the default features and structures of the standard form that is a part of the System.Windows.Forms Type. In this chapter, I do not want to digress into how you use this wonderful new power in Visual Basic, but you will hear plenty about it in just a few short chapters.

Portable Executables

When all of the coding is done and it comes time to compile your code, the resulting file is known as a Portable Executable (PE for short). PEs are not something new, though you may not have heard of this concept before. One major difference is that, previously, a PE was machine (native) code, whereas a .NET PE is not. Outwardly, it appears to be what you're used to seeing, an EXE executable or a DLL component. But under the hood, this is a very different beast. A PE is a combination of two things: MSIL and metadata. What is MSIL? This stands for Microsoft Intermediate Language and is sometimes simply called the IL. The MSIL is the result of a compiled CLS-compliant Project that will later be used by the CLR runtime. It's not source code, and it's not a native code executable. It is a file in an intermediate format that is something in between, and it's the CLR that finally converts your MSIL into native code at runtime.

When the compiler creates the MSIL, the resulting code is processor-independent. Your MSIL code will run on any processor, not just the type you created it on. Microsoft promises that MSIL should be easily portable from a 32-bit to a 64-bit system, making MSIL semi-architecture-independent as well. This is a new take on the write once and run anywhere paradigm once made popular by Java. The other half of this equation is the CLR. MSIL code will only run on a platform that has a Common Language Runtime created for it. To sum this up in an example: You could code your project in Visual Basic on a Pentium III, compile it to MSIL, and later be able to use the exact same PE modules on a Pentium 4 running Linux (assuming a Linux version of the CLR was created). Neat, huh?

The second part of the PE is the metadata. Metadata is stored within the PE in binary format and is read-only (so forget about editing an Assemblies metadata after compilation). This piece describes everything about the PE, from its properties and methods to the resources it references. Up until now, you needed to reference a DLL's type library to learn about its contents. But with a .NET PE, there are no type libraries or IDLs (a C++ type-library equivalent). Each PE is self-describing through its metadata, so there is no need for type libraries in .NET components. A second critical feature of the metadata is that it exactly describes the resources used by the component. If you reference a dictionary.dll in your project, the exact version of it will be listed in the metadata. When you deploy your project, that exact version of the DLL will be included with your project. If more than one version of the dictionary.dll exists on the target system, your Project will know which one to use.

In the past, if a user installed a different program that came with a DLL of the same name (but with a different makeup), your Project would break due to an incompatibility with the new DLL. This commonly happened with sloppy install programs that allowed users to install older versions of DLLs, thus breaking applications that required features not available in the older version. DLL compatibility was a big issue when creating COM components, and developers had to go to great lengths to ensure that any changes they made to their components would not break a compatibility link with an older version of their application. DLL incompatibility worked both ways against the COM developer. Improperly uninstalled programs could wipe out a DLL that was being used by a different program, thereby breaking it. A newly installed version of a DLL could cause older programs on a user's system to stop working, or an older version of a DLL mistakenly installed over the top of a newer DLL would cause problems in the newer programs expecting the latest component's features. While COM DLLs could be backward-compatible, this was not always the case. This ongoing nightmare was affectionately known as "DLL Hell" in developer circles. But that was then, and this is .NET. Let's take a quick look at the metadata generated by the compiler in Exercise 1.2.

Exercise 1.2: Exploring a PE and Its Metadata

1. Start Visual Studio .NET.

2. Choose Create New Project from the Developer's Home Page.

3. Choose the Class Library Project from the Visual Basic Projects folder.

4. You now have a Class1.vb showing in your Project Explorer. If you right-click this Class and pick View Code, you'll see that some code is already in there. Because your goal here is only to get a quick peek at the metadata, you won't add any code to this Class.

5. Click the Build menu at the top and pick Build from the top of the list. This will create a classlibrary1.dll.

6. Open a Command Prompt and change to the directory your DLL is in. Visual Studio .NET should be storing projects in a folder named Visual Studio Projects located under your My Documents folder. An easy way to get there is to type "cd<space>" at the command line and then drag the Visual Studio Projects folder onto the Command

Prompt window. Now hit Enter and you'll be in the Visual Studio Project directory. Use the **cd** command to get to the directory with your project's name and use it again to go to the bin directory. The bin directory is where the compiled PEs are saved during a build.

7. Type the following on the command line: "ILDASM classlibrary1.dll". ILDASM is the IL Disassembler. You will now have a tool open with a tree view of your DLL and its contents (see Figure 1.4). If you expand the tree next to Class1, you see references to some of that automatically generated source code you saw in Step 4.

8. Press Ctrl-M and a new window opens, showing you the metadata file embedded in your PE. Check out all the references and version numbers generated for an empty class.

Note
The ILDASM is included with the .NET Framework SDK.

Under this new development framework, DLL Hell becomes a thing of the past. Now everything you create in .NET holds a direct reference to the exact version of a component that

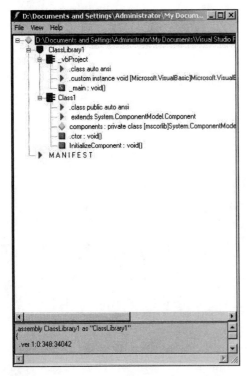

Figure 1.4
The IL Disassembler (ILDASM.EXE) tool showing one Class.

it was compiled against. This removes the problem of compatibility by linking and deploying an Assembly with all of its correct parts and using these for the lifetime of the program. The downside of this concept is that you can now have many versions of a component installed on the target platform at the cost of used-up hard drive space. But at a time when storage space is dirt cheap, this is a small price to pay for the piece of mind you will get as a developer knowing that your program will continue to run no matter what the user installs or deletes.

Assemblies

The basic building block in the .NET Framework is the Assembly. An Assembly can be one or more PE files, or a combination of PE files and various other resources like graphics and multimedia. One logical Assembly can be one or more physical files that could possibly be in more than one location. Picture one COM component separated into many parts and located on multiple servers, and you are on your way to seeing what's cool about Assemblies. To a client, the Assembly appears as one big package, and the actual deployment of its parts are kept hidden. When I later cover deploying applications, Assemblies will play a major role in the grouping and distribution of your files, depending on the settings you assign each piece.

At runtime, it is the Assembly that carries the versioning identification for that bundle of items and dictates the security settings for using those items. Just as a PE has its metadata, each Assembly carries a manifest that contains its versioning and describes the Assembly's contents. Through the manifest, the CLR will know whether the Assembly is being shared with other Assemblies or is a private Assembly that stands by itself. When an Assembly is shared, it presents a digital signature to the client that verifies its identity. This cryptographic key is also a part of the Assembly manifest and is known as the Assembly's "strong name," due to its protective encryption. Figure 1.5 shows how an Assembly can contain many different files, and how one Assembly can be separated into multiple locations.

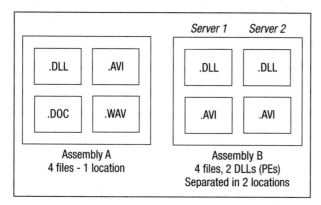

Figure 1.5

Examples of two different Assemblies.

In past Visual Basic versions, the developer had to worry about backward-compatibility. In .NET you are freed from those chains because Assemblies contain references to other Assembly version IDs, and this means more than one version of an Assembly can be on the system. You can have a two-month-old version of widget X, update its code and completely change what it does, and not affect a program using the original widget X because that program will maintain a reference to the older Assembly. Meanwhile, any new programs you create with widget X will hold a reference to that version and will never be affected by changes to the older version.

Looking at the PE metadata in the previous exercise, you will see, near the top, an MVID followed by a code that may remind you of a GUID. This is the Module Version ID, which is unique to that compilation of the PE. Under .NET, GUIDs are no longer used. If you close the metadata subwindow and look at the main ILDASM window, you see a gray text area at the bottom and *.ver* followed by a set of numbers. This is the Assembly's unique version ID. Remember that Assemblies you build in .NET that reference another Assembly will do so through the version ID, and even though you may update this Assembly and recompile it, a previous version of it will continue to exist and all older references will still point to the older version. One thing to note here is that if you compile your DLL but never deploy it, the next compile will overwrite the one in the \bin directory. If you close the ILDASM now and recompile your test DLL, and then reopen it in ILDASM, you will see that the version ID has changed.

Deployed Assemblies can reside in three main locations. The first is in the same directory as your application. This would be acceptable for a private Assembly that will never be reused, but if you wish to allow someone to reuse your code, you will probably want to place it somewhere more accessible. The majority of Assemblies are installed in the \Windows\Assembly directory, also known as the global cache. This is a system-wide repository for publicly available Assemblies. The Assembly cache is capable of holding multiple versions of the same Assembly and will continue to connect the correct version of an Assembly with its associated programs. The final major Assembly location is the Transient cache directory. This is a protective area where downloaded Internet Assemblies go to prevent them from damaging your trusted local installations. In Chapter 14, I will cover how you can plan out which Assemblies go where and how Internet Assemblies work.

Running Your Application

What happens when you run your application or reference as a newly created .NET Class? Now you are calling on the CLR, the cornerstone of the .NET Framework. At runtime, the CLR creates a special *domain* or isolated memory area for your program to run in, and then uses just-in-time (JIT) compiling to load your PE into its domain. JIT means that only the code for the method that you are calling gets loaded into memory, not the entire PE. For later calls to this same method, the JIT compiler uses an existing copy in memory, thereby avoiding having to reload and recheck any code. The performance gain here is that for any

PE, a lot of code may not be used in one particular session. Only the code being called is loaded, saving both time and system resources.

Before running a piece of code, the JIT compiler tries to optimize the code for execution and checks the code for Type safety. Type-safety checking verifies that your code is using the correct memory addresses and ensures that your objects will not corrupt other objects due to mismanaged memory assignments. This also prevents code from bypassing the system's security checks by using unapproved memory blocks (a problem coders have seen in the past in the form of "buffer overrun attacks" on their software). Most importantly, Type-safety checks ensure that when your object is called, there is an exact match between your parameter types and the callers. A systems administrator can disable the Type-safety checks on a server, but this is not recommended. If the code passes the checks, it will be run. Otherwise, the JIT compiler raises a runtime exception error to the user.

You may be thinking that there has to be a price to pay for all of this checking going on before your code is run, and this is correct. For most systems, this cost is minimal, and the performance gains realized with JIT compiling should more than make up for it. But for smaller systems, such as portable devices running Windows CE, you may desire to bypass these checks in favor of smarter resource usage. .NET includes two JIT compilers: a normal version that runs the checks, and an economy version that compiles all code directly without checking it first. Besides bypassing the optimization phase and Type-safety checks, the economy compiler also uses a little trick called *code pitching*. If a method compiled to memory goes unused for a long period of time, the compiler frees up the memory by unloading the method. The downside to this is if the method is again called upon, the compiler must again load it from the MSIL. For most applications, you should stick with the normal compiler. The errors you avoid will more than make up for the clock ticks you might save without it.

As you may have guessed, a great deal more overhead is involved in running your code through a JIT compiler versus the old language-specific runtimes. But when you consider that a JIT compiler is a part of the operating system and not a standard one-size-fits-all runtime distribution, you'll start to see where JIT truly shines. When the runtime has an intimate knowledge of the operating system and the platform, some incredible optimization techniques become available. Remember optimizing your Visual Basic 6 code for the Pentium Pro, or removing checks during compiling that prevented the "floating-point integer bug" in the earliest Pentiums? This is no longer an issue for you as a developer. The JIT compiler knows what chip it is running on and how it can best run your code. Developers seeking high-performance returns from their objects used to have to manually free up resources in the code. Not any more. The JIT knows when resources are running low and frees them up as necessary. Imagine that you deploy an Assembly, and a few months later a new processor is released that has some nifty new optimization features that you really wished were available when you wrote your program. All that would be required in the .NET world is for someone to release the latest version of the CLR that is knowledgeable on this new chip and its features. You now have the ability to write code that is forward-compatible with any future hardware changes.

Managed Code

After a piece of code is loaded, the CLR manages it. This includes all calls made to the code or from it, as well as memory handling and security checking. When accessing an Assembly, the CLR reads in its associated metadata through a process called *reflecting* and sets aside blocks of memory from the available memory heap. The CLR is also responsible for marshalling data between Assemblies, commonly referred to as data serialization. Your application's threading is also managed by the CLR, and because of this, all languages that can use the CLR can now use threads. Finally, the CLR handles resource management. This is when a resource being used is no longer needed and can be released and freed up. Previously, developers had to release their resources in their code, but now, under CLR, this is completely out of your control (for better or worse). For advanced developers, this loss of control might make you feel uneasy, but for the newer developer, this is just one less thing to worry about. You will read more about this new resource management feature in Chapter 2.

Because of all the work that the CLR is doing on the code's behalf, .NET compiled code is referred to as *managed code*. This means that the actual administrative tasks of running and managing the code are handled by the CLR. Visual Basic's .NET compiler, VBC.EXE, is only capable of producing managed code. The COM components you are used to working with are now labeled as "unmanaged code" because they do not require the CLR to run. With the older Visual Basic 6 compiler, you can only produce unmanaged code. But fear not, the CLR can handle unmanaged code, too. In fact, not only can your application call an unmanaged COM component, but you can also make calls to a .NET managed component from your Visual Basic 6 COM components.

Unmanaged Code

Let's take a look at how the CLR deals with your unmanaged COM components. Assemblies are designed to talk to other managed code Assemblies. They do not know how to look in the Registry to learn about COM components, nor do they know how to read in type libraries to learn of those components' interfaces. When an Assembly makes a call to a COM component, the CLR creates a wrapper for this component and generates the metadata in memory containing the information that your Assembly expects in the format that it is comfortable with. To your new .NET Assembly, that old COM component will appear to be just another .NET Assembly. Take a look at Figure 1.6. You will see that managed code will produce one common PE file, while unmanaged code will produce a separate PE file for each language used.

The flip side of this scenario is when a COM component wants to use a .NET Assembly. Again, the CLR steps in as the mediator and generates a GUID for the Assembly and makes the appropriate entries in the Registry by using a program called RegAsm.exe. Next, the CLR creates a type library from the target Assembly, using the TlbExp.exe program, thereby fooling the COM component into thinking that it's talking to just another COM component. Once again, you should note that there will be a slight loss in performance when

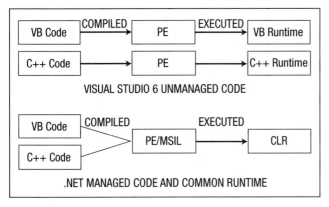

Figure 1.6
CLR-managed .NET code vs. unmanaged Visual Basic 6 code.

mixing components and Assemblies versus using a pure .NET or COM environment. If performance becomes an issue, then you should consider upgrading the components to .NET if at all possible.

Stop for a moment and reflect. I know that is an awful lot to lay on you in one sitting, sort of like drinking from a fire hose. The following is a quick list of all the terms just discussed:

- *Common Language Runtime (CLR)*—An operating system–dependant runtime module that interprets and runs the PE.

- *Common Language Specification (CLS)*—A set of rules defining the languages that can be used.

- *Common Type System (CTS)*—Languages share data types in .NET. These rules help enforce component interoperability.

- *Portable Executable (PE)*—The result of compiled code, made up of MSIL and metadata.

- *Microsoft Intermediate Language (MSIL)*—Compiled source code in the PE.

- *Intermediate Language (IL)*—See MSIL.

- *Just-in-time (JIT) compiling*—Loading and executing an assembly on a method-by-method basis.

- *JITted*—Another name for JIT compiling (the Assembly is JITted by the CLR).

- *Managed code*—Pieces of code that require a CLR to load and manage.

- *Unmanaged code*—Your compiled modules created in Visual Basic 6, usable but not editable in .NET.

- *MVID*—Module Version ID, similar to a GUID for a PE compilation.

♦ *Reflecting*—The CLR reading the metadata of an Assembly.

♦ *Assemblies*—The major building block of .NET. Versioning and security are set at this level. An Assembly can be one or more items, such as PEs, graphics, or multimedia.

♦ *Types*—Formerly known as object or data types, now everything is a Type.

♦ *Namespace*—A method of dividing up a source code file into different areas; previously only possible by adding different files to your project.

Those Other Programming Languages

Because the rest of this book will be dedicated to the Visual Basic portion of .NET, I'll take a moment to show you the new features that the developers across the hall will have to play with. After you are comfortable with using Visual Studio .NET, you may even want to expand your talents into another language. Why not? It could happen.

What's New in Visual C++

When it comes to fast and powerful code, Microsoft's high-level development tool Visual C++ still can't be beat. C++ developers have a very low-level control over their programs, including setting pointers and manipulating where variables are physically stored in memory. If you have an Assembly that has to be high speed and low drag, then C++ is the language to use.

C++ developers will have one extra option available to them that you won't, and that's the choice between creating managed code to run under the CLR or creating unmanaged code capable of running outside the CLR. C++ developers will also have the shortest learning curve when it comes to picking up the newest language, C#. Through a new Active Template Library (ATL) Server, C++ developers will have access to the same Web services and ASP technologies that Visual Basic developers enjoy. A select few developers are capable of writing in both Visual Basic and C++. This is a terrific combination of skills to have, but can be very difficult to combine. If you are looking to add a second programming language to your list of talents, I recommend you read the upcoming description of the new C# language.

What's New in Visual FoxPro

Visual FoxPro is a database-centered development tool that bears a lot of resemblance to Visual Basic. This is about as RAD of a database tool as you can get, and it even allows you to create applications that run on Unix and Macintosh. In Visual Studio .NET, FoxPro developers will enjoy a much-improved IDE, featuring IntelliSense (a blessing that Visual Basic coders already had), numerous language enhancements, and the ability to access their FoxPro databases from outside the FoxPro environment.

.NET will be a big step up for the FoxPro developer group. They will now have access to many of the same features available to Visual Basic and C++ developers, such as the new shared programming classes and the one-environment-for-everyone Visual Studio IDE. The next version of FoxPro will also offer developers improved access to the features of the Windows 2000 operating system as well as the COM+ object model. A greatly improved OLE DB provider will allow for better access to a FoxPro database from outside applications such as Microsoft's Office suite. For a small business wanting to quickly and easily create a database application that provides a bit more power than Access (but is not as powerful or expensive as SQL Server), then FoxPro may be the answer.

Announcing the Birth of C#

As the most-touted language to hit the programming scene since Java, C# (as in C-sharp) was designed from the ground up to be fully object-oriented, and it seeks to attract developers from all of the other languages. C++ and Java coders, in particular, will be interested to learn about this new tool that so closely resembles the ones they are used to using. For Visual Basic developers, C# will be easier to pick up than C++, yet it still offers much of the power and control that makes a high-level language so useful. The syntax is very close to C++, yet simplified. Like Visual Basic, this sharp new language is easy to use and hides all of the complexity that's associated with C++. At the same time, C# offers a great deal of power over the operating system that Visual Basic often lacks. C# is almost as RAD a language as Visual Basic, yet it offers significantly more power at runtime.

One of Microsoft's goals for C# was to remove some of the C++ functions that could easily be misused or cause application errors. Many of the more difficult coding decisions of C++ have been removed in C#, such as knowing which pointers to use in your code, picking the correct data type for your variables, and cleaning up after your Class when it is no longer being used. C# now internally handles memory allocation, and coders no longer have to worry about manually setting pointers. All of the new .NET code features in Visual Basic that you will soon learn about are also available in C#, such as the Garbage Collection and Type safety. In the last few years, C++ has seen very little change, nothing at all like you are going through right now. As a result, while still a very powerful language, it is also somewhat outdated. C# can be viewed as a radical evolution of the C++ language to such a degree that Microsoft gave this language a new name. Even though C# is entering the development world just as COM is being replaced by the new Assemblies concept, you will still be able to access and support your COM and COM+ objects from this new language.

I recommend that you wait to take a closer look at C# until after you have a good grip on the new version of Visual Basic. Then, when you view some code written in C#, you will immediately see the similarities between the two and you will feel right at home in its environment. Throughout this book, I will continue to point out that Visual Basic is not always the best tool for every job. If you have to write an Assembly that needs to perform many complicated operations in the quickest time possible, then you should consider writing it in a more powerful language. Your Visual Studio choices would be C++ or C#, and between these two complicated languages, you will have a far easier time picking up C#. Keep this handy tool in the back of your mind should such an occasion arise (and I guarantee it will).

Gone, but Not Forgotten

Two major tools of Visual Studio have been retired from the lineup. Visual InterDev is no longer available as a standalone tool because all of its functionality and features have been merged into Visual Studio as a whole. You can now create Web projects and code ASP.NET Web forms from any language in Visual Studio. InterDev's legacy is now a part of ASP.NET, and will be covered in depth in Chapter 10. The other tool missing is Visual J++. This language has gone missing-in-action as a result of the Java war between Microsoft and Sun. But Java developers will not be left out in the cold. At least one company at the time of this writing has announced that it is developing a CLS-compliant Java compiler. Microsoft has not ruled out a later standalone version of Java designed for .NET, but due to litigation and Microsoft's uncertain future in the Java arena, it will not be a part of the initial family of .NET tools.

Is Visual Studio 6 Gone for Good?

I highly recommend that you do not treat this new version of Visual Studio as simply an upgrade. Typically, when you buy a new version of software, you uninstall all of your copies of the old version and put the CDs in the closet (or use them as Christmas tree ornaments). For most development teams, this will be unthinkable with Visual Studio .NET. Remember that Visual Basic .NET only creates managed code components, and when you migrate your projects to .NET, they will not be able to be opened in version 6 without a significant effort to "unmigrate" them. The key factor you need to consider are all of your old projects that need to be maintained and updated. If your team is still tracking bug reports and issuing patches on a software release that is already on the street, you will need to maintain a few copies of Visual Studio 6 to take care of these. I suspect that for the next year, there will be a lot of side-by-side development going on.

Side-by-side development with version 6 will not be a problem. Visual Studio .NET can install onto a workstation that already has version 6 on it, and both versions will work perfectly. This was a major concern when Beta 1 was released to the public, but coders quickly discovered that the two development tools could coexist peacefully. You will even be able to maintain two different MSDN library installs so that you can continue to reference version 6 programming information.

Opponents of .NET will point to this reliance on the older version as another reason to shun the new version and continue to use version 6. This is a sad knee-jerk reaction to something that is so radically changed that it makes you feel uncomfortable and doubt your ability to adjust. Companies that take this stance will quickly find themselves falling further and further behind the technology curve, and they can expect to soon see their customers taking their business elsewhere. You, on the other hand, are already on the right path to upgrading your skills to .NET just by reading this book.

The .NET Family of Servers

Microsoft has taken an all-encompassing approach to its .NET initiative. Not only is .NET a framework for developing applications, it is also a hardware architecture aimed at providing application services to support any business need. Like the .NET Framework, these servers were built with a focus on interoperability. As you will see throughout this book, XML plays a big part in creating .NET applications, and so too with this new family of Microsoft servers. Many pieces of this group of services were formally packaged as BackOffice Server. Each of these applications can now be purchased separately or as a group. As a developer or team leader, you may already be familiar with most of these applications, but let's take a look at all eight of them in the overall context of "The .NET Family of Servers." As you read about each server, you can refer to Figure 1.7 to see where this server will fit into your existing network architecture.

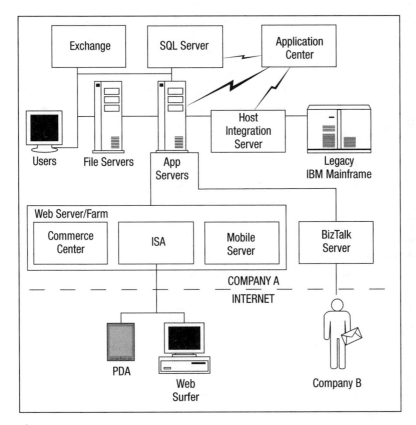

Figure 1.7
An example network layout diagram using .NET servers.

SQL Server 2000

This is Microsoft's enterprise-level database server, positioned to go head to head with the reigning king of databases, Oracle. SQL Server 2000 comes in three editions (Enterprise, Standard, and Personal) and is capable of running on a Windows CE portable device in its most compact form. With its Data Transformation Services (DTS), you can easily create reusable packages that read in data in any format, put that data through a transformation, and load that data into your database. SQL Server 2000 security is certified at the United States Government level C2, the highest available certification in the industry. If you have ever used an English Query Web site that allowed you to ask "Where is the nearest airport to my house?" you will be excited to learn that SQL Server 2000 comes with English Query, which you can use in your projects. For the first time, XML is fully supported within the database. With previous versions, you could transform your query results into XML, but now XML is SQL Server's native language for communicating data. I will explore this in depth in Chapter 8.

Exchange 2000

Exchange is designed to be at the heart of an enterprise's messaging center. From routing and managing email to collaborative newsgroups and document sharing, Exchange is wildly popular with businesses using the Windows NT/2000 platforms. Exchange fully integrates with Windows 2000's Active Directory, allowing you to manage many different server resources from one central location. You can also access Exchange through a Web interface via Microsoft's Internet Information Server (IIS). Communication via HTTP and XML is supported in Exchange, making this an excellent starting point for customized solutions.

BizTalk Server 2000

If you are getting tired of hearing about XML, then skip this part, because BizTalk is all about XML. This is the messaging language of the future, and Microsoft envisions all businesses talking to one another in XML streams. Because XML is self-describing, a large chunk of the complications of business-to-business communications has been solved, but still the question of format remains. One company's inventory messages will probably be in a completely different format from another company's, from the tag order to its naming conventions. This is where BizTalk fits in. By providing a middleware service, BizTalk Server maintains a database of schemas, describing how messages are formatted. Now when company A sends its inventory to company B, a BizTalk Server in the middle takes in the message, compares it to a known format from company A, and translates this into the format that company B's software expects to see. This is what's known as Enterprise Application Integration (EAI). These transformations could go between databases, messaging systems, or business applications. If your application solution requires any interaction with another company's systems, then XML and BizTalk Server could be just what the doctor ordered.

Application Center 2000

In the last few years, technologies such as COM have allowed you to break apart your large and cumbersome applications and disperse them to the far corners of the world, all in the name of scalability. From the developer's perspective, this is a terrific idea. But if you have ever had to maintain a widely fragmented business solution in the real world, this could be seen as a horrible curse. A high-traffic e-commerce Web application could consist of maybe three machines serving out HTML, five machines holding the business objects that support the Web servers, and at least one back-end database server (quite possibly farmed out onto many servers). Things could be humming along smoothly when suddenly the developers kick down the door saying they have numerous updates to post immediately. You may ask yourself, "Self, what's the quickest and easiest way to handle this problem?" Sorry, but "Bury the developers somewhere where they'll never be found" is not a valid answer on this test. But Application Center 2000 is.

With App Center, you can treat your entire farm of servers as one platform for deploying software, and the server will handle all the difficult stuff. You can also track different versions of deployed software, allowing you to differentiate between a testing and a development install. The big hardware push these days is scalability. If you can't make the server do more, add more servers. When more than one server holds a copy of something, yet all the servers appear as one resource to a client, this is what's known as *clustering*. Proper load balancing is knowing when one server is bogged down with requests and routing new requests to a different, more available server. With App Center at the heart of your system, setting up your load-balanced clusters and managing the applications deployed to them becomes a simple task that even a developer can handle.

Commerce Server 2000

Formerly known as Site Server, Commerce Edition in the BackOffice family, Commerce Server 2000 provides many ready-built pieces you can implement in your e-commerce applications. Developing online retail sites involves many areas, such as registering and tracking users, accepting payments, figuring out the local tax rates, calculating shipping charges, and maintaining a current inventory of products for browsing. Commerce Server 2000 seeks to deliver all of these functions so you can simply drop them into your project, customize where needed, and go public with your site in the fastest time possible. This server also provides administrative tools to control the solution after it's been deployed, and management functions to analyze how the solution and your business are performing. If you have an e-commerce project with a short timeline, Commerce Server 2000 is for you.

Host Integration Server 2000

Microsoft's SNA server is a middleware solution to provide connectivity between Microsoft applications and an organization's older legacy systems, such as mainframe databases. Host Integration Server 2000 is the follow-up to SNA. Often, a business will have a substantial investment in an older mainframe database server, but will still want to take advantage of the latest and greatest technologies. Not only can you use Host Integration Server to continue to access these resources, you can also use it to access the mainframes and their bits of data in an object-oriented fashion that you are used to.

Internet Security and Acceleration Server 2000 (ISA)

ISA is designed to support modern-day e-commerce applications at the Web server. The two main pieces of ISA are a firewall to protect the Web site from unwanted intrusions and a Web cache to hold data at the Web server, thereby greatly improving the site's performance. Caching data in a Web application can have huge benefits. For example, suppose 4,000 customers just saw your TV ad for widget X, and they all decide to read about it on your Web site. Without caching, this would mean 4,000 separate calls to your business objects and 4,000 redundant hits on your database for the exact same unchanging piece of information. Add to this equation some network time, because your Web server, application server, and database server are probably on three different machines. With ISA, you could cache your up-to-date product information at the Web server and cut your response time dramatically. Caching equals happy customers, and firewalls equate to happy management. You do the math.

Mobile Information Server 2001

Last but not least, Mobile Information Server 2001 is designed to hook in the mobile user to your enterprise. As mobile phones and PDAs become more and more common, so will a need to get information and messaging down to these tiny platforms. With Mobile Information Server, Microsoft is providing developers an easy way to add mobile support to the solutions. At the heart of this system is Outlook Mobile Access, a trimmed-down version of the popular desktop messaging software. Mobile Information Server extends the power of Exchange Server to support any device your users want to message with. This is the last piece of the .NET family of servers and is still under development at the time of this writing (hence the 2001 in the name).

Microsoft Windows DNA 2000

When I first heard of Microsoft's DNA, it stood for Distributed interNetworking Applications, meaning three-tier or *n*-tier application designs. You remember: a data tier, a business tier, a presentation tier, and any other tier in the middle that you could dream up. Today, DNA stands for . . . well, nothing. You don't spell DNA out anymore, and it's not about application tiers either these days. Microsoft has sort of shanghaied this popular term and is now using it to illustrate the close bonding and interwoven relationships of the .NET Framework and all of Microsoft's supporting servers. You can now refer to the old tiered component development methodology as just plain old *n*-tier development, but as you read on, you'll learn about Services and how a services-oriented project doesn't always fit into a nice, neat application-tier diagram.

Developing Services

Where .NET development really differs from all of the past models of software development is in the fact that Microsoft does not expect you to be developing software in the near future. No, it is not time to start planning an alternative career path, but instead you need to change the way that you think about the applications you design. Microsoft's vision of the future of development lies in Services. In traditional software development, if customers want a word processor built, you develop all the pieces and deliver this as one complete package to run on their desktop. If the customers want an upgrade to their system, you develop this and then redeploy the new solution to the field. In a Services development environment, each of the parts of this word processor could be built separately and sold as a service to enhance the software the customer might already have installed. You can also build complete applications as a service and offer these via the Internet on a pay-per-use basis.

Enter the Internet

The Internet is the key factor behind the Services concept. In a simple sort of way, your daily Web surfing is a type of Services function. You want the latest news headlines, and you get them by surfing to your favorite news agency's Web site. It provides news in the form of HTML that is readable by the human eye. The idea behind Services is that servers, not unlike the news agency's Web server, will provide interfaces to their code modules that will provide you with a service, whether it be distributing information or running a calculation. If you wanted to calculate all of your loan payments over a period of time, you would probably look for a software package that could do this work. In a Services-oriented world, you would send your data (the loan amount and terms) across the Internet to a bank's component that would crunch the numbers and return you a chart with the information you need. You could build a personal finance application that makes use of the bank's services, thereby simplifying your work.

Examples of Services-based ideas have appeared on the Internet before .NET hit the scene. When email first became popular, everyone had to have their own email programs to read and compose their messages. Now all you have to do is to surf to an online email provider, and you can read your messages and write new ones all within the browser. The functions of your email program are handled remotely by the Web server. Also appearing on the Internet is a growing number of online file storage sites where you can store your bits and bytes and access them from any Internet-enabled terminal. E-commerce has been at the heart of the Internet's growth spurt, and Services that can provide identification and payment options for Web surfers are sure to be among the most popular Services.

Implementing Services

One example of a traditional application being ported to the Services concept would be a weather information service. You could host this Service on your Web server, allowing customers to subscribe to your service and access it across the Internet. In a corporate environment, you could host these Services within your intranet for improved performance. Web browsers have continually become smarter and more powerful over the years. Microsoft's vision is to make the user's Web browser a super-smart thin-client platform. Within this framework, you can host any application you wish to build, and all the user will need to do to use your great new "killer" application is to surf to your Web site and click a link. No more running to the stores to buy software; you will simply go online and click a link to start it. When your version 2.0 is ready for release, you'll simply install it on the Web server and you are done. You do not even have to have a customer at your doorstep to make a Service; you can create a service on your own and provide it to paying customers across the Internet on demand.

Further examples of Services would be a Web-based file system that can integrate with the applications you already own, or a messaging service that is capable of communicating with any platform. Developing for different platforms requires you to take different approaches in the traditional software development paradigm. If you take a Services-oriented approach to this problem, you can break away all of the common pieces and treat them as plug-ins to the platform or calling application. Maybe the most shocking thing about Services and the .NET platform is that Microsoft has developed it all around an open standards solution: XML. This gives you the freedom to develop for any platform, whether it is Windows-based, Unix, or Apple. You develop the Services and host them on your server (preferably a Windows 2000 Server, of course), and your clients can use whatever operating system and platform they have to access your Service. XML and SOAP (Simple Object Access Protocol) make this all possible, and these two open standards play such a big role in .NET that they have earned their own chapter in this book.

What Ever Happened to COM?

When developers talk about .NET concepts, you will hear very little mention of the term COM. This has caused many people to panic and wonder if COM has been laid to rest.

COM throughout the Years

COM was a very important step in application-development history, and the Assemblies of .NET are the next step up on the component ladder. Before COM, there was a concept called object-oriented programming (OOP). This was a great concept, but kind of hard to implement in the older development tools. Microsoft's solution to this problem was to create COM as a packaging to go around your object-oriented code and make your interfaces accessible to the rest of the Windows world. COM provided the wrapper for your objects and made it possible to communicate between them. Distributed COM (DCOM) improved upon COM by allowing you to put your components on separate computers and still be able to use your objects remotely. The next step above DCOM was Microsoft Transaction Server (MTS), an add-on to COM to facilitate transactional processing by your objects and to provide a component manager for your COM components that could manage issues such as database access threads and interface-level security checks. When Microsoft released its Windows 2000 product line, it also released COM+, which was a combination of COM and MTS with a few minor features thrown in.

COM was wildly popular among Windows developers. Even teams that were slow to take up the object-oriented programming concepts still used COM to wrap their method-laden classes in. The Java community developed its own version of COM, known as Common Object Request Broker Architecture (CORBA) and later as Enterprise Java Beans. CORBA objects only worked with other CORBA objects, and COM only worked with COM. The nature of these two object models made communication between the two incompatible.

A Better Kind of COM

In .NET, COM and COM+ have evolved into something bigger, yet less complicated. This could be the first time in development history that the latest version of something has turned out "less complicated." A lot of the concepts behind "What is COM?" had to do with complicated issues such as GUIDs and Registry entries, or making remote procedure calls (RPCs) to other COM objects. You would still be correct if you called your .NET components COM, but all of the complexity and administrative issues have been worked out of COM, so what is left is simply called an *Assembly*.

How Assemblies talk to each other is very different from how the older COM plumbing worked. When the CLR needs to talk to a remote Assembly, it uses SOAP and XML to communicate (again embracing those open standards). Unlike the COM and CORBA models previously described, Assemblies now have the ability to be used by any object, no matter what language it is written in or how it is packaged. When Microsoft replaced RPCs with XML, it tore down the walls that surrounded an objects developer in a Windows environment and opened up a new world full of possibilities.

All of the features you knew and loved in COM and COM+ are available in .NET, including transactions, object pooling, and message queuing. In the "New Features" column, you'll enjoy things such as application partitioning and component recycling, plus improved administrative and debugging facilities for your components. The result of all of this improvement is far greater power at the developer's disposal with a greatly simplified implementation model. COM is neither dead nor has it been replaced. COM has evolved into the form of Assemblies, and the world will never be the same again.

Summary

As a senior developer, project manager, or team leader, you are expected to have an expert's understanding of the environment you are planning to develop in. Your team members, fellow developers, and customers will look to you to know how to harness the latest technologies, and for the next few years, .NET is the way. After reading this chapter, you should now be able to answer "What is .NET?"; "How does it work?"; and "What goals was Microsoft aiming for when it planned everything all out?" Like many Microsoft initiatives, .NET was initially greeted with a cold shoulder, because developers thought it was merely a new marketing push. But as you can now see, this is a very broad and deep plan, one that seeks to address all the needs of all the developers and any projects they may think of. Your mind may be full at this point, but I hope that your eyes are wide open to the possibilities that .NET delivers to the developer. This chapter was both a satellite eye-in-the-sky view of the .NET big picture as well as a microscopic examination of how it truly works. Now you will continue your journey and learn how to create solutions within the .NET Framework and how you can incorporate your newfound knowledge into your future projects and proposals.

Chapter 2
Planning and Designing for .NET

Every year, businesses around the world develop more and more new application needs, each one more complex than the last. The paperless office will soon be a reality, and the race is on to get company products and information on to the World Wide Web so that businesses can compete on the global market. Companies are striving to streamline their processes and reduce their operational costs before their competition beats them to it and wins the day. Businesses want applications that work across the Web, and they desire application infrastructures that communicate with their suppliers and shippers. Companies want to develop business-to-customer (B-to-C) and business-to-business (B-to-B) solutions as fast as they can. In the middle of this whirlwind of new development projects are the humble applications developers, analyzing business processes and harnessing cutting-edge technologies as fast as they can to make those companies' dreams come true.

If you have been a developer for at least five years, consider a few questions. Are you developing today's business applications using the same application architectures you did five years ago? Were your customers asking for the same features and functionality five years ago that they are begging for today? Only a select few people were developing for the Web five years ago, and they were not using Visual Basic to do it. In the mid-1990s, applications that communicated with another company's system were rare. Over the last five years, you have seen your customers' requirements grow to take advantage of the latest applications developments, such as the Extensible Markup Language (XML) and the Internet. You also have seen an evolution in the way that applications are designed, from simple client/server applications to fully distributed component-based software. Visual Basic 6 did an admirable job of helping the developer satisfy customers' requirements, but this trusty tool has long been overdue for an upgrade that makes it better suited to create today's application types. Now you have Visual Basic.NET, designed for the Web-enabled world and ready to take on new design challenges.

Today's Applications

Without a doubt, the single most important technology driving and shaping application development today is the Internet. This great tangle of wires, fibers, and cables is connecting businesses, homes, schools, and governments all around the world, and everybody wants to get interactive. Development projects are no longer simple enclosed systems, separated from the rest of the world. Software is now capable of selling, informing, and sharing information. Even customers that are not sure how they can take advantage of the Internet in their company will be itching to find a way to do it. Microsoft's .NET initiative fully embraces the Internet and takes distributed computing to a whole new level. This section looks at some of the most common application types being developed today.

Web-Based Interfaces

More and more, customers want their applications to have Web-based interfaces. These application types are often referred to as *thin clients* because the only piece of the application installed on the user's machine is the Web browser. If the application is overhauled or upgraded, no one needs to visit all the client machines in the company to make these upgrades. When users navigate to the application on the Web server, they will automatically see the latest version. For many companies, the browser interface solves another problem that has frustrated project managers since the dawn of the computer age. Web-based applications are platform independent. This mean that if half of your employees are using Windows NT workstations and the other half are using Unix boxes, and everyone has a Web browser installed, they can all use your application. You don't need to develop a Windows-specific version and a separate Unix-specific version of your application.

The choice to go Web-based is all about cost. One development effort costs less than two. Almost all the processing for a Web-based application takes place on the Web server, which means the users will not need the latest and most expensive desktop systems to use these applications. Maintenance of Web-based applications is centralized to the Web server and supporting application servers. This means that fewer support personnel are needed, which translates into a decreased total cost of ownership (TCO) for the company. With all of these money-saving benefits, it's no wonder companies are abandoning their platform-specific application requests in favor of Web-based applications.

If you are new to Web development, you will be happy to hear that no other development tool today makes creating a robust Web application any easier than Visual Basic.NET does. You will soon learn how to create advanced Web interfaces using powerful server-side controls. You will also learn how Web Services are taking the concept of distributed components and code reuse to a global scale. The Web is the application platform of the future, and you can start developing for the Web today using .NET.

E-Commerce

The Internet started out as a means of sharing information among universities and government agencies. When the general public was introduced to the Web, it became a place to share information about one's hobbies and interests. When businesses stepped into the Web, they immediately wanted to know how they could turn this wonderful worldwide information distribution system into a money-making machine. Thus was born the age of e-commerce. If you are an experienced Web developer, then you are probably already familiar with this application type. E-commerce applications make a company's catalog of products available over the Internet, and allow customers to select and purchase these items from the comforts of home.

E-commerce applications have a Web-based interface served out by a Web server. On the back end is a database that houses the company's inventory, which customers can search through. Visitors may have a shopping cart in which they can electronically place their selected goods as they wander about the system. The final and most critical stage of the e-commerce process is the purchase. Customers provide the Web site with personal information, such as their mailing address and credit card number, so that the application can complete the purchase, pull those electronic items out of the shopping cart, and send the real items to the customer through a shipping company. E-commerce sites have been around for many years now, and although this is not exactly a new application type, it still remains a popular request from customers.

Many issues surround the development of e-commerce applications. Customer privacy and data security are often focused on and sensationalized in the media. Users want to know who is seeing their information, and what kind of protection e-commerce sites are providing for their sensitive data. Who is seeing your credit card information and purchasing preferences? Security is the biggest issue you will tackle in an e-commerce project. Another important design consideration is the user interface and its purchasing process. On the Web, users are not restricted to one local store. They can shop anywhere in the world, and they will buy from the company that makes the purchasing process as simple as possible. Web Services, which you have already been introduced to in Chapter 1, promise to make e-commerce even simpler by allowing users to skip those annoying personal data request screens, making one-click shopping a reality.

The Database Application

Nearly every business application can be categorized as a database application. Every company has information that it needs to store and manage, such as data about its products, customers, suppliers, and much more. The e-commerce application is essentially a database application with a Web-based front end, and online purchasing transaction pieces added.

The database management system (DBMS) forms the heart of the database application, with interfaces connecting to its data stores, allowing users to add, delete, modify, and search its contents. Interfaces to databases can take on many forms, from the older text-based console interfaces to the newer Web-based interfaces. Database interaction has been overhauled in Visual Studio.NET with the latest version of Active Data Objects (ADO), called ADO.NET. Like .NET itself, ADO.NET was written with the Web in mind, and focuses on dealing with databases in a disconnected fashion. Chapter 8 will introduce you to ADO.NET and show you how to use it in your Visual Basic.NET database applications.

The Electronic File Room

You have been hearing about the paperless office for nearly a decade, yet if you go to buy a car, you are still assaulted with a mound of paperwork. Want to buy a home? You could almost build a storage shed with the piles of paper you will have to sign. Slowly, companies are developing applications to take in all of this data electronically, but they are still plagued by the boxes and boxes of historical paperwork they have collected over the years. Many companies rent entire warehouses to store their paperwork in. Paperwork is bulky, expensive, and impossible to run a keyword search against. Nearly every company today has some sort of initiative in place to convert those boxes of papers into electronic files that they can easily store, reuse, and search through. Electronic file systems can be enhanced with a document management system that allows users to electronically make annotations and pass a document along to a co-worker. Even 10 years from now, companies will still be looking to migrate their files to an electronic file room, and they will need applications that let them access and manipulate those files on their PCs.

Business-to-Business

Not only has the Internet revolutionized how businesses can connect with their customers, it has also changed the way that businesses interact with other businesses. Nearly every company's network is hooked into the Internet, making communications going from one business to another a snap. Even with the physical connections in place going from one company's server to another company's server, data formatting is still an issue. In the past, before two companies could share data, both companies needed to agree upon a standardized format for their data. XML solved this problem by tagging the data in a way that describes what each individual element is. Businesses no longer have to agree upon a messaging format; they simply have to interpret the XML messages they receive using the self-describing tags contained within the message.

Now companies want to extend the reach of their business applications and interface with their suppliers and partner companies. E-commerce applications often communicate with shipping companies to arrange the shipping of their products and to obtain the latest shipping rates as part of the ordering process. Inventory management systems may communicate with suppliers when product stores are low, to automate the reordering process. One company may wish to access another company's database or make its own database publicly available to other companies. Business-to-business interactions can greatly streamline a company's processes and eliminate a lot of paperwork and human interaction that was once needed to handle cross-company requests. Chapter 12 will go into depth on how to use XML and the Simple Object Access Protocol (SOAP) to communicate across the Internet in a way that makes your messages universally understandable.

Mobile Applications

Since the day that the computer was invented, users have been chained to a desk with a keyboard and screen glaring at them. Were humans really put on this earth to sit at a desk eight hours a day and speak using their fingertips? For years, movies have teased you with visions of spacemen walking around, waving their flashy handheld devices about, talking to computers in conversational tones. But suddenly, in the last two years, there has been an explosion of mobile platform creations. People are walking down the street and talking into phones. Businesspeople are consulting handheld Personal Digital Assistants (PDAs) to check their schedules or to record information. Warehouse workers are wearing mini-computers on their wrists with barcode scanners attached that let them roam freely among the inventory, scanning boxes and then uploading electronic records of what they find to the computer system. The most amazing thing about the mobile platform boom is that it is only beginning.

For application designers, mobile platforms present yet another challenge to include in your designs. Your job is to make your customers' jobs easier, and if enabling them the freedom to move about as they do their job can make them more efficient, then you need to work this into your designs. Your applications may need to integrate with a wireless network, or you may need to design an interface for your application that can be used by a wireless platform, such as a digital phone or a pocket PC handheld computer. Many phones and handheld computers can surf the Internet, enabling you to develop Web-based interfaces for your applications and avoiding platform-specific interface development. Imagine a single interface for your application that can be used by a desktop computer, a handheld PC, and a digital phone. Mobile platform technology is almost at the point where this vision will be a reality, and when that happens, you will need to be prepared for a whole new set of users for your applications.

Hybrid Applications

As the customer's needs become more and more complex, so will the types of applications they will require. Often, you will encounter a development project that involves creating an application that is a hybrid of many different types of applications. Imagine a golfing equipment company that builds an application with a database on the back end containing the company's inventory data. That company may access that data from within its own office using a Windows-based front end. The company may also create an e-commerce Web site that accesses these very same data stores and enables customers to search its inventory

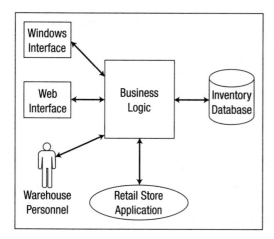

Figure 2.1
The golfing equipment supplier's hybrid application.

from the Web. The company's warehouse personnel may be required to update the inventory using wireless devices such as scanners and handheld PCs. Another company running a retail operation may wish to access this database to locate and order products to stock its own shelves with. Figure 2.1 illustrates a fictional golfing equipment company and the interactive connections these various systems have with the centralized databases.

.NET Projects

To create these different types of applications, Visual Basic.NET enables you to create many different types of Visual Basic.NET projects. By creating different types of projects and grouping them together in a single Solution, you can create hybrid applications that support multiple interface types. This section introduces you to the project types available in .NET that you will use to build these modern-day application types.

Windows Application

Despite .NET's focus on the Internet as an application platform, you will still be able to create Windows-based applications with traditional Windows interfaces. While the interface forms in Visual Basic.NET look almost exactly like they did in Visual Basic 6, these forms are completely new and redesigned for .NET. Now known as Windows forms, these redesigned interfaces are better suited to take advantage of the latest platform and operating system features that have been made available since the release of Visual Basic 6.

If all of the customer's client machines will be Windows-based, then you can design the application's interface using Windows forms. Using Windows forms instead of a Web browser as the user interface gives you a lot more freedom and power on the client end. You have a larger set of form controls to choose from, and you can enhance your form using Visual Basic code to assist the user or provide form field validation. Class Libraries can also be installed on the client machines to offload some of the processing from the application servers to the users' desktop terminals.

Web Application

New in Visual Studio.NET is the Web Application Project. This project type provides users with a Web-based interface using ASP.NET's Web Forms. Web Applications are designed to run within a Web browser on the client's machine, and all the actual code behind these interfaces is centrally located on a Web server. As discussed earlier, in the "Web-Based Interfaces" section, using a Web interface in your application has many advantages, such as lower costs and faster development times. Every few months, a new Web browser is released that features even more functionality than the last. Microsoft sees the Web browser as the application container of the future, and it has been enhancing Microsoft Internet Explorer with features that will make this vision possible. Still, some application functions will be better off hosted in a Windows-based interface, because a Web application requires that most of the processing be performed on the server and not on the client's machine.

What's really great about the Web Application Project is that creating for Visual Basic developers is a snap, even if you have no experience at all with Web development. By making it easy to create Web-based interfaces, Visual Basic.NET enables developers to choose the right interface for the job, Windows or Web, and makes both of these interfaces equally easy to develop for. You don't need to run out and hire a Web-development expert to take advantage of ASP.NET, because your Visual Basic developers will have no trouble creating these interfaces. Designing a Web Form is just as easy as designing a Windows form, and the code behind the Web Form is the exact same version of Visual Basic you will be using all throughout Visual Studio.NET.

Class Library

The Class is the basic application building block that you use to create all application types in .NET. Even the Windows forms are Classes behind the scenes that include code to handle the display and processing of their interfaces. The Class Library Project is the Visual Studio.NET equivalent of the ActiveX DLL (dynamic link library) and ActiveX EXE Projects you created in version 6. The purpose of a Class Library is to provide a service to another component, so another project must call your Class Library and use it in some way. For this reason, Class Library Projects are not standalone applications, but are instead a part of the overall design of a larger application.

The business objects you design and create for your application should be packaged into a Class Library Project, just as you previously placed your business objects into an ActiveX DLL Project. Although you can add classes to Windows and Web Application Projects, doing so does not support the concepts of application tiers and distributed components, and thus should be avoided. When creating business objects, do so in a Class Library Project, and place all of your interfaces in either a Windows or Web Application Project.

Windows Service

The Windows Service is a new kind of project for Visual Basic developers. A Windows Service is a program that is run by the operating system in the background, such as the Windows operating system's print spooler program that waits for users to send jobs to a printer or a Web server service that waits for Web page requests to arrive at a Web server. Previously, only C++ developers could create these services, but now in .NET, Visual Basic developers have this ability as well. Windows Services are designed to run on the Windows NT and Windows 2000 operating systems only, but if your application has a need for a program to be constantly running in the background to monitor resources or process information behind the scenes, then you should consider making this component a Windows Service. Creating a Windows Service is very similar to creating any other Visual Basic program, but testing a service will provide some new challenges to the developer. Chapter 6 discusses the development issues surrounding Windows Services, and you will learn how to create and test a service of your very own.

Web Service

One of the most exciting new developments in .NET is the Web Service Project. A Web Service is basically a Class Library that makes its interfaces available across the Web. This means that you can host your Web Services on a Web server and allow other applications to call your code from anywhere in the world. This new project type takes distributed components and reusable code to new extremes. You can create a Web Service and charge other developers a fee to access your service, and never have to distribute your code to them. Instead, their applications will call out across the Web to your awaiting Web Service using XML-formatted messages transmitted via SOAP and the TCP/IP protocol.

You can use Web Services in your development projects to distribute pieces of your application to Web servers anywhere on the Internet or the customer's network. You can also use other developers' Web Services in your own applications and save a lot of time and money by reusing someone else's code. Just like the ActiveX control market that sprang up to sell developers custom-made controls for their forms, you will also be able to shop for and buy access to Web Services to support your applications. Web Services are the perfect compliment to Web Applications because they both use the Internet as their communications medium, but you can also take advantage of Web Services from your WindowsApplications. If you develop a component for your application that you feel some other developers may wish to use, you should consider building it as a Web Service and market that service for reuse. That way you can get paid more than once for your hard work.

Control Libraries

Interfaces require controls for the users to interact with. Visual Studio 6 has ActiveX controls, which are designed to work with the forms in version 6 but no longer are supported in .NET due to the significant changes made to the Windows forms. The new Windows form controls are called Windows Controls, and you still can create your own controls in Visual Basic.NET. Often, a form will require a special user interaction that is not available using the standard controls provided with the Visual Studio.NET development tool. Developers can look to the third-party market and purchase a control that suites their customized needs, or they can strike out on their own and develop a new control from scratch.

The Web Forms you create using ASP.NET have their own unique type of controls known as Web Controls. Traditional HTML Web pages use a small set of basic controls that all browsers are familiar with. This is very limiting for Web developers, and often Web pages with advanced functions such as sortable data grids require a lot of customized server-side coding to create. You cannot create a customized control to work in the browser because each browser supported a different set of interface standards. Web Controls overcome this limitation by detecting the browser's type on the Web server and sending that browser a version of the control that is compatible with the browser's standards. Because Web Controls are processed on the Web server, they are often referred to as *server controls*.

Creating Solutions in .NET

A .NET Solution is a grouping of one or more projects in the Visual Studio.NET environment. You can create a Solution that contains different project types, such as a WindowsApplication, a Class Library, and a Windows Control. This is a great way to develop your application's pieces separately, yet still group them together so they can be run and tested in one single environment. Solutions can also contain projects created in different programming languages, so your WindowsApplication may be created using Visual Basic.NET and your Class Library may be created using the new Visual C#. One great advantage of this ability is that when you are testing your multilanguage Solution, you will be able to step through your code from one language to another without skipping over any code. For development teams creating applications using multiple languages, this feature is a godsend.

.NET Architectures

In this section, you will learn about application tiers as applied to the logical design for your application. The tiers you identify and design will form the overall logical architecture of your application. Because Visual Basic.NET is now a fully object-oriented programming language, a proper application architecture design is crucial to your application's success. You will learn about the different types of application architectures, how they are used to organize and distribute your components, and the different classification of tiers that make up these architectures.

Standalone Architecture

A standalone application is one complete package. The machine that this application is installed on will not have to communicate with any other machines during its execution. This application type can have an interface, business logic, and database logic, but because the application is built to run on one machine only, it is considered a standalone self-sufficient program. Applications built for home PCs typically use this design style, because the home PC is usually not a part of a network, so component distribution is not an issue. Standalone applications are rare in the business environment, because employees typically need to share data and interact with each other in some fashion to get their jobs done.

Two-Tier Architecture

Also known as the client/server application, a two-tier application stores all the presentation and business logic on the client's machine, while the database is housed on a centralized server somewhere on the network. All of the processing in a two-tier application takes place on the client's machine, with only database queries going out over the network. This application layout gives each client their own independent copy of the application, but allows all the users to access the same database to share the same data elements. Client/server application designs were popular in the early years of Windows development, before applications were designed to place separate business logic components on a network server to reduce the client machines' workload and the application's maintenance needs.

Because a copy of the application is installed on every client machine, maintaining a two-tier application can be very difficult. A change to the application's business logic requires that the maintainers visit every client machine to install the latest updates. Client/server application design places all of its processing demands on the client machines, which will require that the users have a powerful enough desktop computer to handle all of this processing. In contrast to today's thin-client Web-based applications, a client/server application is considered a *fat client*, because the bulk of the application's business logic is on the user's machine. Code reuse between different client machines is nonexistent, so every client machine must have its own copy of all application components. As the number of client machines using the database increases, the application's performance will dramatically decrease. Adding additional database servers to support the increased workload typically means updating the client-side components, which makes the two-tiered design very difficult to scale.

N-Tier Architecture

Two-tier application designs evolved into three-tier designs, which places some or all of the application's business logic in its own separate tier. The three-tier design model quickly grew to a less-limiting design model known as *n*-tier, which acknowledges that an application can have many tiers scattered all over the customer's network. A large-scale business application could very easily have four, five, or even more tiers. Figure 2.2 illustrates the three application architectures described: standalone, two-tier, and *n*-tier.

N-tier application design is the basis of the modern-day distributed application. By designing your application's components to fit neatly into a defined tier of your application, you are breaking up the pieces of your application into manageable components that can be easily

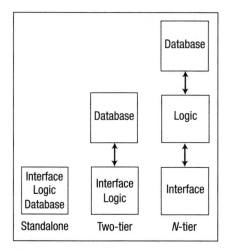

Figure 2.2
Application architecture tiers.

moved from tier to tier and from machine to machine. When a part of your application is updated, only the affected components need to be replaced, instead of triggering a company-wide application rollout. To address increased application demands, components can be load-balanced and farmed out to multiple servers with little effort. For example, a busy set of components containing business logic can be copied to a second application server and managed by a component load-balancing software package. By managing two duplicate sets of components on the network, the application can improve its response time by routing user requests to the least-busy server. Distributed applications offer a significant advantage in both scalability and maintainability over the two-tier and standalone application designs.

Application Tiers

Using tiers is a way to divide your application's logical design into functionally-oriented sections. The three basic types of tiers correspond to the three major portions of a typical business application: the presentation tier, the business logic tier, and the data tier. As you read about each application tier, take a look at the *n*-tier application in Figure 2.2 to see where that tier fits into the overall application design.

Presentation Tier

The presentation tier contains the user interface that the users of your application will interact with. The two most common interface types today are the Windows interface and the Web interface. The surface of these interfaces contains an assortment of textboxes, buttons, and combo boxes to allow the user to navigate and communicate with the application. The sole purpose of the presentation tier is to manage these user interfaces. Both a Windows Form Project and a Web Form Project belong in the presentation tier, because these components draw the interfaces that the users see, and process input from users.

One common mistake is to lump business logic in with the presentation logic. Including a function within a Windows form to calculate the sales tax for the item the user selected on the form is a misuse of the presentation tier. A sales tax calculation is really a piece of business logic and ideally belongs in the business tier. If the sales tax calculation is embedded in a Windows form, which is later installed on every client machine on the network, then updating that calculation will require visiting every machine that has the Windows form installed on it. Separating your business logic from your presentation logic enables you to change your application's interface without having to change any of the logic behind it. You can also change or update your application's business logic without having to modify the components that are responsible for drawing the user interfaces. Any computations or logical functions that are not directly related to the drawing of the user interface should be moved out of the presentation tier.

Note

Functions that can be described as presenting, drawing, or soliciting input and feedback all belong on the presentation tier. Windows forms and ASP.NET Web Forms will reside in this tier.

The best way to think about the presentation tier when designing your application is to ask yourself how you would design these tiers if you were using both a Windows and a Web interface to access your business logic. If you can design the application to work equally well with both interfaces, and not duplicate any functions between these two interface types, then you have succeeded in properly identifying which components belong on the presentation tier and which belong in the business logic tier. Even if you only use one interface type in your actual application, you will be leaving the door wide open to add additional interfaces to your application at a later date as an expansion project. If the customer wishes to convert a WindowsApplication over to a Web Application, or use mobile devices to access your application, then you will only need to re-code the presentational components to make this happen.

Business Logic Tier

The majority of your business application code will be located in the business logic tier. If a function does not directly deal with the user interface, and it does not directly work with a database store, then it belongs in the business logic tier. Business logic consists of the Classes that you develop to represent the objects in your system. The methods and the properties of your objects will enforce the business rules your designers define for your application.

Note

If your function processes or calculates something, or a component contains one of the business objects you design, then this component belongs in the business tier.

The objects located in the business tier act as a go-between connecting your presentation tier interfaces to the raw data that your users will be working with. The presentation tier should never directly communicate with the database, because this violates the interface-only concept of the presentation tier. A lot goes on in the business logic tier, and you can further separate this tier into additional tiers by grouping your components by function or purpose. This idea is discussed further in the upcoming "Additional Application Tiers" section.

Data Tier

Any interaction with your data stores, to include relational databases and the computer's file system, should be handled separately from the business logic by partitioning these functions off into a data tier. Calls to a database are often repetitive and redundant, which gives the developer a great opportunity to reuse their data access functions. The database itself resides on the data tier, on the far right of an *n*-tier design diagram.

Note

Functions that query, update, delete, insert, or add to your databases and file systems should be located in the data tier. All ADO.NET-specific code should live here.

Besides performing all of the inserts, adds, deletes, and updates to your database, your data tier can be used to monitor and check the validity of the data in your database. In a relational database, a row of data deleted from one table can affect many other tables in the database. If you modify a table that is being referred to by another table, you can damage your data structures. You will learn more about the relationships between database tables in Chapter 8, in which ADO.NET and .NET data access methods are discussed. If your application requires special functions to verify the integrity of your database when changes are made, you can consider these checks to be a part of the data tier as well. Only checks and verifications should be done in the data tier. Any calculations your application will perform based on the data returned from the database will be located in the business logic tier.

Additional Application Tiers

Presentation, business logic, and data are the three basic tiers you work with when designing your application. Each of these tiers can be further partitioned off to create additional specialized tiers. Because the bulk of your code is located in the business logic tier, this is where you start when identifying additional application tiers. For example, if you have a component that performs validation on the inputs made in the user interface, you can move these components closer to the presentation tier and create a new tier named "presentation services" to house this component. You would not want to abuse the presentation tier by moving these functions in with your presentation code, but you can move them closer to the interfaces by starting a new tier. When it comes time to deploy your application that has a presentation services tier, you will have the freedom of installing these components on the same machine as the interfaces, or moving them to an application server as a detachable piece.

Your object designers can choose to create special data encapsulation objects that closely resemble your database. The benefit of data encapsulation is that developers will work with the database tables and properties in the same way that they would work with your business objects. The actual database calls will be encapsulated inside of your data objects, hiding the complexity required to communicate with your database to add to, delete from, insert into, or update your tables. If your application has a Customers table, then you can design a **Customer** data object that exposes the table's attributes of **FirstName**, **LastName**, **Phone**, and **Address** and properties of the **Customer** object. This object will also have methods such as **Add** and **Delete** to perform database interactions. Developers working with these database objects will not need to write SQL commands to modify the database. They will instead interact with your data-encapsulating objects and let the object handle the dirty work of establishing the database connection, sending the SQL command, and closing the connection.

Web Services introduce a new tier to the application architecture model. Think of a Web Service created by another company and housed on a Web server in Paris. The Web Service encapsulates its own application architecture that is independent of your own, which includes business logic and possibly a database behind it. Because this service exists independently of your new application, and your architecture does not need to account for the Web Service's architecture, you should not map out the individual pieces and tiers of the Web Service in your own design. Instead, you can isolate the Web Service components of your application into their own Web Services tier in your architecture. Figure 2.3 shows an *n*-tier architecture designed to include a Web Services tier, a data services tier, and an additional presentation tier.

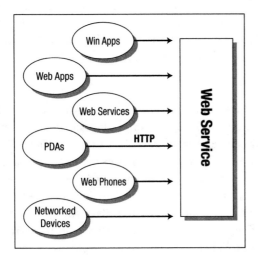

Figure 2.3
N-tier design with additional tiers.

Designing Solutions

Application design takes a set of goals and requirements and turns these into diagrams and plans that the coders can use to gain a clear understanding of the application they are creating. If you brought together a team of the finest homebuilders and told them verbally what kind of house you wanted built, the results of their building efforts would be disastrous. Each builder would have their own ideas on how to get the job done, and without a common frame of reference, the individual pieces would never fit together. Home builders always draw out what they want to build first, starting with some outside views to show the customer, and eventually finishing their designs with a detailed top-down view that tells the builders exactly where things go and what size they should be. Software should also be designed in this way, starting with a high-level conceptual view of the application and increasing in detail until your designers have modeled the objects your developers will finally code.

The Oceanside Resort Project

Throughout this book, a fictional development project for an imaginary company called Oceanside Resort is used as an example. This beautiful resort located in sunny Breezeway Beach has decided that it wishes to jump into the Internet headfirst and take advantage of the Web's global reach to boost its sales, while at the same time simplifying its business processes with a new software package. When Oceanside Resort first hired a development team to develop its application, it had a long list of different kinds of ideas that it felt could enhance its hotel's operations. At the center of its plans was a new reservation system that could be used by the hotel's staff, customers visiting the hotel's Web site, and travel agents using their own customized software. The hotel had recently installed a Fast Ethernet network throughout the building, and purchased three new Windows 2000 Advanced Servers in anticipation of its new reservation system. The hotel staff is using Windows NT Workstation on the desktop to access network resources.

The Requirements

The hotel management provided the following list outlining the application it is envisioning:

♦ One centralized reservations database housed on a newly purchased Windows 2000 Advanced Server located in the hotel's server room.

♦ Hotel employees will interface with the reservations system using Windows NT Workstations.

♦ Hotel customers will be able to log in to a Web site to check room rates and availability. They will also be able to make reservations online and confirm these reservations by providing a credit card number.

♦ The hotel will make the rate and availability information in the reservations database available to travel agents via the Internet. Only travel agents that sign an agreement with the hotel will have access to the reservation system. The hotel is not providing travel agents with software to use the database, only access to their reservations data.

♦ The reservation system needs to be scalable enough to grow with the company, which hopes to expand to other locations one day. This could mean an increase in online bookings as well as an increased demand on the server from added hotel workstations.

♦ The system design needs to be well documented to allow for future capability additions and application upgrades. The customers wish these designs to be deliverables in case they later decide to use in-house developers to create these additional new features.

Initial Software Architect Analysis

Often, your initial set of application requirements will be as vague as Oceanside Resort's. These requirements will need to be fleshed out considerably by the team's business requirements analysts so that the team can better understand what the customer needs. From the initial application overview provided, you can begin to envision an application that provides both a Windows interface to the hotel employees and a Web-based interface to potential customers via the Internet. You should immediately recognize that a lot of common functions will be shared by both the Windows and the Web-based interfaces, which should be located in a separate tier and shared by these different interface types. You can also see how a Web Service can be used in this application to provide access to travel agency applications to the hotel's reservation data across the Internet. By designing this application using components broken up into separate application tiers, the architect will be addressing the customer's scalability and future enhancement requirements.

Conceptual Design

The first design model for your application that you need to create is a conceptual model. This drawing provides a high-level satellite view of the subsystems that make up your application. A subsystem is a large-scale collection of functionality one step below the overall application. For an e-commerce Web site, your subsystem list might include the online catalog, order processing, and customer information processing. Each subsystem will contain a group of functions that are in some way related to each other. If properly designed, a subsystem can be pulled out of one application's architecture and plugged into another application's design. Another e-commerce application could reuse the conceptual designs from another application's catalog subsystem. Your conceptual design should include application resources, such as databases and file systems, and user end points, such as Web browsers or handheld computers. Conceptual designs should be kept simple and abstract to communicate to customers only the "big picture" of what the application will look like, without all the technical details.

Figure 2.4 shows a simple conceptual design for the Oceanside Resort application. This design illustrates the different interfaces to the reservation system, such as the employee's desktop system and the customer's Web browser. Also note how travel agents can interface with the reservation system via a Web Service provided to registered travel agencies. The

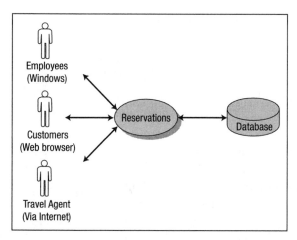

Figure 2.4
The Oceanside Resort conceptual design.

conceptual design should include stick figures representing the users of your application, which are often referred to as "actors" during the design phase. Showing the actors in the conceptual design diagram helps illustrate where the human interaction occurs within your system.

The conceptual design phase also includes the scenarios and use cases you develop that describe the customer's processes, which are discussed a little later, in the "Process Analysis" section. When the conceptual design is finished, you should show it to the customer to verify your understanding of the application they have requested. After your designs progress past the conceptual stage, the details of your design may become too technical for most customers to understand, so you should seek their feedback before moving to the next stage of application design.

Logical Design

The logical design takes the subsystems defined in the conceptual design and breaks these into objects and interfaces. Your logical design also shows the relationship between the objects in your system. All of your object identification and analysis takes place during this phase. It is in the logical design phase that you design the application tiers that your objects will be divided into. Each subsystem defined in the conceptual design can have its own logical design to describe it. Looking at your conceptual design diagrams and use cases and identifying the objects your application will require can be quite tricky and time-consuming. Later in this chapter, you will find out how to recognize the processes within a subsystem and identify objects from those processes.

Each actor who uses your system will interact with your application through an interface. Applications and databases outside of your application will also need an interface that your code can use to talk to these outside resources. Later, when you model your objects, those objects will also have interfaces that allow them to connect to other objects. If you encounter an object that does not clearly fit into one single tier, then you should consider reevaluating that object and separating it into multiple objects. Objects that try to do too much or skip over the middle tiers can corrupt an application's design and adversely affect the software's maintainability and scalability.

Physical Design

When designing a distributed application, you must be able to envision the physical locations of the various components that make up your system. A physical design diagram maps the individual objects in your application that are described during the logical design phase to specific components or Assemblies. An Assembly can be physically located in one or more locations, such as servers or workstations within the company's building, or it can be mapped out to remote machines, such as a customer's home computer or a Web Service hosted on the Internet. Matching the physical design to the logical design will give your developers a more complete picture. When it comes time to plan the deployment phase of your application, you can turn to your physical design diagram to decide how to go about deploying the individual components.

Physical design in .NET is a bit more complex than in past versions of Visual Studio. The Assemblies you will be creating can contain many pieces, such as Classes and resource files (graphics, for example). An Assembly is more of a conceptual package than a physical one insofar as one single Assembly containing many different elements can be located in more than one physical location. One Assembly can contain multiple objects identified in the logical design, and can be located on two different servers in the physical design diagram. When an Assembly is broken up in the physical design diagram, you should annotate that Assembly with a tag to indicate that each piece is only a subset of a larger Assembly, and not the entire Assembly.

Managing the Design Phases

Figure 2.5 shows the relationship between the conceptual, logical, and physical design diagrams. You should always start with a conceptual, high-level diagram that displays the subsystems and actors in an application. Create your use cases and process analysis diagrams

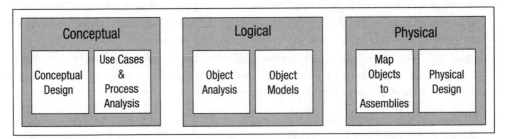

Figure 2.5
Design flow from conceptual to logical to physical.

during the conceptual design phase as well. Next, you will develop the application's logical design by identifying the objects within those subsystems and the relationships between those objects. This is the design phase in which you create your object models that will enable your developers to begin coding. Finally, you will map those objects to packages and Assemblies, which will dictate the physical locations of those objects.

Design Issues

Software architects have many issues they need to consider to design the best application possible. Sometimes, the project requirements address some of these design issues, such as a requirement stating minimum performance metrics or requirements for security mechanisms in the software to provide data protection and activity logging. If your application does not have a specific requirement that addresses a particular concern or design issue, you should still address all of these concerns during the design phase of your application.

Code Reuse

The initial design phase is the best time to start thinking about designing your application to maximize code reuse. If two or more functions need to perform the same calculation, then this common piece of code should be moved off into a new function so that it can be reused. Data access routines are often redundant, so you can centralize your data access code in one location and reuse it from all over your application. One nice advantage of this approach is that you will only need to update your code in one location if a connection string or database server name changes. The opposite of code reuse is code redundancy, which means the same lines of code appear more than once in the source code. Redundancy wastes a developer's time, and if a defect is discovered in one version of the redundant code, your coders will need to perform the same fix for this problem in multiple locations instead of in one spot. Identify the actions your application will be performing over and over, as well as the calculations and functions you will need to isolate into reusable chunks.

Scalability

Designing an application to be *scalable* means that your application has the ability to grow and adapt to greater demands, such as an increase in the number of users. As more users access your application, the demand on your application's resources increases. Assemblies providing business objects will experience increased demands, and more connections to the database will be required. Designing your application to be component-based enables you to distribute busy components to new servers or place multiple copies of a component on the network so that your application can take advantage of load balancing.

Design your application to adjust to increased demands over time. If the initial application design is using an Access database to store its data, consider what application changes will be required if the customers need to migrate their database to a large server, such as SQL Server 2000. If you can design your data access components so that they can easily be switched from one database type to another, and place all of your business logic in distributable components, your application should have no problem scaling to increased customer demands.

How the CLR Improves Scalability

Scaling up refers to when you upgrade a machine by adding additional processors or more RAM. Before .NET, the applications you developed needed to be upgraded and modified to take advantage of new hardware features or upgraded server capabilities. For example, applications built to run on the first generation of the Pentium processor were not capable of taking advantage of the improvements made to this processor when the Pentium Pro was released. In .NET, the Common Language Runtime (CLR) dynamically detects the executing machine's capabilities and uses what it finds to execute your application as efficiently as possible. This means that if the customer scales up the application server with new hardware, your application can automatically adapt to those upgrades. When a new processor is developed a year after your application has been deployed, the customers can simply upgrade the CLR on the server to the latest version that understands this new processor's features, and your application will automatically benefit from this upgrade. A good term for this ability is "forward-compatible," because, through the CLR, your .NET applications will be able to use new hardware features that have not even been developed yet.

Maintainability

As the size of your application grows, so does your application's maintenance needs. A single user application installed on one machine is fairly easy to maintain and upgrade. In a client/server two-tier configuration, if you release a new upgrade to the customers, then someone will have to visit every client machine to install the upgrade. In an n-tier application, you can limit the maintenance required by issuing updates by tier. For example, if only one component in the business logic tier changes, then the maintainers only need to install that one component on the application server. If multiple copies of that component exist on the network and are being used in a component load-balancing scheme, then each copy needs to be updated.

Distributed application administration software, such as Microsoft Application Center 2000, can simplify this process for the administrator by handling all the remote installation tasks from a single computer. If you are not using special software to manage your distributed application, provide the systems administrators with a clear understanding of the location of each component with a physical design diagram. Building your application using logically grouped components greatly improves your application's maintainability, but as applications are scaled out to multiple servers, it can be difficult to comprehend and maintain all of those distributed pieces. Ask yourself how the systems administrators will maintain this application after it has been deployed, and provide them with a detailed physical design diagram to help them understand the geography of the application.

Performance

Even if your application successfully meets every single customer requirement, if the application is painfully slow to use, then the users will label it a failure. Application performance can be affected in many ways. The programming language your developers use to create their Assemblies will have an impact on the overall system performance, as will the developers' individual coding styles. For example, using the **Case** statement to detect a variable's current value will execute far faster than a series of **If** statements. (Coders can check out Chapter 5 for other performance tips and coding best practices.)

When designing a distributed application, you need to be aware of the performance costs of making calls from one remote Assembly to another. Whenever the network gets involved in the application's execution, a slight performance loss results. If your code makes a request of a Web Service located on a remote Web server, the network cost can be quite high. Physically locating components on the same server and limiting your code's interaction with remotely hosted Web Services can reduce these performance losses to acceptable levels. As your components become increasingly more distributed, your application's performance will decrease in response. Components within a single subsystem should be collocated in the same physical location, and calls between subsystems should be kept to a minimum in order to maximize the application's performance.

Database Performance Issues

Making calls to a database can also slow down your application. Complex queries that involve multiple tables joined together can take extra time to execute. If your application executes the same queries over and over, you can greatly improve your database access times by turning your queries into stored procedures. A stored procedure is a compiled query stored within the database itself that your code can execute and receive the results from. Stored procedures can accept parameters, which can be used to dynamically change the query's results. An example would be a stored procedure that returns information on a customer stored in multiple tables. You could send the stored procedure the **CustomerID** as a parameter to cause the stored procedure to only return a specific set of data. Calling stored procedures involves less network traffic going to the database server, and the query itself will execute faster than a SQL command that the database would have to process.

Fat Client vs. Thin Client

A fat-client application places some of its processing demands on the client's machine. A thin-client application performs most, if not all, of its processing on a server. A Web-based application is a terrific example of a thin-client application. You can enhance a Web-based application with a client-side technology, such as JavaScript, to perform some minimal client-side validation and processing. A little extra code embedded in your Web page can save the client a communications roundtrip to the Web server to get a simple answer or validate a form input. Avoiding network communications with client-side scripting is a great way to improve Web application performance without demanding too much processing of the client.

Windows interface applications normally are considered fat-client applications. Business objects may need to be installed on the client's machine, and the client can perform many calculations locally. Assuming that the client machines are powerful enough to handle this increased responsibility, adding components to the client machine is a great way to offload from the application server some of the application's processing requirements. An application that performs some of its processing on the client machines will adapt well to an increase in users, because the increased processing demands those users will place on the server will be smaller than a thin-client application's server-side processing demands. The downside to fat-client applications is that your objects are dispersed all over the network, greatly decreasing the maintainability of your application. If you need to implement another application server to balance out the server's workload, you will also have to update your client-side code with new connection information.

Security

The issue of application security can encompass many different areas, including protecting corporate data, performing user authentication, scanning for viruses, and even logging events. During the requirements-gathering and business analysis phase, your team should gain a clear understanding of the customer's security concerns and issues. Every issue raised by the customer needs to be addressed in the high-level designs of your application so that security is an integral part of the overall application. Trying to insert a security feature into an already built application is a recipe for disaster. For a more detailed overview of some of the security issues you should take into account when designing your application, read Chapter 13 of this book.

Durability

An application is said to be *durable* when it can recover from unforeseen circumstances. Call them glitches, bugs, weaknesses, or acts of nature, but whatever you call them, design your application in a way that accounts for these problems. The simplest example of durability is an application that writes to a floppy disk drive. If the application crashes when a method writing to a floppy disk raises an exception because a disk has not been inserted, then this application is not durable. Handling exceptions, such as a missing floppy disk, in such a way that the application can continue to operate despite the unexpected problem makes your application durable. Problems can occur with network connections, files on the hard drive, and remote operations. Incorporating Web Services into your project can save you a lot of development time, but how does your application react when the Web server hosting the Web Service is shut down? If your server-based components fail, your application can be taken offline for the entire company. Lost data and application downtime directly translates into financial losses.

Designing a durable application can also include systems administration procedural planning. Databases and file systems that your application uses should be regularly backed up so that data is not lost when a natural disaster strikes. Floods, hurricanes, tornados, curious users, and underpaid systems administrators all fall into the "natural disasters" category. Always consider the worse-case scenarios when designing your application and develop plans to deal with life's unexpected challenges. If you can avert disaster within the application itself, make it a part of the overall design. If you come up with an administrative procedure, such as backing up the database regularly, then make that a part of the application's maintenance procedures and educate the customer on how to perform these actions.

Integration and Interoperability

Your application's conceptual design should include any interfaces to the world outside of your application. These interfaces will include links to outside databases, Web Services, applications such as Microsoft Word, and COM components integrated into your .NET application. *Integration* is the process of making applications work with other applications. A COTS (commercial off-the-shelf) software project involves purchasing multiple software packages from other vendors and plugging all of these solutions together to form one complete customer solution. Sometimes your development team will need to create some "glue" code to piece these individual projects together to form one solid application.

Many applications and components that were written as COM objects will not be ported over to the .NET Framework. This is not a problem, because your .NET Assemblies can use COM components just as Visual Basic 6 does. *Interoperability* is the process of connecting one development framework to another, such as .NET to COM. Visual Studio.NET will make this very easy to do, as you will learn later in this book. If your .NET application uses COM components, then you will need to perform interoperability testing to ensure that your COM and .NET components are working together as planned.

Development Language Selection

Visual Studio.NET makes it easier than ever to integrate a team of developers using a mixture of programming languages. You should consider both the application and your available pool of programmers during the design stage and decide which components of your application should be written in which language. Typically, you will have a standard language the majority of your team develops in, such as Visual Basic. For starters, you can assume that all of your application's components will be built in Visual Basic. This would be a wise choice for any project, because of the large number of available Visual Basic developers and the fact that no other development language can touch Visual Basic's rapid development, enabling ease of use and simplicity.

If you have any developers who are familiar with C++ or C#, you should reassess each component in your design and ask yourself whether that component should be developed in a more powerful language such as Visual C#. Developing your application's more processor-intensive components in Visual C# will result in a performance boost for the application. If your team does not have any programming skills other than Visual Basic, encourage developers to branch out into Visual C#, which should be easier to learn than Visual C++ and will give developers the ability to create even more efficient Assemblies for their .NET Solutions.

Developing Objects

As you now know, Visual Basic.NET is the first release of the Visual Basic language that can truly be said to be an object-oriented language. If you are new to the world of object-oriented programming, now is definitely the time to learn about it. This section is meant to provide an introduction to designing object-oriented applications, and is by no means a complete description of all the analysis and modeling techniques available to you, the developer.

The tools and methods used to perform process and object analysis range from simple tools, such as team meetings involving whiteboards, to complex design tools, such as Rational Software's Rose modeling tool and the software architecting tools found in the Visual Studio.NET Enterprise Architect (VSEA) edition. You can use these tools to record your object models, which can then be used to provide guidance for your developers to prevent them from digressing from the designs you worked so hard to build. Using a professional object-modeling tool is highly recommended, because it not only makes creating and maintaining your designs easier, but also enables you to generate some skeletal code from your object models that will provide a great starting point when you start coding the application. At this time, few details have been made available on the VSEA edition, so object-modeling techniques are presented here at a basic level that you can use both in a complex tool and in a whiteboard environment.

An object-oriented application is all about objects interacting, just as they do in the real world. A person can drive a car, and can also reserve a hotel room for their vacation. Applications not designed in an object-oriented fashion are generally function-oriented, meaning the application executes by calling a chain of nonrelated functions. If you designed the reservation system without analyzing the objects in that system, you would probably end up with functions like **MakeReservation** or **AddNewCustomer**. Notice the object names **Reservation** and **Customer** inside of those function names. These two unrelated functions could both be located in a single Class, defying any organized design principles. In an object-oriented application, these two functions might be named **Customer.Add** and **Reservation.Add**.

The objects that you design will form the logical structure of your application. This means that you will perform your object analysis during the logical design phase discussed earlier. To begin your object analysis, will need the conceptual application design, which lays out all the envisioned application subsystems. You also need experts in the customer's process, either a customer representative or a business-requirements analyst that is intimately familiar with the processes.

UML

The art of describing customer processes and translating those processes into application objects has a language all of its own, called the *Unified Modeling Language (UML)*. UML is a graphical language that uses boxes, human stick figures, and lines to communicate information to customers and developers. These graphical elements are often referred to as *notations*. Before UML, many different notation languages were available to describe processes and objects. The most popular of these notation languages were finally merged together to form the UML language, which is by far the most popular set of notations in use today. Many different tools are available today that support UML drawings, such as the Visual Modeler tool that came in Visual Studio 6 Enterprise Edition, Rational Software's Rose modeling tool, and Microsoft's Visio 2000 drawing tool, which lets you model everything from office layouts to network diagrams, Windows interface designs, and UML diagrams.

If UML and modeling are new to you, then it will feel kind of odd and a little silly at first to be drawing stick figures of your users with arrows pointing to ovals and squares. The purpose of these seemingly infantile drawings is to develop a deep understanding of the application you are about to develop. This analysis process is designed to counter the developer's natural instinct to go straight to the keyboard as soon as they have been told an application's objective. Writing code before you fully understand a system will almost always end up a disaster. Application code started before the team's understanding of the customer's processes is complete will be marred by unorganized spaghetti code, abandoned and unused functions, poor application performance, a lack of scalability, and, in many cases, a failure to meet the customer's needs. Resist that urge to start pumping out code, and start your development projects by drawing pictures of the envisioned application. You will be surprised at how different your understanding of a system is at the end of the design phase.

Process Analysis

Since the days of the caveman, humans have loved to tell stories with pictures. It is so much easier to understand what someone is telling you when you can actually see pictures describing what they are talking about. Before you can identify the objects that will make up your application, you must translate the customer's requirements into diagrams that describe the customer's processes. The better you understand the customer's processes, the better your application design will be, so use plenty of diagrams and use different types of diagrams to describe processes. The most important thing to remember during the process analysis stage is to keep it simple. Your customers should be able to comprehend all of your process diagrams, because it will be their responsibility to let you know if you got it right after the analysis is finished. Process diagrams should not be technical and should not include any mention of programming terms.

You can use many different types of diagrams to describe and capture a business process. *Use case diagrams* that illustrate the actors and activities a system will work with are the most common form of diagram. Figure 2.6 shows a simplified use case diagram that illustrates the

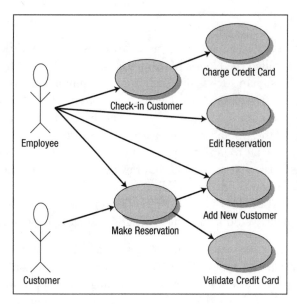

Figure 2.6
Use case diagram of the reservation system.

actors and activities associated with the Oceanside Resort reservation system. *Collaboration diagrams* are a useful way to analyze how users interact with each other and what types of data are passed back and forth. A collaboration diagram uses stick figures to show the various users and their roles within a system, and uses blocks that represent data or artifacts that are passed from one user to another. A third type of diagram is the *sequence diagram*, which provides a timeline-like view of a single process. A sequence typically starts with an actor, which provides some information or application input, which in turn triggers the next step in the sequence. You can think of sequence diagrams as graphical recipes that show how a process is accomplished step by step.

Object Analysis

When you feel that you have a strong understanding of the business processes you are going to create code for, you can dismiss the customers and the business analysts and begin to get technical. Using the copious diagrams created in the business analysis phase, your development team must identify the objects that will make up the application, along with the features of those objects and their relationships to other objects. First, you will find out what an object is and what pieces of information you need to discover about an object.

What Is an Object?

The most important thing you need to know to design your objects is how to identify an object when you are looking at all of those process diagrams. The easiest way to identify an object is to look for the nouns in your process diagrams. If one of your use cases illustrates a customer reserving a hotel room, you can easily detect both a customer object and a hotel room object in that diagram. Employees who interact with your application often have objects dedicated to them as well. During the object analysis phase, write down anything you think could be an object and then discuss these potential objects as a team. As you add detail to these objects, you will better be able to identify which objects should stay in the design, and which should be deleted or merged with other objects.

Properties, Methods, and Events

To bring your objects to life and give them meaning in this world, you need to decide what these objects know and do. If you think of a computer as an object, you could describe it to someone by listing its processor speed, amount of RAM, and hard drive size. These are said to be *attributes* of the computer. In object design, attributes are also known as *properties*, meaning the processor speed is a property of the computer. In code, a reference to the computer's processor property would look something like **Computer.Processor**. A property describes an object or tells a consumer of that object what that object knows. An object can also perform actions. A computer can start, reboot, and execute programs. These actions are known as *methods* in the object design world. To programmatically trigger the rebooting action of a computer object, you would make a call to the **Computer.Reboot** method.

An *event* is like a notification coming from the object that tells a consumer of that object that something happened. When you place a button control on a Windows form, you can write some code that will execute when the button is clicked by placing this code in a **Click** event within the form. The button is a separate object that lives on the form, so you are not placing this code directly inside the button's code. The button's code will raise an event whenever the button is clicked. Your Windows form code will listen for this event and execute that event code whenever a **Click** event is raised. You can create events for all of your objects to call back to the consuming piece of code to let it know something special has occurred. It is up to the consuming code to listen for that event and include some code to react to it, just as the Windows form included code to react to the button's **Click** event.

Object Relationships

Your application objects will have relationships to other objects within the system, just as objects have relationships to other objects in the real world. A developer can program their computer, and a customer can make a hotel room reservation. Your object diagrams will communicate these relationships by connecting lines from one related object to another. Those lines communicate not only which objects are related to each other, but also what kind of relationship they have. You can describe the relationship in words such as "programs" or "creates." You can also describe the relation in terms of multiplicity. For example, one customer can create one or more reservations. This relationship can be described as a *one-to-many relationship*, and you can show this in your object diagrams. Figure 2.7 shows the example **Customer** and **Reservation** objects, including the word "creates" to describe

Figure 2.7
The relationship between two objects.

their relationship. The number 1 appears by the **Customer**, and 1 followed by two dots appears by the **Reservation** object. This describes the one-to-many relationship these two objects have.

Approaches to Object Analysis

Object analysis is where application design can get really difficult, and no two developers will identify the exact same set of objects for a system. Two ways exist to get through the object analysis phase. The first is to assign one senior developer the task of identifying all the objects and creating your object models by her- or himself. This method normally is the fastest way to get through this stage, because no discussions or disagreements on the object selections take place. Of course, the downside to this approach is that the final product will be one developer's vision, and it will probably not be the best design possible.

A team-based approach to object analysis is recommended. It takes longer, and you may get into some heated discussions and disagreements during the process, but the more great minds you can focus on this task, the better the final product will be. Even if you use a software-modeling tool to create your object models, you should first lock your team in a conference room with the process diagrams and a whiteboard and let them sort out their thoughts the old-fashioned way. Only when a final object model has been agreed upon should one or more of your developers commit this model to electronic form. Encourage open discussions of all ideas, and try using a balloting system to pry ideas out of the less vocal developers. These sessions can also provide a great object-oriented design training opportunity for your junior developers.

When using the development team open-forum approach to discovering and designing objects, buy one or two packages of 3-by-5-inch cards and hand out a decent size stack to each team member. At the top, they can write their object name nominations and then place these cards onto the table. As your analysis progresses and it comes time to decide the properties, methods, and events for your objects, you can divide your object cards into three vertical sections: the leftmost section for properties, the middle section for methods, and the rightmost section for events. One advantage of using object cards instead of a whiteboard or computer program is that your team can easily move these cards around the surface of the table when it comes time to discover the relationships between these objects. When the session is done and you feel you have a workable object model represented by the cards on the table, be sure to preserve their layout and order so that you can properly transfer this information to the final object design.

Inheritance Design

One new feature of the Visual Basic.NET programming language that has received a lot of attention is the addition of inheritance. Inheritance is covered in greater detail in Chapter 4 in the discussion of all the latest language enhancements, but it is important to think about inheritance during the object analysis phase, so it is discussed briefly here. To design your applications to use inheritance, you must first identify objects that share common properties and methods. If your team decides to create a **DeluxeRoom** and a **BargainRoom** object to represent specialized styles of hotel rooms that can be reserved, you can see that these two objects are both a type of hotel room and therefore will share many commonalities.

To design objects for inheritance, you need to create a parent or "superclass" for these common objects. In a real-world example, a brother and a sister will both have inherited many features from their parents. Both the brother and his sister will have arms, legs, eyes, and ears. They will both be able to run, eat, and sleep, just like their parents. However, every person is unique in many ways, so the brother and sister will have attributes that only apply to them. Maybe the brother is an excellent soccer player, and his sister prefers mountain climbing. If you model this little family as objects, the **Parent** object will hold all the properties and methods that are common among the entire family. The **Brother** and **Sister** objects will only display properties and methods that are unique to them. Take a look at Figure 2.8 to see this family Inheritance Tree. The arrows going from the **Brother** and **Sister** objects up to the **Parent** object indicate inheritance. Notice that the **Brother** has a **PlaySoccer** method that is unique to only that object and none of the others in the family.

When an object inherits a property or method from a parent, that object is not locked into using the parent object's implementations. For example, if the **Parent** object has an **EyeColor**

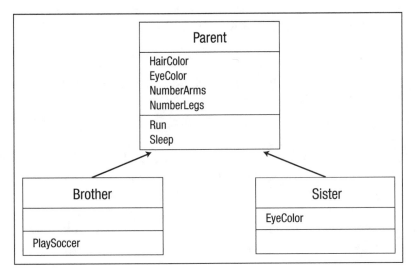

Figure 2.8
The family Inheritance Tree with a parent, a brother, and a sister.

property that is hard-coded to always say **Blue**, the **Sister** object will inherit this property but she can customize her **EyeColor** property to say **Green**. This is called *overriding*, because a child object is overriding the implementation of a parent object's property or method. Notice in Figure 2.8 that the majority of the properties and methods are listed under the **Parent** object, but the **Sister** object has an **EyeColor** property, which matches a property found under the **Parent** object. Because this property duplicates one that is inherited from the **Parent** object, the **Sister** object's **EyeColor** property is said to override the **Parent** object's **EyeColor** property.

When you later learn how to create the inheritance superclass and child classes, you will see that the child classes do not have to create code for all the properties and methods they have inherited from the parent object. Whenever the **Brother** object needs to run its **Sleep** method, it will redirect the application's execution to the **Parent** object. Child objects will maintain pointers to all the properties and methods of the parent object that have not been overridden, and redirect calls to these inherited methods to the parent object. Inheritance is a terrific form of code reuse, and using inheritance can save you a lot of time when you are creating your child objects. The only code that you will need to type for a child object is the unique properties and methods, and the overriding functions for that object. All inherited functions will not be visible in the child object's code because the actual implementation of these functions is contained in the parent object.

Overloading

Another wonderful new feature in the Visual Basic.NET language is called *overloading*. Be careful not to confuse this with overriding, just discussed. Overloading is a way to create a single method within your object that can perform many different functions, depending on how it is called. For example, suppose you design an object that has three methods named **AddCustomer**, **AddRoom**, and **AddEmployee**. You can replace these three separate methods with one single method simply named **Add**. This method will have code within it that will be able to detect by the passed-in parameters and object types which type of **Add** the calling code wants to use. This is known as overloading because you are designing a single method to perform more than one function.

Look for overloading opportunities toward the end of your object analysis phase. If you can group your object methods alphabetically, you will be able to easily spot methods that have similar concepts, such as those starting with **Add**, **Delete**, or **Search**. Consider turning these separate methods into one single overloaded method. The advantage of overloading is that it simplifies the interface for the user. If the user of your object wants to add something to your object, they only need to deal with one single **Add** method for all of their adding needs. It is also easier to maintain your object's code because all of your **Add** code will be collocated and centralized instead of dispersed throughout the object.

Summary

Designing Visual Basic.NET applications will take a lot of time and thought when done properly. Even though you can still get away with creating applications in .NET that are not object-oriented, this would be a gross misuse of such a complex and powerful tool. Visual Basic.NET has a lot of great new features that you can take advantage of in your designs, such as inheritance and overloading. If you do not consider these features during the design phase, it will be all but impossible to implement them during the coding phase. Whether you are designing a small application for a single user or a massive business application that will be used around the world, take the time to consider all the design and architectural issues mentioned in this chapter. If you wait until the middle of the coding phase to address a critical design issue, then it may be too late to properly include it in your designs. Planning is the key to success, so take your time and do not miss any details.

Chapter 3
Using the .NET Interface

Never before has there been a development environment with so many bells and whistles attached to it. Visual Studio.NET is without a doubt the most powerful tool ever created for programming, and in order for you to reach your full potential as a .NET developer, you will need to spend a little bit of time learning about all of the new tools available to you. The Visual Studio.NET interface was developed to run on top of the .NET Framework discussed in Chapter 1 and combines all of the best features of each of the previous Visual Studio language environments into one integrated tool. You will feel right at home using the Visual Basic RAD GUI development tools, but now you will also benefit from features such as the Task List that was previously only available to Visual J++ and Visual InterDev developers. A writer could devote an entire book to the subject of learning and using this interface, but because you have some experience using a prior version of Visual Studio, I am just going to give you the 25-cent whirlwind tour. Please watch your step while boarding the tram, and keep your head and arms inside the car at all times!

Interface Overview

Like all Microsoft products, the .NET interface is fairly intuitive to navigate. If you have never formally studied proper GUI design, you could learn a lot from the .NET interface. Looking at Figure 3.1, you will see the familiar menu items across the top of the screen, and below these, you will find the toolbars. In the center of the interface is the main working area. From here you type your code or design your forms just as you did before. Some

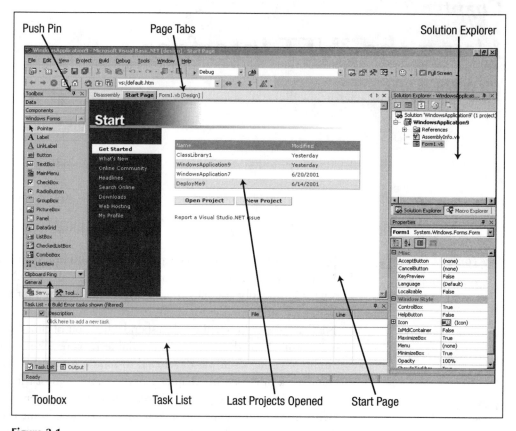

Figure 3.1
The Visual Studio.NET environment.

serious improvements have been made to this benign-looking area, which I will cover in due course.

The first major improvements that will jump out at you as you look at Figure 3.1 are the view windows to the left, right, and bottom of the main area. Instead of a fixed location and size for your toolbox and the old Project Explorer, .NET offers a lot of flexibility as to how you set up your supporting views. By the end of this chapter, you will have a good feel for which tools and views you will use the most, and this will be the best time for you to set up your Visual Studio.NET environment. Customizing your environment based on your newfound knowledge will pay off quickly as you begin to code your Solutions.

Setting up the .NET tools is an art unto itself, but if you are worried about someone else logging on to your system and messing up your layout, don't. The Visual Studio layout is now tied to your logged-in user's account, and someone else logging in will start out with his own default environment. I recommend that at the end of this chapter, you start a Visual

Studio session, lay out all the tools exactly how you want them, and then exit the session. This saves your layout and restores it when you restart Visual Studio. Any changes you make in later sessions will also be saved upon exiting.

Many of the descriptions here will be brief, because these features are used in examples in later chapters. Other interface features will go unmentioned because you will have no problem figuring out what they do or will remember them from past versions of Visual Studio.

Menus

Interfaces can change dramatically from program to program, but every good application will follow the same pattern of menu options to help you find certain options where you are used to seeing them. Visual Studio.NET is no exception, and I will not waste any time on the common features that you will remember from past versions. The Edit menu, for example, is completely standard, but there are notable changes elsewhere that I want to point out. Other menus will appear and disappear during your session depending on what type of item is in the Design view, such as a Schema menu for editing an XSD Schema, or a Table menu and an Insert menu for designing a WebForm. These item-specific menus appear to the right of the Debug menu when you are in the respective environment in the Design view. Let's take a look at the standard set of menus.

File Menu

The File menu is relatively unchanged, but keep in mind that .NET uses the new term *Solutions* in the same fashion that Visual Basic 6 did the term Project Groups. That is, a Solution is a grouping of one or more Projects. When you want to add a second project to your current Solution, you go to the File menu and pick Add Project. Instead of looking for an Open Project Group menu item, you use the Open Solution item. The really big change for the File menu is that this is now the home base for your software versioning controls. Previously, Visual SourceSafe was considered an add-in to Visual Studio and fell under the Add-Ins and Tools menus. Because Visual Studio.NET seeks to create a totally integrated environment, the SourceSafe items are automatically included in the interface and are now located under the File menu. All of the functions you might need to use are here, including Check In and Check Out, History, Share, and Compare.

View Menu

This is the main menu for opening up views and different tools in your environment. The most commonly used views are all located directly under this menu, but because there are so many tools to choose from, you might have to look in a few submenus. Each of these available views is covered in the "Views" section of this chapter.

Project Menu

This menu is the same as it is in version 6 in that this is where you can go to add a new item to your project, such as a Windows form or a Class. It includes a nice menu option called View All Files that will cause your Solution Explorer to show all the files in the Project directory, and not just the code files you would normally see. In Chapter 1, you explored the Project directory at the file system level and saw that it has two subdirectories named bin and obj. These directories and their files are now visible and accessible in Solution Explorer if you choose View All Files.

The most interesting change for the Project menu is the Reference menu item. As before, this is where you go to set a reference to a COM object to use in your program. Because COM is now an outdated technology, the Reference window has been expanded to three tabs. The first, .NET Framework Assemblies, lists all available .NET Framework Assemblies you can use; the second, COM Objects, lists COM objects, and the third, Project File, enables you to set a reference to another Project file. Setting a reference to an object here is often referred to as *early binding* and will make that object's properties and methods available to you both in the Object Browser window and through the coding window's IntelliSense feature. This reference also directly affects the metadata contained in your Assembly, because you now hold a reference to an exact version of another Assembly.

Build Menu

This menu is a result of merging the old version 6 Run menu with the concept of *Solution deployment*. Once again, a Visual Studio external tool, formerly known as the Packaging And Deployment Wizard, has been merged into the interface. Besides being able to run and test your application from within the interface, you also can plan and execute a deployment of your Solution here. The concept of deployment in an Internet world is far more complicated than the old one-install-package-fits-all scheme, so now there is a Configuration Manager menu item that will help you plan this out. An entire chapter (Chapter 14) is devoted to this phase of .NET Project development and will show you some examples of uses of this feature.

Debug Menu

Many of the familiar debugging tools and windows are controlled from the Debug menu. One new menu item of particular interest is the Processes item. This is another exciting improvement that will enable you to find an already-running process on any available system (not just your own) and attach that process to the Solution for debugging purposes. If you cannot wait to hear more about this superpower, you can jump over to the debugging chapter (Chapter 9) to read more about it.

Format Menu

The Format menu is an environment-dependant menu. If you are in Design view, the Format menu is available. Otherwise, you will not see it listed. Just as in Microsoft Word or PowerPoint, you can format and change items in the Designer view from the Format menu, such as set a text box's alignment or the order that items are stacked on your form from front to back.

Tools Menu

The Tools menu provides a varied set of tools, such as those to configure your overall Visual Studio environment (through the Options menu item), add or configure third-party add-ins to Visual Studio, and customize a toolbox or create a new toolbar. The few Visual Studio tools that are still external from the environment, such as the Visual C++ Spy++ tool or the Trace utility, can be launched from here. You also have the ability to add any external tool to this menu you desire from the External Tools item and set up customized command-line parameters to launch this tool. Add-ins, on the other hand, cannot be added manually to Visual Studio. The install program for your add-in introduces itself behind the scenes to make the needed settings changes and then is available for startup from the Add-ins menu. Finally, the Tools menu enables you to connect to a database (Tools | Connect To Database) or a server (Tools | Connect To Server), which you also can do from Server Explorer, discussed later in this chapter, under "Views."

Windows Menu

I really appreciate this new environment's tabs above the Design and Code view that let you flip between the different open items. I found it so annoying to have to click the Windows menu in version 6 to change from one open Class code view to another. You can still do that in the Windows menu, but I think you will appreciate these new tabs as much as I do. You also might use some other Windows menu items that relate to the display of your views windows. With a viewing window selected, you can turn off and on its Dockable setting or use the Hide property to remove that window from this menu. Of course, you also find these options by right-clicking the title bar of the view window you are working with.

Warning

Let me caution you against closing a view window by clicking the X button on its title bar. This will close the window, but it will also close any window that is sharing a pane with it. For example, Solution Explorer and Model Explorer might be sharing the same pane, and if you click the X button on one view, they will both go away. Use the Hide option to unload a view from your work area and retain the other views.

Help Menu

Everybody needs a little help sometimes, and those that are afraid to admit it need it most of all. Included under the Help menu are the familiar links to the MSDN Library, as well as the standard About item (which, by the way, is a great place to find out more about your current computer system, by clicking the System Info button under the About selection).

The top item in the Help menu is a new .NET feature called Dynamic Help. This handy item sends you directly to a Help item based on whatever it is you are doing when you pick it. Dynamic Help senses where your cursor was last placed or what item you have high-lighted and presents you with links to help on that item. Are you writing an ADO command and need to verify the syntax? Select the Dynamic Help window and avoid those painful steps of having to search and sort through MSDN. The Dynamic Help window tries very hard to be your best buddy. It even ranks the links it finds for the currently selected item and lists them with the most relevant at the top. These links also are in groups, such as Actions or Samples, so you know before you click a link what type of help you can expect. Figure 3.2 shows the Dynamic Help window, displaying available help on a selected Windows form.

The MSDN Library of information can be run externally of Visual Studio by launching it from the system Start menu, or it can now be integrated in the IDE by starting it from the Help menu. By picking Help | Search, you open a view in which you can enter a string to search MSDN for help. If you also open the Search Results item, you get a second view pane that lists all the matching items from your search. Double-clicking a search result item opens it in Visual Studio's Web browser in the main area. The Edit Filters menu item enables you to set up a search filter so that you only get back the information you need. You can use this to filter out coding help for Visual C++ and C# from your results list so that

Figure 3.2
The Dynamic Help window displaying help on a Windows form.

only Visual Basic–related information appears. The Index Results menu item opens yet another window pane that lists any items directly associated to an item you select in the MSDN Index view window.

Finally, under the Help menu you find all the support services that Microsoft provides for Visual Studio. You also find a Check For Updates item that initiates a connection with the Microsoft Web site and checks for updates and service packs for Visual Studio. And this menu contains links that take you to the Microsoft Technical Support Web site, a Customer Feedback form, and many other Web pages of programming interest.

Toolbars

Visual Studio.NET has 26 toolbars at your disposal. And even though it has so many toolbars doing so many different things, this section names only a few of the most useful and commonly used ones. Toolbars appear below the menus at the top of your environment. .NET uses the "Coolbar" toolbar style, which enables you to slide these toolbars left and right, move them up and down in the toolbar stack, and even combine them on one line with other toolbars. You can manipulate a toolbar by grabbing it at the far-left edge where you will see a raised vertical ridge. Combining toolbars is a really great option if you like to have a lot of toolbars loaded, because they do not retract out of site like the views windows do to give you more working space. Toolbars can also be detached from the top area to float around the screen freely in tiny windows of their own, by clicking their left edge and dragging them down away from the other toolbars.

Data Design and Database Diagram

The Data Design toolbar is an excellent toolbar to have open if you are working with ADO.NET Datasets. You have two buttons that enable you to quickly generate a Dataset and to preview the data. The Database Diagram toolbar gives you all the database functions that you find in the SQL Server tools, all readily accessible from within Visual Studio. This is a wide toolbar offering many options, such as table creation, database script generation, and table relationship settings. For developers wanting to create databases and change their architectures quickly or without having to jump over to a DBMS application, this is a great toolbar to have loaded.

Debug and Debug Location

You definitely want to add the Debug toolbar to your environment. From this toolbar, you can run your application, add break points and watches, step through your code, and control all the windows you might use to monitor the Solution's execution. The functions available from this toolbar are discussed in greater detail when I cover debugging of .NET applications in Chapter 9. Along the same lines as the Debug toolbar, the Debug Location toolbar can be used when your application is in Break mode to quickly examine the programs being executed, the various threads it has spawned, and the current call stack. These items are presented in handy drop-down menus that enable you to switch between them for quicker troubleshooting navigation.

Designer Toolbars

The majority of the toolbars are intended to assist you in your form designing chores, just like the toolbars in PowerPoint or Word. These toolbars help you quickly do tasks, such as change an item's alignment, create or modify tables, resize items, or make a group of items match in dimensions. Designing good interfaces has become more of an art form and less of a matter of simple text box placement. With the merging of Visual InterDev into the .NET environment, you now see more visually oriented design tools than you had before.

Diff Merge

Now that Visual SourceSafe is integrated into your environment, you have access to many of its functions on the toolbar. Diff Merge enables you to manage two different versions of code, examine their differences, and effect a merging of the two into a single file on a piece-by-piece basis. This toolbar works in connection with the Compare Versions menu item found under File I Source Control.

Full Screen

Full Screen is a one-button toolbar that I think is a "must have" in your environment, because it is so handy and takes up very little space. With one click you can expand your Design or Code views to the full dimensions of your screen with only the menu items across the top visible. This button also stays visible, and with one easy click puts you back into full-blown Visual Studio mode.

Query

This is yet another wonderful toolbar for developers who are working with databases. Using this tool, you can quickly generate SQL queries against your databases with only a few clicks. Even complicated SQL joins and **where** clauses become a piece of cake when you use this tool. SQL Server developers already are familiar with this tool, but now it is available for use with any database you connect your Solution to.

Source Control

If your project is under Source Control, you need this toolbar to manage all the checking in and out of your working files. From this toolbar, you also can share your files with other projects (Files I Source Control I Share), view a file's history while under code control (Files I Source Control I History), or compare one version of a file with an older version to see exactly which lines have changed (Files | Source Control | Compare Versions). This can be a life saver when a developer starts pleading "but it worked last week." You can use the Source Control toolbar to examine what has been changed over time or simply roll back the file to a pervious version. The items on this toolbar are shortcuts to the items under the File/Source Control menu.

XML Data and XML Schema

By the end of this book, XML will seem like an old friend to you. With these two toolbars, you can easily manipulate XML Datasets and design Schemas that dictate how those Datasets are formatted. These tools help to give you a visual perspective on your textual XML files and make working with them a breeze. In the past, developers working with XML had to purchase third-party tools to do their jobs, but now these tools are just another fine part of the Visual Studio tool chest.

Customized Toolbars

After looking over all of these tools, you will probably find a few buttons on each one that you might consider "must haves." Because you do not have the room to load all the toolbars, why don't you just create your own customized toolbar containing whatever buttons you prefer? Exercise 3.1 walks you through creating a customized toolbar containing buttons from many different toolbars.

Exercise 3.1: Creating a Customized Toolbar

1. Choose View | Toolbars | Customize.

2. On the Toolbars tab, click the New button and give your toolbar a name.

3. A new empty toolbar appears on the screen.

4. Click the Commands tab of the toolbar window.

5. Select the Project item in the left pane and then locate the Add Windows Form item in the right pane and drag and drop it in the gray space of your new toolbar.

6. Do the same procedure with the Add Class icon.

7. In the left pane, switch over to the File menu and add the Check In and the first Check Out icons to your customized toolbar.

8. Your new toolbar is now available from the list of toolbars to turn off and on at will.

The Main Area

The main area is where you do all the "real" work for your project. Let's face it, the rest of these tools are just the supporting cast of this show. The true craftsmanship of a developer is performed right here, center stage in the Design and Code area. This area has the wonderful ability to think in two very different modes: graphical design and text-based coding.

The tabbed view is an excellent new way of looking at a multidocument project. As more files are opened, more tabs are added to the top row of the main area. If you want to look at two different files at the same time, you can do this by right-clicking a tab you want to break away from the set and selecting either New Horizontal or New Vertical Tab Group. This opens the file associated with that tab in a second coding area with its own set of tabs. Now whenever you open a new file, it will be added to whichever set of tabs is currently active. You can also right-click a tab and opt to move it to a different tab grouping. If this new layout scheme doesn't thrill you, you still have the ability to go to the Tools | Options menu and, from the Environment folder, set the display setting to MDI, which gives you that old familiar floating child window environment you used in version 6.

Design View

Design views are graphical environments, such as the Windows Form Designer. In these windows, you will mostly use the mouse to drag and drop items and to resize them. Some Design views, such as a Dataset or XSD Schema, start with a message in the middle of it, prompting you to drag an item from the toolbox over to the Designer page. Other Design views, such as forms, have pixels in the background to help you place and align your controls and decorations. Many items in your project will have both a Design view and a Code view. To switch between these two views, simply right-click the main Design view and pick View Code (or vice versa).

When you are on a WebForm Designer screen, you have an extra set of tabs at the bottom edge that enable you to change between the Design screen and the HTML code behind it. This feature was inherited from previous Web development tools, such as Microsoft FrontPage and InterDev. Using these tabs is a little different than looking at the code behind a Windows form, because that view opens in an entirely new window with a tab at the top, whereas a WebForms HTML Code view and the Design view share the same window.

Another great benefit for the Web designer is the ability to switch the Web page's layout from Linear to Grid mode, enabling the designer to place controls anywhere on the form, just as you would on a Windows form. This feature uses absolute positioning tags to override HTML's natural tendency to draw pages in a top-to-bottom "linear" fashion. These tags use coordinates to tell the browser where an item will be placed on the screen. This feature opens many possibilities for Web designers, including the ability to place overlapping items in the Web browser.

Code View

In Code view, you will immediately notice a cool new feature along the left side of the window. Your code is now divided into expandable and collapsible segments, just like a Tree View control. You do not have to do anything different in your code to use this feature; the interface can tell what lines of code belong together and automatically provides these groupings. No more having to page down a long module looking for the right section. Now you can click the plus (+) and minus (-) symbols to expand and collapse each segment for an easily navigated bird's-eye view of your code.

While looking at code in the main area, you may want to be able to look at two different areas of the same module simultaneously. You can do this by clicking and dragging down on the thin gray bar located directly above the vertical scrollbar in the coding area. This enables you to split your coding area in two and view the same code module at two different lines. As you type in one pane, you will be able to see the changes take place in the other pane, keeping them both in sync.

One feature you may want to enable is word wrapping in the Code view. In the past, if your line of code was wider than the window pane, you had to scroll horizontally to see everything. The new Visual Studio code window enables you to turn on a word-wrap function. This does not break up your line of code, but merely makes it more readable in one view. Previously, coders could add an underscore (_) at the end of a line to indicate a hard return before the same code line was continued. No longer do you have to manually add breaks to your code to improve readability.

Even your good old Copy function has a new trick. You are used to copying lines of code in "stream" mode, in which the stream starts where you first hold down the mouse button and ends where you let go. Microsoft has added a new Copy mode known as Column Select. By holding down the Alt key, you can click your code and move your mouse up and down to select items vertically. Pretty fancy, huh? Highlighted blocks of text are now dragable also. Just highlight something so that its background turns blue, and then click and drag the text somewhere else. The code relocates to wherever your cursor is when you release the dragged text.

How you format and indent your code greatly affects its readability. A true programming guru's code is neat and organized so that anyone looking at it can easily follow the logic patterns. Visual Studio.NET helps you out here by offering a "smart" indenting option. With smart formatting enabled, you no longer have to think about tabbing in your code. The IDE can tell by the type of syntax you are using how the line should be indented. Smart formatting is turned on by default, which you can change by going to Tools | Options. In the Options window, this setting is located under the Text Editor folder, the Basic subfolder, and then the Tabs folder. To see this in action, start a **Public Sub** section, add a **While** statement, and then add a **Select** statement. Without ever having to hit the Tab key, your code will be neat and organized.

IntelliSense

IntelliSense has always been a godsend for the Visual Basic developer, and Microsoft has even found a little room for improvement here. Many coding areas that have never before benefited from this feature now have the autocomplete boxes popping up as the user is typing. Web designers coding in HTML and scripting languages will greatly appreciate this tool that Visual Basic developers already know and love. Just type an object's name and then a period, and you get a drop-down menu of all available properties and methods. IntelliSense also works when you are developing XML Datasets and Schemas.

Tip

I personally like to type one or two letters after the period, which causes the drop-down list to scroll to the matching items, and when I get to the one I'm looking for, I just hit the Tab key, and the typing is completed for me. This is a great technique because it avoids having to reach for the mouse. If you are not sure what you are looking for, you can always use the mouse or arrow keys to explore the list box and learn more about your chosen object.

The Visual Studio Start Page

By default, at startup you see the Visual Studio Start Page in the main area. If you right-click this area and choose View Source, you see all the HTML code behind this Web page. From the Web toolbar, you can enter a URL and navigate to any available Web site in this window. The default Start Page features links to many Microsoft resources, such as its Communities (newsgroups), the latest news from the MSDN Web site, and the ability to search the Internet from within Visual Studio. The last few projects you opened will be available on this screen for quick one-click launching, along with links to create a brand-new project or to launch the Open Project dialog box.

The Start Page has a My Profile link that gives you access to your user-specific settings. Here you can customize the Help filters, window layout, and keyboard scheme to your preferred programming language so that Visual Studio.NET feels a little more familiar to you. The first time you start Visual Studio.NET, you are given a chance to set the My Profile options to the language of your choice. The layout options here include Visual Basic 6, Visual Studio 6, Visual Studio Default, Visual C++ 6, and Visual C++ 2. Choose the one that is closest to your past development environment.

Warning

Changing the top-level Profile setting rearranges all of your views and toolbars—do not do this if you have put a great deal of effort into setting up your current environment!

On the surface, the Start Page looks like a fairly simple Web page, but behind the scenes is a masterpiece of HTML blended with XML data and styling. I strongly encourage you to right-click the Start Page and study the code behind it. Editing this code haphazardly could break many of the Start Page's wonderful features, but in the hands of a skilled Web programmer, this Start Page could blossom into an awesome Development Team home page with customized links to team news items or the current Microsoft Project file. To give you an idea of how complicated and advanced the code behind this Start Page is, you will not be able to get it to run correctly in Internet Explorer 5.5. This makes your Visual Studio.NET browser the most powerful browser at this time (though I expect that the next version of Internet Explorer will be ready to take on the improvements introduced in your .NET projects).

In Exercise 3.2, you learn how your team can customize the Visual Studio Start Page to include a page full of information and links related to your team's development project. Now your team members cannot complain about not having enough information or not knowing when the next milestone is due, because it will all be right there in their IDE.

Exercise 3.2: Customizing the Visual Studio Start Page

1. Open Windows Explorer and navigate to \Program Files\Microsoft Visual Studio.NET\ Common7\IDE\HTML.

2. Create a directory named "Custom" if one does not already exist.

3. Using Windows Notepad, create a file named "Team.xml" with the following text in it:

```
<CustomTabs>
<tab>
<name>Team Home Page</name>
<defaultTab>Welcome to the Team Home Page</defaultTab>
</tab>
</CustomTabs>
```

4. Save this file and open Visual Studio so that the Start Page is showing. If you already had the Visual Studio Start Page open, right-click it and pick Refresh.

5. You now see a Team Home Page menu entry on the left side. This menu name comes from the <**name**> tag in the XML.

6. If you click the Team Home Page item, the main information area of the Web page displays your title "Welcome to the Team Home Page" from the <**defaultTab**> tag.

This home page is a very empty example. You will want to create content to be listed here, such as links to the project schedule, a calendar of events, and maybe a chart of accomplished and planned milestones. To do this, you need to create an XML file containing these links and information bits in a tagged format. You will also create an XSL file that will style and display your XML data on the Team home page. Post these two files on an accessible Web server in the company and add links after the **</name>** tag in each developer's Team.xml file, like so:

```
<xml>http://teamweb.mycompany.com/TeamA/TeamHome.xml</xml>
<xsl>http://teamweb.mycompany.com/TeamA/TeamHome.xsl</xsl>
```

Whenever the content in the XML file is updated on the server, developers will see these updates on their individual Visual Studio Start Pages by clicking the Team Home Page item. You learn more about creating XML data pages and XSL styling pages in Chapter 12.

Views

What I refer to as a "view" can really take on many forms, such as an Explorer or an Output window of some type. Each view has an entirely different function, and I will cover these one by one. What they all have in common is their dockable and hideable frame and the ability to relocate to any of the four docking edges of the .NET interface. Wrangling with these floating windows can be somewhat tricky, and this is the main area you should focus on when optimizing your development environment. Visual Studio.NET also features multimonitor support. For developers who are lucky enough to have a second monitor on their desk, they can configure this in the operating system's Windows Control Panel via the Display settings. After it's configured, you can drag your views over to the secondary monitor area, freeing up space in the main area for designing and coding.

Docking is not a new feature, because you could do this in version 6. If the view is docked, it is a part of the border (left, right, top, or bottom). To undock the view, simply double-click its title bar. Now you have a moveable window that will try to dock with an edge if you move it close enough. This was always a great feature, but didn't that toolbox on the left and Project Explorer on the right really bite into your working space? In .NET, you can click the push-pin icon on the Views title bar to make these slide out of view when you are not using them. If two views share the same border and frame, and you activate the Hide feature on one of them, they both slide out of view. The fastest way to make a panel slide away is to click once in the main Designer area. When the views are hidden, a thin gray bar appears on that border with the names of the contained views visible. Clicking one of the view names causes it to slide back out for you to use.

Different views can be grouped together so that they retract as one when they are not needed. Two views share a display area when they are *tab-linked*, which happens when you drag one view over another and release it so that the title bars overlap. When two views are tab-linked and they are pinned down (not retractable), they share the same display area and offer a set of tabs along the bottom of the frame for you to switch between the views. If two views share a border but are not tab-linked, they appear one on top of the other like the Project Explorer and Properties windows did in version 6.

When you first open a view, it appears on a default border. Undocking the view and moving it to another border can easily change this. The order of views from top to bottom (or left to right) along a hidden border bar is based on the order in which you added the views to the border. When more than one frame is sharing a border, you can click the borderline between these two windows and resize them to your satisfaction. Now that you know how to deal with these creatures, let's examine each view more closely.

Solution Explorer

This is the file-level view of your Solution, just like the old Project window. One excellent new improvement is that if you decide to delete a file, it will be placed in the system's Recycle Bin, as opposed to it just disappearing for good as occurred in version 6. To add an item to a Project, just right-click the Project's name in Solution Explorer and select the Add menu item. You can now add project References in Solution Explorer as well. No more going to the Project menu and adding References there. Directly underneath the Project name in Solution Explorer is a References folder that you can expand to quickly see your current "early-binding" reference settings. Right-clicking items in a project reveals source code options, such as Check-In and Check-Out. If you right-click the Solution name all the way at the top, you will see some build and deployment options available here. All of these right-click menus duplicate features already discussed in the "Menus" section of this chapter, but enable you to access them quickly in Solution Explorer.

Solution Explorer displays all projects that currently make up the open Solution. As you learned earlier, your Solution can be made up of projects created in different programming languages. Take a look at two different projects contained in one common Solution in Exercise 3.3:

Exercise 3.3: Adding a Second Project to a Solution

1. Open Visual Studio.NET and click the New Project link on the Start Page.

2. Under the Visual Basic Projects folder, create a Windows Application project.

3. In Solution Explorer, right-click the Solution name at the top, select Add, and then select New Project.

4. Under Visual C#, select any available item to add to your project.

Solution Explorer now displays two projects and all of their associated files. This is pretty much just like what you were used to in version 6 when you created Program Groups, but now you have the ability to view and debug code written in other languages. This is a great time to take a peek at some C# code. Looking at it in an environment you are now starting to feel comfortable with might help you to see the possibilities that exist in multilanguage development projects.

Solution Explorer also enables you to copy or move files from one project to another. If you simply drag and drop a file from one project to another, it is moved (the file no longer is in its original project). To make a copy of a file in a new project, hold down the Ctrl key while you drag and drop that file, to retain the file in its original project. If you have more than one project loaded in a Solution, one of them must be designated as the Startup Project. You can set this by right-clicking one of the Project headers and selecting Set As Startup Project from the pop-up menu.

Class View

Because Classes are no longer directly tied to a physical file (remember that you can now have more than one Class in one code file by using Namespaces), it is a big help to have a special view window that lists all the available Classes in your Solution and their associated properties and methods. By double-clicking an entry in this list, you can open the file containing this Class and jump directly to that property in the code window. Each item in this list has a helpful icon to its left that lets you know what type of item it is and what kind of access setting it holds, such as Protected or Public. At the top of this window is an icon on the mini-toolbar that enables you to sort this tree by name, type, or access for easy reference. Another great feature of this view is that it enables you to drag the name of a Class or its interface over to the coding area to instantly fill in its full name on a line of code you are working on.

Server Explorer

Possibly the most powerful view of them all is the new Server Explorer. From this window, you can view all the resources on your system to include databases, messaging queues, system logs, services, running processes, and performance counters. Better yet, you can add a reference to any computer on your network here and view the resources on that machine remotely. To add another machine on your network to your Server Explorer, click the Add Server item and just enter the server's name or URL. In order for you to be able to access the resources on that server, your user account has to have sufficient permissions on that server. Figure 3.3 shows a Server Explorer window, displaying the resources available on the developer's machine. The types of resources listed will vary from one machine to another.

After you have your Server Explorer setup with all of the resources you need for your current project, you can save your configuration by picking View | Server Explorer View | Save Current View. Be sure your Server Explorer window is active before you select the Save Current View option. By saving this view, you have the ability to create multiple configurations that you can switch between in different projects or within the same project, as needed. All of your saved Server Explorer configurations show up as selectable menu items in the Server Explorer View submenu.

Figure 3.3
The Server Explorer window displaying a machine's resources.

Many of the tasks you previously had to leave the Visual Studio environment to do are now accessible from this window. You can use Server Explorer to kill a hung process by looking for it under the Loaded Modules tree. You can also stop and start system services such as a Web server from the Services tree. The System Event log and other log files are now at your fingertips under the Event Logs tree. This is a great shortcut to the log files when you want to verify that your application is making the proper entries or you are debugging your application and need to check the system log files for clues.

Having a single point of control for all of these resources on any machine you have access to is terrific, but wouldn't it be nice if you could work these resources into your project somehow? While some items, such as processes, are purely informational, others, such as a system's services or tables from a database, can be dragged over to the Designer view to quickly add a reference and the initialization code to your project. Exercise 3.4 walks you through an example of using Server Explorer to quickly add a reference to a server's resource in your code.

Exercise 3.4: Using Server Explorer to Add an Event Log to a Class

1. Start a new Class Library project in Visual Studio.

2. Load and select the Server Explorer window.

3. Expand the Event Logs tree.

4. If you are not already in Design view for your Class, right-click the Class name in the Solution Explorer window and select the View Design menu item.

5. Click and drag the System item from the Server Explorer window to the Designer window and drop it anywhere on the page (the System item is located in the Event Logs tree you expanded in Step 3).

6. You now have an EventLog1 item in your Class Design view window.

7. Right-click the Class Design view window and pick the View Code option.

8. Click the plus (+) symbol to expand the section of code labeled Component Designer Generated Code.

9. Note the automatically added code in the Class declaring EventLog1 as an instance of the **System.Diagnotistics.EventLog** type.

10. Scroll down to below the EventLog1 declaration and note the properties of EventLog1 already set to the server instance that you picked this component from in your component's Initialize event area.

11. Scroll up to the top of the Class. Put your cursor below the **End Sub** statement of the **New** subroutine.

12. Start a new subroutine by typing:

```
Public Sub WriteEntry()
```

13. Press Enter. The **End Sub** tag is added for you and your next line will be automatically indented.

14. You can now write code to place an entry in the System Event log by entering a line like so:

```
EventLog1.WriteEntry("Hello World")
```

This quick example illustrates how much time and effort Server Explorer can save you when working with server resources. You can just as easily add items such as MessageQueues and database connections to your Classes and immediately start to use them without having to declare them and set up their default properties.

Properties View

This view is very similar to the one in version 6, with a few improvements thrown in. Like the Code view, the properties listed can be expanded and collapsed for easier viewing and navigation. This view window now features the ability to group properties in different categories, and each of these categories will have a gray header area. If you do not like to see your properties grouped or are having a hard time finding a property, you can switch to the traditional alphabetically ordered properties list by clicking the A-Z icon at the top of this window.

Many of the form fields feature new properties that you can set in the Properties view, such as the Layout section that enables you to turn on a Dock property for an item and pick a border to dock this control to. When you set the Dock property, you see the control jump over to that border in the Design view window. This property is better used at runtime. You can trigger a control's Dock property at runtime to make your control jump over to a border. If you next set the Dock property to None, that control will return to its original position as defined at design time.

Another great property is the *Anchor* that you can set to help your form fields adjust their position during form resizing. When you pick the Anchor property in the Properties view, you see a small graphical form with a box in the center and four lines connecting it to each of the four sides. By clicking and highlighting these connecting lines, you tell the control to maintain its current distance from the chosen border. Try adding a text box to your form, then select its Anchor property under the Layout Properties group. Next unhighlight the left and top bars in the Anchor settings window and instead pick the bottom and right bars. Now run your form and resize it to a bigger dimension. When you let go of the border, you will see your text box adjust its position. If the control is set to anchor to all four of the borders, resizing the form causes the control to grow and shrink to maintain its distance from all four edges of the form.

You also see this repositioning happen when you are in Design view. The Anchor property is always set for a control, and by default it targets the top and left borders to decide its position. The Anchor is a very nice option that many developers previously either had to code for themselves or buy as a custom ActiveX control to use in their projects. If you have ever created a Windows form that had a resizable border, then you already know the grief of relocating your controls to adapt to the form's new dimensions.

Toolbox

Your old familiar toolbox has some great new features in .NET, too. This is your main source for controls for your Windows forms, your WebForms, and your modeling diagrams. When you are in Designer mode, you will also find Dataset items and components, such as a MessageQueue that you can drag into your project. The toolbox is organized by a set of vertically sliding tabs, to which you can add your own customized tabs with whatever items you prefer on it. Instead of right-clicking and picking Add Component to load a new tool, you instead right-click and select the Customize Toolbox item. In this window, you can add new controls, new shapes for your models, new graphical shapes, and special components such as an ADO data connection. When you are editing a WebForm, you get a different set of controls that are compatible with the WebForms.

How can you place a MessageQueue component on a Windows form? Go ahead and try it! When you drop a component or data item onto your form, it ends up in a separate window below the Designer area. If you flip over to your Code view and expand the Windows Form Designer Generated Code area, you will see that declarations for these items have been automatically added here. Now I will direct your attention to Solution Explorer's References folder, in which you will see a newly added reference to the **System.Messaging** Type. Imagine all of this functionality added to your project with a simple drag and drop.

The toolbox takes on another interesting function when you are looking at your source code. You now see a Clipboard Ring tab in the toolbox window. This contains a rolling log of anything you highlight and copy in your project. Highlight a procedure and press Ctrl+C. Highlight a Type name and copy that. Each time you will see that an item is added to the Clipboard Ring along with some text that gives a short description of its contents. With these items loaded onto the Clipboard, you can now click and drag any of them over into your code, and they will paste themselves in at whatever point your mouse cursor is at when you let go of them. If you are having a hard time telling the difference between different items in your Clipboard Ring, you can right-click them and pick Rename to give them a better description.

The New Tools in Your Toolbox

The toolbox has a few new exciting tools for you to use. In place of the Common Dialog control you have used before, you now find that each Dialog control is separate. One exists for OpenFile, PrintDialog, PrintPreviewControl, and more. A cool NotifyIcon control lets you place an icon in the system's tray at the bottom-right edge of the screen along with the clock. You have seen other applications use this, such as SQL Server's stopped/started icon or the dial-up activity icon. Drop the NotifyIcon on your form and you will see it added to the form's component frame below the design area. Double-click the NotifyIcon item and you can code what happens when someone clicks your system tray icon.

The LinkLabel control should already look familiar to you. This enables you to add a Web-style hyperlink to your Windows form, complete with the blue-colored text and an underline. Just like a Web browser's hyperlink, the LinkLabel control changes colors when activated and appears in a different color after it has been used, all customizable from the Properties window. The link flashes when clicked, giving the user feedback that his or her click was registered. Think of this control as a Button without walls. In the age of the Internet, the LinkLabel control has become a more common form of navigation than the Button.

A very simple control named NumericUpDown can provide a quick and easy number-based control that the user can increase or decrease with the up and down arrows. Just drop this control on your form and declare its upper and lower bounds, and you are all set. You can customize how many decimal points are visible in this tool as well as what the increment value is, such as 1 or .55. It is kind of a simple tool, but one that developers have been creating manually for years and years.

The CheckedListBox is an alternate version of the old classic, the ListBox. Instead of users having to select multiple items in your ListBox by holding down the Ctrl key, they can now put a checkmark next to the items they want selected without touching the keyboard. This is a cool new way to group a long list of checkbox items in one tiny viewing area.

Web Browser

Listed under the View menu you will notice a Web Browser view. You have actually already experienced this view when you explored the Visual Studio Start Page. If you close the Start Page during your session, you can simply select the Web Browser view to get it back. When you have the Web toolbar showing, you can use this browser just as you would any other browser to surf the Internet from within Visual Studio.

Model Explorer and Model Documentation

When you have a UML model associated with your project, you can view all the objects and their attributes via a tree view in Model Explorer. The Model Documentation window is a separate modeling window that displays the textual narratives attached to whatever UML object you select. Model Explorer enables you to select an attribute from one Class and drag it over and into a different Class to duplicate its function in this new Class.

Macro Explorer

Macros have been around for many years and are very popular among the "power" users of Microsoft's Office series. Finally, this automation feature has been made available to developers as well. A macro is a type of script you can execute that automates a function or group of functions for you. Each macro script contains one or more functions. In Macro Explorer, you can double-click a script to edit it, or expand that macro's tree view to see its function list. Double-clicking a function below a macro causes it to execute. Visual Studio includes many macro examples, such as one that turns on and off line numbers in your code editor. Take some time to examine the sample macro scripts, and you might think of some new macros that will save you hours of hard work.

In Exercise 3.5, you create a customized macro that is based on one of the Visual Studio sample macros named CommentRegion.

Exercise 3.5: Creating a New Macro

1. Ensure that your Macro Explorer window is loaded in Visual Studio.

2. In Macro Explorer, expand the tree named MyMacros.

3. Right-click the Module1 item in this list and select New Macro.

4. This opens the Macro Editor, which looks very much like Visual Studio. Your cursor will be in the middle of an already-created subroutine named Macro1.

5. In the Solution Explorer of the Macro Editor, right-click the Module1 entry, and in the Properties window, change its name to "Comments".

6. Change the subroutine name from Macro1 to "FixMeComments" in the code window.

7. Enter the following source code into the subroutine:

```
Sub FixMeComments()
    'This macro is based on the sample macro: CommentRegion
    Dim selection As TextSelection
    selection = dte.ActiveDocument.selection()
    Dim Start As Editpoint
    Start = selection.TopPoint.CreateEditPoint()
    Dim endpt As TextPoint
    endpt = selection.BottomPoint
    Dim undoObj As UndoContext = dte.UndoContext
    undoobj.Open("Comment Region")
    'Loop through the selected area and insert our
    'customized TODO comment at the beginning of each line
    Do While (Start.LessThan(endpt))
        Start.Insert("' FIXME")
        Start.LineDown()
        Start.StartOfLine()
    Loop
    undoobj.Close()
End Sub
```

8. Click the Save icon, and then exit the Macro Editor.

9. Open a Class file in Visual Studio and view its code.

10. Highlight an entire subroutine in the Class.

11. In Macro Explorer, double-click your FixMeComments function located beneath the Comments macro.

12. Note that all lines of highlighted code are now commented out with your customized FIXME tag inserted at the beginning.

If you add a Task List tag named FIXME, these lines of code will now be listed in your Task List to remind you to come back here later to fix the problem and re-enable whatever feature you decided to turn off. Refer to the upcoming section "Task List" for details on how to add a customized task tag.

Object Browser

The new Object Browser opens in the main Design area. Microsoft has improved the Object Browser layout by moving it to a tree-view design that you can expand and collapse to discover objects and their attributes. If you are running a multiproject Solution, you can narrow down the objects listed in the browser by selecting which projects you wish to explore using the Customize button. The Object Browser is another tab along the top of your Designer window so that you can switch over to a piece of code and then jump back to the Object Browser in the same state that you left it. Double-clicking an attribute in the right-hand pane takes you to its associated block of code in your Solution. Figure 3.4 shows the new Object Browser displaying information on the System.Diagnostics.EventLog used in my Server Explorer example earlier.

Document Outline

XML Datasets were created to communicate in hierarchical Datasets. The Document Outline window enables you to view the tags and data in your Datasets in a tree-view style. By clicking an item in the Document Outline window, the corresponding section in Design view is highlighted. This cool tool also works when looking at other tagged files, such as HTML pages, Script files, ASP.NET pages, and XSD Schemas. At the top of this window are two buttons that change the style of the outline between HTML and Script. The Script option is only available with Web pages and Script files to provide a code-level view of your file without all of the surrounding HTML tags. This is also a great place to view all the

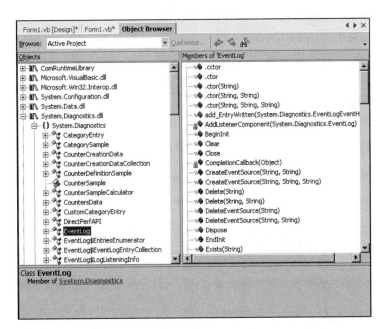

Figure 3.4
The Object Browser displaying information on the System.Diagnostics.EventLog.

events that are associated with a particular Web item to decide which one you want to use. By double-clicking an event in the Document Outline window, you add a section of script to your Web page where you can now create some code for this event.

Task List

Developers have always used comments in their code to form an outline of things to do or to make notes to themselves about issues or problems in that particular section. To later find these notes, they would have to do a search for some key word used to identify them. The Task List view provides a better way to make notes and leave a trail of breadcrumbs so that you can easily find your way back to these points. By simply starting your comment lines with **TODO**, the contents of that comment are added to the Task List view window. You can later view your Task List and double-click any line to jump back to that comment.

Visual Studio also adds lines to the Task List view to draw your attention to empty coding areas, such as Class initializers, or to point out an error in your code. The icon in the second column of the Task List indicates whether this task was added by a comment line or by an error. Often, one error generates many tasks because you have violated more than one rule. If you do not have the Task List open, you can still spot these errors in the code window by the blue squiggly underline in your code. You can hover your mouse pointer over the item to get a ToolTip description of why Visual Studio does not like this item. After you fix the error, the task automatically removes itself from the list. Even if you do not use commenting in your code, this feature can really help you avoid errors before you try to run your project.

Figure 3.5 shows two different tasks listed in the Task List window. The first task was added here by the IDE to warn you that a Type name used in the subroutine was not declared beforehand. Notice the squiggly line (which is blue on screen) underneath the offending

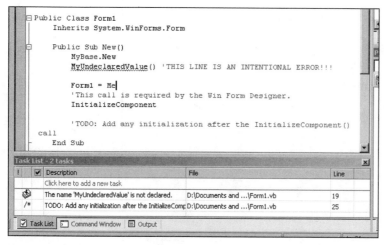

Figure 3.5
The Task List and two examples of taskings.

Type name. The second task was generated when the developer typed a comment line beginning with the **TODO** tag inside of the code.

You do not have to stick with the default **TODO** tag that Visual Studio provides. If you click the Tools menu and select Options, a Task List area enables you to define your own tags and set what their default priority icon will be. Now you can make a tag call **BADBUG** and give it a high priority in your Task List (denoted by an exclamation mark in the icon column). If your entire team has the same set of definitions, this is a great way to quickly communicate code problems or features from one developer to another. The Task List is a terrific tool for team-based development and can even be integrated with Microsoft Project or Outlook with a little custom coding.

Command Window

With so many features, views, menus, and tools, you might wish a simple way existed to just fire off a function without a series of mouse clicks. The Command Window may at first seem like a throwback to the days of terminal-based applications, but this is really a neat shortcut feature. Open the Command Window, type this line in, and press Enter:

```
File.SaveAll
```

This command provides the same function as clicking the Save All icon on the toolbar. That was an oversimplified example, and of course you would rather click the icon on the toolbar than type this command. Did you see the IntelliSense window pop up while you were typing? It's everywhere now, including in the Command Window. This is a great way to explore the realm of possible commands you can use in Command mode and discover other great shortcuts you can create.

Tip

Use the up arrow key to cycle backward through the commands you entered previously. If you want to execute a command that you entered three lines ago, just press the up arrow three times and press Enter.

Let's make the preceding example a little bit more complex. Suppose you want to add a Windows Application project to your current Solution without clicking the mouse. In the Command Window, you could type the following line and press Enter:

```
File.AddNewProject "Visual Basic Projects\Windows Application"
```

Now you have a second project added to your Solution with a Windows form in it. This still seems like a lot of typing to do for something that you could do in just four clicks, doesn't it? To solve this problem, the Command Tool enables you to create aliases for your commands so that you can execute them quickly and with minimal typing. For my last example, I could create an alias like so:

```
alias AddNewProj File.AddNewProject "Visual Basic Projects\Windows Application"
```

Now you can just type your alias name (AddNewProj in my example) in the Command Window and press Enter to execute it. You can also delete an alias in the command tool by typing the following:

```
alias alias_name /delete
```

Your new aliases will persist from one Visual Studio session to the next along with your screen layout information. To make some of your own commands, try typing in a menu name and then typing a period to view all of the available options. After typing a command, you can add one space and a /?. When you press Enter, you will get a description of this command and its available parameters in the Web Browser view.

The Command Window also doubles as the new Immediate window during runtime debugging. While your Solution is in run mode, you can switch between these two modes by entering either "cmd" for Command Window or "immed" for Immediate at the command line. This can be very handy, because you can alias a long command, put the Command Window in cmd mode, and fire off your alias. You learn all about using the new Immediate window in the debugging chapter (Chapter 9).

Output Window

The Output window is what the Visual Studio environment uses to try to communicate important information to you. At the top of the Output window is a drop-down menu box that lets you select different channels of information available, such as the Solution Builder channel for messages stemming from an initiated Build/Run. The Debug channel shows you messages that you have triggered in your code using the **Debug.Write** command (yes, the **Debug.Print** command is now called **Debug.Write**). This is a "must-have" window unless you like to be in the dark about things, such as why your program did not build and run as you told it to do. Other tools also send their output here, such as messages resulting from a request to validate a new stored procedure you created.

The New Menu Editor

The old menu editor just was not cutting it. It was such a hassle to have to break away from the form itself and open a separate window to lay out your menus and adjust their settings. Then you had to go back to the form and click on the menu item to enter some code for it. In Visual Studio.NET, the menu editor has been completely rebuilt to make adding menus to your forms a snap (or in this case, a click).

In the toolbox, you now see an item called Main Menu. Drag this over to your form or double-click the Main Menu icon in the toolbox, and a menu will be added to your form. At the top left of your form, where you would expect to see the File menu, a white box saying Type Here appears. Click this box, type the word "File", and then press Enter, and you see a white box to the right, waiting for you to add a second menu to the top-level menu items, and a white box below the word File, in which you can add menu items subordinate to the File menu. If you click the box below File and enter some text, such as "New", you will have a new menu item. Then, if you click the menu item New, you get a white box to the right that will create a menu item subordinate to the New item. Menu creation could not be any more natural than this. In Figure 3.6, you see a menu being created on a form. New items are easily added to the menu by clicking once on a Type Here box and entering your menu item's label.

Click the word File that you first typed in and look at the Properties window. You see the settings for this menu item that you previously had to open the special menu editor to get at. Instead of putting an ampersand (&) in front of a letter of the menu name to make it a hot key, you instead set this in the Properties window. To enter some code for a menu item's **Click** event, double-click the menu item while in Design mode. Menu items still have the familiar **Checked** property that shows a checkmark next to the item if turned on. If **Checked** is set to **True**, you can also set the **RadioCheck** property to **True** to add a circular dot instead of the traditional checkmark for a saucy new look for your menus.

The Main Menu item has two properties. The first is its **Modifier** property, which specifies whether the menu has a Private, Protected, or Public scope. Each separate menu item can also have its scope set in the same way. The other Main Menu property is called **RightToLeft**. When set to **Yes**, the menu begins on the right side of the form at runtime, and menu items appear right-justified. This menu structure is intended as a form of localization that will feel more natural to Latin-heritage users.

To create a dynamic form that will have a different set of menu items if an action occurs, you can add additional Main Menus to your form. You can add a unique set of menu items to each instance of the Main Menu. If you look at the properties for the parent form itself, you will find a **Menu** property that dictates which menu is currently displayed. At runtime, you can change this value to another menu's name, and the menus will instantly change. You can still dynamically add and remove items from a menu at runtime, but you may find creating an additional menu quicker and less cumbersome.

Menus have the ability to merge with other menus at runtime. Each menu item has two properties called **MergeOrder** and **MergeType** that decide how they sort themselves out. The default for these are **0** and **Add**, respectively. After adding two menus to your form, you could create a method in your code to merge the two menus, like so:

Figure 3.6
Enter menu items in the new menu editor.

```
MainMenu1.MergeMenu(MainMenu2)
```

This code assumes that you stuck with the default names for the menus and that MainMenu1 is showing presently. This code merges all the items in MainMenu2 with the calling menu, MainMenu1. A good use for this feature is when you are creating a Multiple Document Interface (MDI) form. When a child form is opened within the parent, you can call this method to make both the child's and the parent's menu items merge into one all-inclusive menu. The **MergeType** property decides whether the menu item will add itself to the new combined menu, replace an already existing menu item with the same name, or remove itself from the menu altogether. You learn more about this and all the changes made to Windows forms in Chapter 6.

IDE Configuration Options

If you select Tools | Options, you will see a wealth of features that you can set up for each facet of the interface. This is where you can really fine-tune your development experience and customize the behaviors of each area. Literally hundreds of options are available, so I will cover only a few of the most useful under each area.

The Environment section is where you can switch between the new tabbed layout for the coding and design area and the old MDI child windows format. For the Visual Studio startup action, you can define whether you see the new Start Page or the traditional Select A New Project window. You can also define how many of your past projects show up as hyperlinks on the Start Page. Other options here include the option to disable the autocomplete, and the option to enable or disable menu animations, as well as a slider to set the speed at which these animate.

Tip

If you prefer a no-frills environment, you may want to disable the animations for a small performance gain.

The Environment section has a Dynamic Help submenu that enables you to select in which areas this window will provide help. Disabling a topic, such as Training, will help the Dynamic Help window react a little quicker to your selections, by narrowing down the list of things it needs to research and display. You will find the language localization and international settings under the Environment folder for you to customize the IDE for your nationality. As mentioned in the "Task List" section, you can go to the Options page to define custom Task List tags that indicate a comment line should be added to your list. Finally of note is the Web Browser submenu. If you do not want to use the Visual Studio built-in HTML editor, you can define an external one here. You can also change the settings here for the default Start Page and Search Page.

The Source Control menu is important if you work in a team environment that uses source code control software to track your projects. From here, you can choose which source code tracking software your IDE talks to, whether it is the default SourceSafe or a third-party solution. You will also find a text entry block for your login ID that identifies you to the tracking software. This can be handy if you need to interact with the software as the administrator instead of through your operating system login account.

Under the Text Editor submenu, you will see a long list of programming languages. You can set many features here that affect the Code view of your project, such as the aforementioned Word Wrap to make your code more readable. Each language has its own set of options so that you can have Word Wrap enabled in Basic, but have it disabled in T-SQL or elsewhere. You will also find options here to customize the layout and appearance of the tabs at the top of the coding area.

If your project involves working with a database, you will want to visit the Database Tools settings folder, which has boxes for you to set the login and query timeout values and change the default query type for the Query Designer. Under the Database Designer submenu, you can customize the default data type lengths for the database. Both SQL Server and Oracle data types are represented here. For help deciding what some of these options should be set to, consult with your local database administrator.

For advanced debugging and testing options, developers should look to the Debugging menu. For the majority of developers out there, the default settings will work just fine. The HTML and Schema Designer menus simply enable you to set what the default startup view is when you add a new Web or Schema page to your project. If you work with UML models in Visual Studio, you can change the default color and drawing styles for your stereotypes on the Modeler menu. Finally, the Projects menu is for Web developers who are communicating with remote Web sites. You can go here to define how Visual Studio connects with the remote Web server and gives you development access to the pages it is serving. Past users of FrontPage and InterDev will already be familiar with these settings.

Setup Recommendations

Now that you have a general idea of all the tools and features available to you, the time has come to set up your environment with the features you think you will use the most. With all the views and toolbars available, it will be impossible to load everything into the IDE and expect to keep them in good order. The following setup description is my take on the most useful tools that you can use as a baseline to create your own IDE masterpiece. The details of your custom setup largely depend on what role you play in development, whether that be a UML modeler, a Web developer, or a database expert. The setup I prescribe will feel familiar and comfortable for developers upgrading from Visual Studio version 6.

Right-Side Setup

The first two must-have views are the Solution Explorer and Properties windows. I prefer to have these in the traditional location on the right-side border, with Solution Explorer at the top and the Properties window below it. If these two windows are merged and sharing a pane, simply double-click the Properties window on the title bar, drag it to the middle of the screen, and then drag it back to the right, dropping it in the lower-right corner of the screen. To help navigate files that contain more than one Class in them, I have Class Explorer loaded and sharing a pane with Solution Explorer so that I can click the tabs below this pane to select the view I want. I also have the Dynamic Help window sharing a pane with the Properties window. I do not need to see this window at all times, but it is nice to know that context-sensitive help is just one click away.

If your specialty is UML modeling, you certainly want to have Model Explorer loaded, possibly sharing a pane with Solution Explorer in the top-right area. For developers who can appreciate the new macro functions in Visual Studio, they can load Macro Explorer onto one of these panes, as well. For the right-side windows, I prefer to leave them showing most of the time to provide me information and help at a quick glance. The push-pin should be at an angle to lock down these windows and prevent them from sliding out of view when not in use.

Left-Side Setup

I still like to think of the left side as my toolbox, and that is the first thing that should be loaded here. The toolbox can take on many different functions, depending on what you are designing. To this side, I also recommend adding Server Explorer. This window has so many great uses to aid in component design and troubleshooting that I consider it a must-have for all but the most basic projects. Because the toolbox and Server Explorer have so much information to give, they should each be allowed to use the entire left border and not share a split border. I set Server Explorer to slide out of view when not in use, but I often keep the toolbox pinned down for easy access.

Bottom-Edge Setup

This is your main informational area. The controls I place here are largely text-based. The Output Window is a must-have because it provides you feedback from the IDE on errors encountered during development. The Task List is also a great feedback mechanism. Even if you have the horrible habit of not commenting your code, you will still see tasks added here by the IDE to draw your attention to errors in your code. As you start to write code in the next chapter, you will quickly see that much has changed in Visual Basic, and the Task List will help you out by highlighting code that does not conform to the .NET standards.

If you are writing actual code, you should pin down the Task List to see these error messages appear as you type. In Design mode, you will want to hide this window to give you more room to manipulate the form. The Output Window can be retracted during normal coding and then displayed during project testing. If you feel comfortable with the Command Window and like this feature, you should add it to the lower area as well, in a hidden state alongside the Output Window.

Toolbars

Toolbars offer a great many detailed features for your development, and what you display on your toolbars greatly depends on your development specialty. For everyone, I recommend loading the Standard toolbar with the familiar Open and Save buttons, along with both the Debug toolbar for running and testing your project and the Full Screen toolbar to quickly enlarge the Designer area for better viewing. The Full Screen toolbar is really just one button that can fit to the right of the Standard toolbar. Sliding it left or right or dragging it up and down can change the location of a toolbar. You should keep the Standard toolbar in the top-left slot because this is where every program puts the Open and Save buttons.

Database coders may want to load the Database Diagram and the Query toolbars to help them manipulate tables and create data queries within Visual Studio. The UML modelers in the audience will prefer the Modeler toolbar, to manipulate their stereotypes and create new objects in their models. The UI designers have the most toolbars to choose from that offer them numerous formatting and layout adjustments. The combinations are endless, and so are the different development scenarios you might encounter. Pick the ones you find the most useful on a day-to-day basis and load the others as needed. You can see an example of my recommended Visual Studio.NET IDE layout scheme in Figure 3.7.

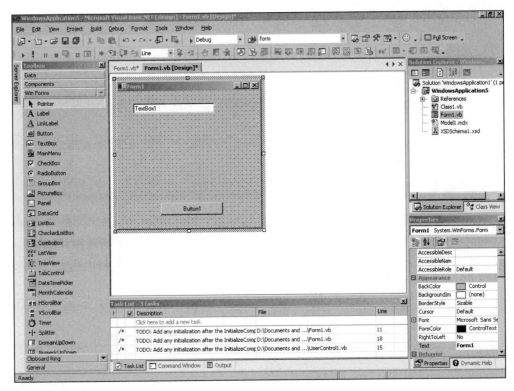

Figure 3.7
Recommended IDE layout for Visual Basic developers.

Summary

Now that you have your Visual Studio environment fully customized, save any files you have open and exit the environment using File | Exit. When you start Visual Studio again, your customized layout will return for you to use. Saving this current state is a good idea, because changes you make to your environment will be lost in cases of computer lockup or application crashes.

You should now feel comfortable moving about in the .NET interface and should have a good understanding of all the tools available to you in your tool chest. I bet that you are itching to dive into the deep end and start examining all the changes to the Visual Basic language, so turn the page and take that leap!

Chapter 4

Visual Basic.NET Language Enhancements

V isual Basic.NET (also known as Visual Basic 7) is without a doubt the most radical change ever made to this popular programming language. Looking back to when Visual Basic 4 was released, you can see that the general population of developers was slow to accept the strange new concept of object-oriented programming. Visual Basic was always about making development easy and simple, and having to think of your code as an object was a big leap. As a result, developers stuck with version 3 for some time as they learned the new concepts and language changes. Even after adopting Visual Basic 6, many developers still shunned the object-oriented concepts introduced way back in version 4. For this group, .NET will seem like the end of their world because these object-oriented concepts are so unavoidable.

Why Has So Much Changed?

At the risk of sending you into an all-out panic, Visual Basic.NET makes the transition period between version 3 and 4 look easy— but you likely already realized that this is going to be a long road. Why did Microsoft choose to rearrange and restructure your beloved Visual Basic so much? Looking back over the history of Visual Basic (you did read that part in Chapter 1, didn't you?), you will see that while it started out as a simple learning language and adopted many of the coding features of other languages at that time, the language eventually took on a life of its own and set out along a different path. Every language starts with a lot of similarities to other languages that are popular at the time, and later grows to become something unique. But now you have the .NET Framework, and the funniest thing has happened to all of these unique and different languages—they are converging! The Tower of Babel is coming down around us. As the languages have evolved, the commonalities between them have shrunk. When a C++ module talked about a **Long** data type, a Visual Basic module couldn't understand it because the data type **Long** meant something else in the Basic lexicon.

The short answer to the question of *why* is interoperability. The only way to make languages truly interoperable is to base them all on one common standard, which (as you learned earlier) is called the Common Language Standard (CLS). Change can be painful, and the sad truth is that Visual Basic has bore the brunt of these changes in .NET. That's understandable if you look at the big picture of what it took to plan a common standard for all of these languages. Would you have used the specifications of the lowest-level language or the most powerful language in the bunch? Many parts of Visual Basic were getting outdated and out of sync with development. Developers could still use **GoSub**s in their code and the **Integer** was based on an outdated 16-bit operating system. Someone had to change their ways, and Visual Basic was the language that could benefit the most from the CLS changes.

My advice to you is to take your time and don't skip any parts of this chapter, because many small details may surprise you later on. What may feel weird and unwieldy at first will eventually come naturally. You may get really tired of seeing blue squiggly lines. Whenever you type some code that does not match the new programming specifications, that piece of code will have a blue line under it. Hover your mouse over the problem text to find out what did not compute. Unlike version 6, .NET will not stop you when you make a mistake on a line. When you press Enter at the end of a line containing an error, you will be able to continue to type while .NET underlines the error and adds a task to the Task List for later reference. When you first start using .NET, you will see these blue underlines everywhere, but over time, the dreaded squiggles will become extinct and you will then be a .NET guru. You will look up from your monitor with a silly grin on your face and say, "Why didn't they do this sooner!"

Working with Data Types

The simplest place to start this grand expedition is with the old familiar data types. Writing a program without using a variable in it somewhere is almost impossible. Alas, some pretty hefty changes have been made in this area that you need to become familiar with quickly. When a fellow developer talks about using a *type*, this is .NET-speak for data types or objects. A piece of data could be of a **Type String** or an object could be of a **Type Customer**, derived from a Class named **Customer**. The Common Language Runtime supports four major types: the Class, an Interface (such as a form), a Structure, and an Enumeration.

Primitive Data Type Changes

I'll start this tour with the dearly departed Visual Basic data types: **Variant** and **Currency**. You may or may not have used **Currency** to hold your dollar amounts, but most of you have used **Variant** at one time or another in your code. These data types offered the developer a lot of flexibility when working with primitive data types. A **Variant** was capable of holding **Null** values that the **String** data type could not deal with. **Variant**s were also resource hogs, an unpleasant side effect of their flexibility. To replace **Currency**, you should now use the **Decimal** data type, which is capable of handing even more digits than the old **Currency** type.

> **Note**
> *R.I.P.: The **Variant** and **Currency** data types have cashed out.*

In place of a **Variant**, you now use the **Object** data type. The **Object** has become a very flexible data type that can handle all sorts of data to include primitive values. When the brain says you need a **Variant**, be sure that your hands type "Object" into your code until using it becomes natural. An **Object** can hold ordinary **String** data, or it can be set to equal **Nothing**. The **Nothing** value indicates a variable has no value. Previously, you had to check whether a variable was **Empty**, **Null**, or set to **Nothing**, depending on the data type you were dealing with. Now, you simply check for a **Nothing** value or use **Nothing** to clear a variable's value. Because **Empty** is no longer needed, the **IsEmpty** keyword you used to use in your **If** statements has also been laid to rest.

> **Note**
> *R.I.P.: **Null**, **Empty**, and the **IsEmpty** keyword have vanished into nothingness.*

A few of your data types have taken on new identities in .NET, namely **Long**, **Integer**, and **Short**. These three data types are still available for use, but their bit sizes have changed and you will want to use them in different circumstances than you had in the past. **Long** has reappeared as a beefy 64-bit data type, **Integer** has stepped up to the 32-bit job, and now you have **Short** playing the role of your 16-bit data type.

New in .NET is the **Char** data type. This type can store one single Unicode character. Both the **Char** and **String** data types are based upon the Unicode international standard that stores each single character in two positions. By storing the data in Unicode, you allow your data to be localized into different languages without having to use complicated translation software to do it. A Unicode-encoded **String** in English could be easily displayed in the Russian language because the characters can now be directly mapped to a different language's fonts. The **Char** data type has a small memory footprint and is best suited for one-letter variables such as flags and initials. Table 4.1 lists the new data types, their memory usage, and their data sizes in .NET.

A Boolean is a true or a false value in your application. Every language in Visual Studio.NET equates a Boolean's value of **True** to the numeric value of 1. If you are familiar with binary numbers this will make sense. Binary is made up of 1s or 0s; the bit is on or off. Off is equal to 0, and on is equal to 1. To keep Visual Basic.NET consistent with past versions of Visual Basic, Microsoft kept the value of **True** equal to –1. When you pass a Boolean **True** from a

Table 4.1   New data types.

Data Type	Data Size	System Name	Memory Used
Char	16-bits	System.Char	2 bytes
Short	16-bits	System.Int16	2 bytes
Integer	32-bits	System.Int32	4 bytes
Long	64-bits	System.Int64	8 bytes

Visual Basic module to one written in another language, the –1 will be translated automatically to a 1 for cross-language compatibility. To avoid all the confusion as to what the value of **True** is equal to, I highly recommend you stop using the –1 value and simply use the constant **True** in your code. That way if the value of **True** changes in the future, your code will continue to work.

Fixed-length **String**s are also out of the picture. You used to be able to fix the length of a **String** like so:

```
Dim CustomerAddress as String * 50    'This is no longer supported!
```

For cross-language compatibility, **String**s will always have unbound lengths up to two billion characters.

The **Date** data type now plays a larger role in your development. Previously, you could assign a date value to the **Double** data type. This no longer works in .NET and results in a type mismatch error. If the value you are working with is a date, store it in a **Date** data type. **Double** is still available in .NET, but does not support dates anymore. While the **Date** data type is as important as ever, the **Date** and **Time** functions are now gone. You now use the **Today** keyword to get the current date, and the **TimeOfDay** keyword to get the current time.

Note

R.I.P.: The **Date** *and* **Time** *functions are no more.*

VB6 Data Type Converters

Because the **Option Strict** watchdog does not allow you to mix and match your variable types anymore, you need to utilize the conversion functions in Visual Basic if you need to compare or combine unlike data types. Suppose you declare a variable to be an **Integer** containing the age of a customer. You may want to include this **Integer** value in a message stored in a **String** variable. Here is an example:

```
Dim MyAge as Integer = 31
Dim Message as String
Message = "Dave's age is " & CStr(MyAge)
```

Table 4.2 **Available converters and their outputs.**

Converter	Converts To	Converter	Converts To
CStr	String	CDec	Decimal
CBool	Boolean	CInt	Integer
CByte	Byte	CLng	Long
CChar	Char	CObj	Object
CDate	Date	CShort	Short
CDbl	Double	CSng	Single

This **CStr** function converts whatever data type that it is working with to a **String** and allows you to combine it with another **String** data type. Table 4.2 lists available converters and their outputs.

Arrays

How Visual Basic.NET handles arrays differs greatly from how the other languages in Visual Studio.NET handle them. Take a look at the following example:

```
Dim Counter (50) as Integer
```

In Visual Basic.NET, this array would have an upper bounds of 50 and would include 51 elements ranging from position 0 to 50. This has always caused some confusion among VB developers, since many expect that declaring an array to 50 would give it 50 elements. In the other Visual Studio.NET languages, your **Counter** array would indeed have only 50 elements, ranging from 0 to 49. The Visual Basic.NET arrays were allowed to be different to help VB developers migrate to .NET and minimize the changes they have to endure. You should keep the differences in array definitions in mind when you are working in a cross-language environment, because an array in C# will not exactly match up an array declared the same way in Visual Basic. One array issue that has change in .NET is the **Redim** statement. You no longer can declare an array using the **Redim** statement. Before you can use the **Redim** statement to change the bounds of an array in your code, you must first have declared that array with a **Dim** in your code.

Like the arrays, everything is now zero-based in .NET. You can no longer declare the code's base to be 1 or 0 by using the **Option Base** statement. The base is always 0.

Note

*R.I.P. The **Option Base** statement is longer applicable.*

Option Strict

Why did all of these version 6 quirks work before, but not now? Up until now, Visual Basic was very forgiving with data type conversions. If you wanted to put a date in a **Double**, Visual Basic made it fit. If you wanted to add a value of an **Integer** to the end of a **String** variable, it was no problem. The result of all this variable mismatching was a lot of confusing code. One minute a variable is a number, and the next it is some text. Often, this led to an error in your code, such as when a numeric value got converted to a **String** and then you tried to perform a mathematical operation on it. Whoops! This will not continue in .NET, because Visual Basic now enforces very strict Type safety. That **Integer** will no longer work with your **String**, and the result will be a type mismatch error.

You now have **Option Strict** to thank (or blame) for all of this safety. Before .NET, you could add the statement **Option Explicit** to the top of your code to enforce explicit declaring of variables within the code. **Option Explicit** is now automatically in effect without you having to type it at the top of your code, and its partner, **Option Strict**, is enabled by default as well. In your .NET code, you have to explicitly declare all data types before you use them, and you cannot mix your types. This will take a little more thought than was required for older versions, but the end result will be more reliable code that is also easier to trace and read. **Option Strict** is turned on by default, but you can turn it off by typing the following at the very beginning of each source code file:

```
OPTION STRICT OFF
```

This feature also applies to the **Option Explicit** command if you do not want to have to declare all of your variables before using them. If **Option Strict** is set to **Off**, you can declare a variable without using the **As** statement to set its data type. This results in that data type becoming an **Object**. This ultimately results in less efficient code, and you will not get the same IntelliSense feedback on your data type as you would if you were to explicitly declare what type of variable it is. Keeping these two features enabled is the smartest route to take. A little more effort now will mean a lot less hassle at runtime.

Declaring Variables

Even the way you declare your variables is a little different in .NET. Now that you are declaring all of your variables, you need to know how to declare them properly. Here is an example of something you could do in Visual Basic 6 that was basically broke but now works in .NET:

```
Dim FirstName, LastName as String
```

In version 6, **LastName** would be a **String** data type and **FirstName** would have become a **Variant**. In .NET, both of these would now be a **String** data type. Even with this improvement, the very best choice for variable declarations is to place each one on a line of its own. This will greatly improve your code's readability and neatness. The key to code readability is proper format (i.e., tab spacing) and clear declaration of variables. Readable code not only makes you look smarter to your peers, but it also makes troubleshooting and maintaining your code so much easier down the road. Imagine trying to fix a class with a bug in it that was completely flushed against the left border, used X and Y for variables, and never declared what data types they were. Readability is your friend!

Joining the dearly departed is the entire family of **Def**-type declarations. This includes **DefInt**, **DefBool, DefDbl,** and **DefDate**. These statements allowed you to define a group of variables in one statement. You can no longer use a **Def**-type declaration statement in .NET; you must explicitly declare each single variable.

Variable Scope

The scope of a variable defines what parts of your code can see that variable. Visual Basic.NET introduces one new level of scope for your variables, named **Protected**. Because you can now derive multiple Classes from a base Class through inheritance, you need this extra level of scope. The introduction of the **Protected** scope now boosts and supports the familiar **Private** scope. **Private** variables are only available to procedures within the same module as the declared variable, whether that module is a Class or a WebForm. **Protected** variables have an "original-class-only" scope, and are not for use by Classes that are derived from this original base Class. If you are not familiar with using derived Classes, this will sound odd right now, but in just a few pages, it will make a lot more sense. Table 4.3 illustrates the available levels of variable scope.

You will notice that the **Friend** scope has also been promoted. Because an Assembly can have a broader definition than just the one set of project files you declare a variable in, those declared with the keyword **Friend** will be available to any module that is packaged in the same Assembly. This means your **Friends** can be used beyond their current Project. Any Assemblies or COM components that reference the containing Assembly and do not belong to it will not be able to see this variable. You can also combine the **Protected** and **Friend** scope on one declaration, like so:

```
Protected Friend FirstName as String
```

The **Dim** declaration can still be used at the top of your code in place of the **Private** declaration, but this is strongly discouraged. This is one of the few backward-compatibility features that Visual Basic.NET has kept, but the proper syntax is to use the **Private** keyword in the General Declarations area and use the **Dim** only inside a procedure.

Table 4.3   Available levels of variable scope.

Variable Scope	Who Can See This Variable
Dim	Procedure level: value will reset upon next **Dim** execution
Static	Procedure level: set value will persist through the next execution
Protected	Class level: only the original or "base" Class can use this
Private	Module level: all procedures in the same module can access it
Public	Project level: all modules in the same project can use it
Friend	Assembly level: all modules in the same Assembly can use it

Structures

A User Defined Type (UDT) is a way to combine a set of data types under one parent to form a customized data type that has properties. This is a very powerful feature that advanced developers have used a lot, and can continue to use in .NET with a few minor changes. Previously, your Visual Basic 6 UDT would look like this:

```
Public Type Customer      'This is an outdated VB6 UDT!
    FirstName as String
    LastName as String
    Items as Integer
End Type
```

The first change in .NET is that UDTs are now referred to as *Structures*, one of the four major managed types. .NET no longer supports the **Type** keyword for declaring a Structure. A Structure is normally declared in the General Declarations area at the top of a module. Your **Customer** UDT should now look like this:

```
Public Structure Customer     '.NET UDT declaration
    Public FirstName as String
    Public LastName as String
    Private Items as Integer
End Structure
```

Note that not only is the Structure as a whole given a scope (**Public**, in my example), but also the contained items will each have their own scope as well. You may omit the scope keyword on the Structure itself, making it default to **Public**. Members within a Structure can take on any data type, including arrays and objects. A member of your Structure can also be of another Structure's type. Structures look and act a lot like Classes do. Two features of the Class that you cannot take advantage of in a Structure are inheritance and Initializers, both of which are covered shortly. You can access the data in your Structure in your code like so:

```
Customer.FirstName = "George"
If Customer.Items > 0 then GenerateInvoice = True
```

You can also pass a Structure as a parameter of a procedure. This is a terrific way to serialize your data and send it to a procedure. If your Structure contains a huge amount of data, you may want to avoid passing the entire Structure and opt to pass only the values needed by the procedure. A procedure can also return a Structure as its output parameter. Here is an example of a **Sub** and a **Function** that both use the Customer Structure:

```
Sub CreateInvoice(ByRef NewCustomer As Customer)
    InvoiceName = NewCustomer.FirstName & " " & NewCustomer.LastName
End Sub
```

```
Function LookupCustomer(ByRef CustomerID as Integer) As Customer
    LookupCustomer.FirstName = "Bill"
    LookupCustomer.LastName = "James"
End Function
```

Structures are a very powerful method for passing groupings of data around your modules. If you intend to make the data accessible as an interface to your Assembly, you should use the **Property Get** and **Set** methods to control read and write access to these values and not a Structure. The **Property** approach also allows you to validate data before assigning it to the object, which you cannot do to a member of a Structure. If a **Public** member of a Structure named **PhoneNumber** is declared as a **String**, any valid string can be assigned to it. If you created a **Customer** Class with a **Property** named **PhoneNumber**, you would be able to validate any new values in the **Set** statement and control the changes any calling procedures might try to do to your **Property**. With Structures, you are at the caller's mercy. For this reason, I recommend you keep the Structures **Private** or **Protected** in scope.

Initializers

You now have the ability to both declare a data type and set its initial value all in one line of code. Previously, this took two lines of code, one to **Dim** or declare the variable, and another to give it a value. This made it possible to hold off declaring a variable's initial value until it was first called in a procedure, making the code harder to follow. The old way often resulted in errors in cases of a variable being called out of order before a value was assigned to it. In .NET, an initialized variable could look like this:

```
Public ManagersName As String = "Jack Peters"
```

On the very first use of **ManagersName**, this variable will already have a value. A pleasant side effect to this new feature is that it greatly improves your code's readability. When someone looks at the declaration statement, they will also be able to see what the starting value of the variable is. Initializing your variables is optional in .NET, but should be used if the initial value is known at the time of declaration.

Exploring the Namespace

When you were introduced to .NET in Chapter 1, you briefly read about something called the Namespace. For the majority of Visual Basic developers this will be a whole new concept, but one that is relatively easy to pick up. You should be used to using Classes to define your objects, such as an **Employee** Class or an **Inventory** Class. Your objects will be made up of properties and methods that expose what the Class knows and the functions it can perform. In version 6, if you wanted to group multiple classes together that had related functionality, you would do so in either a single Visual Basic Project file or by adding multiple DLLs to a MTS/COM+ Package.

Creating Your First Namespace

In .NET, you can now gather all of your related Classes under a Namespace. Here is a very basic example of a Namespace that you might see in a Class named class1.vb:

```
Namespace Warehouse
    Public Class Employees
        'properties and methods for the Employees class
    End Class
    Public Class Inventory
        'properties and methods for the Inventory class
    End Class
End Namespace
```

This is a cool feature! In one single source code file, I now have two Classes with an explicit relationship in that they both belong to the **Warehouse** Namespace. Previously, if you had multiple Class files in a Project, you would reference the Project as the parent, and then reference the Class as the child object. In the new Namespace world, your single Project can have many Namespaces to further organize your Classes. Directly under this Namespace, in the very same file, you could see this:

```
Namespace Front_Office
    Public Class Reports
        'properties and methods for the Reports class
    End Class
End Namespace
```

You should now be able to see how one source code file can hold many classes, and how you can also group these classes in an intelligent and meaningful way. You are probably so excited about this that you are just itching to create your own Namespace, but here is one more cool thing you should know about before you go nuts on the Namespaces: The boundaries of a declared Namespace do not stop at the edge of your source code file. You could add a second source code file named class2.vb to your Project and enter this:

```
Namespace Warehouse
    Public Class Machinery
        'properties and methods for the Machinery class
    End Class
End Namespace
```

Two separate files in one Project make reference to the **Warehouse** Namespace. In the overall **Warehouse** Namespace domain, you would now have three Classes (**Employees**, **Inventory**, and **Machinery**). If you define a Class within the same Namespace and within the same Project that tries to use a Class name already defined, then you will get an error and the Project will not compile.

The System Namespace

In .NET, one Namespace rules over all the other Namespaces in the realm: the almighty System. From the **System** Namespace, is derived any other object you could use, from the Windows forms you drop your controls on, to the data types you store your data in. Previously, a **String** was just a **String**, but now its full name is **System.String**. This does not mean you have to do a ton of extra typing in your code, because the **System** surname is assumed in many cases. The two lines in the following example both accomplish the same declaration:

```
Dim MyCounter as System.Integer
Dim MyCounter as Integer
```

A Namespace can also have a sub-Namespace subordinate to it. This is how the System Namespace organizes everything under its control. No matter what Namespace you are using, if you could follow it backward through the hierarchy of Namespaces, you would finally reach the System at the top. Here is an example of a new Namespace within my **Warehouse** Namespace:

```
Namespace Warehouse

    Public Class Employees
        'code for the Employees class
    End Class

    Namespace Crates

        Public Class CrateContents
            'code for the CreateContents class
        End Class

    End Namespace

End Namespace
```

A Namespace allows you to have two Classes in one Assembly with the same name, provided that they are both in different Namespaces. If you were to add a **FrontOffice** Namespace to the project, you could create an **Employees** Class under it that will not conflict with the **Employees** Class under the **Warehouse** Namespace.

As you add Namespaces within Namespaces, the fully qualified path to your components becomes longer and longer. If the project containing the preceding Namespaces were called **WidgetKing**, then the full Namespace path to the properties of one of their crates would be **WidgetKing.Warehouse.Crates.CrateContents** followed by whatever property of that Class you wanted to use. As you can imagine, typing the full path of every Namespace just to get at one property can be a chore, but there is a shortcut.

Imports Statement

Building on the Warehouse example, suppose that you add a Windows form to the WidgetKing Project and that you wish to display crate information on it. Typing that long Namespace path every time you reference the Class would be unthinkable. The correct way to add this path to the pool of knowledge that your Windows form has is to use the **Imports** command. To make the **Crates** Namespace easily accessible, you would add the following line to the very top of your Windows form source file:

```
Imports WidgetKing.Warehouse.Crates
```

This line of code needs to precede any of your Classes or Namespaces in the source code file. After this declaration, you will be able to directly reference the **CrateContents** Class in your form's code. Namespaces always have a **Public** scope, meaning that everyone can see them. You can still create Classes within your Namespace with a **Private** or **Friend** scope that limit who can see these individual Classes. If you do not specify **Public**, **Friend**, or **Private** before a procedure in a Namespace, it will take on the **Friend** scope. The Assembly that contains your Namespace will be the parent Namespace that users of your components will reference. In the preceding **Imports** statement, WidgetKing is the Assembly, and **Warehouse** is a Namespace within it.

The **Imports** statement also allows you to set up an alias for a long Namespace path that you can later use in your code. The following line of code placed at the top of your file sets up a shortcut to the Windows Registry settings:

```
Imports RegSettings = Microsoft.Win32.Registry
```

With this alias in place, you can then write code to easily make a new Registry subkey entry, like so:

```
RegSettings.CurrentUser.CreateSubKey("MyNewKey")
```

With an alias in the **Imports** statement, you type the alias name to get to the subcomponents. If you create the **Imports** statement without the alias name, you will directly access the subcomponents in your code. Here is the preceding example without an alias declared:

```
Imports Microsoft.Win32.Registry
    'next line appears later in a subroutine
    CurrentUser.CreateSubKey("MyNewKey")
```

Imports will quickly become a very familiar statement in .NET. When you add a new file to your project, many of the needed **Imports** will already be there, such as a Windows form's reference to the **System.Windows.Forms** Type.

Regions

The new enhanced IDE does a great job of identifying different parts of your code and allowing you to expand and collapse these parts. Subroutines, Classes, and Namespaces can all be collapsed to minimize the code in your viewing area and to help you locate the section you wish to change. You do not have to do anything special to get this feature; the IDE will do it for you. But if you have a special area or group of procedures that you wish to group together, you can create a **Region** in your code that the IDE will treat as one collapsible segment. If your **Region** contains other Classes, they will be individually collapsible by Class, or you can close the entire **Region** in one click. Here is an example of a **Region** containing two Classes:

```
#Region "My Special Code"
    Public Class Customer()
        'code for my first class
    End Class
    Public Class Inventory()
        'code for my second class
    End Class
#End Region
```

You would be able to collapse both of the Classes in this example, and you would also be able to collapse the entire **Region** and all of the contained items. **Region**s are merely a way to section off your code within the IDE, and they have no meaning at runtime. If you wish to group a bunch of like Classes under a common heading, you should consider using a Namespace to do this.

Procedure-Level Changes

Many procedure-level changes have been made that you need to learn about. This is one area that will cause even the most experienced of developers to reach for a reference book. Coding is all about attention to detail, and many of the details of creating procedures have changed dramatically. This is a key area for you to learn to truly become a .NET developer. These changes are also the primary reason that your old code will not work in .NET without a Migration Wizard and a lot of reworking.

Logic Flow Changes

I want to start with two minor changes before jumping into the deep end. Here is a change that I hope does not cause anyone a heartache: You can no longer use **GoSub** or **On-GoTo** to call a subroutine in your code or to redirect the flow of your code. These coding relics date back to the days of QuickBasic and have no role in the modern object-oriented development arena. Goodbye and good riddance.

*R.I.P.: The **GoSub** and **On-GoTo** redirectors have gone away.*

The second change is that the **WEND** statement with which you used to end a **While** loop is now an **End While** statement. This should be easy to remember, because everything else terminates with an **End** statement, such as **End Sub** and **End If**.

*R.I.P.: **WEND** has met its end.*

Get and Set

If you have ever created an object in your code, then you surely are familiar with the **Get**, **Set**, and **Let** properties. Until I learned about .NET, I never thought about these procedures as being redundant, but now I do. Here is a Visual Basic 6 code example that exposes a **FirstName** property that can be read and changed by the client:

```
Public Property Get FirstName() As String
    FirstName = "Steve"
End Property

Public Property Set FirstName(NewValue as String)
    myfirstname = NewValue
End Property
```

It took two **Public** procedures to give a client code both read and write access to your property. The **Set** procedure lets the user change this property, and the **Get** procedure lets the user read it. If only the **Get** procedure were provided, this property would be read-only. If the property were an object and not a primitive data type, you would use the **Let** procedure in place of the **Set** procedure to give it a value. However, the **Let** property procedure is no longer used.

*R.I.P.: The **Let** statement is gone—let it rest in peace!*

These property procedures are ingrained in every object-oriented VB developer's daily routine, and getting used to the new way of coding will be tough. Here is the **FirstName** property example in .NET format:

```
Public Property FirstName() As String
    Get
        FirstName = "Steve"
    End Get
```

```
     Set
         myfirstname = FirstName
     End Set
End Property
```

One property now has one procedure, simple and straightforward. Previously, the **Get** and **Set** procedures could have been placed in different locations in the Class, making it really hard for someone not familiar with that Class to understand it. You declare the property as a **String**, and this covers not only the output of the property but also the variable that this property will take in to change its setting in the **Set** section, preventing a mismatched input and output of a property. This new method is also semi-intelligent in that it knows by the **As** declaration on the first line what data type you are using and does not need to be told to use a **Let** or use a **Set**. You simply use **Set**, and the code does the rest.

If your property is going to be read-only, you would omit the **Set** statement, like so:

```
Public ReadOnly Property CustomerID() As String
     Get
         CustomerID = "VITO01123"
     End Get
End Property
```

Note the **ReadOnly** keyword on the declaration line. When you type "ReadOnly," the IDE reminds you that you only need a **Get** statement. Similar to the preceding example, if your property is going to be write-only and will not be readable by the caller, then you substitute **WriteOnly** for the **ReadOnly** keyword and use a **Set** statement in place of **Get**.

ByRef and ByVal

Your subroutines and functions can declare input parameters that they need to perform their calculations. A parameter can be passed to a procedure either as **ByRef** or **ByVal**. Confusion often occurs over the **ByRef** and **ByVal** keywords and their proper usage, so let me clear this up once and for all.

You pass a parameter by its value (**ByVal**) if you do not wish to change that value within the procedure. If your form has a value named **GrossIncome** and you want to call a Class to perform a calculation on the **GrossIncome** value but not change it, you should pass it as **ByVal**. The **ByVal** keyword ensures that only a copy of your data is sent to the procedure, and not the original. The enlisted procedure can modify the copy of data it receives, but your calling module will not see the changes.

Passing a value by reference (**ByRef**) means that you are opening your data to possible changes to it within the called procedure. Using **ByRef** would be the correct choice in situations where you wish to allow the called procedure to permanently change the value of the variable you are passing in. This would avoid having to make the **ItemizedDeductions** procedure a function that would return a new data value that you would then have to add or subtract from the **TotalTaxDue**. Returning data as function output would result in a slight loss of performance due to the data having to be marshaled from the function back to the calling procedure. The following example is a subroutine with two parameters specified. The first parameter is permanently changeable by the subroutine's code, while the second can be changed within the procedure, but this change will not be reflected in the calling procedures data type.

```
Sub ItemizedDeductions(ByRef TotalTaxDue As Integer, ByVal NumberDependants As_
    Integer)
```

Some of the confusion over **ByVal** and **ByRef** centers on which one is more efficient for passing data back and forth. The surprising answer is: both! Neither **ByVal** nor **ByRef** will pass the full value of the data type to the procedure. What they do pass is a pointer to where that data type is stored in memory. The difference between the two is that **ByVal** first makes a copy of the data in a new memory location and passes a pointer to that new copy over to the procedure. All pointers are 4 bits per parameter, no matter what the data type. It could be a tiny **Integer** data type or a gigantic **Object** Type; either way, the resources used will be the same. With this worry out of the way, you need only concern yourself with whether or not you want the called procedure to be able to change the underlying data value. If you wish to protect the original data value, pass it as **ByVal**; if you want to change the parameter, pass it as **ByRef**.

Tip

*Do not worry about efficiency when deciding between **ByVal** and **ByRef**. Simply decide what kind of protection your data value needs! There is a very slight performance hit when using **ByRef** due to the fact that the processor is making a copy of your data, but unless you are making many repeated calls to a function, this loss is minimal.*

Now that I have set the record straight on that subject, it's time to find out what has changed about **ByVal** and **ByRef** in .NET. A lot of Visual Basic 6 code does not even bother to declare **ByVal** or **ByRef** in the parameters area. No set default keyword existed in these cases; the parameter's protection depended on the data type that was being passed. This led to a lot of uncertainty and confusion when values changed or didn't. In .NET, the default is **ByVal**, offering your data automatic protection from any unexpected changes. If you omit the **ByVal** or **ByRef** keywords, .NET inserts **ByVal** when you press enter at the end of the line, making it clear to everyone what the protection level is. If you wish to allow a data value to be changed in the procedure, you have to explicitly state that the value is passed **ByRef** on the declaration line.

One twist to be aware of concerns properties. All parameters passed into a **Property** procedure must be passed as **ByVal**. When you pass a value to a **Property**, you are telling the procedure, "Here is your new value. Set the property to this and be done with it." **Property** procedures should not perform any operations or changes on passed-in parameters, which is why .NET requires that they be passed as **ByVal** only.

Optional Parameters

Parameters declared for a procedure can include the **Optional** keyword in front of the parameter name, which indicates that the caller does not have to pass that value to your procedure. Just as in version 6, your **Optional** parameters must be declared last, and all parameters declared after an **Optional** parameter must also be **Optional**. In version 6, you could check whether or not an **Optional** parameter was passed in by using the **IsMissing** keyword. This is no longer available in .NET.

Note

*R.I.P.: The **IsMissing** keyword is now missing from .NET.*

Because you cannot check whether a parameter **IsMissing** anymore, you are now required to give all **Optional** parameters a default value for the procedure to use if the caller omits a value. Here is an example of a procedure with an **Optional** parameter:

```
Sub SaveReservation(ByVal CustomerName as String, Optional ByVal Country As_
    String = "Belgium")
```

In this example, the **CustomerName** parameter is required, but not the **Country** parameter, which defaults to the value **Belgium** if the calling procedure does not pass a value in its place.

Default Members

Visual Basic 6 allows you to declare one method as the default method for a particular Class. You can also access a default property of an object implicitly simply by entering the object's name and setting it equal to some value. The Command button has a default method of **Click**, and the Textbox's default property is **Text**. In version 6, you can set the text value without naming that property, like this:

```
Textbox1 = "My text"     'VB6 default property usage
```

.NET does not support the concept of default methods and properties. All references to methods or properties must now be made explicitly with their full names. Here is how the preceding setting would be made in .NET:

```
Textbox1.Text = "My text"
```

This is a very minor change, and if you are not in the habit of using default properties and methods, this should not bother you at all. Once again, your code will be more readable in .NET. In the preceding version 6 example, it might be unclear what property of **Textbox1** is taking on this string value, but it is plainly understandable in the .NET example.

Shared Members

The concept of shared members is completely new to Visual Basic, and is also long overdue. Shared members are variables, properties, or methods declared in a Class that are shared with all instances of that Class. In programming languages that had the shared members feature before .NET, these are called static or Class members. If your project has an **Employees** Class, you could give it a shared property named **EmployeesOnline** that gets incremented whenever the **Sub New** runs during initialization. You would also want to subtract one employee from the counter in either the **Destruct** or **Dispose** method. This is what the **Employees** Class might look like:

```
Public Class Employees
    Public Shared EmpCount As Integer

    Public Shared ReadOnly Property EmployeesOnline() As Integer
        Get
            EmployeesOnline = EmpCount
        End Get
    End Property

    Sub New()
        EmpCount = EmpCount + 1
    End Sub

    Sub Dispose()
        EmpCount = EmpCount - 1
    End Sub
End Class
```

An interesting side effect of shared members is that you can reference their values in your code without instancing the Class. You could add a form to your project with a **CommandButton** on it and add this code to its **Click** event:

```
Msgbox(Employees.EmployeesOnline)
```

Without ever declaring the **Employees** Class, you will be able to pop up a message box with the current value of **EmployeesOnline**. Every time someone creates an instance of this Class, the count will go up one. If this Class is on a server and used by employees all over the building, they will all be able to access this shared member and see the same value. In past

Visual Basic versions, you had to create an external storage dump to keep track of global values that you wanted to share in a multiuser project, but now you can simply declare a member as **Shared**. Keep in mind that this entails a bit more controlling code, just as the **Employees** Class had to increment and decrement the count in its **New** and **Dispose** methods. Shared members can be used to share information between users of a system or to track statistics, such as how many users are online or which methods are currently being called.

Overloading

Some definitions of what a true object-oriented programming language is say that the language has to be able to *overload* its members. This is not to be confused with overriding, which is associated with inheritance. Overloading enables you to create multiple procedures that all have the exact same name but that implement different functionality. The result of overloading your procedures is increased flexibility for your objects by giving one interface more than one possible function. The best way to get a grasp on the overloading concept is to look at an example. Here are three **SearchReservations** methods from one single Class:

```
Overloads Function SearchReservations(ByVal Name As String) As String
    'search the database for a Customer Name
End Function

Overloads Function SearchReservations(ByVal CustID As Integer) As String
    'search the database for a CustID
End Function

Overloads Function SearchReservations(ByVal ReserveDate As Date) As String
    'search for the date a reservation was made
End Function
```

Look closely at the parameters passed to these three methods. One is an **Integer**, another is a **String**, and the third is a **Date**. Without showing you any of the underlying code, you can see that these three methods differ on the surface only by their parameters. The caller will see only one **SearchReservations** method. The caller will have the ability to pass in either a **Date**, a **String**, or an **Integer** to this one interface, and the runtime will know which method to run by the type of parameter supplied to it. In past versions, you may have implemented three different methods, such as **SearchName, SearchReserveDate,** or **SearchCustID**. You may have used **Optional** parameters or used a **Variant** and tried to figure out the caller's intention through complicated coding. Now you can create multiple copies of the same procedure and code each one differently based on the passed-in parameter. When you are looking at someone else's code and you see the **Overloads** keyword before a procedure, you need to be aware that more than one version of this procedure exists and the version you are looking at may not be the one that you want to examine.

Throwing Exceptions

The entire concept of error handling has changed in .NET so that all languages now use the same framework for raising and handling errors. The first change I want you to adjust to is to start calling your errors *exceptions*. When you think of your code, you think of all the possibilities and situations you could encounter and try to write code to handle these scenarios. If something happens in your code that you did not plan for, it is known as an exception.

While you can still use the unstructured exception handling method using **On Error GoTo**, you should now use the more powerful structured exception handling method that uses **Try**, **Catch**, and **Finally**. This is a big departure from the **On Error** concept, and I am devoting an entire chapter (Chapter 7) to handling exceptions, and another chapter (Chapter 9) to debugging your applications in .NET. To raise an exception in your code to be passed back up the call stack, you will use the **Throw** statement in the same way that you are used to using the **Err.Raise** statement.

The New Component Life Cycle

.NET presents a whole new way to create code to initialize and destroy your object classes and forms. No more using the **Initialize** and **Terminate** events, because these are no longer recognized events. You need to learn an entirely new component life cycle, and change the way you create and destroy your objects.

> **Note**
> R.I.P.: The **Load**, **Unload**, **Initialize**, and **Terminate** events have been terminated.

Sub New

The new method for initializing your components is the **Sub New** event. This is where you will put your code that is run when a caller first creates an instance of your component. Because forms now take on the structure of a Class, you will no longer use the **Form Load** and **Unload** events and will instead start using the **New** and **Destruct** events. When the instance of your component is destroyed, you can create some cleanup code in the **Sub Destruct** event. In version 6, a caller could explicitly execute your **Initialize** and **Terminate** code without creating your object. With **Sub New**, your startup code can only be run when your Class is created. Placing code in the **Sub New** event is commonly referred to as creating a constructor in .NET. It is here that you will be able to assign default values and construct your object before it is used by a calling procedure. Here is a form with a constructor:

```
Public Class Form1
    Inherits System.Windows.Forms.Form

    Sub New()
        MyBase.New
```

```
        Text1.Text = "Form1 New Event Fired"
        Debug.Write("Form1 instance created")
        'set initial properties and construct the object here
    End Sub

End Class
```

In this example, you see some code behind a standard Windows form. The first line inherits all the **Windows.Form** features from the **System.Windows.Forms** Type. The **Sub New** section is run when an instance of **Form1** is created, writing its message to the Output window of Visual Studio when the form is first created and setting the value of **Text1.Text**. All **Sub New** events should have **MyBase.New** as their first line. The **MyBase** keyword is a shortcut name for the parent Class of your component. Calling **MyBase.New** ensures that the **New** event for the parent or "base" Class is run before the initializing code for the instanced Class. This is critical when you are inheriting Classes, because this command ensures that your inherited Classes are initialized before your current Class is. Even if the Class you are creating is the base Class for your project, it is still ultimately derived from the **System.Object** Type in .NET and should make a call to **MyBase.New**.

A parameterized constructor enables you to create an instance of an object and pass it some default values all on one line of code. The instanced Class will take in the parameter you pass during the **New** event and use it to initialize itself. Here is a constructor for a **DeluxeRoom** Class that uses an initializing parameter to set up a property of its Class:

```
Sub New(ByVal RoomID as Integer)
    MyBase.New
    CurrentRoomID = RoomID
End Sub

Public ReadOnly Property RoomNumber() As Integer
    Get
        RoomNumber = CurrentRoomID
    End Get
End Property
```

The calling procedure could call this Class and immediately check the value of **RoomNumber**, like so:

```
MyRoom = New DeluxeRoom(105)
Msgbox(MyRoom.RoomNumber)
```

This code would open a message box with the number 105 in it, the initialized value of the **RoomNumber** property based on the parameter that was passed into the **GenericRoom** Class upon instancing it.

Sub Destruct

The **Destruct** code will not be run immediately when the user is done with your component, because of a new feature called the Garbage Collector. This is the new resource manager in .NET that determines all by itself when the proper time is to unload an instance of an object. This means that you cannot control when the **Sub Destruct** event fires, and you should not count on the **Destruct** event to clean up your object's resources in a timely manner. I will go into more depth on how Garbage Collection works, under "The Garbage Collector" later in this chapter, so that you understand why your object is not being cleaned up immediately. The operations performed by the **Sub Destruct** code are referred to as a component destructor in .NET. Both the **Sub New** and **Sub Destruct** events can be placed anywhere in your component in any order.

Finalized and Disposed

While the Common Language Runtime (CLR) and the Garbage Collector handle the disposal and destruction of your components, you can create code to handle the cleanup of the resources that your component enlists. For example, your component may create a database connection that you wish to keep open during the object's lifetime. You should add the line **MyBase.Dispose** to your object's **Dispose** event if your component references other components during its lifetime. This will trigger their **Dispose** events before finishing your objects **Dispose** event, ensuring that objects you referenced also have the chance to clean up their enlisted resources. **MyBase.Dispose** should be the last line of your **Dispose** event. The **Dispose** event gives the users of your object a means to trigger a cleanup in their code when they are finished using your object. Because you do not have control over when your object will be destroyed by the Garbage Collector, you should not close the database connection in the object's **Destruct** event. When the caller determines that he no longer needs your object, he should call the **Dispose** event, like so:

```
YourClassname.Dispose()
```

This runs your object's cleanup code and frees up any resources the object created. It will not destroy the object. References to objects will no longer need to be set to equal **Nothing** to destroy an instance. The Garbage Collector will handle the final destruction at an undetermined time in the future. Your **Dispose** event will be declared with the **Public** scope so that calling components can access it.

You should also create cleanup code in your object's **Finalize** event. The Garbage Collector will call this code when it determines that all references to your object have been closed and that the system needs to free up some resources by destroying your object. You should consider the **Finalize** event the backup means of cleaning up enlisted resources and the **Dispose** event as the primary means. The **Finalize** event has a **Protected** scope and cannot be directly triggered by users of your component. Users of your objects should trigger the **Dispose** event, but in case they don't, you need to back them up by doing a complete cleanup in the **Finalize** event. Like the **Dispose** event, you should include a reference to the base Class's **Finalize** event as the last line of your **Finalize** code.

Some overhead is associated with using the **Finalize** event, and it should be used only for critical resource cleanup and not as a place to print debug messages or change variable values. As you will learn in the section "The Garbage Collector" later in this chapter, objects with **Finalize** events take longer to be destroyed than those without **Finalize** events. Any objects that your object holds a reference to will also hang around the system a little longer while your **Finalize** event is being processed.

Class Instancing

Here is a change that should make life easier for you. Previously, you had a confusing list of options for declaring the **Instancing** property of your Class. You had **Private**, **SingleUse**, **MultiUse**, **PublicNotCreatable**, and **GlobalMultiUse**. This property was associated with the Class file that you added to your project. Classes in .NET do not have an **Instancing** property.

Note

*R.I.P.: Class Instancing properties (**MultiUse**, **SingleUse**, **GlobalMultiUse**, and **PublicNotCreatable**) no longer exist.*

The access scope that you declare for your Class determines who can use your class. Classes can be **Public**, **Private**, or **Friend**. The old **Private** instance can be accomplished by setting your Class's access scope to **Private**. To create a Class that is **PublicNotCreatable**, you would declare the Class as **Public** but set the constructor to **Friend**, preventing components outside of your project from creating a new instance of this Class. Any other Classes can be declared as **Public** and their individual properties and methods scoped accordingly.

Inheritance

Without a doubt, the most exciting new feature of Visual Basic.NET is the addition of inheritance to the language's tool chest. In the eyes of some snobbish developers, prior versions of Visual Basic could not be considered a "true" object-oriented development platform due to its lack of inheritance. The textbook definition of an object-oriented language includes three major features: polymorphism, encapsulation, and inheritance.

An example of *polymorphism* is two different objects that present the same interfaces to the user, such as a **Shipment** and an **Invoice** object both containing an **AddItem** method. To the caller, the function of this method might appear to be the same, even though the underlying code is different. This is a familiar concept to most developers and was already available in Visual Basic before now.

Encapsulation is the ability of an object to hide the underlying code, presenting the user with only a set of interfaces. An object contains many properties and methods that are encapsulated inside of this one object. The code required to add a new item to the customer's invoice is encapsulated in the **Invoice.AddItem** interface presented to the user. Like polymorphism, this too was previously available in Visual Basic. The last piece of this puzzle, inheritance, comes in two forms: interface inheritance and code-based inheritance.

Interface Inheritance

Interface inheritance is also available in Visual Basic 6 in the form of the **Implements** statement. You can create an empty interface Class that lists all the methods and properties contained in the object without any code associated with them. Another Class could declare an **Implements** of that interface Class at the beginning of its code, and it would then inherit all of those empty properties and methods. Before you could use this new Class, you would have to add empty procedures for each property and method from the interface Class to the implementing Class. Creating an interface Class is like creating a template that could be used for other Classes that would share its makeup but might contain different code executions. The calling Class inherited all the interfaces defined in the interface Class. This is a very weak form of inheritance, because you do not gain any code or functionality from the implemented Class, only its outline. This level of inheritance is insufficient to meet the full definition of a proper object-oriented development tool.

Interface inheritance is still available in .NET, though the way you define your interface has changed. Instead of creating a separate Class, you create an area in your code outside of any Classes or procedures by using the **Interface** keyword. Here is an example of a defined interface:

```
Interface IGenericRoom
    Property NumberBeds() As Integer
    Sub ReserveRoom()
End Interface
```

Later on in your code, you could create a Class that implements this basic interface, which would look like this:

```
Public Class DeluxeRoom
    Implements IGenericRoom
    Property NumberBeds() As Integer Implements IGenericRoom.NumberBeds
        Get
        End Get
        Set
        End Set
    End Property
    Sub ReserveRoom() Implements IGenericRoom.ReserveRoom
    End Sub
End Class
```

Every property and method in the interface must be represented in the implementing Class, whether you write code for it or not. The capital *I* at the front of **IGenericRoom** is a notation format that marks this item as an interface. Notice that both the property and subroutine in the implementing Class make an explicit reference to the matching **Property** or **Sub** in the interface. This explicit reference is because you can name the properties and methods in the implementing Class something different from the name in the **Interface** definition, and the **Implements** statement on the **Property** or **Sub** line will point back to the original interface names. I could have called the implemented **ReserveRoom** method **ReserveGuestRoom** if I wanted to. You can also implement more than one **Interface** with one **Implements** command, separating the interfaces with commas. Again, all the properties and subroutines from all the implemented interfaces need to be represented in your Class. Interface inheritance is sometimes called a "has a" relationship. My **DeluxeRoom** example "has a" **NumberBeds** property just like the **Interface** template. Now I'll show you how the new code-based inheritance differs from what you used before .NET.

Code-Based Inheritance

True code-based inheritance is the big star of Visual Basic.NET. You now can create Classes that are "derived" from other Classes and implement their functionality. This form of inheritance is known as *implementation inheritance*. I know that sounds confusing, because you just learned to use the **Implements** keyword in the preceding section. For implementation inheritance, you use the **Inherits** keyword to reference another Class. This is a new feature for Visual Basic developers that the Visual C++ crowd is already familiar with.

The Class that you inherit from is known as a *superclass*, and any Classes that implement a superclass are known as *subclasses*. The superclass represents a common set of features and functionality that different subclasses can implement and add to. The relationship between a subclass and a superclass can be called an "is a" relationship. For the Oceanside Resort project, you can develop a superclass named **GenericRoom** and implement it in a **DeluxeRoom** and a **BargainRoom** Class. The relationship could be stated as follows: The **DeluxeRoom** is a **GenericRoom** with added features. Figure 4.1 illustrates the superclass and subclass relationships.

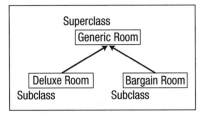

Figure 4.1
A superclass and its associated subclasses.

In Visual Basic.NET, you can implement only one superclass in your derived Class, meaning only one **Inherits** statement is allowed per Class. If the superclass has a pubic property named **RoomNumber** and a public subroutine named **ReserveRoom**, both of these will be available in the **DeluxeRoom** Class, complete with all of their code. You will not even have to type a procedure stub in your derived Class to use this functionality; it will be available automatically. Here is an example of the **GenericRoom** superclass:

```
Public Class GenericRoom
    Private IRoom As Integer
    Private Status as String
    Public Property RoomNumber() As Integer
        Get
            RoomNumber = IRoom
        End Get
        Set
            IRoom = RoomNumber
        End Set
    End Property
    Public Function GetRoomStatus() As String
        If RoomIsReserved = True then
            GetRoomStatus = "Reserved"
        Else
            GetRoomStatus = "available"
        End if
    End Function
    Sub ReserveRoom
        RoomStatus = "Reserved"
    End Sub
End Class
```

The **DeluxeRoom** subclass can inherit all of the **GenericRoom**'s features like this:

```
Public Class DeluxeRoom
    Inherits GenericRoom
End Class
```

If you instanced the **DeluxeRoom** Class, you would see that it contains a **RoomNumber** property and a **ReserveRoom** method, even though the **DeluxeRoom** Class does not contain this code itself. When you run the **DeluxeRoom.ReserveRoom** method, the runtime will jump through the **DeluxeRoom** Class to the **GenericRoom** Class to implement its functionality. You can add additional properties and methods to the **DeluxeRoom** Class as long as they do not match any found in the **GenericClass**, adding to the derived Class's interfaces. Your **DeluxeRoom** Class could have a **HotTubCapacity** property that is all its own and not available within the superclass.

Protected Access

Superclasses also can have properties and methods that belong only to themselves. These are known as **Protected** members. By declaring your property or method with the **Protected** scope (in place of **Public** or **Private**), you are saying that this member is not available to classes that are derived from this superclass. Variables declared in a superclass can also have a **Protected** access scope. You will see **Protected** members when you are creating a Windows form and you add code for a **CommandButton Click** event. This code is **Protected** and only available to this form, because this code is highly specialized and would not apply to a derived version of this form. A **Click** event could look like this:

```
Protected Sub Button1_Click(ByVal sender As Object, ByVal e As_
    System.EventArgs)
    Msgbox(DeluxeRoom.RoomStatus)
End Sub
```

Another Windows form derived from this form will not have access to the original's **Button1_Click** event and will have to create its own event for this action. This brings up another cool use of inheritance: form-based inheritance. Because forms are now classes in .NET, you can create a form with whatever common fields and layout you desire, and then derive other forms from this base form. You will see an example of this in Chapter 6.

Overrides

What if a superclass method or property does not do exactly what you want it to do? Are you stuck with it? Of course not! Derived classes have the ability to override their superclass's functions to make the implementation more customized. Before you can do this, the superclass must declare these members as either **Overridable** or **MustOverride**; otherwise, you cannot override this member. In my **GenericRoom** example, you can add the keyword **Overridable** to the **RoomStatus** function like this:

```
Public Overridable Function GetRoomStatus() As String
```

Now my **BargainRoom** Class can implement its own custom code in place of the default **RoomStatus** code. Your new property could look like this in the **BargainRoom** Class:

```
Overrides Function GetRoomStatus() As String
    GetRoomstatus = "First Come, First Served"
End Function
```

When you do a **GetRoomStatus** on the **BargainRoom**, you will always get back the preceding message instead of the calculated **Reserved** or **Available** status. Superclass members that are declared **MustOverride** must have a matching **Overrides** member in the derived subclass before you can run your code. This enables you to have some localized code for the superclass, and the very same member will be available in the subclass but it will have to implement its own code for this function. Creating new or **Overrides** members in a subclass is referred to as "extending" the functionality of the superclass.

The Garbage Collector

The name of this new .NET feature reminds me of an old saying my high school computer sciences teacher once told me: "Garbage in, garbage out." Her point was that I should spend more time planning my code and less time winging it in the lab. Almost two decades later, no matter how well I plan my code and design my objects, they will still be considered garbage by the .NET Framework.

Introductions

Okay, maybe this isn't as bad as it sounds. By now, I'm sure you have some idea as to what the Garbage Collector does in .NET. This is the cleanup crew that examines the piles of unwanted and unreferenced objects that your code has left behind, and destroys them to clear up memory space for more objects. The Garbage Collector is often referred to as the GC, and can be found under the **System.GC** Type.

The direct benefit of the Garbage Collector for you, the developer, is that you no longer have to worry about destroying your objects when they are finished. In the old COM world, this task sometimes became a huge headache for developers. If your code destroyed an object too early and some errant code came along trying to reference the object—boom! On the opposite end of the spectrum, forgetful developers sometimes failed to destroy their objects, leaving them in memory to hog much-needed resources. The third "really bad thing" that sometimes popped up was the dread "circular reference." This is when one object holds a reference to a second object, which in turn holds a separate reference to the first object. You can't destroy either object for fear of breaking an operation in the remaining object. It took a lot of planning and sometimes extra coding to destroy your objects correctly. The infamous memory leak problem was a result of undestroyed objects piling up and hogging all the system resources until your computer slowly ground to a halt. Ah, the good old days!

Those days are gone, and the Garbage Collector is here to save you all of this trouble. You do not have to give any thought at all about the proper time to destroy an object. You are not even allowed to destroy objects in .NET. No more will you set your object equal to **Nothing** in your code. Memory leaks will not happen when the Garbage Collector is on duty. This is a huge weight off your shoulders, but it does come with one small price. With the Garbage Collector handling the job, you have no say as to when your objects are destroyed. In fact, in all likelihood, they will remain in memory for some time after you are done using them.

As discussed earlier in the section "Finalized and Disposed," Class deconstructors will require a new way of thinking about cleaning up after yourself. The references that your object makes to resources, such as file systems and databases, will need to be cleaned up somehow. To refresh your memory, you will use the **Dispose** event to give the caller a means of triggering this cleanup, and use the **Finalize** event to give the Garbage Collector a means to clean up in case the caller forgot to call your **Dispose** event. And as I told you before, if you do not use a critical resource, leave the **Finalize** event alone. Now I will tell you why.

How the Garbage Collector Works

The CLR has a resource pool called the Memory Heap available to it that it uses to assign blocks of memory to your instanced objects. When an object is created by the CLR, it is added to the top of a stack of other created objects. This stack is in order from oldest objects on the bottom to the newest objects on top. The stack is divided into generations, from the oldest generation (numbered Generation 0) up to whatever the highest allowable generation number is, as defined by the read-only property of **System.GC.MaxGeneration**.

The Garbage Collector runs at certain intervals and whenever it senses that memory needs to be cleared up for more objects. The Garbage Collector examines each object starting at Generation 0. It looks for open references to any items in the object, and it looks to see if the object is currently being used in an active call stack. If the object is completely unreferenced, then the Garbage Collector marks it for destruction. In the COM world, the runtime kept a count of references made to an object, using valuable system resources to continually watch this object. The Garbage Collector sits back and waits for when it's needed and then gives each object in the generation an examination to determine what's needed and what's not.

If an object marked for destruction has a **Finalize** event defined, then it is marked as **IsFinalizing**. The difference is that objects marked for destruction are thrown out at the end of the Garbage Collection, whereas objects that need to **Finalize** themselves do so and remain in memory until the next collection cycle. Any objects that a **Finalizing** object references also stick it out with this object a little while longer. This is why I caution you to use a **Finalize** event only if you have to. But if your object uses resources, such as database connections, the **Finalize** event will be unavoidable and the extra time in memory is a fair tradeoff for properly cleaning up these connections.

Controlling the Garbage Collector

The Garbage Collector is fully automated and will do its job without any intervention from the code. With that said, there is a way you can trigger the Garbage Collector to go through a cycle on a certain generation. If you want to force a cleanup of objects in Generation 0, you can do so like this:

```
System.GC.Collect(0)
```

This is not a recommended action for most projects. For the majority of objects, allowing the Garbage Collector to examine and determine the proper time of destruction will always be the best bet. You can use the **System.GC.GetGeneration** method to determine which generation your object currently belongs to. Only in the most extreme circumstances would you want to go through this trouble. If your object is still referenced, the Garbage Collector will leave it be no matter how many times you tell it to go look.

Threading

Visual Basic.NET has an entirely new threading model called free threading that is everything you have ever hoped for. Finally, you will be able to spawn functions off onto their own threads so that they will operate independently of your application's thread. A good example of a program using threads is the Internet Explorer browser. When you click a file and start a download, you can minimize that download window and continue to surf the Internet in the browser window, because the download has its own thread. If the download window were launched in the thread of the browser, you would be unable to control the browser until the download operation is complete. Another great use of free threading is for operations that you want to be able to pause or cancel. If you have a form that allows a user to search the file system for a file name, you will want to give them a Cancel Search button in case they change their mind and do not want to wait for this long operation to finish.

Tasks on different threads act independently of each other. A long pause on one thread does not affect the operations in the other. If you are writing a server-based component, you can use threads to spread out the workload as the number of users increases on your system. And as you saw in the Internet Explorer example, threads can give the users more control over the application and avoid unnecessary idle time. Take a look at an example of a form that spawns off a long-running process onto a new thread. First, you could create the Class that contains this long drawn-out process:

```
Public Class InfiniteLoop
    Public Sub RunLoop()
        Dim q As Integer = 1
        While q < 5
            'This loop will never end!
        End While
    End Sub
End Class
```

When you execute the **RunLoop** method, it will run indefinitely. If you are not using threading, then your calling form will be locked up and the only way to kill it will be to use the Windows Task Manager. Here is a **CommandButton Click** event that starts this infinite loop on its own thread. The first two lines that would be in the General Declarations are at the top of the form's Class:

```
Private MyLoop As New InfiniteLoop()
Private MyThread As System.Threading.Thread

Protected Sub Button1_Click(ByVal sender As Object, ByVal e As_
    System.EventArgs)
    MyThread = New System.Threading.Thread(AddressOf MyLoop.RunLoop)
    MyThread.start()
End Sub
```

When this button is clicked, the **RunLoop** method will start on its own independent thread, allowing the user to continue to interact with the calling form. You could add a second button to this form with the label "Cancel" and add this code to it to cancel the **InfiniteLoop's** thread:

```
MyThread.Stop()
```

The thread has many other helpful properties and methods, such as an **IsAlive** property that tells you if this thread is still active, and a **Sleep** and **Resume** method, so you can both pause the thread's execution and restart it. This new feature offers a lot of great possibilities, and I am sure you have already thought of a dozen of them.

Summary

At this point, you probably feel a little overwhelmed with all the changes. You might now understand why some developers have called Visual Basic.NET an entirely new language and not version 7, as Microsoft has labeled it. If you read through all the details in the text and tried all the coding examples, you should feel a little more at ease using Visual Basic in the .NET environment. You have plenty more to learn about in .NET, and have yet to discover many other cool features that I know you're going to love. Now that you have the hang of the changes to the Visual Basic language, I'll take some time to talk about how you can best implement these features in your projects.

Chapter 5

Visual Basic Best Practices

In the software industry, you hear a lot of talk about *Best Practices*. I'm sure this term is widely used in many other industries, as well. Managers and team leaders love to talk about Best Practices, especially around the customers. The meaning of the term is fairly obvious: A Best Practice is something that is considered a good idea or the ideal way of doing something. Typical Best Practices are the direct result of years of experience and learning. Often they are discovered only after doing things the wrong way for a long period of time. Like the term itself, a Best Practice is usually something obvious that may make you think "Doesn't everybody know that?" The surprising answer to that question is: No, they don't.

Why Do You Need Best Practices?

Programming offers the most flexibility of almost any profession I can think of. The customer doesn't know if you used all of the object-oriented principals in your development project; they just know that the result works—or doesn't. A customer will never say "Jim, you did a great job commenting your code, and boy is it readable!" Behind the scenes you have a lot of flexibility as to how you create your software, and every programmer has their own unique style and methods. Just as there are many ways to paint a sunset, there are just as many ways to create a requested piece of software. In contrast, a surgeon or an architect would follow a more stringent set of steps when working on a task, because they do not have the luxury of the trial-and-error approach that programmers often employ. While I have never had the opportunity to attempt one, I'm fairly certain there are very few ways to perform a successful triple heart bypass.

What Is a Best Practice?

Everyone has heard of a few Best Practices before, but often this term is only mentioned in conferences, books, and sales pitches. The two most talked about areas in software development are Process and Best Practices. But when you visit the developer dungeons where the real work is being done, you may see very little evidence of either one of these in the day-to-day operations. By nature, software development work is solitary and intellectually intensive. Strong developers have the ability to focus and see a solution in terms of data types and structures. Programmers do their best work alone and have intellects on par with those of doctors and architects. So, if all the developers in this world are so smart, and there are an infinite number of ways you could code a solution, why would you need a list of Best Practices?

Remember that customer I was talking about? Well, it needs that solution in four weeks. And, oh yeah, the delivered product must be easily maintainable. Did I mention that the customer wants the application to scale too? If you didn't have customers to answer to, you could code this project any way you want and take as long as you want to write it. It wouldn't matter if the final solution were a mess under the hood, because no one would have to maintain it. And so what if it was delivered in one EXE file, because no one asked for it to be scalable.

The truth is, everyone has a customer, and customers have some pretty big needs. Blame it on the last generation of development projects, but these customers are a lot smarter than their predecessors. Not as smart as you (wink), of course, but they've learned a few things from some of the god-awful projects that have been unleashed onto the world. This is the reality of your project, and in an age where the complexity of the solutions is increasing and the time frame to accomplish these feats is decreasing, you need an edge to get the job done. Maybe even a prayer, but that book is in another aisle.

By not only paying lip service to Best Practices but also implementing them in your projects and daily coding chores, you are ensuring that you are on the best path possible to meeting these demanding requirements. Taking a few extra seconds to do something right may make you think that those seconds can add up and make the project take longer to accomplish, but the sad result of a job done too quickly is that it will be overrun with bugs and five times as hard to troubleshoot than the carefully coded project. Using Best Practices directly translates into a less buggy product and, surprisingly, a faster time to market than the sloppy method. If being on time and bug-free is not enough to impress the customer, your projects will also be easier to scale and maintain if you follow industry-recognized Best Practices.

Here is a list of key areas where your project will excel if you implement Best Practices on a daily basis:

♦ Maintainability

♦ Scalability

♦ Fewer defects (in other words, bugs)

♦ Shortened development cycles

Best Practices stem from experience, like the old wise man on the mountain who's "been there, done that." Youngsters might scoff at his recommendations ("Ha, commenting code is such a waste of my time!"), but in time they will learn the painful truths behind his wisdom and wish they had sat and listened longer to his tales. This chapter is about Best Practices that apply to the Visual Basic developer sitting in front of the monitor churning out code. Some of these practices are general programming practices, while others are specifically tailored to the new Visual Basic .NET language you are learning about. You can put these to good use each and every day in your project. Encourage your fellow developers to form good habits, as well, and you will be the wise man on your mountain.

Enforcing Standards

Everyone has their own ideas as to what a good practice is, and no two people strive to meet the exact same standards in their work without outside influence. To ensure that everyone on your team understands the standards that you expect their code to meet, you need to publish these standards in a public place, such as in a directory on the project share drive or on a development team Web site. Another good idea is to publicly review these standards with the team to clarify any misunderstandings and to get the team's buy-in to these ideas. Developers might react negatively if you tell them "these are the rules, follow them," but if you present the rules as guidelines or as a list of "highly recommended" practices, you will find that your developers are more willing to adapt to the standards.

An excellent way to follow up your guidelines and further encourage developers to follow them is to have peer code reviews. When a module is complete, a fellow developer should review all the code and note any areas that do not meet the guidelines. You can make this a required part of your project-development cycle, and, over time, the developers' bad habits should die off and be replaced by good habits.

Readability

When you mention the term *readability*, many developers groan and roll their eyes. Does a neat layout affect how efficient your code runs? Of course not, but code that is readable and neat can affect all four areas previously mentioned under "What Is a Best Practice?" Writing code that is easy to follow and well documented greatly improves its maintainability. Rarely is the developer who wrote the original module the person who has to maintain it after it has been deployed. You may find yourself having to fix some of your own code that you haven't seen for some time. By making your code readable, you could be saving yourself hours of work in the not-so-distant future.

Producing neat code requires a little extra thought and planning that could directly result in less bugs during the first test cycle. Testers will often pour over your code to spot inconsistencies or errors, and making their job easier will help the project along. Fewer bugs plus easier testing cycles equals faster development times. Let's look at some key areas where you can maximize your code's readability.

Code Layout

The first thing you notice when you open a source code file is the layout. If everything you see is flush against the left margin, your brain will not be able to quickly determine how the code flows or which areas are separate from the others. When you see a neat and organized piece of source code, you immediately assume you are viewing the work of a professional. If you work on a team of developers, it is almost a given that other developers will look at the coding you've done. By making your code as organized as possible, you set the standard for everyone to aspire to as well as position yourself as the "guru" of the team.

The Visual Studio .NET IDE goes a long way to help you make your code look neat by detecting what you are typing and indenting and color-coding it. The collapsible blocks of code also make organization a breeze in .NET. You should use at least one return between procedures to help a reader easily detect where one procedure ends and another begins. Carriage returns in your code are a great neatness feature, and do not affect your code's size or efficiency at runtime. Although the .NET IDE handles the indenting for you, you still need to use the proper vertical spacing (carriage returns) to make your code presentable.

Use the Namespace feature of .NET to organize your Classes into groups of related Classes within your assembly. Because a single file can now contain many Classes, a reader will not use the Solution Explorer as much as they did before to navigate your project. The compiler may not have a hard time finding its way around, but humans need organization to help them find things. If you had to locate the **Invoice** Class, would you look in file class1.vb, class2.vb, or class3.vb? But if the project had a **Shipping** Namespace, this would immediately seem like a good place to locate the Class you want to change. The order of procedures in your source code can also lend itself to readability. By putting the most frequently used procedures or Classes at the top of a source code file, reviewers will have to spend less time looking for them.

In past versions of Visual Basic, it was common practice to break up really long lines of code by using an underscore (_) at the end to signify a line break. This was a good idea and it really helped out the code's readability. In .NET, this is no longer necessary, because you can set your Code view window to word-wrap just like a word processor. The full line of code is always visible and still appears as one line to the compiler. If you are in the habit of using the underscore, you should drop this when developing in .NET and let the IDE do all the hard work.

Data Type Naming Conventions

I remember when I first learned how to program and used variables such as x and y or a and b in my programs. I would be typing along and suddenly have a hard time remembering if this value should be x or y. Modern code should read almost like a book, and the meaning of each variable should be clear to both the developer and an onlooker. With publicly scoped variables, the original declaration statement might not be readily available to help you figure out that value's meaning. This is why proper naming of your procedures and variables is the second most important area of readability after proper layout.

Short, nondescriptive names should be avoided. Long names are not a problem for the IDE, though I caution you against using names that are too long, because you are the one who has to type it over and over. I once had a boss who wanted all the office computers named something descriptive so that users on the network would know by a machine's name where it was located and what its purpose was. Unfortunately, he went overboard with this idea and we ended up with machines named *AdminPentiumInManagersOffice* and such. Likewise, a Class named **CalculatesTotalTaxesAfterDeductions** may be very descriptive, but it is also ridiculously long.

So, what constitutes a good variable name? Names should have two parts: the first part tells the reader what type of variable it is, and the second part tells what it does. If you have a **String** data type that will hold the customer's first name, a great name for this is **strFirstName**. Notice the *str* at the beginning, letting everyone know this is a **String** data type. This helps a lot in .NET, where mixing and matching your data types will not be as easy as it was before. For data types, the first one to three characters of the name denote the type and are in all lowercase letters. The rest of the name should have capital letters at the beginning of each word in place of the traditional space, to help readers see the different words.

Using commonly used abbreviations is also acceptable as long as everyone understands them. These naming rules are by far the most commonly used in the industry and are called the *Hungarian naming conventions*. I prefer the three-letter prefixes because they give you a better description of the data type than a one-letter prefix. It can be confusing having a **CCustomer** Class in the project and a **cMiddleName** for a **Char** data type. Table 5.1 lists commonly used abbreviations to place at the beginning of your data types' names.

When you read each of the preceding examples, you can immediately determine what data type is being used and what the contained value represents in the code. In .NET, you know that when you have an **intNumDependants**, you need to do a conversion to combine it with your **strLastName** to say "The Smith family has three children." Notations vary from one organization to another, and that's fine as long as everyone within that organization agrees to use the same notations in their code.

Table 5.1   Commonly used abbreviations.

Data Type	Abbreviation	Example
String	str	strLastName
Char	ch	chMiddleInitial
Short	sht	shtNumDeductions
Integer	int	intNumVisits
Long	lng	lngTaxesDue
Double	dbl	dlbGrossIncome
Date	dat	datBirthDate
Single	sng	sngGrossPay
Decimal	dec	decAvergeGrade
Object	obj	objCustomer

Class Naming Conventions

Variables are not the only thing that should be properly named. Your Classes and their members should also have descriptive names given to them to indicate their function. Naming Classes is usually easy, because these represent your objects and will have obvious names like **Customer** or **Inventory**. Properties also have obvious names that are discovered during the object's design session, such as you learned in Chapter 2. You should pay particular attention to how you name your methods and procedures. These typically have action names starting with a verb. An example would be **CalculateTaxDue**. Again, the first letter of each word is capitalized. The name should describe what this method does. Simply naming my last example **Calculate** would not be sufficient explanation of what this procedure does. What does it calculate and why? Properly named procedures enhance code reuse, because other developers see that a **CalculateTaxDue** routine already is available and that they do not have to write their own.

Commenting

Most developers do place some comments in their code, but often not enough. You may use comments to remind yourself of an issue or to mark an incomplete routine, but do you leave enough comments to help a complete stranger figure out what is going on in your code? Proper commenting can make the reader's job a breeze by pointing out the intention of each block of code. Poor commenting seeks to clarify things that would be clear if the other Best Practices were being followed, such as a comment saying "The X variable=number of hours." If this variable had been properly named, this comment would not be necessary. The best comments simply say what the purpose is, such as "this section calculates the employee's gross pay." You do not have to tell the reader how you will accomplish this task, because they should be able to tell that from the code itself.

The best time to make sure your procedure is properly commented is when you first create it. This is contrary to what many developers practice, which is going back and adding comments to their code after it is fully written. How can you create comments before a single line of a procedure is written? You should create an outline of what you plan to do in that procedure before you start writing the code. You would have a hard time writing a book without an outline to help you plan it, and you should use the same approach with your code. This not only helps you leave better comments behind, but it also forces you to think through the procedure from start to finish before you start coding and maybe find a better way to get the job done. Here is an example of an outline for a subroutine:

```
Public Function CalculateDeductions(ByVal TaxUser as UserStructure) As Integer
    ' TODO: Add code to the CalculateDeductions function
    ' Validate the input parameters
    ' Figure out deduction for dependants
    ' Lookup deductions for disabilities
    ' Lookup standardized deduction for user
    ' Total all deductions
End Function
```

With the preceding outline accomplished, you can now go back and fill in code between the lines. You can even go take a long lunch and come back to this piece and you will not have a hard time figuring out what is left to do. A code reviewer can open your file, jump directly to this subroutine, and be able to quickly figure out what is going on from the clues you left behind. If you are having a problem with a piece of code, you should leave a note to remind yourself and to point out this feature to other users of your code. This may save a lot of explaining later on! Use comments to talk to other developers and point out features they need to be aware of. This does not mean telling them how a **For** loop works or what the **If** statement is checking for, because this should be obvious to them from the code itself.

The .NET Task List window adds a new spectrum to the old commenting arena. By creating and using customized tags, as discussed in Chapter 3, you can add special notes to the Task List to highlight areas of code. You can use this to point out special features of your code, or to leave reminders to yourself that something needs to be changed. Code still in development often has workarounds or "stubs" (sections of code that fake a functionality that will be added later) still in them. Task List comments can point these out to other developers and help you remember to replace the stubs when the features are finally ready. This is a great way to let reviewers and your fellow team members know about bugs or workarounds in your code. While pointing out bugs and coding shortcomings may not seem like a great idea, it is far better to admit to the problems in your code and let people know you are aware of them than to have someone run your code and form a poor opinion of its creator.

Module headers are very important in team development environments, but should be kept to a modest size. You do not need to write an epic description of the module you are creating, because the meat of the story will be in the code and the comments you place throughout the code. In the header, you should include your name, the module name and containing Assembly, and a brief one-sentence description of the purpose of the module. I find it useful to add a date when the module was first created, for historical reference. Some development teams append to the header a new line with the latest date of changes and a summary of any changes made to this module. This is a great way to let team members know what's changed in the code when they open the module.

If you generated your code from a UML modeling tool, you probably have comments already inserted in your code. The models of your code will have comments embedded in their objects and members during design time, and these will be translated into code comments when the designer generates code from the model. Typically, these are just summaries of the object's or member's purpose. Leave these comments in the code, and add your processing outline below these. If your models were generated from Use Cases (graphical or textual models that describe the customer's process), you should refer to the Use Cases when creating your process outlines. They step you through the process you are coding and remind you of key features that need to be in your code.

Readability Best Practices

The following is a list of Best Practices to improve your code's readability:

♦ Use the .NET IDE's code indenting feature, and indent more if it helps.

♦ Generous use of the carriage return helps separate procedures and ideas.

♦ Do not use the underscore (_) to break up long lines of code.

♦ Use the Namespace to group like Classes logically in your source code.

♦ Place frequently used Classes at the top of their Namespace.

♦ Place frequently used procedures at the top of their Classes.

♦ Give data types descriptive names using Hungarian notation.

♦ Give your procedures descriptive names that tell what they do and what they are doing it to.

♦ Create comment outlines of your procedures before you begin coding them.

♦ Use comments to explain the purpose of a section, rather than explain the code itself.

♦ Add a header to each module with your name, date, project, and module summary.

♦ Use comments starting with keywords that show up on the Task List to point out problem areas or special sections of code.

Variables

Every program uses variables. A lot of thought needs to go in to your variables, from the best names to give them to the data type you decide to assign them. In .NET, you now have the ability to initialize your variable immediately, and this requires even more planning. Here are some Best Practices for dealing with the variables in your code.

Choosing the Right Data Types

Now more than ever, when defining a variable, you need to be sure to use the right data type for the job. With such a large selection to choose from, it is sometimes hard to know which one you should use. The decision should be based on what the maximum and minimum values are that you expect the variable to take on. Choosing the best data type for the job improves your application's performance and memory utilization. Picking the biggest and bulkiest data types for a variable may give you a lot more flexibility, but it increases the memory storage footprint of your application immensely.

If your variable can have only two possible values, then use the **Boolean** data type. Its **True** and **False** values can also be translated to **Off** and **On**, **Complete** and **Incomplete**, or **Open** and **Close** by your code. If you made this variable a **String**, you would be using almost three times the memory storage space you would have used with a **Boolean**. For this reason, a **Date** data type is also better than storing a date in a **String**, because a **Date** uses only 8 bytes versus the 10 bytes plus 2 bytes per character size of the **String**. Examine all of your **String** data types carefully and ask yourself whether each one would be better off as something else. If its value can only be one of two values, make it a **Boolean**. If your **String** is holding a date, change it to a **Date** data type. If your **String** will be holding one single character value, such as a flag or an initial, then you should definitely switch it to the new **Char** data type. The **Char** uses only 2 bytes, a mere shadow of its bulky **String** cousin.

When dealing with numbers, it is common to declare most numbers as an **Integer**. Now that the **Integer** is a 32-bit data type in .NET, it is capable of holding numbers up to a little more than two billion. If you have a variable in your project that is being used on a smaller scale, such as those in your **For** loops and counters, consider using the **Short** data type. This has half the memory footprint of the **Integer** (2 bytes versus 4 bytes), and holds values up to 32,767. For most uses, I think the **Short** should now be your workhorse number type.

Scope

Every piece of data will have its own access scope associated with it. Using a variable that is not in scope will result in a runtime error. When deciding the proper scope to assign your variable, think about how far out it needs to be seen. Making your data type available to everyone can have some nasty side effects on your own code if the value gets changed. Never give a user of your code more information than they absolutely need to use your object properly.

If your variable is for local procedure use only and should not be viewed by any other routines, make it **Private** or declare it within its procedure with the **Dim** statement. If you want to use your variable all over your Assembly but do not want it to be available outside the Assembly, you should make this a **Friend** data type. Use the **Protected** scope if your variable is in an inheritable Class and you do not want this particular variable to be included in the inheritance. **Public** variables are the easiest to deal with but leave your data wide open for abuse by everyone. Before making a data type **Public**, take an extra moment to determine whether you could assign it a more protective scope and still get the job done.

Where you declare a variable within a procedure affects what parts of the procedure can see that variable. This is a new kind of a scope within a scope that would not have given you a problem in Visual Basic 6. Take a look at the following code example:

```
Public Function CalcOccupancy(ByVal RoomType As String) As Integer
    If RoomType = "Deluxe" Then
        Dim TotalBeds As Integer = 3
        Msgbox("There are " & TotalBeds & " in this room")
    End If
    CalcOccupancy = TotalBeds * 2      'Error on this line!
End Function
```

As you can see from the comment, you would get an error on the second line that references the variable **TotalBeds**, because the variable was **Dim**med within an **If** block, which is below the level of this second reference. You can look at the code indentations to get a visual cue as to how deep a variable was declared. This limited scope would also occur for variables declared within **For**, **Do**, and **While** loops. The fix for this is to declare all of your variables at the very beginning of the procedure, or declare them in your module's General Declarations area.

Initializers

This is a great new feature in .NET and one that you should take advantage of with about 98 percent your variables. Do not rely on the first module that uses your variable to set its initial value. If your variable is accessed by a routine other than the one in which you placed its initial value, your variable will be uninitialized and could certainly result in a wrong answer from your procedure or even a crash. A data type that has not been initialized assumes the value of the constant **Empty**. If you know the starting value of a data type at declaration time or have a value you would rather use in place of **Empty**, you should initialize the variable with it, like so:

```
Public SavingsAccount As Integer = 0
Public MonthlyFee as Double = 8.5
```

By looking at the declarations, you can immediately know a variable's starting value before any processing is done. If the very first procedure to use the **MonthlyFee** variable tries to add $12 to it for a purchased box of checks, you will be adding this to the $8.50 used in the Initializer and not the $0 you would have had if you had not initialized this value.

Converting Data Types

Due to the **Option Strict** constraint placed on your code by .NET, you need to be more careful now when mixing and matching variables of different data types. Sure you could disable the **Option Strict**, but that would be about as smart as driving a race car without a helmet. The crashes will hurt a lot more! Hopefully, you follow an intelligent naming convention that lets you know by the variable's name what data type it is, such as a **strFirstName** and an **intAge**. You may have written some customized procedures to evaluate a piece of data or format it in a way that you can use. You will find the conversion functions much easier to use, and they certainly run faster than having to pass your data to a procedure for the same results.

Sometimes, you can get away with mashing two data types together, but from a Best Practices point of view, this is sloppy work. If you combine a **Short** and an **Integer**, you will be okay as long as the **Integer** is small enough to fit into the range of **Short**. If it isn't, then I hope you had your helmet on! When using conversion functions on variables with decimal points, they round up values (for example, .5 would be rounded up to 1). Keep this in mind while coding. If you convert a bunch of **Decimal** data types to **Integer** data types, you could be loosing pennies on the dollar each time! If you do not care about decimal amounts and rounding up or down during conversion, you can use the **Int** function, which simply lops off any decimal values and returns a straight **Integer** to you.

If you take in a **String** value and want to convert it to a date using the **CDate** function, you should first use the **IsDate** keyword to check if the value can be converted. This prevents an error if you try to convert something that just cannot be considered a date. I find that it is best not to give users a freeform textbox to enter a date into, but instead use either a date picker ActiveX control or a series of Month/Day/Year combo boxes (great for the Web). You will have to later combine the combo box values to form a proper date, but at least this way you know you have a proper date.

Constants

Because a constant does not change and is not considered a variable, I want to briefly touch on constants here and offer some advice. Any item that you use in your statements that will never change should be a constant. This improves your application's performance, because constants are more efficient than variables. When the application first starts up, all constants are loaded into memory. Variables, on the other hand, are loaded as needed and may change often during the application's lifetime. Your **If** statements will be a popular place to use constants and a good place to look at your code to determine if a new constant is needed. If there is a number in your **If** statement, consider making it a constant. By replacing a number with a word, your code will make more sense. Here is an example of a statement with and without a constant:

```
If intNumItems > 10 then bolDiscount = True
If intNumItems > MaximumItems then bolDiscount = True
```

On the first line, the number 10 is what's called a "magic number." By replacing it with a constant, you make the code easier to understand, and this line reads more like a sentence. Visual Basic uses many constants, such as **Blue** for the red-green-blue (RGB) color 0xFF0000, or **Monday** for the day value of 2. Be sure to always use the Visual Basic constants in your code and not the true values. You should place all of your project's customized constants in one central place, such as a constants.vb module. An advantage of using global constants is that if you wish to change a value that is used all over the project, you only have to make the change in one place. Here is a constant declaration:

```
Public Const MaximumItems As Integer = 10
```

This is a bit different from the old version 6 **Const** declaration. Like your other data types, you need to give this constant a scope of **Public**, **Private**, **Friend**, or **Protected** and then declare it **As** some data type before initializing it. If you do not give a constant a scope, it will be **Private** and unavailable outside the current module.

Structures

Formerly known as user-defined types, or UDTs, **Structures** give you the ability to create complicated combinations of data that closely resemble a Class. While using **Structures** to communicate data outside a Class is usually a bad idea, due to the inability to validate values before accepting them, **Structures** are a great method for creating internal globs of information and can help you organize your data intelligently. Within your Class, you may want to group a set of variables, constants, and even functions under a single roof with a name such as **Customer**. Instead of creating separate variables, such as **CustomerFirstName** or **CustomerAddress**, you could create a **Structure**, like this:

```
Private Structure Customer
    Public FirstName As String
    Public LastName As String
    Public Address As String
    Public Phone As String
End Structure


Dim MyCustomer As Customer
```

Within your code, you can now make a reference to **Customer.FirstName**. This gives your variables more identity. If you do not define a scope for your **Structure**, it defaults to **Public**, which may make your variables more vulnerable than you might want. You can also pass the entire **Structure** to another procedure, thereby serializing or packaging all of these variables into one neat and efficient box.

You could create a **ReserveRoom** procedure that asks you to pass in **FirstName**, **LastName**, **Address**, **City**, **State**, **Zip**, **PhoneNumber**, and credit card information, or you could simply ask for the **Customer Structure** that contains all of this data. Which sounds easier to code and will make your code look neater? Here are two procedures that illustrate this concept. The first initializes all the values of the **Structure** and then passes the entire **Structure** to the second procedure, which could be in a different module.

```
Private Sub MakeReservation()
    MyCustomer.FirstName = "Steve"
    MyCustomer.LastName = "Smith"
    MyCustomer.Address = "432 Main St."
    MyCustomer.Phone = "(804) 555-1234"
    Result = ReserveRoom(MyCustomer)
End Sub

Private Function ReserveRoom(ByVal Cust As Customer) As Boolean
    Room.ReserveName = Cust.FirstName & " " & Cust.LastName
    Room.ReserveContact = Cust.Phone
    ReserveRoom = True
End Function
```

The **ReserveRoom** procedure is so much easier to code when you use a **Structure** to pass in variables. One instance in which I do not recommend passing an entire **Structure** to a procedure is when you only need one or two pieces of data. In this case, make each piece its own parameter, to minimize the data you have to deal with. Because a pointer to the data, and not the entire **Structure**, is passed to the procedure, you do not make the application any more efficient, but you do make it a little more understandable.

Do not use a **Structure** if you want to present these variables to the outside world. You should instead make these properties of a Class so that you can implement validation checks on changes made to them or make certain values read-only. **Structure** values can be freely changed without limits by anyone within their access scope. Another downside to **Structures** is that you cannot initialize their variables within the **Structure** statement. Only constants within a **Structure** can be given an Initializer value. **Structures** do not have constructors and destructors, like a Class does, and cannot take in a parameter to help set it up. One final drawback to **Structures** is that they cannot be inherited like Classes can, so you cannot design a super-**Structure** for reuse elsewhere in your project. Despite these limitations, within a single Class, **Structures** are an excellent choice for packaging your variables together and passing them around.

Variable Best Practices

The following is a list of Best Practices that apply to the variables you will use in your code:

- Choose the best data type for your variable—avoid the **String** if you can use a **Boolean**, **Date**, or **Char** instead.

- Give your data types the proper scope (**Public**, **Private**, **Friend**, or **Protected**).

- Declare all variables at the very beginning of the procedure.

- Use the **Short** data type for counters and **For** loops using numbers under 32,767.

- If you know the starting value of a variable at declaration time, initialize it.

- Centralize your constants in one section of your project, giving them **Public** scope.

- Never use numbers in your **If** statements; replace these with constants.

- Use a **Structure** to group variables, constants, and simple functions under one title.

- Use a **Structure** as a single parameter for your procedure to serialize a large amount of data.

- Do not use a **Structure** to present data outside of your Class.

Planning Procedures

Creating procedures that are durable and allow for maximum reuse takes a lot of extra planning and coding. Validation plays a big part in procedure *durability*, meaning how well does your procedure hold up when it is subjected to abuse and misuse. Reusability is the

Holy Grail of object-oriented programming. The more reusable your code is, the less work you have to do in the long run. If you are confused about whether to use a function or a subroutine in your procedure, remember that a function always returns a value to the caller, whereas a subroutine does not. If you start a subroutine and later realize there will be an output from this procedure, you can simply change the subroutine statement at the beginning of the procedure to the word *function* and add an output variable to this line. Let's look at some guidelines for producing great procedures in your projects.

Designing for Reuse

Reuse refers to a piece of code's ability to be used by more than one caller. If your program has a function that calculates the sales tax for an item, this would be a great candidate to separate from the rest of the code into its own procedure. Then, any module that needs to calculate the sales tax can call this procedure and reuse the code. Maximizing code reuse minimizes code duplication and has a long list of benefits to both the developer and the project. Less duplication means there is less code for you to type and troubleshoot. Your project benefits from all of this reuse through improved maintainability, because you only have to fix a problem or make a change to a procedure in one place.

A lot of code has been written that is not optimized for reuse. If you have a procedure that does more than one thing, then it is very likely that this procedure could be separated into two procedures for better reuse. Take the example of my **CalculateDeductions** procedure; this could be broken up into three procedures: **CalculateDependantDeductions**, **CalculateDisabilityDeductions**, and **CalculateStandardDecutions**. The **Calculate-Deductions** procedure can be the controlling parent that enlists the other subprocedures to come up with a final result. If you have a module elsewhere that wants to estimate the deduction for a number of dependants, you will not have to rewrite this bit of code, because it is now broken away from the larger function and available for reuse.

Code that connects to the database can get a lot of reuse mileage by creating a special **GetRecordset** method in a **CData** Class. This can be your single point of connection to the database. The way I like to implement this is by passing in a SQL string to a **GetRecordset** method that I build specially in a separate Class in my project. If the datasource or the data consumer account changes, you only have to go to one place to make an update.

You should think about coding your project in small parts and single functions when you are looking for ways to improve your code's reusability. If you encounter a line of code that gives you a sense of déjà vu, then it is probably duplicating the functionality from another procedure you wrote and it could be a prime candidate for a new procedure. Breaking your code into many smaller fragments may seem to make the project less manageable, but the payoff in time saved rewriting redundant code more than makes up for the added complexity.

Constructors

As you learned in Chapter 4, you can use a Class's **Sub New** event to construct it and set some initial values. Previously, you would have used the **Initialize** event in Visual Basic 6 do this. One great new improvement in .NET is that the calling procedure can now pass parameters in to the **Sub New** constructor that you can use to initialize its values. This method is called a *parameterized constructor*. For variables that will always start out with the same value, you should use a declaration statement to give them their values, which is known as an *Initializer*. For a Class, you may have many properties that you wish to give an initial value to before the caller sets these. This should be done in the Class's constructor or **Sub New** event. A great example of using the constructor and a passed-in parameter is setting up a **User** object based on a login ID. The calling code will pass your **CUser** Class a **UserID** that you can use in the **Sub New** event to query the database and fill in the properties of the Class with the results. The **CUser** Class's **Sub New** event might look something like this:

```
Public Class CUser
    Private MyLogin As String

    Public Property LoginName() As String
        Get
            LoginName = MyLogin
        End Get
        Set
            MyLogin = LoginName
        End Set
    End Property

    Public Sub New(ByVal UserID As String)
        'lookup user in database here using ADO.NET!
        'Fill in properties with data returned from the database
        MyLogin = UserID
    End Sub
End Class
```

This Class requires that the calling code pass in a **UserID** so that it knows how to initialize itself. This example only shows one property, **LoginName**, and I initialize this in the constructor with the value of the passed-in **UserID** parameter. If you called the database within the constructor, you could initial the entire object with data. Calling the database in the **Sub New** event prevents you from requiring the user to trigger a **Load** event to initialize this Class's properties before it can be used. As soon as the Class is instanced and passed a proper **UserID**, it will be fully usable. Here is some code that goes in a Windows Form's **CommandButton Click** event that will create an initialized instance of the **CUser** Class and **Msgbox** the initialized value of the **LoginName**:

```
Dim MyUser As CUser
MyUser = New CUser("dvitter")
Msgbox(MyUser.LoginName)
```

Notice how the parameter is passed in to the **CUser** Class at the time of instancing (the line with the **New** keyword). Immediately after instancing the Class, its **LoginName** property has a value that you can see, and the **Msgbox** will respond with **"dvitter"**. Constructors are a very powerful tool that you should spend a lot of time planning to use. A fully constructed Class means less coding for the caller, because they will not have to trigger the Class's loading and setup anymore.

Procedure Validation

For your code to be durable, it must be able to deal with anything the caller throws at it, and that can include some pretty off-the-wall parameters being passed in to your procedure. In .NET, you can be certain that your parameter and the value passed will be a good match due to the Type-safety checking that the CLR performs. But can you be sure that the data passed in will not cause your code to crash unexpectedly? The best way to avoid an error due to unexpected input parameters is to validate all parameters at the very beginning of the procedure. These checks enable you to gracefully fail the procedure and pass back an intelligent error to let the calling code know it did something wrong.

Never trust the calling code to use your procedure correctly. Likewise, you should never trust the output value of a procedure to be exactly what you need. If your code calls a procedure that returns a value to your code, be sure to check that value before putting it to use. These checks may verify that a number does not exceed a certain value, that a string length is not longer than you need, or that the string does not contain any illegal characters that could cause your code problems. Being able to trust procedures and calling code unconditionally would be really nice and save you a lot of hassle, but the reality of programming is very different. Like the spy movie says: "Trust no one." Or from a politically correct point of view: "Trust, but verify."

The testing phase of your project should be capable of spotting procedures that cannot deal with unexpected parameters. A good tester spends a lot of time trying to break your code, and when they do, you can be sure to hear about it. Think like the tester when planning your parameter validations and ask yourself: "What are the worst possible parameters that someone can pass in and how should I deal with these?" If your testing phase is not trying to raise bugs with bogus parameters, then you may want to point this out to the team leader as a process deficiency. Testing is a very critical phase, and missing these potentially catastrophic errors is unforgivable.

Using Overloads

Being able to *overload* a function in Visual Basic .NET is an exciting new feature, but how to best implement this feature may not be immediately obvious to Visual Basic developers. Visual Basic .NET is now a strongly typed language, and procedures can only accept parameters of a specific type. But by overloading these procedures, you enable them to accept different data types for different circumstances, making them more flexible. You may want a method to perform a mathematical computation on a data type that could be a **Short**, but could also be an **Integer** or a **Long**. You have three options here:

♦ Accept only one data type and force the caller to convert his data type.

♦ Write three different procedures, named **CalcLong**, **CalcShort**, and **CalcInteger**, and force the caller to pick between them based on his data type.

♦ Use overloading on a single method to accept all three data types (by far the easiest option).

On a broader scale, you may want to create a general **Delete** function that can take in different data types and know by what was passed to it what it should do. Deleting a **Customer** from the database and deleting an **Employee** would be two very different procedures, but in a general sense, they are both **Delete** functions. You could also delete an item from the gift shop **Inventory** or delete a canceled **Reservation**. In the past, each of these tasks would have been their own procedure, such as **DelEmployee** or **DelReservation**. You will identify the methods that are best suited for overloading during the design and modeling phase of your project. Look for repeating keywords, such as **Add**, **Delete**, **Remove**, **Update**, and so on. By making these repeating methods share an overloaded function, you are greatly simplifying the use of your objects. Instead of having to decide which function is the right one to use, the caller will simply pass his or her object to one single **Delete** method and let the code figure it out.

An overloaded function can span many Classes. My **DelEmployee** and **DelReservation** methods would be related to both the **Employee** and **Reservation** Class, respectively. Because of its neutral design, the new overloaded **Delete** method would not belong inside either Class, but rather in a more general location, under the same Namespace. Think of these as global methods for the entire Namespace, allowing callers to add, delete, and otherwise manipulate all the items in your Namespace from one single method. Instead of a method named **Hotel.Employee.Delete**, you would have a higher method named **Hotel.Delete** that can handle **Employees**, **Reservations**, and many other objects subordinate to the **Hotel** Namespace.

In Chapter 4, you saw an example of an overloaded function that performed a calculation based on different primitive data types. For the **DelEmployee** and **DelReservation** example, you would make the parameter a Class or a **Structure** data type containing the needed information. Here is what the **Delete Overloads** function would look like for these two situations:

```
Overloads Sub Delete(ByVal Employee As CEmployee)
    SQLString = "DELETE * FROM Employee WHERE (EmpID = " & Employee.EmpID & ")"
End Sub

Overloads Sub Delete(ByVal Reservation As CReservation)
    SQLString = "DELETE * FROM Reservation WHERE (ReserveID = " & _
        Reservation.ReserveID & ")"
End Sub
```

The callers use the same subroutine to delete either object, and, based on the object type passed in to this overloaded function, the compiler knows which function to use and executes the proper code. Each version of **Delete** can have its own unique functions that allow you to handle each case differently. You still have to write a separate routine for each possible passed-in data type, but on the outside, your code will appear to have one function that can do it all. Remember that each **Overloads** procedure must differ by parameter data types from other **Overloads** procedures of the same name.

Controlled Crashes

Any crash that the calling procedure can walk away from is a good crash. A good procedure has exception-handling code in it to deal with these little surprises. Because the exception-handling model is entirely new in .NET, you should read Chapter 7 very carefully so that you understand how this works. The trick to planning your exception-handling scheme is to role-play through all the possible uses of your procedure and spot the places where things can go wrong.

You will deal with two main types of exceptions: those that you can recover from, and those that you can't recover from. An example of a recoverable exception is when your code is trying to read from the floppy drive but the function reports back that a disk has not been inserted in the drive. You can pop up a message box to let the user know to insert a disk and then continue on with your procedure as if the exception never happened. You will be using the new **Try . . . Catch . . . Finally** model in .NET to trap these recoverable errors and try to resolve them before "finally" bailing out of your code gracefully.

For those exceptions that you just can do nothing about, you often need to do a little more than just raise the right error. If you were connected to a database and were in the middle of a financial transaction, you would probably want to roll back all the completed work before reporting an error. If you were writing a BankTeller application, the customer would not be pleased if the **SubtractFromChecking** function worked but then the **AddToSavings** function failed, and the code just popped up an error and did not put the funds back in to checking. Working with file systems can also be a mess if things are not put back the way they were before things went bad. If the exception is so severe that the entire application could crash, you should make every effort to save any open files and user settings before the whole program goes down the tubes. Although a crash probably won't make the user's day, getting back their data and files in tact will help smooth over any hard feelings they may have.

After you have tried everything you can to recover from the exception and have put back everything to the way it should be, you must **Throw** a meaningful error to the caller so that they know that things did not work out. Their code will almost certainly be expecting some result from your code, such as output or a completed function. If you are creating custom exception codes, you need to communicate them to the team or package them with your product so that the users will be able to interpret them. Along with meaningful messages, you may want your code to output its problem to a log file for later review. This is a terrific place to put the really technical details of what went wrong so that you can get a better grasp on the exception and troubleshoot it more efficiently. The users do not want to see technical jargon in the returned error message, but you definitely want these details in a log to help you track down the problem. I recommend including an exception handling procedure that your code can call and pass the exception off to, so that it can make the proper log entries for your code in a nice, neat, reusable way.

Procedure Planning Best Practices

The following are some Best Practices to keep in mind when you are planning out your procedures:

♦ Separate your procedures into smaller, reusable parts.

♦ Centralize your database connections in one **Data** Class to be used by all.

♦ Use overloading to make reusable components more flexible.

♦ Use constructors to initialize your Class properties, and allow the user to pass in a parameter so that you can build your object intelligently.

♦ Validate all parameters passed in to your procedures.

♦ Validate the output of all procedures before using them.

♦ Test all procedures to verify they can handle bad parameters.

♦ Design you methods to share functions such as **Delete** and **Add** through overloading.

♦ Plan your procedures to recover from expected exceptions.

♦ Raise meaningful exception messages to callers.

♦ Roll back transactions, save files, and crash gracefully to avoid data loss.

♦ Write exception information to a log file for later troubleshooting.

Logic Functions

This section covers the Best Practices associated with creating logic statements and functions within your procedures. This includes **If** statements, **Case** statements, and mathematical computations. How you arrange and calculate your logic plays a large role in your application's overall performance, and by tweaking and refining your code, you are ensuring that it will run as fast as possible.

Making a Case for the Case Statement

The **If** statement is a Basic logic statement from way back in the old days. No, I'm not going to tell you that this statement should be thrown out, because it is firmly planted in the Visual Basic lexicon and is as needed today as it was in the beginning. But I will tell you that sometimes you should use the **Case** statement in place of **If**, and for good reason. If you find yourself writing a chain of **If/Else** statements trying to match a variable with a value, you should strongly consider moving this to a **Case** statement. When the **If/Else** statements execute, each line of code will be considered and processed in order, slowly and painfully. When you use a **Case** statement, the runtime skips through the code faster looking for a match and executes quicker. You will not have the advanced comparisons available as in the **If** statement, such as when you use the **Or**, **Not**, or **And** keywords, but if you are dealing with a single variable and a set list of possible values, the **Case** statement is the best way to go to quickly figure out the value. Here is an example of a **Case** statement:

```
Select Case RoomType
    Case "Standard"
        RoomRate = 75.50
    Case "Bargain"
        RoomRate = 39.95
    Case "Deluxe"
        RoomRate = 150.75
End Select
```

Not only is this quicker than a similar **If** statement, but it also is a lot easier to type and makes your code far more readable than having to follow the logic in an **If** statement. You can further improve the performance of a **Case** statement by listing the cases in order from most likely to least likely. The faster the **Case** statement finds the matching value, the faster it executes.

Looping through Arrays

Visual Basic.NET will continue to dimension its arrays by having you declare the top element in the array. If you **Dim** an array to 10, then the highest element in your array will be 10. The lowest element will be 0 since everything in .NET is zero-based, giving you a total of 11 elements in your array. This hold-over from past versions of Visual Basic may cause some confusion when working with the other languages in .NET. If you **Dim** an array to 10 in C#, this would mean that the array has 10 elements in it, ranging from 0 to 9. Be aware of this inconsistancy when passing arrays from Visual Basic to other languages.

Also remember to never **Redim** an array unless you are sure that it has already been **Dim**med in the code, because you are no longer allowed to declare an array with the **Redim** statement, only resize it. If you carefully **Dim** all of your arrays in the General Declarations area or at the top of your procedure, you should not have any troubles with out of order **Redim** statements later on in your code.

If Statements

The **If** statement is the backbone of any application logic. This was probably the first logical statement you learned in Basic and you will still use it a lot today. Besides the earlier tip about changing some **If/Else** structures to **Case** statements, a few other tricks will make your **If** statements both more readable and more efficient. The first thing you should avoid in your **If** statements are calculations. The proper way to use a calculated value in an **If** statement is to calculate it beforehand and simply use the result in your statement. Here are two **If** statements: the first performs a calculation within the **If** statement, and the second performs the calculations prior to executing the **If** statement:

```
'This If statement does calculations and is hard to read
If (RoomFee + HotelTax) > MaxPerDiem Then TotalFee = (RoomFee + HotelTax) * _
     Discount

'Here is the same code broken out in to understandable lines
TotalFee = RoomFee + HotelTax
If TotalFee > MaxPerDiem Then
    TotalFee = TotalFee * Discount
End If
```

Not only is the second example easier to follow, it will process faster as well. Note that my **If** statement does not check if the **TotalFee** is greater than some set dollar amount but instead uses a constant called **MaxPerDiem** here. If this value changes at a later date, you need to update it only in the constant's module, and not everywhere the dollar amount appears in the code. In the second example, I also broke away the computed result of the **If** statement to its own line to enhance the readability of the code. A good way to spot poorly written **If** statements is by the length. If the statement stretches all the way to the right margin and contains any mathematical operators, then I urge you to break this out and precompute your values.

Another thing you should avoid is calling a function in your **If** statement. This can also slow down your application and should be done before the **If** statement checks the results. Here is the right and wrong way to use an **If** statement to check a function's value:

```
'Wrong way
If CalcOccupancy(MyRoom) > MaxOccupancy Then Overbooked = True

'Right way
TotalOccupancy = CalcOccupancy(MyRoom)
If TotalOccupancy > MaxOccupancy Then Overbooked = True
```

The second version requires an extra variable to hold the result of the function, but the **If** statement will execute faster and the code makes more sense. The real performance payoff comes when you execute more than one **If** statement against the result or include this **If** statement in a loop. If you precompute the value outside this loop, then you will not be calling the function over and over and causing your application to bog down with unnecessary recalculations of something you already knew.

Logic Functions Best Practices

The following is a list of Best Practices that apply to your procedure's logic statements:

♦ Use a **Case** statement in place of an **If-Then-Else** pattern if you can.

♦ Place the most common matching values at the beginning of your **Case** statement.

♦ Do not use the **Redim** statement unless you are sure your array has been **Dimmed** first.

♦ Do not perform calculations in your **If** statements—precompute the values.

♦ Do not call functions from inside your **If** statements—call them beforehand.

Threading Issues

Now that you have the ultimate power of spawning off processes on to their own threads, how do you plan to use it? *Free-threading* is not a tool that should be used just for the sake of using it, and many issues and complications can arise from having many threads going simultaneously and communicating between items on separate threads. Two restrictions on free-threaded processes are that they cannot be functions and they cannot use **ByRef** parameters, meaning anything you pass in to the thread will be a copy of the original. Because you can only use subroutines and not functions, you have to find another way of getting something back when the thread is done processing.

Warning

*Free-threaded processes cannot be functions and cannot use **ByRef**.*

The key thing to ask yourself when you are considering using a new thread is "why?" Does the process you are starting onto its own thread cause your application to lock up or pause when it is run on the same thread as the application? Do you wish to allow your users to continue to use the application on the original thread while the new thread performs a long, intensive process? If the answer to either of these two questions is "yes," then free-threading should indeed help you out. But if the answer to both is "no," then you should reevaluate whether or not you really need the added complexity of another thread to manage.

Threading Events

In most cases, you will not want to simply launch a process onto its own thread and forget about it. Because your application will continue processing on its own thread, you need a mechanism to listen to the new thread for feedback. You could continually check whether the thread is still alive with the **IsAlive** method of the spawned thread, but this would be a continuous loop of checking that would bog down your application despite using a thread. You could get feedback from a thread by using global variables, which the threaded process could change and the caller could access. Using Global variables is a messy way of going about this, and you would have to continually check whether the value has changed to know that the threaded process has done its job. The preferred method of getting feedback from a threaded process is through events. The Class that contains the routine you wish to free-thread will have to declare an event in its General Declarations area, like this:

```
Public Event SearchComplete(ByVal NumberFilesFound As Integer)
```

Somewhere in the procedure you plan the spawn off on to a new thread, and you will need to raise this event to let the creator know that the work has been completed successfully. Raising events back to the calling procedure is often referred to as raising a *callback event*. This line will probably be at the very end of the procedure and will look something like this:

```
RaiseEvent SearchComplete(TotalFilesFound)
```

Upon completion of the routine, it will fire off this event and cease processing, causing the thread to close as well. The caller will need an event handler to hear this callback and be able to do something about it. Without an event handler, the caller will be oblivious to the raised event and will never know the result. The caller could still check the **IsAlive** method for the thread to see if it is gone, but the result of the search will be lost when the thread closes. Here is the event handler the caller will implement to hear the result of the threaded processes:

```
Sub SearchCompleteEventHandler(ByVal NumberFilesFound As Integer)
    Msgbox("Your search located " & CStr(NumberFilesFound) & " files.")
End Sub
```

Unless you do not need to know the result of a free-threaded process, be sure to implement an event and matching event handler. Some processes that are spawned off will not need to report back their results, such as maintenance or cleanup functions. I still recommend fitting these with events, even if they only return a **True** or **False Boolean** to let the caller know they succeeded or failed. You may also want to pass more than one message back to the caller to let them know how things are going. These status messages can also be events, fired off at multiple times by the thread. These can act as checkpoints to let the caller know that something is done and they can now do something special.

Controlling Threads

When you create a new thread, your code has the ability to manipulate and control that thread with commands such as **Abort, Sleep, Suspend, Resume,** and **Start.** If you are happy with just spawning a thread and waiting for the result, then things should be fairly simple for you. If you are one of those type A personalities who just can't leave things alone and feel that you have to assert your authority over this new thread, then you are opening yourself up to a world of complications.

You use the **Start** method when you first create the thread, to get it going. The **Abort** method simply kills the thread, a very handy command for threads you suspect have gotten hung up. The **Sleep** method pauses the thread for a certain amount of time, and then the thread continues processing. **Suspend** stops a thread's execution until you finally call the **Resume** method to get it going again. Be very careful when telling threads to **Sleep** or **Suspend** their actions. This can cause locked-up threads and resources with all sorts of horrible results you never intended to cause. If your thread manipulates a database connection or items in your project, such as a form or its controls, do not try to **Sleep** or **Suspend** it. In these situations, if you can't resolve a problem, then **Abort** the thread to avoid further problems.

Threading Best Practices

The following are Best Practices to keep in mind when using the new threading feature in an application:

♦ Give your Classes callback events if they will be launched onto their own threads.

♦ Create event handlers in Classes that create and spawn new threads.

♦ Use thread events to communicate the results of a thread's processing or to relay the thread's status back to the caller.

♦ Use the thread-controlling commands carefully.

♦ Never **Sleep** or **Suspend** a thread that manipulates a database, form, or control.

Delegates and Multicasting

Multicasting refers to sending the same message to many recipients on one command line. Imagine being able to type one line in your code that sends a description of an error to three subroutines; one to write it to a log file, one to email it to the systems administrator, and one to pop up a message letting the user know what happened. You could also use multicasting to string together a group of delegates and send them all a single message. Raising events to more than one receiver can also be done through the use of *delegates* and multicasting. These scenarios are very simple examples of what delegates can do for you, and I am sure you will think of some more uses for this advanced feature.

A **Delegate** acts as a pointer to the real function, and many delegates can be combined into one single **Delegate** that you can pass a value to and trigger all the combined delegates. A **Delegate** is defined at the top of one of your modules as a **Delegate Sub**. Any subroutines in your project that have the same input parameters as your **Delegate** subroutine can be used by a delegated object. Here is an example of a file that defines a **Delegate** named **delError**, followed by a module that contains three matching subroutines:

```
Delegate Sub delError(ByVal ErrDescription As String)


Module ErrorHandler
```

```
    Sub LogError(ByVal Description As String)
        'some code here to log an error
        debug.Writeline("LogError: I logged this error = " & Description)
    End Sub

    Sub SendEmail(ByVal Description As String)
        'some code here to email error to sysadmin
        debug.Writeline("SendEmail: I sent an email about " & Description)
    End Sub

    Sub MessageBox(ByVal Description As String)
        'read in error and come up with a user friendly translation
        MsgBox("The error was " & Description)
    End Sub

End Module
```

The **Delegate** is named **delError** and will always accept one parameter of the **String** type. The three subroutines within the module all accept the same **String** parameter type. A subroutine in a separate module that uses the same **String** parameter could also be enlisted by my **Delegate Sub delError**. Each subroutine can take in the very same parameter and perform a different operation on it, such as write it to a log file, send the systems administrator a friendly email, or format and display a helpful message box to the user. Your project may also have a Windows form that you wish to have use the **Delegate** functions. Within this form, you could set this up like this:

```
Dim MyErr1, MyErr2, MyErr3, SendAll As delError
MyErr1 = AddressOf LogError
MyErr2 = AddressOf SendEmail
MyErr3 = AddressOf MessageBox
SendAllErrs = CType(System.Delegate.Combine(MyErr1, MyErr2), delError)
SendAllErrs = CType(System.Delegate.Combine(SendAllErrs, MyErr3), delError)
```

This set of code first declares four delegates of type **delError**. Next, the code defines which routine each **Delegate** refers to by using the **AddressOf** keyword followed by one of the subroutine names within the module. The first three delegates point directly to one subroutine. The fourth object is a combination of the first three that enables you to multicast your error. The **System.Delegate.Combine** function enables you to merge two delegates into one new one. Because I wish to call three subroutines, I have to use a second **Combine** statement to add the third **Delegate** to the combination of the first two. Now that I have this set up, I can make one simple call anywhere on this form to all three subroutines, like this:

```
SendAllErrs("The Data Server is offline")
```

You can now see that a **Delegate** calls a portion of code for you, based on the **AddressOf** you pass it. Like a delegate in Washington, D.C., this guy is your code's connection or middleman to the subroutine's code. This might seem kind of ho-hum on the surface, but not only can you combine calls to multiple procedures into one statement, you can also change the pointer of a **Delegate** dynamically in your code. Based on the type of message you have to send, you may want a **SendMessage Delegate** to point to different places. By changing its **AddressOf** pointer setting, you can change where this **Delegate** points. The **AddressOf** can be changed many times, and you can make these decisions in an **If** statement, like so:

```
If MyVal = "X" Then DelegateA = AddressOf Sub1 Else DelegateA = AddressOf Sub2
    DelegateA("Your message here")
```

The **DelegateA** function pointer acts as a switching hub and can direct your call to whichever function you point it at with the **AddressOf** statement. This is why delegates are also referred to as function pointers. Between the dynamic pointers and its multicasting abilities, I am sure you will find new ways to put delegates to good use.

Delegates Best Practices

The following are some Best Practices to keep in mind when working with delegates:

◆ Use delegates for events and multicasting.

◆ Use the **Delegate** to point a delegated object to any subroutine that has a matching input parameter.

◆ Group **Delegate** objects together using the **System.Delegate.Combine** method.

◆ Use more than one **Combine** statement to add more delegates to a grouping.

◆ Use the **AddressOf** statement to change the function pointer of an object dynamically in your code.

Using Inheritance

Now that you have this wonderful new power called *inheritance*, how can you best use it? I strongly caution you against using inheritance excessively without proper planning and object design. The goal of code-based inheritance is to reduce redundant code and enhance code reuse. By deriving your Classes from a superclass, you are reusing the code from the superclass, thereby saving you a lot of time now, and even more time later when it comes to troubleshooting or changing these functions.

When to Use Inheritance and When to Avoid It

If you find yourself overriding nearly all the superclass's functions, then you are probably guilty of inheritance abuse. In cases like this, you may want to switch over to interface inheritance by using the **Implements** keyword. This gives you the procedure outline of the superclass with none of the included code and functionality. If all the subclasses are overriding the superclass, then code-based inheritance may not be the way to go. If the objects you are modeling at first appear to be similar but you discover that each has unique implementations of nearly all of its attributes, then you may want to avoid the inheritance path for these. If you did try to create an unnecessary superclass and inherit it, you will have a lot of code redundancy in your objects, and troubleshooting will not be easier because each subclass will be implementing its own version of the procedures. Instead of looking at one superclass attribute, you will have to locate the subclass that had overridden this attribute and troubleshoot it there.

How will you know when to use inheritance and when not to use it? This decision should be made in the modeling phase of your project. As you study the collection of potential objects that you are going to code, look for objects that resemble each other and have the same names for attributes and methods. The best candidate objects will have some relationship to each other, often through a parent object.

Here is an example of some object analysis uncovering similarities between proposed objects that Team A will be creating for the Oceanside Resorts reservation system: In the Oceanside Resort project, we have decided to create an object for each type of room we offer. Room choices include Deluxe rooms, Standard rooms, and the no-frills Bargain rooms. Every room will have attributes that hold the number of beds, the reserve status of the room, the room number, the floor number, and the building number. Deluxe rooms have a number of extra amenities, depending on the room, such as hot tubs, tanning beds, and kitchenettes. The Bargain room's reserved status is always "first come, first serve" because these rooms cannot be reserved. Every room will have an **Add** and **Delete** method to add new rooms and remove rooms that no longer exist.

From the information you have on the room objects, you can see that all rooms share a group of similar attributes. In this example, it is obvious that each room will be inherited from a generic room superclass. Some rooms will have extra attributes that are not in the superclass, and some rooms will implement the attributes differently than the superclass. Another example you could think about is a car dealership. If you create an object for each car model, you will find a lot of similar attributes, such as number of doors, color of paint, number of tires, and many others. But each car will also have unique attributes, such as CD changers, premium speakers, V8 engines, and so on. In this project, you would certainly want to create a generic car superclass that each model will inherit from and further customize.

Multilanguage Inheritance

Because Visual Studio .NET is capable of handling source code files written in different languages, you can write a superclass in any language you choose and then create a subclass in Visual Basic that derives itself from that superclass. As long as the Class you wish to inherit is within your Assembly and in scope, you can inherit from it the same way you would any other Visual Basic Class. This is great for development teams that have coders who do not code in Visual Basic. They can still create usable superclasses that your VB programmers can use in their projects. The project also benefits if the superclass has a procedure that performs some intensive processing that is better off written in a more powerful language. With this form of inheritance, your Visual Basic objects now are multilingual insofar as their internal procedures will be written in VB and their inherited procedures will be in another language. The CLR in .NET handles the switching of gears behind the scenes that makes all of this possible.

Overrides

When designing the base Class, you must make a few decisions for each procedure that you create. The first decision is whether or not this procedure will be inheritable. You may want your superclass to have private procedures that only it can use. These are given a scope of **Protected** when declaring the procedure. Subclasses do not inherit **Protected** procedures. The second decision is whether or not you wish to allow the derived Classes to override your procedure. Often, you will want to give the subclasses the freedom to override a procedure and implement their own custom functionality, and for these procedures, you need to declare them as **Overridable** on the declaration line. Without this keyword, subclasses are forbidden from overriding the superclass's function. You can also mark a superclass's procedure as **Must Override**, which requires the subclass to create its own implementation before it can run. This is a good strategy if you wish to have a special superclass implementation that a subclass cannot use directly but must instead make up its own. You make all of these decisions during the modeling and design phase of your component.

Inheritance Trees

As mentioned in Chapter 4, your derived Class can only inherit from one superclass. But what you can do is form an *Inheritance Tree* where your derived Class inherits from a superclass, which in turn inherits some of its functionality from a higher superclass (a super-superclass, if you will). You create an Inheritance Tree when the superclass can be considered a child of another parent. In the car dealership example, the top-level superclass could be a **Vehicle** Class, from which you could derive **Car**, **Truck**, and **Minivan** Classes. From these subclasses, you could further derive another level of subclasses for each specific model. Figure 5.1 is a diagram of a possible car dealership Inheritance Tree.

In Figure 5.1, the **Vehicle** superclass has all the attributes that are common to every single vehicle on the lot. The second level superclasses inherit these attributes and add attributes that are unique to a car, truck, or minivan. The lowest-level subclasses inherit from the **Car**, **Truck**, or **Minivan** superclass, thereby inheriting all the attributes of a **Vehicle** and the added attributes of the second-level superclass. When you are looking for parent-child relationships between your objects, look for hierarchies of relationships that you can use to promote code reuse and efficiency.

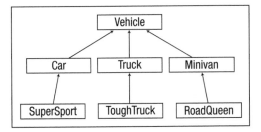

Figure 5.1
Car dealership Inheritance Tree.

Inheritance Best Practices
The following is a list of Best Practices for inheritance:

◆ Examine your objects for parent-child relationships to identify possible superclasses to derive your subclasses from.

◆ Look for multiple levels of parent-child relationships to build an Inheritance Tree.

◆ You can write superclasses in other languages, such as Visual C++ and C#, and derive new Classes from these in Visual Basic.

◆ Override attributes in the derived Class when the inherited functionality does not fit your needs.

◆ If you are overriding most of the inherited functions, then this Class probably is not a good candidate for inheritance.

◆ When modeling, decide which superclass functions can be overridden and which must be overridden, and declare these as **Overridable** or **Must Override**.

Summary

Best Practices are more than a sales pitch for the customers. They are a set of guidelines derived from experience that you can use to get the most out of your development projects. After reading about all the new and radically different changes in .NET, you and your team need to assess how these changes affect the way you code and design your applications. The big selling point of the new Visual Basic .NET language is all the great new powers it gives to the developer. But with added power comes additional responsibility (as well as the ability to abuse these new features in new and scary ways). Be sure you understand each new feature before you try to harness its power and use it in a customer's project. Remember, before something is considered a Best Practice, a whole lot of developers have to do it the wrong way first. Don't become an example of the wrong way to do something in next year's Best Practices speech.

Chapter 6
Windows Development

Visual Basic was created for the sole purpose of developing Windows-based applications. Before there was Windows on your screen, there was blackness (and sometimes greenness). Text would print out painfully line by line from top to bottom on your screen. While Visual Basic was not the first language to allow you to make Windows, it was arguably the first development tool that made creating sophisticated graphical user interfaces (GUIs) easy. If you wanted to create a new windowed form, you just added one to your project. If you needed a text box on the form, you just dragged a textbox from your toolbox and dropped it on the form. No complicated drawing statements were necessary. All you had to do was to write some code that reacted to what the user did with the form. This form of development is known as *event-driven programming*, meaning the form is mostly inactive until the user clicks something or types something. Then, your code reacts to this event and decides what should happen next.

Nearly a decade after the birth of Visual Basic, Windows applications are still in high demand. When you first build a form in Visual Basic.NET, it looks almost exactly like it always has in Visual Basic. But behind the scenes, things have changed substantially. The Windows form, which has remained fairly constant over the last decade, has been completely redesigned in .NET. I will cover what's changed, and how you can take advantage of its new features. The exiting ability to inherit Classes also reaches into the realm of forms, and you will learn how to use inheritance in your projects. You will also learn about Windows Services, a new application type you can create in Visual Basic.NET that previously was unavailable.

155

Windows Form Types

The forms you create in .NET are no longer just plain old forms; they are now called Windows forms in .NET. The reason behind this subtle change is that .NET is not just a Windows application development tool. With the addition of ASP.NET and the ability to create Web applications, Microsoft saw the need to differentiate between these different types of interfaces. Henceforth, the traditional Win32 forms will be called Windows forms, and the new forms that you create for Web-based users are called Web Forms. These are some of the new terms that will make you appear to be "in the know" when talking about .NET.

Forms As Classes

While the Add menu says that you are adding a Windows form to your Solution, what you are really adding is a Class. When you are dragging-and-dropping controls and editing their properties in the visual designer, you are really creating code within the form's Class that remembers all of these settings and initializes your form at runtime the way you designed it. Behind the scenes, a form is now a Class and includes a lot of extra code you never saw before. In past versions, you could drop a control on the form and set its properties in the visual designer and never see the code that actually did this (you may not have even realized that there was code behind all of these form settings). Now, you can see this code in the forms Class and even set the form's properties in code as opposed to using the traditional Design mode settings. You can create an entire form along with all of its controls and layout in the code window without ever seeing it in Design mode. Of course, this would be a very painful way of going about this task, but knowing you can do it is kind of cool.

The Windows form is derived from the **Forms** Class in the **System.Windows.Forms** Namespace. This is the parent of all Windows-based forms, no matter which development language you are using. Previously, many models were used to create interfaces, such as the Visual Basic Forms model, the Visual C++ MFC, and the Win32 API calls. Visual Basic forms were always the easiest to create, but lacked many advanced features. Some VB developers ventured into the world of the Win32 API to make complicated calls that accomplished these advanced features. You no longer have to be a "black-belt" programmer to use these features, because all of these types of forms have been merged into one universal framework for creating GUIs in .NET. Any controls you place on your form will also be derived from a Namespace Class. Now that you are familiar with inheritance, this should not be so shocking. The **System.Windows.Forms** Namespace is also home to many other GUI-related Classes, such as the **Clipboard**. A **CheckBox** control is really a derived Class coming from the **System.Windows.Forms.CheckBox** Class.

The new Windows form is a lot more powerful than the old VB6 form you are used to, yet is just as easy to create. The visual designer was based on the wonderful tools you had in version 6, yet the form itself has inherited many of the traits and features of the old C++ and Win32 API forms. Windows forms will introduce you to a new graphical drawing tool named GDI+

(Graphical Device Interface). This is the follow-up to the original GDI that introduces many neat drawing capabilities, such as texture brushes and transformations. You will be able to do so much more than just "flood fill" an item with a chosen background color.

The Code behind the Scenes

You already took your first look at the code behind a Windows form earlier in the book. You saw that code already exists behind it in the form of a Class. The basic unedited Windows form starts out with three **Imports** statements: **System.ComponentModel**, **System.Drawing**, and **System.Windows.Forms**. These **Imports** commands enable you to quickly access items in these Namespaces. The **ComponentModel** Namespace controls the components you use on your form; the **Drawing** Namespace is part of the GDI+ family that enables you to create graphical displays on your form; and the **Windows.Forms** Namespace is where all of your Windows forms will be derived. Your starting **Windows.Form** Class, which starts out named **Form1**, already contains a **Sub New** and **Sub Dispose** event for you to place your constructor and destructor code in. Remember that forms no longer have **Form_Initialize**, **Form_Load**, and **Form_Unload** events. You will treat the code behind a form just like any other Class, which means you will use the **Sub New** and **Sub Dispose** events to initialize and clean up your forms.

Finally, a section of the **Windows.Form** Class is labeled Windows Form Designer Generated Code. If you peek in this section, you see all the settings needed to instance a WinForm from the **Systems.Windows.Forms.Forms** superclass and set its initial values. The settings for the controls are here as well. Note the **Inherits** keyword at the very beginning of the Class referencing the **Forms** superclass. This means a lot more code is behind this form than what you see, because the superclass holds much of the implementation of the Windows form. The comments warn you not to make changes to this code because you can destroy or override the settings you made in the form designer. All of this code was hidden from you in Visual Basic 6 to keep things simple, so remember how long you got by without tinkering with this code, and try to avoid making changes directly to this section.

Windows Form Inheritance

A lot of your form's behavior is handled by the **System.Windows.Forms.Forms** superclass at this point. If you click the left drop-down menu at the top of your coding window, you see an item named Overrides. Select it, and the right drop-down menu will be populated with all the procedures in the superclass that can be overridden. Nearly every event you know of is in there. That means, without you ever having to code anything, a form **OnClick** event and a form **Finalize** event are already included. Of course, that doesn't mean you'll want to stick with the default events. On the contrary, in most cases, you want your own **OnClick** event code, to deal with certain situations in your own special way. If you select the **OnClick** event from the right drop-down menu, a **Protected Overrides Sub** is added to your form's Class. Because the **Forms** superclass has defined this event as **Protected**, your **OnClick** has to be **Protected** too, and by declaring this event locally, you are overriding the superclass's implementation.

Also note that the **Sub New** event first makes a reference to **MyBase.New**, which calls the **System.Windows.Forms.Forms'** **New** event first before running your form's **New** code. Imagine that another form is derived from your form, making your **Form1** the superclass. If you had some great setup code in the **New** event, you would want a derived form to run this first before running its own setup code, wouldn't you? That is how **Sub New** proliferates down the Inheritance Tree. The **Dispose** event also makes a reference to its base Class by calling **MyBase.Dispose** first thing and then doing its own cleanup afterward. This is a neat and proper example of inheritance programming, and should always be followed in the same manner as this form shows you.

MDI Forms

Multiple Document Interface (MDI) applications were created so that you can make a window within Windows to contain a group of related child forms. You can still create MDI parent and children forms in .NET, but how you go about this has changed a bit. For starters, you do not have to create your project as an MDI Project, nor do you have to add a special MDI form to your project to play the part of the parent. You just add a regular Windows form to the project and then set its **IsMDIContainer** property under the Window Style grouping to **True**. You immediately see your form turn into an MDI parent frame, within which you can load child forms. You can still place controls on the surface of an MDI parent, which gives them an interesting effect of floating on top of any open child forms. For example, if you place a button on the surface of the parent and at runtime open a child form within the parent, the button will still be visible above the surface of the child form.

Menus and toolbars are the preferred way to control child forms from an MDI parent form. Exercise 6.1 walks you through the steps of creating an MDI parent form and launching a child form within it.

Exercise 6.1: Creating an MDI Parent and Child Form

1. Start a new project and select Windows Application from the available projects list.

2. Open Form1.vb in the designer by double-clicking it.

3. Left-click the surface of Form1, and in the Properties window, set IsMDIContainer to **True**.

4. Drag a **MainMenu** control from the toolbox and drop it on to Form1.

5. Click the first block of the **MainMenu** control and type "File".

6. In the menu block below your File item, click once and type "Open Child".

7. Right-click the Project name in the Solution Explorer window, select the Add menu item, and then Add Windows Form. Pick the Windows Form from the Add New Item window and click the Open button.

8. Drop a **Label** control onto this new form and set its **Text** property to "Hi There!".

9. Note the name of this form (it should be Form2) and switch back to the Parent MDI form in Design mode.

10. Click somewhere in the middle of Form1, click the File menu, and then double-click the Open Child menu item.

11. Enter the following code in this menu item's **Click** event:

```
Dim MyChild As New Form2
MyChild.MDIParent = Me
MyChild.Show()
```

12. Save the project and run it. Click the File/Open Child menu item and observe your Form2 opening as a child window of Form1.

The main settings to remember are the parent's **IsMDIContainer** setting, and the child's **MDIParent** setting. Once these are both set, you can start spawning child forms within your parent. If you do not set the **MDIParent** property, your Form2 will launch outside of the parent's frame as its own standalone form. In the preceding example, if you continue to click File/Open Child, you will open multiple copies of Form2 within the parent, because the **New** keyword in the **Dim** statement gives you a new copy of the Form2 Class every time it runs. When dealing with MDI applications, your parent form should have a menu named Window that lists each individual child window that is currently open. This enables users to change child forms even when a top-level form covers one up.

The parent form has an **MDIChildActivate** event that fires off whenever one of its children is activated. The parent can also reference the properties of the currently active form via the **ActiveMDIChild** object. Here is an example of an **MDIChildActive** event that pops up a **MessageBox** with the active child's **Text** property whenever that form becomes active:

```
Public Sub Form1_MDIChildActivate(ByVal sender As Object, ByVal e As _
        System.EventArgs) Handles Form1.MDIChildActivate
    MessageBox.Show(Form1.ActiveMDIChild.Text)
End Sub
```

With a few adjustments, you can continue to make MDI applications in VisualBasic.NET. MDI projects are still a great way to group and control many related child forms under one parent, similar to grouping multiple documents within a word processor application. You may have noticed that Microsoft's Office suite of tools has moved away from the MDI application model in favor of a more standalone-type model. If you open Word 2000 and then click the New Document button, a second Word window opens. Instead of two documents sharing a parent, you have two instances of Word 2000, each with its own document. I believe many former MDI applications will also follow this new application model and abandon the parent/child form relationship.

Modal Forms

A modal form is one that demands your attention and stays as the active form until you satisfy its needs, usually by clicking an OK or Cancel button. This type of form is often used for application About boxes and pop-up Options or Settings dialog boxes. This is a great form-display mode to use if you absolutely must get the user's input on something before they can go on. A form that allows you to click another form and move the application's focus away from it is known as a *modaless form*. How you make a form modal has been greatly simplified in .NET. It's all a matter of how you show your form. If you do want the form to be modal, you use the **ShowDialog** method of that form. If you want the form to appear as a normal form that can loose focus, you just use the **Show** method. Here is an example of a form named **CustomerData** being shown as modaless:

```
CustomerData.Show
MessageBox.Show("Please fill in the customers data")
```

And here is a form being shown as modal:

```
Options.ShowDialog
MessageBox.Show("Thank you for your inputs")
```

Besides the obvious difference in how you show the form, another important difference exists between these two methods. The first nonmodal example would open the **CustomerData** form and continue processing to the next line that pops up a **MessageBox**. The second example would show a modal form and not proceed to the following **MessageBox** until the modal form has been closed. This causes a pause in the code for the calling form, because it will want to wait until the modal form receives its input before moving on in the code.

The **ShowDialog** method can be used without a parameter, or it can be passed the name of a form, which could be the keyword **Me** for the current form or the name of another form currently showing. This form becomes the parent of the modal form, but the new modal form is still on top and demands attention. The **MessageBox** is a type of modal form that forces you to click a button to make it go away, but you only need to use the **Show** method for this form.

The MessageBox

Until now, the **MessageBox** seemed more like a utility to pop-up messages than it did a real Windows form. Previously, you used the **MsgBox** function to launch your pop-up messages. You can still use this function as a shortcut in .NET, but what you are really doing is instancing a special forms Class and passing parameters to its constructor. The **MessageBox** in .NET is derived from the **System.Windows.Forms.MessageBox** Class and behaves just like a normal form. You use its **Show** method to make it visible, and pass it some parameters to set up its features. Here is how you would call the new **MessageBox**:

```
MessageBox.Show("Please insert a disk in to Drive A", "User Error",
MessageBox.IconError + MessageBox.OKCancel)
```

The first parameter is the text that will be inside the **MessageBox**, the second parameter is the **MessageBox**'s title, and the third parameter decides what style the **MessageBox** takes on. The style decides which icon is displayed within the **MessageBox** as well as what types of buttons the **MessageBox** provides the user with. To specify both the icon style and the button style, you need to separate these two parameters with a plus sign, as in the preceding example.

Although **MessageBoxs** are just another Windows form Class, you cannot declare them using the **New** keyword. Obviously, you do not want to have multiple **MessageBoxes** open at one time, so you only need this one instance to get the job done. The preceding example simply pops up a **MessageBox** control that goes away when the OK or Cancel button is clicked. Many times, you will want to know which buttons on your **MessageBox** were pressed. You can use either the **If** or the **Case** statement to trap this button and react to the user's selection. Here is an example of a **Case** statement that will trap an **AbortRetryIgnore** **MessageBox**'s button selection:

```
Select Case MessageBox.Show("Can not save file - share drive unavailable", _
      "Network Error", MessageBox.AbortRetryIgnore + MessageBox.IconError)
    Case DialogResult.Abort
        'Abort the Save procedure
    Case DialogResult.Ignore
        'Skip saving this file and move on
    Case DialogResult.Retry
        'Retry the failed file save
End Select
```

You could also use an **If** statement, which would look like this:

```
Dim UserExit As Boolean
If MessageBox.Show("Are you sure?", "Exiting", MessageBox.YesNo) =
DialogResult.Yes Then UserExit = True
```

Notice that the style parameters all pass in a property of the **MessageBox**, such as **YesNo** or **IconError**. The result of the **MessageBox** can be checked via constants in the **DialogResult** Class, which is also derived from the **System.Windows.Forms** Namespace. The result is a statement that reads just like a sentence and can be clearly understood by anybody.

Designing for Windows Forms

Throughout the years, the number of types of applications that you can create has grown considerably. You started out with those dry and colorless character-based applications, and graduated from there to GUIs and forms with Visual Basic. Then, you had to decide if your form would be an MDI or an SDI (Single Document Interface). Recently, the Web has moved to the forefront of development, with coders using CGI scripts, JavaScript on the client side, or ASP-based server-side scripting. Advanced Web developers have learned to implement COM components in their ASP projects to remove and reuse much of their logic. Now you need to know when is the right time to use a Window form, and how you can take advantage of these new Web Services being hosted on the Internet from your Window forms.

When to Use Windows Forms

The first decision to make is whether to use a Windows or a Web interface. Many traditional Windows developers may sneer at the thought of using a Web interface for their project, but the increasing demand for these applications cannot be ignored. The lure of server-based Web interfaces is strong due to the ease of deployment and maintenance. With browsers becoming more and more powerful all the time, they will soon be the ideal container for almost any project you can build. Windows form projects typically require greater deployment planning, and having to maintain hundreds of client installs of your application can grow to become a nightmare. If your client machines are not on a network, then you will have no choice but to go with Windows forms for the project. You may also choose to go with Windows forms if a lot of processing needs to be done on the client, such as a graphical design tool.

If you choose to go the Windows forms route, you need to make some more decisions, such as whether to use SDI or MDI. Proper design of your Windows forms is essential for maximizing code reuse and application scalability. How much processing you plan to do on the client will decide how much code is housed on the client versus on a server somewhere else on the network. You now have the ability to use Assemblies over the Internet in the form of Web Services, which adds a whole new level to the *n*-tier deployment paradigm if your application will have access to the Internet.

Windows Forms on the Presentation Tier

If you are following proper *n*-tier architecture and coding principles, then your Windows forms will contain as little, if any, business logic code as possible. You will not want to run a query against a database directly from a button control's **Click** event, nor would you want to validate a business rule here either. If you did, you would be smashing all the tiers of a good *n*-tier design into the presentation tier, making your application single-tiered, or possibly two-tiered at best. This can have a horrible effect on your application's scalability and maintenance planning. What if the database connection has to be changed, or the business rules are changed? You would have to redeploy the updated Windows form pieces to every single user. As discussed in Chapter 2, a Windows form should only be used for displaying information to the user and getting input back from them.

I do a lot of Web development, and I like to think of interfaces as "thin clients." By creating your Windows forms "thin," you should be able to create a duplicate Web interface for a browser that can reuse the exact same logic that is contained in the business tier. Interfaces should be used only for creating the visual environment, and nothing else. When you are thinking about thinning out your Windows form code, think about what code you could move to the business tier that you would want to take advantage of from a mirror Web interface. When in doubt, move the code out.

With that said, you certainly will find some instances of code that is better off contained in your Windows form. This specialized code usually performs a function directly related to the display and intake of data, such as a top-level input validation formula. You might want to tell a user before they click the Save button that such-and-such a field is blank or that the phone number they entered is missing a digit. This Presentation-level code will save the application a network round trip. You will also have a happy customer if your Windows form tries to help them enter data, instead of letting them make a load of mistakes and then laughing at them after the **SaveData** routine comes back with a long list of errors. You, the developer, can laugh at the customers all you like, but your interfaces really shouldn't.

Calling Web Services from Windows Forms

While you may not know what Web Services are at this point, it is important that you know that you can use them in your Windows forms. You have already read a few examples of what a Web Service can do, such as the weather service example in Chapter 1. A Web Service will host a function or service that your applications can call on to do some work for them. One of the great things about Web Services is that you do not have to be writing a Web application to take advantage of them. Your front end to the application can be a Windows form. Behind the scenes, your form may wish to call upon a Web Service to do some of its processing or provide it with some data, such as a weather report or some movie times.

Calling a Web Service is very similar to calling upon any other Assembly. The main difference is in the reference you set. Instead of adding a regular reference to your project, like you would a DLL or another Assembly, you right-click the project's name in the Solution Explorer and select the Add Web Reference menu item. The form you use is very similar to a Web browser. The left side offers you hyperlinks to locate the Service you want, and the right side gives you more information on the items you select. You are asked to enter the URL address of the Web Service you wish to use. If you do not have the exact URL of the Web Service, you can use the Web Service browser to surf to the hosting Web site and locate the Service or read more information about it. Your library of available Assemblies just grew considerably. Now, instead of being limited to the Assemblies installed on your system, you can incorporate code in your project that is housed anywhere in the world. Literally. Anybody that puts a Web Service out on the Internet is making it available to anyone who wants it, provided of course that you meet the proper licensing or fee requirements.

I expect that soon there will be search engines and master lists of available Web Services you can search. This is an incredible new concept that Microsoft is banking on becoming the next wave in application development. After you read Chapter 11 on Web Services, remember that you can harness the power of these Assemblies from traditional Windows applications. When you are designing Windows applications, you should also keep in mind the ability to use Web Services, and think about how you can centralize certain functions that the forms can use via the Internet. This is by far the best implementation of code reuse yet.

Windows Form Properties

A form has a bundle of complex settings that you can use both at design time and during runtime to change its appearance. So many great settings are available that you should try to not use the default form appearance and come up with something new and exciting.

General Forms Settings

You can still modify the border of your form to allow it to be resizable or fixed. The **BorderStyle** setting is found under the **Appearance** grouping, and along with the old familiar settings, it also offers a new look called **Fixed3D**, which gives your form a really cool "sunken-in" look with the border of the form appearing to be a frame. Your form can have fixed or sizable borders, and can appear as a normal window with a full toolbox or as a Dialog window with only the Close button showing. What I really like about the form's **BorderStyle** property is that it is not locked down at runtime. Here are two functions that will change the form's **BorderStyle** property whenever the mouse pointer enters and leaves the form's display area:

```
Public Sub Form1_MouseEnter(ByVal sender As Object, ByVal e As _
     System.EventArgs) Handles Form1.MouseHover
   Form1.BorderStyle = Windows.Forms.FormBorderStyle.Fixed3D
End Sub

Public Sub Form1_MouseLeave(ByVal sender As Object, ByVal e As _
     System.EventArgs) Handles Form1.MouseLeave
   Form1.BorderStyle = Windows.Forms.FormBorderStyle.FixedSingle
End Sub
```

This code has a neat effect on your form, making it come to attention when the user moves his or her mouse into its area. These functions show off the form's ability to change its style at runtime. The **MouseEnter** and **MouseLeave** events can have many other uses as well, such as changing the mouse's pointer icon whenever a user hovers over a special area on your form.

When you add a form to your project, the source code file you add will have a generic name, such as Form1.vb. Changing this is a little different from what you are used to. If you click the form in the designer window, its Properties window will be filled with a long list of properties related to the form's layout and appearance. A **Text** property is included that sets what the text says on the form's title bar. This was formerly known as the form's caption, and all captions having to do with forms or controls are no longer used in .NET. To change the name of the form's source code file, click the form name in your Solution Explorer window. The Properties window now displays a different set of properties from those associated with the display of the form. Here you will find a **FileName** property that lets you change **Form1.vb** to something else, such as **frmReservation.vb** (a proper Hungarian name for one of my Oceanside Resort reservations desk forms).

Visual Studio.NET no longer features a starting position placement window in which you can tell a window what portion of a screen it should start in. Instead, you set the window's **StartPosition** property to one of five settings: **Manual, CenterScreen, WindowsDefault-Location, WindowsDefaultBounds**, or **CenterParent**. The two **WindowsDefault** settings base their starting positions on an internal operating system setting of where a window should start. If your form has a border style of **Sizeable** and you select the **Windows-DefaultLocation** setting, your form is the same size as it was in the designer and appears near the upper-left corner, and the OS decides what the best location is to place this form. Because this is such a flexible and adaptive setting, Visual Studio has made this the default **StartPosition**. If you select the **WindowsDefaultBounds** setting, your **Sizeable** form is resized to a default form size as decided by the OS. **CenterScreen** centers your form in the exact middle of the screen, and **CenterParent** centers the form within its parent form's area. If the form is an MDI child, the parent is its MDI container. If your form is standalone, then the parent is the screen itself. The **Manual** position starts your form flush against the top and left edges of the screen, and allows the user to manually position your form as desired.

Window Positioning

Besides the window's **StartPosition** property, you have other means of placing or moving a window about the screen. A form is located by its **X** and **Y** properties or its **Top** and **Left** properties, which state how far over from the left and how far down from the top the form is displayed. In .NET, you use GDI+ to draw your forms where you want them. You use the GDI+ **Point** command to set the form's position, and it allows you to use this method at runtime as well as during form initialization. Here is how you use the **Point** command:

```
CustomerData.Location = New Point (10,10)
```

Like the **Top** and **Left** commands, the two parameters passed to **Point** dictate the distance, in pixels, from the left and right edge of the screen. The first parameter is the X (left to right) coordinate, and the second is the Y (up and down) coordinate. You must use the **Location** property for the initial placement of the forms you add at runtime, but after they're placed, you can reference a form's location by its X and Y coordinates. You can change one of these coordinates at a time, like so:

```
CustomerData.X = 80
```

This line of code would jump your form to the right 80 pixels. The same format works for the Y coordinate. The X and Y coordinates can be increased or decreased instead of being set to an exact value, by using the plus or negative symbol in front of the value you see in the following example:

```
CustomerData.X += 20
```

Your form would move 20 pixels to the right with this command. You could also use the negative sign in place of the plus sign to move the form left or up. You also can read the values of the X and Y properties to determine where your form is currently located on the screen. Checking these values first before trying to manually locate the form is a wise move.

An interesting alternative to the **Location** property of your form is the **DesktopLocation** property. It works exactly the same way, except instead of using the exact top and left corners of the screen, this property takes into account where the Windows taskbar is located and adjusts accordingly. If you place the taskbar at the top edge of your screen, a form placed at coordinates (0,0) would be partially obscured by the taskbar. If you set the **DesktopLocation** property to (0,0), your form would smartly locate itself directly below the taskbar and flush to the left. The same intelligent location settings hold true if the taskbar is on the left edge of the screen.

When manually placing your form on the screen, remember that all users do not use the same monitor resolutions. Whereas you may use 1024x768 and a form looks fine located at (700, 500), another user may use 800x600 and your form will be displayed halfway off the edge of their screen. The new **DesktopLocation** property might be the best choice of them all to help you compensate for the users' placement of that troublesome toolbar along the edge of the screen.

Window Sizing

Like the **Location** property, you must first set the full dimensions of a window added at runtime in one statement. Logically, this has two parameters: the first for your form's width, and the second for its height. You again use the GDI+ with the **Size** command, like this:

```
CustomerData.Size = New Size (400,200)
```

Your form would be 400 pixels wide by 200 high in this example. After you give the form its initial size, you can adjust either the width or height separately by using the form's **Width** and **Height** properties. A form resizing might look like this:

```
CustomerData.Width = 500
CustomerData.Height = 300
```

Again, be careful that you do not expand your form beyond the resolution of the users' screens. The width and height should be adjusted only after knowing what the form's current

X and Y coordinates are. You can also increment the **Width** and **Height** properties just like the X and Y coordinates, but you cannot increment the **Size** or the **Location** properties. Both the **Size** and **Location** properties of a form can be reused to reposition or resize a form after it has been placed, and this is the best choice if you plan to change both settings at once.

Layering

Forms and the controls hosted on a form can be layered, where one is on top of another. Many times, you will want to manipulate the order of items within the layers to bring something to the front of the order or send it to the bottom. Previously, you used the **ZOrder** property to assign an integer value that represented the order of an item, but now forms and controls have methods you can call to simplify the process. To bring a form or control to the very top layer, you call the **BringToFront** method. To send it to the bottom layer, you call the **SendToBack** method. A form that is brought to the top layer becomes the new active form in the application. If you call the **Show** method of a form you are opening, you can use the **BringToFront** method on the calling form to bring it back to the top of the order after the new form opens.

Opacity

Forms now have a property named **Opacity** that can have an interesting effect on clients using the Windows 2000 platform. The default value is 100 percent, meaning that a form is 100 percent solid and not at all transparent. You can set this property at runtime or in the form's Properties window to something less than 100 percent, and your form will take on a semitransparent appearance. This feature works only for users with Windows 2000, due to the advanced graphical nature of this property. Try out the following code in the **Sub New** event of a form:

```
Dim FormOpacity As Double = 0.5
CustomerData.Opacity = FormOpacity
```

The 0.5, or 50 percent, setting has a really nice effect, and the form along with its controls is mostly readable. Down around 0.2, or 20 percent, the form becomes extremely ghostlike and hard to read. You can change this at will at runtime, such as for a situation in which you want a form to fade out after a selection has been made and to fade back in when needed again. Here is a cool "gee whiz" routine that makes the form disappear and reappear when **Button1** is clicked:

```
Protected Sub Button1_Click(ByVal sender As Object, ByVal e As _
        System.EventArgs)
    Dim q As Double
    'Make the form disappear
    For q = 1 To 0 Step -0.01
        Me.Opacity = q
    Next
```

```
    'Bring the form back
    For q = 0 To 1 Step 0.01
        Me.Opacity = q
    Next
End Sub
```

This routine simply fades out the form and then fades it right back in. The form never unloads, and all controls maintain their settings. Try splitting these two loops between two different buttons, one for fade out and one for fade in. You can also make the lower bound of the loop something like .2, so that the form is almost gone but not quite. Now you can move the semi-invisible form around the screen and see what is going on behind it. This is a cool effect to use on small forms that are processing on a separate thread, such as downloads or file searches. You can see what is going on there, and you can also see the form beneath this one. You could use this feature for some pretty cool effects in your next program, but, of course, be sure you use it wisely. A cool effect can become an annoyance if abused.

TopMost Property

You will want some forms to stay visible on top of other forms, even when they are not the focus of attention. The floating toolbars feature in the Visual Studio environment is a prime example of just such a case. Even when you are not using the toolbar, it is still visible on top of the main form you are using. Setting the form's **TopMost** property to **True** has this effect on a form. A slight difference exists in how this executes on a Windows 98 system versus a Windows 2000 system. For Windows 98 applications, the form stays on top of every form you have loaded, even those outside of your current application. The Windows 2000 **TopMost** property behaves a little better, in that it only applies to the owning application and not to others.

Windows Controls

The code behind the controls you drop onto your forms also shows up within your form's Class. Within the form's **Sub Initialize_Components** procedure, you see all the settings for your controls that you set while in Design mode. Again, these settings were always there, you just didn't get to see them. You should get used to calling your controls Windows Controls, or just simply controls. The term "ActiveX" has been replaced along with the term "COM." Once again, I salute this change, because hearing about "ActiveX this" and "ActiveX that" was starting to get kind of old and overdone. Now you can just call a control a control and be done with it.

Control Properties and Methods

.NET has done away with default properties and methods, and this includes those associated with the controls on your form. You will no longer be able to trigger a button control's **Click** event simply by calling the button's name, nor will you be able to assign a value to the

Text property of a textbox control without calling it by its full name of **TextBox1.Text**. This makes the code neater and clearer because it removes any doubt about which property the code is referring to. You will get an error in the coding window if you try to reference a default property or method. By referencing all control properties explicitly using their full names, you will not run into any trouble.

Every control has a **Locked** property you can set to **True** or **False**. This is a handy property that locks the control down at its current size and location and prevents you from changing it. This is great if you get a form set up perfectly and want to prevent an accidental control repositioning. A locked control cannot be moved or resized. This lock protects the control only during design time, and does not affect the control's **Anchor** setting at runtime.

New Settings for Old Controls

Many of your favorite controls have some new settings in .NET that will add to the style and sophistication of your projects. The button control now has a **FlatStyle** property that, along with the **Standard** button look, enables you to make your buttons appear flat or popped-up. The flat look is in these days, especially with Web designs. The pop-up style has a kind of reverse effect from the standard look in that it appears flat until it gets focus, and then the control pops up for emphasis. This **FlatStyle** property applies to most of the controls, so you can give your interface a uniform appearance.

Many controls like the button now feature a **TextAlign** property, which gives you excellent control over which part of the button your **Text** label appears on. The top, bottom, left, right, and the corners of a control are now reachable with this property. Instead of giving your button a picture to display, you now have a **BackgroundImage** property that can be used with any style of button control. The **Image** property gives you even more control over a graphic on the button by allowing you to use an **ImageAlign** setting or pull the image used from an associated **ImageList**.

The textbox has a list of **Behavior** properties that you can set. These control what is and is not acceptable within a textbox, such as **AllowReturns**, **AcceptTabs**, and **PaswordChar**, the latter of which is the character this control uses to mask from prying eyes whatever the user types. Setting the **AllowReturns** property to **False** might be a good choice if you have a multiline textbox that you do not want to have hard returns in. These returns do not translate properly into a database field, and preventing these can really simplify your job.

The **Option** and **CheckBox** controls both have **Image** properties that can place a picture on their backgrounds, just as the button control can. The **CheckBox** control also has a property called **CheckedState**, which not only allows you to specify whether this box is checked or unchecked, but can also be set in an Intermediate state. With this setting, the box has a check in it, but it also has a faded-gray background color. If you have ever seen an install program like the one with Visual Studio 6 that puts a checkmark next to packages that are installed, and a faded checkmark next to packages that are partially installed, you have seen one possible use for this feature already.

The Anchor Property

If your form has a sizeable border or can be maximized to fill the entire screen, then you definitely want to set some anchors for all the controls on this form. An **Anchor** property is simply a reference to one or more of the borders on the form that tells the control to always maintain its current distance to that border. If you tell a textbox to anchor to the left border, it will always stay the exact same distance from the left border, no matter how you resize the form. If you tell a button to anchor to the top and bottom borders, it will maintain its current distance from both borders. When you pick a pair of opposite borders to anchor to, the control will have to resize its dimensions to maintain its distance. If the form is resized to be taller, the button will also have to become taller to maintain its distance from both the top and bottom borders.

The easiest way to set anchors for a control is at design time in the Properties window. When you select the **Anchor** property of a control, you get a special visual tool to click, shown in Figure 6.1. By selecting the bars that connect the center square to the four edges, you set an anchor to each border. The white bars are unselected, and the gray ones are selected.

You can also set or change an **Anchor** property at runtime in your code. Suppose that you have a button control that you set to anchor to all four borders while in Design mode. When you run the application and expand the form, the button will expand as well. Somewhere in your code, you could change this button's **Anchor** property to only anchor to the left and top borders, like so:

```
Button1.Anchor = Windows.Forms.AnchorStyles.TopLeft
```

When this line of code runs, nothing immediately changes about your button. But if you again resize the form, you will see that the button is no longer resizing itself, but only

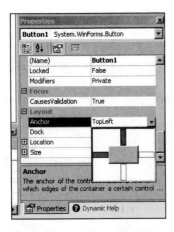

Figure 6.1
The control's **Anchor** property selector.

relocating itself to keep its distance from the top and left borders. Sometimes, you will want a control to get bigger if the form is maximized. Other times, you will not want it to get bigger, but rather only relocate itself to account for the change in the form's size. Picking the **TopLeft Anchor** style is equal to no anchor at all, because the top left corner of the form is where your control would have anchored itself to without the **Anchor** property. Picking the right and bottom borders could help your controls spread out on the form, to prevent a lot of unsightly empty space when the form is enlarged. Watching the form's dimensions is a wise choice that enables you to stop a user from resizing your form smaller than a preferred setting. Anchored controls may eventually shrink so far that they become unusable, and you can prevent this from happening by preventing the form from shrinking past a certain size.

The Docking Property

A control's **Dock** property is a familiar idea with a new twist. Everyone should be familiar with docking toolbars that can merge with one of the borders of the application or separate itself from the border to float freely on top of the application. Now you can use this docking ability with all of your controls. At runtime, you can set a control to dock with either the left, right, top, or bottom border. You can later set the control's **Dock** property to **None** to send it back to its original position before it was docked. The **Dock** property is available at design time, but you should leave it to **None** here. If you do set a control to dock to a border, it immediately jumps to that border in Design mode. At runtime, if you then tell this control to set **Dock** to **None**, it stays along at the border because that is its starting position. So, leave **Dock** set to **None** until runtime.

When a control docks with one of the borders, it fills up that border. If you dock a button to the top border, it becomes the width of the form. If you dock a second control to this same border, the two controls both are the width of the border and are displayed stacked one above the other. Because a control takes up so much space when docked, I do not recommend doing this with smaller controls, such as **CheckBox** and **OptionBox** controls. Besides the four borders, you can also set the **Dock** property to **Fill**, which causes the control to fill the entire form. Any control that is below this docked control in the stacking order will disappear. You can set which controls will be displayed on top by right-clicking a control and selecting the Bring To Front menu item.

Here is a simple example of control docking. You need to create a Windows form with four buttons on it. The first button, **Button1**, is the control that you will **Dock**, **UnDock**, and **Fill** using the other three buttons. Here is the code for those three buttons' **Click** events:

```
Protected Sub Button2_Click(ByVal sender As Object, ByVal e As _
        System.EventArgs)
    Button1.Dock = Windows.Forms.DockStyle.Top
End Sub
Protected Sub Button3_Click(ByVal sender As Object, ByVal e As _
        System.EventArgs)
```

```
      Button1.Dock = Windows.Forms.DockStyle.None
End Sub

Protected Sub Button4_Click(ByVal sender As Object, ByVal e As _
      System.EventArgs)
      Button1.Dock = Windows.Forms.DockStyle.Fill
End Sub
```

Your form will look something like Figure 6.2. When you click **Button2**, **Button1** will **Dock** to the top of the form and expand its width to fill the form, and maintain its previous height (see Figure 6.3). Clicking **Button3** undocks **Button1** and returns it to its original position. Clicking **Button4** causes **Button1** to expand to fill the entire form (see Figure 6.4). You should right-click and select Bring To Front for buttons two, three, and four while in Design mode so that they will not disappear when **Button1** fills the entire form.

Figure 6.2
The docking control, with **Button1** undocked (**None**).

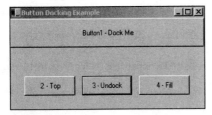

Figure 6.3
Button1 docked at the top.

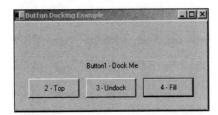

Figure 6.4
Button1 set to Fill.

Setting the Tab Order

A properly set up control tab order on a form is a thing of beauty. You can tell that the designer really put in the extra effort to make this form as usable and as sensible as possible. Visual Studio.NET has a terrific new feature that makes your tab-setting job so much easier. No more having to pick one control, set its tab order, pick the next control, set its tab order, and so on. Now, you only have to look under the View menu and check the Tab Order menu item. A little blue box with a number in it will appear to the left of each control on your form.

To set the tab order, you click each little blue box in order, starting with the control you want to be first. When you click a blue box, it turns white and the number reflects its new tab order index. After you click the last box, all the little boxes turn blue again and your tab order is set. If you make a mistake, just go back to the View menu and turn off the tab order, and then turn it back on to start over. Only controls that have a **TabIndex** property and are capable of getting focus get a blue box in Tab Order mode. If you need to remove a control from the tab order, you should set its **TabStop** property to **False**. You will still be able set the index of this control in Tab Order mode, but it will be skipped over when someone tabs to it. While you are in Tab Order mode, you can't alter or move controls or add new controls to a form, so be sure to uncheck the View | Tab Order menu item when you are done.

Ambient Properties

Controls often have **Ambient** properties that read a property of the container that is hosting the control. A label's background color can change when the container changes its background color. In VB6, if you place a label or option box on a form, the label's background color sets itself to the default gray. Changing the form's background color has no effect on a label's background color. The controls in .NET are far more intelligent now. Change a Window form's background color and the controls adjust by picking up on the **AmbientChanged** event. Drop a new control onto a colorized form and it initiates itself with the form's current background color as its own. When designing your own controls, keep the **AmbientChanged** event in mind and make your control react to changes in the container, such as a new color or a resizing.

Group Resizing

This little trick may save you some time when you are trying to resize a bunch of controls on a form. If you select one control, hold down the Alt key, and select all the other controls you wish to change; they are grouped together and all are highlighted. Now, just pick the resizing dots on one of these controls and start dragging. All the controls in the group resize themselves along with the one you are controlling. This may save you some time when dealing with a page full of **CheckBox** controls or a group of button controls. You also can move the entire group as one selection, just as you could before in version 6.

With the whole group selected, look under the Format menu at the top. A few handy menu items here can help you make a group of controls more uniform. Choosing Format | Make Same Size makes the sizes of all grouped controls match. You also can match all of their vertical and horizontal spacing. Drawing controls by hand can sometimes be imprecise, but by grouping them together and selecting a few Format options, your controls will look like you spent hours setting them up.

Control Event Handlers

At the top of the Designer region of your form's Class code you will see where the controls are declared. Notice that they are declared using the **WithEvents** keyword. This is done so that you can write a **Button1_Click** procedure, which will run whenever the **Button1** is clicked and raise this event. This is important to note if you decide to add controls dynamically via code. If you do not declare a control **WithEvents**, then the event-handling code you write for that control will never get triggered. A cool alternative exists to writing a separate event for every single action. You can group a collection of events together to go to one procedure by creating a handler. A handler is based on the **Delegate** you learned about in Chapter 5. Suppose you have a form with two button controls on it named **Button1** and **Button2**. You can add the following code to the **Initialize_Components** procedure to redirect each control's **Click** event to a single handler event:

```
AddHandler Button1.Click, AddressOf Me.Click_Handler
AddHandler Button2.Click, AddressOf Me.Click_Handler
```

The handler named **Click_Handler** will be somewhere within your form's Class (hence the **Me** keyword) and might look like this:

```
Protected Sub Click_Handler(ByVal sender As Object, ByVal e As _
      System.EventArgs)
   MessageBox.Show("You Caught Me!")
End Sub
```

If you compare the handler's arguments to those of a normal **Click** handler, you will see that they are the same. Just like the **Delegate**, the parameters must be a match when redirecting events to a handler. The **AddHandler** points the control's event to the handler you specify, which the **AddressOf** keyword will point to. A nifty variation on this theme is dynamically pointing an event to different handlers based on a special circumstance. If you have a customer information form that has a Close button, you may point that button's **Click** event to a simple close handler until something on the form changes. Then, you may wish to redirect the **Click** event to a save procedure to save the form's values back to the database.

Event handlers can be used for any event, and they are particularly well suited for handling events being raised by form controls. If you no longer wish to redirect an event to a handler, you can remove that handler by using the **RemoveHandler** command. If you remove a handler, be sure this is an event your code can live without.

ActiveX Controls

Visual Studio.NET now uses Windows Controls as its preferred interface control. This does not mean that you can no longer use your library of ActiveX controls in .NET. If you right-click the Toolbox window and select the Customize Toolbox menu item, a window opens showing four tabs. The first tab, named COM Controls, lists all of your old ActiveX controls that are currently registered (remember the old days when you actually had to register these things?). The last tab, called .NET Framework Controls, lists the native Windows Controls that come with Visual Studio.NET.

It is highly recommended that you use the native .NET controls instead of the older COM controls whenever possible, because the .NET controls have been designed with the new framework in mind. Microsoft is planning to offer an upgrade tool to help you migrate your old ActiveX controls to the new Windows Controls format, though from what you have learned here, you should know that this will not be an easy transition and may require a lot of recoding.

Adding Controls in Your Code

Dragging and dropping controls is as easy as can be, but now that you can have form Classes that you create purely in code and not in the designer, how will you get a control onto them? The same way you made the form: by coding it. Here is an example of how you would add a button control to your form at runtime:

```
Dim MyButton As New Button()
MyButton.Text = "New Button"
MyButton.Size = New Size(100, 40)
MyButton.Location = New Point(50, 50)
Me.Controls.Add(MyButton)
```

You first declare **MyButton** as a new instance of the **Button** Class. Next, you set up its starting properties, such as its **Text, Size,** and **Location.** The **Point** and the **Size** functions are a part of the GDI+ drawing collection. Finally, you add **MyButton** to the current form's Controls collection. Depending on the control you are adding, you may have other properties you wish to set up before adding the control to the form. Always be sure to set a form's or control's **Size** and **Location** properties before showing it.

This is where the event handlers can really come into play. When your application first runs, you do not have a **MyButton** on your form, and you won't have a **MyButton_Click** event handler. After you add the new control to your form in the code, you will want to point that control's **Click** event to a predefined event handler, just like you learned to do a few pages ago. Here is what the next line of code in the **MyButton** example would look like:

```
AddHandler MyButton.Click, AddressOf Me.Click_Handler
```

Now your brand-new button has a **Click** event handler. The whole event handler thing might have seemed a bit overboard when you read about it previously, but now you can see where setting these up becomes necessary.

Controls Collection

Adding dynamic controls to your forms at runtime required a trick in older versions of Visual Basic. You had to have that type of control already on your form named as an array so that you could add a new one to it. Your **CommandButton** would be named **CommandButton(0)**, and you could then add **CommandButton(1)** to the form. Without a control array, you could not add dynamic controls at runtime. All of your dynamic **CommandButton** controls would be under one array, and all of your dynamic **CheckBox** controls would be under another array. It could become very confusing to maintain all of these controls.

The Controls collection was introduced in Visual Basic 6, and in .NET, this is the only method you have to remember. No longer do you have to deal with clunky control arrays. You are not even allowed to create a control array. The Windows forms all have a Controls collection to which you can add any control you like, whether it is already on the form or not. Here is some code that adds a new **CheckBox** to **Form1**:

```
Dim MyCheck As New CheckBox()
MyCheck.Location = New Point(10, 10)
MyCheck.Text = "I like pizza"
Form1.Controls.Add(MyCheck)
```

You simply declare a new instance of the control, set its starting properties (such as its labels and coordinates), and then **Add** it to the **Form1.Controls** collection. The Controls collection has a **Count** method that tells you how many controls are currently loaded on the form, both those added at design time and those added dynamically at runtime. Because all of your controls are stored in a single collection, you can manipulate and scan through them with ease. Try creating a form with an assortment of controls on it. Add at least five or more controls, and make at least one of them a **CheckBox**. Using the following code, you can sift through the collection and spot which controls are **CheckBox** controls and what their **Text** values are:

```
Dim q As Integer
For q = 0 To Form1.Controls.Count - 1
    If TypeOf (Form1.Controls(q)) Is CheckBox Then
        Messagebox.Show(Form1.Controls(q).Text)
    End If
Next
```

As you learned in Chapter 4, all arrays are zero-based. If you have five controls on your form, then your **For** statement needs to search from 0 to 4, or **Form1.Controls.Count −1**. Checking a control for its **TypeOf** can be very handy if you wish to weed out all controls but a specific type.

Validation

Introduced in version 6, the Validation model makes checking the values of textbox controls and other controls a lot more efficient. The actual implementation of the **Validate** event was a bit confusing until you got used to it. Whenever a control loses focus, the next control selected or appearing next in the tab order responds with its **Causes Validation** property. If the property value is **False**, then the next control gets focus and the program moves on. If the next control says **True** to **Causes Validation**, then the **Validate** event of the control losing focus fires. While this seems odd at first, the reasoning is sound. If the control losing focus were to trigger the **Causes Validation** event, then you would never be able to leave this control until you entered a valid item. But, if the other controls on the form trigger its **Validate** event, then you can have controls, such as a Cancel or a Help button, that do not trigger the validation event and allow the user to escape this box without fixing the error.

A similar validation model is in effect in .NET with a few minor changes. How controls use **Causes Validation** is unchanged, but the events you place your code in have changed. Instead of a **Validate** event, you use the control's **Validating** event, as in "Hold on, I'm validating something." Here is an example of a **Validating** event for a textbox:

```
Private Sub Text1_Validating(ByVal eventSender As System.Object, ByVal _
      eventArgs As System.EventArgs)
    If Len(Text1.Text) < 2 Then
        Throw New System.Exception
    End If
End Sub
```

In the **Validating** event, you do not need to have a **Cancel Boolean** data type, though you can use one if you wish. If you use the VB6-to-.NET code-migration wizard, you will see that it carries over your **Cancel** variable into the new .NET project. But, because **Cancel** does not have any immediate relevance to the **Validating** event, the migrated code will have to manually check the **Cancel** variable's value and throw an exception if it is **True**. When you find the control's value to be invalid, you need to raise an exception using the **Throw** command, which replaces the **RaiseErr** command. This sets the focus back to the control.

You may want to pop up a message or give the user a ToolTip to let them know what is wrong with the value they entered. A user can get frustrated quickly if a control does not let them leave and does not have the decency to tell them why. Also be sure to set some control's **CausesValidation** properties to **False** to give the user an escape route. Help and Cancel buttons are a good place to do this.

Controls now have a second event associated with validation called **Validated**. This event will fire if the **Validating** event passes successfully, as if to say "Yippee, I'm validated!" If you wish to trigger an action on your form whenever a certain field is successfully validated, this would be a great place to do it. You might want to enable the Save button as soon as a certain field is changed and validated so that users see that they need to save their changes before leaving the form.

Visual Inheritance

So far, you know about two forms of inheritance: interface and implementation. Those are the two official types of inheritance, but with .NET, Microsoft is introducing a third form called *visual inheritance*. You know that inheritance involves referencing a premade Class to take advantage of its properties and methods in your new Class. This gives you an excellent way to reuse your code. You also now know that Windows forms are really Classes behind the scenes. So, why can't inheritance apply to Windows forms as well? Well, it can.

Adding an Inherited Form

You can design a form generically and build it into an EXE or DLL file. Maybe you have one form that could have many different uses, such as my **GenericRoom** example. I can build a **Generic Room Data Entry** form with all the textbox and **CheckBox** controls for a standard room, and then I can inherit from this form a **Deluxe** and **Bargain Room** form from which I can build on or override the generic form's functions. The layout and the graphics you place on your superclass (or as I like to call it, "superform") will appear in the new derived form. Exercise 6.2 shows you how to create a superform and how to inherit it in another project. You will be referencing the **GenericRoom** superform in Figure 6.5 during the exercise.

Exercise 6.2: Visual Inheritance

1. Start Visual Studio, select the New Project link, and then create a new Class Library project named "GenericRoom" (be sure to name this in the text box of the New Project selection window).

2. Right-click the project's name in the Solution Explorer and select Add | Add Windows Form.

3. Lay out your form in Design mode to resemble the form in Figure 6.5.

4. Select each item on the form and set its **Modifier** property to **Public**. By default, all form controls are **Private**. If you inherit a form with all **Private** controls, you will not be able to override most of their properties.

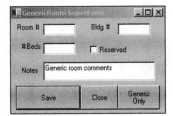

Figure 6.5
The **GenericRoom** superform.

5. Keep one button control on the form set to **Private** to prove that this control will not allow you to modify some properties in the derived version of the form (I named this button "Generic Only" in Figure 6.5).

6. Make sure the Notes **TextBox** control has some text in it, such as "Generic room comments".

7. Double-click the form's Save button and add a **MessageBox** line to pop up a message saying "I'm saving your data".

8. Right-click the project's name in the Solution Explorer and select Properties. Verify that both the Assembly Name and the Root Namespace text boxes say "GenericRoom".

9. Right-click the Class1.vb file in the Solution Explorer and delete this from the Project.

10. Save the Project, and then select Build | Build.

11. Click File | New and pick Project.

12. Select the Windows Application project and call it "RoomDataEntry".

13. Right-click the project name in the Solution Explorer and select Add | Add Inherited Form.

14. Type the form name "Bargain.vb" in the text box at the bottom of the form. Be sure the Inherited Form is the highlighted project type and click the Open button.

15. The next window asks you to locate the Class that contains your superform. If the GenericRoom project is not displayed in the list of inheritable forms, click the Browse button and navigate to the same directory where you found the GenericRoom.dll and select that file. Double-click the DLL and you should get a line in the list with a project name of GenericRoom.

16. Select the GenericRoom item on the list and click the Open button.

17. Your project now has a Bargain.vb item in it. Even though the icon next to it denotes a Class and not a form, if you double-click this item, you should see the **Bargain** form in Design mode.

18. Open the Bargain form in Design mode. Notice that the controls have a different coloring scheme than they did in the superform. The Generic Only button control that you left as **Private** is a dark-gray color, and the rest of the controls are a medium gray (slightly darker than the form's surface). This tells you visually which controls are **Private** and which are **Public**.

19. Click the form's Generic Only button control and observe the Properties window. Most of the properties you see are not editable, except for the Image List and Context Menu.

20. Click each control on your form and verify that each has its **Visible** property set to **True**.

21. Click the Bargain form's surface and set this form's **Text** property to say "Bargain Room Data Entry".

22. Select the empty Form1 that was created when you started this new project. Add a button control to it with a **Text** property saying "Add Bargain Room". Double-click this button and add the following two lines of code:

```
Dim MyBargain As New Bargain()
MyBargain.Show()
```

23. With Form1 as the startup form for the project (it should be already), save the project and then run your application.

24. On the starting form, click the Add Bargain Room button to open the Bargain form. Notice that the textbox contains text that you set on the initial GenericRoom form.

25. Click the Save button and you see the pop-up message you placed in this button control's **Click** event in the GenericRoom project. You will not see this code in the Bargain.vb file, because the code is inherited from the form's superclass, **GenericRoom**.

Exercise 6.2 shows not only how you can create a template form and reuse it throughout a project, but also how you can set certain controls to **Public** or **Private** to affect their editability, and how you can override an inherited form's setting, such as by changing the form's **Text** property to something new. You saw how the code behind a control's events in the template form appeared in the derived version through implementation inheritance. Visual inheritance is really implementation inheritance performed on a form, which is more visual in nature than a typical object Class. By adding an inherited form in the manner described, you gain the ability to open this form in Design mode and edit its appearance there. You can also inherit a form through your code, though this requires a lot more work to change something on the form, because you will not be able to open the form in Design mode.

Adding Visual Inheritance by Code

To see this code-based visual inheritance, add a second button to the main startup form of the **RoomDataEntry** project and set its **Text** value to say "Add Deluxe Room". Double-click this button and add the following lines of code:

```
Dim Deluxe As New GenericRoom.Form1()
Deluxe.Text = "Deluxe Room Data Entry"
Deluxe.Show()
```

Without using the GUI to add an inherited form to your project, you are able to declare a derived form based on a Class you have referenced. The tricky part here is that many of the edits and changes you made earlier via the designer window, such as setting the control's **Visible** property to **True**, now have to be made in the code. The upside is that code is more flexible than the designer, and enables you to create derived instances of this form dynamically based on variables and conditions you set.

Windows Services

This is a new application type for Visual Basic developers that previously only Visual C++ coders could create. This is also a change in terms for the Windows platform that everyone else will have to adjust to. Windows Services were formerly known as NT Services. These were the programs running in the background that were controlled via the Server Manager's Services interface. The Print Spooler is one example of an NT Service that most people have encountered. This program starts when the system boots and stays resident waiting for print requests. An administrator of the server can set whether or not the NT Service starts up automatically at bootup. Choosing this startup setting is a good choice for items like the Print Spooler or a Web Server, which is another great example of an NT Service running in the background.

When a service hangs, an administrator is able to select it from the Service Manager and tell it to stop and then start again, in hopes of jump-starting it and resolving the problem. If you are running a Windows 2000 machine, you will find Windows Services under Start | Programs | Administrative Tools. For NT 4 users, look under Administrative Tools for the Server Manager, and then check the first menu on this tool to locate Services. These interfaces list all the Services that are installed on the server and their current status. In Windows 2000, you can right-click a service to find its control options, and in Windows NT, you click a service's name once and then use the buttons to the right of the list.

Developing Windows Services

Developing Windows Services is an entirely different form of application development. These typically are not GUI-driven, nor do they want input from a user. These Windows Services are supposed to live at the system level and respond to system-wide events on a scale grander than a single user application. You cannot run a Windows Service from the Visual Studio environment to test it. Once you create the Windows Service, you need to install it on a test server and attach a debugging program to it or view log files to spot errors. Obviously, this can be a dangerous project to deploy, so do not try this at home or on a production server.

Because this is a program written for the server and not a user, you will not develop GUI interfaces for it, nor will you use feedback mechanisms such as **MessageBox**es. If your Windows Service has something important to say, write it to a log file. Because services often fail quietly and these failures are not discovered until much later, the log file is the smartest way to leave a trail of bread crumbs behind to figure out what went awry. A system tray icon is a good indicator to a user that the system is running, and thus should be used for most add-in services. You can probably see a whole family of icons in your system tray right now to let you know that some services are running in the background.

In Exercise 6.3, you walk through creating a very simple Windows Service that simply adds an entry to the Event Viewer's Application log every five seconds to let you know it is online. Once you understand how to create a Windows Service, you will find hundreds of more-complicated and exciting uses for this new Visual Basic application type.

Exercise 6.3: Creating a Windows Service

1. In Visual Studio, pick the New Project link on the Home Page.

2. Under the Visual Basic Projects folder, select the Windows Service icon; then, in the Name text box, call this "NETServiceTest". Click OK to create the project.

3. The service will start in Design mode. On the Visual Studio Toolbox, click the Components tab, and then drag an **EventLog** component over to the services designer and drop it. You should now see an EventLog1 box here.

4. Next, drag a **Timer** component over to the services designer.

5. Right-click the designer area and select View Code.

6. Enter the following lines within the services **OnStart** event:

```
EventLog1.Source = "NETServiceTest"
EventLog1.WriteEntry("I'm started")
```

7. Enter the next line within the **OnStop** event:

```
EventLog1.WriteEvent("I stopped")
```

8. Switch back to Design mode.

9. Set the **Interval** property for the **Timer** to 5000.

10. Double-click the **Timer** to access its **Tick** event.

11. Enter the following line in the **Timer** control's **Tick** event:

```
EventLog1.WriteEvent("The clock goes Ding!")
```

12. Switch back to Design mode for the service.

13. In the Properties window, change the **ServiceName** property to "NETServiceTest".

14. Click the Add Installer hyperlink at the bottom of the Properties window.

15. A new designer screen opens for the installer portion of your service. Click the ServiceInstaller1 component.

16. In the Properties window, change the **StartType** property to "Automatic".

17. Save your project, and then select Build from the Build menu.

18. Open a command prompt window, change directories to where your project is installed, and then use the **Cd** command to change your directory to the Bin subdirectory.

19. Run the InstallUtil.exe program to install your service on the system. The command line will look like this:

```
InstallUtil.exe NETServiceTest.exe
```

20. Open the Services Manager interface, and you should now see a service named NETServiceTest with Startup Type set to Automatic.

21. Right-click this service, and select the Start menu item (or in NT4, click the item once and then click the Start button).

22. Now your Windows Service is running. Right-click the service again and you will see a Stop and Restart command. Do not stop this service until the end of the exercise.

23. Open the Event Viewer under Administrative Tools.

24. Switch over to the Application log file. You will now see a list of entries made here by NETServiceTest. The oldest one on the list says "Test Started", and all the ones after this say "The clock goes Ding!", which is added every time the **Timer** on your service completes a cycle.

25. Switch back to the Services Manager, right-click the service, and pick Stop.

26. You may want to disable this service so that your "The clock goes Ding!" messages will not flood your log file. Windows 2000 users can right-click the service, pick Properties, and set the Startup Type to Disabled.

27. Go back to the Event Viewer and check the last message entered by the NETServiceTest. It will be your Stopped message.

28. To uninstall this service, go back to the Bin directory where you installed it, and type this:

```
InstallUtil.exe /u NETServiceTest.exe
```

This new application type has some really cool possibilities. Remember that the **OnStart** and **OnStop** events only occur at service startup and shutdown, and should only be used for setup and cleanup. The **Timer** will be your main tool for reoccurring checks, though you will find other ways to make your service respond to actions or listen for events, such as HTTP requests sent to a Web server. You will be able to pick the system account that your service acts as when performing its actions. In Design mode, you will be able to turn on two useful properties: **CanPauseAndContinue** and **CanShutdown**. These are off by default, but you may have uses for them in your project, and they will give the administrator some extra options for running your service. If you try to create a Windows Service on your own and find that it does not show up in the Services Manager after installation, check whether you added an **Installer** component to the Services project. Without this piece, the InstallUtil.exe does not have enough information to get the Windows Service checked into the operating system.

I think the Windows Service project will be a very popular new feature in .NET for VB programmers who have never had this power before. If your platform is Windows NT or 2000, Windows Services play a major role in the overall operation and administration of the computer. If you are developing for Windows 9x platforms, sadly, you will not be able to harness the power of Windows Services. Services typically listen or monitor for something, such as a print request, an HTTP request, or a change in the file system. Maybe you wish to monitor a message queue for traffic and want to be able to respond to new messages any time of day. With Windows Services, your prayers have been answered.

Summary

Visual Studio.NET does not just introduce a few changes or upgrades to the Windows application type; it throws out the whole framework and adopts a stronger, more powerful framework based on over a decade's worth of experience. A lot of great little features are included here along with all the major changes, and I think you are going to see some really snazzy interfaces in the coming year. The latest versions of Microsoft's Office suite and its operating systems are prime examples of this framework in action, and now you too can take advantage of these features in your projects.

Chapter 7

Exception Handling in .NET

Of all of the new features in Visual Basic.NET, the new model of exception handling is by far the least avoidable. You could easily forgo the new inheritance features and still be able to write a decent project in .NET, just as you could avoid using many of the other new and exciting tools that have been made available to you. I am not recommending that you avoid these great new features in any way, but you could conceivably write a working application without them. But, this is not the case with exception handling, because a program written without any exception-handling code is far from passable, and to write your exception routines in .NET, you have to learn the new .NET way of doing things. By now, you should be used to learning about new and strange things in .NET, so I will just dive right in and start covering the new exception handling model.

Introduction to Exceptions

The new exception handling model is quite different from the old way of handling errors. If you have some experience in Java or C++, this might not be a shock to you, but for the traditional Visual Basic developer, this new model will take some getting used to. Before I discuss how you will code for these new handlers, let's review a few common exception concepts and terms.

Types of Errors

When creating a program, you can encounter only three types of errors. Of course, for each type of error, there seems to be thousands of things that can cause that error to occur and send your application down the tubes. The three types of errors you can encounter are the following:

♦ Syntax errors

♦ Logic errors

♦ Runtime errors

The *syntax error* is a problem with the code created by the programmer. Often, a line is a missing character or a parameter that causes the compiler to quit and complain to the developer. Although .NET does not fix your typing quirks, it does help you to spot these errors immediately via the squiggly blue-line feature and the Task List. The IDE immediately spots a syntax error and points it out to you by placing the squiggly blue underline below it and by adding a notification line to your Task List letting you know a problem exists that needs your attention. This is why I recommend that you keep the Task List in view at all times. With it, you know long before you try to run the application whether or not the program will compile successfully, because of the presence or lack of errors entered in the Task List. Using the Option Strict setting in your modules helps a lot in spotting these tiny errors. Sadly, the new structured exception-handling framework cannot work around your syntax errors. Only you can prevent syntax errors.

A *logic error* happens in a piece of code that compiles and seems to run just fine. The bad part of this error is that the result you get is not the one that you wanted. This could happen due to an incorrect value in a variable or a mistaken calculation. If you have 10 students in the class, and you multiply the total of all of their grade point averages, you will indeed get a number back, but it will not be the classwide GPA you were hoping for. Again, this type of error is caused by the developer, and for the most part cannot be resolved with any form of exception handling. I say "for the most part" because often a logic error also results in a runtime error type, which can be resolved through exception handling, structured or unstructured.

The *runtime error* is by far the most dreaded and deadly of all errors. A syntax error becomes obvious very quickly when you try to compile your project, and a logic error can be spotted and resolved through even a casual application testing session, but the runtime error will come back to haunt you months after your product has been deployed to the field. While the occurrence of runtime errors is almost inevitable, how you deal with these can mean the difference between an ugly crash and your program continuing to function despite the bug. This is where exception handling comes into play. These errors are tricky because a block of code may run correctly over and over, and then suddenly crash when it encounters a situation it can't account for. As an example, consider a missing floppy disk error. The **SaveFile** code could work for months until some silly user forgets to put the floppy disk in the disk drive. With proper exception-handling code, you can catch this error and deal with it neatly to avoid that embarrassing crash altogether.

Trouble Areas in Your Code

Although it's true that an error can happen just about anywhere in your application, the vast majority of your errors will come from three different sources in your code. By recognizing these sources as problem causers and treating them accordingly, you are taking a huge step in making your application more durable and less likely to crash from these errors. The three main areas you should focus on when looking for troublemakers are your mathematical computations, data-access routines, and file-access routines.

Computations

Mathematical and computational errors include those pesky "overflow" and "divide by zero" problems. Often, the areas surrounding the computation might be clean and exception-free, but when you have a line that performs a calculation, the results can often be unexpected. You should try to partition off all of your computations and include exception-handling code near them to deal with any unexpected results that could crash your program. The following function would create a computational exception:

```
Public Sub BadMath()
    Dim StartVal As Short = 32760
    Dim q As Short
    For q = 1 To 10
        'add q to the StartVal
        StartVal = StartVal + q
    Next
End Sub
```

The **StartVal** and **q** variables are defined as a **Short** data type, which can only go up to 32,767. When the loop runs and starts adding to the **StartVal** variable, it will quickly exceed this limit, raising an **Overflow** exception to deal with. Anticipate problems like this and trap their errors before they pop out to the caller and cause more problems.

Databases

Dealing with a database is a complicated process that can result in numerous exceptions. Even if a routine worked last week against a database, things can change that will cause your queries to stop working and crash your application. Databases are outside sources of data that are often beyond your control. If a database administrator (DBA) makes a change to a user's access permissions, your code might be temporarily shut out. Any changes to a table in the database often result in an error if your code is not aware of these changes. Separate any and all database connections in your project from the rest of your code so that you can deal specially with their quirks and problems. You may further separate the queries from these connections, because even though a connection to the database can be made, sometimes the commands you send to that database can fail for their own set of reasons.

File Access

Working with files on the hard drive can be the most troublesome area, because the hard drive is subjected to user interaction and error. Your code may expect a file to be in the logical place, but if the user decides they don't need that file and delete it, your code is out of luck. Your code might open a file for input and expect 10 lines of code but only get back 5 because the user thought they could edit this file in Notepad. You might expect the user to know that a floppy disk needs to be inserted before they can save anything to it. This assumption would make you guilty of underestimating users and their abilities to wreak havoc, which is probably the worst mistake a coder can ever make. When working with the file system, always verify a file's existence first before proceeding with file read and writes. Code your procedures with the assumption that the file you want may not be there. Also be prepared to deal with those **End of File**, or **EOF**, errors coming up sooner than you may have expected.

When Is an Error Not an Error

In the Visual Basic community, using the term *error* is more traditional than using the term *exception*. I think the word *error* has been greatly misused in VB, though the intention of incorporating the term was to simplify things for you in a typical VB fashion. The word itself, "error," should make you think of such things as syntax errors and array out-of-bounds errors. In other words, errors are caused by things that the coder messed up or did not take into account. A commonly used example is a function that tries to read or write to a floppy drive. If the user fails to put a floppy disk into the drive, your application will raise an exception when it tries to write some data to the missing floppy. Sure, users are "error-prone," but users do not cause errors in your program. They instead cause "exceptions" to your code to happen.

An *exception* is a problem that pops up during the normal flow of events. Trying to write a file to a floppy disk that is not available is the exception to the function. You have certainly heard the old expression "the exception to the rule." Well, the normal flow of your routine would be the "rule" of the code, and a problem that occurs outside of this normal flow would be an exception. All too often the users of your program will cause these exceptions in your code. Never underestimate the user, and never assume that they will do the obvious or intelligent thing. If you ask them to insert a floppy disk, then your code better be prepared to deal with an empty disk drive. When you ask them to enter their first name, then you certainly better check what they entered for numbers or odd characters. I'm sure you could think of a million other things the users could do to foul up your code, and you should be checking and avoiding for every last one of those occurrences.

Not every exception is an error, but every error is an exception. I know it sounds like a riddle, but it's true. The first change you need to make is in your terminology. When you are writing code, anything the compiler does not like and points out as being wrong is an error, probably a syntax error as previously discussed. Any problems that your code encounters at runtime will be known as an exception. Think in these terms, and speak about your code in these terms, and you will be ready for the next step.

Dealing with Exceptions

Now that you know the types of exceptions and what to pay extra attention to when coding your project, you next need to understand how exceptions behave when they pop up and how you should go about dealing with them before they get out of hand.

The Exception Hierarchy

What happens to an exception if your procedure fails to handle it? It is passed out for the calling procedure to deal with. If that routine receives an exception from the routine that originated the exception, and fails to deal with it as well, it will again be passed up the call stack to the next-highest calling procedure, until finally it will pop out of the last process in the stack, causing your application to crash with an error. The call stack is a stack of processes that are currently in use on the thread. Your application might start with a Windows form that at some point calls a **CalculateFee** function in an outside Class, thereby adding this new function to the call stack. This function may in turn call other functions to do the job, such as a **FigureStateTax** function. These would be stacked on top of the calling process, and so on.

If an exception occurs in the **FigureStateTax** function, such as an array being referenced outside of its boundaries, that exception goes looking for some code to handle it. If the **FigureStateTax** function does not have any exception-handling routines in it, or the routines that it does have do not cover this type of exception, then the function closes and an exception is raised in the **CalculateFee** function. Once again, this exception looks for some error-handling code to deal with its problem, and if it finds none, the **CalculateFee** function closes and the Windows form gets the exception. This Forms Class is the startup piece of your project and your top-level Class, so if it can't handle this exception, the application crashes and the exception is raised to the user. Those poor unknowing users are always the last line of exception handling in all applications, and you know they won't know how to deal with this error either.

After reading the preceding example, it might seem like a bad idea to let any exceptions pop out of your functions, but often this is not a bad idea. You certainly want all of your procedures to have some form of exception-handling code, but you shouldn't try to handle every single possible exception here. The most important ones to catch are the ones that you can recover from, such as uninserted floppy disks or an array being out of bounds. Some loops in your code use exceptions to discover when something is finished, such as an **EOF** exception popping up after the last line of a file is read. Handle all the exceptions you can as close to the cause as you can. If your procedure cannot recover from the exception, then let it pop out to the caller and let them deal with it.

When you choose to **Raise** or **Throw** an exception manually from within your code, you are doing so to communicate to the calling procedure that a problem has occurred. Unless you catch your own exception, it will cause your procedure to exit and pass the exception along to the caller. This is a clean and professional way to pass errors out of a function. Sometimes, you may see a function that tries to use its output parameter to communicate that an error has occurred. This can be a very sloppy way of doing things, and requires that both the raising and handling functions have extra code created to implement this. Here are two examples to look at. The first is the wrong way to notify users of an exception, and the second is the right way:

```
'This is the WRONG way to pass an exception
Public Function ValidateCreditCard(ByVal CCNum As String) As String
    Dim q As Integer
    'Check for dashes in number
    For q = 1 To len(CCNum)
        If Mid(CCNum, q, 1) = "-" Then
            ValidateCreditCard = "Error! Do not include dashes in number"
            Exit Function
        End If
        'Send CCNum to credit bureau's Web Service
        ValidateCreditCard = CreditCardService(CCNum)
        Next
End Function


'This is the RIGHT way to pass an exception
Public Function ValidateCreditCard(ByVal CCNum As String) As String
    Dim q As Integer
    'Check for dashes in number
    For q = 1 To len(CCNum)
        If Mid(CCNum, q, 1) = "-" Then Err.Raise(2021, "ValidateCreditCard",_
            "Do not include dashes in credit card numbers")
    Next
    'Send CCNum to credit bureau's Web Service
    ValidateCreditCard = CreditCardService(CCNum)
End Function
```

The **For** loop in both examples checks for the presence of dashes in the credit card number passed to it. If it finds any, the first function places the error message in the output parameter. This function then exits via the **Exit Function** line, not raising any errors up the call stack to the calling procedure. The caller then has to examine the output of this function to look for the "Error" message, instead of seeing the expected results. The second function illustrates the proper way to communicate this problem to the caller, by using the **Err.Raise** line to raise the customized exception number 2021, complete with a **Source** property of **ValidateCreditCard** and a **Description** property. The caller will not have to look at the output parameter at all, because this exception triggers the caller's exception-handling code and forces the caller to deal with the problem.

The problem of how to raise an error becomes more pronounced when you are writing code that might be used outside of your development team. Everyone on the team might understand the code in the preceding bad example and know how to check the returned value for the word "Error" before using it. But, if you sell your function to an outside developer, they will be expecting the cleaner method of exception handling shown in the second example.

Resolving Exceptions

You have a few options available to you when dealing with exceptions that have been raised:

♦ Resolve the problem and try the operation again

♦ Allow the exception to pop out of the procedure to be handled by the caller

♦ Log the exception for later troubleshooting before letting it pop out

Fixing the problem or working around it is the optimum way of dealing with it, if at all possible. Many exception handlers expect errors to happen, such as an error caused by a disk not being available for read or write. You resolve this situation by letting the user know they need to insert a disk and then retry the operation. If the problem is not resolvable within the procedure but will not cause that application to come to a halt, then you want to let this error pop out to the calling procedure. Often, these errors are the result of improper use of your procedure by the caller, and letting them know about a problem allows them to fix it or work around it.

Letting exceptions pop out can work for you until you reach the top of the call stack and the parent module. If the top-level module can't handle an exception and chooses to let it pop out, the result is an application shutdown. For this reason, your parent modules, whether they are forms or controlling Classes, should have exception-handling routines capable of dealing with any and all errors so as to prevent unwanted crashes. The second option in the preceding list just isn't feasible for the top-level module. If an exception can't be resolved, then you need to log it, let the user know something bad has happened, and make every effort to shut down the application gracefully and save any changes or data that the user is working with. Because logging these exceptions is the key to fixing them, I'll cover that topic next.

Logging Exceptions

When an exception happens out in the wild after an application has been deployed, rest assured you will hear about it. Bug reports from the field should not come as a shock to most developers, and these bugs will inevitably happen. If your project has a well-run testing cycle, then you should be able to greatly minimize the number of uncaught bugs in the released versions of your product. If you don't test your code thoroughly, then be prepared for an avalanche of trouble calls.

Nothing is less helpful to a developer than a bug report that says "Somewhere on this screen, I clicked a button and the program crashed." Vague reports without details of the user's actions and the resulting exception type can leave a developer almost helpless to find and correct this problem. If you are thinking that a little user training can alleviate this problem, think again. Users tend to think in simple terms; click a button and get a response. More often than not, the details of an error are completely lost on them (I suspect that 99 percent of the time, they never even read the error message you give them).

As a result, the responsibility is yours to track these critical errors for later diagnoses. If your application encounters an unexpected error that it cannot recover from, you should log this error to the hard drive for later examination. If the details of the error have been properly recorded, then you will be able to call back the user who reported it and, with a few simple directions, get them to open the log file and read the message to you. It doesn't matter that this message will mean nothing to them, because it will mean everything to you. Message boxes should be kept simple and written in user-speak, while log entries must be detailed and technical.

Log files should contain as much detail as is available at the time of the crash, and can be as technical as you need. You should always include the exception name or number as well as the source procedure that raised the exception. You will find many other pieces of data that are useful and that should be added to your logging functions, such as the values of certain variables at the time of the exception, and what the user's last actions were before the error occurred. It would be extremely helpful to know that the user was on screen X and clicked button A right before the bug occurred, because then you know where to start to duplicate this error. Many logging functions lack this extra data because it is often difficult to figure out at the time of the crash. The use of global variables to hold a copy of this data can make the last-known user action or variable value easily accessible from your logging functions.

Unstructured Exception Handling

The old way of handling exceptions ("errors") is known as unstructured handling. From now on, when I mention unstructured handlers, you should think about the **On Error** statement. In this method, you tell the procedure at the beginning that if anything bad happens, it should jump to some predetermined line in your code. Because this is such an open-ended way to trap errors and causes your code to jump around a lot, it is considered to be an "unstructured" method. The example in Listing 7.1 shows how you would typically create unstructured exception handlers in Visual Basic 6.

Listing 7.1 Unstructured exception handling in Visual Basic 6.

```
Public Function CountUp() As Integer
    On Error GoTo CountUpErr
    Dim MyArray(10) As String
    Dim q As Integer
```

```
    For q = 1 To 20
        'assign values to each array element
        MyArray(q) = "New Value"
    Next
    Exit Function

CountUpErr:
    Err.Raise 2020, "CountUp Function", "Something bad happened"
End Function
```

The function in Listing 7.1 would indeed result in an error, because the array was only **Dimmed** to 10, and the **For** loop goes up to 20, resulting in an **Array Out Of Bounds** error. Let's look at the various parts of the unstructured method. At the beginning of each function or subroutine, you have to have an **On Error** statement to tell the function where to go if something bad happens.

On Error GoTo

By placing the line **On Error GoTo** at the top of your procedure, you tell the procedure to jump to this one special section of code if any exceptions occur. This is the only instance of the outdated **GoTo** command that you will encounter in .NET, which should tell you something about the entire unstructured method (that it, too, is outdated). Because this method is still an option in .NET, I cover it briefly, and for most of you, this will be a simple review. Two alternatives exist to the example in Listing 7.1. The following **On Error** line at the top of a procedure would completely disable the exception handling in this procedure:

```
On Error GoTo 0
```

The procedure with this **On Error** line would execute as if no exception-handling code were available. If you substitute this line for the one in Listing 7.1, the code would raise an error and break at the **MyArray(q) = "New Value"** line where it occurred. While disabling your exception handling might not seem like the best of ideas, you might find an instance in which you would want to see a procedure run unhandled to spot hidden errors. Here is a similar use for the **On Error GoTo** statement:

```
On Error GoTo -1
```

This version is a little odd, but it erases an exception that has been raised. If you use the example in Listing 7.1, in which processing is passed to the **CountUpErr** section, and then add this new **On Error GoTo –1** line to the error handler, the result is that your exception is raised and sent to the handler, which then promptly erases the error and exits the procedure without complaint. The **CountUp** procedure does not report an error, and the caller will never know it happened.

A second form of the **On Error** statement is commonly referred to as "inline error handling" and looks like this:

```
On Error Resume Next
```

This line acknowledges that an error might happen, but tells the compiler to continue to the next line of code. You could misuse this line to ignore any exceptions that happen in your procedure, but the true intention of inline handling is to place the code that deals with the error right after the line that might cause the error. If you substitute this line for the **On Error** line in Listing 7.1, the procedure runs straight through without stopping, even though it encounters numerous errors, one for every instance of **q** outside the dimensions of the array. This could result in a great deal of logic errors in your code. Look at the following subroutine:

```
Public Sub ReadDisk()
    On Error Resume Next
    Err.Clear()
    System.IO.File.Open("A:\MyFile", IO.FileMode.Open)
    If Err.Number = 57 Then
        'No diskette inserted error
        MessageBox.Show("Please insert a diskette and try again")
        Exit Sub
    ElseIf Err.Number = 53 Then
        'File not found error
        MessageBox.Show("I could not find MyFile on the floppy")
    End If
End Sub
```

This subroutine uses the new .NET method of file access via the **System.IO** Namespace. The procedure starts by stating that it will **Resume Next** if it encounters an exception. If you do not put a disk in the drive, or you put one in that does not have MyFile on it, an exception will occur at the **System.IO** line. When using **Resume Next**, the line immediately after the line that could cause an error should check the value **of Err.Number** and try to deal with it. In my example, if the **System.IO** line raises either an error number 57 or 53, a **MessageBox** control will be displayed, instructing the user how to resolve this problem.

Despite the exception, the procedure continues to run. If the **System.IO** line raises any other exceptions, they will not be handled at all in this example. I use the **Err.Clear** method to erase the current value of the **Err** object before running a line that could result in an error. This prevents the inline error checking from detecting an error that was caused prior to the intended line you are checking. The benefit of inline error checking is that the code that fixes the exception is directly beneath the line that causes the error, making this procedure a little more readable and efficient. The downside is that you may be checking for errors in many cases where none exists, which has a negative effect on efficiency.

Resume

You have already seen one use of the **Resume** statement on the same line as the **On Error** statement. You will also use **Resume** within your unstructured exception handler to send the control back to the main body of code after a problem has been resolved. If you fix the problem and want the line that raised the exception to run again, you would simply call **Resume**. If you want the line immediately after the line that caused the error to run next, you would use **Resume Next**. A third option is to follow your **Resume** statement with either a line number or a section label to redirect control to that particular area. You could use this option if you wish to jump backward or forward within the procedure to retry something or skip something.

Drawbacks of the Unstructured Method

The problem with unstructured exception handling is that anything bad that happens within the code ends up with the error in the **CountUpErr** section. You have to have some extra code in the error-handling section to detect the **Err.Number** and decide what went wrong. If you have a really long routine, then a lot of things could have gone wrong. After you figure out what happened (or didn't happen, in some cases), you either deal with the problem here within the module or raise an error back to the calling routine using the **Err.Raise** method. An alternative flow for the error-handling function I just described is to change the **On Error** statement to **On Error Resume Next**. This enables inline error handling, meaning that if the code has an error, it continues to the next line, because some code would be included there that would check for this error.

Although using the old **On Error** statement may seem familiar and comfortable right now, this is a really sloppy way of handling exceptions. Any error would send the code down to the single point of exception handling, the **CountUpErr** section, where you would have to figure out the error before dealing with it. The inline method of exception handling is a little better, because you know the error happened on the line preceding your handling code, but it is still sloppy, because you are checking for exception conditions even when they do not exist.

You will still be able to use unstructured exception handling in Visual Basic.NET, and continue to use **On Error** and **Err.Raise** in your code. But, if you truly want to be on the cutting edge, I urge you to give the new structured exception-handling framework a try. I think you will be really impressed with it, and realize how backward and unstructured the old way was. I mean, come on. The **GoTo** statement dates all the way back to the birth of Basic itself. It is time to move on to a more powerful means of trapping errors. If you think you can have it both ways, you're wrong. A function that uses **On Error** or **Resume** will not be able to use the new **Try, Catch, Finally** method. You might as well make the change now, because these old and outdated methods always seem to drop out of the Visual Basic language sooner or later.

Structured Exception Handling

In .NET, you will be introduced to structured exception handling. In contrast to the old unstructured method, you will now intelligently trap and deal with errors closer to their cause. Similar to a class's procedure, the exception handling is done in the form of a code structure. When you look at structured exception handling, which areas are being handled by what code will be very clear. If this is your first exposure to the **Try**, **Catch**, **Finally** method of exception handling, then these names probably sound pretty funny. An odd combination they are, but these are also very descriptive terms that indicate how this new method works. I'll examine each phase in this section.

A Structured Exception-Handler Example

To help you get started, take a look at Listing 7.2, which shows a .NET version of the **CountUp** function, complete with structured exception-handling code. If you want to try this code out, start a new WindowsApplication project and add one button control to it. Then, add the code from Listing 7.2 to the **Form1** Class.

Listing 7.2   A simple structured exception handler.

```
Protected Sub Button1_Click(ByVal sender As Object, ByVal e As _
     System.EventArgs)
   Dim Result As Integer
   Result = CountUp
End Sub


Public Function CountUp() As Integer
   'This is my Structured Exception Handler Demo
   Try
       'try to do this
       Dim MyArray(10) As String
       Dim q As Integer
       For q = 1 To 20
           'assign values to each array element
           MyArray(q) = "New Value"
       Next
   Catch
       'if the Try section fails, do this
       Debug.WriteLine("CATCH exception = " & err.description())
   Finally
       'Do this before Try finishes up
       Debug.WriteLine("CountUp FINALLY ran")
   End Try
   MessageBox.Show("CountUp function exiting successfully")
End Function
```

Don't worry if this all looks sort of alien to you, because I am going to break this example down piece by piece and explain everything that is going on here. Try running this example in Visual Basic. Start the form and click the **Button**. The **Button** will trigger the **CountUp** function. When the **q** loop tries to set the value of **MyArray(11)**, an exception will be raised, causing the code to jump to the **Catch** area. Because I am not dealing with the exception in this example, after the **Catch** block's **Debug.WriteLine** outputs its message to the Output window, the **Finally** section will run and write its line to the Output window as well. Now you have seen a function **Try**, **Catch**, and **Finally**.

After seeing this function run through once, change the upper bounds of the **For q** loop to 5 and then rerun the project. Because this loop does not exceed the array's dimensions, an exception will not be raised. After the **Try** block completes, the **Finally** block runs, and then the function will be completed. Because no exceptions are raised, the **Catch** block is never used.

Now, let's walk through each section slowly, to look more closely at what is going on in this example and how this simple function can be enhanced.

Try

The concept behind the **Try** section of code is that you are going to try to run through the normal flow of code. In my **CountUp** example, I am going to try to assign values to an array. I know that this is going to fail because the array was only Dimmed to 10 and my **q** loop goes all the way up to 20. The main body of this function is within the block of code marked by the term **Try**. Notice the **End Try** toward the bottom of the example. This marks the end of this **Try** block. The **Catch** and **Finally** blocks within this **Try** block apply only to this **Try**.

Below the **End Try** line, you could start another **Try** block to handle a different piece of your code. This is useful if your procedure performs more than one function, such as processing an input and then writing it to a floppy disk. You want to separate these sections and deal with their possible exceptions separately. If you didn't separate these two, your **Catch** routines would have to be a little bit smarter to tell where the error came from. Here are three important rules to remember when dealing with **Try** exception-handling code:

♦ Every **Try** must end in an **End Try**

♦ One **Try** section must have either a **Catch** or a **Finally**, or both

♦ Each **Try** section can have no more than one **Finally** section

If at any time you wish to get out of a **Try** block and move on in the function, you can issue an **Exit Try** command on a line all by itself. Just like the **Exit Function** command, this causes the processing to jump out of this block of code and move on to the same level of code that the **Try** was at. If the **Try** block you are exiting is followed by another **Try** block, then your project will proceed into the next **Try** block. When calling an **Exit Try**, the **Finally** section of code will run, so do not put any code here that you hope to avoid by using an **Exit Try** call.

Catch

Just as the name implies, the **Catch** section is where you catch the exception. If an exception never occurs in the **Try** area, then the **Catch** code is never used. A **Try** block does not need a **Catch** area, but without a **Catch** section, you rely on the **Finally** section to clean up the mess and exit gracefully (remember that a **Try** block does need either a **Catch** or **Finally** section, but not both).

What is really neat about the **Catch** section is that one **Try** block can have more than one **Catch** section. This is intended to save you the trouble of having to decipher the exception and decide which code to run or how you should gracefully exit the function. **Catch** works a lot like the **Case** statement. Like the **Case** statement, these **Catch** values will be examined in order from first to last. Because of this, you want to place the most likely **Catch** routines at the top to speed things along, just as you would place the most common **Case** values near the top.

Replace the **Catch** section in Listing 7.2 with the following segment of code. Be sure to remove the old **Catch** section, because you have a new one in this piece of code.

```
Catch e As System.NullReferenceException
    Debug.WriteLine("NullReferenceException CAUGHT")
Catch e As System.IndexOutOfRangeException
    'if Try fails, do this
    Debug.WriteLine("IndexOutOfRangeException CAUGHT")
Catch
    Debug.WriteLine("Some other exception has been caught")
```

With the upper bounds of the **For q** loop set back to 25, run the project and click the button. Because this is writing to the array outside of its dimensioned bounds, it will raise an **IndexOutOfRangeException**. Notice that the first **Catch** will be skipped, the second will be run, and the third will never be evaluated. This is why you put your most generalized catchall **Catch** statement at the bottom of the order. This will catch all unhandled exceptions that make it through your more focused **Catch** routines that came earlier in the **Try** block.

If you wish to trigger the first exception, add the following line of code before the **For** loop:

```
Throw New System.NullReferenceException()
```

Now, your function has two exceptions in it. The **Throw** statement is not truly an exception; you are just raising this statement to manually trigger your first **Catch** section. This is the .NET equivalent of the **Err.Raise** statement, and I will cover it in more detail shortly. Notice that when the project runs now, you get a **Debug** line from the **NullReferenceException** section, and not from the **IndexOutOfRange** section, even though the bug is still in there.

Three ways exist to use the **Catch** statement. The first is to name an exception type that you want to **Catch** with this section. If the raised exception does not match this type, then the error keeps looking for a handler. The other two ways are "catch-all" methods. The first catch statement creates a variable named *e* of a **Type Exception**, which gives your **Catch** section the **Exception** object from which it can learn more about the error. The least usable form of **Catch** is to use it without any parameters. In this case, you will not be able to detect what kind of error occurred, only that something did go wrong. Here are examples of the three **Catch** uses:

```
Catch e As System.DivideByZeroException
    MessageBox.Show("Caught DivideByZero error")
Catch e As exception
    MessageBox.Show(e.Message)
Catch
    MessageBox.Show("Something bad happened")
```

The order in which you place these **Catch** sections is critical to the outcome of your handling. Because the last two versions are open-ended and will **Catch** any exception passed to them, you do not want to place these above your detailed exception handlers. Like the **Case** statement, after a match has been found, the rest of the cases will not be checked, which is why the **Case** structure is a lot faster than a series of **If** statements. Always put your detailed and most likely **Catch** statements at the top, and save the catchalls for last.

You need to be really careful when coding your **Catch** sections to ensure that you do not introduce more unwanted exceptions to the **Try** block. If your **Try** raises an exception that is caught, but then the **Catch** section mistakenly triggers a new exception, the new exception will pop out of the **Try** block unhandled and go looking for someone to **Catch** it. The original exception will then be lost, and you will never know about the true cause of the crash. These extra exceptions are certainly unwanted, so take extra care when coding your **Catch** sections so that you do not introduce further errors into your code.

Finally

If **Try** is where you try to run the code, and **Catch** is where you deal with the errors, then what is the **Finally** section for? This is another clever feature of structured exception handling. Just as your Class has a destructor to clean up after, so too does your **Try** block, in the form of the **Finally** section. Suppose that the **Try** section has created a database connection and is in the process of executing a **SQL INSERT** command when the error occurs. If your **Catch** statement chooses to bail out of the procedure and let the error pop out to the calling procedure, you still are left with this hung-up connection to the database. If the caller were to run this procedure a few more times, you would end up with a whole lot of tied-up database threads, wasting precious system resources.

But never fear, it's **Finally** time to neatly clean up these problems. As you saw in my .NET **CountUp** example, the **Finally** section of code runs regardless of whether the **Try** block succeeds. Even when you bail out of the **Try** block with an **Exit Try** statement, the **Finally** section still runs. This is important to remember, because anything you put in here will run no matter what the results are.

When designing your **Try**, **Catch**, **Finally** structure, you want to always use the **Finally** section to clean up after your code. Never rely on the **Try** section to close database connections or reset variables, because if an exception occurs, those lines of code may never run and you will be stuck with a mess. When placing code in the **Finally** section, think through the **Try** block as if everything worked perfectly and now it is time to clean up. After you code the cleanup for a successful run, reevaluate the **Finally** section to see whether it will clean up properly if the **Try** section has an exception. Does the **Finally** section try to close a connection that may possibly never be opened in the **Try** section due to an exception being raised beforehand? Use this knowledge to make your **Finally** code as flexible as possible so that it will do a complete cleanup no matter how the **Try** block exits. Remember that the **Finally** block will always execute no matter what happens in the **Try** section.

Besides cleanup, you can also use the **Finally** block to run a special line of code, even if the **Try** block has an exception. If your procedure can possibly recover from an exception, then the **Finally** block is where you can make it happen. You can set the output parameter here to some value, even if an exception occurred. You can also use this area to give the user a **MessageBox** or to write a line to the Output window to improve your code-tracing and debugging phase.

The **Finally** is not mandatory unless your **Try** block does not have a **Catch** section. Even if you do not want to **Catch** an exception, you can utilize the **Try** . . . **Finally** structure to ensure that your block of code is cleaned up after, no matter what happens. The following example shows a **Finally** section that is being used to **Close** a file that is opened in the **Try** block. This would be a clean way of ensuring the file gets closed, even if an exception is raised and the **Try** block suddenly passes control away before it can close the file.

```
Dim MyLog As StreamReader
Try
    MyLog = File.OpenText("c:\Windows\System.ini")
    FirstLine = MyLog.ReadLine
Finally
    MyLog.Close()
End Try
```

You should always put your **Close** or disconnect statements in the **Finally** block when working with files or databases.

Using Multiple Try Blocks

The real beauty of the new structured exception-handling framework is that you do not have to rely on one single **Try**, **Catch**, **Finally** block to handle the whole procedure, whereas previously you had to rely on a single **On Error** statement for all of your code. You can, and you should, partition off blocks of your function into separate **Try** blocks so that you can deal separately with the different types of exceptions that might occur. If the first part of your function reads data from a file on disk, and the second part opens a connection to the database to save this data, then you will be dealing with two entirely different actions that could each result in many different and unique exceptions. By breaking these up, you can make the **Catch** and **Finally** code highly specialized, which will help you deal with problems more precisely. The example in Listing 7.3 shows a single function broken up into multiple **Try** blocks. Notice how the **Catch** sections of each block look for exceptions that are specific to that block only. This is important, because a **Catch** section cannot catch exceptions that are raised outside of its containing **Try** block.

Listing 7.3   A single function with multiple Try blocks.

```
Public Sub TryMe()
    'Multiple Try block example
    Dim MyLog As StreamReader
    Dim NewLog As FileStream = New FileStream("C:\NewLog.txt", _
        FileMode.OpenOrCreate, FileAccess.Write)
    Dim WriteLog As StreamWriter = New StreamWriter(NewLog)
    Dim FirstLine As String

    Try
        'Read in FirstLine of System.ini
        MyLog = File.OpenText("c:\Windows\System.ini")
        Debug.WriteLine("Reading System.ini section")
        FirstLine = MyLog.ReadLine
    Catch e As Exception
        Debug.WriteLine(e.Message)
    Finally
        MyLog.Close()
        Debug.WriteLine("Read section finished")
    End Try

    Try
        'Open a file to Write out the FirstLine value
        Writelog.BaseStream.Seek(0, SeekOrigin.End)
        WriteLog.WriteLine("The first line of System.ini said " & FirstLine) _
            Catch e As Exception
        Debug.WriteLine(e.Message)
```

```
    Finally
        Writelog.Close()
        Debug.WriteLine("Write section finished")
    End Try

End Sub
```

Listing 7.3 will look a little odd, because besides showing you how you can utilize more than one **Try** block in a procedure, it also introduces the **Stream** method of reading and writing to a file. Instead of the traditional **Open** statement followed by some **Input** and **Print** statements, you now use the **StreamReader** and **StreamWriter** to read and write to files. The reason for this change is to bring Visual Basic more in line with the other languages in the .NET family and how they read and write to files.

Notice in Listing 7.3 that the first **Try** block seeks to open a file, read a line from it, and then close it, whereas the second **Try** block opens another file, writes the line I read in during the first **Try**, and then closes the second file. If an exception occurs in either **Try** block, there is a **Catch** section to write the exception's description or **Message** to the Output window. I put the **Close** commands for both files in the **Finally** sections to ensure that no matter what happens in the **Try** blocks, good or bad, the files will be closed properly and will be ready for use again. If I had failed to **Close** the files and the program kept running, the files would be locked and unopenable the next time a procedure tried to access them.

Use these **Try** blocks liberally, and separate all of your major functions and calculations so you can better deal with their exceptions. Also, be sure to utilize the **Finally** section. You could easily get away with never using the **Finally** and placing all of your cleanup code at the end of the **Try** block, but if something causes your code to exit the **Try** unexpectedly, you will be leaving a big mess behind that is sure to trip up your program in the long run.

Nested Try Blocks

You have just seen how you can place one **Try** block after another to break up your procedures into clearly separated sections. Now let's see how you can nest a **Try** block within another **Try** block to further isolate exceptions within that block. Here is what a **Try** block with a nested **Try** block looks like:

```
Public Sub NestedTry()
    Try
    'This is the OUTER Try block
        Try
        'This is the INNER Try block
            Throw New System.NullReferenceException()
        Catch e As Exception
            Debug.WriteLine("Exception in INNER Try")
        End Try
```

```
    Catch e As Exception
        Debug.WriteLine("Exception in OUTER Try")
    Finally
        Debug.WriteLine("End outside Try")
    End Try
End Sub
```

In this nested example, any exceptions that occur within the nested **Try** block will first look for a nested handler. In my example, I have a handler that handles all exceptions, so the exception will be caught at this level. If none had been found, the **NullReferenceException** I threw in the nested **Try** block would pop out to the outer **Try** block and look for a handler. If an exception occurs in the outside **Try** block, it will only be caught by the **Catch** statements in the outside block, and never by a nested **Catch** statement.

Variable scope comes into play when creating nested **Try** blocks. If you declare a variable within the nested, or inner, **Try** block using the **Dim** statement, this variable will only be in scope within or below (inside another nested **Try** block below the current block) this **Try** block. If you were to try to reference this variable above this block, such as in the outside **Try** block or in another **Try** block below the outside one, you would get a "variable not declared" compiler error. I find that it's best to declare all variables at the very beginning of the procedure and not inside any **Try** blocks. This prevents all out-of-scope problems within the procedure.

You would use a nested **Try** block to break up a **Try** block into subsections. You might encounter a **Try** block that you feel should not be broken up into two separate vertical blocks, yet you have a section of code in the middle of a block that can cause its own unique problems or exceptions. You can place that section into a nested **Try** block to handle it in a special and unique way, and still keep all the code before and after this section in the same **Try** block. Be aware that exceptions within a nested block will pop out just as they would pop out of a procedure if a suitable handler is not found.

Constructor Exceptions

In Chapter 4, you learned about a wonderful new way to initialize your Classes, called the *constructor*. Whenever a caller creates a Class, the constructor initializes the Class's settings and places data in your properties so that the Class is completely ready for action. This is done via the **Sub New** event, which allows coders to pass input parameters to the constructor to customize the initialization. But because the constructor is a subroutine, it will not have an output parameter to tell the caller that everything was initialized without error. It is impractical to create a separate property, such as a Class **Status**, for the user to check after initialization to tell them everything is fine or something went wrong. For this reason, it is extremely important that you use exception handling in your constructors that will **Throw** an exception back to the caller if a problem occurs. Here is a Class's constructor that will **Throw** an encountered exception back to the calling procedure:

```
Sub New()
    Try
        'Initialize the class here
    Catch e As Exception
        'If there is an error, throw it back to the caller
        Throw e
    End Try
End Sub
```

If a problem occurs during Class construction, the Class that created it will get an exception. If no exceptions are raised, then the creating Class can safely assume that no problems were encountered and can immediately start using the new Class instance.

Identifying Exceptions

When working with unstructured and structured exception handlers, you will be using two different objects to read and analyze the errors. You will continue to use the **Err** object when working with the unstructured **On Error** statements, and you will use the new **Exception** object when creating structured handlers. How you raise your own errors will differ between methods as well. The **Err** object still has a **Raise** method, while you will now use the **Throw** command in your structured handlers to create errors in your code. Let's examine each method separately.

The Err Object

You will continue to use the **Err** object's two main properties: the **Number** and the **Description**. Your code can call on the **Err** object to identify an exception by its number so you can create a **Case** structure to deal with the most common of these codes. Because the **Description** field is text-based and often long, you only want to use this when you are logging the exception or when presenting the user with a message describing the exception. To sort and identify an error, you use the **Err.Number** property.

The **Err** object only remembers the very last error that occurred. If you resolve an error and the code continues to process, the next error that occurs will erase all the data from the previous error and replace it with its own. If you are interested in keeping a history of errors or values in the **Err** object throughout the run of your program, be sure to store these off into a file or array somewhere before they get erased. As you saw in the **On Error Resume Next** example, sometimes you will want to clean out the values in the **Err** object manually by calling its **Clear** method. This prevents inline error-handling code from detecting an old occurrence of an error that is no longer applicable.

The **Err** object has a third useful property, named **Source**. When you are troubleshooting errors within Visual Studio, it usually isn't too hard to figure out exactly where the exception occurred. But if your application is deployed and you have a logging function that keeps track of exceptions that it encounters, then it would really be helpful if it also made a note of which Class encountered this problem. By using the **Err.Source** property, you will find this information easily accessible. I highly recommend that you log the **Source** of any errors along with the number (the **Description** is probably unnecessary for logging, because you are smart enough to know what these error numbers mean).

Raising Exceptions

The **Err** object also gives you the ability to create your own errors. Although dealing with more errors within your own code may not seem like a good idea, raising a special error to the calling code that is outside your control is a good idea. If a problem occurs in your code that does not fit any of the standard Visual Basic errors, you can create your own error and raise it within the code. Then, the caller will catch this error and realize that something specific to your procedure had a problem. Be sure to document any customized errors you create so your users will know when to expect them and how to deal with them. Here is an example of an **Err.Raise** statement that sets a customized error number of 2020, and also sets the **Err** object's **Source** property and **Description** property:

```
Err.Raise vbObjectError + 2020, "MyClassName", "The Phone Number was not
    properly formatted"
```

When raising a customized error, you need to add the constant **vbObjectError** to it so that the receiving code can properly decode it. You do not need to use this constant when using the standard errors that come with Visual Basic. You can still raise an error from within a structured exception handler, and you will want to use this when creating customized exceptions, such as my earlier 2020 example. Your **Catch** statement would still look the same and would catch this error in the **e** variable, which is of Type **Exception**. The following code example shows a **Try** block that raises a customized error for the **Catch** sections to deal with:

```
Try
    Err.Raise(2020, "CCChecker", "Dashes in credit card number")
Catch e As Exception When Err.Number = 2020
    MessageBox.Show("Please do not put dashes in your credit card number")
Catch e As Exception
    MessageBox.Show(e.Message)
End Try
```

My customized **Err** number is 2020, which will be caught by the first **Catch** statement that checks the numerical value of the **Err** object using a **When** statement. If you change the **Err** number in the **Raise** statement to 2021, the first **Catch** statement will not catch this error, and your catchall last section will. The preceding example is very important if you wish to use structured exception handling in your project, and also plan to raise customized errors. You should **Raise** an error whenever a value passed into your Class does not validate, which will return to the caller an exception instead of an incorrect Class return parameter, or a parameter that holds the bad validation message instead of an output value. If things go right in your procedure, give the user what they want. If things go wrong, give them an exception.

Structured Exceptions

When creating structured exception-handling routines, you will not be dealing with the **Err** object, nor will you be identifying exceptions by their associated numbers. Looking back to Chapter 5, I advised against using raw numbers within your code, because their meanings are often unclear. Only the programmer would know what error number 53 is at a glance. But when a **Catch** section of a **Try** block traps an **IndexOutOfRangeException**, it is obvious which exception is being dealt with. All of these exception values can be found directly underneath the **System** Namespace. As long as your module has **Imports System** at the top, you will be able to directly reference the exceptions by name in your code.

Because you are now expected to remember a bunch of constants and forget about all the numbers you memorized, it would be very helpful to have a reference for all of these exceptions that you might encounter in your code. Table 7.1 lists some of the most common **Exception** values that you will encounter in your code.

Throwing Exceptions

When you are using the new structured exception-handling framework in .NET, you will be "throwing exceptions" instead of "raising errors." This is a change in both concept and terminology that you must get used to. Remember that if you **Throw** an exception, you are also using the **Try**, **Catch**, **Finally** structure, just like when you throw a football, you hope someone will try and catch it. When you are using the **Throw** command, you do not use error numbers. Instead, you throw constants that you have declared as exceptions or that are built in to the Visual Studio system. You will be using many of the constants listed in Table 7.1 to identify the exception that you are throwing. Here is an example of a **Throw** statement:

```
Throw New DivideByZeroException()
```

You use the **New** keyword when the **Throw** line makes a direct reference to an exception constant that is a part of the **System** Namespace. The full name to the preceding exception is **System.DivideByZeroException**, but if you put **Imports System** at the top of your module, you can reference your exceptions without using their full names. You can declare a variable to be the exception type you desire, and use that in place of the long exception name. If you declare the variable with the **New** keyword, you do not have to use **New** in your **Throw** statement. Here is how you would declare a variable as an exception and then **Throw** it:

```
Dim DivError As New System.DivideByZeroException
Throw DivError()
```

The first way, while requiring a bit more typing in the long run, appears neater and more understandable to someone reading your code, and is the format I recommend.

Table 7.1   Common exceptions.

Exception Value	Description
DivideByZeroException	A math equation is trying to divide some value by zero
IndexOutOfRangeException	You are trying to access an element of an array that is outside its **Dimmed** boundaries
AccessException	An attempt to access a Class member failed
ApplicationException	A nonfatal and nonspecific exception occurred in your application
ArgumentException	An invalid argument was passed to a procedure
ArgumentNullException	This procedure cannot take an argument that is null
ArgumentOutOfRangeException	An argument passed to a procedure was outside an allowable range
ArithmeticException	The result of a calculation is either infinite or cannot be stored in the designated data type
ArrayTypeMismatchException	The code tried to place a data type into an array that does not match the array's data type
EntryPointNotFoundException	A Class has failed to load due to a missing starting method
ExecutionEngineException	A CLR internal engine error has occurred
FieldAccessException	An attempt to access a field's value has failed
FormatException	An argument's format does not match the method it is associated with
MethodAccessException	The code has failed to access a Class's method
MissingFieldException	You are trying to access a field that does not exist
NotSupportedException	The method you are trying to use is not supported
NullReferenceException	You cannot dereference a null object reference
OutOfMemoryException	The system does not have enough memory to finish the operation
OverflowException	A calculation has resulted in an overflowing variable
RankException	Too many or too few arguments were passed to a method
StackOverflowException	A call stack overflow violation has occurred
SystemException	A general nonfatal exception
TypeInitializationException	An exception was thrown by some Class initializing code
WeakReferenceException	Your code has tried to access a weak-reference object after it has been destroyed

Relaying Exceptions

If you use a general-purpose **Catch** section to pull in all errors that occur, you may catch some that are better off handed off to the calling procedure. Let's take another look at that example of a nested **Try** block:

```
Try
    'some code here
    Try
        Throw New System.NullReferenceException()
```

```
        Catch e As Exception
            Debug.WriteLine(e.Message)
            Throw e
        End Try
        'some code here
Catch e As Exception
    Debug.WriteLine(e.Message)
End Try
```

The exception is first raised by my code within the nested **Try** block, and first caught by the nested **Catch** section. If I **Catch** the exception here and do not do anything about it, control will be handed back to the outer **Try** block without any exception being noted. This is a bad idea if the nested **Try** block did not succeed at what it was supposed to do. In the preceding example, I chose not to deal with the **NullReferenceException** in the nested block, and instead relayed it to the outer **Try** block using the **Throw** command. Because the variable **e** has the value of the initial exception, you simply **Throw e** out of the nested **Try** to be caught by the outer **Catch** section. If the nested **Try** block did not have a **Catch** section at all, this exception would then be passed out to the outer **Catch** statement. I like to call the passing of unhandled exceptions "popping out" and the re-raising of a previously handled exception as "relaying."

Cross-Language Exceptions

The exceptions you will be throwing are a part of the .NET Framework and are available to all the languages within the framework. This means that if you **Throw** a **NullReferenceException** in your procedure, and the caller is a Class written in Visual C++ or C#, then they will have no problem understanding the exception and dealing with it. The same thing goes for your Visual Basic procedures that instantiate or inherit from a Class written in another language. When an exception pops out of that Class and into your VB Class, it will be in a format you are already familiar with and are capable of identifying. If you open up a C++ and C# Class and look at the code, you will see the same familiar **Try**, **Catch**, **Finally** structures that you have just learned about. This common exception-handling framework is absolutely necessary to make cross-language development possible in .NET.

Testing Exception Handlers

Developing a strong exception-handling framework does not happen on the first try. Even if you spend days planning and thinking about how you will deal with the unexpected, and even expected, errors that might occur, you are sure to miss a few. Proper testing is the key to improvement of your routines and to reducing the number of bugs in your deliverables to an acceptable level.

The team tester should not be the same person as the coder. Like love, a closeness to your code can prevent you from seeing its defects and shortcomings. The coders should always hand off their work to an experienced tester, preferably a really nasty one who takes great joy in breaking things. Don't hate them because of it, though. Their job is to find the weaknesses and help the team get as close to perfection as possible. Without their dedication to destruction, application quality would certainly suffer. Here are a few areas that your testers should be concentrating on.

Test the Limits

For procedures that accept numeric variables, the possibility always exists that a value can be passed in that is either out of an acceptable range or will cause your calculation to fail. Testers should use a full range of numbers that the parameter type will allow, from the highest to the lowest. Even if the parameter is not a direct user input, a calling procedure can still pass a value that is out of range and cause an exception.

Bad Data

Depending on what type of procedure you are testing, bad data can take on many forms. Validation of input parameters will help you assure that an improper variable does not make it far enough to cause an exception in your code. As a tester, you should try using all sorts of horrible data in all the wrong places, such as pasting in a page full of characters into a box that accepts a **String**, or placing more than the appropriate number of digits in a telephone or social security number input box. If the form asks for your age, try typing a letter at the end of your age to see if the code can deal with it.

User Error

Never trust a user. They will be the source of all of your bad data, and they have the ability to foul up just about any function they participate in. When I perform code testing, I find that it is almost fun to run my application and try to think of all the things I can do wrong that the coder wasn't expecting. If you tell users to click button A, odds are that they will click button B. If you ask them to insert a diskette, there's a pretty good chance they'll ignore you and click the OK button without the disk inserted. Think like a user and not like a developer, and many of the exceptions will become painfully obvious to you.

Best Practices for Handling Exceptions

With so many options available to you for dealing with exceptions, you need a plan of attack to help you conquer these bugs. Knowing when to catch a bug and how to resolve it is the difference between a reliable application that the users love and a buggy application that the users despise. The list here summarizes key practices and tips given throughout this chapter:

♦ Use the new structured exception-handling framework and stop using **On Error GoTo**.

♦ Break up your procedures into multiple **Try** blocks to partition off possible error-causing code.

♦ Use multiple **Catch** sections to check for known exceptions, just like you would use a **Case** structure.

♦ Put the most likely and detailed **Catch** statements first, and save the general catchall statement for last.

♦ Use the **Finally** section to clean up after your **Try** section and to close all database and file connections.

♦ Use **Throw** to raise exceptions in your code or to relay exceptions outside of your procedure.

♦ Use **Try** and **Catch** in your Class constructors to trap Class initialization problems.

♦ Use nested **Try** blocks within **Try** blocks to further separate troublesome code.

♦ Never assume that the user will do the right thing.

♦ Always include exception-handling code when you perform a calculation, access a database, or read/write to the file system.

♦ Log the exception Type and source for later analysis. Consider including other data tidbits, such as the user's last known actions or values of certain variables.

♦ Only allow unresolvable exceptions to pop out to the calling procedure.

♦ Test all procedures to verify that they are stable. Use all kinds of data, and seek to break the procedure any way that you can until it appears to be invincible.

♦ Do not use a function's output variable to let the caller know that the function failed—raise an exception.

♦ Declare local procedure-level variables at the top of the procedure before you start any **Try** blocks.

Summary

Think back on all the business applications that you have used over the last few years. Which ones did you think were poorly developed? No doubt it was the ones that crashed often and lost all of your data. By taking the extra time to account for the unexpected, you are helping your application to join the ranks of the trusted few, and helping it to avoid being labeled as unstable and unreliable. The users will never know the pains you went through to make your code bulletproof, but they will definitely know an error the second that they see it, and that is the thing they will remember the most about your application. Even one little critical bug can be a horrible smear on your team's reputation. Take exception handling seriously. You can never have too many exception handlers.

Chapter 8

Data Access in .NET

Most of the Visual Basic applications you encounter will have some sort of database behind the scenes providing data to the user. Visual Basic's primary use is for the development of business applications, typically of the data-handling sort. Database applications have been created to track a company's customers, employees, information on other businesses, and those all-important inventory items. In the business application development arena, data is life. Even computer games often use a lightweight database to keep track of a player's high scores and statistics. Learning how to access and manipulate data is a must for almost any Visual Basic developer.

Data Access Concepts

Before I jump into all the technical details of how to use ADO.NET and Visual Studio.NET's database tools, it will be helpful to understand the uses for databases and some common database terms that you will encounter in this chapter. If you do not have a lot of experience working with relational databases, then this section will teach you the basics that you need to know to start accessing these data stores in your VB applications.

A Short History of Data Access

Database stores come in many forms, from the largest enterprise-level database servers, such as SQL Server and Oracle, down to the smaller office-sized Access databases. When you were first learning Visual Basic, you probably learned to write code that read in some data from a text file, a very simple form of a database.

Along with Visual Basic itself, the methods you have used to access these databases have matured over time and taken on many forms. Throughout the years, you have used many methods to access your data stores, such as Data Access Objects (DAO), Remote Data Objects (RDO), Remote Data Services (RDS) for Web-based projects, and most recently Active Data Objects (ADO). All of these methods fall under one big umbrella called Universal Data Access (UDA). This large family of three-letter abbreviations is kind of confusing, but luckily the ADO method has stuck with us for the last few years and has replaced all prior methods. ADO has provided a flexible and powerful means of dealing with databases, and should be used as the primary data access method for almost any project you choose to create.

Types of Data

Data can take on many different forms, from a flat, text-based file that you read in line by line, to a large relational database that you can run queries against, such as SQL Server. Relational databases are the primary data stores in most companies, and are what most developers consider traditional forms of data. More and more, you will encounter new forms of data in nontraditional formats that you will need to have access to. Microsoft's Exchange mail servers can provide a wealth of data in the form of email stores and newsgroup entries. Data can be mined from spreadsheets and documents, such as a file system populated with Microsoft Word documents that your application can pull data from. With the growing presence of the Internet, you will find many more examples of nontraditional data stores that you will want to access.

An Internet Web site that allows you to search through text found on Web pages is a great example of harnessing the data found in flat-text HTML Web pages. Your queries to these search engines do not actually visit all the sites that they list. Instead, their search engine locates and sucks in the data from all of these Web pages, creating one centralized database with links back to the original source of the data. The actual Web pages do not live in the database, only their textual data elements do. This is an example of a traditional data store at the heart of the system, which gets populated by robots and scripts that access nontraditional data stores throughout the world. Document management systems are growing in popularity among businesses wanting to organize all of their electronic files. Like the search engine, a document management system keeps a database of metadata on each individual document, along with a pointer to the file system location of the document. When you locate a document you want to read, the database tells you where to go to see it.

Relational Databases

Understanding how relational databases work is very important if you plan to access their data. If you have some experience with relational databases, then you can skip over this small section. A relational database is made up of tables, such as a database containing a Customers table, a Purchases table, and an Inventory table. What makes it relational is that the tables often link to each other. For example, each purchase in the Purchases table will have a reference to a customer in the Customers table, and a reference to one or more items in the Inventory table matching the items that the customer has ordered. You will not actually see the customer's information in the Purchases table. Instead, you will see a reference to the line of the Customers table where this information will be found.

These relationships are done through "keys." Every table has a Primary Key, which is a unique (never duplicated) identifier for each item in the table. Every item in the table must have its own Primary Key. For the Customers table, you could assign each customer a special **CustomerID** as its Primary Key. When the Purchases table makes a reference to the customer that made the purchase, it simply lists the **CustomerID**, which will link that purchase back to the Customers table and all the necessary data. This reference in the Purchases table to the Primary Key in the Customers table is known as a *Foreign Key*. A Primary Key field must be unique in the table, but a Foreign Key field can repeat itself, such as the case in which one customer makes more than one purchase, thereby producing more than one purchase line referencing the same **CustomerID**.

Introducing ADO.NET

Along with the release of Visual Studio.NET, Microsoft is releasing the next iteration of the ADO data access method, now named, appropriately, ADO.NET. Early .NET documentation referred to this new version as ADO+, so if you see this name, recognize that it is the same as ADO.NET. While the name implies that this is just another upgrade to the ADO line, this data access method has undergone so many changes in this version that Microsoft probably could have given it a new name. This chapter covers all of those changes, and gives you some examples of how to use Visual Studio to create connections to your database and manipulate the data within those databases.

Data Providers

Past versions of ADO were built on top of the object linking and embedding (OLE) DB layer of interfaces. OLE DB is a set of data providers that was created to be a COM-based follow-up to open database connectivity (ODBC). Similar to a driver that your computer uses to connect the operating system to a CD-ROM, a provider is a means to connect your code to that actual database. A provider must be capable of talking to the type of data stores you wish to access. OLE DB is really a group of providers, and which one you use depends on the data store you are accessing. Specialized providers exist for SQL Server and Oracle databases, a provider named Jet exists for Access databases, and numerous other specialized providers are available. ADO acts as the consumer of the data that was provided by the OLE DB. You use ADO to issue commands through the OLE DB to the data source, and then manipulate the data that is returned to you.

ADO.NET now uses a concept called *managed providers*. Because OLE DB is a COM-based interface, ADO.NET connects to it through a COM wrapper, which is similar to what your program would use to call a COM component from your .NET Assembly. The two major categories of managed providers are the ADO provider and the SQL Server provider.

Obviously, if you are not dealing exclusively with a SQL Server database, then you want to use the ADO general-purpose managed provider. If you are using a SQL Server 7 or later database, then you can gain some performance enhancement in your database calls by implementing the specialized SQL Server provider, which bypasses the older OLE DB providers and takes advantage of the native Microsoft capabilities of SQL Server. This provides a more direct route to the data you want.

When you were developing COM-based database applications, you had the ability to pool your database connections by using either the Microsoft Transaction Server (MTS) or COM+. This is a great way to manage these resources, because connections to your database can become scarce on a busy server. When you pool a connection, a limited number of connections are kept on standby in a "pool," and as calls to the database are made, the pool manager issues them a pooled connection. As soon as the call is complete, the connection is held open by the manager and issued to the next call to come along. Enabling this feature in MTS and COM+ took a little extra work on the developer's part, but now, with managed providers, this is all done automatically behind the scenes. Once again, a really great feature is enabled automatically, removing yet another worry from the developer's mind!

Both managed providers have four objects you can use: the **Command**, the **Connection**, the **DataReader**, and the **DataAdapter**. If you have used ADO before, then you already know that the **Connection** object is what connects your code to the database, and the **Command** is the object you use to tell the database what you want or what action it should take. The new **DataReader** object takes the place of the old "fire hose" forward-only and read-only cursor. If all you are looking for is a set of uneditable data delivered as quickly as possible, then the **DataReader** is the object you should use. When I put all of this information together and show examples of code, I show you how to use the **DataReader** object.

The fourth object, the **DataAdapter**, is now your main source of communication with the database, and actually takes the place of your **Command** and **Connection** calls. When you implement a **DataAdapter** and activate it with the proper parameters, it creates the **Connection** object for you, issues the **Command** you desire, and then closes the **Connection** to the database upon completion. I think that you will find that the new **DataAdapter** takes a lot of the complexity and worry out of accessing a database. The **DataAdapter** is actually a part of the managed providers layer that sits between your Dataset and the database. You will be formally introduced to the **DataAdapter** in the second example in Exercise 8.2. But before you see this in action, you need to understand a few more concepts.

Both of the managed providers have these four objects, but they are named differently depending on which managed provider you are using. Table 8.1 lists the objects' names based on which provider you are using.

It is pretty easy to see the difference between the two. The tricky part here is that if you choose to go with the SQL Server provider and its associated objects in your code, you cannot quickly change your code over to another database without some rewriting. If you

Table 8.1   Managed provider objects.

ADO Provider	SQL Server 7+ Provider
OleDbConnection	SqlConnection
OleDbCommand	SqlCommand
OleDbDataReader	SqlDataReader
OleDbDataAdapter	SqlDataSetAdapter

think you may need to keep the code flexible to deal with other database types, then you should choose the ADO provider and sacrifice a little bit of performance in favor of a great deal of flexibility. Figure 8.1 illustrates the data access layers of managed providers and their associated objects.

Another advantage of going with the ADO provider based on OLE DB is that future OLE DB drivers can be created for new databases or updated database releases. To migrate your application to a newer database, you simply need to obtain the latest OLE DB driver for it and update your **Connection** or **DataAdapter** object.

Disconnected Data

Older, traditional forms of data access were done in a "connected" fashion. Your application would call the database with a query, and you would get back one record at a time. By pressing the Next Record button or by issuing a command, the application would call back to the database and ask for the next record in the set. Every time you changed a record and then moved to another record in the table, the change you made would be reflected immediately in the database. The problem with this old method is that a large amount of network traffic was associated with it. All of this back and forth communication may work well on a private company LAN, but now, with the advent of the Internet and varying connection

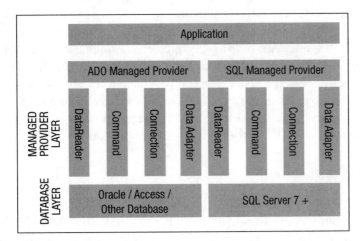

Figure 8.1
Data access layers.

speeds of remote users, you don't want to make them wait a few seconds (and certainly not minutes!) between records while you go and get the next record.

ADO fixed this problem by allowing you to create disconnected Recordsets, where the entire set of returned data was passed down to the client to navigate and change without talking to the database. After the client was done with this Recordset, the application would then upload the Recordset back to the database to be merged back in. While this did present a few new complications, such as conflicting database updates, generally this was the most efficient way for remote users to access Recordsets.

In past versions of ADO, the disconnected Recordset was one of the options you could select when creating your Recordset. The new ADO.NET Datasets are entirely disconnected from the database after creation. The days of connected record-by-record data accesses are now gone, along with all of those old mainframe data stores.

Tip

If you must work with databases in a connected fashion, you can still use old versions of ADO via a COM wrapper to make these calls.

As soon as the **DataAdapter** fills your Dataset, it is automatically disconnected from the database. It may take a few extra seconds to fill your Dataset with all the returned data, but once it is disconnected, no more calls to the database occur until you decide it is time to use the **Update** command to update the database with any changes that were made to the Dataset as a whole.

Using Old Versions of ADO

If you have a special case that requires you to stick with the older versions of ADO, you can continue to use these in .NET just as you would any other COM-based components. For projects that you are migrating to the .NET Framework, you may want to use the older version of ADO to avoid a lot of code rewriting to fit in with the new ADO.NET usage. For any project that uses COM or is migrating from a COM project, continuing to use an older ADO version is the smart way to go. But if you are creating a new project in .NET, I highly recommend you start using the new ADO.NET to access your data stores. At first, you will have a slight learning curve to overcome, but after you get used to it, you will find that you have a great deal more power and flexibility with the new data access model. As you learned previously, using an older version of ADO is the only way to go for working with Recordsets while staying connected to the database.

The Dataset

Until now, ADO always returned you a Recordset with which to work. In ADO.NET, the Dataset has replaced the Recordset as the new way of packaging the data you work with. Because data can be more complicated than a simple record or row-based Recordset, ADO had to evolve to better present this data to the consumer.

XML in Data Access

The last few versions of ADO began to introduce new XML-based features that developers can use in their applications. Generally, these features enable you to convert or stream your Recordset into an XML format, but the initial Recordset generated by ADO is still a relational table and not natively XML-friendly. Whereas old versions of ADO added in the XML support, ADO.NET was designed and created from the ground up based on XML and its ability to display and describe data. Like Visual Studio.NET, all the latest Microsoft products are now XML-based, such as SQL Server 2000, which now natively talks in XML Datasets. In the past, XML was an option you could convert data over to. Now XML is the standard, with which you will become intimately familiar very soon.

A big difference exists between a hierarchical XML file and a relational Recordset. A Recordset returns rows and rows of data, each sharing the same attributes or columns. Each record in a Recordset is related to another, because they are all the same type of record, such as a Recordset of customers from the database. For example, every row from a query of the Purchases database represents a unique purchase in the system, which has attributes that include customer information linked in from the Customers table. When these two tables are queried and formed into a Recordset, the relationship between them is lost and all you get back is a merged table of the results.

In an XML file, you can represent a hierarchy of items and their relationships, such as purchases, items within an order, and the customer associated with those purchases. You can imagine these relationships as a tree, where you can track a customer's relationship to his or her purchase or purchases, and follow that purchase to the multiple items that were requested. Figure 8.2 shows the difference between a Recordset and an XML file, and the relationships they represent.

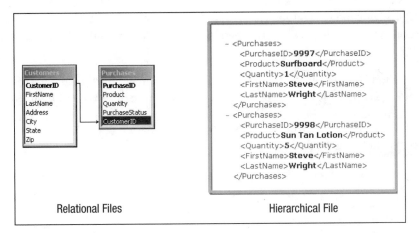

Figure 8.2
Relational vs. hierarchical records.

Characteristics of a Dataset

A Dataset is comprised of one or more tables of data. Each table can be referred to as a DataTable, another object in the ADO.NET object model that can be added to a Dataset along with other DataTables. The DataTable is closely related to the Recordset you are used to using, and is made up of DataRows and DataColumns. You can deal with a Dataset as a whole, and you can also work with an individual DataTable as a standalone object or as part of the Dataset's **Tables** collection. Figure 8.3 illustrates a Dataset that contains two DataTables, each with its own sets of DataRows and DataColumns. This Dataset also illustrates a relationship between these two tables based on the **CustomerID** attribute.

How you work with a Dataset differs greatly from how you are used to dealing with those older ADO Recordsets. A Dataset and all of its returned data now form an object you can work with. Continuing with the example Customers Dataset, after this Dataset is created, you can access its attributes as properties, such as **CustomerDataset.FirstName**, where **CustomerDataset** is the name of your Dataset, and **FirstName** is a column or attribute returned from the database. Previously, you had to access Recordset values in one of these two fashions:

```
'The old ways of reading data in an ADO Recordset
CustomerName = CustomerRS.Fields(0).Value
CustomerName = CustomerRS("FirstName")
```

Neither one of these two access methods was very object-oriented, except for the **Value** property of the Recordset, which had no relation to the data it contained. Now the **FirstName** field from the database is a property of the Dataset. An added bonus of this feature is that the attributes you specify for a query will now be available via IntelliSense drop-down menus after you type in the Dataset's name. This is terrific, because I always found myself going back to the SQL command to remind myself what the exact column name was that I asked for or which column the value would be in when I used the **Fields** property of the Recordset (boy was that painful!).

Just like Visual Studio.NET, a Dataset you create will be strongly typed. If the **FirstName** field of the database is character-based, then the **FirstName** property of your Dataset will be the same matching data type. Disconnected Recordsets were not strongly typed, so if you

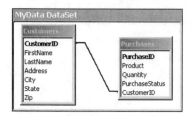

Figure 8.3
Examining the contents of a Dataset.

assigned a **String** data type to a Recordset field that over in the database could only be a number, the Recordset would not give you any warnings about this. But, when you went to update the database with the Recordset, boom! You would get back a mismatched data type error from the database, and ADO would simply fail the transaction.

Your Datasets have the ability to do so much more than the older ADO Recordsets. An ADO.NET Dataset is not just one table; it is a collection of tables. Actually, your Dataset will have two collections, one to hold all the tables, and a second that holds the table relationship information. These collections are aptly named **Tables** and **Relationships**. You could fill a Dataset with the results of one query, and then add to this Dataset the results of another query, each with completely different attributes and data.

Goodbye to Locks and Cursors

In past versions of ADO, you had to be familiar with the many types of database cursors and data-locking mechanisms to properly use ADO. You had both server-side and client-side cursors, such as the dynamic, static, forward-only, and keyset cursors. You also had to decide whether to use an optimistic or pessimistic lock on your data, which always threw me for a loop because I always like to be optimistic about my programming. When you use ADO.NET, all of these decisions are removed from your code. Because the Dataset is inherently disconnected and client-side, both the locking and the cursor issues are resolved.

You do have one choice that you can make that's similar to those old choices, and that is to use the **DataReader** object in place of the Dataset. You would do this in the same circumstances in which you previously used the forward-only, read-only ADO connections. A little later in this chapter, I will show you how to use the **DataReader** and explain why you might want to use it. Again, if you find that you must work with your data in a connected fashion and just cannot live without cursors and locking, you can still use ADO version 2.6 or earlier to do this.

Using Data Components to Create a Dataset

Now that you have learned the concepts of disconnected Datasets and managed providers, it's time for you to put these together and create your first Dataset. For starters, you need a database to play with. For this exercise, you will create an Access database with two simple tables in Exercise 8.1. Next, in Exercise 8.2, you will use the Visual Studio.NET data components to quickly and easily add a data connection to your project and fill a Dataset with data.

Note
The steps in the exercise are for Microsoft Access 2000. If you have Access 97 (or another database), modify these steps as necessary to create this database.

Exercise 8.1 Creating a Simple Database in Access

1. Open Access 2000 and under the "Create A New Database Using" head, select the Blank Access Database option.

2. Call this database Purchases and select a location on your hard drive to save it in. Remember this location, because you will need to relocate this Access MDB file in Exercise 8.2.

3. You need to create two tables: Customers and Purchases. Double-click the Create Table In Design View item in Access to start a blank table.

4. For the Customers table, create the following field names with the associated data type:

   ♦ CustomerID: Number

   ♦ FirstName: Text

   ♦ LastName: Text

   ♦ Address: Text

   ♦ City: Text

   ♦ State: Text

   ♦ Zip: Text

5. Right-click anywhere on the row containing the **CustomerID** field and select the Primary Key menu option. This makes the **CustomerID** attribute this table's Primary Key.

6. Save the table, and be sure to name it Customers.

7. Create a second table for your purchases data. Create the following field names and their associated data types:

   ♦ PurchaseID: Number

   ♦ CustomerID: Number

   ♦ Product: Text

   ♦ Quantity: Number

   ♦ PurchaseStatus: Text

8. Right-click the row containing the **PurchaseID** field and select the Primary Key option.

9. Close this table, and be sure to name it Purchases.

10. Select Tools | Relationships. A gray window will open, asking you to add some tables to this window. Add both the Customers and the Purchases table here, and then close the Add Tables subwindow.

11. To create a Foreign Key relationship between these two tables, click and drag the **CustomerID** attribute in the Purchases table on top of the **CustomerID** in the Customers table. When you let go of the mouse button, a pop-up window will verify that you are adding a relationship between these two tables.

12. This table relationship will be one-to-many, meaning for every one customer, zero-to-many purchases could be placed (I might place three purchases or I may have none in the system, but I'm a legitimate customer either way). At this time, do not change any relationship options, and simply click the Create button. Now, a line connects your two tables, and both ends of that line should point to the **CustomerID** attribute.

13. Save all changes to this database and proceed to Exercise 8.2 to create an application that queries your new tables.

If you do not have Access available and you have some experience with designing databases, you can create these two tables on your own. In Exercise 8.2, when you are asked to select the OLE DB provider driver and the path to your database, substitute the appropriate driver type and locate the correct database file or server to complete the connection.

Exercise 8.2 Using Components to Quickly Create Datasets

1. Open Visual Studio.NET and select New Project. Select the WindowsApplication Project type and name it ADOForm.

2. You now have a new Project with a blank Windows form open. In the Toolbox window, select the Data tab so the data components slide into view.

3. I am working with an Access database in this example, so I am using the ADO providers. Drag and drop an **OleDbDataAdapter** component over to the form.

4. A wizard helps you set the connection string for this **OleDbDataAdapter**. Click the Next button on the opening page, and then click the New Connection button on the connection page.

5. You now see a Data Link Properties window. Click the Providers tab, select Microsoft Jet 4.0 OLE DB Provider near the top, and click the Next button near the bottom of this form.

6. Click the button to the right of the Select Or Enter A Database Name text box. You are prompted to browse the file system for the Access database you created earlier. Locate it and double-click it.

7. Click the Test Connection button to verify that your Project can read this database. Be sure that Access is closed so that it does not interfere with your Project's connection.

8. If the connection test is a success, click the OK button at the bottom of the form.

9. You are now back on the **OleDbDataAdapter** Wizard window. Click the Next button at the bottom of the form.

10. The next page asks whether you want to use SQL commands, create stored procedures, or use already-existing stored procedures within your database. Select the Use SQL Statement option and click Next.

11. Now you need to build the SQL command. Start with a simple query that just requests all the data from the Purchases table. Enter this query in the text box:

```
SELECT * FROM Purchases
```

12. Click Next, and then click Finish on the last form.

You now have both an **OleDbDataAdapter** and **OleDbConnection** component added to it, which you can see in the Component view area below the form Design view. The **OleDbDataAdapter** created this **OleDbConnection** object for you.

13. In the Toolbox view, click and drag a **Dataset** object over to your form. A window should open, asking if this will be a Typed or Untyped Dataset. If you see this window, you can select the Untyped option and click OK.

14. In the Toolbox, select the Windows Forms tab, and then drag a **Button** control over to your form.

15. Double-click the newly added button to access its code. Enter the following line of code in this **Button** control's **Click** event area:

```
OleDbDataAdapter1.Fill(DataSet1, "Purchases")
Msgbox(DataSet1.Tables.Count)
```

16. Save and run your Project. When you click the button, a brief pause occurs as the **OleDbDataAdapter** connects to the Access database, runs the query you provided, and then fills the Dataset with the returned data.

Exercise 8.2 illustrates how quickly and easily you can create a Dataset simply by dragging and dropping a few components. The first time through this exercise might be a little slow, but after you are comfortable using the data components, you'll be able to create data connections and Datasets quickly. You may be interested to see what is going on behind the scenes in Exercise 8.2. Because the Windows form no longer hides any code from you, you can switch your form to Code view and look at how the components are set up. You will find these in the Windows Form Designer Generated Code section of your form. In this section, you will see many pages of code setting up your connection and the parameters of the Dataset—far more lines of code than you are used to seeing in ADO connections. The majority of this code defines parameters for the table, such as column names, their data types, and any constraints they have. When you next learn how to create a Dataset in your code without the benefit of the data components, you will see that you do not need all of this extra code to accomplish a simple query.

Creating a Dataset in Code

You saw the quick and easy way to create a Dataset in Exercise 8.2, and now I want to show you how you can create the same Dataset without using the data components. This will take a little more typing to accomplish, but it will help you better understand the relationship between your **DataAdapter** and the Dataset itself. To see how you can bypass the data components to code a connection to the database, add a second **Button** control named **Button2** to the form in Exercise 8.2 and add the code in Listing 8.1 to **Button2**'s **Click** event.

Listing 8.1   Creating a Dataset with code.

```
Protected Sub Button2_Click(ByVal sender As Object, ByVal e As _
 System.EventArgs)
    'Declare your variables
    Dim MyData As DataSet
    Dim DSAdapter As OleDb.OleDbDataAdapter
    Dim ConnectString As String
    Dim SqlString As String
    'Initialize variables
    ConnectString = "Provider=Microsoft.Jet.OLEDB.4.0;Data _
        'IMPORTANT NOTE: Substitute the path to your Access .mdb file below!
        Source=C:\Oceanside\Purchases.mdb;Persist Security Info=False"
    SqlString = "SELECT * FROM Customers"
    MyData = New DataSet()
    'This next line sets up the DataAdapter complete with
    'our ConnectString and SqlString query
    DSAdapter = New OleDb.OleDbDataAdapter(SqlString, ConnectString)
    'Use DSAdapter to fill MyData with data from your query
    DSAdapter.Fill(MyData, "Customers")
    'Let us know how many tables are now loaded
    MsgBox(MyData.Tables.Count)
End Sub
```

After you complete the code for **Button2**, save and run your Project. Click **Button2** and you will get the same results you got from **Button1**, with a message box popping up to let you know that one table has been loaded into the Dataset. Either way works just fine. Some developers like to do things the hard way, and others prefer to use the speedy RAD tools that allow them to drag, drop, and go. The choice is up to you.

The advantage to using the code in Listing 8.1 is that you can get a better feel for how ADO.NET really works. You start by declaring a **Dataset** and a **DataAdapter**, which, because you are accessing an Access database, will be an **OleDbDataAdapter** using the Jet OLE DB provider to connect to the data. In my code, I created two **Strings**, one to hold the query and the other to hold the connection string. I could have just as easily placed both of these long values directly into the **OleDbDataAdapter** in place of the variables, but by making these variables outside of the command, I have the flexibility to modify them and reuse them. If you make your **ConnectString** a global constant, you can use it in all of your database connections, and only have to visit one line of code if something changes, such as having a new driver installed.

The **DataAdapter** handles all the details of connecting with the database. Simply tell it what **ConnectString** to use and what query to pass in, and let the **DataAdapter** handle the rest. You do not have to mess with the **Command** and **Connection** objects anymore because the **DataAdapter** does this for you. After I initialize the **DataAdapter** with my two variables, I only have one thing left to do, which is to pour the results of my query into the **MyData** Dataset. Appropriately, you use the **MyData.Fill** command to tell it which **DataAdapter** will feed it and what the source table will be. In my simple query, the source table is the same one I named in my SQL statement, Customers.

As soon as the Dataset has been filled, the **DataAdapter** closes the connection to the database, removing yet another worry from the developer's mind and freeing up a precious resource. In the past, sloppy ADO code might have neglected to close a database connection, leaving the connection locked and unusable by other queries and applications. Every time you ran this sloppy function, another database connection would be lost to the world, and slowly (or sometimes quickly) your database performance would drop off and users would have to wait longer and longer for their data. With ADO.NET, this is no longer an issue.

After the **Fill** command is run, your Dataset will be disconnected from the database. Any changes you make to the Dataset values will not be reflected in the database itself until an **Update** is called. You are free to change, edit, manipulate, or move the data around as much as you like without damaging the real data on the server. Another advantage of working with a disconnected Dataset is that you can modify the tables to fit your needs, such as by adding a new column to the Dataset that is not available in the real database. A little later on, I will cover the issues surrounding the **Update** method of sending your changes back to the database.

Because the **DataAdapter** maintains the **Connection** and the **Command** objects separately, you can change the SQL statement in your **DataAdapter** and simply reexecute the **Fill** command using the same preestablished connection. Following the code in Exercise 8.1, you could change the **DataAdapter** object's SQL query and add a second table to the Dataset, like so:

```
DSAdapter.SelectCommand.CommandText = "SELECT * FROM Purchases"
DSAdapter.Fill(MyData, "Purchases")
```

The preceding two lines of code would change the **DataAdapter** object's SQL query to pull all the data from your Purchases table, and the **Fill** command would execute this query. This is a handy way to reuse the **DataAdapter** you create and assign a connection.

Now that you have seen the beauty of ADO.NET Datasets and the **DataAdapter**, the time is right to break the news to you: Most of the old ways of working with your database connection are gone! In ADO.NET, you no longer use the **Open** method of a Recordset to execute your commands. Instead, you rely on the **DataAdapter** to do all the connecting and querying. All the Recordset navigation commands are also obsolete now, such as the **MoveFirst** and **MoveNext** commands. These were holdovers from days gone by when your Recordsets would stay connected to the database and you were required to issue cursor-movement commands to get things done. Because your Datasets are both disconnected and object-oriented, you no longer need these old commands.

Note

*R.I.P.: The Recordset, along with its **Open**, **Close**, **MoveNext**, **MoveFirst**, **MoveLast**, and **MovePrevious** commands, is gone.*

Adding DataTables to Your Dataset

After you have a Dataset with a table loaded, you can rerun the **DataAdapter** object's **Fill** command to add more data to it. If you run the same query against the Customers table and add this to the Dataset, you will have one table with two copies of the same data. When adding a table to a Dataset, if the table already exists, then the returned data is appended to the end of that table. If the table does not already exist, a new table and its returned data is added to the Dataset. One Dataset can have one or more tables in it, which will be stored within the Dataset's DataTable collection.

A great way to dissect and learn more about the makeup of a Dataset is to use the **DataGrid** control in Visual Studio.NET. If you create a blank Windows form and add a **DataGrid** control to it, you can quickly display a Dataset in that control, like this:

```
DataGrid1.DataSource = MyData
```

The **DataGrid** is a wonderful and powerful tool for viewing Datasets. If you run the **Fill** command twice with the same query both times and then load the Dataset into a **DataGrid**, you will see that one table with duplicate data currently exists in your Dataset. If you change the SQL string for the second run of the **DataAdapter** to now pull data from the Purchases table, and also update the source table to say Purchases in the **Fill** command, your Dataset will now have two tables in it. When you tell the **DataGrid** to display this Dataset, the control will allow you to switch between these two tables at will, showing you that two separate tables exist within this one Dataset.

If you execute a SQL query that brings back data from many different tables, you are still creating one single table, just as you did with the Recordset. Take a look at the following SQL string:

```
SELECT Purchases.PurchaseID, Purchases.Product, Purchases.Quantity, _
   Customers.FirstName, Customers.LastName FROM Customers INNER JOIN _
   Purchases ON Customers.CustomerID = Purchases.CustomerID
```

If you are not used to dealing with SQL commands, this might look a bit intimidating. What this query wants to do is create a table with columns for **PurchaseID**, **Product**, **Quantity**, and the customers' **FirstName** and **LastName**. The first three columns will come from the Purchases table, and the last two will be pulled from the Customers table based on which **CustomerID** is associated with this purchase. This is how a Foreign Key to Primary Key relationship works, and that is what the **INNER JOIN** part of this command is doing—joining these two tables by their **CustomerID** attributes. The result of this query is one table, even though the data was pulled from two separate tables.

Multitable Datasets and Relationships

A few pages ago, I mentioned that you could add tables to your Dataset's **Table** collection. If you add the following lines of code to the end of **Button2**'s **Click** event (from Listing 8.1), your form will run a second query on the database and add its results to **MyData**:

```
'Add a second table to MyData
SqlString = "Select * FROM Purchases"
DSAdapter = New OleDb.OleDbDataAdapter(SqlString, ConnectString)
DSAdapter.Fill(MyData, "Purchases")
MsgBox(MyData.Tables.Count)
```

This second query pulls all the data from my Purchases table and adds a second table to the Dataset collection. These extra lines of code closely mimic those you used earlier, with only the **SQLString** being changed and the source table in the **Fill** command changing. When you run this code, the second message box will report that you now have two tables loaded in the **MyData** Dataset.

Because both the Customers and Purchases tables were loaded into the Dataset separately, they will have no relationship to each other. Tables within a Dataset do not have to have a relationship of any kind. You may simply want to use one Dataset as a vehicle to hold and transport many different tables. This can be a fast and efficient way to move tables of data from one Assembly to another, because this creates one nice, neat package of all the needed tables, as opposed to many smaller Recordsets that you created before.

Because both of the tables you have loaded in your Dataset are related to each other, you should add this relationship to the Dataset. The Purchases table has a Foreign Key relationship between its **CustomerID** attribute and the **CustomerID** Primary Key in the Customers table. The following line of code will manually create this relationship between the two tables within your Dataset:

```
MyData.Relations.Add("CustomerPurchases", MyData.Tables("Customers")._
 Columns("CustomerID"), MyData.Tables("Purchases").Columns_
 ("CustomerID"),_
 False)
```

The makeup of your Dataset will now exactly resemble the Access database you created, complete with a Foreign Key relationship between the two tables.

Creating Customized DataTables

Datasets and DataTables are a great way of handling large amounts of data that are related to each other in some fashion. Sometimes, passing all of this data piece by piece from one procedure to another can be kind of tricky. By passing the data as a Dataset or DataTable, you can package all of this data into one container. When you fill a Dataset using the **DataAdapter**, the Dataset is automatically given a schema to define its structure and is then filled with data. Your Dataset container is complete and ready for passing as soon as it has been filled.

But what if you want to create a package of data that is not coming from the database? You can still do this, by creating your own DataTable from scratch. First, you need to define its schema or structure. After you have defined the container, you can start filling it with data. The following code example shows how you can create your own customized DataTable and place some data in it:

```
'Declare your variables
Dim CustomTable As DataTable
Dim MyNewRow As DataRow
CustomTable = New DataTable("Rooms")

'Add columns to your table
CustomTable.Columns.Add("RoomID", System.Type.GetType("System.Int32"))
CustomTable.Columns.Add("RoomNum", System.Type.GetType("System.Int32"))
CustomTable.Columns.Add("Status", System.Type.GetType("System.String"))
CustomTable.Columns.Add("NumBeds", System.Type.GetType("System.Int32"))

'Fill NewRow with data to add to your table
MyNewRow = CustomTable.NewRow
MyNewRow("RoomID") = 1
MyNewRow("RoomNum") = 101
MyNewRow("Status") = "Available"
MyNewRow("NumBeds") = 2
```

```
'Add NewRow of data to your table
CustomTable.Rows.Add(MyNewRow)
MsgBox(CustomTable.Rows.Count())
```

You start by declaring a new DataTable called Rooms, and then define the column names and data types contained within this table. Next, you define one single row of data and then add this to your table. Obviously, you will want to add more than one row of data to your table, which you can do by using a **For** loop to add data row by row. Now you can simply pass your CustomTable from one procedure to another, and all of this data, along with its schema, will be easily accessible.

A DataTable can work as a standalone table, similar to the old Recordset, or it can be added to an existing Dataset, which may contain other tables. By adding your DataTable to a Dataset, you can then add other tables to the Dataset and set up relationships among these tables, just as you would create a relational database. Here is the line of code that will add your customized DataTable to your Dataset in Exercise 8.2:

```
MyData.Tables.Add(New DataTable("CustomTable"))
```

The ability to add some new and customized tables to a Dataset containing other tables created via SQL queries opens up a whole new world of possibilities. You can now create relationships between these database-derived tables and the ones you created from scratch. You can also use the **Tables.Add** method to add table queries from different databases together to one Dataset. For any application developers who deal with two or more databases in a Project (such as a mobile application with an Access database that syncs up with a SQL Server database when connected to the corporate network), being able to bring data from these two different sources together under one roof can have a lot of useful benefits.

Changing Data

Looking at data is fine and dandy, but if the data never changes, then what is the point, right? Databases are all about change. New records are added all the time, and obsolete records are deleted for good. Attributes of existing data change to keep up to date. A new customer may be added to the database. That customer might make a new purchase, change his or her address after a move, or even cancel an existing purchase. All of these changes need to be accounted for and recorded within your database. Because ADO.NET works in a disconnected fashion, you do not make these changes directly to the database you are working with. Instead, you bring the data you need to change, delete, or add into a Dataset, make the changes that need to be made here, and then update the database to match your Dataset. Let's take a look at how you will perform these functions using ADO.NET.

The Dataset Update

All of your actions will involve the Dataset and not the database directly. You can change a value in a row, add a new row, or delete a row in the Dataset, all without immediately affecting the back-end database. The benefit of being disconnected is that all of this Dataset interaction requires no network traffic at all. Let's look at an example procedure to see how this works. The following example creates a new Dataset and **DataAdapter** and executes a query to pull in all the purchases from the Purchases table. After the Dataset is full, I add a new line to the Purchases table within the Dataset and set this new row's attributes. At this point, the new line is not in the database, only in my local Dataset. At the end of the procedure, I execute the **DataAdapter** object's **Update** command, which takes in the Dataset specified and sends all changes made to it to the database.

```
'Declarations
Dim ConnectString As String
Dim SqlString As String
Dim MyData As DataSet
Dim DSAdapter As OleDb.OleDbDataAdapter
Dim MyNewRow As DataRow
'Setup DSAdapter and fill the Dataset
ConnectString = "Provider=Microsoft.Jet.OLEDB.4.0;Data _
 Source=C:\Oceanside\Purchases.mdb;Persist Security Info=False"
SqlString = "SELECT * FROM Purchases"
MyData = New DataSet()
DSAdapter = New OleDb.OleDbDataAdapter(SqlString, ConnectString)
DSAdapter.Fill(MyData, "Purchases")

'Add a new row to Purchases and define some new data
MyNewRow = MyData.Tables("Purchases").NewRow
'Fill in attributes here
MyNewRow("PurchaseID") = 33
MyNewRow("Product") = "Surfboard"
MyNewRow("Quantity") = 1
MyNewRow("CustomerID") = 1
MyNewRow("OrderStatus") = "New"
MyData.Tables("Purchases").Rows.Add(MyNewRow)

'Save data back to the database
DSAdapter.Update(MyData, "Purchases")
```

The first section is very straightforward. I simply load **MyData** via the **DataAdapter**. The second section looks like the code I used to create a customized DataTable. Here, I add a **NewRow** to the Purchases DataTable within the **MyData** Dataset, and then define the values for each field in that row. The last step is to send these changes back to the database through the **DataAdapter**. The **Update** method takes two parameters, the first being the

Dataset you wish to update, and the second being the source table this Dataset is working with. These parameters are necessary because your **DataAdapter** can be used for more than one Dataset in a session.

The real power of using the **Update** method of the Dataset is that it can handle any and all changes made to the Dataset, to include updates to values, deletion of rows, and insertion of new rows. To make these changes through SQL statements would require at least one SQL statement per operation, each one being a separate call to the database. Writing **INSERT**, **UPDATE**, and **DELETE** SQL queries can be quite complicated, too. But if you perform all of these actions on a Dataset and call the **Update** method, all of this complexity is hidden from you and handled automatically by the **DataAdapter**.

RowStatus and Accepting Changes

Rows within a DataTable have a **RowStatus** associated with them that you can check to see if anything has happened to this row since you filled the Dataset. A row's **RowStatus** property can be **Unchanged**, **Modified**, **Deleted**, **New**, or **Detached**. All of these statuses are obvious except for the last one. In the previous example, when I first set **MyNewRow** equal to the table's **NewRow**, this became a **Detached** row. It was defined, but not completed and not formally added to the table until the **Rows.Add** line. A row is also considered **Detached** if it is marked for deletion but the table has not had its changes committed. This row is technically gone, but it is still hanging around in case you change your mind.

A really convenient feature of working with the Dataset is that you can change your mind about the edits you made. Each DataTable and DataRow has two methods for this: **RejectChanges** and **AcceptChanges**. If you execute the **RejectChanges** method for a table before you execute the **Update**, any modifications you made to that table are reset to their original form. The **AcceptChanges** method commits your changes at the table level. The way in which this works is that three copies of your data actually exist: an original copy that contains the data provided by the **DataAdapter**, a proposed copy that includes all uncommitted changes to the table, and a current copy of the table that holds the values of the latest committed changes. By calling the **AcceptChanges** method, you move your proposed copy of the table into the current copy, and by calling the **RejectChanges** method, you remove any changes made in the proposed copy and start over with the last current copy of that data.

The DataReader

In past versions of ADO, you had the forward-only, or "fire hose," cursor that you could use to quickly fill a Recordset with uneditable data. This was commonly used for quick jobs, such as filling a **ListBox** with a set of lookup values from the database. The resulting data was not editable, but if you only wanted to read the data, then the forward-only cursor provided the fastest performance of all the cursors. In ADO.NET, you now use the **DataReader** object to accomplish these tasks.

How you use the **DataReader** object is quite different from how you used the Dataset. You do not use the **DataAdapter** to fill the **DataReader** with data. Because the **DataAdapter** was handling your **Connection** and **Command** objects for you, you have to create your own **Command** and **Connection** objects when working with the **DataReader**. The **DataAdapter** also has that nice feature whereby it closes the connection after your Dataset has been filled. This, too, you have to manually handle when working with the **DataReader**. Unlike the disconnected Dataset, the **DataReader** works in a connected fashion, and is the only connected data object you will be able to work with in ADO.NET.

In the following example, I use a **DataReader** object to pull out all the state names from a table named States and use this data to fill a **ComboBox** on the form. Forms often have these handy drop-down boxes filled with data that the user can pick from. When your values exceed more than a few lines, you should consider moving this information to a table in your database. One great advantage of this approach is that if any values are added or deleted from this list, you only need to update the database table and not the application itself, which would require a complete rebuild and redeployment. Here is the code I am using to fill my **ComboBox** with state names:

```
'Declare variables
Dim MyDataReader As OleDb.OleDbDataReader = Nothing
Dim ConnString As String = "Provider=Microsoft.Jet.OLEDB.4.0;Data _
 Source=C:\Oceanside\Purchases.mdb;Persist Security Info=False"
Dim MyConn As New OleDb.OleDbConnection(ConnString)
Dim MyCmd As New OleDb.OleDbCommand("SELECT StateName FROM States",MyConn)

Try
    'Open my connection
    MyConn.Open()
    'Execute the command, attached to the DataReader
    MyCmd.Execute(MyDataReader)

    'Read in the data and fill ComboBox here
    While (MyDataReader.Read)
        ComboBox1.Items.Add(MyDataReader("StateName"))
    End While
Finally
    'Close the DataReader connection if still Open
    If MyConn.State = Data.DBObjectState.Open Then MyConn.Close()
End Try
```

Notice that this example uses the **Try...Finally** framework you learned about in Chapter 7. Because the **DataReader** object's connection must be closed manually, you will want to do it in the **Finally** section of your **Try** block to ensure that this connection is closed, even if the **DataReader** fails somewhere. Because the failure can possibly happen on the **Open** line, before the connection is even opened, you should check the connection's **Status** to see if it is actually open, before you try to issue a **Close** command. Trying to close a connection that was never open will result in an exception within the **Finally** area, which, as you know, will not be caught within this procedure.

To get this **DataReader** to work, I had to declare separate objects for my **DataReader**, **Command**, and **Connection**. Notice that the **Dim** statement for my **Command (MyCmd)** has a reference at the very end of the line to the **Connection** that you wish to associate this with. When you fire off the **MyCmd.ExecuteReader** command, this will make the connection between the SQL command and the connection string I specified. After the **Execute**Reader command, **MyDataReader** is hooked into the database and ready to start reading in data.

I used a **While** loop and the **DataReader** object's **Read** method to start the database pointer and move it down through the States table. You no longer use the move commands as you did in past ADO versions; you simply call a **Read** method that knows this is a forward-only object and simply moves to the next line in the table. Because my objective was to fill a **ComboBox** with the data pulled in by the **DataReader**, I do this within the **While** loop by adding the current value of the **StateName** column to the **ComboBox**. Every time my **While** loop does a **MyDataReader.Read**, a new value will be pointed to and added to my **ComboBox**.

SQL Inserts, Deletes, and Updates

No matter how easy and powerful the Dataset is to work with, sometimes you will want to deal directly with the database. It wouldn't make sense to fill a Dataset with the entire Purchases database just to delete a purchase you already knew the **PurchaseID** of. Doing so would be a waste of bandwidth, because you would have to issue a **Fill** command, have the database respond with the matching data, modify the returned data in the Dataset, and finally issue an **Update** command to send the contents of the Dataset back across the network minus the one little record that you wanted to delete. Simply executing a SQL **DELETE** command against the database makes a lot more sense. The same logic may hold true when adding new records to a table, and possibly even when updating some table values.

You do not have to use the Dataset to pull data out of the database before you can make any changes to it. ADO.NET still allows you to issue SQL commands directly to the database. By harnessing the **Connection** and **Command** objects, you can issue other SQL commands, or even run a stored procedure in your database.

Issuing Commands

Running a SQL command against a database very closely resembles how you are used to doing it in prior ADO versions. Take a look at this example:

```
Dim DirectCmd As OleDb.OleDbCommand
Dim DirectConn As OleDb.OleDbConnection = New OleDb.OleDbConnection("_
 Provider=Microsoft.Jet.OLEDB.4.0;DataSource=C:\Oceanside\Purchases.mdb;_
```

```
    Persist _
    Security Info=False")
Try
    DirectConn.Open()
    DirectCmd = New OleDb.OleDbCommand("DELETE * FROM Purchases WHERE _
        (PurchaseID = 33)"_
        , DirectConn)
    DirectCmd.ExecuteNonQuery()
Finally
    DirectConn.Close()
End Try
```

Similar to the old ADO methods, you are working directly with a **Command** and a **Connection** object, as opposed to letting a **DataAdapter** do this for you. I placed the **Open** and **ExecuteNonQuery** methods inside a **Try** structure to allow for future exception handling, and so that I could place the **Close** method for the **Connection** in the **Finally** area to ensure closure. After setting up your **Command** and **Connection** as in the preceding example, you can issue any SQL command, such as **DELETE** or **INSERT**. The **ExecuteNonQuery** method used in the preceding example should not be used for **SELECT** queries. You instead use the **Execute** method to indicate that this is a query and that data will be returned from it.

Running Stored Procedures

A *stored procedure* is a compiled operation stored directly in the database. Because these have already been compiled, they run much faster than a SQL command passed into the database. Stored procedures can take in parameters, which allow you to customize the actions of that stored procedure. A **DeleteEmployee** stored procedure might have an **EmployeeID** parameter that you can use to tell it who to delete.

You can execute a stored procedure in much the same way you execute a **DELETE** or **INSERT** command. Here is an example that runs a stored procedure inside a SQL Server 2000 database named GiftShop:

```
Dim ProcCmd As OleDb.OleDbCommand
Dim ProcConn As OleDb.OleDbConnection = New OleDb.OleDbConnection("Provider=_
    SQLOLEDB.1;Integrated Security=SSPI;Persist Security Info=False;Initial _
    Catalog=GiftShop;Data Source=MasterServer;Use Procedure for Prepare=1;Auto _
    Translate=True;Packet Size=4096;Workstation ID=MasterServer;Use Encryption _
    for Data=False;Tag with column collation when possible=False")
ProcCmd = New OleDb.OleDbCommand("DeleteAllPurchases", ProcConn)
ProcCmd.CommandType = Data.CommandType.StoredProcedure
ProcConn.Open()
    'Execute the query
    ProcCmd.ExecuteNonQuery()
ProcConn.Close()
```

Like the other directly executed commands, you define the **Connection** and the **Command** objects yourself. For a stored procedure, you see the **Command** object's **CommandType** property to **StoredProcedure**. The name of the stored procedure is **DeleteAllPurchases**, and is declared along with the **Connection** name. Remember to use the **Execute** command instead of the **ExecuteNonQuery** if your stored procedure returns data to your code.

Accessing Data with Server Explorer

Two ways exist to create your data connections: the hard way, through lines and lines of code, and the easy way, by dragging and dropping data components onto your form and setting their properties. But, believe it or not, an even easier way is available to access data in your Projects. You were introduced to Server Explorer in Chapter 3, and saw how it gave you quick and easy access to all the resources on your computer, as well as on any other computer on the network. Without having to type a lot of complicated code, you learned how you could quickly access a system's log file in just a few clicks. Working with data can be just as simple!

The following exercise assumes that you have an Access database somewhere on your system. It could be any database, such as the Purchases database created earlier, or the Northwind database that is always included with Microsoft Access. If you wish to use another data source, such as a SQL Server, doing so will be just as easy as using a simple Access database. I'll indicate in the exercise where you will want to deviate from the Access example I am using. Exercise 8.3 shows you how you can create a Windows application that enables you to view and manipulate a table of data by typing only two lines of code.

Exercise 8.3 Accessing Data Using Server Explorer

1. Start a new WindowsApplication Project.

2. Drop a **Button** at the top of your form, and then add a **DataGrid** to the form. Resize the form and the **DataGrid** to be at least half the width of your screen.

3. Open the Server Explorer view. At the very least, you have two expandable tree views in this window. The main tree is called Servers, which lists your computer and all of its resources. Other computers may be listed beneath Servers if you have added them. You also have a tree called Data Connections. If you have accessed any data in Visual Studio.NET, you should see this data source under this tree.

4. Expand the Data Connections tree by clicking the plus symbol to its left, and then double-click the line that says Add Connection. A window named Data Link Properties opens. Click the Provider tab.

5. Select the Microsoft Jet 4.0 provider for your Access database (if you are not using an Access database, pick the appropriate driver).

6. Click Next at the bottom of this tab. Click the button to the right of the text box below the label that says Select. Browse for your Access database file and select it (non-Access users should make your own custom settings on this tab).

7. Click the Test Connection button to verify the settings, and then click OK to finish adding this connection.

8. You now have a data connection in Server Explorer that is always available for use in your Projects. Expand the tree view for the database connection you just added and you should see subtrees for Tables, Views, and Stored Procedures. Expand the Tables view, and you will now see which tables are in the database you picked.

9. Drag and drop any table over your Windows form. Both an **OleDbConnection** and an **OleDbDataAdaper** are automatically added to this form, with all the proper settings. Even the query to **SELECT** all data from this table will be completed for you.

10. Open your Toolbox view, select the Data tab, and drag a Dataset over to your form. Select the Untyped option after you drop the Dataset component. This component will now be displayed in the component area below your form.

11. For the finishing touches, double-click the button and enter these two lines of code within its **Click** event:

```
OleDbDataAdapter1.Fill(DataSet1)
DataGrid1.DataSource = DataSet1
```

12. Save and run your Project. When you click the button, **DataSet1** will be filled with all the data in the table you picked. **DataGrid1** will then display **DataSet1** for you.

How easy was that? A few clicks, two lines of code, and you have a functional database application that pulls data from a table and displays it in an editable and sortable format. All of the hard work was done for you (even those two little lines of code were short and simple). More complicated queries take some extra work to perform, but for a basic "show me everything" query, Server Explorer cannot be beaten as a RAD development tool.

You can also add database connections to Server Explorer by selecting Tools | Connect To Database, which presents you with the same Data Link Properties dialog box you saw in Step 4 of Exercise 8.3. You may find it handy to add connections to all of your databases so that you can get at their data almost immediately. Just because a database connection is in Server Explorer does not mean it is a part of your Project. Only connections you create in code or by adding data components are included in the final Assembly you deploy.

Using the Query Designer

Creating complex and useful SQL queries is an art form. Coming from the graphical-driven world of Web development, I have often felt the frustration stemming from a homespun SQL query that did not have the proper joins defined, resulting in nothing at all being returned to me. Luckily, I have a database "guru" sitting next to me at work who I can turn to and beg assistance from. If you have never used a Microsoft Query Designer, such as the ones that come with SQL Server and even Visual Basic 6's data environment, then I'm sure you've felt this pain, too.

Visual Studio.NET also includes a Query Designer tool, and this is an absolute lifesaver when it comes to dealing with multitable complex queries. After you have discovered this great tool, you may never want to manually type a query again. The first thing you need to do before you check out this tool is to set up a Database Project. Exercise 8.4 has you start an entirely new application based on the Database Project template, which is very similar to the old data environment project. From there, you can open a Query Designer and see how wonderful it is.

Exercise 8.4 Creating a Database Project and Using the Query Designer

1. Start a new Project in Visual Studio.NET. Under the Other Projects folder, select the Database Projects folder, and then the Database Project icon. Name this Project MyDBProject and click the OK button.

2. Because this Project is intended to deal with databases, a window pops up asking you to set up a database reference to get started with. If you have already defined some database connections in Server Explorer, then these will be listed in this window for a quick selection. If none are available here, click the Add Reference button and set up a data connection to any available database, such as the Northwind database that comes with Microsoft Access.

3. In Solution Explorer, you will see that your Project has numerous data-related folders, including one for Queries. Right-click this folder and select the menu option Add Query.

4. You now see an Add New Item window asking what type of query item you wish to add. Select the Database Query item and click Open.

5. Another window opens asking you which database reference you wish this query to work with. Select the reference you picked in Step 2 and click OK.

6. In the main Design view, you see four horizontally divided areas. On top of this view is a pop-up window asking you to add one or more tables to the query. Go ahead and just click the Close button on this window for now.

7. I am building a query that calls to both the Customers and Purchases tables I have been using since Exercise 8.1. To add a table to your query, right-click inside the top horizontal section within the gray area and select the Add Table menu item.

8. From this window, I highlight the Customers table and click the Add button, and then do the same for the Purchases table. Click the Close button when two or more tables have been added.

9. Because my Customers and Purchases tables already have a relationship within the database, a line joins these two tables. One end points to the Foreign Key **CustomerID** in the Purchases table, and the other end points to the Primary Key version of **CustomerID** in the Customers table.

10. The third section from the top now has some SQL query keywords in it. This is where you see the actual text version of the query you are creating. The lowest section of the Query Designer is where you see the data that is returned from your query when you run it.

11. I want to build a query that returns all the purchases I have in my database, and that includes the first and last name of whomever made those purchases. In the top section, I click the checkboxes next to **PurchaseID**, **Product**, and **Quantity** in the Purchases table, and the checkboxes next to **FirstName** and **LastName** in the Customers table. Notice that a line has been added to the second section of the Query Designer for each attribute I selected. Also notice that the SQL string in the third section now includes all the attributes I selected as well.

12. In the top section, right-click the diamond in the middle of the line joining the two tables. Here you can define what type of join this query is using. Because you are interested in getting all the purchases, and only the information on the customers who made those purchases, the Purchases table will be your master table. Choose the menu option Select All Rows From Purchases.

13. By either using the Query toolbar or right-clicking in the top section, select Run. The bottom section will be filled in with all the data that is returned by your query. You can look at Figure 8.4 to see what my Query Designer looks like at this point. Because I had three purchases in the Purchases table, I got back three rows of data. The same customer placed two of those purchases, so not all of my customers are represented in the returned data.

After you get the hang of using the Query Designer (and it won't take long), you will want to use it for all of your SQL designing. This tool can make even a database novice look like a seasoned data-access veteran. I highly recommend that you have the Query toolbar open when you are working in the Query Designer. From this toolbar, you can run your query, validate your query (check to see whether the SQL syntax is valid), and show or hide the four sections if you find that you do not need all of them showing. A Change Type drop-down button on the Query toolbar enables you to change the default **SELECT** query to an **UPDATE**, **INSERT**, or **DELETE** query.

You also can do a lot with the second (the Grid Pane) section of the designer. Here, you can enter special criteria that an attribute has to meet to satisfy the query, such as **PurchaseID**

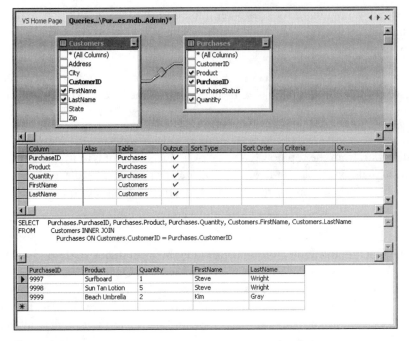

Figure 8.4
The Query Designer window.

is equal to 99887. If you set this as a criteria, only purchases with that **PurchaseID** are returned. You can also use the Grid Pane section to select a column to sort the data by. You will often want your data to be sorted before handing it over to some code or a control to display. A list of 50 state names can be very hard to traverse if the names are not in alphabetical order.

When you tell the Query Designer which database connection you are working with, you are also telling it which dialect of SQL you will be using. Anyone coming from an Oracle background knows all too well that Oracle's PL-SQL query language is vastly different from SQL Server's T-SQL queries. Only the most basic SQL queries work with both databases equally well. But not to worry, because the Query Designer can tell from the type of database connection which version of SQL you will be using. As the designer, you only have to worry about clicking the right attributes, and typing a few criteria values.

The Database Project has many other useful tools you may want to investigate. From here, you can design database scripts, triggers, and stored procedures. These also have handy designers for you to use. If you like the power of the Database Project, you can incorporate it into another project by adding a Database Project to a different Solution, such as one containing a WindowsApplication Project. These tools are really handy and should be kept close by whenever you are working with database connections.

Working with XML

XML is the format of choice for exchanging data in this new millennium. Prior to XML, two different applications had to agree on an exact data format to talk to one another. But now with XML, the data files are "self-describing," meaning that the data is identified with meaningful tags that allow any application to immediately understand the context of the data. You do not have to build your XML file in a specific format as long as you are using a tagging scheme that is meaningful to both you and any other application that wishes to use the data.

While prior versions of ADO allowed you to convert your ADO Recordsets to an XML file, these features were added on top of ADO and took a little work to use properly. ADO.NET was designed to work with XML natively, and not as an afterthought. More and more of the applications you will be building will use XML to communicate, so let's take a look at how you work with XML using ADO.NET.

Creating XML Files

If your application requires that you exchange data in XML format, you either build the XML structure manually or create a Dataset and output this in an XML format. For example, your application may have to send data to an outside application, such as a file that describes today's product purchases. You have already developed a query to pull this information from your database, which looks like this:

```
SELECT Purchases.PurchaseID, Purchases.Product, Purchases.Quantity, _
  Customers.FirstName, Customers.LastName FROM Customers INNER JOIN _
  Purchases ON Customers.CustomerID = Purchases.CustomerID
```

After you run this query and fill a Dataset with the results, you will want to write this out to an XML file for transmission. Here are a few lines of code that create this file for you:

```
Dim XMLOut As FileStream = New FileStream("C:\Purchases.xml", _
  FileMode.OpenOrCreate, FileAccess.Write)
Dim WriteXML As StreamWriter = New StreamWriter(XMLOut)
MyData.WriteXml(WriteXML)
```

This block of code uses the new **Stream** object to write your file to the hard drive. You start by defining the **FileStream** and where the file will be, and then declare a new instance of the **StreamWriter** that will write to this file, and finally pass this **StreamWriter** to the Dataset's **WriteXml** method. Run this code and look on your hard drive. You now see an XML file named Purchases. Open this in Internet Explorer 5, and you will be able to view the data within the file and expand or collapse its different segments. The top portion of the XML file is not your actual data, but rather a description of the data contained later in the document. This is why XML is so cross-platform and cross-development-language friendly.

You could create an XML data file manually, but look how easy it is to just dump your Dataset and have all the tagging and defining done for you. This is yet another good use for customized DataTables. Even if your data is not queried directly from a database, you may want to build your data into a DataTable as shown earlier, and then add this DataTable to a Dataset. The benefit here is that you can now quickly translate your data to XML and back again to a Dataset.

Reading XML

Creating an XML file is only half the job. If your application is on the receiving end of the XML file, you need a way to pull the data out of an XML file so that the data can be easily viewed and changed by your application. Again, you could write a complicated parser to walk through all of those tags and figure out what to do with the data within, or you could quickly and easily suck all this data into another Dataset. Using the XML file you created in the **WriteXml** code, here is how you could read this file into a second Dataset:

```
Dim XMLFile As StreamReader = New StreamReader("c:\Purchases.xml")
Dim MyPurchases As New DataSet()
MyPurchases.ReadXml(XMLFile)
```

To read the file in, you declare an instance of the **StreamReader** and tell it where the file is. You also declare a new instance of a Dataset, and then execute its **ReadXml** method on the **StreamReader** you created. The process of reading in an XML file is referred to as "shredding" the data, a colorful term that describes the parsing of tagged data fields being ripped and separated from a flat, text-based file. After shredding the XML file, your data is loaded into a Dataset and is fully updateable. With XML and ADO.NET, you can exchange data with anyone, from Windows to Linux platforms, and from Visual Basic to Java applications.

For each major item of data in the XML file, the Dataset will create a new table. If your XML file contained objects for Customers and Purchases, then you end up with two tables in your Dataset, one called Customers and the other called Purchases. Because XML is really good at describing relationships between objects, your Dataset will also be able to interpret these relationships and make the proper links between your new tables in the Dataset. This is a new level of complexity that past versions of ADO could not deal with. With ADO.NET, your Datasets are now just as intelligent as any XML file you can create.

Data Access Best Practices

Continuing my tradition of offering tips on how to best apply your new-found knowledge learned in this chapter, I offer the following Best Practices for you to consider when dealing with databases in Visual Studio.NET.

Data Access Best Practices

◆ Get used to dealing with disconnected Datasets and give up the old connected commands.

◆ Use the **DataReader** to fill drop-down boxes with simple lookup data.

◆ Use **Try...Finally** when working with the **DataReader**, and always close its connection in the **Finally** section.

◆ Reuse **DataAdapter** by changing its **SelectCommand.CommandText** value to a new SQL string and reexecuting the **Fill** command.

◆ Group related DataTables into one Dataset and add relations to these tables.

◆ Create customized DataTables to enhance your application or package-related data into one tight, easily marshaled package.

◆ Utilize Server Explorer for ultrafast data-access programming. Add commonly used database connections to Server Explorer to keep them easily accessible. Remember the "two-lines-of-code" example and how easy it is to create a database application using Server Explorer.

◆ Use the Query Designer to develop and test complex SQL queries. Add a Database Project to your Solution to harness all of its advanced database development tools.

◆ If you are working exclusively with SQL Server 7 or above, use the SQL managed providers. For all other cases, use the ADO managed providers. If a chance exists that your current SQL Server database may change, use ADO to be on the safe side.

◆ Use older versions of ADO, such as version 2.6, for dealing with databases in a connected fashion.

◆ Use the **WriteXml** and **ReadXml** methods of the Dataset to exchange XML data files with other applications. Loading XML files into a Dataset is quick and makes working with the data a snap.

Summary

We live in the information age, and what a glorious time it is! At a basic level, information is really data, and a program that does not deal with data in any form is just about useless. Avoiding data access in Visual Basic is nearly impossible, so every developer's top goal should be to learn the latest and most efficient ways to grab the data you need and mold it into something useful. In most programs, data takes center stage and should be treated as the star of any datacentric application.

Chapter 9
Testing and Debugging in .NET

As perfect as you would like to think your code is, the testing and debugging process that immediately follows the creation of a new component is unavoidable. Nobody creates code and hands it off to the next team member without first checking whether that code does what it's meant to do. Sometimes, you discover that it doesn't do the right thing, a discovery that is often accompanied by a mournful sigh followed by minutes (and sometimes hours) of debugging. Do not despair when you find out that you are human after all. The real trick here is to find those bugs and squash them before others in your office discover that you are only human.

This chapter will help you to use the tools provided by Visual Studio.NET to locate and fix those bugs in the shortest time possible. Before there were debugging tools, you almost had to take a "back to the drawing board" approach to locate a bug. You would print out a listing of your source code and, with pencil in hand, go line by line looking for that little defect within those pages and pages of spaghetti code. I can't even imagine how the programmers of yore found defects hidden in stacks of programming punch cards that the early computers used for storage. (If you are too young to know what a punch card is, picture a stack of hundreds of thin cardboard cards about the size of an airline ticket with hundreds of dashed holes punched in them that represent code to an old mainframe computer.) Ouch.

.NET Debugger Overview

With the invention of visual programming tools came a set of heaven-sent visual debugging tools. No more printing out the code and spending long nights looking through it to locate a defect. These new tools immediately tell you where the crash occurred and exactly what the exception was.

Sometimes, however, you still will not have enough data to fix the problem. I will show you how to use the visual debugging tools to find out all that you can about the program's environment, which should help you to quickly spot what went wrong and repair the problem. Some of these tools have been in your toolbox for a few years, while others are new in .NET. Learning how to use each and every tool available can shave hours off of your debugging process, and possibly even preserve a little bit of your sanity.

All of the debugging features you will learn about in this chapter are part of the Visual Studio.NET debugger. A *debugger* is a program that attaches itself to your application and lets you view and troubleshoot the program as it is running. When you start your application in Debug mode, you are really starting both your application and the Visual Studio.NET debugger. You can opt to run your application without the debugger by selecting Debug | Start Without Debugging. Although your application will start a little quicker, choosing this option does not give you any debugging tools to work with, and you will not be able to pause the application's execution to examine the code in Break mode.

Although the debugger will run alongside your application, it will not run in the same process as your application. The debugger runs as an out-of-process program, tagging along with your application and reporting back the details of its execution to the Visual Studio environment. A debugger can actually be attached to any program, which you will learn more about later when I show you how to attach the Visual Studio.NET debugger to an application running outside of Visual Studio.

The debugger featured in Visual Studio.NET looks very similar to the one you used in Visual Basic 6, but this version is actually a descendant of the Visual C++ version 6 debugger. Because the .NET debugger will be used for all of the languages being developed in .NET, Microsoft chose the most powerful debugger available for incorporation into the .NET suite of tools. But don't worry, this new debugger is everything you remember the Visual Basic debugger to be, and more.

Breakpoints

When the runtime compiler encounters an exception that is not handled in the code, it will break at the line of code where the exception was encountered. Often, this is not the best place to start when you need to figure out what has caused this problem. You may want to see what was going on a few lines before this line raised an exception to trap where the real problem occurred. To do this, you need to add a *breakpoint* to your program, which is an intentional break in your code. When the program is going through its normal operations, it is said to be in Run mode. When you put a program into Break mode, it is like pressing the Pause button on your VCR. All processing stops at the breakpoint, but the application can pick up again exactly where it stopped. Break mode enables you to examine all aspects of the code at that point in time, just as the VCR Pause button enables you to closely study that one frame of film it stops on.

Adding Breakpoints

The quickest and easiest way to place a breakpoint in your program is to click the gray vertical edge to the left of your code. This adds a red dot to the gray area exactly to the left of the line you wish to break on. You can add many different breakpoints to your program, and as each one is encountered, the program will enter Break mode. You can also add breakpoints to your program by using Debug | New Breakpoint. By using the menu, you have to provide a little more information, such as the name of the file or function you wish to place the breakpoint in, as well as the line number and character column within that file or function. By clicking the gray area of Code view to add the red-dot breakpoint, you are setting all of this information for the breakpoint with just a click of the mouse.

When you are debugging some code using breakpoints, you should have the Debug toolbar showing. Among other handy features, this toolbar offers some VCR-like controls that look like your standard Play, Pause, and Stop buttons. Sure enough, these buttons can cause your program to stop and cease processing altogether, or pause into Break mode. The Play button starts your program from scratch, if you are not in Break mode, or causes the program to pick up again where the code entered Break mode. Figure 9.1 shows a program in Break mode. Notice the red dot indicating where I inserted my breakpoint. You can also see the Debug toolbar at the top of the screen. The compiler's current position in your code will be indicated by a yellow arrow in the left margin. If you turn on the highlighting option for the current line of code, the line that the arrow points to will have a yellow background to make it easy to locate.

When you have multiple breakpoints in a program, the runtime compiler will pause whenever one of them is encountered. You can get the program running again by clicking the Play button on the Debug toolbar. The code will continue to process until it encounters another breakpoint, which will again cause the runtime compiler to pause. You can get pretty carried away with adding breakpoints to your code, and you may suddenly want them all to go away. Instead of hunting down each and every breakpoint you created, you can simply select Debug | Clear All Breakpoints to remove all of them from your code for a break-free run.

You can also use the Debug toolbar to pause your program while it is running. To do this, simply switch to the main Visual Studio.NET window and click the Pause button on the Debug toolbar. This pauses the program's execution where it is currently at, just as a breakpoint

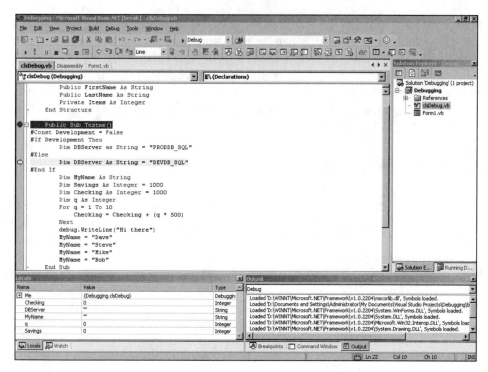

Figure 9.1
Break mode and the Debug toolbar.

would. You may find this useful when your program is performing a long, drawn-out operation and you wish to pause it to look under the hood for a moment. The keyboard shortcut to place your application into Break mode is Ctrl+Break. After you are in Break mode, many tools and features are available that you can use to examine the state of your code. These tools and features are covered later in the chapter. First, I want to show you how you can make these simple little breakpoints a bit more powerful.

Breakpoint Properties

Each breakpoint is more than just a stop sign at the side of the road. In .NET, breakpoints are more akin to a railroad switching junction which, depending on its settings, can allow you to continue along on your trip or divert your path in to a station (a "Break mode" for trains). You can give your breakpoints intelligence by adjusting their properties. To access a breakpoint's properties, right-click the breakpoint in your code and select Breakpoint Properties from the pop-up menu.

The Breakpoint Properties dialog box opens, which has three tabs that correspond to the three ways in which you can place a breakpoint in your code. Each breakpoint's position is relative to a certain function, a position within a source code file, or an address at which your program runs. Accordingly, the three tabs are named Function, File, and Address.

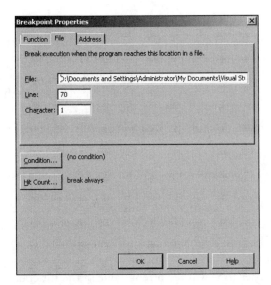

Figure 9.2
The Breakpoint Properties dialog box.

Breakpoints that are added by clicking the gray bar to the left of your code are file-based. Figure 9.2 shows the File tab of the Breakpoint Properties dialog box.

Each breakpoint is associated with a certain line number and a certain character position within that line. From the Breakpoint Properties dialog box, you can move a breakpoint simply by changing its line or character number. Previously in Visual Basic, breakpoints were simply associated with a line, and not an exact position within a line. By manipulating the character property, you can set the exact location within the breakpoint's line where the pause will occur. For all but a few debugging cases, this is more detail than you may need, but you might find this fine detail handy when you are testing some really long statements or logic statements chained together with multiple **and**, **or**, and **not** operators. How detailed you want to get is entirely up to you.

Breakpoint Conditions and Hit Counts

Each breakpoint can have an associated Condition or Hit Count that you can set in the Breakpoint Properties dialog box. A condition can be a check of a variable's value, such as the following condition for a breakpoint in a banking program:

```
Withdrawal > Savings
```

If this statement is true when this breakpoint is reached in the code, then the program will enter Break mode. Otherwise, the code continues to execute as if no breakpoint had occurred. The value you check does not have to appear in the line of code you are breaking at either, as long as that variable is in scope when the code evaluates the breakpoint's condition property. This form of condition applies to the Is True option box for the condition's type setting.

Conditions can also be just a variable name that you want to monitor for a change. To do this, set the condition property to the variable's name, and select the Has Changed option box for the type of condition. The first time this breakpoint evaluates the variable, it will make a note of the variable's value and continue with the execution. During the same execution of your program, every time this breakpoint reoccurs, it will reexamine whether the variable's value has changed. If it has changed, the breakpoint pauses the code. This can be a very handy setting for functions that run over and over that you only want to break out of when a variable changes value.

You can also select the Hit Count property to allow your function to execute a set number of times before breaking. This feature keeps track of how many times the breakpoint has been evaluated, and stops when the counter reaches a certain value. This counter can be checked against a set value, or a multiple of a value. If the value is set to 5, and you select the Break When The Hit Count Is A Multiple Of option, the breakpoint will pause the code on its fifth run, tenth run, fifteenth run, and so on. When you enter Break mode, you can right-click the breakpoint and access its properties to view the current value of the hit counter. This page even has a button that enables you to reset the hit counter without stopping the program fully. Stopping your program automatically resets the counter for the next run.

To allow for maximum flexibility when troubleshooting, the properties of your breakpoints are editable while in Break mode. This means that you can start a program, put it into Break mode, and change the conditions of the breakpoints to adjust for special circumstances. Using this feature, you can run more than one test on a function's values without fully stopping the program to change the conditions you are checking. Simply pause the program, set a new condition, and click Play.

Breakpoint Disabling and Saving

One other neat feature of the breakpoint is the ability to disable it without removing it totally. If you spend a lot of time setting up the conditions of your breakpoint, but find that you want to see your program run without breaking, it's nice to be able to simply disable the breakpoint temporarily rather than delete it for good. When you right-click the red breakpoint dot, you see a Disable Breakpoint menu option. When you disable the breakpoint, the dot appears as a black, unfilled outline, kind of like a "ghost breakpoint." To re-enable this breakpoint, simply right-click it and select Enable Breakpoint from the pop-up menu. As with the breakpoint's properties, you can disable and enable a breakpoint when in Break mode without bringing your program to a full stop.

If you previously used breakpoints in Visual Basic 6, you may have been annoyed by the fact that whenever you closed Visual Basic, all of your breakpoints disappeared for good. This is no longer the case in Visual Basic.NET. When you close Visual Basic.NET, all of your breakpoints are saved for you. This is where the disabling can really be useful. Now you can create many useful breakpoints in high-traffic areas of your code and simply disable them when they are not needed. This will save you a lot of time, because you have to create these breakpoints only once per program instead of once per session. Use this great feature and avoid removing breakpoints that you might need later in your testing and debugging process.

Viewing Variable Values in Break Mode

Now that you have a breakpoint, you need to know what you can do with your code to try to spot the exceptions or abnormal circumstances that will lead to an exception. In just a few pages, you will learn about all the special view windows you can use when debugging your code, such as the Output and Watch windows. But first, a terrific debugging feature needs to be addressed that's available as soon as you enter Break mode. This feature is not new to .NET, and you were probably already using it in version 6. But this feature is so powerful and yet simple, I want to make sure everyone knows that it is available to them.

When in Break mode, you can hover your mouse pointer over a variable that is in scope to see its current value. The value will appear in the form of a tooltip, which is a small yellow message box that pops up over the variable. I love to use this feature as soon as my breakpoints are triggered and the program pauses. A quick look at your variable's values can tell you a lot about what is going on, and helps you to spot situations that you may not have accounted for in your code.

You need to remember two important things when using this feature. The first is that the variable you want to check needs to be in scope. If the **MyName String** variable is declared in a different procedure than the one you entered Break mode in, then you will not be able to view its value. Variables **Dimmed** within a procedure are only in scope when that procedure is active. **Private** variables within the Class and all **Public** variables will be in scope when you trigger a Break mode within their Class. If you hover your mouse pointer over a value and the tooltip reports the variable's declaration statement but not its value, then the variable is out of scope. **Public** and **Private** variable contents are viewable within procedures that are not currently in scope, as long as the variable is within scope.

The second key thing to remember when viewing variable values is the location of the breakpoint in relation to your variable. If you pause your code before a variable is initialized with its first value, you will see its uninitialized value, such as zero for an **Integer** data type. Any changes that happen to the variable after the breakpoint are not represented in the tooltip value that you see. The breakpoint is a "snapshot" of what is happening at that point in time within your code, and cannot account for changes made later in your code.

Breaks Caused by Exceptions

Some settings in version 6, such as Break On All Errors or Break On Unhandled Errors, are not included in Visual Studio.NET, but you can configure some similar settings that decide how the application deals with exceptions in Run mode.

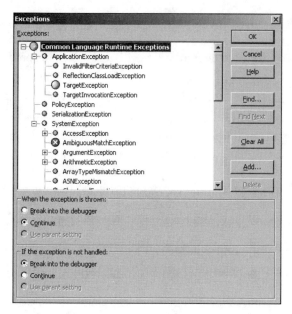

Figure 9.3
The Exceptions dialog box.

If you select Debug | Exceptions, an Exceptions dialog box opens, shown in Figure 9.3. In this dialog box, you can define how each and every possible exception is handled by the application, or you can simply select one set of options to apply to all the exceptions in the system.

The list of exceptions in this dialog box is an expandable tree view. You can highlight a single exception in this tree and make some associated handling settings at the bottom of the window. To configure exception handling globally for all exception types, select the top-level tree object named Common Language Runtime Exceptions and make your settings for this item. As you change the handling settings for each exception, the icon by the exception's name on the tree will change. A large silver ball indicates that this is the default normal setting. The large red ball with an X in it means that normal exception handling is disabled. A tiny red ball with an X in it means that this exception inherits the handling setting of its parent object on the exception tree. You can change the settings for this item so that it has its own handling instructions separate from its parent's settings.

Two simple settings are made for each exception:

♦ *When The Exception Is Thrown*—The default setting is Continue, because this forces your code to handle the exception through **On Error** or **Try**, **Catch**, and **Finally** structures. If you change this setting to Break Into The Debugger, the application automatically breaks whenever this exception is raised. This setting is similar to the old Break On All Errors setting in version 6.

◆ *If The Exception Is Not Handled*—The default setting is Break Into The Debugger, which matches the normal application result of exiting with an error when no exception handler is found. You can change this setting to Continue, which avoids exiting the program with an error, but could have unpredictable results in your project. Unless you are trying to ignore a specific error, you should not use the Continue setting.

All objects below the top-level tree-view objects have the Use Parent Setting option available for both settings. This option tells the exception to inherit its handling instructions from the object above it.

Stepping through Code

Being able to pause your program and view its current state is really helpful, but tricky problems may be hard to spot simply by looking at snapshot values at the breakpoints. You need a way to run your code in slow motion, just as you would use a VCR to view that winning field goal in overtime frame by frame (or, when discussing debugging examples, perhaps "that missed field goal" is more analogous). In Visual Studio, this slow-motion execution of your code is referred to as *stepping* through the code. The stepping modes you are about to learn are available via shortcut keys, the Debug toolbar, or the Debug menu in Visual Studio.

Step Into

The simplest form of code stepping is to simply step forward to (or Step Into) the next line of code. You can do this quickly by using the F8 key. When your program enters Break mode, you can use the Step Into (F8) key to step through your code line by line, enabling you to closely examine the code each step of the way. This is great when you are not sure exactly where the problem is occurring in your code. The downside to this method is that for really long programs, viewing every line can be slow and painful. Whenever your function calls another function, you step right into the called function and go line by line through its code until you are returned back to the calling function. Loops can also be slow and painful to look at when using the Step Into feature. If you encounter a loop that can run over and over again, you may want to add a conditional breakpoint within the loop to stop when a certain value has been reached, saving you from endlessly pushing the F8 key to find the results you want. When you are stepping through your code, your current position is noted by a yellow arrow in the gray bar to the left of your code. This yellow arrow is the Next Statement indicator which you saw in Figure 9.1.

Step Over

The Step Over method of stepping is a lot like the Step Into method, with one key difference. Whereas the Step Into command follows the code execution into called functions, forcing you to step through all of those lines of code as well as the function that you are troubleshooting, the Step Over command enables you to go line by line within a function, and when it encounters a line that calls another function, it runs that function in full and then steps you to the next line within the function you entered Break mode in. Thus, with Step Over, you can avoid having to look at the code in the called function completely. This is a great choice if you have a high degree of confidence in the functions outside of the one you are troubleshooting.

You can continue to use the F8 key to step through your code, and when you are about to Step Into a line that you see is going to call an outside function, you can switch to Step Over using Shift+F8 and avoid having to step through that function. Be careful when using Step Over, because the cause of the exception could very well be the called function and not the function that you initially were checking.

Step Out

If you do use Step Into to step from the Break mode function into a subfunction, you have the option to Step Out of the subfunction to quickly get back to the calling function. Like Step Over, this causes the subfunction to execute fully, placing you back in the calling function at the next line of code after this subfunction was called. Use Step Out to indicate that you've seen enough of a subfunction and to return quickly to the function you really want to examine. The shortcut key for Step Out is Ctrl+Shift+F8, or you can use Debug | Step Out.

Run To Cursor

When in Break mode, you may wish to fast-forward the code to another line of code without having to continually press F8 to step through every last line until you get there. This is a really simple feature that you can use to jump ahead in the code. Simply click the line of code you wish to fast-forward to, which places your blinking cursor on this line as if you were going to edit it. Next, press Ctrl+F8 or select Debug | Run To Cursor. All code between your current breakpoint and the location of the cursor will process, and then the application will enter Break mode again at your cursor's location. When using this feature, you must keep in mind that if the line of code where you placed your cursor is not encountered in the natural processing of your application, your program will simply start running again until it encounters this cursor or enters Break mode for a different reason.

Set Next Statement

You may encounter a few rare instances in which you enter Break mode and want the procedure to resume processing in an entirely different location. This Set Next Statement feature should be used with care, because it causes your code to skip everything in between your current breakpoint and the line that you decide should be the next statement to execute. Any calculations or variable changes made in the middle of these two lines will not be processed, possibly giving you erroneous results.

To use this feature, click the line of code that you wish to execute immediately following the line of code where the processing is currently at, as indicated by the yellow arrow in the left margin. Select Debug | Set Next Statement or press Ctrl+F9 as a shortcut to indicate that this line should be next to process. Another shortcut for this feature is to drag the yellow arrow in the margin to the left of your code to whatever line you wish to be processed next. This arrow is known as the Show Next Statement indicator, and tells you where in your code the processor is currently looking. When you click the Play button or press F5, processing immediately jumps to the indicated line of code, and the application continues to process until another breakpoint is encountered.

When you are jumping around through Classes and up and down files of source code, you may become lost and need a way to quickly get back to the breakpoint where your application paused. You can use the Debug | Show Next Statement feature to jump right back to the current line of code. You can also trigger this feature by clicking the yellow arrow on the Debug toolbar. If you do not see the yellow arrow to the left of your code, then you cannot see the next statement of code that the application will process.

Step by Line, Statement, and Instruction

So far in this section, I have been stepping through my code line by line, just as I did in version 6. In Visual Studio.NET, you now have three levels of stepping available to choose from. The default and the one that you are used to using is the Line option. When you enter Break mode and press F8, you step forward one line of code. Every piece of code on that line will execute as you move on to the next line. If that one line of code has three statements on it, then all three of them will be executed.

The next level down from the Line setting is the Statement level, which executes each statement on a line of code individually every time you step forward using F8. If more than one statement is on a single line of code, then you have to press F8 one time per statement to step through that entire line. If color coding is turned on, you see each individual statement highlighted separately from the rest of the line while you step through each one.

The lowest and most detailed level of stepping is the Instruction level. One statement can have many instructions in it. Consider the following simple variable setting as an example:

```
MyName = "Nick"
```

If you start your stepping on the line above this statement and step down into it, you have to press F8 twice to get through this line. The first step evaluates the variable name **MyName**. At this point, the value is not set to *Nick*, but instead retains its previous value. The next step evaluates the *Nick* part of the statement, and it is at this point that the **MyName** variable is assigned this value. Generally, you want to step by Instruction only when you need to walk through a single statement piece by piece to see exactly what is happening. For the vast majority of your debugging sessions, you should stick with the Line mode of stepping.

Color-Coding Breakpoints and Next Statements

It really helps to color-code the lines you are working with while in Break mode. If the entire line of code associated with a breakpoint does not have a background color of dark red, then the debug line coloring setting is turned off. You can turn this feature on in the Tools | Options menu. You will find this setting under the Debug folder's General settings section. Check the box next to the item that says Color Text Of Current Statement And Breakpoints. Now when you enter Break mode, the lines that are breakpoints have a red background, and the line where the processor is currently looking has a yellow "highlighted" background. This setting makes debugging in .NET feel a lot more like what you were used to in version 6.

Edit And Continue

When you enter Break mode, you can do a lot more than simply look at the code and try to spot the errors. You also can change the code while in Break mode, and start application execution right where you left off with the new code being applied. A few limits exist as to what you can change and still be able to continue executing your application without having to stop and restart it. The following are the most common situations in which a change to your code requires you to halt your application and restart it:

♦ Changes to exception handling **Try**, **Catch**, and **Finally** structures

♦ Changing a data type, such as a **Double** to an **Integer**

♦ Deleting an entire function

♦ Any changes to a read-only file

These changes have too large of an impact on the application's execution, and the application will exit from Run mode if such changes are made. Your changes are also limited to less than 64 bytes worth of new variables being added to a function. Despite these limitations, you have a lot of room to make changes and fixes to your code without bringing your application to a full stop. The biggest benefit here is that you can immediately test these changes by telling your application to continue its processing instead of starting the application all over. Any changes you make to the code that come before the line where the breakpoint is located will not be processed during the current pass, because this line of code has already been processed.

Depending on the extent of the changes that you make and their proximity to the last breakpoint in your code, the next statement to execute may change. If this happens, Visual Studio presents a pop-up window that tells you the next statement has changed. You can select Debug | Show Next Statement to jump to the line of code that Visual Studio is now considering the next statement in line. If this statement is not correct, you can use the Set Next Statement feature to correct it.

You may encounter something called *stale code* when you are editing your code in Break mode. This happens when a piece of code is edited that is outside the scope of the function currently being executed, or when too many changes have been made for Visual Studio to safely apply them all when you tell the application to continue. In these circumstances, the application continues to process when you tell it to, but it continues to use the older, unedited version of the code you edited until that block of processing is complete. After the application is done with that code, it will then try to apply the changes you made while in Break mode. The older, unedited code that the application starts using is what's referred to as stale code.

Before the new edits are applied, your stale code appears in gray, to let you know that it has been changed but that the new code has not been applied yet. If you wish to disable the Edit And Continue feature, you can do so under the Tools | Options menu. Uncheck the Enable Edit And Continue option under the Debugging | Edit And Continue section.

The Stop Command

You can enter the word **Stop** on a line of code all by itself to force your program to quit and exit. This differs from a breakpoint because your application shuts down completely, preventing you from debugging it or checking the values of active variables. For this reason, the **Stop** command should be used sparingly or not at all when you are trying to locate and resolve bugs in your application.

Debugging Windows

Numerous windows are available to the programmer in .NET for viewing and analyzing your code. These windows are available only when the application is in Break mode. You do not receive any live data from these windows while the application is running, so you need to either use breakpoints in your code or manually place your application in Break mode by pressing Ctrl+Break or by using the toolbar's Break button.

All of the debugging windows discussed in this section can be loaded via the Debug | Windows menu. When your application is stopped and you are working in Visual Studio.NET, only the Breakpoints, Exceptions, and Immediate windows are available on this list, because these are the only windows that can be of any use to you when the application is not running. After you run the application, all the other debugging windows are available on this menu. Most debug windows do not display data when the program is running, but rather only when it enters Break mode. The one exception to this rule is the Output window, which provides messages for your review while the program is running, enabling you to track the application in realtime. This is also the only window that you will not find under Debug | Windows. Instead, you open this all-purpose window via the View | Other Windows menu. Let's take a look at each window and see how you can use it to track down bugs.

Debugging Mode Layout

Because debugging windows are of no use to you when your application is stopped, Visual Studio.NET maintains two different window layout schemes for you. The first scheme is the normal design layout that you use to write the program with. When you start an application, Visual Studio.NET switches your layout to Debug mode, which includes all the special debugging windows that you will soon learn about. All the parts that are useless in Debug mode, such as the Toolbox and Server Explorer, slide out of the way to make room for the debugging windows. If you make changes to the window's layout while in Debug mode, your changes will be in effect only in Debug mode. When the application is stopped, your layout will return to your normal design and coding layout.

Tip

Build a really information-rich debugging layout and don't worry about ruining your normal coding layout. All of these debugging windows are really useful and you should not be afraid to use every last one of them if you think that they can make your job easier.

Disassembly Window

The Disassembly information appears in the same central window as your Code view. When you enter Break mode, a new tab called Disassembly appears along the top of your Code view window. I am covering this window first because if you enter Break mode manually, the Disassembly window is the first thing that you see in Visual Studio.NET. If the data contained in the Disassembly window looks like Greek to you, you're half right. This strange and complicated language is actually Assembly language. The Disassembly window shows you the currently active function after the compiler has run it. This is the output of the Common Language Runtime (CLR) compiler. What's really cool about this code is that it should look the same for both a Visual Basic and a C# routine that perform the same functions. After these two different languages are run through the CLR, the output should basically be the same lines of Assembly code, with only a few minor differences.

You will see many light-gray lines of code, which represent the Assembly language translations. Above each batch of lines of Assembly code you will see a single line of code in dark text. This is the code directly from your source code file. Each line of source code translates into many lines of Assembly language. Aren't you glad you're not an Assembly programmer? You may be able to pick out all of the memory addresses and pointers within the Assembly code. Ah, the beauty of Visual Basic. No need to worry about addresses and pointers, because VB handles it all for you.

The one feature that the Disassembly window enables you to manipulate is its Address setting at the very top. This Address box acts as a quick lookup feature that will scroll the listing of code to the line that holds whatever memory address you enter into it. Because most VB developers are not familiar with using memory addresses, this feature can safely be avoided. For all but the most adventurous of VB developers, the Disassembly window provides little more than a "gee whiz" thrill (or maybe more confusion than excitement).

Breakpoints Window

Now that your breakpoints will be saved along with your application's code, you should add breakpoints all over the place and disable the ones that you are not using at this moment. You might be hesitant to do this, though, because it might seem difficult to keep track of all of those breakpoints and their current enabled or disabled states. This is not the case at all—not with the super-handy Breakpoints window in Visual Studio.NET. In fact, with all the information that is tied to your breakpoints, this window is almost a must for anyone wanting to get the most out of their debugging sessions.

Each breakpoint you add to your code is listed in the Breakpoints window, indicating in which source code file and at which exact line number each breakpoint is located. To the left of the breakpoint's location is a checkbox. Simply uncheck this and your breakpoint is disabled. The red dot next to the checkbox in the Breakpoints window is always red, even when the breakpoint is disabled, and appears as a hollow circle in Code view. Using the Breakpoints window is much quicker than trying to locate that one breakpoint in Code view and right-clicking it to disable it. By default, you also see the Condition and Hit Count properties associated with the breakpoints.

At the top of the Breakpoints window is a Columns drop-down menu that enables you to add other useful information to this view, such as the programming language being used where this breakpoint is located (very useful for multilanguage projects), the name of the program this breakpoint is in (great for when you attach your debugger to programs outside of Visual Studio as well as to your current program), and the name of the function that contains this breakpoint.

Need to jump to the line of code that has this breakpoint? Just right-click the breakpoint's line in the Breakpoints window and select Go To Source Code. Your breakpoints also make great bookmarks. The properties of each breakpoint are directly accessible from this window by right-clicking a breakpoint. You can even add a new breakpoint or delete a highlighted breakpoint from here via the New and Delete buttons at the top of the window. You can now add, edit, delete, disable, and enable all of your breakpoints from one all-knowing window without ever looking at a single line of source code.

Tip

If you plan to use a lot of breakpoints and save them along with the code, use the Breakpoints window to manage them all.

Output Window

Use of the Output window is a must, because this is where your application and Visual Studio will try to communicate with you behind the scenes. You open the Output window by selecting View | Other Windows | Output Window. This is the only debugging window that does not appear under Debug | Windows. When you first start an application, you see a list of messages from Visual Studio indicating that it is loading all of the necessary pieces for your project. Any unhandled exceptions that are encountered during Run mode also show up here, so if you dismiss the pop-up window with the exception's name in it, you can still look to the Output window while in Break mode to see that message again. If you wish to use the **Debug** object to write messages to yourself for debugging, then you look to the Output window to read those messages. You will use either **Debug.Write** or **Debug.WriteLine** to send messages to the Output window. I will cover the **Debug** object in more detail later in this chapter.

You can filter the messages being displayed by the Output window by using the drop-down menu at the top of this pane. You can choose to see only the debug messages that are produced by both your Debug lines and the Visual Studio environment by choosing the Debug filter, or you can switch to the Solution Builder filter to view messages that are the result of your application's build phase. If any errors occur when Visual Studio tries to build your project before running, you will see these listed as items that were failed or skipped during the build process. If your application fails the build process, it will not start in Debug mode and the Output window will report to you via the Solutions Builder messages that problems have occurred.

For debugging, the Debug view of the Output window is your main source of information. If you do not see your **Debug** object messages and exception messages in the Output window, check to be sure that the drop-down menu at the top of this window is set to Debug. Every time your application starts, Debug view lists all the modules that were loaded at startup, such as the **System.Windows.Forms** object that is always loaded at the start of any Windows application. You can use this output to verify that all the proper modules are loaded for your code to work correctly.

Locals Window

You probably remember this window from past versions of Visual Basic. The Locals window's job is to display all the variables that are currently in scope. If the **MyName** variable can be accessed by the currently active procedure, it will appear in the Locals window. If a variable cannot be accessed by the procedure, such as **Private** variables declared in a different Class, the Locals window will not display it. From the Locals window, you will see the variable's name, current value, and data type. The variable's value is editable from the Locals window and is shown in red if you change it, and it will remain red until the application runs again and applies the changes. No values are shown in the Locals window while the program is running; values are shown only during Break mode.

Autos Window

The Autos window is similar to the Locals window, but on a smaller scale. The Autos window only displays variables in use on the currently active line of code and those for the line that came immediately before it. If the value of the variable changes between those two lines of code, the most current value is shown in the Value column. All other variables that are in scope but not on these two lines of code will not be displayed. For really busy procedures with a lot of items in the Locals window, you may want to use the Autos window to filter out any variables not currently being affected by your code. As in the Locals window, values are editable in this window and are applied after the application re-enters Run mode.

Modules Window

This debugging window lists all the modules that are currently loaded in your application. These will include the System modules, such as the Windows.Forms.DLL that your WindowsApplications are derived from. Along with the names of the modules, you will see their current address in memory, the path to the module on the hard drive, the order in which your application loaded these modules, and the version number of the module you are using. Now that you are dealing with managed Assemblies, it really helps to know which version of a module your code is working with, because your system can have more than one version installed.

The Modules window also has a column named Information, and for most of your modules, the line here will say Symbols Loaded. *Symbols* refers to the debugging symbols that are associated with each module. These symbols assist in the debugging of the module's code, and without them, you will not be able to debug that module from within Visual Studio.NET. Working with debugging symbols is a C++ concept, and the .NET debugger came from C++ roots. If a module is indicating that its debugging symbols were not loaded, you can right-click the module's name and select Reload Symbols. A file browser will pop up and ask you to locate a PDB file, which is a Program Database file containing debug information that can be generated for a C++ module. If a PDB file is not available for that item, you will not be able to debug the module directly.

Me/This Window

You may be familiar with the keyword **Me**, which you can use in code to refer to the currently loaded module and items contained within it, without specifically naming that module. Within a Windows form, you can access a button on that form by using the **Me** keyword:

```
Me.Button1.Text = "It's good to be me"
```

The **Me** keyword takes the place of the form's name. The Me window lists all the items that currently fall under the **Me** keyword. This window displays the information in a tree-view format, and includes all components, variables, and objects that are associated with the current Class. You may see this window change its name to This occasionally, because C#

uses **This** in place of the **Me** keyword. When you enter Break mode in a Visual Basic application, the window's title will say Me, and if your source code's next statement line is in a Visual C# module, the window's title will be This.

The variables listed within the Me window are editable here. Simply double-click the variable's value under the Value column and enter a new value for it. New values are colored red in this window until your application continues to process again. When processing continues, all changes are committed and the variable values go back to their default black color.

Call Stack Window

As one procedure calls another and those called procedures complete their jobs, your application's call stack grows and shrinks. Your call stack starts with your main Class, such as a Windows form. If that form calls a procedure in Class1, then a call is added to the stack and the processing leaves the form and enters the new procedure in Class1. If you enter Break mode at this point and open the Call Stack window, you will see that both the calling form Class and the called Class1 procedure are listed, with a yellow arrow indicating that the procedure in Class1 is currently being executed. Along with the names of all the active procedures in your application, you will see a column indicating in which language each procedure was written. Visual Basic procedures are labeled simply as Basic. The Call Stack window lists the procedure calls with the most recent call at the top of the list. All calls made by your application are represented here, including those made to procedures written in another programming language.

By right-clicking any line in the Call Stack window, you can determine what pieces of information are shown here. You can customize this window so that along with the module's name and the procedure's name, you also see what line of code was last executed and any of the procedure's associated parameters listed by name, type, value, or any combination of the three. By right-clicking any line in this window, you can also set the window to display any calls to and from threads other than the one your application is running on.

Breakpoints can be added from the Call Stack window by right-clicking a procedure in the stack and selecting Insert Breakpoint. After a breakpoint is inserted, you can again right-click the line and choose Breakpoint Properties to finish setting up the breakpoint. Because the Call Stack window offers a high-level view of what's going on in your code, you may not want to use it to insert breakpoints. When a breakpoint is inserted at the call stack, over in the code, you see the breakpoint appear at the last line of code executed. This is great if that's where you want it to be placed, but for most cases, you should use Code view to locate a line of code and insert a breakpoint more precisely.

Double-clicking a procedure in your call stack jumps your Code view to that procedure and its last executed line of code. If you were to do this to the line for the Windows form that called Class1, you would jump to the line of code that actually called Class1 and passed control to it. If the item in the call stack that you double-click does not have any available source code for you to look at, you instead are shown the Disassembly window, listing the current compiler output for this procedure. If you click a line that lists a Visual Studio.NET superclass, such as the **System.Windows.Forms** Class, you will only see the Disassembly view, because you do not have the original source code for this Class.

Tip

Use the Call Stack window to see how deep your procedure calls go. Viewing the call stack will help you to decide whether to handle exceptions locally or let them rise up the call stack to another procedure.

Threads Window

As you learned in Chapter 4, you now can spawn processes off onto their own threads of execution. This is a very powerful feature, and having a special Threads window to monitor all of these spawned-off threads is a big help. The Threads window lists all currently active threads that your application is working with, including their ID, Priority, and Location. A thread's Location translates to where in the code that thread currently is processing. Running two threads is like running two different applications. When you are looking at the Threads window in Break mode, you can double-click a thread and jump directly to its current processing point in the source code. This is extremely helpful, because debugging a multithreaded application can get seriously complicated as a result of the presence of more than one Next Statement line of code.

You can pause and continue a thread's processing from the Threads window, just as you could do from your code. When you right-click a running thread, you have the option to freeze it, thereby pausing its operation when you return to Run mode. To undo this action, right-click a frozen thread and select the cleverly named Thaw option, which "unpauses" your thread when the application reenters Run mode. If you are working with threads in Visual Basic, you will definitely want to have this window open in Debug mode.

Immediate/Command Window

Before you ventured into the world of .NET, the Immediate window was where you looked for your Debug and Trace output messages. Now in .NET, these messages are displayed only in the Output window. The Immediate and Output windows are closely related, in that the Output window is the way in which the application and code communicate with you, and the Immediate window is the way in which you issue commands back to the application.

The Immediate and Command windows share the same pane, and act as two different modes that you switch between. Generally, if you are working in Design mode, then you use the Command window, because there is no active application to talk to. When your application enters Run mode, you can switch this pane to Immediate mode by selecting Debug | Windows | Immediate. Command mode is for talking to the Visual Studio IDE, and Immediate mode is for talking to the application by way of the debugger. You can use the Visual Studio menus to switch modes, or you can simply type "immed" at the command prompt to switch to Immediate mode, and type ">cmd" at the immediate prompt to switch to Command mode. You can still work in Command mode when an application is being debugged (refer to Chapter 3 for more details on using the Command window). If you would like to get a listing of all the aliased commands available for you to use in the Command window, simply type "alias" at the command prompt (>) and press Enter.

Viewing and Changing Variables

Using Immediate mode, you can query any values in your code by typing a question mark (?) followed by a space and the value you wish to check. You can use this method to check the values of your variables, or to query the settings of a form's item. Only values that are currently in scope can be queried from the Immediate window. If you step from one procedure that has a locally **Dim**med variable named **MyName** into another procedure that does not declare this variable, the value of **MyName** is not retrievable and you instead get back a message saying the variable has not be declared. If you can see the variable in your code window, it is faster to just hover your mouse cursor over that variable to find out its current value.

In the Immediate window, you not only can view a variable's value, but also change its value. For instance, suppose that you are stepping through a **For** loop with a counter named **q**, and its current value is 5, but you wish to skip ahead so that its value becomes 9. You would only need to type this line into the Immediate window:

```
q = 9
```

Your code may have values that you want to see that are not directly accessible in your code, such as the currently selected item within a combo box. Unless you have a statement that directly refers to the combo box's **SelectedItem** property, then you have no way of finding out what its value is. To use your Immediate window to find this out, you could type the following command:

```
? ComboBox1.SelectedItem
```

The Immediate window would come back with the name of the item currently showing as selected in your ComboBox, as well as the data type of that item.

Executing Commands and Procedures

With all of the variable-monitoring tools available in .NET, the Immediate window might not seem all that powerful at first, but here is something you can do in this window that you can't do anywhere else: You can execute whole commands and procedures from within the Immediate window. The results from the procedure or command that you execute from this window become a part of your program's execution. If you wanted to see what would happen if you doubled the value of a variable, you could type a line similar to this in the Immediate window:

```
Checking = Checking * 2
```

Now, within your code, the **Checking** variable's value would be doubled, and would maintain this value as you continue to run the code. For another example, suppose that you have entered Break mode in a procedure, and as you are stepping through its code, you decide that you want to run a separate subroutine named **Class1.AddReservation** to see what the results would be. In the Immediate window, you could run this by typing the following line:

```
Class1.AddReservation
```

The program would temporarily enter Run mode, and the **AddReservation** subroutine would run in its entirety. When it is completed, you would be returned to Break mode at the same location where you left off. The ability to run procedures out of order and on special occasions can be very useful during a troubleshooting session. You should exercise some care with this feature, because running certain procedures outside of their normal order can often have unexpected and unwanted results.

Watch Window

If you are not already familiar with the Watch window, this is a debugging window that you can use to place a spotlight on your variables. When you add a new watch to your program, you add that variable's name to a list of variables that you are currently watching. The Watch window will display your variable's current data only when your application is in Break mode. If you enter Break mode and a variable you have placed a watch on is out of scope, the Value column reports back to you that it is unable to evaluate the expression. If your variable is in scope, then its current value is displayed. As you step through the code, this value stays up to date and changes to red immediately after its value has changed. Take a look at the following code example:

```
Dim MyName As String = "Craig"
MyName = "Bob"
MsgBox(MyName)
```

If you were stepping through these three lines of code, the Watch window would display the name Craig in red when your Next Statement arrow is pointing at the line that sets **MyName** to Bob, because the Next Statement line has not yet been executed, so the value is still Craig at this point. If you step to the **MsgBox** line, the Watch window will report back that **MyName** is now Bob, and its value will be colored red again because it has just changed. Step past the **MsgBox** line and the value will go back to being colored black. Like all the other windows that show you a variables value, you can edit the values in the Watch window. Edited values are red until the program is continued or stepped forward and the new value is applied in the code. You can also place a watch on a constant in your code, but a constant will not be editable in Break mode, because the value of a constant is locked in at application startup and never reevaluated.

To add a watch to your application, run your application and then enter Break mode either through a breakpoint or by clicking the Pause button. Double-click a variable in your code to highlight it or by placing your cursor in front of the first character in the variable's name, and then right-click the highlighted variables and select Add Watch from the pop-up menu. This variable is now added to your Watch window. To remove a watch, click once on the variable's line inside the Watch window and press Delete. Watches are saved along with your code and breakpoints when you exit Visual Studio.NET, saving you the trouble of reestablishing your watches every time you open your code.

A shortcut for adding a watch to a variable is to double-click the variable to highlight it, and then drag and drop that variable name down to your Watch window. This dragging-and-dropping shortcut also works with the variables displayed in the Locals, Autos, and Me windows. If you have the Locals window open and spot a variable that you would like to place a permanent watch on, just drag it over to the Watch window to set this up. You can also use watches to evaluate expressions in your code. Take a look at this line of source code:

```
TotalFunds = Savings + Checking
```

If you highlight from the S in *Savings* to the end of the variable name *Checking*, and then drag this mathematical expression over to the Watch window, you will get a continuous watch on the sum of these two variables. Even when this particular line of code is not being run, the Watch window will continue to evaluate the expression with the current values for the variables listed. Arrays and Structures that are given watches are displayed in a tree view within the Watch window, which enables you to expand the top-level item to get at its subitems. For example, a **Customer** Structure would be expandable to allow access to its **FirstName** and **LastName** variables. For an array, each declared element for the array will be displayed under its tree branch, even if a value has not been assigned to that element. This is a very useful tool for monitoring the values stored inside arrays, which are sometimes hard to keep track of.

Tip

Use the Watch window to keep an eye on the results of your expressions. This will help you to spot an erroneous result before the actual expression is evaluated in the code.

QuickWatch Dialog Box

The QuickWatch dialog box enables you to perform a one-time watch or check on a variable's value or an expression's result. When you are in Break mode, you can open the QuickWatch dialog box by right-clicking anywhere in the code and selecting it from the pop-up menu. In the Expression box at the top, you can enter a variable's name, type an expression such as "Savings – Checking", or select a previously entered QuickWatch expression from the drop-down list of values. Click the Evaluate button and you will get an instant evaluation of the current value of your variable or expression.

Once again, the values you see here for your variables are editable and are applied after you close the QuickWatch dialog box and continue the application. Just enter the new value in the QuickWatch's Value column and press Enter to apply it.

Note

*Enclose **String** data types in quotes when assigning new values in the QuickWatch dialog box.*

The QuickWatch dialog box is a *modal* window, which means you have to close it before you can go back to your troubleshooting or continue your program's execution. If you suddenly want to make the expression you have chosen a permanent watch, you can do so by clicking the Add Watch button, and that expression will appear in the Watch window. QuickWatch is also capable of displaying and evaluating Structures and arrays via a tree view, just as I described for the Watch window.

Tip

Use the QuickWatch dialog box to perform "what if" calculations when troubleshooting.

Breaks vs. Watches

A big difference exists between the watches in Visual Studio.NET and the ones you are used to using in version 6. Previously, you could give a watch a setting to make your program enter Break mode whenever the variable you were watching was equal to True or whenever its value changed in the code. You will not be able to set these conditions on your .NET watches. In .NET, a watch is for watching a value, and a breakpoint is for stopping your code under special circumstances or at a set location. Because breakpoints are only evaluated at set locations, you have to strategically place your breakpoints in meaningful locations to trap and evaluate a variable's value that you are hoping to catch.

Other Debugging Windows

The Memory window is available during debugging, which enables you to view the contents of your computer's memory that is being used by your application. This information breaks down each character into the hexadecimal values that are actually written to memory. This window probably won't interest most VB developers, and can be safely avoided. Along these same lines, if you are debugging a native-code application, you can use the Registers window to view and edit the value of the system's registers. This is another debugging window you will not need open in most cases. Working with computer memory and registers is not necessary to make a great Visual Basic application, and not having to deal with these issues may be the only thing "basic" about the Visual Basic you know today.

Another new debugging window is the Running Documents window, which applies only to Web applications that are using HTML and ASP.NET pages. Because these run within pages or "documents" as opposed to modules, they get their own special window to keep track of them. This window is covered in Chapter 10 when I introduce you to ASP.NET.

Other Debugging Resources

Although you have an army of debugging windows at your disposal, these are not the only tools you have to help you troubleshoot your applications. This section presents a few more resources that can be a big help to you when the code is misbehaving.

Debug Toolbar

This toolbar is so useful that I keep it open all the time—even when I am not troubleshooting my code. Figure 9.4 shows the buttons described here. For starters, the toolbar has some handy buttons to start your application, stop it, or place it in Break mode (those are the VCR-like controls mentioned earlier). Next to the Start button is an exclamation point icon that, when clicked, starts your application without attaching the debugger to it. You will not be able to debug or even enter Break mode when you start your application by clicking this button. In fact, an application started with this icon will be completely independent of Visual Studio, and you can leave the application running and switch back to your code in Visual Studio to continue working. You can also launch more instances of your application by using this icon, or use the Start button to launch the second instance of your application in Debug mode while the first instance continues to run independently of Visual Studio.

If you start an application in Debug mode, you can detach it from the debugger and Visual Studio by using the Detach All button to the right of the Stop button. When you use Detach All, Visual Studio acts as if you stopped your application and places you back in Design mode, but the instance of your application you originally started continues to run independently of Visual Studio. Immediately to the right of the Detach All button is a button named Restart. If you start your application with the debugger attached, you can click this icon to completely shut down your application and restart it with a fresh instance. Instead of clicking Stop, waiting, and clicking Start, you get two clicks for the price of one.

The Debug toolbar also has icons that perform all the stepping actions described earlier, without using the shortcut keys or menu items. It also has a handy drop-down list that enables you to switch between stepping modes, such as the Line, Statement, and Instruction modes. Further down the toolbar, you can add, modify, and delete breakpoints and open any of the debugging windows mentioned earlier. Using the menus often is slow and painful as you search for the item that you want, and who can remember all of those shortcut keys? Use the Debug toolbar and you will find that the tools you need are only a click away.

Figure 9.4
The Debug toolbar.

Debug Location Toolbar

As your applications grow in complexity, so will your debugging needs. In Visual Studio.NET, you can launch procedures onto their own threads, and you can attach your application's debugger to other active programs. If you are working on a complex multithreaded or multiprogram debugging project, you should load the Debug Location toolbar to assist you. From this toolbar, you can jump between programs, threads, and items in your call stack simply by using three drop-down combo boxes. Want to look at the current line of execution on another thread? Simply pick it from the Thread combo box and you'll jump right to it.

Crash Dumps

Visual Studio.NET has the ability to save the state of your application if it crashes. All of this data is packaged into what is called a *crash dump*. This dump enables you to save the erroneous results of a particular run of your application for testing and debugging at a later time. You can even debug a saved crash dump on a machine other than the one where the crash occurred. Large development organizations can use crash dumps to up-channel these bad results to their testing and debugging experts, so even if the crash happens when a user is trying out the application, the results can be saved and passed on to an expert who knows how to examine them.

When you are using Visual Studio.NET in Debug mode and Visual Studio pops up a message reporting an unhandled exception, you should click the Break button to enter Break mode. If you click the Continue button, the application will complete its crashing and the crash dump will be lost. When you enter Break mode from an unhandled exception, you can select Debug | Save As CrashDump to save the application's state. After you have the data saved, you can stop the application by clicking the Stop button on the Debug toolbar. Now you have a permanent record of the application's state at the time of the crash, which can be really useful to the troubleshooters. Far more useful than, say, a simple exception message and a vague description by the user.

If you wish to open a crash dump file, you do so in Visual Studio just like you would open any other file. Select File | Open | File and then browse for the file you saved, which will end with .dmp. Visual Studio.NET can also open and examine crash dumps created by the Microsoft Dr. Watson utility, which I'm sure anyone who has worked on a Windows NT system has encountered. This "doctor" utility creates a crash dump whenever Microsoft Office goes down for the count, enabling you to troubleshoot those crashes as well as your own applications. To debug a crash dump, you need all the source code files for that Project available on the machine that you are using to open the crash dump. You do not need the program's source code to create a crash dump, just the .NET debugger.

Tip

Use crash dumps to debug problems at a later time—some bugs are harder to replicate than others, and by saving a crash dump, you may be saving yourself the trouble of trying to duplicate a tricky bug.

Compiler Statements

You can continue to use compiler statements in your code just as you did in version 6. You use these statements if one version of your application could be compiled into two or more different versions, such as a client and a server version or a development and a production version. One version may have different procedures or variable settings than another, but you do not want to have to maintain two separate versions of your code for this project. Instead, you can simply use the compiler statements to decide which pieces of your code will be compiled based on a constant setting. Here is an example of the three compiler statements, **#Const**, **#If**, and **#Else**:

```
#Const Development = True
#If Development Then
        Dim DBServer as String = "DEVDB_SQL"
#Else
        Dim DBServer As String = "PRODDB_SQL"
#End If
```

Every time this block of code is run, the value of **DBServer** is set to **DEVDB_SQL**, which represents a name of a SQL server inside your development environment. You would keep the **#Const** named **Development** set to **True** whenever you are testing your application locally or when you deploy it to a development server inside your company. When it is suddenly time to ship your product to the customer, all you need to change is the **#Const** **Development** to **False**, and when you compile or run your application, the code after the **Else** statement will be executed.

At runtime within Visual Studio, compiler statements are consulted to decide which code should be run. When you compile your application for deployment, the compiler statements tell the compiler which pieces of code it should compile and which lines of code can be left out of the final product. Using compiler statements is much more efficient than trying to comment out many lines of code to switch between your two development environments. Simply change the value of your **#Const** and let the **#If** statements decide which code to run.

Attaching Processes

With Visual Studio.NET's debugger, you have the option of attaching to your debugger a process that is running outside of the Visual Studio environment, enabling you to troubleshoot that process or include it in the troubleshooting of your application that uses the enlisted process. The process that you want to add must be running, so you can't add a Microsoft Outlook process to the debugger if Outlook is not running. But, if you start Outlook, then you can add this running process to the debugger. What's really nice is that the process does not have to be running locally on your machine to be added. You can add processes from any machine on your network to the debugger for enterprise-wide troubleshooting. To see this really cool feature in action, try out Exercise 9.1.

Exercise 9.1: Attaching Processes to the Debugger

1. Start a new WindowsApplication Project and call it AttachMe.

2. Add one button to your form. Double-click that button and give it the following code:

```
Protected Sub Button1_Click(ByVal sender As Object, ByVal e As _
    System.EventArgs)
  Dim FirstName As String
  Dim LastName As String
  Dim FullName As String
  FirstName = "Dave"
  LastName = "Smith"
  FullName = FirstName & " " & LastName
  Debug.WriteLine("Say Hi to " & FullName)
  MsgBox("My name is " & FullName)
End Sub
```

3. Save your Project, and then select Build | Build.

4. Close Visual Studio.NET completely.

5. Locate and start the AttachMe.exe file you built (it will be in the Bin directory underneath your Project's working directory).

6. Start Visual Studio.NET, but do not start any Projects.

7. With no Projects loaded, select Debug | Processes.

8. Notice toward the top of the Processes window a box for your machine's name. This is where you could specify another machine name to add remote processes to the debugger.

9. Double-click the AttachMe process in the list of running processes.

10. An Attach To Process window opens, asking you what type of programs you will be debugging. Because you wrote AttachMe in Visual Basic.NET, this is a CLR program, and the item with that label should already be checked. Simply click the OK button to finalize the attaching procedure.

11. Click the Close button to close the Processes window.

12. The debugger is now debugging the AttachMe program. Click the button on the AttachMe form.

13. Notice that **Debug.WriteLine** has written a line to your Output window, and now the **MsgBox** is showing. Do *not* click the **MsgBox** button.

14. In Visual Studio.NET, select Debug | Break to enter Break mode. You should now have a Form1.vb tab in your Code view. Click it, and you will see the code for this form with a green arrow indicating that the MsgBox is the current line of code. All of your debugging windows will now be usable. You will be able to add watches or view variables in the Locals window.

You can also detach processes from your debugger through the Debug | Processes window. Recall from Chapter 6, when you created your own Windows Service, that the only way to debug a Service is to install it and then attach it to the debugger, just like you did with the AttachMe example. The Processes window has a checkbox that, when checked, will add all running system processes to the list along with the currently running programs. The Debug Location toolbar can come in handy when you are attaching outside programs, because it enables you to quickly switch between different programs attached to your debugger. Remember, if you attach a process that does not have debugging symbols in it, all you will see is the disassembly information when you examine it in Break mode.

Debug and Trace

The **Debug** and **Trace** Classes can assist you in troubleshooting and monitoring your code. Using these two Classes is often referred to as *tracing*, because they can help you follow along with your program's execution. The **Trace** Class comes from the C++ world, while the **Debug** Class should already be familiar to Visual Basic developers. The main difference between these two Classes is that when you build your application for deployment, only the **Trace** commands are compiled into the final version. This means you should use the **Debug** Class during development testing in Visual Studio.NET, and rely on the **Trace** Class to help you trace a program's execution both before and after it has been deployed. Both **Debug** and **Trace** include all the methods covered in this section.

Write and WriteLine

The **Debug.WriteLine** method sends its message and provides you with some information without you having to place your application in Break mode. This enables you to troubleshoot and trace a program's execution in realtime instead of step by step in Break mode. Here is an example of a typical **Debug** line:

```
Debug.WriteLine("Class1 Initialized")
```

By placing this **Debug** statement in **Class1**'s **New** subroutine, you will see a message written to the Output window every time **Class1** is initialized, helping you to keep track of which pieces of code have been run. **Debug** has a **Write** and a **WriteLine** method, the only difference between the two being that the **WriteLine** method does a carriage return after it outputs its message, and the **Write** method does not.

WriteIf and WriteLineIf

You can give your **Debug.Write** statements some intelligence by using their **If** versions. Say, for instance, that you want to write your message to the Output window only if the value of the **MyValue** variable is equal to 5. You could use the **WriteLineIf** statement like so:

```
Debug.WriteLineIf(MyValue = 5, "MyValue equals 5")
```

If the expression you are checking for is **True**, then the message you specify is sent to the Output window. If the value of **MyValue** is not equal to 5, then no message will be written by this **Debug** line.

Assert

An **Assert** statement can act as a conditional breakpoint within your code. The **Assert** statement evaluates whatever condition you give it as a **Boolean True** or **False**, and causes your code to enter Break mode if the result is **False**. Take a look at the following **Assert** statement:

```
Debug.Assert(MyValue = 10)
```

If your code processes this line and the value of the **MyValue** variable is 10, then the statement is **True** and your code will continue processing. If the value is anything other than 10, the **Assert** is **False** and your application will enter Break mode for you to troubleshoot. You can also use the **Assert** statement to send a message to the Output window if the statement evaluates as **False**. Here is an example of an **Assert** with an output message:

```
Debug.Assert(MyValue = 10, "MyValue does not equal 10")
```

In past versions of Visual Basic, the **Assert** statement was a way to persist your breakpoints, because the breakpoints you added in the code's margin did not get saved when you exited Visual Studio. Because breakpoints are now saved in .NET, you should try to use the real breakpoints instead of **Assert** statements. Not only do they enable you to set conditions and counters, but you can also quickly disable and enable these, whereas an **Assert** statement would have to be commented out or modified manually.

Putting It All Together

You certainly have a lot of tools in your troubleshooting toolbox, and now that you have been introduced to them all, it's time to decide how you can best use these tools to debug the many application types you will create in Visual Studio.NET.

Visual Studio.NET Debugging Layout

Just as you customized the Visual Studio.NET development environment with the most useful tools available, you should also customize your debugging environment. As you switch between a debugging and a development mode, your environment will switch too, giving you two different selections of windows with their own unique layouts based on what mode you are in.

For starters, the Debug toolbar is a must and should always be loaded. The Debug Location toolbar is not as critical unless you are troubleshooting multithreaded or multiprogram environments. In this complex situation, you should load the Debug Location toolbar to help you navigate between all of those separate entities being debugged.

Hands down the most important debugging window of them all is the Output window. If you can't see the messages from the compiler or your Debug messages, then you are troubleshooting in the dark. In my book, the Locals window runs a close second in terms of usefulness. When entering Break mode, you need to quickly evaluate the current state of your program's variables, and the Locals window enables you to do this. If you have placed any watches on your variables, you should also load the Watch window. I allow my Locals and Watch windows to share a pane together. Having windows share a pane can save a lot of space and enables you to make these windows bigger for easier viewing.

Breakpoints now play a much bigger role in your debugging phase. The ability to save them from one session to another enables you to add a whole slew of breakpoints to your code and not have to reconfigure them every time you start Visual Studio. If you do use breakpoints in your code (and you should have no reason not to), then you should load the Breakpoints window to help you track and manage them. I set up my Breakpoints window to share a pane with my Output window. Typically, the Output window is visible, but if I need to check out my breakpoints, that information is only one click away.

As your programs grow in size and complexity, you may want to add other windows to your layout. The Modules and Threads windows both are very useful if your program uses multiple modules and threads. For programs with a lot of nested procedural calls in them, loading the Call Stack window is a smart choice so that you can visualize how these calls are stacking up and what their relationships are. Figure 9.5 shows my preferred Visual Studio.NET debugging layout.

Class Debugging

Your debugging sessions will mostly be triggered by one of two events: a logic error or an unhandled exception in your code. A logic error will not crash your application, but the result you see on the screen will not be what you expect, such as an incorrect savings account balance being displayed.

The debugging difference between an exception and a logic error is that you will immediately know where to start your debugging with the exception, because Visual Studio will point

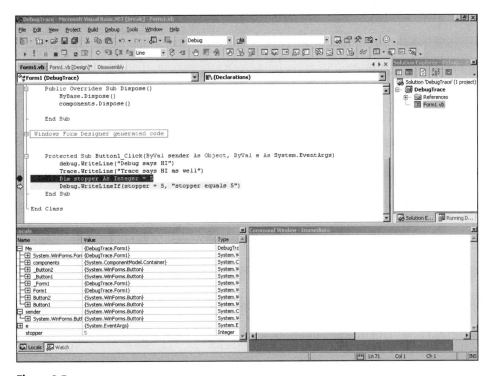

Figure 9.5
A customized debugging layout.

this out to you. Typically, the line that raises the exception is not the cause of the problem, but only a symptom of a bigger problem. Because you cannot step backward through your code from the location of the breakpoint, you should locate a line of code earlier in the function where you can place a breakpoint that takes you into Break mode before something goes wrong. Mentally working backward through your code and deciding where to begin your search is sometimes harder than it sounds. When the exception first places you in Break mode, read the exception's message to get a clue as to where to begin your search. Checking the values of all the variables in scope via the Locals window will also help you to narrow down your search, if you can spot something out of the ordinary.

Logic errors are often more difficult to debug because nothing appears wrong on the surface of the application. To troubleshoot a logic error, you need to decide where in your code is a good place to put a breakpoint to place you in Break mode before the erroneous logic function occurs. After you are in Break mode, you can step through your code and observe the values of your variables by using either watches or the Locals window. A watch can be helpful because you can create a watch that evaluates a mathematical expression and reports back to you the current value, which avoids you having to do this math in your head as you step through the application. When you find the location where the math just doesn't add up, drop another breakpoint or leave a comment so that you can find your way back there should the problem reoccur.

Windows Services Debugging

Because a Windows Service is designed to be run by the operating system, you will not be able to run it within Visual Studio.NET for debugging purposes. To debug a Windows Service, you need to build it and install it on the operating system. Once installed and started, you then can start Visual Studio.NET and attach the debugger to this service, as described earlier in this chapter. For development versions of your service, you should use plenty of **EventLog** entries to report the status and actions of your service to a place where you can view them via the Event Viewer, found under Start | Administrative Tools in Windows. Use this tool just as you would use your **Debug.WriteLine** statements and the Output window when you are troubleshooting your other applications. A lot of care must go into designing and coding your Windows Services, because the only way to troubleshoot these is to actually install and run them on the operating system.

Multilanguage Solutions

Thanks to the new fully integrated .NET development environment, you can add many different Projects to one Solution with each Project developed in its own language. If your team is developing an application using more than one programming language, you should test all of these separate Projects under one unified Solution. Using Visual Studio.NET to step through the code and to follow cross-language procedural calls can cut your debugging time considerably. In the past, a Visual Basic developer could not troubleshoot a failed call to a component written in Visual C++. The developer would merely report to the C++ programmer that such-and-such did not work right. Now with .NET, you can step out of your VB code and into the C++ code and immediately spot the problem.

Class Libraries and Windows Controls

Neither a Class Library nor a Windows control will run on its own. Both of these Projects must be called by another "parent" Project. The best way to troubleshoot these two Projects is to add a second Project to your Solution that will call your Class Library or Windows control. An example of this would be a customized text box Windows control that you have created. You cannot run this simple text box all by itself to see how it works, so to troubleshoot it, you have to add a WindowsApplication Project to your Windows Control Solution.

Because both of these Projects fall under one Solution, you can leave breakpoints in the control's code that will respond whenever the control is utilized on the hosting form while in Run mode. One tricky part about debugging Windows controls is that you can only debug them in Run mode, such as when the WindowsApplication is run and uses your text box. Controls actually work in two modes, Run mode and Design mode. When a developer drags your control to a form in Designer view and then resizes it or changes a property's value, the developer is working in Design mode. The debugger is not running in Design mode, so you cannot troubleshoot problems with your controls that occur in Design mode.

To debug Design mode problems, you need to carefully study your control's behavior and then troubleshoot it without the aid of a debugger.

Threads

Debugging an application that creates new threads can be especially difficult. If your main application starts two processes onto their own threads, this is the troubleshooting equivalent of debugging three separate applications, with each of them doing its own thing. A break or exception in one thread typically does not indicate an error in another thread, and each thread must be treated as a separate entity. Threads also have various states, such as running and paused, and they can often get into trouble, such as a deadlock condition, which occurs when two threads are competing for access to the same file on your hard drive. Excessive use or a buildup of threads can really drain your system's resources, causing even more problems for the developer to look out for.

Using the Threads window is a must if your application is going to create any new threads. Use this window to spot out-of-the-ordinary thread pauses or hang-ups. Stress test your application under extreme circumstances to ensure that your threads will not get deadlocked or hung up after your application is deployed. Spotting threads that are sleeping and never seem to awaken from a code-induced sleep is an indicator of a problem. Threads may linger forever if they are not closed out properly. You may also encounter a thread that closes out prematurely without completing its full function, thereby causing an exception on another thread. Threading is a terrific new feature that is one of my favorite additions to Visual Basic, but you should take a lot of care when using threads, because each one can double your debugging concerns and problems.

Summary

As applications grow more and more complex, so too must the development tools you use to create these projects and debug them. As a result of Visual Basic.NET's addition of so many new features and language enhancements, you can expect to encounter some highly complicated bugs, the likes of which you have never seen before. It's a good thing that Visual Studio.NET is the most powerful development environment ever created, complete with every debugging tool imaginable to help you spot these bugs and squash them quickly. Debugging applications is all about situational awareness: The more you know about the current state of the application and how it got there, the easier it will be to find the error. Use as many of these tools as you can, because you can never know too much about your application.

Chapter 10
ASP.NET Web Development

Inarguably, the Internet has been nothing short of revolutionary, and its sweeping changes have had a direct effect on the applications your clients are asking for today. Even if you have not yet developed an application that uses the Internet in some fashion, odds are good that you have still encountered a customer who was interested in harnessing the power of the Web. The lure of the Web's worldwide accessibility is simply too strong to ignore, both as a developer and as a customer needing a new application built. Not too long ago, an application's reach was limited to the customer's internal network in a client/server configuration. Now that network has been extended, and with the increased capabilities of today's servers and the ever-accelerating speed of the user's connections, the age of the thin-client, Internet-based application is now upon us.

Until recently, being a "Web developer" was an entirely different job title than that of your traditional "applications developer" or "software engineer." When you were job hunting, you were either one or the other, and very rarely both. But now, with Visual Studio.NET, developing an application for the Web is not a job for a specialist, but instead is just another extension of your Visual Basic skills. Even if you have no plans to use the Web in your applications, you should still learn how to do it, because I guarantee that someday you will need to use the Web in an application, like it or not. Not learning how to create a Web interface would be like ignoring the Windows form interfaces. These two interface types are completely interchangeable in today's application projects. The Web interface may take a little more work to create a version that's as powerful as your Windows form, but the Web interface will give you the power of platform independence, meaning that your application can run on any operating system that has a Web browser. Imagine developing applications that users of Unix, Linux, and Mac systems all can use. Tear down another wall, because with the power of ASP.NET, you are no longer confined to being "just" a Windows application developer.

ASP Development Background

If this is your first journey into the world of Web development, then it will help to have an understanding about how these different Internet technologies came to be and what their strengths and weaknesses are. In this section, I will briefly cover how ASP came into being, and then provide a few words on some related Web technologies that you will come in contact with on the Internet.

The History of ASP

At the dawning of the Internet age, Web pages were merely static documents that you could read but not interact with. Talk about humble beginnings. But the early pioneers of the Web soon found a way to develop interactive Web sites using server-side scripting. Common Gateway Interface (CGI) scripts were stored on the Web server and processed submitted data from Web Forms. If you filled out a registration form with your name, address, and phone number, this information would be sent to the CGI script, which would then process it and return to you another Web page. Server-side CGI scripts are created in an interpreted scripting language such as Perl, a popular scripting language used in most CGI scripts.

An interpreted language can be read as text directly off the hard drive and requires a runtime compiler to process it. If you are creating Perl CGI scripts, these scripts will be run by a Perl interpreter installed on your Web server. One of the downsides to using interpreted languages is that they will not run as fast as a compiled programming language. Also, because a script requires that an interpreter be started to run it, a script creates additional processes on your Web server, with one instance of the interpreter for every call being made to a script. The more calls being made to your CGI scripts, the more instances of the interpreter that you have running, thereby slowing down your server. Six simultaneous calls to a single CGI script would result in six instances of the script's interpreter being created, each in its own separate process. Most Unix-based Web servers still rely on CGI scripts for server-side processing.

To overcome the resource drain imposed by CGI scripts, Microsoft introduced the Internet Server Applications Programming Interface (ISAPI), which runs only on Microsoft Internet Information Server (IIS), which in turn only runs on Windows NT and 2000 operating systems. Whenever the Web server needs to run an ISAPI application, it can launch it within the same process as the Web. When six users all try to use an ISAPI application simultaneously, only one instance is loaded into the same process as the Web server, allowing all users to share it. After the first use of an ISAPI application, the Web server keeps it loaded and waiting for the next call, saving even more time for the user. The drawback to the ISAPI approach is that the applications are not easy to create, and you have to be a Visual C++ programmer to do it. The upside to using ISAPI applications is that their code is compiled into a dynamic link library (DLL), which can execute faster than a scripted language that must first be interpreted before it can be executed.

While ISAPI applications are powerful, their complicated nature did not help boost the popularity of the Microsoft Web server. Only a small number of ISAPI applications were developed in comparison to the hugely popular CGI scripts. Microsoft knew that the key to making a Web technology popular was to make it easy to create. CGI script developers do not even need a formal development tool to make their server-side applications—they simply need a text-editing tool, such as Notepad or Unix's Vi, and a Web server set up to support CGI scripts. So Microsoft took this all in and wondered "how can we make this easier?"

Microsoft's answer was Active Server Pages (ASP). An ASP page is created in plain text, just like a normal HTML Web page. Within the page, sections of text are marked with a special tag that indicates to the IIS Web server that some processing has to be done at that point. The code between these tags is a scripting language, often VBScript but sometimes JavaScript, Perl, or some other interpreted language. Take a look at the following example of a basic ASP Web page:

```
<HTML>
<BODY>
<H1>The time is <%=Time%></H1>
</BODY>
</HTML>
```

You could open this page in any text-editing tool, such as Notepad, to view and edit it. My very basic example looks like a stripped-down HTML page, with one little exception: the **<%=Time%>** entry. The **<%** and **%>** opening and closing tags tell the Web server that there is some code in between them to process. If the user were to ask for the preceding ASP page, the HTML output of the Web server would look like this:

```
<HTML>
<BODY>
<H1>The time is 9:51:45am</H1>
</BODY>
</HTML>
```

When the Web server processes the ASP page's code, it replaces **<%=Time%>** with the current value of the system clock. The browser would get the preceding HTML without any of the code in it, and then it would display only the message "The time is 9:51:45am" to the user, leaving out the HTML tags. Within the ASP coding tags, you can do all sorts of processing and calculations, and only the results that are declared as an ASP script's output will leave the Web server. I first started programming for the Web using Perl CGI scripts, which took a lot of effort and time to do correctly. When I first discovered ASP pages, I instantly fell in love with them. Whereas a CGI script feels like a program with a little HTML thrown in, an ASP page feels more like an HTML Web page with a little code thrown in to make it dynamic. Microsoft had truly made dynamic server-side development simple.

What's Wrong with ASP?

Sure ASP is both easy to use and powerful, but it has some downsides and some things that could be improved. Because ASP pages are text-based scripts, they have to be interpreted by the Web server before being processed. The more code you have in your ASP page, the slower it processes. Being restricted to only using VBScript as your programming language has some drawbacks as well, because VBScript is only a subset of the full-blown Visual Basic language. To avoid these problems, and to take advantage of the full feature set of Visual Basic and Component Object Model (COM) development, advanced ASP developers often place their code into COM components, and then call these components from the ASP page. This allows for reusable code and improves the Web site's efficiency by placing as much code as possible into compiled DLLs.

ASP pages are not object-oriented, and the majority of these Web pages are designed in a linear fashion, just like the HTML pages they were born from. Top to bottom, you can read through an ASP page and figure out exactly what it is doing. Although this is simple, it does not allow for code reuse within an ASP page. You can use an **Include** statement in your page to draw in code from other ASP files on the hard drive, but this is a very limiting form of code reuse. Likewise, the objects within a Web page cannot be accessed in an object-oriented fashion. On a Windows form, you can make a reference to a button's property on the form's surface by typing "Form1.Button1.Text", but in ASP, you cannot reference items on the Web page in this manner.

Using script-based ASP has other downsides, such as its reliance on late binding to COM objects, and an annoying habit of locking the DLL after you use it. Whenever I was working on an ASP project and had a new copy of a DLL that I needed to test, I had to shut down the IIS Web server, shut down the MTS server, restart the MTS service, and restart the Web server before the operating system would allow me to overwrite the older version of my DLL. Troubleshooting an ASP page is actually kind of primitive. You are mostly restricted to writing little messages to the user's browser when things go wrong. Without these debugging messages, you would have no idea what the value of a certain variable is before the crash. And, if your ASP page works with a COM component, you can forget about stepping through your code. Your ASP pages and the code in your component classes are in two entirely different worlds. Finally, your code in an ASP Web page can't use strongly typed variables. This means that you can't **Dim** a variable specifically as a **String** or any other specific data type.

Even if you can live with all of these shortcomings, ASP still suffers from the lack of a decent development tool. Although you can visually create a beautiful Web page in Microsoft FrontPage, you can't edit your ASP pages in FrontPage, because it was not designed to understand ASP and thus will break your ASP code. Visual Studio 6 comes with Visual InterDev, which closely resembles the Visual Basic environment but with a focus on ASP development. Whereas FrontPage is strong in layout, InterDev is fairly weak. I find InterDev to be a very useful tool for working with ASP code, because it offers limited IntelliSense and code-coloring features, which sure beats working in Notepad.

Many abilities have been added to ASP pages since InterDev was released, including new ASP tags that the interface previously could not understand. If you didn't have a fancy ASP editor available, you could always use Notepad, which is a pretty painful way to write code. Upon its release, ASP was a terrific new technology, and it has helped a great many developers create terrific Web sites that use server-side scripting. This powerful and easy-to-use technology gave a big boost to Microsoft's IIS Web server's popularity, but ASP is a technology that could be a lot better. Now ASP is all grown up and it's ready for the big time.

Client-Side Technologies

Whereas technologies such as CGI scripts, ISAPI applications, and ASP pages work on the server side to provide a rich, dynamic Web experience, still other technologies are available to the Web developer to enrich the user's surfing session right at the browser. Even a terrific page generated on-the-fly by the Web server is still just a static, unintelligent Web page when it reaches the browser. You can use client-side programming to assist the user who is using your Web page and to make the page both interactive and entertaining. Client-side enhancements can be placed in one of two categories: scripting languages embedded in the HTML, and miniprograms that are downloaded along with your page and run by the browser.

Multimedia and Applets

A Java applet is a program written in the Java programming language that is downloaded to the user's machine and run inside the browser by a Java Virtual Machine (JVM). Applets can be small, supporting programs that enhance a Web page, such as an animated scrolling marquee displaying a friendly message for the user, or they can dominate the Web page, as is the case with many online games that are delivered within an applet running in your browser. A Web page that has an interactive loan calculator built into it is another example of a Java applet. Because the code for this calculator is contained in the applet, the Web page does not have to communicate with the Web server to figure out the answer to your equation. Because an applet represents a whole program, applets sometimes are slow to download and require a Java Virtual Machine (JVM) installed on the user's system to run.

You will also encounter multimedia-based enhancements on the Web, such as Macromedia's Flash and Shockwave, which provide movies and animation to enliven an otherwise dull Web page. Creating multimedia enhancements requires special tools, and these development projects often involve graphic artists and animation specialists. In most development shops, the role of the applications programmer and that of the multimedia specialist are filled by two differently skilled people.

Client-Side Scripting

Closer to your own skill set are Web page script enhancements. A Web page can have small scripts embedded in it to respond to changes or events that take place in the browser. For example, if you would like to ensure that the user has entered a properly formatted email address on a Web Form, you can check this by running a script immediately after the user clicks the Submit button. If the email address does not validate, you can cancel the form's submission and immediately tell the user to fix this problem, all without sending a single bit across the Internet. Without a client-side script, you would have to allow the user to send the form all the way to the Web server, catch the error there, and then send back all of the user's data along with the error message. While validation scripts may not be a flashy enhancement to your Web page, helping out the user and providing immediate feedback is far more important than providing them with some "eye-candy" fireworks animations.

Netscape vs. Internet Explorer

When developing for the Web, you need to remember one important thing: two distinct "tribes" of users are out there. Approximately half of the world's Web surfers are using a Netscape browser to surf the Internet, and the other half of the world's Web surfers are using Microsoft's Internet Explorer. At the time of this writing, Netscape still has a respectable but shrinking percentage of the users out there using its products. Because these two competing browsers are developed by two distinct companies, each has its own unique capabilities and supports different sets of enhancement technologies. Netscape, for example, supports the JavaScript language for client-side scripting, but not VBScript. Internet Explorer supports both VBScript and JavaScript, but Microsoft has developed its own version of JavaScript, known as JScript, which differs in many ways from the Netscape version. With Internet Explorer, you can use ActiveX controls in your Web pages to add to the somewhat-limited set of form controls that come standard in HTML. Sadly, Netscape does not natively support ActiveX controls.

The job of the Web developer often involves some tough decisions about which technologies to use, and which to forego. If you are developing for a client that will only use Internet Explorer, then you are free to use either JScript or VBScript for your client-side scripting and you can include ActiveX controls in your Web pages. If any chance exists that a customer could use Netscape to look at your Web site, you are forced to bypass ActiveX controls and VBScript on the client side. You will also have an added responsibility of double-checking your JavaScript code to ensure that it works the same for both browsers, due to their different interpretations of this language. Despite some hard decisions, you should seek to maximize the use of these client-side technologies and make it a personal goal of yours to make the interface as helpful as possible for the user.

Introducing ASP.NET

If .NET has a recurring theme about it, then it must be the saying "This is not just another upgrade." Well, you can certainly apply this to ASP.NET, too. Like the changes to the Visual Basic language, the changes made to ASP go straight to its core, with the result being an entirely new way of creating dynamic Web pages. The entire definition of what an ASP page is has changed in .NET. Before, you could have defined an ASP page as a text-based Web page with pieces of VBScript inserted in it. With .NET, this has completely changed. In fact, the changes between ASP and ASP.NET are so severe that even experienced ASP developers will have to spend some time learning this new Web development model.

ASP.NET pages are no longer text-based, as are the old familiar HTML pages. Your ASP.NET code now is compiled, which means that you can't edit it with Windows Notepad. The upside is that it will execute much faster than its interpreted predecessors. The second sweeping change is that VBScript is out of the picture. When developing your ASP.NET Solutions, you will write the code in one of the .NET languages, such as Visual Basic or C#. This change can only be seen as a plus, because VBScript was really just a subset of the features found in Visual Basic, and why play with only half a deck when you can use the whole deck of cards?

ASP.NET includes many details to learn about, and I could write a whole other book about it. To cover ASP.NET in one chapter requires that I brush through some topics kind of quickly and leave out some of the more detailed points of this application type. But, what I want you to take away from this chapter is that creating an application that takes advantage of ASP.NET and Web Forms is incredibly easy to do with the skills you already have. Web development is not a job for somebody else in the company, it's just another application type that you can easily create in Visual Basic. If you can do it in Visual Basic, you can now do it in ASP.NET. If Visual Basic is not your thing, then feel free to write those Web pages in whatever .NET language you feel comfortable with; because this book is being written for the VB crowd, though, that's the language I am going to stick with here.

Note

The ASP.NET Web Application Project that you are creating in this chapter needs to talk to an IIS 5 Web server to create itself. This should be configured for you already during the Visual Studio.NET installation. The IIS Web server can be installed on your machine, or on another machine on your network. IIS5 comes with the Windows 2000 Server installation, and should be a part of your default server install.

ASP.NET First Look

No better way exists to learn about a new development tool than to fire it up and start playing around with it. To get you familiar with ASP.NET as quickly as possible, I'd like to start by creating a really basic example. Try out Exercise 10.1 to see how easy it is to create your first ASP.NET Web Form, and then read on as I dissect the example and explain how it all works. Working through Exercise 10.1 is very important, because I will build upon this easy example as the chapter progresses.

Exercise 10.1: Creating Your First ASP.NET Web Form

1. Open Visual Studio.NET, and click the New Project link on the Home Page.

2. Under the Visual Basic Projects folder, click the ASP.NET Web Application Project icon, and then call this Project "MyFirstWeb" in the Name textbox.

3. Your ASP.NET Web Application Project was created directly in the Web server's path, which by default is \Inetpub\wwwroot. Underneath this directory, you should now see a subdirectory named MyFirstWeb. Your Solution now has five files in it: Web.config, Global.asax, MyFirstWeb.vsdisco, Styles.css, and your Web Form, named WebForm1.aspx. The Web Form will open in Design view when the Solution is done loading.

4. Click the Web Form's Design view window, and then, in the Properties window, change the PageLayout property to GridLayout.

5. From the Toolbox's Web Forms tab, select the textbox control and draw a textbox in the center of your Web Form. Next, select the button control and place a button directly below the textbox. Place these two tools in exactly the same way as you would when working on a Windows form.

6. Double-click the button to access its **Click** event. This will look just like a button's **Click** event section in a Windows form. Place the following line of code inside the **Click** event:

```
TextBox1.Text = "Hello Internet!"
```

7. Save your Solution, and then select Debug | Start to run your application. Your Web Application will start in Internet Explorer. When the Web page is done loading, click the button to see your message appear in the textbox. Your Web page will look something like the one shown in Figure 10.1.

8. Make a note of the URL for your Web page (substituting the name of the Web server you are using for *yourmachinename*):

```
http://yourmachinename/MyFirstWeb/WebForm1.aspx
```

9. Stop your Web Application by selecting the Debug | Stop menu item. The Internet Explorer window will close and you will be returned to Design mode in Visual Studio.NET.

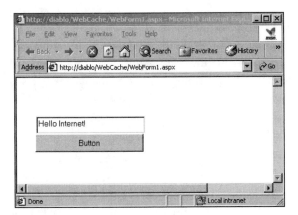

Figure 10.1
The Hello Internet sample Web page.

Except for a few extra files in your Solution, and the fact that your application ran inside of the Internet Explorer browser instead of a Windows form, creating this simple little Web Application probably felt a lot like all the Windows-based applications that you have been creating for years. Even if you are an experienced ASP developer, I'm sure you are shocked at the improvements that have been made here. But, I must warn you that the aftershocks will be even stronger, because some serious "coolness" is going on behind the scenes of my simple little "Hello Internet!" Web Application. Let's start by picking this example apart to see what's going on.

Using Web Forms

You should no longer think in terms of Windows applications and Web applications, because, as you can see, these two distinct types of interfaces are now easily interchangeable. Creating a Web Form is just as easy as creating a Windows form in .NET. You can drag and drop a control from your Toolbox over to a Web Form and then set its properties or enter code for the control's events just as you would when creating a WindowsApplication.

Both the layout information for your Web page and the code behind your page are stored in the single compiled ASPX file on the Web server. Notice that ASP.NET Web Forms now end in .aspx instead of the older .asp extension. This difference in file names enables you to continue to use older ASP pages on your Web server. One Web Form ending in .aspx represents one Web page that you will serve to a user. When a user requests a page, the Web server will know by the file extension whether this is a compiled ASP.NET page or a script-based ASP page that it must process. One limitation that you should be aware of is that you cannot mix ASP and ASP.NET pages in one Web-based application. Because these two pages operate differently, they can't coexist in the same application session, and will not be able to talk to each other. Despite this limitation, you can still host your old ASP Web sites on the same IIS servers that you host your new ASP.NET applications on.

Web Application Configuration Files

When you first create a Web Application, your Solution has its first Web Form (the one ending in .aspx) as well as a few extra files that are included to help you configure the environment. The first file is the Computer.config file, named Web.config. This is the central configuration file for your entire Web Application, and you can make settings here that will define how your application handles exceptions and security issues.

The next file is the Global.asax file, which can contain code to handle application-wide events. The Global.asax file is consulted every time a user requests a page, so you can use this file to create some code that runs whenever a user first starts a session on your Web site, or to create a piece of code that runs every time a user requests a page, no matter which page they ask for. The application-wide events that you can code for include **Session_Start**, **Application_Start**, and **Application_BeginRequest**, as well as ending versions of these events, such as **Session_End**.

The file in your Web Application named Styles.css is your Web Application's style sheet. Having a style sheet enables you to define some HTML display tags in one central place and then use them throughout all of your Web pages. If you later decide to change something about that tag, such as the size of the font being used, you only need to do it in the style sheet and not in every page that uses the tag. When you first open the Styles.css file, you see many of the basic HTML tags already defined in here. Defining tags in a style sheet and then using these tags throughout your Web site will help keep your pages looking neat and orderly.

The last file you will notice in your Web Application is the oddly named VSDISCO file, an abbreviation for "discovery." Your VSDISCO file is where you can set up dynamic discovery for your Web Application. This file is responsible for making any Web Services you create discoverable or usable by other applications. I will boogie down with the VSDISCO files and talk about Web Services and the details of their discovery in Chapter 11.

Web Forms Design Interface

Similar to a Windows form, a Web Form has two sides: the interface, and the code behind it. Visual Studio lets you look at the interface code in two different fashions: graphically in Design mode, and textually in HTML mode. At the bottom of the Web Form's Design view are two tabs named Design and HTML to switch between these two views. Because the layout Design mode is fairly powerful, you will not need to deal with the HTML mode very often, if at all. This is a great benefit to the developer who previously had to worry about creating properly formatted HTML. Poorly formatted HTML would have opening tags such as the **<CENTER>** tag but no matching **</CENTER>** tag to close the statement. If you stick with Design mode, Visual Studio.NET will handle all of this coding for you, and your HTML code will be neater than it's ever been. Figure 10.2 shows a Web Form in Design mode in Visual Studio.NET. Note the layout grid showing on the face of the Web page, indicating that this page is being created in GridLayout mode, which you will learn about in the "Web Forms Layout" section.

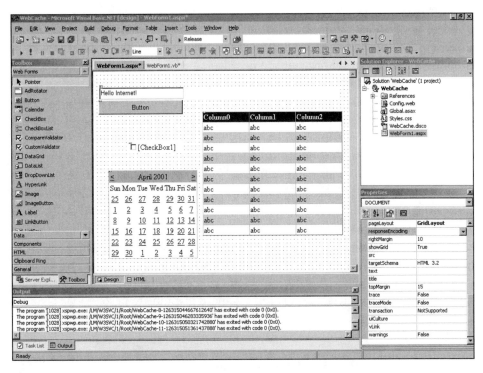

Figure 10.2
Visual Studio.NET Web Form in Design mode.

Code-Behind

As you saw in my example of a script-based ASP page at the beginning of this chapter, past versions of ASP mixed their HTML layout tags with their script-based coding. The interface and the logic were mixed together, with special tags indicating where the HTML ended and the script coding started. In ASP.NET, the HTML code for your layout and the code behind your form are completely separate. To view the HTML, you would pick the HTML tab at the bottom of the Design view window. To view the Visual Basic coding behind your Web Form, you select the Web Form in the Solution Explorer and click the View Code button at the top of this pane, or right-click the Web Form itself in Design view to find a View Code menu item. The Visual Basic code will open in its own separate Code view tab, allowing you to switch back and forth between the code and the interface.

Because the code is separated from the interface, it is referred to as the *code-behind*. By keeping the code separate, you can modularize and reuse your code in ways that were never possible in past ASP versions. If you look at the very top line of your HTML view of a Web Form, an interesting tag sticks out from the rest of the HTML tags. This tag declares the Page Language to be "vb", indicates that the code-behind is stored in a separate source code file (in Exercise 10.1, this file would be named WebForm1.aspx.vb), and includes an **Inherits** statement. This tag contains the page directives, which the compiler will reference when it creates a final compiled version of your Web Form.

Web Forms Layout

A Web Form can be laid out in two different ways, which you will set using the Web Form's **PageLayout** property. The first method is called *FlowLayout*, in which you develop your Web pages from top to bottom. This is the way in which Web developers traditionally have created their pages. If you first add a textbox to your page, and then a button, the textbox will always come before the button, either above it or to the left of it. Designing a page in a linear fashion takes a little bit of advanced planning. To develop really elaborate layouts in this traditional Design mode, Web developers often turn to the **<TABLE>** tag to design an invisible table containing many cells, much like an Excel spreadsheet. You can then place your content into different cells to give your site a neat newspaper-like layout. Designing a layout table in a Web page can be extremely time-consuming, but the results are well worth the effort. The FlowLayout mode is the default **PageLayout** setting for a Web Form.

The second method, *GridLayout*, will feel a lot more natural to seasoned Visual Basic developers. Your Web Form has a layout grid on it, and allows you to place and size controls anywhere on the face of the Web page you desire. Creating a professional-looking Web page in this mode takes both less time and less advanced planning to make it look organized.

Tip

Use the GridLayout option. This will feel more natural to VB developers, and gives you the most freedom to create fancy Web pages.

The trick behind this mode should make every seasoned Web developer gasp in amazement. A Web browser will want to draw your Web page from top to bottom, just like a page created in FlowLayout mode. The GridLayout page does all the hard work for you by creating invisible tables within the browser to help place your controls exactly where you want them. Select the HTML tab at the bottom of your Design view area to see the raw HTML code behind a page that is using GridLayout. You will see a whole lot of table tags, which include the top level **<TABLE>** tag, the **<TR>** tag to define a row, and the **<TD>** tag to define a column within a role. All of these tags are added for you by the Web Form Designer to help the browser precisely place your controls on its surface.

If you have ever labored at creating a complex Web page using a table to control your layout, you will immediately recognize the brilliance behind this trick. Sadly, if you have never worked with Web page tables, then you will probably never realize how awesome Web Forms are compared to what Web developers are used to using. Take a look at Figure 10.3, which shows a Web page displayed in the browser. This page was designed in GridLayout mode, and has elements all over the page. Next, take a look at Figure 10.4, which shows the exact same Web page with the **Border** property of the **<TABLE>** tag set to two instead of zero. The **Border** property is what defines the thickness of the lines between the cells of a table. To create an invisible table, Visual Studio sets the **Border** thickness to zero, so the lines are there but you can't see them. When I turn these lines on in Figure 10.4, the effects of the table on my Web Form's layout become easily apparent.

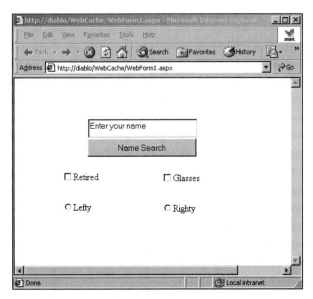

Figure 10.3
A Web Form created in GridLayout mode.

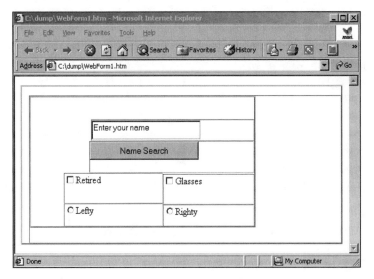

Figure 10.4
A Web page created in GridLayout mode with its borders showing.

How ASP.NET Works

When you see a Web Form in action from a user's perspective, it will appear to operate a lot like a Windows form does. You will have an interface with buttons and textboxes on it that react to your input. But many significant differences exist between the Web and the Windows interfaces. Let's take a look at how an ASP.NET application works, to learn more about these differences.

A Typical Web Session

A user will open a Web browser and start your Web Application by navigating to one of your pages. Unlike the WindowsApplication that always starts with the same form showing, a Web user can bookmark any page on your site and use that as the entry point for their session. In many applications, this could cause problems if the requested Web page is expecting some input or settings from a previous Web page that the user did not go through. You will want to add some extra code to your sublevel Web pages to ensure that the user has not missed a crucial step in getting there, if any chance exists that this will cause your page to fail.

When the browser requests a page from the Web server, an HTTP request string is sent across the Internet to the waiting Web server, which locates the desired page and processes it. This could involve dynamically drawing up the HTML layout code or communicating with compiled Classes and database stores that lie outside the requested Web page. When the page is ready, the Web server sends it back over the Internet to the user's browser. Here is an example of a simple single-page request:

```
http://servername.com/registration.html
```

If the Web page you are working with in your browser allows you to enter data, such as a registration form, it needs a way to send this information back to the Web server for processing. This data will accompany the request for the next Web page as one long concatenated string. Here is what the request string would look like if the submitted form had two textboxes on it:

```
http://servername.com/saveregistration.asp?FirstName=Rich&LastName=Jones
```

Because an HTTP request is sent as one single string, the values of the fields on a Web page need to be included in that string as shown in the preceding example. The Web server will break these values apart so that your code can work with them. The receiving Web page or script processes these field values and returns yet another HTML page across the Internet. Understanding this back and forth, ask and receive interaction between the browser and the Web server will help you better envision how your Web Forms will fit in with your overall application's architecture.

Runat

Look back to that simple Web Form you created in Exercise 10.1. You had one textbox, one button, and one line of code in the button's **Click** event written in Visual Basic. That line of Visual Basic code, along with any other coding you add in the Web Form's View Code window, is all a part of the code-behind section. When you run this Web Form and view it in the browser, none of this code is sent to the browser. Go ahead and run the Web Form, and then right-click the surface of the browser and select View Source. A Notepad window will open, showing you all the HTML that the browser has received from the Web server. A browser is not capable of dealing with Visual Basic code, only HTML and client-side scripts. None of your **Click** event's code is there. So, how does this Web Form work?

Look at the Web page's HTML code in Notepad, and then switch over to the Visual Studio environment and view the raw HTML version of your Web Form. You should notice that the first line of HTML in the Visual Studio's version does not appear in the browser's version. The reason is that this line of HTML is a directive for the compiler, and would not mean anything to the browser. Next, scroll down both versions of HTML and look for the **FORM** tag. In the Visual Studio environment, it should look something like this:

```
<form id="WebForm1" method="post" runat="server">
```

Over in the Web browser's version of the HTML code, this line will look like this:

```
<form name="WebForm1" method="post" action="WebForm1.aspx" id="WebForm1">
```

The reason for the difference between these two lines is the **runat** part of the Visual Studio's **FORM** tag. That data from a form within a Web page will be processed by the Web server, just as it was before with CGI scripts and ASP pages. My Web Form contains some code-behind to react to the button's **Click** event. The Web server will process all the code-behind on behalf of the browser, so any coding you do in Visual Basic behind the Web Form will process on the server and not on the client. The Web Form knows this, so it sets the **runat** tag to **"server"**. When the Web server processes this page, it replaces the **runat** tag with an action tag that the browser will understand. When you click the button in Example 10.1, the form named WebForm1 submits itself back to the Web server and to the ASP.NET component named WebForm1.aspx, where the form's values will be processed and a new page returned to the browser. **Runat** plays a very large role in ASP.NET, and you will encounter this tag again shortly when I talk about Web Form controls.

Postback

The first time a user requests a Web Form, they will get back the default Web Form, complete with whatever data you placed in the Web Form during Design mode. If that Web Form has a dozen textboxes on it and the form has to do some processing on the server, the user will not appreciate having all the textboxes sent back to him with their default values (what happened to all my typing?). In past versions of ASP, maintaining the value of the form fields took some extra coding on the developer's part, but these values are now maintained automatically in ASP.NET by using a concept known as *postback*. A postback is a request made to a Web page from that very same Web page. If Web page A makes a request to Web page B, then it is not a postback, but if page A sends a request to page A on the server, then it is a postback. When Web page A is returned from the postback, the values the user entered in it will still be showing. Try out Exercise 10.2 to see the postback feature in action.

Exercise 10.2: Postback Example

1. Using the Web Form from Exercise 10.1, add a second textbox to the form.

2. Save and then run your Web Application.

3. The browser will start and show you two empty textboxes and a single button.

4. Type some text into the new textbox added in this exercise.

5. Click the button.

6. The Web Form will post itself back to the Web server, which will process the code in the button's **Click** event and then place your "Hello Internet!" message in **TextBox1**. The Web server will know that this is a postback and that it should maintain the values in all the other form fields, so when the new Web page is returned to the browser, the text you entered in Step 4 will still be there.

For Visual Basic developers who are new to Web development, maintaining the values of these form controls may not seem all that exciting, and on your development machine, this may look deceptively easy. But the disconnected nature of the Web can make maintaining a form's state very difficult. The user's Web browser does not maintain a connection with the Web server throughout their session. They simply ask for one item or Web page at a time and then disconnect from the Web server until another request is made. The Web server does not maintain a record of what is provided to each and every user; it simply processes the requests and then closes the connection on the Web server's end. Being able to easily handle postbacks without any extra coding removes a lot of the complication involved in dealing with the disconnected Web environment.

ASP.NET Controls

A Web page form and the controls it contains are the user's means of communicating data back to the Web server. Without controls, a Web site will not receive any data to process, and the user will be able to use only simple static hyperlinks to move from one page to the next. For a truly interactive site, you must get some feedback from the user, whether it is their name or a selection from a drop-down list picking which inventory item they want to order. I will start this discussion of controls by looking back at the controls used by HTML pages in the past, and then I'll compare those controls to the new Web controls that are available in ASP.NET.

Browser-Based HTML Controls

Traditional HTML introduced a set of controls early on that gave developers the ability to seek input from the user. These controls, which have been a part of HTML since the beginning, are referred to as HTML Controls to help differentiate them from the newer Web Controls ASP.NET prefers. Here is a line of HTML that draws a simple HTML textbox control in the browser:

```
<INPUT TYPE="TEXTBOX" NAME="FIRSTNAME" VALUE="Enter your name here">
```

These control tags were used, long before there was ASP, to help the users send data to the Web server. Besides the textbox, you could also place buttons, option buttons, checkboxes, drop-down list boxes, pictures, and scrolling multiline textboxes on your Web page's form. The Web server only had to send the tag previously shown to place a textbox on the browser's surface, because the browser understood what a textbox was. In the past, you were limited to this core set of only a few HTML Controls, because these were the only controls you could be sure a Web browser could display. You could not create an **INPUT** tag asking the browser to show a DataGrid control, because the browser had no idea what this was.

You can still add an HTML Control to your Web Form by editing the HTML code in Design view or by selecting these controls from the HTML tab of the Visual Studio Toolbox window, but you should avoid using these with Web Forms. The reason is that when you add an HTML Control using the **INPUT** tag, you are preventing the code-behind from seeing this control, because HTML Controls are client-based and your code-behind is server-based.

> ### Tip
> I recommend that you do not use the older HTML Controls in your Web Forms. This means you should not add controls to the raw HTML using the **INPUT** tag or use the controls on the HTML Toolbox tab.

ActiveX Controls

Microsoft's Internet Explorer introduced the concept of the ActiveX control to the browser, which allows the developer to use the same ActiveX controls on a Web page that they use in their Visual Basic applications. The HTML tags that declare this control are different from the HTML Control tags, and the control itself has to be downloaded to the browser along with the HTML page, to be displayed properly. ActiveX controls execute on the client side within the browser, just as they would when they are hosted on a Windows form.

ActiveX is a super-powerful addition to the world of Web development, but it has one major drawback. Only Internet Explorer browsers can use ActiveX controls. If any of your users are using a Netscape browser, they will not see the ActiveX control, because Netscape does not support this control type. The ability to use ActiveX controls in your Web pages is a beautiful gift to Web developers, but this gift spends most of the time sitting in the closet unused. Only a lucky few developers working inside controlled intranets are able to make use of ActiveX. The rest have to worry about Netscape incompatibilities, and to support Netscape browsers, they must forego ActiveX controls.

Server Controls

The selection of useful controls has always been a limitation of Web development. HTML Controls were limited to a very small set of common controls understood by all browsers, and ActiveX controls could only run in Microsoft's browsers. The developers of ASP.NET were faced with the challenge of how to create powerful interfaces with useful data that would work in any browser, Microsoft or not.

The key to solving this problem lies within the Web server itself. Because you typically have no control over the browser your users are using (with the possible exception of some intranet developers), you need to be able to detect the browser type at the server and dynamically create your pages with the highest level of technology that the browser will support. Because these controls are processed on the Web server, they are known as *Server Controls*. Both the Server Controls and the code-behind part of your Web Forms exist only on the server side, so your Server Controls will be a part of the Web Forms object model and can be accessed in an object-oriented fashion. For example, you can access a textbox's **Text** property like so:

```
Me.TextBox1.Text = "My Message"
```

You will see more ways to utilize controls in an object-oriented Web Form when I talk about the code-behind a little later, but I want to first introduce the three types of Server Controls available to you: HTML Controls, Web Controls, and Validation Controls.

HTML Controls

The most basic type of Server Control is ASP.NET's version of the HTML Control, which allows you to use a simple textbox or button and still be able to access its properties and methods in your server side. All the controls that browsers are familiar with can still be used as a Server Control through their HTML Control counterparts. These controls are just like their browser-based versions, except that the server is aware of these controls thanks to special tags within the HTML. The Web Form will create a wrapper around the control by using special tags and attributes. Take a look at a line of HTML from a Web Form that declares a textbox:

```
<asp:TextBox id=TextBox1 runat="server"></asp:TextBox1>
```

This is the line of HTML you will see within Visual Studio's HTML view of your Web Form. Instead of an **INPUT** tag, Visual Studio adds this special **asp:TextBox** tag to the HTML. Note the **runat** tag, which indicates to the Web server that this is a server-side control. The **id** attribute identifies the name with which you reference this control from your code. When the Web server processes this page and encounters this tag, it substitutes a tag equivalent for HTML Controls, so that the browser sees this line of HTML:

```
<input name="TextBox1" type="text" id="TextBox1" />
```

Using the Web Forms version of these controls works out great because the browser gets an HTML tag that it is comfortable with, and the developer is able to work with this control in the code-behind methods and procedures. If you are working with HTML that uses the old form of specifying controls, you can easily convert these to their server-side versions by changing the **INPUT** tag to the **asp:controlname** tag and adding a **runat="server"** attribute to this tag.

Using the Web Forms version of the HTML Controls is really very simple to do. Just design your Web Form in Visual Studio and add the controls from the Toolbox window's Web Forms tab. Now you can work with your Web Form controls just as you do the Windows form controls. These controls even have changeable properties showing in the Properties window in Visual Studio. Table 10.1 lists the most common HTML Controls that are derived from the **System.Web.UI.HtmlControls** Namespace. When creating an ASP.NET Web Form, you should have no reason at all to use the old **INPUT** tag.

Web Controls

Using a simple HTML Control has always been necessary to ensure that your Web page will work on every browser. Advanced Web page controls were available before now, but they did not work on every browser. Form controls in a Web environment have always been fairly limited. You have your trusty textbox, Select (a ComboBox equivalent), Option buttons, CheckBox, and button, but that's about it. When Visual Basic developers gained the ability to create their own customized controls for their Windows forms, the ActiveX control development market exploded with rich and powerful tools that you could use in your projects. It's taken a little extra time, but this boom has finally reached the Web development sector as well.

Table 10.1   HTML Controls.

Object Name	Web Control Tag	Old HTML Tag
HtmlButton	**<asp:button>**	**<INPUT TYPE="BUTTON">**
HtmlImage	**<asp:Image>**	**<IMG SRC="mypic.jpg">**
HtmlInputCheckbox	**<asp:CheckBox>**	**<INPUT TYPE="">**
HtmlInputRadioButton	**<asp:RadioButton>**	**<INPUT TYPE="">**
HtmlInputText	**<asp:TextBox>**	**<INPUT TYPE="TEXT">**

Visual Studio.NET introduces Web Controls to overcome the limitations of the small set of intrinsic HTML Controls. Learning from past Web development efforts, Microsoft realized that the only controls that would gain a wide acceptance are those that can support all of the popular browsers, and not just Microsoft's. Web Controls accomplish this by detecting the browser being used and generating the most powerful format of the control it can get away with within the limits of that browser's capabilities. If the user is visiting your site using Internet Explorer 5 or above, then the Web Control will know that this browser is capable of using Dynamic HTML (DHTML) client-side coding to enhance the control. If a user is using Netscape, their browser does not support DHTML, so the Web Control will smartly send its output in pure HTML format. In .NET lingo, this is referred to as the ability to detect and adapt to up-level and down-level browsers. By default, your Web pages will try to support all types of browsers and adapt to their needs, but you can customize this behavior with properties such as the Web Forms **ClientTarget** property, which can be set to **Auto**, **UpLevel**, or **DownLevel**.

Web Controls will continue to get smarter in .NET, because while the browsers you are using on the desktop are slowly starting to share some standards, other browsing platforms are becoming more and more popular and will require greater flexibility from your Web site. Handheld PCs are a rapidly growing area that developers should pay attention to. The Pocket PC operating system comes complete with a miniversion of Internet Explorer to surf the Internet. Digital phones are another example of a new platform for viewing Web sites that is gaining ground. Keep these technologies in mind, and ask yourself not only *who* will be looking at your Web site, but also *what* will they be using to browse with.

The DataGrid Web Control

To truly understand the power of a Web Control, it helps to see one in action. Probably the best example of an extremely powerful control that previously was only available to the WindowsApplication developer is the DataGrid control. If you've used the DataGrid control before, you know that this is a great way to display your data, and it handles all of the display and manipulation functions for you. Simply pass it a DataSet, and the DataGrid control will create a table with the right number of columns and rows, and it will even allow users to sort and edit this data.

In the Web world, developers have spent countless hours creating CGI and ASP scripts that painfully draw out these tables to display their data. Advanced Web developers found ways to make their tables sortable and pageable. A pageable data table display is a single page that may show only 5 or so records out of maybe 20 or more that were returned by the initial query. The page will provide you with Next and Previous buttons to move to the next or previous page and the next or previous set of five records. This was a great feature to minimize the amount of data traveling over the Internet during each request, because you could send only a portion of that data and let the user decide whether he or she wants to see more. The downside to this feature is that it took a lot of custom coding to make it a reality.

Wouldn't it be nice if you could just use that DataGrid control from the Visual Studio Toolbox? Well, now you can.

The Web Forms DataGrid control is an excellent example of a Web Control. This control handles all of the display and manipulation of your data for you, leaving you to just run the query and pass the results to the DataGrid. The Web Control is processed on the Web server, and the output is pure HTML that any standard browser will understand. This avoids the problem of browser-specific controls, such as the ActiveX controls that were sent as compiled code to the browser. I like to think of these Web Controls as mini-HTML generators. When your DataGrid gets a DataSet that it's supposed to display, it will figure out the DataSet's schema and generate a set of **TABLE** tags to display the data. You'll see rows and columns on your Web page, and there will even be a header row at the top of the table showing the column names.

In the old ASP script world, I spent days writing a script that would parse out a Recordset and dynamically create a table to display it. When I added paging and sorting functions, it took another few days to create. Now these features take just minutes. If you try out Exercise 10.3, you'll see how easy it is to use the DataGrid control and other Web Controls just like it. The Web page that you create in Exercise 10.3 has the same complexity as the page I spent almost a week creating last year, and the ASP.NET version takes only a few drag-and-drop actions and three lines of code.

Exercise 10.3: Using the DataGrid Web Control

Note

This exercise accesses a database to display some data. Any database that you can add as a data connection in Visual Studio.NET's Server Explorer window will work just fine (Access, SQL Server, or Oracle).

1. Start a new ASP.NET Web Application Project in Visual Studio and call it "WebDataGrid".

2. With the Web Form open in Design view, drag a DataGrid control from the Toolbox's Web Forms tab over to your Web Form and drop it. Resize the DataGrid to fill most of the page.

3. From the Server Explorer window, expand one of your Data Connections until you can see a list of all the tables it contains. Drag one of those tables to your Web Form and drop it anywhere on the form. A Connection and a DataAdapter object will appear in Components view below your Web Form.

4. From the Toolbox's Data tab, drag a DataSet to Components view and drop it. Select the Untyped option if you see a window asking you to "Choose A DataSet." Click OK on this window to finalize this component.

5. Put your mouse cursor over an empty portion of your Web Form, right-click, and select View Code.

6. Scroll down and locate the **Page_Load** event. Place the following code inside the **Page_Load** event:

```
If Not(IsPostBack) Then
        OldDbDataAdapter1.FillDataSet(dataset1)
        DataGrid1.DataSource = DataSet1.Tables("TableName").DefaultView
        DataGrid1.DataBind()
End If
```

Note

If you are accessing a SQL Server database, your DataAdapter will start with Sql instead of OleDb.

7. Save this project and then run it. Internet Explorer will start, and you will see the DataGrid displaying the contents of your DataSet. Right-click the surface of the browser and select View Source. Look through the HTML behind this page and you will see dozens of lines of **TABLE** tags that were generated by the DataGrid Web Control on the Web server.

You can turn on advanced DataGrid features, such as column sorting and data paging, by clicking the DataGrid in Design view and looking at the Properties window. Dozens of features are available that you can customize so that your Web page does not look like everyone else's. You can change the background colors, decide whether or not to show the column headers, turn on the AllowSorting option, or specify how many rows of data will be displayed on a single page by turning on the AllowPaging option and entering a number of desired rows in the PageSize box.

One terrific advantage of using a control such as the DataGrid control is that it will maintain the data held within its table during round-trips to the Web server. This means that every time the form containing the DataGrid control has to communicate with the server, it will not have to requery your database. This results in much faster response times and far less calls made to your database from your Web pages—and on a busy Web server, these extra few seconds can really add up.

Validation Controls

Validating your data is a must when working with user input. You could rely on your Web page's **submit** function to validate all of the user's input on the form, but this would leave the user waiting for the server's response to know whether the input was right. A better way to validate data on a Web page is to do it on the client side by using JavaScript. As previously pointed out, JavaScript is the only reliable means of coding some form of dynamic interaction with your users on the browser end of the application. Until now, the only way to write some JavaScript validation code was to learn JavaScript and create your own functions. If you are expecting me to tell you to go out and get a JavaScript book, you might be surprised.

Web Forms enable you to use another new kind of control called a Validation Control. The name is a bit deceiving, because these are not controls in the traditional sense, such as textboxes or buttons are. But you place the Validation Controls on your form just as you would place a textbox and set some properties for it. This control's job is to lie in the background in wait, looking for a chance to validate one of your Web Form's controls within the browser. When the browser loads your page, all of your Validation Controls will be invisible to the user. Only when the control validates another control and finds that the data is not valid will it appear to the user to give a message. Because of this off-and-on appearance, I think of Validation Controls as intelligent warning lights, like those on the dashboard of your car. When everything is fine, you never know they are there, but when something is wrong, they light up to let you know about the problem and hopefully avert a disaster (yes, that "check engine" light on your dashboard *could* be a bad sign).

So you're wondering what a Web page control has to do with JavaScript? Well, the control part that you see on the Web page is really just the warning light that turns on and off. When you look at the HTML behind a Web page that has some Validation Controls on it, you will see JavaScript functions created for the sole purpose of validating the form's data. Voila! You've created client-side JavaScript functions to validate your control's data without ever typing a line of JavaScript. Pretty cool, huh?

Validation Controls come in many flavors, and which ones you use depends on the type of validation you need to perform. The set of Validation Controls includes the following:

♦ **ReqularExpression Validator**—Validates the control's value within a defined expression

♦ **Custom Validator**—Allows you to create your own custom validation code

♦ **Compare Validator**—Compares one control's values to another's values

♦ **Range Validator**—Ensures that the control's value falls within a set range of values

♦ **RequiredField Validator**—Ensures that a required form field is filled in

♦ **ValidationSummary**—Gives you one centralized place to look to see whether all the validator controls on the page are satisfied or if any errors remain on the form that still need to be corrected

Each control is implemented using the same method, and you only need to work with the control's properties to customize their actions.

Let's take a look at a Validation Control in action. Try out Exercise 10.4 to become familiar with using this powerful control in your Web Applications.

Exercise 10.4: Using the Validation Controls

1. Create a new ASP.NET Web Application Project and name it WebValidator.

2. With the Web Form open in Design view, add one textbox and one button to it. Change the **Text** property on the button to say "Calculate Sale Price".

3. Place a Label control below the button.

4. In the Toolbox, under the Web Forms tab, drag a RangeValidator control to your Web Form and place it below the Label control. Change this control's **ErrorMessage** property to read "Please enter a dollar amount".

5. Change the **RangeValidator's ControlToValidate** property to "TextBox1", and its **Type** property to "Currency".

6. Add the following code to the button's **Click** event:

```
Dim SalePrice As Double
SalePrice = CDbl(TextBox1.Text) - (CDbl(TextBox1.Text) * 0.1)
Label1.Text = Format(SalePrice, "$#,##0.00")
```

7. Save and run your Web Form. Try entering some text in the textbox and clicking the button. The Web Form does not submit itself to the server because this error is caught by the Validation Control, which will become visible below the button to let you know that you need to enter a dollar amount.

8. Change the value of **TextBox1** to a dollar amount and click the button. The sale price (10 percent off) will be calculated and displayed in **Label1**.

Using a Validation Control is a snap; just drop it on the form, set a few properties, and don't worry about it again. These controls are smart enough to stay invisible until some value is wrong, and then pop up to warn the user about it. If the user fixes the problem and then submits the page, the validator will turn itself off again. If multiple validators are being used on a form, they will turn off and on independently all by themselves, and will only let the form submit itself when all validators are satisfied with their data elements. Some key rules to remember are that one validator can only validate one control, and that some controls cannot be validated, such as a button, a CheckBox, or another validator control. Of course, you would have no reason to validate those controls. The textboxes will cause 99.99 percent of your data troubles, and that is where you should focus your form field validation efforts.

Custom Controls

Just as you can create your own customized controls for your Windows forms, you can also make controls for ASP.NET. You will do this by creating a Web Control Library Project. How you actually create this control will differ greatly from the Windows form controls you may have some experience creating. Remember that the new Web Form controls pump out pure HTML to the browser, and are also capable of adapting to different browser types. Because of this, creating a customized Web Control does not involve working in Design mode, but instead is based purely on code that will output HTML statements instead of graphical drawing information.

Look back at the Web version of the DataGrid used earlier and examine this control's output by viewing the source code that the browser receives from it. The output of this control is in HTML, with a lot of **TABLE** tags used to make it appear neat and orderly. The DataGrid control's intelligence is far superior to any of the original HTML Controls, because now you can bind data and manipulate it through sorting and paging functions. No longer are developers limited to the core set of boring HTML Controls. Nor do they have to stick to the set of Web Controls that ships with Visual Studio.NET, because pretty soon there will be a new market out there for Web Controls, just like the industry that supports Windows form controls now.

Coding Your Web Forms

In the past, to create a Web site, you had to know a lot about HTML. If you wanted to make your pages dynamic, you had to know a scripting language such as VBScript or Perl. If you wanted your pages to be interactive and intelligent on the client's end, you had to create some client-side scripts in JavaScript. Generally, these diverse skill sets did not fall inside the realm of the Visual Basic programmer. Some VB developers ventured into Web development as it became clear to them that the Internet was the wave of the future, but only a select few took on these new challenges. Now that you no longer need to learn another language to create a Web site, you have no reason to not start using Web Forms. As you read this section, you will see that coding a Web Form is almost exactly the same as coding a Windows form, with only a few small differences.

Object-Oriented Web Forms

The code behind your Web Form will be written in Visual Basic, and it will look so much like the code that you have been writing for your WindowsApplications that you might forget you are creating a Web page. If you put a textbox on a Windows form, and a textbox on a Web Form, within those forms' code, you could refer to the textbox like so:

```
Me.TextBox1.Text = "My new value"
```

Web Forms are now object-oriented. In past versions of ASP, you could not reference a Web page's control properties in your VBScript. Often, you relied on variables to pass values around and to perform your calculations with. When you use the server-side controls on your Web Forms, the Visual Studio.NET IDE becomes aware of your controls, along with all of their properties and methods. You'll be able to access a textbox's **Text** property, or code an event for a button's **Click** event, just as you always have in VB.

The top-level class for a Web Form is the **System.Web.UI.Page**, from which all of your Web Forms are derived. Your Web Form is the parent for all the controls on your Web page. These controls are a part of the **Page.Controls** collection. Your Web Form's controls will have events associated with them, such as the **TextBox1_TextChanged** event. You will be able to create code that runs on the Web server to handle events that are fired from within the browser. Creating the code-behind for a Web Form should feel natural to anyone who has ever created a Windows form in Visual Basic.

Web Form Events

Like a Windows form, your Web Form and its controls have events that you can code for. I think everybody will find the Web Forms **Load** event useful, and to make a page truly interactive, you should learn how to work with the control events as well. Remember that unlike a Windows form, the interface for a Web Form and the code that handles its events are separated, maybe by as much as thousands of miles.

Some events are raised on the server while the page is being processed. Any events that are raised by a user's interaction with a Web page are raised in the browser, which then must communicate with the Web server to handle the event. Events occurring on the server side will work just like a Windows form's events, but events that are raised within the browser will initiate a round-trip communication with the server, which is where the event's code is housed.

Tip

If you are developing for dial-up Internet users, you may want to minimize your control events, because they require a round-trip session to the Web server and back to execute the event's code.

The Web Form's **Load** Event

The Web Forms event that you will find the most useful is the **Load** event, whose name will remind you of the old Visual Basic 6 form's **Load** event. The **Load** event will be used to set up your Web Form with its initial values, which may be pulled from a database or a data-aware class. A Web Form's **Load** event will fire every time its Web page is called. This can be a problem, because often a Web Form will communicate back to itself on the Web server to run a chunk of its server-side code. But, a way exists to figure out whether this is the first

Load event or a follow-up **Load** event, and change the code you execute accordingly. Take a look at the following Web Form's **Load** event:

```
Protected Sub Page_Load(ByVal Sender As System.Object, ByVal e As _
  System.EventArgs)
    If Not IsPostBack Then    ' Evals true first time browser hits the page
        Dim MyUser As New clsUser("Mike Wilson")
        TextBox1.Text = MyUser.FirstName
        TextBox2.Text = MyUser.LastName
        If MyUser.IsSupervisor = True Then CheckBox1.Checked = True
    End If
End Sub
```

The **WebForm1**'s **Load** event first checks the value of the page's **IsPostBack** setting. Earlier, you saw how a Web page can retain the values of its form fields after a button is clicked, and the Web page submits some data to the server. For the first request for a Web page, the **IsPostBack** variable is equal to **False**, because the user is not posting any data back to this form. But, if the user submits a form to that very same form, they will expect to keep the data they entered on the form when it comes back to them. If you check the **IsPostBack** variable and see that it is **True**, then you do not want to refill these form fields with fresh data, but instead want them to maintain their current values. So, the **IsPostBack** block of code runs only for a first-time query of this page, and not for subsequent requeries. This makes repeated calls to the same Web Form run faster than the initial call.

The preceding **WebForm1** example references a Class named **clsUser**, which initializes itself upon creation by using its **New** event. Because the data is loaded when I **Dim** the **MyUser** object, I can immediately start pulling values out of the **MyUser** object and placing them into my Web Form's controls. When the **Load** event is complete, my **WebForm1** will have all the necessary user data from the **clsUser** Class loaded into its interface, and the Web server will forward this to the user.

The Web Form's **Unload** Event

Again, thinking back to Visual Basic 6, you will remember that a form not only had a **Load** event, but also had an **Unload** event that fired when the form was closing. The Web Form has an **Unload** event as well, but its use is very different from that of VB 6's **Unload** event. The Web Form **Unload** event fires on the server side when the Web page is done processing, right before the Web server sends the page out. In a typical Web environment, once the Web server sends the page, its instance is destroyed on the Web server (of course, I am talking about the dynamically generated version of your Web page, and not the file full of code that you worked so hard to create).

Like a Windows form, you need a way to clean up after your code. In a Windows form, you used the **Destruct** and **Finalize** events, but in a Web Form, you use the **Unload** event. Use this event to close database connections and file streams. Like the **Load** event, the **Unload** event fires every time the Web Form is accessed, both in the initial calls and the postbacks. Use this event as a centralized cleanup location for any code inside your Web Form.

If you leave your Web Form's resources open, the Garbage Collector eventually cleans these up, but on a busy Web site that has tens of thousands of hits an hour, you cannot afford to leave these resources tied up. If you have any sort of Web page caching scheme enabled, you can also use the **Unload** event to cache your Web page for later use. This event, used along with the Web Form's **Load** event, could help you save a complicated Web page to a cache and then quickly re-institute it during another caller's **Load** event, thereby bypassing all of that costly processing.

Web Control Events

Often, you want to know immediately when a button has been clicked or a control has changed its value. In the Web environment, clicking a button often means that you are submitting the data contained on a form back to the Web server (but this is not always true). Because buttons play such a prominent role in Web interfaces, a button's **Click** event will fire right away, causing the Web page in your browser to communicate back to the Web server. All of the data currently showing on the Web page will also be sent back to the Web server so that the server-side code can see the full picture of what is going on with the page. After the button's **Click** event is executed, if the user is not redirected to a new page, the old Web page will return to them complete with all of their data still in place. You should remember that control events are raised by the Web page hosted in the user's browser, but they are handled on the Web server in the code-behind piece.

To see a round-trip event in action, simply add a button to your Web Form and then put a little code in its **Click** event (or you can simply use the Web Form from Exercise 10.1). When you run the Web Form, it will load in your browser with the button showing. Click the button, and the **Click** event will be triggered, causing your Web Form to submit itself to the Web server, run the **Click** event's associated code, and then return the same page in its exact same state to the browser. This may seem like the page is going a little out of its way to get the job done, but you have to remember that the browser is not capable of executing Visual Basic code, so it is up to the Web Form and the Web server to make this magic happen. Note that as soon as you click the button, the **Click** event fires and the round-trip is initiated.

Delayed Control Events

If you are a hockey fan, you know that sometimes the referee will throw a flag but not immediately blow his whistle. He does this to allow the team that will gain from the penalty to continue its attack on the goal until its momentum has been stopped. Most Web Form controls throw their events just like that referee throws his flag: The event is raised, but not immediately processed. The Web Form waits for a break in the action, often caused by another event such as a button's **Click** event.

For Visual Basic developers who are used to events firing immediately, this may come as a surprise. You may create an event for one of your controls and then become confused when the expected result doesn't happen right away. To better understand what is going on, try out Exercise 10.5 to see a delayed event in action.

Exercise 10.5: Delayed Event Handling

1. Start a new Web Application and call it DelayedEvents.

2. Place one button and two textboxes on your Web Form.

3. Double-click **TextBox1** to access its **TextChanged** event. Place the following line of code here:

```
TextBox2.Text = TextBox1.Text
```

4. To further illustrate my point, add a breakpoint on the line of code you just entered for the **TextBox1_TextChanged** event.

5. Run your Web Form.

6. Enter some text into **TextBox1**, and then press the Tab key to switch to the second textbox. Note that your event did not fire.

7. Click the button. This triggers the button's **Click** event, which will immediately start a round-trip to the server.

8. In Visual Studio, your Web Application will enter Break mode inside the textbox's **TextChanged** event. If you had entered any code for the button's **Click** event, this would process after the **TextChanged** event.

9. Select Debug | Continue and look at your Web page to see that **TextBox2** now has **TextBox1**'s value, and **TextBox1** retained its value even though you made a round-trip to the server. The first time your Web Form loads, **IsPostBack** will be equal to **False**, but during the round-trip event, **IsPostBack** will be equal to **True**.

Delayed events are stored by the controls within the browser, and all stored events will execute when the next round-trip to the Web server is initiated. All **Change** events will execute first on the server, followed by the **Click** event. Unfortunately, you can't control the order in which your fired **Change** events are processed, so do not rely on their order of occurrence when trying to synchronize these events. Also remember that you will not be able to immediately detect a changed value in a control. Although the event will be raised, it will not be processed until a later time. Control values are changing all the time, and you have to pay a high price in terms of wait time when the browser has to make a round-trip to the Web server to find something out. This is why ASP.NET chooses to store these events, to avoid wasting bandwidth and slowing down the application. Imagine a Web Form with a dozen textbox controls on it calling back to the server every time you enter a value in a box. The user of this form would not be too happy with its performance.

Now that I have gone into depth on how delayed events work, I'll explain how to override this delay. Each control has a **AutoPostBack** property that defaults to **False**. If you set this to **True**, the control's events will not be delayed and will instead trigger immediately. Just envision that annoyed user waiting for the round-trip to complete when you decide to enable this feature.

Caching

Caching refers to saving some data in a special holding area for later use. In a Web environment, caching can be used to save bits of data closer to the Web server or to maintain a state for a user. Without caching, you do not have a means to locally store information about a user and their session unless you write this data to a database. Because repeatedly accessing a database can really slow down your application, this is not such a wise choice for short-term state storage. You could also use cookies, which are files written to the user's machine that store data about their activities, but not only are cookies hard to work with, many users do not take lightly to the idea of strangers writing data to their hard drive.

In the past, developers were able to create caches of data on the Web server by using custom-built code. Often, this data was written to a file on the server's hard drive, commonly in XML. ASP.NET makes caching data easy by offering the **Page.Cache** object for your coding use. No longer do you have to write long output and input functions to save and read cached data; simply call the **Cache.Insert** to save something, and then the **Cache.Get** to retrieve it. Picture a Web Form with two buttons on it—or better yet, go ahead and create one. Add the following code to **Button1**'s **Click** event:

```
Page.Cache.Insert("MyName","Bryan")
```

When you run the form and click the button, you trigger a round-trip to the server that runs the button's **Click** event. The value of *Bryan* is saved to the page's cache using the key **MyName** to identify it. You can now stop your Web Application and add some code to the second button's **Click** event, like so:

```
Dim HisName As String = Page.Cache.Get("MyName")
If HistName = Nothing Then
    Button2.Text = "Nothing"
Else
    Button2.Text = HisName
End If
```

Start your Web Form again, and this time click **Button2**. The form will take a round-trip to the server and pull the value from the page's cache with the matching key, **MyName**. I first check to see whether the value I brought back is equal to **Nothing** because if the **Page.Cache** is not currently holding anything under the **MyName** key, then the value of **Nothing** is returned to my **HisName** variable. You can use this in your Web Form's **Load** event to test for the existence of a data cache on the Web server, and if **Nothing** is returned, then you can switch to plan B and run a database query or set your own data values. To see a **Nothing** returned in the preceding example, just change the key's name to "YourName" and run your Web page. Because no key with this name exists in the cache, your **Button2** will end up saying **Nothing** on its face.

If you ever want your pages to remember pieces of data from one request to the next, use the **Cache** object to help you out. You cache not only simple data types like **Strings**, but also objects or even whole pages of generated HTML. If your Web site is an online retailer with a catalog that rarely changes, instead of requiring your code to continually query data from a database, you could store your latest catalog in either a DataSet or in XML format within the Web server's cache. The closer the data is to your Web pages, the quicker your server's response time will be, and, more importantly, the happier the users will be.

Page Objects

Experienced ASP developers may wonder what has happened to the objects they are used to using in their ASP pages, such as **Response**, **Request**, **Server**, **Session**, and **Application**. All of these objects now fall under the **Page** object, and are still accessible from your code. These objects form the heart of the script-based ASP world. The **Response** object is a way to write to the browser from within your code, and the **Request** object is how you read in the form values that a browser has submitted. Because you should now be using the Web Control form fields to read in values, you should not need the **Request** object. Instead, you simply query the control values on the server side, such as **TextBox1.Text**.

The **Server** object can provide useful information about the Web server your page is hosted on, such as its **MachineName** or the **ScriptTimeout** setting the server employs. More importantly, the **Server** object is how an ASP page creates an instance of a COM object for its use. You use the **Server.CreateObject** in the same way that you used the **CreateObject** command in Visual Basic 6. The **Application** object encompasses the entire Web Application, to include all of its parts and all of the users using it. In contrast, the **Session** object holds information on a user's session, such as the unique SessionID the Web server recognizes the user by.

My coverage here of these objects is short because they do not play as prominent of a role as they have in the past. Developers should no longer use the **Session** object for caching their data, which was a bad idea to begin with due to poor system resource utilization by the **Session** object. You will most likely begin using .NET Assemblies with your ASP.NET Web

Applications, and will hopefully no longer need to late-bind COM objects to the Web page using the **Server** object. Still, these objects do have some uses, and they are a great source of information about the Web server's and user's environment that you can access from your HTML and Visual Basic code.

Using Web Forms or Windows Forms

One issue to keep in mind when designing your application is whether to use Windows forms or Web Forms. This is a fairly simple issue, but I want to bring it up to let you know that it's a one-or-the-other choice. If you create a Web Application, then the user is accessing your application through a Web server from a remote machine. The key thing to remember is that you cannot mix your form types within a single Visual Studio Project. A Web Form cannot open a Windows form, nor can you use **MessageBoxes** or dialog forms to enhance your Web Form, as you do with Windows forms. You need to find other creative ways to pass messages to users and supply them with setting screens within the confines of a Web browser.

What you can and should do, though, is place as much of your business logic as possible into separate Class Library Projects. This will give you the ability to create both WindowsApplication and Web Application Projects that can share the same business logic classes. This is the purest form of separating the presentation logic from the business logic for creating *n*-tier applications.

Tip

I like to use JavaScript on the client side to create pop-up windows to act as my **MessageBoxes***, dialog boxes, and even input forms. These minipages can act independently of the main browser window, but they can also communicate back to the main Web page through JavaScript.*

Debugging ASP.NET

Anyone who has ever developed a script-based ASP page knows that debugging these is a nightmare. ASP debugging practically takes you back to the programming Stone Age, with most developers utilizing skillfully placed **Response.Write** lines of code to send debugging information to the browser window. You create your page, drop a few checkpoints in it using **Response.Write**, and then run the page in the browser. If it works, great, but if it doesn't, good luck figuring out why. The browser window displays the line of code the ASP page has a problem with, along with an extremely short explanation of why. If this line of code calls out to an external DLL, then you won't be able to tell what the DLL's problem is, but instead see only the value or message returned by the DLL. You can now debug your Web Application just as you would a WindowsApplication. You no longer have to write your debugging messages to the browser, nor do you have to use the try-fail method of testing to spot the problems, because now you can step through your pages.

Stepping through ASP.NET

The code that you are creating for your Web Forms works just like the code in a Windows form. Because of this, you can debug your ASP.NET code just as you would any other Visual Basic project. If you wish to add a breakpoint to the code, go right ahead. Need a watch placed on one of your variables? You can do that too. Remember that the code-behind will run when the Web server is processing, and not when the user is viewing your page in the browser. For client-side debugging, you need to rely more on your talents of observation and pure brainpower to find those bugs (and when brainpower isn't enough, a little client-side JavaScript can provide you with some clues, as well). But for server-side debugging, all of the Visual Studio.NET debugging tools are at your disposal. Exercise 10.6 is a simple one-button Web Form that shows you how you can debug your Web pages using breakpoints and watches.

Exercise 10.6: Debugging ASP.NET

1. Start a new Web Application and name it WebDebug.

2. Add one button to your Web Form.

3. Double-click the button to access its **Click** event. Add the following lines of code in this event:

```
Dim MyName As String
MyName = "Alex"
```

4. Add a breakpoint to the second line of code by clicking the gray border to the left of the coding area. You will see a red dot to the left of this line of code.

5. Save and run your Web Form. The browser will start, with your button showing.

6. When you click the button, the Web page will make a round-trip or postback to the Web server, where it will encounter your breakpoint in the **Click** event. Processing of the server-side code will pause as you enter Break mode.

7. In the WebForm1's Code view, double-click the **MyName** variable to highlight it, and then right-click it. Select Add Watch to place a watch on this variable. Be sure that your Watch window is visible so that you can see this watch.

8. Press F8 to step forward one line of code to the **End Sub** statement. Your watch value for **MyName** will now show a red value of **"Alex"**.

The ability to step through your code does not end within the code-behind. If your Web Form's code calls another Class, you can step right over to that Class and continue debugging. That Class can be written in any language, and as long as Visual Studio.NET has the source code for it, you can follow your application's execution from beginning to end. This removes all of the guesswork that is involved with the script-based ASP pages that do not allow VBScript-to-COM debugging sessions.

All the normal debugging windows are available to you when you are working on Web Applications. You can keep track of your threads in the Thread window, or view the call stack to see all the calls that your application is making. Your Web Form can even use the Locals window to display all of its variables that are currently in scope.

Web Application Tracing

Veteran ASP developers no longer have to use those clunky **Response.Write** statements to print debugging information to the Web page they are testing. When you are developing within Visual Studio.NET, you can use **Debug.WriteLine** statements in your Visual Basic code, which send their messages to the Output window during debugging sessions. By using this method of troubleshooting, you do not have to worry about your messages being seen by the user within the browser. Use the **Debug** object to test your code on the server side.

You can't use the **Debug** object in your HTML presentation code, because this code runs on the browser side, away from the server-side Output window. You need a debugging method that will print some messages to the browser window to help you follow your code's progress. The **Trace** object does this for you. Within your HTML, you can embed a **Trace** object as follows:

```
<%Trace.Write("My Title","My Message Here")%>
```

Be sure to surround your **Trace** statements with the **<%** and **%>** brackets, which tell the Web server that this is some script to be processed and not HTML. Just adding a **Trace** line alone will not enable tracing on your Web page. In Design view, if you click a Web Form and then look at its Properties window, you will find a **Trace** property that defaults to **False**. Setting this to **True** enables the **Trace** statements within your Web page, plus a whole lot more. The Web Form also features a **TraceMode** property, which sets how the information you see displayed in the browser is sorted, whether by time or by category.

Go ahead and enable **Trace** and then run your Web Form in the browser. You will see a treasure trove of information at the bottom of your page, including a list of the controls on your form, cookie information, all of the server variables defined, and the current header values that are stored for this form behind the scenes, such as the browsers type being used, which is stored in the User-Agent header. Your **Trace** output messages are listed in order of occurrence in the Trace Information Table. The **Trace.Write** command takes two parameters: the first parameter names the category of the message, and the second is the actual message. You can create any category name you desire. Figure 10.5 shows my **Trace** output line from the preceding code example, along with all the other tidbits of **Trace** information made available for your use.

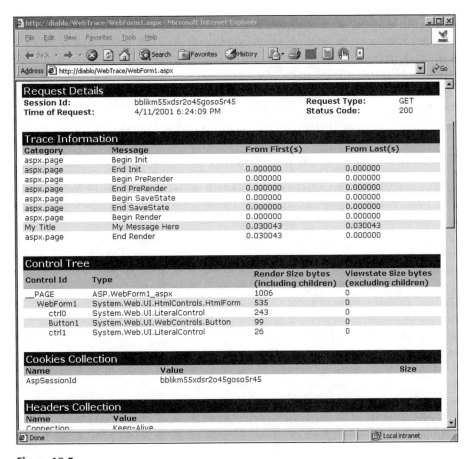

Figure 10.5
The Web Form's **Trace** output.

Summary

At the dawning of the Internet age, very few Web developers existed. Over time, as people realized that HTML pages were really just simple, raw text that anyone with a text editor could create, the number of Web page authors grew exponentially. To make a Web site stand out from an amateurish collection of static pages, developers found ways to dynamically create their pages and display data from data stores. The Web had reached a new level of complexity that only a select few mastered. Due to the technical nature of professional Web development, a wide gap was again established between the amateurs and the pros. Even the introduction of ASP as a simple way to create dynamic server-side pages only succeeded in creating a niche for specialized ASP developers separate from the mainstream programming languages.

Now with ASP.NET, any developer can create a Web Application without learning a new skill set. You can continue to write your code in Visual Basic, or C#, or any other .NET language and still take advantage of the world-wide reach of the Internet. You don't even have to be an HTML guru, which should now be evident, because none of the exercises in this chapter required you to type any HTML to create your Web pages. If a downside exists to all of this power that ASP.NET brings to the table, it's that Web developers who previously were experts in their field may need to start expanding their skills to other application types. To those developers, I give the same advice that I give Windows developers who are just now learning about ASP: seek to expand your world, and don't be afraid of change.

Chapter 11
.NET Web Services

Visual Studio.NET introduces a new Project type called Web Services to the applications development arena. Although the name of this new Project type is new to Visual Studio developers, you may be surprised to learn that Web Services is not a brand new concept, but rather is a melding of many previously introduced concepts. To use this new Project type, you do not have to radically change how you program. You just need to learn a few new concepts that you may even already be familiar with.

The big change to your applications that will result from the introduction of Web Services is in the way that you plan your applications. Because you need a thorough understanding of any new technology before you can properly work it into your latest projects, I'll start by discussing what a Web Service is and why you may want to use one. I will discuss both the pros and cons, because although you will find a natural fit between this new technology and some projects, you will have other projects for which this technology is not useful. After describing what a Web Service is, I will show you how to create a few simple services, and then how to incorporate these examples into other projects you are already familiar with.

Introducing Web Services

Every .NET developer needs to understand what a Web Service is and how it can be used in today's applications. Like ASP.NET, even though you may not see a use for this new Project type in your current applications, someday you will encounter a project for which Web Services fit the bill. For project managers and lead developers, it is imperative that you understand all of the technologies available to your teams so that you can plan and design the best applications possible as quickly as possible. As you read about Web Services, think about how they might fit into your current projects. The only real challenge about developing Web Services is finding the best way to harness this new technology, a chore that will fall mostly on the planners and software architects in your organization.

What Is a Web Service?

A service is something that is provided to you by someone else. The local phone company provides the phone line and the maintenance associated with it to your residence so that you can call other people by using the phones that you have bought. Internet service providers (ISPs) allow you to dial in to their computers to hook up to the Internet. These are two examples of service providers, both of which expect a little money in return for the services you are consuming. A consumer is someone or something that consumes or uses a service, and in the phone and cable examples, that consumer is a person.

In Web Services, the consumer is a piece of software. It could be a WindowsApplication installed on your PC, or a Web site that taps into a Web Service to help complete a function. Web Services are consumer-oriented, and your service will be designed to provide something useful to the consumer. One example is an authentication Web Service. Your application could call on this service to authenticate and identify a user for you. Your application would be freed from the responsibility of providing a secure authentication method and storing the credentials for all of your users.

I'll expand on the authentication service example to see how you could use a Web Service. Suppose that you have created a membership-based Web site. Only users with authorized accounts can access your Web site's information. You could include in your plans a login and authentication module, which would require extra development and testing, thereby increasing the cost of your project. An alternative would be to enlist the support of someone else's Web Service to perform this function for you. The host of this supporting service would maintain the user accounts and handle the administrative tasks of identifying users and granting them access. Using third-party Web Services is like using any other off-the-shelf package in your application. You only need to worry about the licensing or usage fee, and compared to what it would cost for you to develop your own services, the price could be a real bargain.

Application service providers (ASPs; not to be confused with ASP and ASP.NET Web pages) have been available on the Internet for some time now. ASPs can be seen as a predecessor to Web Services on a larger scale. ASPs seek to provide a whole application to a user, such as a word processor or billing system. Instead of having an application specially developed or buying a shrink-wrapped application off the shelf, a company would pay a subscription fee to an ASP and access the program across the Internet. Your application would always be up to date because the developers could continually update it on the ASP server. Whereas ASPs attempt to provide the whole application, Web Services only provide small packages of functionality and services that can be utilized by other applications. In general, a company will use an ASP if they are looking for a whole, complete application, whereas developers will work with Web Service providers if they need to purchase a single feature to support one of their projects.

Communicating with Web Services

The Web communicates via Hypertext Transport Protocol (HTTP). Whenever your Web browser navigates to a Web page, it sends out a request for that page via HTTP, and the Web server responds with the Hypertext Markup Language (HTML) and graphics, also sent using HTTP. HTML is a great format for describing layout, such as the location and size of fonts on a Web page. You would not want to use HTML to pass data such as customer listings back and forth across the Web. Instead, you can encode your data into Extensible Markup Language (XML) packages. XML was made to package and describe data in a way that anyone can understand. Anyone with access to the Internet can use the HTTP protocol, and anyone can interpret an XML package of data.

Consumers communicate with Web Services by using HTTP. Anything capable of communicating via HTTP can access your service, from complicated WindowsApplications all the way down to a simple Web browser. To make the data universally understandable, the Web Service packages it in XML. You don't even need a program to read XML. You can pick through a file of data using something as basic as Microsoft Windows Notepad, which enables you to see all the data along with its identifying tags. Because the way that you send and receive data with a Web Service is based on open standards, any applications written in any language and running on any platform can use your service. In fact, the concept of Web-based services itself is not limited to just Microsoft development tools. Java 2 Enterprise Edition (J2EE) developers can also create their own versions of Web-based services that should be compatible with the Projects you create in .NET, thanks to open-source standards. Figure 11.1 shows a few examples of consumer platforms communicating with a Web Service via HTTP.

Throughout the years, applications have become increasingly more distributed. Programs started out as single compiled files, and then evolved into a single main executable supported by multiple resource files. Later, with technologies such as Distributed COM (DCOM), developers were able to distribute their application's files across many different computers, further enhancing their application's scalability. Web Services can be seen as distributed components taken to the extreme. You do not have to be in control of the server that hosts the service code your application uses. You don't even have to program in the same environment in which the service was written to use it, nor do you have to communicate with the service using special platform-specific or vendor-specific protocols. The more computers that are hooked into the Internet, the more distributed your applications can be.

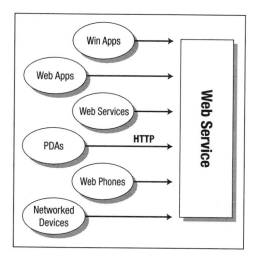

Figure 11.1
Consumers communicating with a Web Service by using HTTP.

Examples of Web Services

Even before .NET existed, examples of Web Services were available on the Internet. Service providers are available on the Internet that will track your Web site users for you and handle the authentication chores for you. Some of these providers will also provide monetary services that allow your users to shop on your Web site without filling in pages and pages of personal information and credit card numbers. Because they are authenticated through a service provider, and that provider already has its financial information, the user can more easily make purchases. For e-businesses, shortening the path to the users' wallets has always been the top priority. A major problem for online stores is "abandoned purchases," referring to users who have already picked out an item to buy but, due to confusing Web pages or annoying requests for information from those pages, decide to click away and take their business elsewhere. High abandonment rates are often a sign that something is wrong with the Web site's design. If users can shop with an e-wallet provided by a Web Service, then the chances of them completing their purchases increase tenfold.

Some of the most popular functions on the Internet involve email, chat, and instant messaging, all of which can be provided as a service to consumer applications. For example, an email service will handle the user accounts and storage of their messages, and the consumer will only have to access these stores as needed. Chat and instant messaging can be incorporated into a project to improve user interactions and information sharing. Imagine that you are developing a company's billing application, and the client wishes to give its employees the ability to quickly share information and ask questions of other departments. You could answer these needs by augmenting the application with a chat and messaging service. How much longer will that take to develop and how much more will it cost the client? It won't take long at all, and the price will be minimal, because somebody out there has already done the work and is making it available to your development team in the form of a Web Service.

Those are some of the obvious examples of services that can be provided over the Internet. Internet file storage is an up-and-coming area you will encounter on the Internet. Instead of filling up your local hard drive with files, you can store them on the Internet. This not only saves you space on your home computer, but also makes these files accessible from any other platform with Web access, such as from work or a friend's house. Group collaboration tools are a great match for Web Services. A calendar that is created as a Web Service can be used not only by all the employees in the office, but also by employees based around the globe. Companies can also share documents on a global scale by using Web Services.

Web Services can be used to create information providers, which provide consumers with data on weather, news, and traffic. A consumer application can obtain the latest information from your service for its own use. Already, cars are available on the market with navigation systems installed that help drivers find where they are and where they are going. A system like this can access a Web Service that provides traffic information so that the mapping software can help the user avoid congested areas. Travel agency software can access Web Services that provide flight information and lodging availability information direct from the airlines and hotels. Games can use Web Services to save a user's character settings, connect users with other players for multiuser matches, and provide a global high-scores section where you can see how you stack up against other players.

Currently, the Internet is a cold and impersonal place. The Web sites I visit know very little about me and the things I am interested in. Web surfers are assaulted with banner ads for things they'll never buy and pieces of news and information that they'll never read. The Internet is crying out for a Web Service that allows sites to customize the user's experience based on a personalized profile that the service maintains. If the Web site knows that I love pizza and my favorite sports are lacrosse and soccer, it will be able to put in front of my face any items that might interest me, making both me and the company I purchase these items from much happier. Taking personalization one step further, when I go to a friend's house and use their computer, the computer doesn't know what my favorite Web sites are, or what toolbars I prefer to use when I am working in a word processor. But, if I am working on a computer with Internet access, it could acquire my personalized settings and Favorites list from a Web Service that knows about me. This would be the ultimate example of a roaming profile.

End-Points

Simply stated, an end-point is any object that can use a Web Service. An end-point can be seen as both a hardware- and software-based user of a service. A traditional WindowsApplication may be the first end-point that you think of. You might think of a Web Application, which is a great example of a possible end-point for a Web Service because both services and Web servers rely on the HTTP protocol as their main form of communication. From the smallest application to the largest operating system, software end-points are everywhere.

As the Internet continues to grow, you will see more and more hardware devices that can communicate across the Web. The PC is the king of the hardware end-points, but everyday it seems that another device with Internet capabilities is introduced to the world. Already, digital phones and personal digital assistants (PDAs) are becoming popular alternatives to the cumbersome PC for mobile Internet viewing. Automobiles are starting to enter the marketplace, too, touting Web-enabled capabilities such as navigation aids and messaging. I even saw a movie recently in which the main character's refrigerator informed him that he was running low on an item and offered to place an order at the grocery store for more. Many manufacturers are already looking at their home gaming systems as potential end-points that can hook into the Internet and provide the gamers with worldwide access to other gamers. Microsoft's XBox, which will be available in the fall of 2001, may be the first home gaming system to truly take advantage of the Internet and Web Services.

As you walk through your house, look at all the items that run on electricity and think about how that item might be seen as an end-point. Imagine that the clock next to your bed is hooked up to the Internet, and can synchronize itself with the United States Naval Observatory's (USNO) atomic clock and automatically adjust itself for daylight savings. As Web-enabled devices get smaller, the need for Web Services will grow. By placing your code and services out on the Internet, you are lightening the load on your device. If the device uses a Web Service to store all of its information, then the device will not need a hard drive or onboard RAM. The uses for Web Services might seem limited now, but in the next few years, these uses will explode into a whole new development market.

The services that you develop now for your WindowsApplications may be used a few years from now to support that alarm clock or refrigerator I mentioned. You might develop an address book Web Service, which could make its information available to a user at home, at work, from their phone, or even from an Internet-enabled kiosk in the mall. Right now, you can access a Web Service from any operating system, any Internet-enabled device, using programs created in any language. When designing a Web Service, keep all of these potential end-points in mind, and realize that you are working with the ultimate form of code reuse that goes far beyond anything you have ever used before.

Hailstorm

Half way through the beta-testing phase of Visual Studio.NET, Microsoft introduced the world to its own planned implementation of its Web Services concept, code-named Hailstorm. Unfortunately, much of the media reacted to this announcement as if they truly were caught in a hailstorm. Naysayers pointed to Hailstorm as proof that Microsoft was out to rule the world. Its planned Web Services include the ability to store user information, preferences, and even online purchasing information, such as credit card numbers. Fueling this fire was the news that Microsoft had plans to charge for these services. Could this truly mean the end of the world as you know it?

Like many of the opinions you will read about Microsoft in the press, the initial reaction to Hailstorm was overblown and driven by the anti-Microsoft crowd. Now that you understand what a Web Service is, it should not come as a big shock that a company would seek to provide a collection of these services for both users and developers to simplify their Internet development projects. While the early years of the Internet were marked by an "everything should be free" mentality, the true reality of this world is that developers have to eat too. Providing Web Services should be seen as a business, and not as a give-away. You would not expect to be able to use the top-of-the-line Windows control created by another company without licensing it first, and you should think of Web Services in the same way.

Hailstorm evolved from the Microsoft Passport service, which most of you may already be familiar with. Passport provided a centralized repository of user information for all Microsoft sites. You could log in to access your Hotmail email account or sign on to a limited-access Microsoft Web site using the same Passport account. Hailstorm expands on the Passport model, and seeks to provide a collection of services to both Internet surfers and application developers. These services include an e-commerce wallet, user identification, and instant messaging. Development projects can incorporate Hailstorm services into their designs and save considerable development time. Not only can you get your projects to market faster, but, because you do not have to develop these features on your own, you also can share these features with other projects throughout the world, which will make your users even happier. Currently, every time you go to a different e-commerce Web site, you have to fill out some forms to tell the site who you are. If all of your favorite Web sites used the same identification and payment service, you would be able to skip these annoying steps and simply point and click your way through the checkout phase. Web Services make it easier on the user, which in return can equal more customers and more purchases to the business.

Of course, you can see why allowing one company to maintain everyone's information would worry some people. If any one company can position itself as the center of the universe for all personal information and financial transactions, competing with that company would be nearly impossible. You're no dummy, I'm no dummy, and Microsoft certainly isn't run by dummies. I don't see the possibility of having one company in control of all my personal information as a bad thing, because the alternative to this vision is a world filled with dozens of information providers competing with each other. In this alternate universe, one of your favorite Web sites may recognize you, but another one may not. You might be required to sign up at a dozen services, thereby fragmenting your profile into a dozen copies that you will need to maintain and update. This fragmented market is hardly better than what you have right now. This is not the way to achieve customer satisfaction, and I believe this fragmentation would hinder the Internet's growth potential. The Internet as a form of information sharing has been a huge success, but the next big step for the Web will be conquering the consumer world. So far, reactions to online purchasing have been mixed, and the key to winning over fickle consumers is to make it as easy as possible for them to find the items they want and to lay down their cash with little or no effort. The only way this will become universally possible is through the use of information services such as those Hailstorm hopes to provide.

Microsoft is pushing forward with its Hailstorm initiative by incorporating these services into all of the products it is currently developing. Soon, you will be able to take advantage of Web Services from within Microsoft's Office XP, in games created by Microsoft, and even in future versions of its XP operating system. Without a doubt, other competing Web Services will spring up in the next few months. Competition is terrific and it helps to push companies to develop better and better products. In the next few years, expect to see a lot of services competing with Hailstorm, with the strongest competitor eventually being adopted as the Internet's preferred service provider.

Web Services Pros and Cons

By now, the pros and cons of Web Services should be readily apparent. By purchasing or licensing a Web Service, your development team can save a lot of time and effort incorporating an application feature that you would normally have to develop on your own. Developers are not cheap, so the savings to the project can be considerable. Development also takes time, and testing your products (you do test, don't you?) takes even longer, to ensure that you got everything right. By purchasing and integrating a service that was already developed and tested elsewhere, you can shave days and even months off of your project's timeline.

For e-commerce applications, being able to accommodate users that have profiles and e-wallets hosted by popular Web Services can mean increased sales and profits for your site. These services will inevitably create networks of supporting online shops that accept these credentials. As competing Web Services pop up, your application developers will have to do their homework to ensure that they support the most popular and robust of these services. Over time, as the competition withers away, a clear winner in this category likely will emerge that all e-commerce sites will seek to support.

The one obvious downside to Web Services is the question of availability. Since Web Services communicate across the network, what will happen if this connection is lost? Every year, networks become more reliable with faster connections, but outages do still occur. If your client's application cannot reach out to the Web Service, that function will be unavailable. The host of your Web Service will also play a large role in your customers' overall satisfaction. If the hosting server frequently goes down, has a slow connection to the Internet, or is so overwhelmed with requests that the response time is unacceptable, customers will blame you for including a feature in the application that fails frequently or appears to be broken. When licensing Web-based services, be sure to research the service's host as thoroughly as you research the service, to avoid such an embarrassment.

Hosting Web Services

Like a Web site, your services need to be hosted on a server that makes them available to the Internet (or intranet if you are working on an internal network). If the server goes down or looses its connection to the Internet, customers will not be able to access your work. Whereas not being able to navigate to a Web site can be an annoyance to Web surfers, not having your application work because the Web Service it relies on is offline can be catastrophic, depending on how big of a role that service plays in your application. For this reason, the hosting of your Web Services is not a topic to be taken lightly.

If your Web Service simply provides the latest weather forecast, then it is pretty likely that applications that use your service could continue to work with outdated data or even no data, assuming of course that the developers take into account an unavailable Web Service. If the service you are creating plays a crucial role in some application, then you need to take every step possible to ensure that the service will be online 24 hours a day without fail. If your company controls the server, then take every precaution available to keep that server online, including backup power and redundant servers that will take over if the primary server fails. If your service is hosted by an outside agency, then be sure to research its hosting services, paying special attention to its uptime percentage, system failure procedures, and any availability guarantees it might offer you. Even if a server is up 100 percent of the time, if that server is overloaded with visitors or has a slow connection to the Internet, then your users will still be disappointed in the results. If the Web Service host fails, it will still be the developers who take the fall.

The hosting aspect of Web Services should play a major role in your application's planning process. Ask yourself where your service will be hosted, how much downtime is acceptable, and how your application will react if your service goes offline. Is your service a "nice to have" feature, or a critical part of the program? Unless your company is in the business of hosting Web sites, odds are high that you are not prepared to reliably host a Web Service in your facility. The services you develop may work great on your company's internal LAN, but if your LAN is connected to the outside world by anything less than a T1 line, the response time to outside users will pale in comparison to what your developers see. A well-thought-through hosting plan can be just as valuable as the Web Services themselves.

How Web Services Work

Including Web Services in your application's architecture is a large departure from the familiar client/server network architecture everyone is familiar with. You must understand how your application will communicate with the Web Service, and how the service will provide you not only with the information you desire but also a complete description of itself and its features. You do not have to know every single detail about a Web Service to use it in your application. In fact, if I were simply to tell you that a great Web Service exists on server "X" that I think you might be able to use, you could easily figure out in a few steps what services are hosted on the server and what the interfaces for those services are.

Web Service Communications

Working with a Web Service involves three phases of communications. As you read about each phase, refer to Figure 11.2, which shows a communication flowchart of all three phases. The first phase is communication with the service's host to determine what Web Services that server is hosting. This phase of communication is known as the discovery phase because it is how your application can discover what services are available.

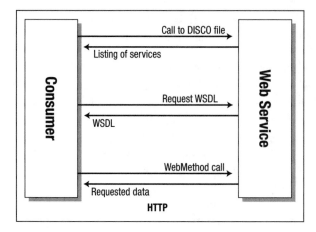

Figure 11.2
Three phases of Web Services communication.

After you know that a certain service is hosted on this server, you need to find out what interfaces that service supports, before you can start using it. This second phase of Web Service communication is a request for the service's Web Service Description Language (WSDL) file. You will also see a WSDL simply called an SDL.

After learning all you need to know about the Web Service's interfaces, you are finally ready to enter the last phase of communication, in which you place requests for information to the service and receive its responses. Let's take a look at each phase in more detail now.

Discovery

Contrary to popular belief, disco is not dead. In fact, it is alive and well in .NET. You have already briefly encountered the DISCO, or discovery, file in Chapter 10 when you created your very first Web Application. You learned that Visual Studio.NET creates this file for you automatically when you start a new Web Application Project, and that its purpose is to help visitors to your site learn about the Web Services that are hosted there. Now I will go into a little more detail on how this file works and how you can use it to make your Web Services available to your users.

The DISCO file in the Project's Web directory is named after the entire Project it was created with, and not each individual Web Service source code file that you create inside the Project. You could create a RoomService Web Services Project that contains multiple services, such as a ReservationService and a RateQuoteService. The actual DISCO file in this Project would be named RoomService.vsdisco. This allows a Project to have more than one service, yet still maintain one single DISCO file that advertises all the services contained in that Project. The DISCO file responds to any requests made to it and returns an XML-formatted file. This file lists the available services that the DISCO file is representing, along with the Uniform Resource Locator (URL) paths to access the WSDL for each service so that the requester can learn more about that service. Here is what the URL would look like to call the DISCO file of the RoomService Project:

```
http://yourservername/RoomService/RoomService.vsdisco
```

An application requesting information from this URL would receive back the following XML file from the DISCO file:

```
<?xml version="1.0" ?>
  <discovery xmlns="http://schemas.xmlsoap.org/disco/">
  <contractRef ref="/RoomService1/Service1.asmx?sdl"
  docRef="/RoomService1/Service1.asmx"
  xmlns="http://schemas.xmlsoap.org/disco/scl/" />
</discovery>
```

If you use a Web browser to query the DISCO file (just type that URL into the browser's Address box), you will see the preceding XML displayed in your browser. An application you create can programmatically query a DISCO file as long as it is prepared to receive and parse the returned XML data. No hard and fast rule exists that says you must have a DISCO file within your Project's directory. You could post one DISCO file on your Web server that describes all the services hosted on that server, giving all of your users one central place to look to discover all the services you provide. A DISCO file does not even have to be on the same server as the services it represents, because it references those services by a full URL path. After you have the service's discovery information, the next step in learning all that you can about a Web Service is to request the service's WSDL by using the URL specified in the discovery's response.

The WSDL

The WSDL file lays out the language of the Web Service, and describes how all communications with that Web Service should be formatted. If you send a message that does not comply with the WSDL, then you are not guaranteed that the service will understand your request and give you the data you desire. The WSDL is known as a "contract," because if a consumer agrees to follow the format described in the WSDL, then the Web Service agrees to provide the data the consumer expects, which is also defined in the WSDL. You don't need a lawyer to interpret this contract, because the WSDL spells it all out in easy-to-understand XML. To request a WSDL from a Web Service, you simply append "?SDL" to the end of the URL pointing to that Web Service. Here is an example of a URL requesting my RoomService Project's WSDL information:

```
http://yourservername/RoomService/Service1.asmx?SDL
```

You can view the WSDL information in Internet Explorer, because the file is XML-based. Internet Explorer is a terrific tool for examining XML files because it indents child tags and allows you to expand and collapse tags based on their groupings and relationships. If you examine a WSDL file, you will notice that it has four major groupings: **httppost**, **httpget**, SOAP (Simple Object Access Protocol), and the Web Service's schema. The schema gives an overall description of the parameter names and their data types in a universally understandable format. The other three sections are each a separate form of message encoding that a consumer can use to talk to the Web Service. Here is an example of the WSDL that would be provided for the RoomService Project:

```xml
<?xml version="1.0"?>
<serviceDescription xmlns:s0="http://tempuri.org/" name="Service1" targetNam_
 espace="http://tempuri.org/" xmlns="urn:schemas-xmlsoap-org:sdl.2000-01-25">
  <soap xmlns="urn:schemas-xmlsoap-org:soap-sdl-2000-01-25">
    <service>
      <addresses>
        <address uri="http://yourservername/RoomService/Service1.asmx"/>
      </addresses>
      <requestResponse name="DeluxeRoomQuote" soapAction="http://_
          tempuri.org/DeluxeRoomQuote">
        <request ref="s0:DeluxeRoomQuote"/>
        <response ref="s0:DeluxeRoomQuoteResult"/>
      </requestResponse>
    </service>
  </soap>
 +<httppost xmlns="urn:schemas-xmlsoap-org:post-sdl-2000-01-25">
 +<httpget xmlns="urn:schemas-xmlsoap-org:get-sdl-2000-01-25">
  <schema targetNamespace="http://tempuri.org/" attributeFormDefault=_
    "qualified" elementFormDefault="qualified" xmlns="http://www.w3.org/1999/_
    XMLSchema">
    <element name="DeluxeRoomQuote">
      <complexType>
        <all>
          <element name="StartDate" xmlns:q1="http://www.w3.org/1999/XML_
              Schema" type="q1:timeInstant"/>
          <element name="EndDate" xmlns:q2="http://www.w3.org/1999/XMLSchema"_
              type="q2:timeInstant"/>
          <element name="NumBeds" xmlns:q3="http://www.w3.org/1999/XMLSchema"_
              type="q3:int"/>
        </all>
      </complexType>
    </element>
    <element name="DeluxeRoomQuoteResult">
      <complexType>
        <all>
          <element name="result" xmlns:q4="http://www.w3.org/1999/XMLSchema"_
            type="q4:string" nullable="true"/>
```

```
        </all>
      </complexType>
    </element>
  </schema>
</serviceDescription>
```

The WSDL contains a lot of information, and its purpose is to give developers and applications alike all the information they need to use this Web Service. I highlighted the headers for the four main sections of the preceding WSDL: **soap, httpget, httppost,** and **schema.** The first three sections are mostly repetitive, so I left only the **soap** section expanded. These sections describe the format of the message encoding that each of these request types will use. I will go into more detail on the protocols in the "Requests Using Get, Post, and SOAP" section. The fourth section, the schema, is like a dictionary to help you understand the terms that the Web Service uses. For example, when the Web Service asks for a **NumBeds** variable, you can tell by looking at the schema that this variable will be an **Integer,** because the schema says that **NumBeds** is of **type="q3:int".** The **StartDate** and **EndDate** are of a **timeInstant** type, which, translated into Visual Studio speak, is a **Date** type. If you are wondering why the schema simply doesn't call them **Date** and **Integer,** remember that these services can be used by any program, and not just those created in Visual Studio, so the data type descriptions are meant to be universally understood. The URLs you see sprinkled about the WSDL act as pointers to Internet references that describe what a WSDL is, and what a schema is.

Examining a service's WSDL information can be very informative and is a great way to understand how a Web Service describes itself. Of course, when you are programming in Visual Studio.NET, the Integrated Development Environment (IDE) requests and maintains the WSDL information for you. When you reference a Web Service in your Visual Studio Project, the WSDL is read in by the IDE, which remembers all of the service's settings and parameter restrictions and enforces them when you are entering your code. Component Object Model (COM)-based DLLs come with type libraries that allow Visual Studio to understand the component's structure, thereby making it easy to work with. WSDL is to Web Services what those type libraries are to COM components, except the WSDL information can be used by any programming language, whereas the type libraries are understood only by COM programming languages.

Requests Using Get, Post, and SOAP

Consumers can send their requests via the HTTP protocol using the Get, Post, or SOAP protocol. HTTP is a transmission protocol whose specialty is moving data back and forth across the Internet. Get, Post, and SOAP are all encoding protocols that take the data you wish to transport via HTTP and encode it into a message for transmission by HTTP. If you have worked with form fields on a Web page before, then you are probably already familiar with the Get and Post methods. All three of these Web-based communication-encoding protocols are open source and available to everyone. In the past, the drawback of communicating with COM and Common Object Request Broker Architecture (CORBA) objects was that you had to use a proprietary protocol to send and receive your data, which left many developers out in the cold. If you were not programming with Microsoft technologies, then you could not talk to the code in a COM component. Likewise, CORBA developers could not communicate with COM objects. With open-source protocols, anyone can talk to your code. Let's next take a quick look at these three forms of Web-based communication that your Web Service can receive requests through.

Get and Post have been around as long as the Internet, and are used every day by HTML Web pages to communicate back to the Web server bits of information. If you fill out a registration form on a Web site and submit it to the server, all of your form data will be encoded in either a Get or a Post process for transport via HTTP to the server. The Web server will know which protocol you used and will use the appropriate method to extract your encoded data from the HTTP stream. You can look at any HTML Web page with a form on it, and inside its **<FORM>** tag, you will see an **Action** attribute that specifies either Get or Post as the transmission protocol. The Get protocol attaches its data to the end of the URL being sent to the Web server so that all the data is communicated in one long string. Here is an example of what a URL would look like with two form fields and their associated values encoded in the URL by the Get method:

```
www.yourservername.com/processer.asp?FirstName=Jim&LastName=Thomas
```

The Get method uses special characters, such as question marks and ampersands, to separate the data and the field names. Other special characters are used for spaces and other such characters that do not translate well into URL strings. The Post method differs from the Get method in that it packages its data inside of the HTTP message, and not at the end of the HTTP address. Data is represented in matched data pairs, with the first part being the form field identifier and the second part being the form field's value.

SOAP is new to the Internet, and is an exciting new way to package data for transmission via HTTP that is far more powerful than the Get or Post methods. SOAP is based on XML, which as you know is a powerful tool for packaging and describing data. Chapter 12 goes into much greater detail on the inner workings of XML and SOAP, but for the current Web Services discussion, you should understand that SOAP is a protocol for transmitting data across HTTP that offers all the power and flexibility of XML messaging without the limiting data pairing of the older Get and Post methods. If you are looking to communicate information that is more complicated than a simple Web form, then SOAP is the robust protocol that can help you out.

Proxy Classes

If you are wondering how you are going to manage to create these Get, Post, and SOAP messages and then extract the data returned by the Web Service from the HTTP transmission, no need to worry, because you won't have to do any of it. Visual Studio.NET handles the transmission medium and the formatting of your messages, by creating what is known as a *proxy class* for the Web Service you are calling. With a proxy class, your application perceives that it has a local copy of the class, complete with all of its properties and methods. It perceives all of this because when your application registered the Web Service, it obtained the WSDL, which describes all of these details. So, even though your WindowsApplication and the Web Service you wish to use are a world apart, your interface knows all there is to know about the service and pretends that it is just another class in the Project.

Besides acting as a local stand-in for the Web Service, the proxy class has an even more important job to do. When your code makes a call to a method of the Web Service, the proxy steps in and says: "Hey, hey, I was only pretending to be that other guy! I better package this request up, send it out to the real Web Service and then un-package the service's response so that the caller doesn't figure out I was faking it!" The proxy class will decide the best way to package your data and will then send it on to the real Web Service. When the response is returned in its XML format, the proxy class will receive the data, translate the XML in to a .NET data type and hand it over to the calling code. As a developer, you don't need to worry about any of the details of Web Service communications and message formatting, and you can treat your referenced services just like you would any other Class in your Project.

Creating Web Services

I suspect that by now you are as excited as I am about Web Services, and I'm sure you are dying to create your own services to see how it's done. If you expect this process to be complicated, then you'll be pleasantly surprised. Read on to see how easy it is to create a service using the Visual Basic skills and knowledge you already possess.

A Simple Web Service

The first example of a Web Service will be a simple information provider for Oceanside Resort. Data consumers will be able to contact this service, provide a few bits of information, and get back a rate quote for one of the available hotel rooms. A travel agency could access this service across the Web using a WindowsApplication. This information could also be useful to a Web site that allows travelers to plan their vacations and search for the best hotel deals available.

When you first create a Web Services Project, you will notice that Visual Studio.NET contacts the Web server to set up your files, just as it does when you create an ASP.NET Web Application. Your main Web Service file name will end in .asmx. Like the Web Application, you will have a few extra files in your Project to help configure the Web environment. You can find a description of what these extra files are used for in Chapter 10. Working with Web Services is a lot like creating a Class. Remember that your service will provide information to the consumer, and not a graphical interface like a Windows or a Web Form Class does. You will be able to develop your Web Service graphically, but only to drag and drop components to your interface from the Toolbox window. Like ASP.NET pages, Web Services use code-behind, which stores your Visual Basic code within the ASMX file.

Try out Exercise 11.1 to see how simple it is to create a working Web Service. This exercise also introduces you to a Web browser informational view of your service, as well as a quick and easy method you can use to test your methods.

Exercise 11.1: Creating a Basic Web Service

Note

Like Web Applications, Web Services will require that you have an IIS 5 Web server either installed locally on your machine or on an accessible server somewhere on your network.

1. Start Visual Studio.NET and create a new Project. Select the ASP.NET Web Service Project and call it RoomService.

2. Your Project creates an ASMX file to house your Web Services code, along with a Global.asax and Web.config file to configure the environment. You will notice a Room-Service.vsdisco file, which will help consumers "discover" more about the Web Services you are creating in this Project.

3. Select the file named Service1.asmx in the Solution Explorer window, and then click the View Code button at the top of the Solution Explorer.

4. The Service1.asmx file looks like a typical Class file, and you will even notice a **New** event in it. Note that underneath the line that says Public Class Service1 is an Inherits line referencing the System.Web.Services.WebService superclass. Although this source code file may look like a normal Class file, it does not share the same parent superclass as a regular Class file.

5. Within the **Service1** Class, add the following function:

```
<WebMethod()> Public Function DeluxeRoomQuote(ByVal StartDate As Date,_
   ByVal EndDate As Date, ByVal NumBeds As Integer) As String
      'Access database here to find out room availability
      Dim RoomRate As Double
      Const HotelTax As Double = 0.1
      If NumBeds = 1 Then RoomRate = 89.95 Else RoomRate = 99.95
      RoomRate = RoomRate + (RoomRate * HotelTax)
      DeluxeRoomQuote = format(RoomRate, "$##0.00")
End Function
```

6. Note the **<WebMethod()>** tag in the function declaration line. Aside from this new tag, your **DeluxeRoomQuote** function looks like any other Class function you have

encountered. Save your Web Class, and then click the Run button on the Visual Studio toolbar.

7. Your Web browser will start and navigate to the Web Service you just created. Because you are not a consumer application making a request of the service, your Web Service will do a little advertising for itself. Take a look at Figure 11.3 to see what your Web Service displays when you point your Web browser at it. What you see is a dynamically generated Web page describing the Web Service and all of its available methods. Notice that your Web Service lists one method named **DeluxeRoomQuote**.

8. Click on the hyperlink labeled **DeluxeRoomQuote**. The browser will display a new page showing information on how to call this method **SOAP**, HTTP **GET** and HTTP **POST**. At the top of this page, you will see a TextBox for each of this method's input parameters. Enter a date in both the **StartDate** and the **EndDate** blanks, and then

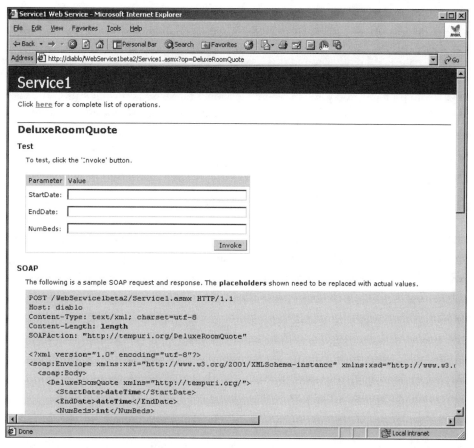

Figure 11.3
Viewing a Web Service's information in your browser.

enter a "2" for the NumBeds parameter. Click on the Invoke button below these textboxes.

9. A new browser window will open. The parameters you entered are submitted to the Web Service just as a consumer's input would be, and the result is displayed in the new browser window. Because the output of a Web Service is in XML, Internet Explorer will display an XML file, which should look like this:

```
<?xml version="1.0" ?>
<string xmlns="http://tempuri.org/">$109.95</string>
```

10. The price of a deluxe hotel room with two beds for one night is $109.95 at Oceanside Resort, including hotel tax. You can use the Web Services information page to test your Web Service to see how it handles different input parameters and to check your service's output values.

Exercise 11.1 shows you many interesting things. The first thing you should notice is how easy it is to create a Web Service. You can create functions just as you would any other Class. Of course, if I really wanted this service to be useful, I would check the user's starting and ending reservation dates against my database to see whether a room really is available, and I would probably also want to adjust the room's rate based on what season the visit was planned for. A Web Service's purpose is to provide some sort of output of information, so your service will depend on functions to calculate and relay your information to the consumer. You can still use subroutines for internal Web Service use, but because a subroutine does not provide any information, a Web Service consumer would have no need to call it.

Browsing and Testing Your Web Services

The Web Service information page offers a very handy view of your service, and it shows you what outside users will see when they access your service. By simply typing the URL path to an ASMX file, you get back that service's information page. Try starting your Internet Explorer browser and typing the following URL in the Address box, replacing *yourservername* with the name of the Web server you are using:

```
http://yourservername/RoomService/Service1.asmx?SDL
```

Your browser will display the information page for the Service1 Web Service. You can use this page to discover all the details associated with the Web Service, which you will need to know if you are going to make use of it. This Web page is a great way for the developer to quickly test the services without building a separate consumer application. As soon as you finish coding your Web Service, you can use your Web browser to enter some test data in the service's input parameters and observe what kind of output your service will provide.

If a Web Service has more than one method available, you will see all available methods listed toward the top of the information page, and then a separate testing area for each method beneath the informational area. Clicking the hyperlinked method name at the top of the information page scrolls the Web page down to where you see this method's testing area. Toward the top of the information page, notice the link to the WSDL Contract, which will return to you the XML-encoded WSDL information you learned about earlier.

Accessing Web Services

A Web Service is not a standalone application. You need a consumer to call upon your service and use the information it provides. A service with no consumer is like a musician with no audience. Though you can access a Web Service from any application with Internet access, no matter what language you use to create it, this section covers the two most common .NET application types, which you are already familiar with: the WindowsApplication and the Web Application.

WindowsApplications Calling Web Services

If you are developing a WindowsApplication that will have access to the Internet through the computer your application is hosted on, then you will be in a position to take advantage of Web Services. Maybe your development team has plans to develop some of the application's functionality as a service, or maybe your Project Manager has included another company's Web Service in the application's architecture. Either way, as the Windows Application developer, you need to know how to call upon this service and use the data it will provide to you.

Exercise 11.2 creates a Windows-based travel agent application. You can imagine this single Windows form as being part of a large application being used in a travel agency. This fictional agency wished to have its application designed to use Windows forms as an interface, but because it often deals with hotels that are not a part of its agency's network, its application needs a way to request the latest data on the various hotels' room availability and rates. This is where the RoomService Web Service you created in Exercise 11.1 steps in. Your travel agency application will ask the user for a few key pieces of data and, upon a click of a button, will query the hotel's Web Service for the latest room rate.

Exercise 11.2: WindowsApplication Accessing a Web Service

1. Create a new WindowsApplication Project and call it TravelAgent.

2. On your Windows form, add two DateTimePicker controls and set both of their **Format** properties to **Short**. Add a label to the left of each control, naming DateTimePicker1 "Start Date" and DateTimePicker2 "End Date".

3. Add a ListBox control, and edit its **Items** property so that the first line reads "1 Bed" and the second reads "2 Beds". Add a label "Number Beds" to the left of this control.

4. Add a button control to your form and set its **Text** property to "Check Room Rate".

Figure 11.4
The travel agency Windows form.

5. Add a Label control below the button control and set its **Text** property to "Room Rate = ". This Label control will be referenced as Label4 in the sample code shown later in this exercise. Your completed form should look something like the one in Figure 11.4.

6. In the Solution Explorer window, right-click the Project name (TravelAgent) and select Add Web Reference.

7. In the Add Web Reference window, enter the URL to your RoomService ASMX file in the Address textbox at the top of the form. Your URL should look like this:

```
http://yourservername/RoomService/Service1.asmx
```

8. Press Enter after you type in the URL. The window will navigate to your Web Service just like a Web browser would. If the service is successfully located, you will see the now-familiar information window in the left pane, and two links in the right pane, one to view the "Contract" (the WSDL) and the other to view any available documentation for this service.

9. If you successfully located the RoomService ASMX file, then click the Add Reference button at the bottom of this window.

10. Your Project will now have a folder named Web References underneath the References folder. Below the Web References folder is a globe icon followed by the name of your service's Web server. If you expand the Web server's name, you should see three files: Reference.map, Service1.vsdisco, and Service1.sdl. These files contain the information that the service provided your application describing its interfaces.

11. Double-click the button back on your Windows Form to access its **Click** event. Enter the following code in **Button1**'s **Click** event:

```
Protected Sub Button1_Click(ByVal sender As Object, ByVal e As _
  System.EventArgs)
    'Call RoomService!
    Dim RateQuote As String
    Dim RoomRate As New yourservername.Service1()
    Dim StartDate As Date = DateTimePicker1.Value
    Dim EndDate As Date = DateTimePicker2.Value
```

```
      Dim NumBeds As Integer = ListBox1.SelectedIndex
      'If nothing selected (-1) then set NumBeds = 0
      If NumBeds = -1 Then NumBeds = 0
      'Add 1 to NumBeds to get true bed count
      NumBeds = NumBeds + 1
      'Call Web Service and pass in parameters
      RateQuote = RoomRate.DeluxeRoomQuote(StartDate, EndDate, NumBeds)
      Label4.Text = "Room Rate = " & RateQuote
   End Sub
```

12. In the line that declares **RoomRate**, be sure to substitute the name of your RoomService's host Web server for *yourservername*.

13. Save and run your program. Pick one of the Number Beds entries and click the Check Room Rate button. The code will gather your input parameters and call the RoomService. The value returned from your Web Service will be assigned to your **RateQuote** variable, which is then displayed in Label4.

Although you will use a special Add Web Reference form to locate and select a reference, after you have that reference in your Project, using the Web Service is just like making a call to any other Class housed in an Assembly. Recall that the output of the Web Service is an XML file, just as you saw in the browser when you used it to test your Web Service. Your WindowsApplication is smart enough to extract the results from the XML and assign that value to your **RateQuote** variable. Because the output parameter of the **DeluxeRoomQuote** function was declared as a **String**, your **RateQuote** function must also be declared as a **String** for this to work.

When your application set a reference to the Web Service, it received a local copy of the WSDL, describing that Web Service. With this knowledge, the Visual Studio.NET IDE is able to verify that the parameters you are passing to the Web Service are of the correct type, and that the variable you use to accept the value returned from the service is also a match. This is some pretty impressive knowledge when you consider that your Web Service can be all the way on the other side of the world.

Web Applications Calling Web Services

Your ASP.NET applications will inherently be a terrific candidate for using Web Services, because both rely on the power of the Internet to communicate. Unless your Web site is limited to a customer's internal intranet, your Web Forms should be capable of accessing Web Services throughout the world, greatly expanding the pool of ready-to-use code at your disposal. Creating a Web Form is very similar to creating a Windows form, and adding a reference to a Web Service is handled in the same fashion.

The Web Application example in Exercise 11.3 creates a Web page hosted by a travel agency that regularly polls a preferred list of hotels to provide visitors with the hotel's current room rates. Participating hotels would have to make their information available through

Web Services for this Web page to be truly useful, but for now, I'll just display the rates for the super-exclusive Oceanside Resort.

Exercise 11.3: Web Applications Accessing a Web Service

1. Create a new Web Application and name it BargainRooms.

2. Click the surface of the Web Form and set its **pagelayout** property to "gridlayout".

3. In the top-left portion of the page, place a Label control and set its **Text** value to "Today's Hotel Room Rate Quotes". Under this Label's Font grouping in the Properties window, locate the **Size** property and set this to X-Large.

4. Drag two labels to the page and place them below your heading label so that the two new labels are side by side. Set the **Text** value of the leftmost label to "Oceanside Resort Deluxe Room", and set the value of the rightmost label simply to "$". Set the width of the right label so that your room quote dollar amount easily fits. You can resize this control by dragging the label's right-side edge to the right a little bit. Figure 11.5 shows an example of the Room Rate Web Form built for this exercise.

5. In the Solution Explorer window, right-click the BargainRoom Project name and select Add Web Reference.

6. Just as you did for the WindowsApplication, add the URL for your RoomService.asmx file in the Address textbox and press Enter. Your URL will look like the following URL, except with your Web server's name in place of *yourservername*:

```
http://yourservername/RoomService/Service1.asmx
```

7. When the Web Service browser shows the information page for RoomService, simply click the Add Reference button at the bottom to finalize this reference.

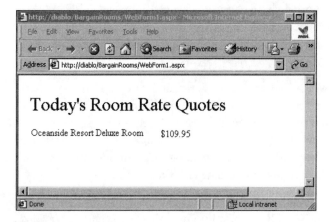

Figure 11.5
The BargainRooms Web page.

8. In the WebForm1 Design view window, right-click the surface of WebForm1 and select View Code.

9. Locate the **WebForm1_Load** event. Because you will want to pull in the quotes for all of the hotel rooms you are advertising for while you are drawing the Web page, you will make these calls within the **Load** event, which occurs before the user gets the page. Place these calls inside the **If Not PostBack** section to ensure that you call the Web Services only during the initial page load, and not during page round-trips. Enter the following code in the **Load** event:

```
Dim TodaysDate As Date
Dim Tomorrow As Date
Dim OSRRate As String
Dim CallRate As New yourservername.Service1()
TodaysDate = Today
OSRRate = CallRate.DeluxeRoomQuote(TodaysDate, TodaysDate, 2)
Label2.Text = OSRRate
```

10. Save your Project and then press F5. Internet Explorer will start and display your Web page. While the page is loading, it will call upon your RoomService Web Service to provide the latest rate quote based on today's date and two beds. When the page is done drawing, it displays the current room rate, and looks something like the Web page shown in Figure 11.5.

Working Web Services into your applications is so easy. The steps you take to reference and call a Web Service are exactly the same, whether you are creating a WindowsApplication or a Web Application. If you are designing an application that will be Web-based, you shouldn't have too hard of a time finding a good use for Web Services. If your application uses a traditional Windows interface, do not overlook the Web Services as a way to compliment your application and easily obtain for your users the latest available data from outside sources.

Advanced Web Services Topics

Building on what you have learned about Web Services, this section covers some more advanced uses for Web Services, such as using them to supply callers with whole DataSets full of data instead of simple primitive data types. The more information a service provides, the more useful it will be to its users. You even can use your Web Service to talk to other Web Services on the Internet and use their responses in your service's response to the caller. A service may seem small and simple to an end-point user, but behind the scenes, a lot of complexity and background processing may be going on to provide the consumer with a helpful response. Like an iceberg, the portion of the Web Service a consumer sees is only a small part of a large object lying just below the surface.

Receiving DataSets from Web Services

More than likely, you will want to do more with Web Services than simply respond to callers with **String** and **Integer** messages. If a bookstore wants to turn its catalog of currently available books into a Web Service that "hard-to-find" book locator services can access, responding with the entire store's inventory in a single **String** would be unmanageable at best. If you were coding this method into a Class, you would want the output to be a DataSet, right? In the Oceanside Resort application, remote end-point applications such as a front-desk clerk using a WindowsApplication or a manager using a Web-based reporting system may want to access the entire Customers list as stored in the database. To see how a Web Service can provide complex DataSets to the client, try out Exercise 11.4.

> ### Note
> *Exercise 11.4 uses the Oceanside Resort database created in Chapter 8. This exercise also assumes that you have this database added to your Server Explorer as a Data Connection for easy access. If you do not have this database set up as a Data Connection, refer to Chapter 8's "Accessing Data with Server Explorer" section to learn how to set this up.*

Exercise 11.4: Providing DataSets from Web Services

1. Start a new ASP.NET Web Service Project and name it CustomerInfo.

2. With the Service1.asmx file open in Display view, open the Server Explorer window, expand the entry for the Oceanside Resort Purchases database, and then expand the Tables tree. Drag and drop the Customers table to Service1.asmx. A Connection and a DataAdapter component are added here for you.

3. From the Data tab of the Toolbox window, drag and drop a DataSet component to Server1.asmx.

4. Right-click Service1.asmx and select View Code.

5. Create the following WebMethod inside the **Service1** Class:

```
<WebMethod()> Public Function OSRCustomers() As DataSet
    'This method returns a DataSet of the OSR Customers table
    OleDbDataAdapter1.Fill(DataSet1, "Customers")
    OSRCustomers = DataSet1
End Function
```

6. Save your Project and then press F5 to run it.

7. Internet Explorer will start and show the information page for your Web Service. No input parameters are listed because I didn't specify any. The Response Type entry shows that this Web Service will respond with a DataSet, which is very important for the

using application to know, because it has to declare a DataSet variable to receive the data. Because I did not specify input parameters, this information form has no textboxes in which to enter test data, but it does have an Invoke button that enables you to test the service's output.

8. Click the Invoke button. A new browser window opens, and the DataSet results are displayed in XML format. Listing 11.1 shows the XML results with two customers returned from the database. The first section of this XML file describes how the rest of the file is formatted and what format the returned data types take on. Because this file is so descriptive, the receiving caller does not have to be using .NET DataSets to use this data.

Listing 11.1   A DataSet in XML.

```xml
<?xml version="1.0"?>
<DataSet xmlns="http://tempuri.org/">
  <xsd:schema id="NewDataSet" targetNamespace="" xmlns=""_
    xmlns:xsd="http://www.w3.org/1999/XMLSchema" xmlns:msdata="urn:schemas_
    microsoft-com:xml-msdata">
    <xsd:element name="Customers">
      <xsd:complexType content="elementOnly">
        <xsd:all>
          <xsd:element name="Address" minOccurs="0" type="xsd:string"/>
          <xsd:element name="City" minOccurs="0" type="xsd:string"/>
          <xsd:element name="CustomerID" minOccurs="0" type="xsd:int"/>
          <xsd:element name="FirstName" minOccurs="0" type="xsd:string"/>
          <xsd:element name="LastName" minOccurs="0" type="xsd:string"/>
          <xsd:element name="State" minOccurs="0" type="xsd:string"/>
          <xsd:element name="Zip" minOccurs="0" type="xsd:string"/>
        </xsd:all>
      </xsd:complexType>
    </xsd:element>
    <xsd:element name="NewDataSet" msdata:IsDataSet="True">
      <xsd:complexType>
        <xsd:choice maxOccurs="unbounded">
          <xsd:element ref="Customers"/>
        </xsd:choice>
      </xsd:complexType>
    </xsd:element>
  </xsd:schema>
  <NewDataSet xmlns="">
    <Customers>
      <Address>123 Main St.</Address>
      <City>Charlottesville</City>
      <CustomerID>11111</CustomerID>
      <FirstName>Jack</FirstName>
      <LastName>Jersey</LastName>
```

```
            <State>VA</State>
            <Zip>22029</Zip>
        </Customers>
        <Customers>
            <Address>9433 Smith Ct.</Address>
            <City>Rapid City</City>
            <CustomerID>11113</CustomerID>
            <FirstName>Kim</FirstName>
            <LastName>Gray</LastName>
            <State>SD</State>
            <Zip>44321</Zip>
        </Customers>
      </NewDataSet>
</DataSet>
```

The steps used to create the function in Exercise 11.4 are exactly the same as the steps taken in Chapter 8 to create a DataSet. The only difference between this function and the one in Chapter 8 is the **<WebMethod()>** tag in the function line. You can very easily take functions you have previously created in Classes and port them over to Web Services by adding this tag to the function declaration. It's the exact same function, but the tag tells the Web server that this function is available as a service. You will not be able to add this tag to your Classes that are outside of the Web Service ASMX file because this file acts as the listener sitting on the Web server. As you read on, you will see how the ASMX file can act as the listener and as the Web interface for an even larger application behind it.

Web Services As Interfaces

As you saw in the previous section, a Web Service does not have to exist on its own. The Customers DataSet example in Exercise 11.4 showed that a database may exist behind your service, and certainly all but a few services will need to rely on some back-end data stores to make them useful. Your Web Service Project can contain much more than just service files. Because this Project is housed on a Web server, you can add Web Forms to it. The Web Forms do not have to interact with your service either. Picture a Project that contains the RoomQuote service in it, and also contains many Web Forms that constitute the hotel's informational Web site. Web surfers can navigate to the Web Forms to learn about the hotel and its amenities, while end-point applications, such as travel agent information systems, can access the Web Service maintained in the very same Project. Of course, to keep the maintenance and design issues as simple as possible, you should not combine Web Forms and Web Services in a single Project if they do not have anything to do with each other, but I wanted to point out that Web Forms and Web Services can coexist in a Project.

Like Web Forms, your Web Services can be the front end to a larger, more complex application. Your service can talk to Classes added to the same Project or make calls to components and Assemblies outside of the Project. If a Web Service Project contains one service ASMX file and multiple Class files, only the interfaces marked as **<WebMethod()>** within the service ASMX file can receive and process HTTP requests. These methods are your application's Web-based interfaces to the outside world. Your Classes will have many interfaces within them, but these will go unseen beyond the boundaries of the Web Service.

What truly makes Web Services interesting is that they can access other Web Services. Because the ASMX file has access to the Internet, it can communicate with other services on the Web during its processing. The book finder example provided earlier could be used to illustrate all of these different access types a Web Service can enlist. When a request is received by the book finder service, the service could make a call to a back-end Class, which in turn could call a database maintained by the book finder's owner. To make the book finder truly global, you would want it to have the most up-to-date information available from multiple booksellers. You could do this by having the book finder service contact Web Services hosted by outside bookstores and ask them if they have such-and-such a book. When the book finder service is all done gathering its data from a multitude of sources, it returns one consolidated response to the calling end-point. That caller will never know that the book finder looked all over the world for the book they requested. Figure 11.6 illustrates the book finder example and shows all of the back-end connections the service can make.

Debugging Web Services
The debugging tips given in Chapter 10 for ASP.NET Web Applications also apply for Web Services. When you start your service from within Visual Studio, the code can respond to breakpoints you leave within your code, which in turn gives you access to all the other .NET debugging facilities, such as Watches and Locals. You can place a breakpoint

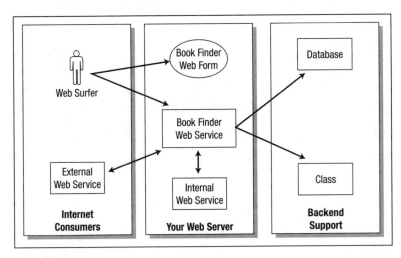

Figure 11.6
Back-end support for the book finder service.

in your **<WebMethod()>** and when the service executes that breakpoint during debugging, it will enter Break mode and take you back into Visual Studio.NET. You will be able to step through your service's code and into other modules, such as Classes, that you have added to your Project.

The **Debug** and **Trace** objects are also available for Web Service troubleshooting and should be used liberally during Web Service development. Using the **Trace** object enables you to leave messages behind in log files even after the service has been deployed to an operational server. This can be a very useful way to log all calls made to your service from within the code, which enables you to track and monitor its usage. Because Web Services, like Web sites, can be made available to everyone on the Internet, being able to maintain statistics on your services can make a manager's dreams come true. You can log all calls made to your methods, and thrill your boss by reporting the service's peak usage hours and the most popular parameters passed into your methods ("Hey boss, did you know that the most popular book requested this month is *Designing Visual Basic.NET Applications?*").

If you have ever created an ActiveX control in Visual Basic 6, you know that they are hard to troubleshoot standing on their own. The hardest way to test a control is to compile it and then start a test Project that includes your control in it. If the control has a problem, you have to close the test Project and go back to the control's Project to try to locate the problem. The smart way to test a control is to add a second Project to the Project Group that references the control. This enables you to test and fix the control in the same environment. The same trick can work with Web Services as well. While the information Web page that Visual Studio launches for your Web Service is very nice, and enables you to test your service, nothing really puts some code through its paces like another Project. Exercise 11.5 shows how you can add a second Project to your CustomerInfo Web Service Solution to test it out. Using test Projects enables you to step directly from the calling code into the Web Service to follow its execution and better locate hard-to-find problems.

Exercise 11.5: Web Service Testing with Another Project

1. With the CustomerInfo Project open in Visual Studio, right-click the CustomerInfo Solution in the Solution Explorer, select Add, and then select New Project.

2. Add a new WindowsApplication Project and name it CustomerTest.

3. Add a DataGrid control to Form1 of the CustomerTest Project, and resize it so that it is the width of the form.

4. Add a button control below the DataGrid control.

5. Your CustomerTest Project needs a reference to the CustomerInfo Project. Right-click the CustomerTest Project in the Solution Explorer and select Add Reference. You will not be using the Add Web Reference item, because the service you are accessing shares a Solution with your test Project.

6. Click the Project tab of the Add Reference window. You should see your CustomerInfo Project listed here, because it exists inside the same Solution as your CustomerTest Project. Double-click the CustomerInfo Project to add it to the lower list box and then click the OK button.

7. Double-click the button on Form1 to access its **Click** event. Add the following code to this event:

```
Dim MyCust As New CustomerInfo.Service1()
DataGrid1.DataSource() = MyCust.OSRCustomers
```

8. In the Solution Explorer, right-click the CustomerTest Project and select Set As Startup Project.

9. Save your Projects and then press F5 to run the Windows form. Click the button, and the Windows form will call your Web Service and display the DataSet it returns.

10. Stop the application and return to Visual Studio.NET. In the Form1 code, place a breakpoint on the second line of the button's **Click** event where it sets DataGrid1's **DataSource** property.

11. Press F5 to run the application again.

12. Click the button. Your application will enter Break mode at your breakpoint. Press F8 to step forward, and you will be able to follow your Form1's call over into the Service1 WebMethod.

Developers of large and complex Web Services need a way to easily test these services without switching between the service and a testing application. By combining your test application and the service under one Solution, you can save lots of time in the testing phase of your software project, and you can step through the entire process from the consumer's request to the service's response.

Summary

The ability to package pieces of your application into services that make themselves available across the Internet really adds a new dimension to distributed application design. The introduction of Web Services will create a whole new market for services that will be made available by developers for quick and easy integration into your projects. The more code that is made available on the Internet for reuse, the less time your projects will take to create. Why write an authentication component when one is already written and ready for use? When you are in the design phase of a project, look at each module and ask yourself if this module would work better as a Web Service. Has someone else already created such a service that you can simply license and use in your project? Could you write this module as a service, and then market it to other development efforts as a licensable service, thereby earning even more money for your work? With just a slight change to the way you design software, you can easily adapt to the Web Services concept and find new and exciting ways to take advantage of these services.

Chapter 12

SOAP and XML in .NET

Key Topics:

- **XML Basics**
- **Schemas**
- **XML in DataSets**
- **Working with XML**
- **Transformations**
- **SOAP**

Throughout this book, you have seen many references to both the Extensible Markup Language (XML) and the Simple Object Access Protocol (SOAP). Before the existence of Visual Studio.NET, the only books you could find that talked as much as this book does about XML and its associated technologies, such as SOAP, were dedicated solely to the topic of XML. Now that .NET is here, XML is no longer a separate entity from your code that you could choose as an alternative to the standard messaging formats. Instead, XML is fully integrated into the code and the development environment, meaning you don't have to take any extra steps to include XML in your applications. Visual Studio.NET was built on a solid foundation of XML open-source concepts, and the key to truly understanding .NET is understanding why XML is such a wonderful achievement and what it brings to the .NET development framework.

This chapter starts by explaining XML in plain English, and then builds upon that description by explaining all the other "X-" buzzwords, such as XSLT (Extensible Stylesheet Language Transformation) and XSD (XML Schema Definition). I will show you how .NET uses XML and how you can use the Visual Studio.NET interface to work with XML from within your applications. By the end of this chapter, you should have a clear understanding of all the XML concepts, including why XML is so important to development projects in the near future, and how you will incorporate XML into your .NET applications from here forward. If you are already very familiar with XML, you may want to skip over the basics and concentrate just on the Visual Studio.NET portions of this chapter, such as how to create schemas in .NET.

XML Basics

When XML burst onto the development scene, onlookers might have concluded from all the media attention that XML was the most important technology created since the birth of the computer itself. Shelves and shelves of books have been written about it, magazines have been devoted to it, and any good programmer's resume is incomplete without the keyword *XML* somewhere on it. The hype on XML was, and still is, somewhat intimidating. Surely, a technology so widely touted as the salvation of applications everywhere must be hard to understand and take advantage of in your projects. Most certainly this is a technology that only XML gurus can work with, and not something every coder needs to learn about to get by. Right? Maybe in the past, but if you plan to use .NET, then you need to know about XML. As for XML being complicated and complex, I think you will be surprised at how simple XML really is. It's time to burst the bubble of hype and find out the truth about what XML is.

Markup Languages

XML arrived at a time when most of the Web design community was starting to get comfortable with Hypertext Markup Language (HTML) as a means of communicating Web pages. In fact, markup languages predate even HTML, which is only a subset of its predecessor, Standard Generalized Markup Language (SGML). What is a markup language? It is simple text surround by tags that identify to the program what that text is. HTML uses tags to identify the layout and display of data within a Web browser, as in this line from a Web page:

```
<B><I>Welcome to .NET!</I></B>
```

A browser would display this message in bold and italic text, due to the use of the **<B>** and **<I>** tags. The opening tags precede the text that is supposed to be bold and italics, and the closing tags, **</I>** and **</B>**, which have the same name as the starting tags except with a backslash after the opening angle bracket, indicate the end of the text that's supposed to be bold and italics. A good, clean tagging scheme has opening and closing tags, with every opening tag having a matching closing tag somewhere after it. The tags "mark up" the text in between them. XML is also a descendant of the SGML family, and uses markup tags to describe the data, instead of describing page layout as HTML does. Boiled down to its simplest form and definition, an XML file is just plain text surrounded by descriptive tags. Here is a very simple line of an XML file:

```
<PhoneNumber>(904)555-1234</PhoneNumber>
```

Both the reader and any application receiving this line of XML easily recognizes that the data between these two tags is a phone number. HTML could not properly describe a phone number, because it is limited to a small set of display-related tags that all Web browsers are capable of understanding. If a Web browser encounters a tag that it does not understand, it ignores it and moves on to a tag that it does know what to do with. XML tags, on the other hand, can be named anything you wish as long as those users and applications that read the XML data understand the tags you are using.

That is what all the hype is about: text and tags. I don't know about you, but when I first looked at XML, I thought "So that's it?" In fact, I was sort of amazed that no one thought of this sooner. Businesses have been exchanging data electronically since humans first hooked two computers together. Before XML, developers had to format their data-exchange files in a predefined format with exact spacing or delimiting. If you strayed from the agreed upon format, the data would be unintelligible outside of the creating application. Without tags, software cannot tell that one field is a first name and another is a last name. In the past, you could read a file of ASCII data into your application and parse out the data, provided you knew in exactly what order the data was written and in what format the data appears. XML tagging removes these strict formatting rules, because the data describes itself. The individual data elements can come in any order within the text file. These tags simplify business-to-business communications, because each team of developers has to agree only on a single set of commonly understood tags, not an entire format. In fact, as you'll learn later, you don't even have to use the exact same tags as another application to exchange data with it.

Describing Data

My simple phone number XML example shows that tags can describe what the data represents. I like to picture database tables when I look at XML files. A table has a name, such as Customers, and each table contains one or more attributes, such as FirstName, LastName, and PhoneNumber attributes within the Customers table. Each field has a data type assigned to it. A **String** in a SQL Server database would be stored in a **VACHAR2** data field. Data integrity is a very important issue when working with data, and by defining strict types for your data, you prevent incorrect data from being inserted into that field. If the customer's age is stored in a field named Age with an **Integer** or **Number** data type, then inserting a **String** value, such as a phone number with parentheses and dashes in it, would be illegal. The integrity of this data field will be preserved, and you are assured that a value read from the Age field will always be a number.

Field names and data types describe the details of data. Take a few steps back from your data and you will see a different way to describe your data: relationships. The FirstName, LastName, and PhoneNumber fields are all attributes of a bigger entity known as the Customer. Your customers can be related to other entities, such as orders they have placed that are stored in an Orders table. Each customer can place zero or more orders for an item in your inventory. Each order that is placed will reference one or more items from your inventory. Those items could be listed in their own separate Items table. In a relational database, objects such as customers, orders, and items could each be represented by an individual table. Each table would have some fields or attributes to describe it, just like the customer's FirstName or an order's OrderID.

Relationships between data elements can be kind of difficult to describe in one single text file, but XML tagging can preserve these relationships and further describe your data to any consumers of your information. Take a look at the entity relationship diagram in Figure 12.1, which depicts the relationship between one customer who has placed two orders, each containing two items.

How can you describe the data in Figure 12.1 in a top-to-bottom flat-text file? A picture is easy to understand, but a file containing the actual data elements needs a little more work to describe how each element is related to one another. Take a look at the following XML file that would package the data depicted in Figure 12.1:

```
<CustomerOrders>
  <Customers>
    <FirstName>Kim</FirstName>
    <LastName>Gray</LastName>
    <PhoneNumber>(804)555-2311</PhoneNumber>
    <Order>
      <PurchaseID>9998</PurchaseID>
      <Item>
        <ItemID>4932</ItemID >
        <ItemDescription>DVD Player</ItemDescription >
      </Item>
    </Order>
    <Order>
      <PurchaseID>9999</PurchaseID>
      <Item>
        <ItemID>4933</ItemID >
        <ItemDescription>Alarm Clock</ItemDescription >
      </Item>
    </Order>
  </Customers>
</CustomerOrders>
```

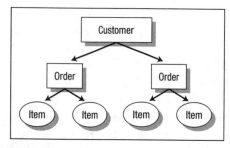

Figure 12.1
The customer-to-orders-to-items relationship diagram.

While not quite as pretty as a picture, the preceding XML data is still easy to understand. CustomerOrders is a major grouping, under which you can include one or more Customers. The tags describe each individual data element, and the placement of the tags helps to describe their relationship. The FirstName tags and their data elements are located inside of the Customers opening and ending tags, which indicates that the FirstName is an attribute of the Customers. The two orders are also within the area enclosed by the Customers tags, indicating that the orders are subordinate to that single customer. Beneath each order you will find a subset of tags describing the Items within that Order. This illustrates how an object with properties can be displayed in XML, and how its relationship to other objects can be described.

The W3C

When reading about XML, you will often see references to the World Wide Web Consortium (W3C). This group is the center of the universe for Web standards, and its board members come from companies all over the industry, representing both software and Internet-related interests. All Web-based technologies, including HTML, XML, and XML schemas, go through W3C for review and approval. Finalizing a standard can take a long time, so you sometimes will encounter early versions of technologies that have been submitted to the W3C but have not yet been formally adopted. For example, when Microsoft was developing the first version of SOAP, it continually submitted its plans to W3C for adoption as an industry standard. It is the W3C, and not any one company, that defines the standards and specifications that all Internet technologies are based on. The technologies that W3C seeks to standardize are open-source and platform-independent technologies. You won't see a W3C standard on any proprietary technologies such as Microsoft's COM.

Over time, technologies will grow and take on new and exciting features. XML is currently only in version 1, even though it is no longer considered a new technology for the Internet. HTML is a widely used markup language that's based on W3C specifications that have been around for over a decade. Every year, a new set of HTML tags is recommended to the consortium for inclusion in the HTML specifications, which is currently at version 4. Some of the recent recommendations to the XML specifications have included adding Namespaces to XML, using XSLT transformations, and the introduction of XML style sheets. Companies such as Microsoft develop these improvements and submit them with the hope of having them recognized as a worldwide standard. You need to be aware of the formal W3C approval process when using a feature that is not formally included in W3C's specification, because you can't be certain that the feature will be approved and widely accepted a year from now. You can read more about W3C's efforts and the current XML specification at **www.w3.org/xml**.

Visual Studio.NET XML Files

You can add individual XML files as code modules within your Visual Studio.NET Project. Select Project | Add New Item. In the pop-up window you will find the XML File module under the Local Project Items | Data folder. When you add an XML File to your project and open that file, you will only see the header line of your empty file, which will look similar to this:

```
<?xml version="1.0" encoding="utf-8" ?>
```

This header declares that you are using XML version 1 and that the characters in this file are encoded in utf-8, which means the characters are stored in the Unicode 8-bit format. By storing your XML data in Unicode format, it not only is self-describing through its tags, but is also internationalized, because nationalities that use different character sets from the ones the file was written in will be able to open and view it in their native format.

The only view you will have of your XML File is a code-like view of the tags and their elements. This manual way of creating an XML message can be very time-consuming, and the resulting message will be static and unchanging when finished. If you plan to add a static message to your project for exchange with other applications, you can add an XML File as a resource for your project to reference at runtime. XML File view has two tabs at the bottom of the viewing window: XML and Data. The XML tab is the default, which shows you the tags and raw data elements just as you would see them if you were editing an XML data file in Notepad. One advantage of entering XML tags into this view is that when you type the ending > character of the opening XML tag, Visual Studio automatically adds the ending version of your tag for you. For instance, if you type **<Customers>**, as soon as you press the > key, the ending **</Customers>** tag is added for you. This helps to ensure that your messages are well formed, with no unterminated tags lying around.

When your XML File has some data elements in it, you can switch over to Data view to navigate through these elements. Data view works a lot like the DataGrid control, displaying your data in rows and columns. After you have the basic elements defined in XML view, you can switch to Data view, in which editing and entering data elements is easier. You can add records in the grid just as you would with a DataGrid, and all the tags will automatically be created for you in XML view. For elements that are related, such as my Customers and Orders example, you can click a plus sign to the right of each row to get a listing of related child elements that you can click to jump to for viewing and editing. The Data view window makes working with XML data a lot like working with a DataSet. The left side of the Data view window lists the DataTables defined in the XML File, while the rest of the view displays the data in whichever table you have selected.

If you are creating an XML File from scratch without first creating an associated schema, you may want to create a schema to describe the format of your message from your XML File to validate future data messages against. This is kind of backward from the way that you should create your messages, which is schema first and then the message. But if you find that you want to create a schema after you have created an XML message, you can do so by right-clicking either XML or Data view and selecting Create Schema. In the Solution Explorer window, you will see an XSD File with the same name as the XML File you were just editing. The original XML File you were editing will have references to the schema you just created. This link between the schema and the message ensures that you are following a special predefined format for your messages. I will cover these schemas in depth in just a bit, and explain why these are so important to use when exchanging XML messages.

Because XML Files are text-based, you can use the Visual Studio.NET Document Outline window to view your XML data. You open this window either by selecting View | Other Windows | Document Outline or by right-clicking the XML view of your XML File and selecting Synchronize With Document Outline. The Document Outline window gives you a tree view of your XML data, with expandable and collapsible items. As you select items within the Document Outline window, their corresponding tags in the actual XML document become highlighted to match. Figure 12.2 shows my simple Customers and Orders XML document with an accompanying Document Outline window.

Schemas

As mentioned earlier, you can conceivably name your XML tags anything you desire. Hopefully, you will use names that help to describe the data, and not some arbitrary labels such as MyValue or Z. If making up your own set of tags is a lot like creating a whole new language, then how can you ensure that others will be able to understand your language and speak it back to you in an understandable way? Schemas are a way to define the language that an XML file uses to tag its data. For the sending application, the schema ensures that you are meeting the tagging guidelines and not creating unapproved tags that could be misunderstood. If two organizations are using the same schema to exchange data, then they can be

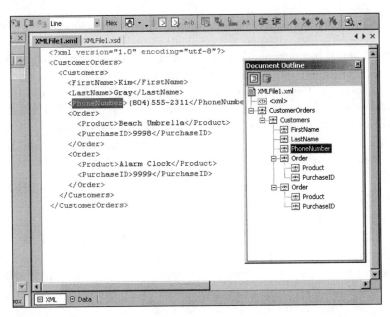

Figure 12.2
An XML file in XML view mode and the Document Outline window.

assured that they are speaking the same language. Schemas are a lot like templates that you use to match your message to a predefined message format.

XML without schemas is a lot like the biblical Tower of Babel: nobody understands what anybody else is saying. For business-to-business communications, agreeing upon a common language is critical. Schemas are such an important piece of data exchange that you will be able to find industry-specific schemas on the Internet already defined and ready to use. Some examples of these area-specific schemas are those that describe chemical, medical, and financial data. If you are developing an application for a company that will communicate with other outside agencies involved in the same major industry, you should find out whether a schema exists that defines the formats your application should adhere to. Often, your application will not fit into any special category and will have its own unique data elements to describe. If you discover that no schema is available that does what you need it to do, you will need to create your own and share it with anyone who wishes to communicate with your software.

XSD Files

XML schemas in .NET are stored in XML Schema Definition (XSD) files. In the Solution Explorer window, these files end in .xsd. These XSD files do not contain the actual data you are exchanging, but instead define the format of the pieces of the message, including the elements, their attributes, and the data types of those attributes. The data types defined in a schema will match the approved specifications put forth by W3C and will not necessarily match the data types you use in the rest of your .NET coding.

Early XML used Document Type Definitions (DTDs) to define the tags that were used within a message. Recently, XSD schemas were submitted to W3C for inclusion in the XML specification, and this recommendation should be approved in the very near future. Schemas and XSD documents are the method of choice now, and DTDs are an outdated way to describe your message's format. Other schema recommendations have been submitted to W3C for approval, such as the Document Contents Description (DCD) and XML Data Reduced (XDR) schema. If you read somewhere about using DTDs or XDRs with your XML, remember that in .NET, XSD is the standard way of defining and describing your XML documents, but other methods are acceptable and will be encountered.

Schema Formats

A schema looks just like an XML file. A schema is a set of tags that defines what tags an XML file can use. You will often find schemas within the actual XML file, but you may also find them in separate files on their own. When the schema and the XML are separated, the XML file will contain a link to the schema file that it is based on, to let the user know where they can find a detailed description of the tags within the XML. Keeping your schemas separated is a really good idea because it promotes code reuse.

Remember that a schema is a template and does not convey actual data to a consumer. It simply defines the tags that the XML files will use to tag their data. Listing 12.1 is an example of an XSD schema file with elements for Customers and their Orders.

Listing 12.1 Customers and Orders schema.

```xml
<?xml version="1.0" encoding="utf-8"?>
<xsd:schema id="XMLSchema1" targetNamespace="http://tempuri.org/XMLSchema1._
 xsd" elementFormDefault="qualified" xmlns="http://tempuri.org/XMLSchema1._
  xsd" xmlns:xsd="http://www.w3.org/2001/XMLSchema">
    <xsd:element name="Customers">
        <xsd:complexType>
            <xsd:sequence>
                <xsd:element name="FirstName" type="xsd:string" />
                <xsd:element name="LastName" type="xsd:string" />
                <xsd:element name="PhoneNumber" type="xsd:string" />
                <xsd:element name="Orders">
                    <xsd:complexType>
                        <xsd:sequence>
                            <xsd:element name="PurchaseID" type="xsd:string" />
                        </xsd:sequence>
                    </xsd:complexType>
                </xsd:element>
            </xsd:sequence>
        </xsd:complexType>
    </xsd:element>
</xsd:schema>
```

All of those tags are required to describe my Customers object and its three attributes and the Orders object with its two attributes. The Customers element is described as a **complexType** because it contains attributes and another object, Orders. The XML messages that you create that are based on a schema must be validated against that schema to be considered valid messages. This prevents messages from being created that contain elements not described in the schema, which would cause problems on the data consumer's end. If your XML message were to reference the preceding schema, you would not be able to add tags to your message that were not first defined in this schema.

Creating Schemas in Visual Studio.NET

Before you create messages in XML format, you should first decide on a schema that your message will adhere to. Hopefully you will have a preexisting schema, either an industry-standard schema or one already developed for use with all the participating data consumers. The downside to creating a new schema from scratch is that it must always be shared with anyone that will be reading your data, and sometimes this schema will have to go through some extra steps to be approved by all interested parties before it is officially adopted for messaging (in other words, office politics will intrude upon your schema design).

Visual Studio.NET allows you to add XSD schemas as modules to your project, and the Integrated Development Environment (IDE) features a wonderful drag-and-drop interface that enables you to easily create a schema and define its elements and their relationships. Try out Exercise 12.1, which walks you through creating your own XSD schema in Visual Studio.NET.

Exercise 12.1: Creating an XSD Schema

1. Create a new WindowsApplication Project and name it XSDTest.

2. In the Solution Explorer window, right-click the Project name, XSDTest, and select Add | Add New Item.

3. Select the XML Schema item and click the Open button.

4. Your Solution Explorer now lists a file named XMLSchema1.xsd in your Project. This file should be open in Design view with a message in the center saying "To start, drag objects from the Server Explorer or the Toolbox". If the schema file is not open in Design view, open it by double-clicking the XMLSchema1.xsd file in your Solution Explorer.

5. From the Toolbox's XSD Schema tab, click and drag an element item to Design view and drop it near the top of the Design area. You should now see a small table in your schema that represents this element.

6. On the top row of the element table, enter the name "Customers" in the left cell. This is the name of your element, just like the name of a table in a database.

7. In the cell to the right of the Customers title is a drop-down list box. Click the down arrow and select Unnamed Complex Type. Because your element will have attributes added to it within this minitable, it is a complex type.

8. In the row directly below the Customers row, enter the attribute "FirstName" in the left cell and set its data type to String in the right cell. Below FirstName, add rows for LastName and PhoneNumber, both of String type.

9. Click the LastName row in your Customers element. Look at the Properties window, and you will see a whole collection of properties associated with this simple **String** type attribute. Changes you make to the properties of your elements will be reflected in the raw XML formatting of your schema, which you will examine in Step 13.

10. Below the PhoneNumber row, add an attribute named Orders and set its data type to Unnamed Complex Type. Click anywhere on the schema surface outside of the Customers minitable and you will see a new minitable added to the schema with the title Orders. A line connects the Orders table to the parent Customers table.

11. Give the Orders table a PurchaseID attribute and a Product attribute. Make both of these String data types.

12. Your XML schema should now look like the one shown in Figure 12.3.

13. At the bottom of the Design window are two tabs labeled Schema and XML. You have been using the Schema graphical design mode to create your schema. Now click the XML tab to see what the actual textual version of your schema looks like. Your Customers schema will look just like the schema in Listing 12.1.

14. Go back to Schema view and change the ReadOnly property for the LastName element in the Properties window to True, and then switch back to XML view to see what changes were made to the raw XML code. At the end of the tag defining LastName will be some extra data defining this element as having ReadOnly set to True.

15. Click the Schema tab to go back to the graphical design mode. Right-click the surface of the schema and select Preview DataSet.

16. The DataSet Preview dialog box opens, giving you a tree view of your schema and its elements. As you select elements in the tree view on the left, that element's properties are displayed on the right side of the dialog box, which will match those properties you examined in Step 9. The DataSet Preview dialog box is for viewing only. To make changes to your schema, you need to close this window and edit the schema itself.

Creating a schema is fairly straightforward, and if you have any experience working with database design tools, then the schema designer should feel natural to you. Database schemas and XML schemas are very similar. Maybe you did not think of the Design views of your databases as schemas, but that's exactly what you are creating when you define the table names, their attributes, and the attributes' associated data types. You are creating the schema that will rule over your database and enforce your data type limitations and table-to-table relationships.

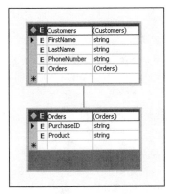

Figure 12.3
The Customers schema in Design view.

Referencing Schemas

When an XML message references a schema, it is declaring that it complies with all the rules and formats set forth in that schema. You can create XML messages with no schema referenced, which gives you the greatest amount of freedom in creating your XML tags. The problem with XML anarchy is that the consumers of your XML data might not understand your tags if your message is not based on a predefined schema. What's worse, if you are not using a schema, your consumers have no guarantee that the next message they receive will be in the same format as the last one they processed. If you use a simple text-editing tool such as Notepad to create your schemas and XML messages, then any schema you reference in the message will not be enforced during the message's creation, because Notepad is just a simple text editor and not a full-blown development tool that understands what all of those tags mean.

Visual Studio.NET can read your schemas and enforce their rules within the XML messages you create. If you are working with an XML File that references an XSD schema, and you try to enter a tag that is not defined in the schema, you will see that familiar squiggly line under your illegal tag, and a message will be added to the Task List letting you know that this tag does not conform with the referenced schema. Prior to Visual Studio.NET, you had to buy a separate XML editing tool to establish this schema-to-message relationship during your editing. Now these features are standard in .NET, and you should not have to buy a third-party development tool to work with XML.

So far, I have focused on schemas that are external to the XML messages I am creating. These schemas need to be stored somewhere the messages can see them, no matter who is reading the message. The Internet is a terrific place for hosting your schemas, because you can reference the schema's location with a URL. Industry-standard schemas have Internet URLs that you can use in your reference tags. If you cannot place your schema on the Internet, you may need to distribute it with your application and with the outgoing messages. A neat and convenient way to include your schemas with your messages is to place them inside the XML files. Here is an example of an XML message with its schema embedded within the message:

```
<?xml version="1.0" encoding="utf-8"?>
<xsd:schema id="XMLSchema1" targetNamespace="http://tempuri.org/XMLSchema1._
 xsd" elementFormDefault="qualified" xmlns="http://tempuri.org/XMLSchema1._
  xsd" xmlns:xsd="http://www.w3.org/2001/XMLSchema">
    <xsd:element name="Customers">
        <xsd:complexType>
            <xsd:sequence>
                <xsd:element name="FirstName" type="xsd:string" />
                <xsd:element name="LastName" type="xsd:string" />
                <xsd:element name="PhoneNumber" type="xsd:string" />
                <xsd:element name="Orders">
                    <xsd:complexType>
```

```
                    <xsd:sequence>
                        <xsd:element name="PurchaseID" type="xsd:string" />
                        <xsd:element name="Product" type="xsd:string" />
                    </xsd:sequence>
                </xsd:complexType>
            </xsd:element>
        </xsd:sequence>
    </xsd:complexType>
</xsd:element>
<Customers>
   <FirstName>Kim</FirstName>
   <LastName>Gray</LastName>
   <PhoneNumber>(804)555-2311</PhoneNumber>
   <Order>
      <Product>Beach Umbrella</Product>
      <PurchaseID>9998</PurchaseID>
   </Order>
   <Order>
      <Product>Alarm Clock</Product>
      <PurchaseID>9999</PurchaseID>
   </Order>
</Customers>
</xsd:schema>
```

Including a schema within your XML message enhances the description the message gives to its readers. Not only do the tags in the message describe the data elements they surround, but the schema included along with the message informs the consumer that you are following a set schema, and any further messages from this source should adhere to the very same schema. Therefore, a good practice is to not change the schema or the format of your messages after they have been made public. If an application is written to read your messages based on a schema you have published, then that application will surely break if you rearrange, remove, or add new elements to the schema for that same message type. Nobody likes to have the rules changed on them in the middle of the game, and for XML messaging, the schemas are the rulebooks that you pledge to follow when formatting your messages.

Exercise 12.2 walks you through referencing an external XSD schema from an XML File added to your project. This exercise also shows you how the schema reference enforces and limits the tags you can use while working in your XML File.

Exercise 12.2: Referencing an XSD Schema

1. Continuing with the XSDTest Project created in Exercise 12.1, right-click the Project's name in the Solution Explorer and select Add | Add New Item.

2. Select the XML File to add to your Project, and click the Open button.

3. The XML File is added to your Solution Explorer window and opens in Design view. You will only see a header tag in your new XML message. If your Task List window is not currently showing, load this window so that you can see its messages.

4. Click anywhere on the surface of your XML message so that the cursor is blinking somewhere in your message. In the Properties window, you will see a target Schema property. Click the down arrow by this property and select the XMLSchema1.xsd file you created in Exercise 12.1. The path to this schema will match the path shown in the schema's **targetNamespace** parameter of the **xsd:schema** tag (line 2 of the schema in Listing 12.1).

5. Your XML File now has a tag referencing the schema that should look like this:

```
<Customers xmlns="http://tempuri.org/XMLSchema1.xsd">
```

6. Note that an opening and ending set of Customers tags has already been added for you. Type "<" between these two Customers tags, and you will see a drop-down list of the available subtags defined for Customers in the schema.

7. Instead of picking one of the schema-defined tags, enter this tag:

```
<MyBadTag>
```

8. Visual Studio.NET will know that this tag does not conform to the schema your message is referencing, and instead of adding a matching end tag, it will place a squiggly line under this illegal tag and add a message to the Task List window letting you know that the schema does not support the MyBadTag element.

Exchanging Schemas

For two organizations to understand the data that they are exchanging, both need to be using the same XML schema. If both companies are using an industry-standard XML schema, then they shouldn't need to exchange schemas, provided that everyone follows the standards precisely. If the schema has any variations, or one of the participating data consumers is using a unique schema, then this information needs to be shared with everybody else who uses the data. Those consumers would use this schema as a translation mapping to figure out data messages and convert them to a format that they understand. One way to convert one XML format to another is with Extensible Stylesheet Language Transformation (XSLT) documents. You will also encounter references to XSL (XML Stylesheet Language), and for the sake of my discussion, XSL is the same as XSLT. You will learn more about transformations in the next section.

A simpler way to translate schemas and XML messages is to use a server-based product such as Microsoft's BizTalk Server, which is an integral part of the Microsoft DNA server lineup discussed in Chapter 1. BizTalk Server stores all messaging schemas used by both your company and the companies you communicate with so that it can understand and communicate with any outside agency you exchange data with. BizTalk Server will handle the complicated tasks of formatting your outgoing data in a format that external users will understand, and then reformatting data received from outside agencies into a schema that internal applications are familiar with.

It's doubtful that every company and every development team in the world will one day soon all agree upon a standard set of schemas with which to format their data. Even within a single business type, such as financial institutions, the lingo and the labels given to data elements vary greatly from company to company. The world itself may be slowly moving toward a universal currency, but there will always be a language barrier to overcome when communicating with people of a different nationality. Schema transformations, and assisting server-side utilities such as BizTalk, can help to overcome these limitations and easily enable business-to-business data exchanges.

XML in DataSets

You read in Chapter 8 that XML is an integral part of the new ADO.NET. The DataSets you create and fill with data will be using XML behind the scenes to move your data. This is a big change from past versions of ADO, which were not XML-based, although the last few versions of ADO did allow you to output your data to an XML file through a conversion method. When you are working with DataSets, you usually will think in terms of DataTables and DataRows, but if you need to pass along the values of your DataSet in XML format, you can do so easily. Let's take a look at the role that XML plays when working with DataSets.

Examining XML and Schemas in DataSets

The DataSet has **GetXml** and **GetSchema** methods that gives you access to your DataSet's data in XML format and the schema that the DataSet has generated to define the data within. To see how you can examine this data, follow Exercise 12.3 to create a DataSet manually in code and then write its XML data and its associated schema to a textbox control on a Windows form.

Exercise 12.3: Examining XML in a DataSet

1. Create a new WindowsApplication Project and name it XMLDataSet.

2. Add two button controls to the very bottom of your Windows form, one to the left and the other to the right. Place a textbox control above these button controls and set its Multiline property to True. Expand the textbox to fill most of the form, because this is where you will be examining the XML and schema outputs. Set the textbox control's ScrollBars property to Both to make viewing this box easier.

3. Set **Button1**'s Text property to XML and set **Button2**'s Text property to Schema.

4. Right-click the Windows form and add the following code to the form's general declarations area right below the Public Class Form1 line:

```
Private CustomTable As DataTable
Private MyNewRow As DataRow
Private myDS As DataSet = New DataSet()
```

5. Add the following code to the form's **New** event:

```
CustomTable = New DataTable("Rooms")
CustomTable.Columns.Add("RoomID", System.Type.GetType("System.Int32"))
CustomTable.Columns.Add("RoomNum", System.Type.GetType("System.Int32"))
CustomTable.Columns.Add("Status", System.Type.GetType("System.String"))
CustomTable.Columns.Add("NumBeds", System.Type.GetType("System.Int32"))
MyNewRow = CustomTable.NewRow
MyNewRow("RoomID") = 1
MyNewRow("RoomNum") = 101
MyNewRow("Status") = "Available"
MyNewRow("NumBeds") = 2
CustomTable.Rows.Add(MyNewRow)
myDS.Tables.Add(CustomTable)
```

6. Add the following code to **Button1**'s **Click** event:

```
TextBox1.Text = myDS.GetXml
```

7. Add the following code to **Button2**'s **Click** event:

```
TextBox1.Text = myDS.GetXmlSchema
```

8. Save your Project and then press F5 to run it. Click the XML button, and you will see
the XML version of the DataSet's data displayed in the textbox. Click the Schema
button to see the schema that the DataSet created on-the-fly when the data was loaded
into it.

Exercise 12.3 shows how easy it is to access the data within a DataSet in XML format, as
well as the schema defining that data. You can use the **GetXml** method to serialize your
DataSet's data into XML format and then pass it to another procedure. When your DataSet
is loaded with data, either manually as in Exercise 12.3 or by being loaded from an
OleDbDataAdapter, it creates a schema automatically based on the data it has received.
You saw the DataSet's schema when you clicked **Button2** on the XMLDataSet form. This
schema has a great deal of detail in it even though you never once told the DataSet how it
should set up this schema, because DataSets understand XML and can figure out the schema
on their own.

Loading DataSets with XML

In addition to pulling XML out of a DataSet (as you just learned how to do), you can just as easily load a file full of XML into a DataSet. A DataSet has **ReadXml** and **ReadXmlSchema** methods that makes this chore a snap to accomplish. Simply point the DataSet to the schema and a file full of XML, and you are set. These XML message and XSD schema files could be a part of your project, or they could be simple text files sitting on the hard drive that you can pull into your DataSet. If you load an empty DataSet using its **ReadXml** method without specifying a schema, then the DataSet will automatically create a schema based on the data it reads in. The following line of code shows how simple it is to pull in a file full of XML and populate a DataSet with it:

```
myDS.ReadXml("c:\DataStorage\MyXmlData.xml")
```

That is all it takes to fill up a DataSet with some data stored in XML format. If you also had a schema file that you wanted to load into your DataSet, you could load that before you load the XML by using the DataSet's **ReadXmlSchema** method in the exact same way you use the **ReadXml** method. After you have a DataSet full of XML, it will act just like any other DataSet. You can add more tables to the DataSet, or perhaps load some more XML files into it.

Defining DataSet Schemas

DataSets can be made to follow XML schemas just as XML files can be. Instead of loading some data into your DataSet and letting it create its own schema dynamically based on the data itself, you can first specify a data schema for the DataSet to use, and then load the data. You will use the DataSet's **ReadXmlSchema** method to load in a schema, which could be stored in a file on your hard drive or within an XSD file within your project. Here is an example of how you would load a schema in an XSD file into your DataSet:

```
myDS.ReadXmlSchema("c:\DataStorage\MySchema.xsd")
```

You can add a schema to your DataSets to enforce formatting rules. If you are not sure that a file you are about to read into your DataSet using the **ReadXml** method is in the proper format, you can first add the correct schema to the DataSet and then try to load the XML file. If you are creating a DataSet manually by adding tables and rows in your code, it is helpful to have a schema defined for that DataSet to ensure that the DataSet you create will adhere to an agreed-upon format that will be exchangeable with other applications.

Working with XML

You can read and write XML without adding special files to your project or creating a DataSet to hold the data. Just as you can read and write to a text file on your hard drive, you can work with XML in a similar fashion within your code. You have a few choices to make when deciding how you are going to read and write your XML messages from within your code. The big choice you will face is which XML access model you should use to work with your data. This section covers all the popular XML models, along with their strengths and weaknesses.

DOM

The Document Object Model (DOM) is how applications created outside of Visual Studio.NET typically will read in a file of XML and navigate through its contents. If you wrote a Java program that received XML messages, you would probably use a DOM to read and manipulate the XML data. .NET has its own navigation engine to work with XML, which you will soon learn about in the "XMLReader" section.

One of the significant differences between DOM and .NET's engines has to do with how efficiently they work with data. To work with an XML document, the DOM engine must load the entire document into memory. If you are working with an extremely large file of XML data, this can really suck up a lot of your free memory. .NET's XML engine does not need to put the entire document into memory, only the portions it is currently working on. You are not restricted to using only the .NET set of XML tools; you can still work with DOM by using the .NET DOMDocument Class, which supports all the standard DOM actions and adds a few new features to DOM, including support for XSL and XSLT. Working with DOM is useful when you need to jump around a file of XML to look for particular items and change their values.

SAX

Simple API for XML (SAX) is used by some developers as a replacement for DOM. The advantage that SAX provides over DOM is that it can handle larger files of XML data more efficiently. SAX also has the ability to cease reading a document when it finds what it is looking for, instead of continuing through the document until the end is encountered. The latest version of SAX, version 2, provides Visual Basic developers with some interfaces for developing with SAX, but application support for SAX is not as widespread as support for DOM is. SAX's main specialty is reading XML data. If you want to create XML messages, you should choose to use the DOM model and not SAX. When you hear the term *SAX*, remember that this is an alternative to DOM that can provide developers with better efficiency when reading large files of XML data.

XMLReader

For reading the contents of an XML message, .NET provides the XMLReader Class, which acts just like the forward-only "fire hose" cursor that you used in past versions of ADO to read data from a database. XMLReader provides a one-way, straight-through method to read through some XML data that avoids saving all the data read to a cache. When you use the XMLReader in your code, you really are using one of its three implemented versions:

♦ *XMLTextReader*—This is the fastest method, because it does not make any effort to validate and check the data that it is reading in. If you are not concerned about the data being well formed, and simply want to read it in as fast as possible, this version is the best choice.

♦ *XMLValidatingReader*—If you do need to work with well-formed XML, this version can check your data against a schema as it is read in, and verify that the data matches the format you are expecting.

♦ *XMLNodeReader*—This version also reads the data in one forward-only pass, but the data will be made accessible through XML nodes. As you look at a raw XML document, you can see how each element within that document can be represented as a node, just like the nodes in a tree-view control. Parent nodes and child nodes are represented within the data. Each node can have properties, such as a type or a value, and each node can be related to other nodes above and below it. By reading your data in as XML nodes, you can explore these values and access their node properties to better manipulate the XML data.

XMLWriter

When you want to create a stream of XML, whether you are passing the XML to another piece of code or simply writing your XML to a file on the hard drive, you use .NET's XMLWriter Class. In your code, the XMLWriter Class is implemented by the XMLTextWriter. You use the XMLTextWriter Class to create your XML messages manually in your code. You do not need to work with the XMLTextWriter if you are using DataSets to form and create your XML messages. You use it only if you wish to manually read and write your XML.

The XMLWriter works in the same forward-only fashion as its XMLReader counterpart. This means you can create a new XML document and write it out from top to bottom, but you cannot jump around within that document and change the values of elements contained within the XML. The XMLWriter contains a collection of **Write** methods that will write specific types of lines and tags to your XML message. It also contains a **WriteComment** method that writes your text string to the XML file, surrounding it with comment tags to indicate that this is not actual data within the message. The very first line of the XML document, which declares what version of XML is being used, can be written using the **WriteStartDocument** method. At the end of your message, you use the **WriteEndDocument** method to place the ending tag for your XML.

The data within an XML message is strongly typed based on the element's definition in the schema, which declares what type of data this element contains. When you are writing XML from your code, you will need to do a conversion of your code-based data types to XML data types by using the XMLConvert Class. Remember that XML messages have their own collection of data types that do not directly match up with the .NET data types, so when you want to write a variable of the **Double** data type to an XML message, you need to use XMLConvert to place it in the right format. The XMLConvert Class can also be used to convert data read in from an XML message to a selected .NET data type for use within your code. Again, because .NET is strongly typed, you need to convert the foreign XML data types to .NET data types before using their values in computations and expressions.

XPath

Short for *XML Path Language*, XPath enables you to write code that talks to a specific piece of an XML message. XML data often represents a hierarchy of information, such as a customer who places some orders, with each order containing one or more items. That information has a path through it that looks like this:

```
Customers/Orders/Items
```

The preceding is an example of both an XPath path and a simple XPath query that is looking for Items listed within the XML message. You can use XPath to formulate queries against a file of XML data. Think of XPath as a SQL query language for searching through XML messages, except that the syntax for XPath is a whole lot simpler to work with than a query language such as T-SQL. For example, here is an XPath query to locate all Customers in the XML message whose **FirstName** attribute is equal to Steve:

```
Customers[FirstName = "Steve"]
```

If you do not want to work with the entire file of XML data, you can use XPath queries to pull out only the information you need from the XML message, just as you would run a query against a table in a database that returns only the rows that match your search.

Which Model to Use

Now that you are familiar with the popular XML access models, which one is right for the job you need to do? No one correct answer applies in every single instance. The choice really depends on what job you need to do, the size of the documents you are working with, and what type of access you need to those documents. You can use Table 12.1 to help you figure out which model will work best in a specific situation.

Table 12.1   Which XML model to use.

Situation	Model to Use
Fast, forward-only reading with no validation	XMLTextReader
Fast, forward-only reading with schema validation	XMLValidatingReader
Fast, forward-only reading with access to node information	XMLNodeReader
Fast, forward-only writing	XMLTextWriter
Reading and writing, jumping around documents	DOM
Reading in extra large files of XML	SAX
Querying an XML message for a subset of data	XPath

Transformations

XML messages adhere to a strict format, and the choice of which format is up to the message's creator. Hopefully, the message format used adheres to a higher power, such as an industry-standard schema or an agreed-upon set of tags. In all but a few circumstances, the messages you receive will probably not be in the exact format you prefer to use. Remember that old party game called "telephone," in which someone whispers a message to another person, who then whispers it to somebody else, and on and on until the message finally gets to the end of the line and typically sounds nothing like the original message? This distortion of the message happens because everyone interprets data differently, and it's human nature to put your own spin on things instead of mechanically repeating a message like a computer. A *transformation* occurs when the receiver of a message changes that message's format to match a format the receiver is more comfortable with. In this section, I will explore some of the reasons you would want to transform a message from one format to another.

Transformation Uses

You may want to interpret or format a message in a way that is different from the way the originator of the message formatted it. The message you receive may have gone through many different interpretations, similar to the telephone game, and may not resemble the original message that was created. Because the chances of getting everyone in this world to conform to one set of formatting standards is near zero, the answer to this problem is transformations. The XML messages that you receive will be self-describing, so you can create a transformation process that takes a message and reshapes it into something you are happier with. XSLT is the technology with which you can create these transformations, and Visual Studio.NET offers tools that can help you set up these transformations.

Transformations have many other uses besides formatting a message in a way that is more acceptable to your application. You do not have to transform an XML message into another XML message. You can transform XML data into other formats such as HTML. Picture a process that outputs a set of data in an XML message. Another process may have the responsibility of sending the application's user an HTML Web page that displays some requested data elements. This process can use transformations to take the XML results of another process and wrap the data elements in HTML, adding layout and graphics tags to make the data browser-friendly. The ability to separate the data from the display code is a terrific idea, because so many types of browsing platforms are on the market. Which makes more sense: write two applications, one to support PC-based Web browsers and the other to support WAP (Wireless Application Protocol) Web-phone browsers, or write one application that transforms the resulting data into either HTML or WAP, based on the detected browser? Call me lazy, but I prefer to write just one application that can utilize the same logic and data elements behind the scenes and dynamically adjust its output before sending the results to the user.

With XSLT, you can also transform messages into other text formats, such as flat-text ASCII files or Adobe PDF format. All of these formats (HTML, WAP, and PDF) are just wrappers around a central set of data. The data will be the same no matter in which format you prefer to look at the data. You don't need to write a special application to produce a specific output; you only need to wrap your data in the appropriate format by using XSLT transformations.

XSLT transformations can also be used as data filters to provide different views of the same data source. If a user does not wish to see all the columns of information in a DataSet, you can use the transformation process to filter and hide data elements at will.

How XSLT Works

Transformations are very simple processes. You start with an XML message in one format, run it through the transformation process, which is controlled by an XSLT file, and end up with a new XML message formatted the way you like it, such as an HTML Web page that displays the data contained in the original XML message. Using XSLT files is often referred to as a *template-driven process*, because you are trying to match a message with your XSLT template to convert it to a new format. Your template may have been based on conversion rules such as "Any tag company A calls FirstName, company B wants it to say CustomerFirst". During the conversion process, the FirstName tags would be converted to CustomerFirst tags to satisfy this requirement. Figure 12.4 illustrates the transformation process from a source XML message to a resulting XML message.

SOAP

XML is now the preferred way of formatting the messages and data you exchange within Visual Studio.NET. SOAP compliments XML as a means to exchange XML messages with remote users via the Hypertext Transfer Protocol (HTTP), the most commonly used transmission protocol on the Internet. The beauty of HTTP is that everyone can use it, not just those users on operating system X or applications that were written using component technology Z. Previously, if you wrote a COM component, your component could only communicate with other COM components, either through remote procedure calls (RPCs) or DCOM. Neither RPC nor DCOM worked if you wanted to call a CORBA object created in Java, and the CORBA object would be equally unable to call your COM object.

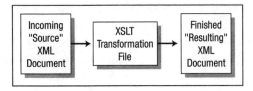

Figure 12.4
The transformation process.

SOAP enables *code remoting,* which simply means you can make procedural calls to modules of code at a remote location. Remoting is a very big concept in .NET, and you will use remoting when you communicate with Web Services or when one .NET Assembly calls another. You can even use SOAP to remotely talk to a COM component. Remoting pretty much takes over for the concept of DCOM, which enabled you to place your old COM components on different servers and communicate between them. With SOAP, you can do far more than communicate between COM objects, and the distance by which they can be separated is limited only by the reach of the Internet.

SOAP Overview

The Simple Object Access Protocol (SOAP) is based on open standards and can be used by developers on any platform using any development environment. SOAP is used to make RPCs across the Internet by using HTTP, which was originally intended to be used for the easy exchange of Web pages over the Internet. Any system that could access the Internet could send and receive HTTP packets. When you use a Web browser to surf the Internet, your Web page requests are sent out via HTTP and the returning Web pages come back to your browser via that same HTTP path. Exchanging simple text-based Web pages is not very glamorous, and may even seem a little too simplified for application use, but that's the beauty of SOAP. The messages that are sent across HTTP using SOAP are just simple text-based packets, and do not require any special vendor-specific protocols to be sent or received. SOAP is often labeled as a lightweight protocol because it is so simple and piggybacks its messages on another protocol, HTTP.

SOAP was created in 1998, only a few years after the birth of XML. Developers knew that XML was a revolutionary way to format their communications, and could very easily be harnessed to facilitate RPCs, thereby tearing down a few walls between the different vendor-specific development environments. SOAP was primarily a Microsoft invention, and it held on to this invention for a few extra years before going public with it (it's now Spring 2001, and the SOAP Toolkit 1 has just been released). Alternatives to SOAP developed by other groups have been proposed, such as a protocol called XML-RPC.

I have already overviewed the topic of SOAP in the discussions regarding Web Services. In my examples, I showed how simple requests are sent across the Internet via SOAP to waiting Web Services, which accept these requests just as your COM object accepts requests from other objects. The results from the Web Services were then sent back across the Internet using SOAP, and the calling application received these results in the form of an XML message. This chapter has gone into depth on how XML messages are formatted, and although reading and writing XML may sound time-consuming, when you use Visual Studio.NET to set up references to your Web Services, all the message formatting and unformatting is automatically handled by the code, making the entire XML and SOAP portion of your component calls invisible to you.

The SOAP Envelope

The XML message that you wish to send across the Internet is always at the heart of the SOAP message. To aide in the transport of your XML message, SOAP creates a virtual envelope around the XML. A SOAP message looks a lot like a hand-written letter. The SOAP message contains an outer envelope that wraps everything up for transmission. Inside the envelope are a header and a body section. The header contains the addressing information, just as a letter's header says who the message is from. The body tags of the SOAP message wrap around the XML message that you are sending. Here is an example of a SOAP envelope enclosing a header and a body with some XML:

```
<SOAP-ENV:Envelope xmlns:SOAP-ENV="http://schemas._
 xmlsoap.org/soap/envelope/" SOAP-ENV:encodingStyle="http://schemas._
 xmlsoap.org/soap/encoding/"/>
  <SOAP:Header>
    <v:From SOAP:mustUnderstand='1'>developer@exploringvb.net</v:From>
  </SOAP:Header>
  <SOAP:Body>
    <CustomerOrders>
      <Customers>
        <FirstName>Kim</FirstName>
        <LastName>Gray</LastName>
        <PhoneNumber>(804)555-2311</PhoneNumber>
      </Customers>
    </CustomerOrders>
  </SOAP:Body>
</SOAP:Envelope>
```

In this example SOAP envelope, you can see the envelope at the top, which encloses both a Header section and a Body section. The envelope contains reference links to Web sites that define exactly what the standard SOAP format and encoding styles are. The Header section stops and then the Body section begins, so the body is not embedded within the header. The XML message in the preceding example is just a small chunk of my earlier Customers example describing one of my customers. The **mustUnderstand** parameter in the Header section sets the importance of this message. With **mustUnderstand** set to 1, the receiver must respond to this response, either with the expected response or with an error. If the **mustUnderstand** parameter is set to 0, then the message is more informational and the sender will not get hung up if they receive neither a response nor an error.

HTTP is also an overly simplified protocol that communicates with simple requests and responses. You use HTTP when you request a Web page to browse, and the Web server responds with an HTML Web page. Requests are packaged using either a **Get** or a **Post** method when transporting across HTTP. When the SOAP message is sent out through HTTP, the SOAP envelope is wrapped in a **Post** message, which adds above the

SOAP message a header that describes the contents as being in XML format (**text/xml** in Post-speak), and includes other needed information, such as the IP address of the machine making the request and the size of the message. Here is my SOAP message wrapped in a **Post** request:

```
POST /Customers HTTP/1.1
User-Agent: Windows2000
Host: 255.255.255.255
Content-Type: text/xml; charset=utf-8
Content-length: 999
SOAPAction: "/Customers"

<?xml version="1.0"?>
<SOAP-ENV:Envelope xmlns:SOAP-ENV="http://schemas._
 xmlsoap.org/soap/envelope/" SOAP-ENV:encodingStyle="http://schemas._
 xmlsoap.org/soap/encoding/"/>
  <SOAP:Header>
    <v:From SOAP:mustUnderstand='1'>developer@exploringvb.net</v:From>
  </SOAP:Header>
  <SOAP:Body>
    <CustomerOrders>
      <Customers>
        <FirstName>Kim</FirstName>
        <LastName>Gray</LastName>
        <PhoneNumber>(804)555-2311</PhoneNumber>
      </Customers>
    </CustomerOrders>
  </SOAP:Body>
</SOAP:Envelope>
```

Notice that my SOAP message is unchanged, but more lines are now at the top of my message. The HTTP protocol is named here, my IP address is recorded in the Host line, and the length of the message is noted so that the receiver will know they got the whole thing. An XML tag was added above my SOAP envelope tag to tell HTTP that the content of this message is in XML format.

Figure 12.5 walks through the creation of a SOAP message step by step from the authoring component all the way to the message leaving the machine via HTTP. The great thing about using SOAP in Visual Studio.NET is that all of this wrapping and describing is done for you. You should never have to look at a SOAP envelope or create a **Post** request because .NET handles all the logistics for you. If you are working with SOAP outside of the Visual Studio.NET environment, you use Microsoft's SOAP Toolkit (currently in version 2) to simplify your work and handle the packaging and unpackaging of your SOAP messages.

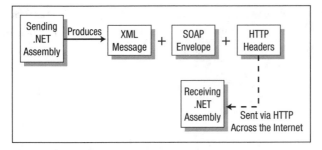

Figure 12.5
SOAP message creation walk-through.

DCOM vs. SOAP

COM lets your objects talk to other COM objects, enabling you to place your code in separate containers. But you are still limited to placing your COM objects on a single computer. DCOM takes COM one step further and enables you to distribute your objects among many different computers and make calls between them. DCOM truly made distributed programming and scalable applications possible for the COM development community. So why should you drop DCOM and take up SOAP as your primary means of communicating between your code Assemblies?

For starters, DCOM has many limitations, not the least of which is that it is a Microsoft technology and does not facilitate communications to and from objects created with non-Microsoft development tools and languages. For years, this was acceptable, and everyone knew you were either a Microsoft developer or one of those other people, and rarely did the two groups ever cross paths. As stated several times, SOAP is based on open-source platform-independent concepts and can be used to talk to and receive requests from anyone, anywhere. The requester does not even need to be running Windows or have a local copy of the .NET runtime compiler to make a request of your objects through SOAP.

The reach of the SOAP protocol far exceeds that of DCOM, which does not use HTTP to transport its requests. When a company places a firewall at the entry to its company server, it effectively blocks all protocols and communication ports that are not absolutely necessary to do business. Often, this leaves every means of communicating with the server shut off, except for HTTP, which allows outsiders to access the company's Web site. DCOM usually finds itself shut out when a firewall is in its path. But SOAP, which uses the widely accepted HTTP to move its messages across the Internet, has no trouble getting through those firewalls to communicate with remote bits of code.

I personally find DCOM somewhat difficult to use and to configure properly. A fair bit of administrative overhead is involved in setting up a DCOM link between two objects. After your objects are communicating via DCOM, an awful lot of back and forth communication goes on, making DCOM a very tightly coupled form of remoting. Using SOAP to communicate between objects is often referred to as *loose-coupling* because, instead of a constant back-and-forth flow of data, a request is sent to the target object, and then one complete response is returned to the requester.

Developers who have used DCOM know that you make a performance sacrifice when making DCOM calls. Obviously, communicating with an object on a separate machine takes longer than communicating with an object on the same machine. Much of this slowdown is caused by the network connections between separate machines. A call across a network cannot be as fast as a procedural call that does not need to use the network. Using SOAP also has a price, because all the calls that you make through HTTP use the network. I'm sure you have heard plenty of talk about Internet bottlenecks and Web slowdowns, and when you send your SOAP messages out into the world, they travel down the same crowded highways as everyone else's Web page requests. When planning your remoting strategy, you need to keep in mind the performance cost of using SOAP and HTTP to connect your objects, and plan for those slowdowns if the requesting and the providing objects have a great distance separating them.

Summary

XML seems a little daunting at first, but after you figure out how all the pieces fit together that make XML work, using it is quite simple. If you are not using XML yet, now is the time to start, because this is the messaging format of choice for the new millennium. I know that working with XML can sometimes be a bit confusing because of all the acronyms that begin with X. After you get all these terms straight in your head, working with XML is extremely straightforward. To help you out, Table 12.2 summarizes all the terms and acronyms that you have read about in this chapter.

Table 12.2   XML and SOAP terms.

Abbreviation	Full Name	Description
DTD	Document Type Definition	An older schema definition format
DOM	Document Object Model	A model for reading and writing XML
HTTP	Hypertext Transfer Protocol	A transmission protocol that moves data across the Internet
	Remoting	Making calls to remote procedures
SAX	Simple API for XML	An efficient model for reading in large files of XML
SOAP	Simple Object Access Protocol	A way to communicate with objects via HTTP
W3C	World Wide Web Consortium	The governing body for Internet technologies
XDR	XML Data Reduced schema	Another document schema definition language
XML	Extensible Markup Language	Using markup tags to identify data in a message

(continued)

Table 12.2   XML and SOAP terms *(continued)*.

Abbreviation	Full Name	Description
XPath	XML Path Language	A query language for searching through XML messages
XSD	XML Schema Definition	The .NET standard for defining document formats
XSL	XML Stylesheet Language	The XML transformation language
XSLT	XML Stylesheet Language Transformations	Files to aid converting one XML file to another format

Chapter 13

Security in .NET

The topic of security is a broad one, one that encompasses many aspects of application development. What's the first thing that comes to mind when you think of security? If you ask five different people, you could easily get five different answers. Someone with a systems administration background, like myself, may first think of crackers (malicious hackers) and viruses that threaten the security of servers everywhere. From an administrative standpoint, security also covers areas such as users and system accounts, which determine what a user can see and do within the system. With the growing popularity of the Web and e-commerce, users are becoming increasingly aware of the vulnerabilities of the information they share with companies on the Web. Even the way in which you transport your information back and forth across the Internet and your networks falls under the domain of security.

For me, the subject of security expands well beyond computers and information technologies. While in the United States Air Force, I worked as both an intercontinental ballistic missile (ICBM) maintenance technician and an electronics intelligence (ELINT) specialist, and constantly had the perils and pitfalls of lax security practices drilled into my head. When I hear the word *security*, little alarms go off in my head and I flash back to those boring hour-long low-budget videos I was required to watch every three months to remind me to be constantly vigilant. Part of getting security right is being aware of all the issues that security encompasses, and sometimes you need to be reminded of issues you once heard about but may have forgotten. In the first section of this chapter, I will go over the many areas of security as they apply to software development. Following my review of security, I will address how these different security issues come into play in .NET and how you can program these security features into your applications.

Before you hastily decide to skip over this chapter, stop and think about why security is a subject worthy of a chapter all its own. Modern-day software applications deal with a wide assortment of data, all of which is valuable to somebody. An institution's financial records would certainly be considered sensitive and worth protecting to that company. On the flip side, if you are a company in competition with another company, having an unauthorized copy of that company's financial data could give you a pretty hefty edge in the worldwide market. Maybe industrial espionage is not a widespread, everyday problem, but without a doubt, it does happen. Even closer to home, the personal data you share across the Web every day is at risk of being intercepted or stolen by crackers. When personal information such as social security numbers and credit card information is at risk, do you think consumers believe security is not an important issue? Sure, learning about computer security issues may not be as exciting as, say, nuclear missiles and stealth fighter technology, but you better believe that computer security is a major issue for software projects today. Avoiding or minimizing your efforts to make your applications secure can have disastrous results for both your clients and your reputation. So remember (holding up a poster of a pointing Uncle Sam), only you can prevent security incidents!

Security Basics

You cannot properly define the subject of computer security in one sentence. Too many areas exist within the realm of security to sum it up so easily. For a developer, security comes into play within your applications in many different ways. For example, you might need to allow certain users a special privilege to maintain user accounts, while restricting other users from accessing a certain file. Before you can restrict or grant access to something, you must first be able to authenticate and identify your users in a foolproof way. You may need to encrypt your application's messages to prevent them from being read by unauthorized parties.

This section covers all the important issues that a software developer must be aware of when working on an application. Many computer security issues exist beyond the scope of software development, such as the physical security and protection of servers or using locking screen savers to protect your workstation while you are on your coffee breaks, but these issues are not of a direct concern to the applications developer, and I will not spend any time covering these issues here. If you see a section header that you feel confident you are familiar with, then you can probably skip ahead to the next section. But if you have the slightest doubt about whether you know enough about a security subject to explain it to someone else, then I urge you to read that section to clarify your understanding, for later discussions within this chapter.

Security Checkpoints

Access to computer resources can be controlled and monitored by a system or an application in many different ways. For companies using a secure operating system such as Windows NT, users are required to have a password-protected account before they will be allowed to log in to the system. These accounts typically are maintained at a central location, such as a server acting as a domain controller for the network, and they provide access control to the entire system or domain. It is possible to log in to a computer with an account locally maintained by that one computer, but if the other computers on the network do not know about this account, then access to network resources will be limited or completely denied. A local account can provide machine-level access control, but these accounts typically will not be recognized beyond the machine they were created on and are unsuitable for enterprise-wide applications.

After a user has an identity within the system, that account can be used to grant or deny access to resources on the system. Restrictions can be placed at many different levels within the system, such as file and directory permissions. Databases such as SQL Server can also use system accounts to decide who can and cannot see certain types of information, such as tables and views within the database. Code can also be protected by access controls, thus preventing unauthorized users from executing methods or accessing properties contained in an Assembly. User accounts enable you to define access permissions at a very detailed level, meaning one user at a time. By creating groups of users, you can define access permissions at a higher level and greatly simplify the administration chores for a given system. User accounts and groups are covered a bit later in the chapter.

Authentication

To enforce security controls on the users of your applications, you must first be able to correctly identify your users. Typically, this is done with a login and password Dialog window, just like the one you see when you are logging on to a Windows NT machine. If you are developing an application for a Windows NT or Windows 2000 machine, you can take advantage of the user's Windows login identity, which they have to enter when they log on to the machine. Integrating your application's user accounts with those of the operating system can save you a lot of development time, and it will make your customers happier because they won't have to remember yet another login name and password for your software (heaven knows everyone has enough passwords to remember already). Later in this chapter when I discuss implementing security in your code, you will see how you can use the already present Windows NT user accounts and groups to provide the security for your application.

Understanding how Windows security works and how you can create user accounts and assign them permissions and privileges can really pay off when you are designing and coding your applications to be secure. Learning about Windows security can give you a glimpse into the world of the system administrator, an unenviable role in which I have spent some time. If you have not had the pleasure of configuring Windows servers or adding user accounts, try to corner your company's systems administrator to gain some insight and experience in working with the administrative tools. Reading about these accounts and their settings is one thing, but actually creating these accounts and manipulating their security permissions will give you a clear understanding regarding how Windows NT implements security and how you can take advantage of NT's built-in security features within your own applications.

Windows Users

The Windows NT OS has a security system built into it that requires all users of the system to log in and provide a password. System administrators create user accounts and groups to identify and organize the system's users. A group is simply a logical collection of users, such as the accounting department or an Administrators group. The user accounts typically relate directly to a single person, such as a user account for Frank Miller with a username of "fmiller". A user account can also define special users such as the anonymous Internet user account, which gives unauthenticated users of your Web site limited access to system resources. On a secure system, everyone must have an identity before they are allowed to see and do anything.

By letting Windows NT handle the complicated chores of authenticating your users, you avoid all the work required to develop your own secure authentication system and the overhead associated with creating and tracking a list of users and their metadata. It could take weeks or even months to create your own login functions, complete with encrypted password transmission and the ability to track a user as they move through your application. After you have created your own customized user accounts, you will need to administer these separately from the Windows accounts, thereby increasing the administration and maintenance requirements for your application. Your application won't win any fans by requiring users to remember one more password needed to access your application.

Windows authenticates users by using Windows NT Challenge/Response. The operating system will handle the tasks of popping up an authentication window, accepting the user's entry, encrypting and decrypting the user's credentials, and finally matching that user with an account in the system. Windows NT can authenticate users against accounts stored locally on the user's machine, or against a set of accounts stored on a server that is associated with an entire domain. By maintaining accounts at a domain level, you are centralizing all the account administration to one location and allowing users to log on to any computer within that domain by using the same centralized credentials. Using domain *trusts,* administrators can set up their domain servers to trust other domain servers and use the accounts housed there, further extending the reach of the Windows user accounts.

User Groups

While every user must have a user account on a secure system, you do not have to define your security settings for each unique individual. The smart way to define what users can see and do is by grouping your users into group accounts. For example, if your sales force can only view a certain form in your application, but the accounting personnel can both view and edit that form, the easy way to maintain this structure is simply to check what group the user belongs to when creating the form and then dynamically hide or lock controls as necessary. As new employees are added to the system, the system administrators will ensure that their user accounts get added to the proper groups to give them the access they require. Figure 13.1 shows an example of how user accounts can be gathered into user groups.

By using user accounts and groups defined at the OS level, you remove the need to provide user administrative functions within your application. If you were to bypass the Windows accounts and use your own customized accounts, you would need to create the authentication module, at least one extra table in your database to store all of the users' information, and administrative interfaces to allow someone to add, delete, and modify the accounts in your system. But, if you choose to use groups defined in Windows NT, you can write your code based on these groups and let the system administrator add new users to the groups defined for the domain without modifying your application or your database.

Making security calls at the group level also helps simplify the coding and administration of your project. If you place some code in your application that works only if the user is fmiller, and then Mr. Miller leaves the company, you have to rewrite the application. But, if you place Mr. Miller in a group, such as accounting, and give permissions to the group and not the user, the system administrators can easily delete the fmiller account and add a new user belonging to the accounting group, who then has the exact same privileges and permissions as Mr. Miller had.

Permissions and Rights

After you identify the user and know which groups the user belongs to, you can figure out which permissions and rights the user has been granted. While using an application, a user may want to access a file. The system must ask the question, "Can this user read, update, or delete this file?" Users often also need to perform actions within a system, such as approving a travel voucher or restoring an old backup of the database. Even the code that your application executes will have a set of permissions and privileges that dictate which other blocks of code it can work with, and what resources your code can use. If code were allowed to

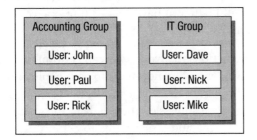

Figure 13.1
User accounts and user groups.

perform any action unchecked, malicious code, such as viruses, or even poorly written applications would be given free reign over the computer to delete and damage files at will. Let's look at how the Windows NT OS restricts what a user or code being executed by a user can do.

File Permissions

Permissions, or *rights*, decide what things your users can see and whether or not they can make changes to those objects. Windows NT prefers to format a machine's hard drive using NT File System (NTFS), which enables the OS to define who owns a file or directory. NTFS also enables the OS to define who can see those files and who can add to or change those items. Because you will often want to allow more users besides the item's owner access to an item, Windows NT creates access control lists (ACLs) to list and track users and groups that have been explicitly granted or denied permission to access an item.

Picture a Microsoft PowerPoint briefing stored in a shared directory somewhere on the network. The creator of that briefing may want the entire accounting department to see it, as well as the head of the HR department, but not the rest of the HR department. Using the File Manager, the creator can right-click the briefing, select Properties, and then click the Security tab to set the Permissions for this file. The creator will add the user account for the head of the HR department, and the group account for the accounting department. To prevent anyone else from seeing this file, the owner needs to remove the Everyone account, which is given access by default to publicly available files. If you restrict access to files that your application uses in this way, you can use the Windows NT accounts to see whether a user has the proper credentials to perform the desired action.

User Privileges and Roles

Users can also perform actions within the system, such as rebooting the computer and manipulating system services such as print jobs. These actions are considered privileges or rights that can be granted or denied to a user. At the OS level, user privileges are defined by the system's policies. The system administrator can define policies that give or take away a user's rights to perform a wide range of actions. Even the user's ability to change desktop wallpaper can be restricted by using policies. Some companies employ very restrictive policies that prevent users from doing the simplest of functions, such as shutting down the computer or changing a screen saver. (You will know you have walked into one of these companies if you see photos of the system administrators stuck to cubical walls with darts.)

Your application may also have many different actions that your users can perform, such as backing up and restoring a copy of the database or adding new users to your application's internal access list. These are not actions that you want to make available to everyone who uses your system, so you must carefully control them and assign them only to the appropriate users. Through your application, you can define and assign rights to certain users in much the same way as Windows NT uses policies.

One way in which I have implemented user rights is to create a table of application users and assign them application-specific roles, such as supervisor or clerk. When the user accesses your application, you can match their NT account username with the entry you store in your table to figure out their role, and then use that role within your code to allow or deny certain operations. I might use a user's role to determine whether I should display a button on the screen that will give them access to administrative functions, or simply hide the button to prevent them from ever seeing these advanced features. During your application-design phase, your business analysts should be able to identify the different roles your application's users can assume in the system, and associate special actions to these roles that the developers will create code to control.

Restrictive Permissions

Each user has a set of permissions in Windows NT, and each group that a user belongs to has its own set of permissions as well. These different sets of permissions are considered and evaluated as a single set of permissions when the OS is deciding whether or not to grant access to a resource. For example, suppose that a user individually has only read access to a PowerPoint file stored on the department's shared directory on the network. With user permissions alone, that user cannot do anything other than read that file. But if the user belongs to a group, such as accounting, that has been given Change access to all files in that directory, the user inherits these permissions and is allowed to edit the PowerPoint file.

Windows NT not only checks whether the user has a certain access through any of his or her group relationships, it also checks whether access has been specifically denied to the user or any of his or her groups. Here is a different twist to the preceding example. Suppose that the user's account has Change access to that PowerPoint file, but in the file's security settings, the accounting group is declared to have No Access. This block on one of the user's groups is inherited by the user, and completely prevents the user from accessing that file. This is an example of NT enforcing the most-restrictive permissions that have been assigned to this user, by association with a group. If you are using NTFS permissions to control resources that your application accesses, you can use groups and restrictive permissions selectively to grant and deny users access.

Code Access

When code is being executed, by default it takes on the identity of the user or the calling piece of code that launched it. As one piece of code calls another, it passes along that identity. This prevents a caller from executing some code that can do more than the caller is allowed to do, such as deleting somebody else's files. Preventing users from exceeding their defined powers is a really good idea, but sometimes your code will need to do more than the user is allowed to do. In these special cases, your code will assert its own permissions over the callers, or masquerade as another user. Typically, the user your code poses as will be a special user account created just for the application, but you could go so far as to pose as any existing account, such as the Administrator account.

Giving your code more power than the absolute minimum it needs to do its job can be an incredibly dangerous thing. While it may be tempting to use an all-powerful account like the Administrator account to do things your user normally cannot do, it would be wiser to create a special application-specific account that has just enough power to do the job at hand, but not so much that the account could be abused and misused. As the noted historian Lord Acton once said, "Power tends to corrupt and absolute power corrupts absolutely." Giving your code free reign over the system will make your development job much easier, but it could come back to bite you if a malicious cracker finds some new and destructive uses for your interfaces that you never considered possible.

Because your code takes on a caller's identity when it is executing, the runtime compiler examines the active code in the applications call stack and determines the appropriate level of access each piece of code should be allowed. If a piece of code is trying to perform an action, such as query a database table, and one of the modules in the call stack lacks sufficient permissions to perform this query, the runtime compiler will disallow this action for the current module, even if that module does have sufficient access. This prevents unauthorized pieces of code from enlisting other pieces of code wielding extra powers that surpass the access level that the system has permitted the application user. Figure 13.2 illustrates a hierarchy of modules in an applications call stack. This figure illustrates how all the modules in the call stack are examined as a whole to determine the appropriate level of access granted to a request made by a piece of code at the top of the call stack.

Encryption

Encryption is the act of encoding a message so that someone who happens to intercept that message cannot easily read it. The art of encrypting transmissions dates back practically to the dawn of time when man first used smoke signals or flags to communicate their messages secretly over a long distance. Any enemy that saw the signal might think, "Puff, puff, puff-puff? What could that possibly mean?" Only the receiver of the message would know that those puffs of smoke translated to "Attack on the left flank." Obviously, military establishments have played a large role in the development of encryption techniques to protect their strategic plans and communications. Recently, along with the worldwide popularity of the

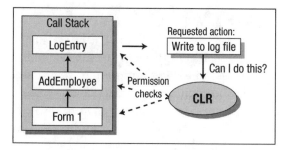

Figure 13.2
Code-based permissions in the call stack.

Internet, public interest in protecting corporate and private messages and data has grown tremendously. Programs such as Pretty Good Privacy (PGP) allow any home user to protect their email messages with powerful enough encryption to fool even the National Security Agency (NSA).

While communications within a single company going from one workstation to another workstation generally do not need strong encryption to protect them, when your application wants to communicate with the outside world, you may easily find a need to protect your messages. Personal medical histories, credit card transactions, and corporate financial data are just a few of the many pieces of sensitive information worthy of encryption and protection. Not affording these pieces of sensitive data is not only a bad programming practice, but can result in legal actions against the application's developers. This section will discuss how encryption works and introduce you to many of the most popular forms of encryption available to developers today.

Public Keys

Public-key (PK) encryption is an encryption method that uses two separate keys to encode and decode a message. One key is known as the *public key,* because it typically is made publicly available, and the second key is the *private key,* which is not handed out but instead is maintained by the message's author. When the message is encrypted for transmission, the sender uses the private key to create the resulting encrypted message. The receiver uses their public key to decrypt that very same message. The public key used must match the private key used by the sender. This method also works backward, whereby the holder of the public key can write a message using their key that only the holder of the matching private key can decode.

Anyone who has a copy of the public key can read a message created with the private key, but they cannot read messages created with someone else's public key, which requires the matching private key to decode. This encryption method works well in the email world. To send secure messages back and forth to your friends, you could provide them with your public key and hold on to the matching private key. I have received email that had the sender's public key listed in the same area as their company name and business phone number.

You will often see mention of both 40-bit and 128-bit encryption. These two common formats determine the length of the key that is used to encrypt your data. Obviously, a 128-bit key will be much longer than a 40-bit key, and thereby far more difficult to crack and compromise. Originally, 128-bit encryption was only available for systems within the United States due to export restrictions that limited encryption software being sold to outside countries to 40 bits. With recent changes to export regulations, all but a few countries now have access to 128-bit systems. The private and public keys use a powerful encryption algorithm to create their messages. RSA (short for Rivest, Shamir, and Adleman, the last names of this algorithm's inventors) is a widely used encryption algorithm that takes the key and the message and formulates an encrypted file for transmission.

Hashing is a term often associated with encrypted transmissions. A *hash* is a numerical value generated by an algorithm based on the string of text you are going to encrypt and transmit. The hash is sent across the network along with the encrypted data. When the user on the other end receives the message, they decrypt the string and then create their own hash based on the resulting string. If their hash matches the hash that was sent with the encrypted data, the receiver can be sure that the data arrived intact and unmodified.

Certificates

On their own, key-based encryption systems are a wonderful thing, but managing and tracking all of those keys can be difficult. Simply having the right key is not always sufficient to give someone access to your information. You want to be sure that the person holding that key is who you think they are. You may also want to issue keys that have expiration dates embedded in them so that users are required periodically to request a new key and reaffirm their identity and their need-to-know status. By packaging your keys into a certificate, you can manage and track the keys you have issued to your users. A system or entity that issues certificates to users is often referred to as a certificate authority (CA). It is their job to determine who should be issued a certificate, and then track the issued certificates and their associated users.

Certificates are a lot like the security badge that I wear around my neck to get into my office. I had to apply for my security clearance with the government, which investigated my background to ensure I was worthy of such an honor. I was next issued a badge with my name and picture on it so that the security guards I pass every day can be sure that the guy wearing the badge is the same one that they approved. Every few years, I must resubmit myself for investigation so that the government can be sure I have been behaving myself, and that I am still a trustworthy employee. It's not unheard of for someone to forget to do some paperwork, and I come to find out on Monday that my badge no longer works. Certificates, like badges, can be used to formally give someone limited access to information for a short period of time. The certificate contains the key needed to access that information, along with the information about the user to whom the certificate was issued, the date the certificate expires, and information on the certificate's issuer.

The certificate you are issued is not a pretty, signed piece of paper that you can frame and hang on the wall. The certificate is software-based and maintained by the application that needs it, whether that is a Web browser or an email program. If you need to access a Web site that requires a certificate, your browser will store the certificate's information and present it across the Internet to the Web server protecting the information you wish to see. You can take a look at the certificates that your Internet Explorer browser is maintaining by clicking Tools | Internet Options and then selecting the Content tab. Internet Explorer allows you to add personal certificates to your browser, and it also maintains a list of trusted CAs. Internet Explorer's CA list is pre-populated at installation with a list of popular authorities.

Software publishers can use certificates to identify themselves and their code securely to Internet users. You may have encountered this already if you have seen a pop-up Dialog window asking whether you always want to trust content provided by such-and-such a publisher. If you respond "yes" to this question, that publisher's name and certificate are added to Internet Explorer's Publisher Certificate list as being trusted, and you will no longer be bothered with that question when downloading content created by that publisher. When discussing certificates, the term X.509 often arises. This is a standard that describes the formatting of digital certificates. The certificates used in Secure Sockets Layer (SSL), discussed next, conform to the X.509 standards. X.509 certificates are not an officially approved standard, so at this time you cannot be sure that all certificates in use today meet the same set of standards.

Secure Sockets Layer

The most common application type that takes advantage of point-to-point encryption is the Web application. Because your Web application's users and the server that hosts your application can be separated by thousands of miles, you want to protect sensitive information that is passed back and forth from user to server. When dealing with the Internet, dozens and dozens of connecting points may exist between the user and the server, and most of these points are out of your control. As packets flow back and forth across this no-man's-land of wires, it is very easy for a third party to set up a *sniffer* at one of these points to intercept and view the packets of data you are sending. Because of this vulnerability, the use of SSL has become a very popular way of encrypting point-to-point communications across the Internet.

Using SSL to connect your users with the server creates a connection between them, which helps overcome the connectionless and stateless nature of the Internet. The client and the server first perform a digital handshake that confirms each other's identity. Both the user's browser and the Web server must be SSL-capable for this to work. Because SSL is a connected form of communication, the server knows when the user closes his or her browser or leaves the Web application. A Web server not using SSL never knows for sure whether a user has gone home for the day or is just taking a long time to read your Web page. After the handshake, the server also knows exactly where the user is, by the IP address and machine ID used during the handshake, which prevent another user from hijacking the secure connection between the real user and the server.

SSL not only enables the server to clearly identify a user and create a connection directly to that user, but also encrypts all messages going to and from that user. An SSL connection can use a certificate containing a public key to encrypt its data, thereby making its communications unreadable to anyone except for the server on the other end of the SSL connection. SSL brings together all the technologies discussed so far to help the server correctly identify its users, create a fixed connection with them across an otherwise connectionless Internet, exchange certificates and public keys with the user, and use those keys to encrypt and transmit data back and forth. If you are designing a Web application that will require secure communications between the Web browser clients and your code housed on the Web server, then SSL is a technology you need to include in your development plans.

The SSL protocol exists on a different layer than the standard HTTP protocol used for communicating information back and forth across the Internet. A protocol named S-HTTP (*secure*-HTTP) was created as a secure extension of the HTTP protocol. S-HTTP is similar to SSL because it provides a way to send information securely across the Internet. Unlike SSL, however, S-HTTP does not create a two-way connection between the user and the Web server, so it is only suitable for simple one-way secure communications, such as the transmission of a user's credit card number to an online bookseller. The S-HTTP protocol is commonly used in e-commerce applications where only one or two pages that the user fills out contain sensitive data. You will know you are accessing a Web page that uses S-HTTP when the URL for that Web page begins with HTTPS:// instead of the standard HTTP://.

Kerberos

When dealing with the authentication of users on a network, you may encounter an authentication protocol called Kerberos. Kerberos authenticates both ways, as opposed to the traditional one-way method of authenticating only the user. Not only does the user have to prove his or her identity to the server, but the server also has to prove to the user that it is, in fact, the correct server. When Kerberos has successfully authenticated a user, that user is issued a ticket, which contains the key the user will use to communicate securely with the server. Like certificates, Kerberos tickets come with an expiration date to limit their usage and to force a user to reapply for access at certain intervals.

Support for Kerberos (version 5) was built into the Windows 2000 operating system and provides stronger authentication and tracking than provided by the traditional Windows NT Challenge/Response method. Kerberos was developed and distributed by the Massachusetts Institute of Technology (MIT) and has been made freely available for use by anyone. If your application and its users are all running in a pure Windows 2000 environment, then Kerberos is an option for your development plans. Older operating systems, such as Windows NT 4 and Windows 98, do not have built-in support for Kerberos, but these older Microsoft OSs can still take advantage of the Windows NT Challenge/Response authentication method.

Virtual Private Networks

SSL can work great on a limited scale, such as when you are working with customers accessing your Web application from machines that you have no control over. However, if you are working with employees of a single company, using SSL for each and every employee can be overkill. When you are working with a group of employees that is physically separated from the company's network, you can overcome that separation by tying in the group's network into the rest of the company. Virtual Private Networks (VPNs) are a way to connect two networks together across the Internet. When a VPN is established, the users on the remote network can use your application just as they would if they were sitting in the same building as your server.

Transmissions between the two networks are encrypted and decrypted to protect their contents from being read by unauthorized persons. Establishing a VPN is usually a task for the

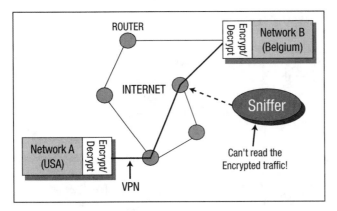

Figure 13.3
Two networks connected by a VPN.

systems administrators and network communications technicians, and is not something software developers directly participate in. But knowing that you can connect remote users using a VPN can be helpful when you are planning and designing an application, because you can suggest this technology to the customer if it will help to solve some of the customer's remote communication problems. Figure 13.3 shows how a VPN can connect two separate networks across the Internet.

IP Security (IPSec) is being developed to use keys to secure the packets that are sent back and forth across the TCP/IP protocol. You may hear this term used when discussing VPNs. Tunneling is also often associated with VPNs, and allows one network to pass its packets to another friendly network through a third network that is outside your control. Tunneling protocols such as Microsoft's Point-to-Point Tunneling Protocol (PPTP) do this by embedding their packets within a TCP/IP packet and by using keys and certificates to encrypt the bits of data they are transporting. Although the packets still travel across unsecured public networks, by encapsulating and encrypting your data into subpackets, your create a secure tunnel from one network to another that observers inside the tunnel will be unable to examine.

The Application Security Plan

When you are designing an application, you must ask yourself and your customers many questions when deciding where and how to implement your security checkpoints. Even if you think that your application doesn't have any security requirements that need to be addressed, it is still a good idea to review these questions. You may discover that you do in fact have a security issue that will require some extra planning. Addressing security issues during the application's design phase will make your job far easier than if you discover a security concern late in the development that you must then try to work into your nearly completed application.

Assessing Your Security Needs

Even before your team's application architect sits down to map out the objects your system will require, your requirements team should assess what the security requirements are for your system. Hopefully, you will be able to review the software requirements and extract the security requirements from there, although unstated or implied requirements often exist that your business analysis team should be able to nail down before the designing begins. Consider these questions when you are planning your application's security designs:

♦ Do I need to prevent certain users from seeing or doing certain things?

♦ Do special limited-access features exist, such as administrative or supervisor actions, that the average worker should not be able to perform?

♦ Should my application integrate with the operating system's user accounts?

♦ Will I need to augment the user's account information with an application-specific User object?

♦ Should I check whether a user can access resources at the file, directory, and database level, or should I decide within my code what a user can and cannot do?

♦ Will my code need to masquerade as another user to perform actions that the user might not normally be allowed to perform?

♦ Do I need to encrypt information going to and from the users?

♦ Will remote networks of users need to access my application?

♦ Will I have users entering my application from the Internet?

♦ Will I need to authenticate users across the Internet and provide them with a local user account?

♦ Should I create an auditing trail for my application, and, if so, what information should I be tracking (user logins, file accesses, deletes and changes, queries, and so on)?

♦ Can my code be used by crackers or viruses to cause damage to the system, and, if so, how can I prevent this from happening?

Security Auditing

If you have ever had the pleasure of working with a security monitor, then you know that they are a stickler for paperwork. Security types can never have too much paperwork lying around their office, and, in their view, if you don't make a record of it on paper, then it didn't happen. The reason for their feverish addiction to recording every detail is that when the time comes to investigate a wrongdoing, all of those records are worth their weight in gold. If your application deals with sensitive data and authenticated users, then your system likely requires some sort of auditing process to be built into its design.

Deciding whether to audit or not can be a simple yes or no question. If you decide that you do need to create auditing log files for your system, you have dozens of more decisions to make, such as where to store these log files, what information is important to record, and what items simply eat up valuable disk space. How often will your log files be backed up, or possibly cleaned out? Remember the five *w*s your elementary school teacher told you to consider when writing your book reports: who, what, where, when, and why. These same five *w*s will help you to figure out what pieces of information you need to audit for your application. Remember that the purpose of auditing is to provide those security folks with enough information to finger the naughty user and possibly prosecute them.

Audits are caused by a *trigger*, which translates into an event worthy of auditing. A method that handles the logging in and authenticating of a user is a good place to audit user logins. Databases can use internal triggers that are set off by certain database actions to create database-specific audit logs. If your auditing plan only focuses on database accesses, then you can utilize these database triggers and the database management system (DBMS) auditing features to save you the trouble of writing a customized auditing method. One thing to keep in mind when planning your auditing feature is the extra storage space your audit files will require. Unix servers are notorious for suffering from filled-up partitions due to excessive system audit logs. If your application is going to do excessive auditing, consider writing these logs to a separate partition so that your application or the OS is not affected.

Auditing for security reasons is very similar to creating log files to track your application's execution. To find out what went wrong with a program, you need to know who did what and when and where they did it to properly track down that bug and fix it. You may even choose to co-locate your security and application logging functions within the same code to simplify your application.

Working Security into the Application Design

After you have a firm grip on what your application's security requirements are, you can then begin to plan the objects, modules, and database tables that your application will require. Your application may require special tables to track information on your system's users and their permissions. Because creating code to query your user's database table from all over your Assembly does not support code reuse, you need to create a User object to encapsulate all of these calls and make the user's information easily accessible throughout your application.

Many security settings will occur during installation, outside of the application's installation program. Special system policies, directory permission settings, and Web server security settings might all be required to make your application as secure as it needs to be. You should thoroughly document all of these settings and include them in an installation guide to help future administrators duplicate the settings that you have deemed necessary. Later in this chapter, I will go over some of the system settings you need to make to secure your applications, such as setting up the Internet Information Services (IIS) Web server to authenticate your Web users and restrict what pages they can view.

The User Table

If you need to record and maintain information that you cannot get from the system's user account, then you need to add a table (or tables) to your database to track this information. Pieces of data such as a user's system role, employee number, or email address might all be stored in your user table. Because you can detect the user's logged-in account from within your application, you can use their system account name as a key to match up the user with your user table data.

The User Object

To package all of a user's information in a neat and organized object-oriented fashion, you will want to create a User object. Within this object, you encapsulate all the user's information that you need to track, along with the security methods necessary to authenticate that user and determine their role and level of access in the system. Your User object can have properties such as **FirstName**, **LastName**, and **UserRole** that you can access from other parts of your Assembly. You might also have methods such as **Add** and **Delete** to allow administrators to manage these users, and possibly an **Authenticate** method if you are handling authentication within your application. Because the user is at the center of all security issues, your User object will play a critical role in your application's design and execution.

You will have all the database calls encapsulated within your User object, so other code modules simply have to instance your User object and check its properties to learn about the currently active user in an object-oriented fashion. You may have some code that will only run if a user is acting in a "supervisor" role. You could check a **User.Role** property to see whether they qualify and decide whether or not to run the code.

.NET Security

Now that you have a good background in security, let's take a look at how .NET implements security when your application is executed. By now, it should come as no surprise that the Common Language Runtime (CLR) is at the heart of the system, monitoring and controlling all actions performed by your code. Understanding how the CLR manages your code from a security-conscience point of view will help you to plan and design your application's security features better.

CLR: The Security Guard

In .NET, security is monitored and controled by the CLR compiler. Because all Assemblies are loaded and executed by the CLR, this is the logical place for .NET to perform all of its security checks and verifications. You have already read in Chapter 4 about how the CLR enforces type safety for data types. Strict type safety enforcement not only makes your code more stable and reliable, but also ensures that code can use only preapproved blocks of memory to store its data, thereby preventing the code being executed from bypassing the CLR's security checks.

The CLR creates an application domain, or AppDomain, that it uses to isolate an application from other applications the CLR is managing. This prevents one application from stepping on or taking advantage of another in a way that could bypass security checks or cause damage to the system. These AppDomains include all executing code and modules for an application, as well as the blocks of memory they are using. The CLR prevents outside applications from accessing the memory blocks contained within another application's AppDomain.

By limiting your application's memory uses to a predefined box, the CLR prevents accidents and security attacks such as the infamous buffer overrun attack. Buffer overrun attacks typically target programs written in C because that programming language allows a great deal of flexibility as to where you can write data values to memory. If a program were to write a value to a block of memory without first checking whether that value exceeds the memory space available, the code would cause a buffer overrun and potentially allow an attacker to write their own executable code to an adjacent block of memory. When executed, that executable code could allow the attacker to take control of your machine or execute mischievous code. The CLR performs its own bounds checking to prevent sloppy code from overrunning its available memory space and allowing outside code to be introduced. COM components are unmanaged, so they do not have a watchdog like the CLR keeping an eye on their actions to prevent mistakes from happening.

Verifying and Checking Assemblies

When the CLR first loads an Assembly, it takes a moment to perform a verification check before actually executing any of that Assembly's code. This first look at the code ensures that the Assembly complies with all the CLR requirements and standards. If you are still thinking of the CLR as a large and grumpy security guard, you can picture the verification stage as the guard's first glance at an approaching employee seeking entrance to the building.

If the employee doesn't look too seedy, the guard will probably let him get close enough to present his ID badge for inspection. The CLR next inspects the Assembly and gathers a set of information that the CLR refers to as evidence. The CLR will ask the Assembly what its strong name is, who is its author, and where it came from. Assemblies can be downloaded to a client's machine from the Internet, so the "where" question is very important because you can trust some sources but not others. The CLR/security guard does not pass judgment based on its own set of rules. The CLR instead compares the evidence it has collected on the Assembly to a set of policies maintained for the system. If the Assembly's information checks out with all the system policies, the CLR will bless that Assembly and finally execute it.

When the CLR compares the evidence to system policies, three separate policies are actually being checked: a policy that covers the user, a policy that addresses the issues that are important to the machine running the CLR, and a policy to cover the application's policy issues. A *policy* is a set of rules that must be applied to the Assembly. To be run, an Assembly's evidence must pass all three policy checks. Figure 13.4 illustrates the CLR/security guard

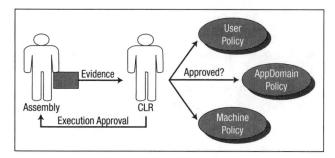

Figure 13.4
The CLR verifying and checking an Assembly.

process, from verification, to evidence gathering, and finally to the policy checks. It is the CLR that grants the Assembly its permissions and rights based on the Assembly's identity.

Microsoft Intermediary Language Security Issues

When you build your application, the final result is not a fully compiled file. With .NET, your Assemblies are built into Microsoft Intermediary Language (MSIL). The CLR reads in the MSIL and compiles this data at runtime. In Chapter 1, you read about all the great advantages to using MSIL instead of compiled code, such as the user's ability to install new and improved versions of the CLR that will benefit and improve your application's performance without you having to change any code. MSIL has a downside, though. Because it is not compiled, users can very easily examine its contents. The IL (Intermediary Language) disassembler (ILDASM) provided with the .NET Framework SDK is one such tool that allows someone to look through the contents of a MSIL file and discover all of its features. This weakness has many in the industry worried that their code will be on display for the entire world to see if they use .NET.

At the moment, this fear is justified to some extent. Hopefully, Microsoft will enhance the MSIL files and allow developers to encrypt or lock them from prying eyes to protect their companies' trade secrets and methods. Until such protection is added to MSIL, ways to mitigate this shortcoming are available. .NET was designed to focus on delivering applications and content over the Internet. To do this, the user will only use a browser to access your application. Your application's code will reside on a server that you control. Because you control the server and the application's code, outside eyes will not be able to pick apart your MSIL files. If you are selling code-based solutions to other companies, or a portion of your application installs onto the client's workstation, then those portions of MSIL will be exposed to possible decompiling, provided the users have the right tools, knowledge, and enough desire to see your code. Unmanaged code is not stored in MSIL, so it is not easily decompiled and examined. In .NET, only C++ can create unmanaged code components.

Developers might worry that if someone can see your code and reverse-engineer your work, then they could feasibly create an Assembly that impersonates your Assembly. If this were possible, all sorts of bad things could be done in the name of your innocent Assembly. But relax, because this won't work. The Assemblies you create in .NET can have a unique name assigned to them, known as a *strong name*. Strong names are encrypted, and each name is created specifically for that one Assembly build. Assemblies that reference your Assembly will do so through that unique strong name. Because your Assembly is referenced by its strong name, another developer will not be able to impersonate your code and cause a security problem for you because they will not be able to duplicate your strong name. Because the strong name is a unique encrypted key, it is a way of signing your Assembly that proves to users of your code that this is the real Assembly they have always counted on, and not an impersonator.

Managed and Unmanaged Code Security Interaction

The relationship between your managed .NET Assembly code and your unmanaged COM components is based on deception. When a COM component calls a .NET Assembly, that Assembly must put on a COM disguise by providing a type library and Registry entries. When an Assembly calls a COM component, the CLR wraps that component in another disguise to make it appear to be an Assembly. Because Assemblies and COM components behave and act differently, the way they handle security issues is incompatible. Because of these differences, .NET allows COM to handle security in its own way, and does not pass any security information back and forth between COM objects and .NET Assemblies.

This disconnect presents a security issue that developers need to be aware of, because an Assembly with limited powers can call to a COM component that is unaware of the Assembly's restrictions. The enlisted component may be able to perform actions that the Assembly developer never intended to allow. When Assembly developers plan to make calls to COM components, they need to take this fact into account and decide whether their component calls can be abused and made to do more than they are intended to do. Your basic COM component provides very little security enforcement outside of the file permissions placed on the component and any internal security checks added by the coder. MTS and COM+ added the ability to assign components to special packages, which could then be assigned users and groups, enhancing the developer's ability to manage a component's security issues. If your Assemblies will be working with COM components, treat those components as independent entities when planning your application's security.

Web Application Security

How you plan and configure the security for a Web-based application is quite different from how you plan a traditional Win32 application. All of the users seeking to access your Web pages and Web Services will be coming in through the Web server using the HTTP protocol. This works in your favor, because that leaves only one doorway that you need to watch and secure. That doorway is actually called a *port*, and although your computer has dozens if not hundreds of ports, by default, only one is the port that your server listens to for Web page HTTP requests. You can have more than one port listening for HTTP if you set up multiple Web server instances, but for the sake of simplicity, assume that your server is running only one copy of your Web server.

To further simplify things, I am going to focus on the IIS 5 Web server that comes with Windows 2000, because this is the server of choice for developing ASP.NET Web pages. Web sites can be hosted on many different types of servers, such as Apache or Netscape, but if you plan to harness all the great new Web development features included in .NET, you need to use a .NET-capable server such as IIS 5. When I go over the steps that you can take to secure your Web server and the sites it is hosting, those steps will differ greatly from the steps that you will use for Web servers created by different companies.

Anonymous Web Users

By default, when IIS is installed, the Web sites are open to the general public. A Web user does not even need to have a network account to access an unsecured Web site. They simply type the correct URL and start surfing your site. Remember that when code executes on a server, it must have some identity to help the server determine what it can and cannot do. You might think that because your Web visitors are unauthenticated, they have absolutely no access or ability to perform any actions on your Web server. In fact, by the rules, they should not even be allowed to look at those Web pages until the server is provided with some ID first.

To overcome your anonymous Web visitors' lack of identity, IIS creates a special account during installation and assigns that account to your unauthenticated Web visitors. If you look at the local list of users on the Web server, this account is named IUSR_*yourservername* (substitute the name of the Web server at the end). This is the IIS guest user account that is used for viewing pages within the Web directories. Any actions performed by the Web server and its Web pages on behalf of the user will be done using the IWAM_*yourservername* account. If, for example, Terry Tate from Texas runs a Web page anonymously, and that Web page calls a dynamic link library (DLL), which in turn wants to write to a file on the Web server's hard drive, the IUSR account will request the Web page, and the IWAM account will make the call to the DLL.

If you do not make any security changes to your Web server or the Web pages in the file system, you will see that users pretty much have free reign within the confines of the Web directories. By default, the root Web directory for IIS is \Inetpub\wwwroot. Any files located in directory trees not under this root directory are considered off limits to Web surfers, so you do not have to worry about visitors browsing through the WinNT directory or any other sensitive places. Also by default, the majority of the directories and files under the Web server's root directory have the Everyone account added to them, which includes all authenticated users and the anonymous IUSR account. Shortly, you will see how you can manipulate these files' settings to restrict access to portions of your Web page. During installation, IIS places some default Web pages in your Web root directory so that the user has something to look at if they type your URL into the browser. IIS also adds some administrative directories under the Web root. Access to these directories should be restricted to only authenticated users with the knowledge and need to perform Web server administration tasks.

IIS Web Server Authentication

If your Web application needs to limit the access of the users that can access it, or you need to be able to identify the users by their NT user account, then you need to configure your Web server to authenticate your users. The first step to securing your IIS Web server is to turn on the authentication mechanisms by using the Internet Services Manager. The IIS Web server allows three types of authentication: anonymous, basic, and integrated Windows.

Anonymous Authentication

By default, the anonymous authentication method is checked, meaning users are not authenticated but are simply given the IUSR identity. Optionally, you can change the default account that the Web server assigns from IUSR to any other account the Web server knows about, though typically the IUSR account is the best account to use for outside visitors.

Basic Authentication

With basic authentication enabled, the Web server requests Web visitors to identify themselves. When the user enters the URL to a Web site that has basic authentication enabled, they get a login prompt asking for their username and password. The credentials they enter are checked against the NT accounts that the Web server knows about. If the user's credentials match an existing account, they are let into the Web site. If they do not match, the user is asked two more times to log in and then is provided with an "Authentication Failed" Web page. Basic authentication is called "basic" because it does not use the built-in login encryption and transmission features that NT uses when a Windows NT workstation transmits its login information to a Windows NT server. Usernames and passwords are sent across the Internet unencrypted. While this may not seem like a very smart thing to do, this is allowed so that Web browsers that do not understand how to securely authenticate with an NT server (such as Netscape Communicator) can still log in.

Integrated Windows Authentication

This level of IIS authentication can help you overcome the unsecured nature of basic authentication by telling the Web server to try and use the Windows NT Challenge/Response mechanism. If the browser the user is using is Internet Explorer and the Web server has NT Challenge/Response checked, then authentication will be encrypted from browser to server. One nice benefit you get from using integrated Windows authentication is that if your user is already logged on to the network, Internet Explorer simply passes that account information along to the Web server and never bothers the user to retype this information. You can set up your IIS Web server to accept both basic and NT Challenge/Response authentications, which enables Internet Explorer users to log in quickly and securely, and still allows

Netscape users to enter using basic authentication. One thing to remember is that if you are using any form of authentication, you should uncheck the anonymous method, to disallow unauthorized users from entering your Web site.

Authentication does not have to be applied at one single point that covers the entire Web server. If you define your security settings at the root Web item in the Internet Services Manager, which should be labeled Default Web Site, then these settings will propagate down to all of your sub-Web pages. An alternative to defining one centralized security setting is to leave the root Web directory set to anonymous access, and instead define security settings for subfolders and virtual directories underneath that Web site. For example, when you create a Web Service or Web Application Project in Visual Studio.NET, a subdirectory is created below the Web server's root directory, and all of your files are saved there. This helps you to keep the Web server organized, and allows you to physically separate your different Web projects. An added benefit of saving Web projects to their own subdirectories is that you can define a unique set of authentication rules and file permissions for each and every project. Later in the chapter, Exercise 13.1 will show you how to define security settings for a single project in a subdirectory or the root Web directory and not affect the rest of the Web server's settings.

File Permissions on the Web Server

Authentication alone is not enough to secure your Web site; you must also adjust the security permissions associated with the files in your Web site's directory and subdirectories. If you are securing a Web site that has the Everyone account attached to all of its directories and files, then you are essentially bypassing the authentication mechanisms, because the operating system thinks that anyone and everyone can look at these files. After turning on the IIS Web server authentication, your next step should be to remove the Everyone account from all of your secured areas. Generally, if you remove the Everyone account from one directory, all directories and files below that should also drop the Everyone account. This happens by default because subdirectories and files are usually set up to inherit their permissions from their parent directories. The Everyone account can still be used at the root Web directory to allow everyone to see a directory of sub-Web sites. For example, the company Web site may allow everyone to see its front page, but the developers can restrict access to subareas of the site by removing the Everyone account and specifying which user accounts can access those pages.

Tip

To adjust security settings for files and directories, you use the File Manager. Right-click the item you are making settings for, select Properties, and then select the Security tab to view which accounts have access to this object.

If you remove all user accounts from your Web site's directories, no one will be able to view your site, including you! The accounts you want to leave alone are the Administrator account that lets you do your job, and the Creator and Authors accounts that allow the users who authored the pieces of your Web site sufficient access to change and update those items. Besides these essential accounts, it is really up to you, the software architect, to decide what accounts need access to what pages. If your system is wide open to all authenticated users, you can simply add the Authenticated Users group to the pages. This account works well if you want to force authentication for users who access your Web site, and then further enforce security access and permissions within your code, and not at the file level. You could add individual user accounts to each file, which would give you file-level access control, but in the long run, this would be an administrative nightmare. As you learned during the discussion of user accounts, using NT groups to allow and restrict access on a larger scale is the ideal way to manage access. If only a subset of all of your authenticated users should be given access to your pages, such as only the accountants in the office, then you should use a specialized NT group in place of the Authenticated Users group to further restrict access.

Figure 13.5 shows a file structure for a fictional Web site that uses NT accounts to grant and deny access to certain sections based on a user's assigned groups. One nice thing about groups is that a single user can belong to multiple groups. A user may belong to both an accounting and a supervisors group, for example, allowing them to access both the restricted supervisors area and the accounting home page.

Page-Level Checking in Web Applications

If you are developing a Web Application that will provide similar functionality to a Windows-Application, it's easy to see how each Web Form can directly represent a Windows form your Project might have. One key difference exists between these two forms that you need to be aware of when creating your Web Application's security plan. In a WindowsApplication, you cannot jump to another form without using a provided navigation mechanism, such as a button or a menu item. Likewise, you cannot start your Windows program at one of the subscreens, because a WindowsApplication has a specified starting form that always loads first when the program is run. WindowsApplication developers can use this fact to implement security checkpoints that hide or prevent users from accessing certain forms if their role in the system is not sufficient to use those forms.

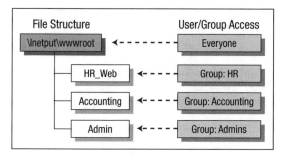

Figure 13.5
Restricting access to Web directories.

Your Web Applications will have navigational elements that allow users to follow the correct path to these limited-access forms, but nothing is preventing the user from going to the Address textbox on the Web browser and simply typing the full path to the form they wish to use. If you place your security checkpoints on the navigational elements and not on the page itself, users will be able to easily bypass your security and get into all sorts of trouble. Along these same lines, you are not guaranteed that the user will enter your Web site at the same page every time. Users have figured out the browser's Favorites feature and will use it to bookmark the pages they use the most.

To prevent this from causing problems for your Web Application, you need to check for such things as authentication, the user's access role, and the page context at the beginning of each Web page. If the user found a shortcut to your page but does not have the correct role attribute, forward them to an "Access Denied" page. If your page is expecting some form data elements to work with, but the user bypassed the form and went straight to the response page, detect those missing values and send the user back to the form. Do not let the free-form nature of the Web and Web browsers provide a user with the opportunity to step around your security checks and access functions they otherwise would not be allowed to use.

Securing a Web Application

Now that you understand how the IIS Web server handles authentication and file access permissions, this section shows you the steps you need to take to make these settings. Exercise 13.1 works with the simple Web Application you built in Chapter 10. If you do not have this exact project created on your system, any other .NET Web Application that exists under the Web server's root directory will work. If you have yet to create a Web Application on your Web server, go ahead and try Exercise 10.1 in Chapter 10 so that you have something to work with. The steps in Exercise 13.1 are for a Windows 2000 server running IIS 5. To learn how to secure a different brand of Web server, consult the Web server's documentation.

Exercise 13.1: Securing a Web Application on IIS

1. Start the Internet Services Manager by clicking Start | Programs | Administrative Tools | Internet Services Manager.

2. In the frame on the right, you will see a tree view with an icon representing your Web server as the top-level item. Expand your Web server and you will see the Default Web Site item. Expand the Default Web Site item to see all the subfolders beneath your Web server's root directory. The folder icons mean that this is an actual folder under the \Inetpub\wwwroot directory. The icons with the globes represent virtual directories, which can be anywhere on your server but appear virtually as a subdirectory of the Web server.

3. One of the folders below Default Web Site is named MyFirstWeb for the Web Application Project you created. Right-click this folder and select Properties.

4. On the Directory tab of this directory's Properties window, be sure that Directory Browsing is unchecked. This is a minor security fix that will prevent casual exploring of your Web site. You probably have seen this on the Internet, where you type in a Web site's URL and receive in return a listing of the directory's contents for you to review. Generally, it is not a good idea to allow users to see behind the mysterious red curtain, and directory browsing can allow hackers to easily spot possible security weaknesses on your site.

5. Click the Directory Security tab of the Properties window, and click the Edit button in the top section, labeled Anonymous Access And Authentication Control.

6. You will see three checkboxes representing the three types of authentication: anonymous, basic, and integrated Windows. Because you want to restrict access to the files in this directory, uncheck the Anonymous checkbox.

7. Check the box by Basic Authentication to require users to log in using an account the server knows about. For this exercise, do not check the Integrated Windows Authentication checkbox.

8. Click the Edit button to the right of the Basic Authentication checkbox. You will see a pop-up window asking you to specify which domain the Web server will query to resolve the login names and passwords. By default, the Web server relies on its own locally defined accounts, but in a multidomain environment, you might want to check logins against another server by entering a different domain name in the textbox. Choosing another domain as the authentication host requires that the outside domain be trusted by your Web server's domain. If the system administrator has not explicitly set up a trust for that domain, your Web server will not be able to ask the target domain server whether a user account is authorized. For the majority of applications, cross-domain authentication will not be an issue, only something to be aware of.

9. Click the Cancel button on the Basic Authentication Domain window to close it. Click OK on the Authentication Methods window, and then click the Apply button at the bottom of the Properties window. Your authentication settings are now applied.

10. Close the Internet Services Manager.

11. Open the File Manager. Locate your Web Application's directory, which should be named MyFirstWeb under c:\Inetpub\wwwroot.

12. Right-click the Web Applications folder and select Properties.

13. Click the Security tab. You will see a list of all accounts that currently have access to this directory. Uncheck the Allow Inheritable Permissions checkbox at the bottom of this window, which will allow you to define access permissions that differ from this folder's parent directory.

14. Remove all the accounts except for Administrators, Admins, and CREATOR OWNER by highlighting each account and clicking the Remove button.

15. Click the Add button. Add the Authenticated Users group by double-clicking the item in the list at the top. Click the OK button to finish adding this account. On the Security tab, highlight Authenticated Users and click the Read & Execute Permission checkbox at the bottom (if it is not already checked). Click this window's Apply button to finish making these changes, and then click OK to exit this window.

16. Start your Web browser and enter the URL to the Web site you just secured. The URL will look something like this:

```
http://yourservername/MyFirstWeb
```

17. The Web server will respond to your page request by asking you to log in with a username and password. First, try out a fake username to see how the Web server denies you access. Next, log in using a username and password that the Web server knows about, such as your standard login account username.

Code Access Security

Security is being monitored and enforced at many different levels in the operating system. Your application's users have a set of privileges and rights that they have been granted within the system. The code they execute can have its own set of permissions and rights that may not match the users. Code that calls your code's methods can have a different set of permissions than your code has. You do not want a caller to be able to run some code that gives them access to your system that they would otherwise not have, such as the ability to delete system-auditing files and to modify the Registry. Unchecked access such as this is the basis for every mean-spirited virus that is terrorizing cyberspace today. You, as the coder, have the ability to check whether the user has sufficient permission to do what your code intends to do, and then grant or deny them the ability to run your code.

Many well-meaning COM components have become the victims of misuse by hostile code that took advantage of a lack of permission checking by the code. By performing access checks in your code and limiting the reach of your code to only what it needs to do its job, you prevent your code from being abused and misused. All of this extra checking may not seem worthwhile, but imagine your code making the five o'clock news as a potential computer security weakness. (If you sit very quietly, you can almost hear the company's stock price falling!)

Demanding Caller Permissions

Code can be made to do some pretty powerful things, all of which can easily be misused. Modifying the system Registry, deleting files, and accessing files the user has no right to look at are all examples of misuse. If your code is going to perform an action that not everyone should be allowed to do, you should check whether the caller does in fact have the proper clearance to execute the action your code performs. Being able to run an application and being able to perform the actions contained in a single method are two entirely different levels of permission checking.

When your code asks whether or not the caller can perform an action, it is done as a **Demand**. A code-based **Demand** checks whether all the code in the call stack has the necessary permission to perform a specified action. If you want to check only the code that called your method and not all the code behind it in the call stack, then you use the **DemandImmediate** method. Take a look at the following code that executes a **Demand** to see whether a caller has **Write** permission to a file on the hard drive:

```
'This code goes at the top of the Module, before the class
Imports System.Security
Imports System.Security.Permissions

'This code goes at the top of a method that plans to write to a file
Dim PS As New PermissionSet(PermissionState.None)
PS.AddPermission(New FileIOPermission(FileIOPermissionAccess.Write, _
  "c:\Private_File.txt"))
PS.Demand()
```

This bit of code introduces the concept of a **PermissionSet**. A **PermissionSet** can be created to act as a collection of permission rules that you wish to define. You can execute multiple **AddPermission** methods to add multiple access rules to your **PermissionSet**. The **PermissionSet** also has a **RemovePermission** method that you can use within your code to dynamically remove and negate a permission you have previously defined in the set. When you execute the **Demand** method, the code asks all the callers in the call stack if they have sufficient permission to perform the actions defined in the **PermissionSet**. If any of the modules in the call stack do not have sufficient permission to write to your file, this method raises a **SecurityException** at the **PS.Demand** line, and the method will exit, never getting to the file output portion.

PermitOnly

You can also use **AddPermission** to add a collection of allowed actions, such as writing to FileA and reading FileB. After these permissions are added, you can execute the **PermissionSet**'s **PermitOnly** method, which tells the CLR that only those actions you defined in the **PermissionSet** are allowed, and all others are not permitted. You can use this to lock down your code and permit it to perform only a small set of approved actions and disallow all others, even if the CLR and the security policies would allow it. Your code is saying, "Yeah, I know I can do all that, but I only need to do this and nothing else." The next code example shows how **PermitOnly** works:

```
Public Sub PermissionTest()
    Dim PS As New PermissionSet(PermissionState.None)
    PS.AddPermission(New FileIOPermission(FileIOPermissionAccess. _
Write, "c:\FileB.txt"))
    PS.AddPermission(New FileIOPermission(FileIOPermissionAccess. _
Write, "c:\FileA.txt"))
    PS.PermitOnly()

    'Dim the logfile parts
    Dim NewLog As FileStream = New FileStream("c:\NewLog.txt", _
FileMode.OpenOrCreate, FileAccess.Write)
    Dim WriteLog As StreamWriter = New StreamWriter(NewLog)
    WriteLog.BaseStream.Seek(0, SeekOrigin.End)
    WriteLog.WriteLine("This is only a test")
    WriteLog.Close()
End Sub
```

This **PermissionSet** has two permissions defined for it, which allow **Write** access to FileA and FileB. The body of the code wants to write a message to a third file, Newlog.txt. Because I specify that the **PermissionSet** will only permit the actions defined in that set and nothing else, this subroutine will raise a **SecurityException** when I try to run **WriteLog.WriteLine**.

Deny

This section introduces a different way to look at the permissions defined in the **Permission-Set**. When I use **PermitOnly**, I tell the CLR that only those permissions explicitly defined in the **PermissionSet** are acceptable. You can instead use the **PermissionSet's Deny** method, which tells the CLR that anything I define in the set is not allowed. Take a look at this block of code defining a **PermissionSet**:

```
PS.AddPermission(New FileIOPermission(FileIOPermissionAccess. _
 Write, "c:\FileB.txt"))
PS.AddPermission(New FileIOPermission(FileIOPermissionAccess. _
 Write, "c:\FileA.txt"))
PS.Deny()
```

If you place this code at the top of your method, your method will be allowed to do anything the policies will allow it to do, except for **Write** to FileA or FileB, because these two actions have been defined in the **PermissionSet** and then explicitly denied using the **Deny** method. This is a more limited form of restricting the actions your code can take, and you will want to use this method only for very limited and well-defined circumstances.

Assert

When code asserts itself, it's saying to the CLR, "I know the user cannot do this, but I do have sufficient privileges and I want to use them." If you again define **Write** access to FileA and FileB in your **PermissionSet**, and then execute the **PS.Assert** method, your code will tell the CLR that the permissions of the callers in the call stack do not need to be checked for these two files, only the permission this block of code applies. Assertions can be dangerous, because they allow code to perform actions that callers and users may not be allowed to perform. In a way, the **Assert** prevents the CLR from doing a full-permissions check of all code involved. Sometimes an **Assert** is warranted, such as when your application is accessing private or hidden files that the user does not have permission to check. If you plan to **Assert** permissions in your code, consider running internal security checks within your asserting code to prevent misuse of your code.

Summary

For many software development projects, the issue of security is often forgotten or glossed over somewhere in the application-design document. However, this issue is becoming increasingly more important to both customers and program managers, and you can be certain that their concerns will be directed to you. As software moves to the Internet in the form of Web Services and Web-based applications, security concerns will play an increasingly bigger role in your projects. Understanding the issues and knowing how you can work those issues into your application designs is more important than ever. Deal with the tough security questions early during the design phase, and ask the questions that might seem unfathomable. What's the worst thing that can happen to my application? Can my code be misused? Is data exposed to unauthorized access? Will a virus be able to take advantage of my code and destroy my company's reputation? When it comes to security, you can't overplan, and the key to a good security plan is to never underestimate the enemy.

Chapter 14

Deploying .NET Applications

At some point in the life of every application, it must leave the nest and venture out into this cruel world. Now that you have created a few simple .NET applications and have a good understanding of .NET development principles, it is time to talk about how you are going to package and deploy your applications out into the world. The concepts and pitfalls associated with software deployments have changed in reaction to the completely reworked application framework you will find in .NET.

The old Package and Deployment Wizard that came with Visual Studio 6 enabled you to create an installation package that included a setup.exe file and a Cab file full of all the necessary resources, such as graphics and dynamic link libraries (DLLs). Although the included Package and Deployment Wizard program was helpful, it was kind of basic and lacking in certain areas. Third-party software developers stepped in and provided even more powerful software packaging suites, which quickly overcame the Packaging and Deployment Wizard as the method of choice for application deployment for software professionals.

Installing a Component Object Model (COM) application is a fragile process because of the weaknesses of DLLs. All too often, a new program's installation would break a DLL dependency for one of your older programs because of differences in DLL versions and interfaces. Poorly designed uninstall programs could do further damage by removing DLLs that other programs relied upon, thereby breaking other companies' applications. These are the well-known pitfalls of "DLL hell." But with the release of .NET, DLL hell has frozen over and the benefits of Assembly paradise have made these problems a thing of the past. To better understand the issues surrounding the deployment of a .NET application, you'll first take a look at the makeup of that application and the many different possible combinations you may encounter out in the world.

Dissecting .NET Applications

To keep up with a modern distributed application environment, .NET applications are designed to be separated into many different pieces and dispersed to many separate locations. You can still install all of your application's files and resources in one single directory on the hard drive and run it as a standalone application, but where .NET really shines is in its ability to deploy pieces of a single application all over the enterprise. In the past, development teams would design and build each physically separated piece as a separate application and then deploy it in parts: install program X on server A, and then install program Y on server B, and then finally configure these two independent entities to work with one another. In .NET, you could build this application as a single Solution and deploy it in a single simplified effort. First, let's break apart a distributed application to understand it at its lowest level.

The Application

The application is the top-level parent object that encompasses all the code and resources it uses. Going back to the fictional Oceanside Resort project from Chapter 11, a single application could be the hotel's reservation system. Included within the reservation system are many Assemblies, such as those that handle the Windows interface that will be used on the desktops of the front desk clerks, and those that house the business objects that are located on a centralized application server on the network. The reservation application can also use Web Services provided by other companies on the Internet, such as a Web Service to validate and process credit card information. Even though I am not creating the Web Service as a part of my reservation system, my application makes use of this service, making it an integral part of the overall application.

Assemblies

The Assembly is the basic building block of all .NET applications. As explained in Chapter 1, one single Assembly can be made up of many different modules, including code-based Class files, graphics, and multimedia resources. An Assembly is also capable of existing in more than one location. For example, one Assembly might contain two Visual Basic Class source-code files located on machine A, and a dozen graphical files stored on machine B. Despite the separate locations of these pieces, they are all housed within a single Assembly. One application may consist of many Assemblies; so, if the application is considered the big picture of your project, then Assemblies are the individual pieces that together form the picture. They are "medium-scale" because you can zoom in on an Assembly and see even smaller details, such as a source-code file or a BMP graphics resource file contained within the Assembly.

Figure 14.1 shows an example of a physical deployment map of the example reservation system. Not all of the necessary components for this reservation system are shown—only enough to illustrate the distributed nature of both an application and an Assembly. Notice that Assembly A is made up of many resource files dispersed among two separate computers, the reservation clerk's desktop computer and the hotel server. Also note the car rental Web Service the application calls to, located on a distant uncontrolled server.

When looking at the Assemblies in Figure 14.1, it is easy to see how a single Assembly fits into the big picture of a single application. But like DLLs, an Assembly can be used by many different applications. The concept of code reuse is not new to .NET. You could create a DLL that contains a Class that exposes a ValidateCreditCard interface that can be used by more than one application. Both the reservation system and a gift shop inventory application could make good use of this handy method, made available through a shared Assembly. Your .NET Assemblies will expose reusable interfaces the same way that COM objects do.

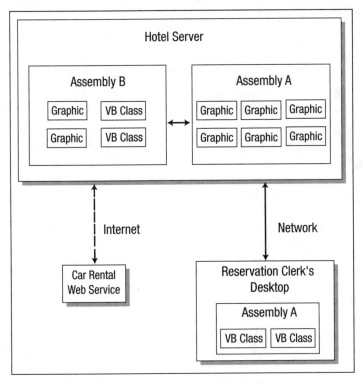

Figure 14.1
The reservation application physical deployment diagram.

Application Installation Locations

A .NET application can be more distributed than a COM application, and the individual application pieces can be scattered literally throughout the world. The car rental Web Service shown in Figure 14.1 could be located on a Web server anywhere in the world, but this Web Service will still play a big part in your application. If you are developing a Web Application, your ASP.NET pages will be located in directories on the Web server. Behind these pages can be other Assemblies located locally or remotely, and your Web pages and Assemblies can also make calls to remote Web Services. The possible combinations of installation locations are endless, but this section will focus on a simple example of a WindowsApplication installed locally.

Your application will have a base directory in which it installs its main executable along with any necessary resource files. Many programs install themselves under the Program Files directory for neatness, though sometimes developers ignore this directory and install the application in a directory at the root drive. With COM, DLLs could be installed any-where on the system as long as they were properly registered using the regsvr32 program. This utility made entries in the Registry that let the system know where a certain DLL was located. A DLL had to have a unique name, because only one version of a DLL name could be registered. The .NET Assemblies you will create will be stored in one of four main loca-tions in the directory structure, depending on what type of Assembly you are installing.

The first location is in the application's base directory. This is where you want to install the first Assembly type, which is a private Assembly that will not be used by any other pro-grams. If only your program uses an Assembly, then you can protect it and limit access to it by making it private and co-locating it with the application's main files. If you wish to allow programs other than your single application to use your Assembly, then the application's directory is an option. Because a private Assembly is used only by the application it is distributed with, .NET doesn't need to assign it a strong name to identify it. Flip back to Chapter 13 for more information about how strong names work.

The second type of Assembly is known as a shared Assembly because it can be shared among different applications. Shared Assemblies are built with strong names that uniquely and securely identify the Assemblies to other pieces of code. Shared Assemblies are installed in a public location on the system, which for a Windows NT/2000 machine would be in the \WinNT\Assembly directory. Locally installed shared Assemblies are placed in a subdirectory under \WinNT\Assembly named GAC (short for Global Assembly Cache). As you will see in just a bit, the GAC is capable of holding more than one copy of an Assembly. All the .NET Framework Assemblies are installed in subdirectories within the GAC. The GAC maintains a database of all Assemblies installed into it. When an applica-tion requests an Assembly with a certain version number, the GAC consults its maps and directs the application to the proper Assembly, or returns an exception to the application letting it know that a requested Assembly version is not installed.

The third Assembly type is similar to the locally installed shared Assembly, except that it requires special controls and restrictions. If you install an application locally, then, to a certain degree, you are trusting that the included Assemblies won't cause damage to your system. Assemblies that users install and trust go into the GAC. Assemblies can also be downloaded from the Internet. Because it would be unwise to install an Assembly downloaded from the Internet with all of the rights and permissions that your local Assemblies have, these pieces of code are quarantined in a special download directory below the \WinNT\Assembly cache, which is often referred to as the Web cache. Assemblies stored in the Web cache are prevented from executing actions, which could damage a user's system, such as by deleting files or using resources you wouldn't want an outsider to use, such as your address book.

The fourth and final Assembly installation location is related to ASP.NET Web Applications. By default, your Web Application will be built and installed underneath the Internet Information Services (IIS) Web server's root directory, \Inetpub\wwwroot, in a directory named after your project. Below this directory is a \bin directory where the Web Application will store its own Assembly. Visual Studio.NET creates this directory, and the directory permissions are set up so that Web surfers cannot browse or examine the contents of the bin directory. Any shared Assemblies your ASP.NET pages reference are stored in the GAC with the rest of the system Assemblies.

Assemblies

At the heart of every .NET application is the Assembly, the building block that you create to use with other Assemblies to form your applications. When you talk about deploying a Visual Studio 6 application, most of the issues you address concern the COM components you have created, which are the basic building blocks of a Visual Studio 6 application. When you are planning your .NET application deployments, the Assembly is at the center of all of your plans. This section discusses how Assemblies are versioned and shared, and how these settings affect your deployment plans.

Assembly Versioning

Unlike COM DLLs, your computer can store and use multiple versions of the same Assembly, each sharing the same name. How does your computer do that? Each Assembly has a subdirectory within the GAC, and below that is a subdirectory named for each version of the Assembly. So, if your system has both a version 1.01.001.1 and a version 1.02.023.3, each of these would have its own directory containing a different version of the same Assembly. Using this storage method, your system can have multiple usable copies of a Customer.DLL file. With COM, your system might have multiple copies of a DLL installed on the hard drive, but only one of them would be the currently registered and active version that client code will reference and use.

When your system maintains multiple versions of an Assembly, all of these copies can be used. Remember that when an application is built, it creates a list of Assemblies that it references and their associated version numbers. The application packages these into its manifest. So, application A can use version 1.01.001.1 of your Assembly, and application B can use version 1.02.023.3 of that very same Assembly, which may have been deployed at a later date than the first version. Because the GAC can maintain multiple copies, you can be assured that when an installed program installs a new version of a certain Assembly, that installation will not break an older application that references a different version of the Assembly. Figure 14.2 shows the GAC directory structure and an example Assembly directory containing two different versions of an Assembly.

Assemblies are given version numbers so that you can distinguish between them. Those version numbers come in four parts. For example, an Assembly could be given version number 1.02.003.4, whereby the first two sections, 1.02, are the version number that you will assign to your work. It is up to you to increment these numbers to match a versioning scheme your organization has defined. The third section of the example version number, .003, is the build number. Every time you build your application, this number is incremented. If you have to rebuild your application, and want to keep the build number the same, you can increment the final piece of the version number, which is known as the build revision number (.4 in the example). If your development team is doing a Friday afternoon smoke

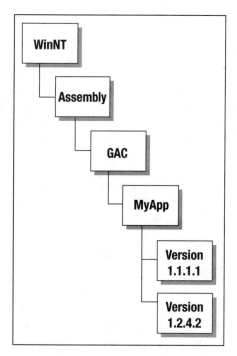

Figure 14.2
The GAC directory and two versions of an Assembly.

test to see whether the application will run as expected, and you spot a bug that is quickly resolved, you can maintain the same build number and instead increment the build revision number when you rebuild the fixed application.

> ### Note
> *To set the version number that your Assembly will be built with, look for the **<Assembly: AssemblyVersion("1.0.*.*")>** tag in the AssemblyInfo.vb file included in your project. You can edit the value of an **AssemblyVersion** tag to be whatever version you would like. The asterisk symbol is a wildcard that the compiler fills in when your Assembly is built. You should change only the first two portions of the **AssemblyVersion** and allow the compiler to set the last two version positions.*

The directories your Assemblies are stored in will be named after their version numbers. The applications that use your Assemblies will maintain a list of the Assembly version numbers so that the applications know which copy in the GAC is the one they need to bind to. .NET not only allows the system to maintain different versions of an Assembly in the GAC, but also allows more than one version of an Assembly to be loaded by the runtime compiler. Application A can run and use version 1.01.001.1 of the Customers.DLL while application B simultaneously runs with a copy of version 1.02.023.1 loaded into memory right alongside its ancestor version. The Common Language Runtime (CLR) will know which application is talking to which Assembly and route those calls accordingly.

Here is an application scenario that will help you to understand how Assembly versioning works at runtime. Imagine that you have created two separate Class Library Projects in .NET, called TestA and TestB. One of the methods in a Class in TestA references the TestB Assembly, and one of the methods in a Class in TestB references the TestA Assembly, forming a nice circular reference. When you build your TestA and TestB Projects, you will have two Assemblies installed in the GAC, both with version 1.01.001.1, and both with manifests that reference the other (A to B, and B to A). So far this is pretty easy to understand. To spice things up, suppose that a month later you add a new method to the Class in TestA and rebuild it. This new version will be numbered 1.02.001.1, and two copies of the TestA Assembly will exist on your system, each in its own directory in the GAC named after its version number. When the second version of TestA was built, it referenced the one and only version of TestB, but TestB has not been rebuilt, so its manifest still points to the first version of TestA.

Confused yet? Now for the final twist. Suppose that version 1.02 of TestA is loaded and calls version 1.01 of TestB, which in turn makes a call to a method in TestA. Because TestB only knows about version 1.01 of TestA, the CLR will load version 1.01 of TestA to make TestB happy. Within this single AppDomain now exist one copy of TestB and two copies of TestA. Figure 14.3 illustrates the relationship between these three Assemblies loaded in a single AppDomain. No need to worry about how you are going to clean up after this circular reference, because the Garbage Collector will handle it for you. Circular reference handling in Visual Basic 6 is hard enough when trying to figure out whether A is done with B and

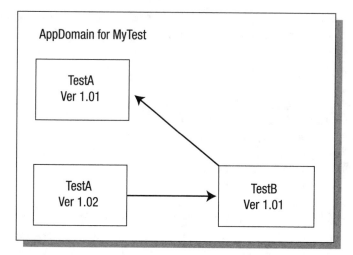

Figure 14.3
Multiple copies of an Assembly in a single AppDomain.

whether B is done with A, but imagine having to deal with A version 1 using B, and B using A version 2. It simply could not be done without that handy Garbage Collector to clean up the mess for you.

Maintaining Assembly Versions

With all the versions floating around the system, you might think that tracking and controlling all the Assemblies would be an administrative nightmare and a headache for developers to contend with. Not so. The ability to store and use multiple versions of an Assembly removes the need to worry about backward-compatibility. You can edit a Class and change all of its properties and methods and affect nothing except for the application you build with that updated Class. An application is distributed with all the Assemblies that it is built with. The downside to this is that you cannot exclude certain Assemblies from your installation package in the hopes that they are already installed on the client. Your applications hold exact references to an Assembly's version, and if the target system has that Assembly but a different version number, your application will not work. As a result, some .NET installation packages will be larger than before, to include all the Assembly versions that are listed in the application's manifest.

Every time you rebuild an Assembly, any application that uses that Assembly that needs to take advantage of the changes made to it will need to be rebuilt as well, because otherwise their manifests will hold pointers to the older, nonupdated version. If any applications do not need to use the updated version of your Assembly, they can be left alone and will continue to work as they always have. When you are updating the components of an application, start your builds at the outlying Assemblies and work your way up to the final build, which will be the top-level application that uses all of those updated Assemblies. If you built the parent Assembly first, and then the child Assemblies, your parent Assembly will be referencing outdated version numbers.

All the settings you used in Visual Basic 6, such as project and binary compatibility, are no longer needed because every application uses the exact copies of the Assemblies it was built with. Administration is not a problem either, because the GAC stores and tracks your Assemblies for you. No more worries about affecting other applications or having other applications ruin your work. The only major price to pay for all of this freedom is storage, and with 20GB drives going for under $150, that is a very small price to pay to ensure your applications will never be corrupted.

Sharing Assemblies

For an Assembly to be shared by multiple applications, that Assembly must be signed with a unique strong name. A strong name is based on a key pair that you generate and assign to your Assembly by using a program named sn.exe, which is included in the .NET Framework SDK. You will run the strong name tool and generate a file containing a pair of matching keys that will be used by your Assembly to generate a strong name. After you have generated a key, you will assign that key to your Solution via the Solution Properties window. Exercise 14.1 walks you through the steps of creating a key pair using sn.exe and assigning it to a Solution so that the Assembly you create can be shared.

Exercise 14.1: Creating a Shared Assembly

1. Open a command prompt window by clicking Start | Run, typing "cmd" into the textbox, and pressing the Enter key.

2. Enter the following command and then press Enter:

```
sn.exe -k c:\mykey.snk
```

If the sn.exe tool is not in your computer's execution path, you need to locate this file using Windows Explorer and then change into the sn.exe file's directory to execute the command. Keep this command prompt window open for Step 8.

3. In Visual Studio.NET, create a new Class Library Project and name it ShareMe.

4. Right-click the ShareMe Project in the Solution Explorer window and select Properties.

5. Under the Common Properties folder in the left pane, click the Strong Name item. To the right of this entry, check the box next to the line that says Generate Strong Name Using.

6. The key file option should be selected by default, with a textbox below it that is currently blank. You will see a Generate Key button here. You can use this button to create

the same key file you manually created in Step 2. For this exercise, I will use the manually generated key file. Click the Browse button to the right of this textbox and locate the mykey.snk file you created on the C drive. When you locate the file, double-click it to indicate that this is the key file you are using. Click the OK button at the bottom of the Project Properties window to close it. You should now see your mykey.snk file listed as a part of this project in the Solution Explorer window.

7. Select Build | Build. Your Output window will report one succeeded build when the job is complete.

8. In the command prompt window, change into your ShareMe Project's directory, and then use the **cd** command to access the \bin directory. Enter the following command:

```
sn.exe -v ShareMe.exe
```

9. The strong name tool will examine the ShareMe.exe file and report back to you that this file has a valid strong name. If you use the sn.exe tool with the –v switch on any Assembly that does not have a key assigned to it, the strong name tool will report back that this Assembly is not a strongly named Assembly.

10. Keep this command prompt open for Exercise 14.2.

When other projects reference your Assembly, they will do so using the strong name you generated for your Assembly. Every time an application that uses your Assembly loads, it will verify your strong name to ensure that it is using the correct version of the Assembly. Without the correct key file, other developers will not be able to create an Assembly with the exact same strong name as your Assembly, which is why assigning keys to Assemblies and generating strong names from those keys is known as *signing* your Assembly. The strong name provides a guarantee to other applications that your Assembly is the exact same version that they were compiled with.

After a shared Assembly has been built, it needs to be entered in to the GAC's database and moved into the GAC directory structure so that other applications can reference your shared Assembly. The GAC is capable of maintaining multiple versions of an Assembly and will direct the calling applications to whichever version their manifest directly references based on the Assembly's strong name. Visual Studio.NET has a utility called GACUtil.exe that you can use to register your Assemblies in the GAC database and move them into the cache directory structure. If you are creating a deployment package containing a shared Assembly, then the Windows Installer will automatically register the Assembly with the GAC during your application's installation process.

Types of Deployments

The type of deployment strategy you use depends on what type of application you are building. Your application may be located completely on a single computer, which will greatly simplify your installation planning. But how do you deploy a distributed application that spans one or more servers, plus the pieces that install on the clients' desktops? This section discusses the issues pertaining to the locations of your installations and the means you can use to get your application's parts to those locations and install them.

Standalone

The standalone application is the oldest and easiest application to deploy. All of your code will go onto one machine and will not need to communicate with any servers to perform its work. While business applications rarely fall under this grouping, most of your home-user applications, such as word processors and games, do. Your application will still have many pieces to it, and can include numerous Assemblies to be installed on the computer, but your deployment package can be distributed as a single package and installed in a single effort.

Client/Server Applications

Almost as old as the standalone applications are the client/server installations. This is a two-part installation with the majority of the code and back-end work being done on a centralized server, with a smaller interface piece installed locally on the employees' desktops so that they can access the system. In a simple client/server deployment, the server includes all the back-end resources, such as the database, so that you can install the server's portion in one complete package and then install a separate client package on each employee's machine. Modern software applications rarely fall into this simple two-tier model because of component distribution and the multiserver environments you will read about next.

Distributed Applications

Modern-day business applications typically are distributed in nature and can be spread across many different servers on your network. One server may do nothing but house the database, while another server acts as a centralized application server. The employees still need to access the application, so either a local client-version installation will be running on their desktops, or they will log in to the application with a browser by contacting the Web server. This Web server can also be a separate machine from the ones holding the database and the business logic.

Originally, creating distributed applications was known as a three-tier development model because designs included a presentation, business logic, and data tier. The three-tier model is more commonly referred to as a n-tier model because the number of actual tiers you can employ can be variable. Within the business tier, there can be many different layers and types of components being used. In a Web Application, presentation logic is present on both the server that creates the Web pages and the client where the Web browser draws out the Web page and implements the client-side logic, which in turn often implements a subset of your business rules.

The real key to designing distributed applications is to break apart objects in your code that are not related to each other, thus creating numerous smaller pieces. Although it may take a little extra work to design and code such a fragmented system, the benefits to your application's distribution are numerous. Maintenance of the application is improved because you only have to update and replace your applications piece by piece instead of fully redeploying the entire package. As the application workload grows, distributed applications can be further distributed to other machines that implement load balancing, which you will learn about next. Finally, componentization better supports code reuse and allows you to take a single component from one software project and use it in another project without bringing along all the unneeded code from the older project.

Farming and Load Balancing

For extremely high-demand enterprise applications and for Web-based applications accessed through the Internet, a single server may not be enough to handle the workload. In these cases, applications can be further distributed among multiple servers deployed in a server farm. For example, a single Web site can be housed on multiple Web servers, each one having its own copy of the Web site. Using either software or hardware load-balancing techniques, the network will route Internet requests for Web pages to the least-busy server. Farming and load balancing can also be used with COM components and .NET Assemblies to distribute their workload among different machines. This is known as *component load balancing (CLB)*. To the applications making calls to components that are being load balanced, there will appear to be only one single copy to talk to. The server performing the CLB administration will accept the calls to the components and pass them along to the most available copy of your component.

In the past, deploying and maintaining multiple copies of the same code spread across the network took a lot of planning and some pretty good timing, but now, with applications such as Microsoft's Application Center 2000, all of these mirror copies can be centrally managed and updated. Application Center 2000 handles the distribution of your code by farming it out to the individual servers for you. This collection of servers that houses the copies of your code is known as a *cluster* to Application Center. The ability to distribute your application among multiple servers is known as *scaling-out*. If you are working on an application that can be used by a large population of users (hundreds or even thousands of users), then load balancing and server farms are issues you will want to consider. If your application is not under quite that extreme of a workload, you can explore less-complicated methods of improving your application's performance, such as upgrading the server's memory or processor. This is known as *scaling-up*, and making a few hardware improvements to a server is far easier than keeping a large server farm and all the components contained in it in sync with each other.

Distribution Media

You will need a way to get your application from the development machine to the customers' machines. To answer the question of what type of media you are going to use to package your application, you must first determine who and where your customer is. Is your customer a large corporation that has asked for a distributed application to be installed across many servers? Will the users need a locally installed interface or will they use a Web-based interface? Are you going to sell your product shrink-wrapped in stores, or will you allow users to download it from the Internet? This section covers the standard distribution media types, from the small-scale floppies to worldwide Internet downloads.

Floppies

I'm sure you remember the days when the box you brought home from the software store was filled with disks. Some of you may even remember 5.25-inch floppies being in the box. Even now, you will encounter this form of limited-distribution media, particularly when dealing with single files such as a Microsoft Word document that you might be taking home with you to work on. Very few applications these days fit on a single floppy disk, and for most applications, the number of disks you would need to store a program is unthinkable. In fact, by some company standards, the disk is such an outdated medium that you may encounter minitowers and servers that do not even have a floppy drive installed (don't laugh, I've seen it more than once).

CD-ROMS

The floppy was replaced as the media of choice by the CD-ROM. Capable of storing up to 650MB of information on a single disk, the CD is the best choice for mobile deployments, meaning those users who are not on a company network or customers who will buy your application shrink-wrapped off the shelf. CDs are also a great choice for archiving your applications or transporting the installation pieces to the customer's location.

CDs are a usable form of resource storage that can save your users' valuable hard drive space. Resources such as help files and multimedia files can remain on the CD and be accessed that way by the application without copying those files to the hard drive. Fast access times for modern CD-ROM drives and their large storage capacity make this a terrific option for application deployment. Now that CD-ROM read/write drives are affordable to the masses, everyone has the ability to easily burn their application to CD for distribution to their customers and clients.

Network

The network is also a form of distribution media. You can store an installation package on a shared drive somewhere on the network and then access it from any computer capable of seeing that shared drive. Using the network is a really wise choice for enterprise-wide client-side installations. Instead of walking around the building with a CD in hand, you can instead direct the users or systems administrators to simply run your centrally located installation program on the client's machine. The real beauty of network installations is that you have to update only one copy of the installation media. No need to recopy disks or reburn CDs when a new version of your application is released. Just copy the new installation program to the share drive and continue installing. This is a great way to distribute updates and patches to everyone on the network, as well.

Network administration packages are available that enable systems administrators to automate the installation of software and update files on remote user machines. With these systems, administrators don't need to personally visit each machine or involve the users in the installation. Just let the software install your application after everyone has gone home for the night and, when they log in the next morning, they will have a new toy to play with. As a developer, you will want to provide the customer with a CD copy of your application to put on their shelves just so they have something to install in case of a catastrophic server failure or a natural disaster that destroys all the network backup tapes.

Not only can you deploy your applications across the network, but you also can use the network to link client-side application pieces with resources stored on a network share. This option cuts down on the hard drive space used on the client's machine, and allows you to store resources in one centralized location where all users can access them. Large files, such as multimedia sound and movies and application help files, can be accessed across the network. Enterprise installations of programs such as Office 2000 that feature an install-on-demand feature can centrally locate a copy of the installation CD on the network and allow all users to install needed pieces across the network, saving the systems administrators a great deal of time and energy. Even a user's working files can be stored on a server and accessed from their desktops across the network using a locally installed program. This is a great idea because typically local desktop machines are not covered in a company's backup plans, but the application servers should be, thereby saving and preserving the users' work from possible disaster.

Internet

The latest and greatest distribution media is the Internet. In fact, it is becoming such a popular and widely used form of distribution that other forms of media, such as music and books, are exchanged and downloaded regularly on the Web. Early in the history of the Internet, developers used this new distribution media to allow users throughout the world to download their applications. The typical Internet software download is a single standalone installation package. Because you do not have a direct connection with your customers on the Internet, software downloaded from the Internet often has a licensing requirement that limits its usage, disables certain functions, or disables the application after a certain number of days.

Some applications and operating systems, such as Windows 2000, are using the Internet as a means to check for updates and patches. This feature is particularly useful for customers who you are not in contact with, unlike those that work in an office building. Instead of using systems administration software to push updates and patches out to the clients, you can build your application with the ability to call back to a centralized server on the Internet and regularly check for updates. If an update is found, your application can easily download it from the server and install it locally, meaning your customers will always be up to date. If you are designing an application that can communicate with the software distributor across the Internet, be aware of customers' privacy concerns. You should give the user the option to disable or limit the actions your software can perform using the Internet. Many users will be fearful that your software is stealing their files and selling their personal information, and, true or not, if users think this is happening, then you aren't going to have much luck trying to sell your software to anyone.

Purchasing and downloading software from the Internet is catching on with consumers and may someday soon replace going to the software store and buying boxed software. Hopefully this will bring software prices down, because publishers will be saved the overhead of creating CDs, boxes, and instruction manuals. Still, I like having a CD that I can turn to in case my system crashes. Home users rarely have a backup plan, and when they have to rebuild their systems from scratch, they do not want to repurchase and redownload your software. One option is to give them lifetime free downloads of the version of the product they purchased. Another option that I like is to offer to mail them a CD copy of the software, for a few extra dollars. Although the Internet is a terrific distribution medium, consumer confidence and trust in the system is not at the level yet that will allow software publishers to completely abandon physical distribution media.

Builds

Before code can be deployed, or even executed, it must go through a build stage. When you build a project, the Visual Studio.NET integrated development environment (IDE) takes all the code in your project and creates Assemblies. Any resources you have included in your project, and any references to other Assemblies, are included in the build phase. The build process glues together all the standalone pieces you have created within your project to produce a deployable package.

You will find the menu items for Solution building under the Build menu at the top of Visual Studio.NET. The very top item, Build, will build your entire Solution based on the currently selected build configuration. As you will learn in the next section, more than one type of build process configuration is available in .NET, and you are already very familiar with one of them, the debug build. The second menu item on the Build menu is Rebuild All. A rebuild first cleans out the directory you are building your Solution to, and then it performs a build from scratch. This keeps the build directory clean and removes old, outdated files from past builds. The different build configurations you can define for your Solutions are described next.

Debug Builds

Every time you create some code in Visual Studio.NET and then run it to see what it does, you are using one of the .NET build types to quickly put everything together for testing purposes. This is known as a *debug build,* which means Visual Studio.NET is building your application with a focus on debugging and testing. Extra information is added into the build to support the testing and fixing of your code, and your application is not optimized for performance with this type of build. Try out Exercise 14.2 to examine the building of a simple application for debugging.

Exercise 14.2: Debug Builds

1. Start Visual Studio.NET and create a new WindowsApplication Project named Deploy1.

2. Make sure that the Standard toolbar is visible. To the right of the Start button, which looks like the play button on a VCR, you will see a drop-down box. Be sure that this is set to Debug.

3. Ensure that the Output window is visible. You can load this window by selecting View | Other Windows | Output. At the top of the Output window is another drop-down box. Click this box and set it to Build to display the build messages.

4. Save your project and then click the Start button. The Build window will scroll a series of messages reporting the results of the debug build. The first line of this output will report that your project is named Deploy1 and that you built it using the Debug configuration. The next few lines will report that the project resources and references have been added and that the compilation of your code has been completed.

5. The last two lines of this report are the summary lines for the Build and Deploy stages. Because you have not deployed this project, the Deploy line will report zero successes, failures, and skipped projects. The Build line should report one successful build, with zero failures and skipped projects. If you added a second project to your Solution and ran another build, the Build line should report two successful builds.

6. Stop the application and keep this project open.

Exercise 14.2 introduced you to the Build information that gets displayed in the Output window of the IDE, and shows that even though you are debugging your project in Visual Studio.NET, your application still goes through a build phase before it starts. The drop-down box on the Standard toolbar lets you quickly select what type of build you wish to use for this run, and when you are debugging, you will want to use the debug build for its added debugging information and features. This build is not a good choice for final building of Assemblies because of the added debugging information it includes with your code and its lack of code optimization steps.

If your code has an error in it that prevents your project from being built, the Output window's Build information reports a failure and the IDE pops up a message letting you know errors occurred during the build phase, and asking you if you wish to continue running the program. In most instances, you will want to respond No to this question and troubleshoot the problem back in Visual Studio. The Build output messages include a line reporting each individual problem encountered during the build. These failures can typically be avoided by monitoring the Task List window, which reports syntax errors in your code that prevent proper application building.

To see a build failure in action, try adding a button to the WindowsApplication in Exercise 14.2, and then add a line of code to that button's **Click** event, adding in a syntax error. Save and then run your project, and you will see the pop-up error message and the reports of errors in the Build output messages. Notice that even though your code has bugs in it that were reported to you in the Task List window and during the build phase, Visual Studio.NET will still try to run your application. If your project cannot be built successfully without error in Visual Studio.NET, then you are not ready to move on to the deployment phase with your application.

Release Builds

When you are confident that your code is ready for the public, then it is time to switch from using debug builds to using release builds. Assemblies built for release will not have any unnecessary debugging information included in the final file, which will often make this Assembly a little bit smaller than the same code built for debugging. Code being built for release will also be optimized and should perform more efficiently than a debug build. Changing between debug and release builds is as simple as changing the value in the drop-down box on the Standard toolbar from Debug to Release. This control ties directly to the Active Config property of the Solution you are working on. Click the Solution at the top of the Solution Explorer window and you will see the Active Config property listed in the Property window.

Customized Build Modes

Building a simple single-project Solution does not require any additional settings, but what if you have multiple projects in your Solution? Each project can be built for either debugging or release, depending on how complete and finished the code is. If you add a project to your Solution that your development team created six months ago and deployed as part of another application, then you may not need to build this project using a debug build. Visual Studio.NET allows you to create customized builds that decide on a project-by-project basis which build to use. You can find these settings by selecting Build | Configuration Manager.

The Solution itself has a debug configuration defined for it that includes all the projects contained in the Solution. If you look at the Solution's Debug configuration, you will see that all the projects listed are set for debug builds. You can change the project-level builds for the Debug and Release configuration here, but it is best to keep all the projects set to Debug in the Debug configuration, and Release in the Release configuration to avoid confusion. If you wish to mix and match build types, you can create your own customized Solution build configuration and assign different projects their own unique settings. Again, you should leave the Release configuration unchanged with all projects set to Release builds and their Build checkboxes checked so that when you do finally want to build up your completed Solution for deployment, you can be sure that all of your code will be built complete with optimizations.

You can also check and uncheck a box for each project to define whether or not the project will be built at all when the Solution is using this configuration. If you uncheck the Build checkbox for one of your projects and then run your application, you will notice that the Build output messages report that one or more projects were skipped during the build process. Try out Exercise 14.3 to learn how to create a customized Solution build configuration.

Exercise 14.3: The Solution Build Configuration Manager

1. Start a new WindowsApplication Project named DeployCustom1.

2. Add a second WindowsApplication Project named DeployCustom2 to your Solution by right-clicking the Solution's name in the Solution Explorer window and selecting Add | New Project.

3. Select Build | Configuration Manager. When the Configuration Manager window opens, select the Debug entry in the drop-down box at the top of the window and notice that both projects are set to Debug build under this Solution configuration. Click the Solution's Release build and note that both projects are set to Release builds here.

4. Click the Active Solution Configuration drop-down box and select the entry labeled New.

5. For the Solution Configuration Name, call it Split. You can leave the Copy Settings drop-down listbox set to Default, and leave the Create New Project Configurations checkbox checked to give your new Solution Configuration some starting settings.

6. You will now look at the Split configuration settings. Change the Configuration setting of DeployCustom1 to Debug, and set DeployCustom2 to Release.

7. Uncheck the Build checkbox for the DeployCustom2 Project and then click the Close button.

8. Ensure that the build drop-down listbox on the Standard toolbar is set to Split, and then click the Start button.

9. Look at the Output window and set the message filter to Build to see the build phase report. You will see a successful report for DeployConfig1, and then a message saying that DeployConfig2's build was skipped. At the bottom of the build report, the final score will be one succeeded, zero failed, and one skipped project build.

When making settings for each project in the Configuration Manager window, you will notice that a drop-down box exists for each project in a column named Platform. At this time, the only value available here is .NET. In the near future, this configuration option will allow you to declare which platform type you are building your code for, which will allow the builder to make platform-specific modifications and optimizations to your code. This is a very exciting feature that I cannot wait to see implemented, because it will enable developers to write once and create multiple platform-specific builds based on one set of code.

Build Order and Dependencies

In a multiple-project Solution, you may want to rearrange the order in which your individual projects are built. You can do so by selecting Project | Project Build Order to open a window named Project Dependencies with a tab named Build Order showing. A list on this tab shows all the projects within your Solution. The order defined in this list is based on the dependencies that are defined on the Dependencies tab of this window. Click that tab and you will see the list of projects in a drop-down list at the top of the window, and a list of dependencies for the selected project in a window below the list.

If one project makes a call to another project, it has a dependency on that project, so that project will have a checkmark next to it. If the checkbox next to a project is gray, then you cannot set a dependency to it because doing so would result in a circular dependency. If you have three projects in your Solution named A, B, and C, then A can depend on B, and B can depend on C, but C cannot depend on either A or B because this would create a circular dependency. Figure 14.4 shows how A, B, and C can form a circular dependency. The Dependencies tab prevents you from creating a circular dependency. The build order will be based on these dependencies so that the items are not built until the items that they depend on are done being built.

Batch Builds

The larger your projects get, the longer a build can take. Small projects can build in just a few seconds, but some builds can take hours. Visual Studio.NET gives you the ability to batch all of your builds together so that you can pick and choose the projects you wish to build and which build configuration to use for each one, and then get out of the office for a

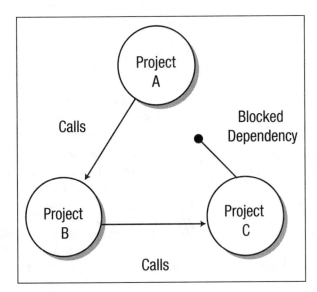

Figure 14.4
Circular dependencies.

break while your projects are built. You will find the Batch Build utility under the Build menu. All the projects in your loaded Solution will be listed in the Batch Build window at least twice, once for every build configuration you have defined for them. By default, every project starts with a debug and release build, so you will have at least two entries for every project here.

You can check the checkbox next to each build you wish to add to your batch, and then click the Build, Rebuild, or Clean buttons on the right to fire off your batch build. Clicking the Clean button will clean out old build files from the target build directories. Clicking the Rebuild button will first perform a cleanup, just as clicking the Clean button does, and then it will perform a build of your selected files. The progress for your batch build will be reported in the Output window for you to monitor. Batch builds are not intended for debugging because they will only create builds of your code, but Visual Studio will not actually run the code when the build is complete. After you have a set of batch build configurations, you can quickly rebuild all of these files using Build | Build BatchBuilds or Build | Rebuild BatchBuilds, which will immediately execute the builds defined in the Batch Build window.

Setup and Deployment Projects

Previously, Visual Studio shipped with an add-on tool named the Package and Deployment Wizard. When your application was ready for deployment, you would save it in Visual Studio, and then start this separate deployment utility and point it to your finished project awaiting packaging. In .NET, the deployment phase is now integrated into the development IDE. .NET introduces many new concepts and ideas to software deployment, such as the Windows Installer, which is introduced in this section. After learning about the Windows Installer, you will learn about the different installation projects you will use in .NET to deploy your applications.

The Windows Installer

The new Windows Installer was first used with Microsoft Office 2000. Windows Installer comes preinstalled on Windows 2000, Windows Me, and Windows XP operating systems, and can be installed as an add-in for Windows NT and 95/98 systems. It's important to remember that Windows Installer must be installed on the computer before your .NET application will be able to install. Software packages created to use Windows Installer can be distributed as one complete file ending with a .msi file extension. This one file includes all the pieces needed for the installation, as well as the instructions that will be given to the Windows Installer engine to tell it what to do with all of those pieces.

Visual Studio 6 installation packages used a Setup.exe file to start and manage the installation, with all the necessary resources wrapped into an accompanying CAB file. The setup programs handled all the installation and registration issues for an application based on another file named Setup1.lst. The problem with this approach was that each setup program was not intimately aware of what was already installed on the operating system. The Windows Installer fixes this problem, because the installation software is a part of the operating system and knows about all the installed software. Your .NET MSI installation files will then tell Windows Installer which files it needs to install and what settings to make, but it will not tell Windows Installer how to do its job. Windows Installer maintains a database of all installed software packages, so it knows what references go with which programs and will prevent the problems that arose from those DLL hell issues mentioned at the beginning of this chapter. Application uninstalls are also handled by Windows Installer so that it can check its database and ensure that the application's uninstall process does not damage another program installed on the system.

The Windows Installer database can be used by administrative programs such as Microsoft's Systems Management Server (SMS) to identify software components and install them on remote machines. One of my favorite features of Office 2000 is the "install on demand" feature. You can install a standard set of Office 2000 programs and utilities on your system and leave uninstalled the pieces you do not think you will need. If you use a function in a program that requires the use of a feature you did not install, Windows Installer launches and attempts to install that piece so that you can keep working. Typically, this results in a message box telling the user to insert the Office 2000 CD into the drive so that this piece can be installed. After the piece is installed, Windows Installer updates the application database with the new settings.

Setup Project

Instead of starting an external program to create your installation package, you will instead add a special deployment project to your Solution. Which project you add depends on the type of deployment you have in mind. The Setup Project is the standard project you add to your Solution for Windows-based applications. Of all the new deployment project types, this one is the closest to the old Packaging and Deployment Wizard installation packages. The Setup Project deploys full applications that have Windows-based interfaces to the default Program Files installation directory.

A Setup Project offers a great deal of options for you to customize the installation of your application. The six major areas of customization that you can adjust within your Setup Project are listed in Table 14.1, along with a brief description of what these different configuration areas are used for. When you are editing these different areas of your Setup Project, you will be working with both the Design window, which displays all the items within that area, and the Properties window, which lists all the properties for each highlighted setting in the Design window.

I strongly support the "learn by doing" approach, so try out Exercise 14.4, which will step you through adding and configuring a Setup Project to a Solution containing a simple Windows-

Table 14.1 Setup Project configuration areas.

Area	Typical Configuration Uses
File System	Define the default installation directory, add folders to the user's desktop, and add menu items to the user's Start|Programs menu
Registry	Create customized entries in the system's Registry
File Types	Declare customized file types that your application is associated with
User Interface	Customize the windows and interfaces users will see when installing your application
Custom Actions	Define customized actions for your application's installation, install commits, rollbacks, and uninstalls
Launch Conditions	Define prerequisites for your application's installation that your Setup Project will check and verify before starting an installation

Application Project. This exercise visits some of the more common configuration areas, such as the file system settings and Registry settings. Windows Installer will perform all the configurations defined within the Setup Project at the time of installation.

Exercise 14.4: Creating and Configuring a Setup Project

1. Start Visual Studio.NET and create a new WindowsApplication named DeployMe.

2. Right-click the DeployMe Solution in the Solution Explorer window and select the Add | New Project menu item. In the Add New Project window, click the folder in the Project Types pane named Setup And Deployment Project.

3. Select the Setup Project icon, name this Project DeploySetup, and click the OK button to add this project to your Solution. Right-click DeploySetup in the Solution Explorer window and select Add | Project Output. The DeployMe Project should be displayed in the drop-down box at the top. Highlight Primary Output in the list and click OK. This adds the DeployMe Project's primary output, which is an executable file, to the DeploySetup Project. You can add additional projects to the Setup Project in the same way. An item now appears under the DeploySetup Project called Primary Output from DeployMe, and a folder appears below DeploySetup named Detected Dependencies that is now full of dependency information.

4. The DeploySetup Project's File System information will be open in the Design window and you will see two panes. The left pane lists four folders: Application Folder, Global Assembly Cache, User's Desktop, and User's Program Menu. The right pane lists items added to each of these folders. At the moment, all of these folders are empty.

5. With the DeploySetup item in the Solution Explorer window selected, look at the Properties window, which is where the general installation information will be defined, such as the author's name, manufacturer's name, the URL to your Web site, and the title for the installation screens. Change the Title and Project Name properties both to

DeployMe, and enter your first name for the Manufacturer field. Notice the properties here that define whether the install program should first look for newer installs and whether it should uninstall older versions of itself before installing your application. Three codes (Product, Package, and Upgrade) also are generated for your Solution so that Windows Installer can uniquely identify your installations. You have the option of selecting these codes and regenerating them if you would like a different ID.

6. Click the Application Folder in the left pane and look at the Properties window. You will see the properties associated with the folder this setup project will install itself to. The DefaultLocation property will be set to [*ProgramFilesFolder*] [*Manufacturer*] \ [*ProductName*]. This path is made up of three variables: the system's preferred place to install programs, the name of the Solution's manufacturer (your first name entered in Step 5), and the Solution name.

7. You can add a subfolder below the main application folder by right-clicking the Application Folder in the left pane and selecting Add | Folder. Go ahead and add a folder and name it Graphics. This folder now appears in the right pane when you click the Application Folder in the left pane.

8. Below the Application Folder you will see the Global Assembly Cache folder. You cannot change the location of a system's GAC, but by right-clicking the Global Assembly Cache folder, you can add the project output of one or more of the projects in your Solution to install the generated Assemblies to the GAC. The next two folders down allow you to customize the user's desktop and program menu entries for your application. Your installation could create folders on the user's desktop or add a menu item to the user's Start | Programs menu tree to let them start your application.

9. To look at another section of setup configuration options, right-click DeploySetup in the Solution Explorer window and look under the View menu. This is where you can switch between the six different configuration areas. Select the File Types menu item.

10. Registry View: In the Solution Explorer window, right-click DeploySetup and select View | Registry. In the Design window, expand the HKEY_LOCAL_MACHINE tree, and then expand the Software tree so that you see the entry your application will make, which will be named [Manufacturer]. Right-click this entry and select New | Key. A new folder will be added below [Manufacturer] that you should name DeployMe after your main project. Press Enter to finish adding this folder. Right-click the DeployMe folder and select New | Environment String Value. In the right pane, a value pair will be added. Name this Database_Server and press the Enter key. In the Properties window, set the Value property to MyServerName. When your application installs, it will automatically make this Registry entry for you, which you can call on in your code to find out the name of the database server. Administrators can change this server name in the Registry if a new server is installed, saving you the trouble of rebuilding your application.

11. Launch Conditions View: Right-click DeploySetup in the Solution Explorer window and select View | Launch Conditions. In the Design window, right-click Search Target Machine and select Add File Search. Name this entry MustHaveFile. Highlight MustHaveFile and, in the Properties window, set the Folder property to Fonts Folder, and set the File property to Roman.fon. This setting causes the installation program to search the machine for this font, and only allows the installation to proceed if the font is found.

12. Select File | Save All to save all of your settings.

13. Right-click DeploySetup and select Properties. The DeploySetup Property Pages will be displayed.

14. At the top of the window, change the Configuration setting to Release. In the panel on the left, click Build. In the Output file name box, you will see the path that your installation file will be saved to. Change this to Release\MyFirstInstall.msi.

15. Because you want all of your resources packaged within the MSI file, leave the Package Files property set to In Setup File. If you select CAB files, further down in the Property Page is an area where you can specify the maximum size of your CAB files. Below that setting is a place where you can authenticate your application by providing a certificate to any users proving the code is authentic. A certificate is not necessary for a deployment. Refer to Chapter 13 to learn why you would want to certify your code with a certificate.

16. At the bottom of the DeploySetup Property Pages, click the Apply button and then click OK.

17. On the Standard toolbar, change the build-mode drop-down listbox to Release.

18. Right-click DeploySetup in the Solution Explorer window and select Build. Visual Studio.NET will now deploy your application based on all the settings you have defined. Watch the Output window to see the Build output messages reporting the progress of your deployment. The last line should report back "Build: 2 succeeded".

19. On your desktop, open the My Documents folder, open the Visual Studio Projects folder, and then double-click the DeploySetup folder. This is the Project folder for your Setup Project. Below that is a folder named Release, in which you will see a file named MyFirstInstall.msi. This is the installation file you will distribute to your customers.

20. Double-click the MyFirstInstall.msi file. Windows Installer asks whether you wish to remove or repair your application, which was installed during your build. Select the Remove option and click the Finish button to clean out the old install, and then double-click the MyFirstInstall.msi file again to start a fresh install.

21. Click Next on the first screen, and then click Next on the Select Installation Folder screen to accept the default installation location (notice how the location variables you saw in Step 6 have been translated into a directory name). On the third screen, click the Next button to complete the installation. When the installer is done, click the Close button to exit.

22. Using Windows Explorer, look under your Program Files directory and you will see a directory named after you. Double-click this directory and you will see a subdirectory named DeployMe. Double-click this directory to see all the installed pieces of your application. My DeployMe directory has more than 12MB of files in it just to make this simple featureless WindowsApplication run. Most of the files you see in the DeployMe directory are copies of the .NET DLLs that are included with the installation package in case the user does not have a copy.

Exercise 14.4 offers a peek at only a few of the settings that can be made for your application installation package. The possible combination of settings is almost endless, and the new Setup Project offers you more freedom than ever before to decide how your software will be installed and what special settings need to be included with the installation. Adding a Setup Project to your Solution is not a simple task, and getting the installation perfect will take a lot of time and experimentation, but the level of control this project gives you should be equal to, if not better than, the software installation utilities you previously had to purchase separately to deploy your product.

Web Setup Project

Because Web-based applications now share the stage with Windows-based applications yet are still fundamentally different from their windowed cousins, Web-based applications have their own setup project. The biggest difference between a Web-based application and a Windows-based application is the location they are installed to. Because visitors to your Web server are not allowed, by default, to look in the Program Files directory, your Web-based application must be installed under the Web server's root directory (\Inetpub\wwwroot for IIS Web servers) so your Web users can use the application.

You add a Web Setup Project to your Web-based Solution the same way you added the Setup Project to your WindowsApplication, and most of the settings available to you will work the same way. The File System settings for a Web Application are more limited than those for a WindowsApplication because your Web Application is limited to the Web server's directory structure. The File System View for your Web Setup Project enables you to define folders below your Web Applications folder on the Web server, and you will be given access to the Global Cache (GAC) directory as a place where you can store your Web Application's shared Assemblies. You will not see any settings for the Start menu or the user's desktop when deploying a Web Application because a browser will always be used to access your pages, not icons or menu items. The other installation Views (Registry, File Types, Custom Actions, and Launch Conditions) will all operate the same as those in the Setup Project.

Installing a Web Application is only half of the job. The other half of a proper Web-based application installation is configuring the Web server and the Web environment for your application. Recall in Chapter 10 being introduced to the configuration files that are included with your Web Application and Web Services Project. You need to configure these files before you package your application for deployment. When your Web-based application is installed on a new Web server, your configuration files are installed as well, providing the Web server with the necessary information to properly run your application. You can refer to the "Web Application Configuration Files" section of Chapter 10 for more information on using these files to customize the Web server's behavior.

The Web Setup Project offers a terrific new way to package a Web Application into one single MSI file for deployment. Previously, because Active Server Pages (ASP) pages were script-based, the Setup and Deployment Wizard would package your DLL code for deployment, and your Web pages would be packaged separately. Someone installing your Web site would have to manually create the folder and the Web server settings, copy your Web pages into this folder, and then install the DLL setup package. Now with the Web Setup Project, installing a Web Application is just as simple as installing a WindowsApplication. Like the Setup Project, creating a Web Setup Project that suits your individual needs takes some time and effort, but you will soon learn how to quickly and easily package your Windows and Web Applications without having to manually define pages and pages of settings.

Merge Module Project

The Merge Module Project is the hardest of the four deployment project types to understand, but after you understand it, you will see why this deployment type is a wonderful new addition in .NET. If you are deploying a Solution that has a Windows front-end interface, you use the Setup Project to deploy it. If your application has a Web-based interface, you obviously use the Web Setup Project. But what if your application does not have an interface because your Solution is intended to be used by other applications? Setup Projects and Web Setup Projects are designed to deploy standalone applications, but if you are creating a Solution such as a code library or a control that can be used by other applications, then you will deploy these by packaging them with a Merge Module Project.

Because the code that your Merge Module Project will be deploying is designed to be used by other applications, that code will need to be built into a shared Assembly. Before you add a Merge Module Project to your Solution, assign the Assembly a key file to generate a strong name from using the steps outlined earlier, in the "Shared Assemblies" section. Merge module installation files have an .msm extension instead of the .msi file extension given to application installation files. When Windows Installer on the user's machine installs your merge module package, it automatically registers your shared Assembly with the system's GAC, making it available globally to all applications. If a version of your Assembly already exists on the system, the GAC will create a separate directory for your new version and maintain both the new and the older copies of your Assembly.

Cab Project

The Cab Project was included in Visual Studio.NET to allow developers to support an older method of installing software across the Web using CAB files. This installation project will create a CAB file for you that can be placed on a Web server and be made available for download over the Internet. If you have ever created a Visual Studio 6 Web installation package, then you are already familiar with downloading CAB files using a browser so that their contents can be installed locally on your machine. Because this project is intended for backward-compatibility, and because any developers who would want to use this feature are already familiar with it, the Cab Project is not covered any further in this book.

Setup Wizard

Always trying to make things easier for you, Microsoft has included a deployment wizard to help you quickly create a customized deployment project for your Solution. The Setup Wizard asks you a series of questions about the application you are planning to deploy, and then configures your Setup Project for you based on your answers. This saves you the trouble of manually going from form to form to make simple setup configuration settings, and if your deployment is reasonably simple, the wizard is a great way to get the job done quickly. You can also use the wizard to make all the necessary settings for your Setup Project, and then adjust the Setup Project manually to further customize the installation. Try out Exercise 14.5 to see how easy it is to use the Setup Wizard to deploy a WindowsApplication.

Exercise 14.5: Using the Setup Wizard

1. Create a new WindowsApplication Project and call it QuickApp.

2. Right-click the DeployMe Solution in the Solution Explorer window and select the Add | New Project menu item. In the Add New Project window, click the folder in the Project Types pane named Setup And Deployment Project.

3. Select the Setup Wizard from the list of Setup and Deployment Projects, and name this project SetupWiz.

4. The first page of the Setup Wizard will appear. Click Next to continue.

5. Page 2 of the wizard asks whether you are deploying an application or a package for redistribution, such as a merge module. Select the first option, Create A Setup For A Windows Application, and click Next.

6. Page 3 asks you which parts of the QuickApp Project you wish to package. Click the checkbox next to Primary Output For QuickApp, and click Next.

7. Page 4 allows you to add additional files to your distribution package, such as help files and graphics. At this time, you do not have any extra files to include, so just click Next to continue.

8. Page 5 provides a summary of your choices. Click Finish to complete the Setup Project creation process.

9. The SetupWiz Project is added to your Solution along with all the settings you selected. You can make additional settings when the Setup Wizard is finished by right-clicking the SetupWiz Project in the Solution Explorer window and opening a View window just as you did during Exercise 14.4.

10. On the Standard toolbar, change the build configuration drop-down listbox to Release.

11. To generate your distribution package, just right-click SetupWiz Project and select Build.

Using the Setup Wizard will feel a little more like the old Package and Deployment Wizard you are used to using, but even though you are using a wizard to decide your installation's settings, you are still adding a new project to your Solution that will contain these settings. The Setup Project is a terrific improvement over the scripts that the Package and Deployment Wizard created, because not only do you have an unbelievable amount of control over your application's installation with the Setup Project, but you also can easily change your settings and redeploy the project without having to again leave the Visual Studio environment, load a script you previously saved, and then make your changes to that script. Changing an installation setting is as easy as changing a textbox control's property value.

The Setup Wizard can simplify your Web Application and merge module installations just as easily as did your Windows Application Setup Project. If your Solution is Web-based, such as a Web Application or Web Service, then pick Create A Setup For A Web Application on the wizard's second page. If you are deploying a Class Library Project to be shared by other applications, then select the Merge Module Project type on page 2. All the other wizard pages will be the same as the ones you saw in Exercise 14.5, but the wizard will make additional settings behind the scenes to customize the deployment project based on your selected application type.

Dispersed Deployments

A single Solution in .NET can contain multiple projects, each of which can be deployed in its own unique way. If you have a Solution with one WindowsApplication Project and one Class Library Project in it, you can add two separate Setup Projects to your Solution and tailor one Setup Project to deploy your WindowsApplication piece and the other to handle the deployment of your Class Library. Each Setup Project could target a different machine to deploy to. The ability to control the deployment of your Solution on a project-by-project basis enables you to build and deploy a single Solution to multiple locations. You will use the same steps as already covered to configure your Setup Project, except that you will customize the location and server settings based on where you wish to locate the project that your Setup Project references. A single Setup Project can also handle multiple projects within a single Solution, so the deployment possibilities are almost limitless.

Summary

Software deployment has come a long was from a simple copy-and-paste installation of a single executable file. DLL components introduced a long list of problems to the issue of software deployment planning, creating a need for smarter installation programs to prevent the corruption or removal of DLLs being used by other programs. COM gave developers the ability to distribute the pieces of their application in different locations on the machine and even on separate machines, further complicating the deployment planning process. The Package and Deployment Wizard included with Visual Studio 6 was somewhat lacking in both customization features and deployment robustness, and most development shops looked to third-party deployment software to package their applications. With .NET, Microsoft has put a great deal more effort into the development of its deployment tools, and like all the other tools that were once separated from the Visual Studio IDE, the tools for configuring and deploying your application are now fully integrated into the Visual Studio.NET environment.

Chapter 15
Migrating Projects to .NET

Every time a bigger and better development environment comes along, you are faced with the question of what to do with your old application code. Consider an example outside of Visual Studio for a minute. If you create a document in Microsoft Word 97 and then install Office 2000 on your system, you will still be able to open your Word document because Office 2000 is backward-compatible with Word 97. Users would be pretty upset if they upgraded to the latest version and were suddenly unable to open their old files. Prior to Office 2000, the idea of forward compatibility was unheard of. Any document created in Office Word 97 could not be opened using Office Word 95 because that document had features embedded in it that Word 95 would be unable to interpret. Luckily, Office 2000 documents can be opened in Office 97, making the bridge between the old world and the new world a two-way road. Prior to .NET, the issue of code migration did not cause too many worries among developers because from version to version, the Visual Basic language only changed for the better, without rearranging how things worked in the past. Migrating a project usually meant just opening it in the latest Visual Basic version and saving it again.

As you near the end of this book, it should be obvious to you that your Visual Basic 6 code is not going to be so easy to migrate to Visual Basic.NET. For starters, not only were new features added to your beloved Visual Basic, but older, outdated code features have been dropped or redefined to such an extreme that .NET will not understand most of the source code files written in version 6. In all but a few cases, you will be unable to simply open a source code file that was written in Visual Basic 6 and run it in .NET without some changes being made to it.

These same migration concerns also apply to ASP Web developers, who will want to migrate their script-based Web pages to the high-speed compiled .NET environment. Although most of this chapter focuses on migrating your Windows applications from version 6 to .NET, oqʃ section is devoted entirely to the topic of ASP-to-ASP.NET migration to support those developers who have created Web-based interfaces using ASP.

This chapter examines the issues surrounding the migration of Windows and Web-based applications into the .NET Framework, including changes you can make to your older projects to simplify this transition, and directions on how to incorporate .NET's newer features into your older Visual Basic 6 Projects.

Planning Your Migration

The most important step you must accomplish before migrating an older project to Visual Studio.NET is to ask yourself why you are migrating it. Unless you are a hobbyist developer writing code on your own free time, taking your code that already works fine in the Component Object Model (COM) world and migrating it to the .NET Framework is costly in terms of time. Face it, developers are not cheap, and migrating your code to .NET will not be as easy as opening your old code in .NET, saving it, and then running it. That old code is going to require a lot of attention, both before and after the migration process. You will encounter many cases in which you should not migrate your code to .NET. You can still use your old COM components from your .NET Assemblies, and this ability can save you a lot of time and money as your development projects move into the new .NET world.

Why Migrate?

Throughout this book, you have read about all the wonderful new features of Visual Basic.NET, including inheritance, free threading, and Web Forms. As you were reading about these features, you might have thought of a few ways you could have used these features in past projects to make your applications even better. Maybe a new feature could have saved you hours of development time if only you had .NET back then. Skim back through this book and recall all of these new features, and think about how they could be used to enhance your old Visual Basic 6 Projects. When you are faced with the issue of migrating a Visual Basic 6 application to .NET, you should first list all the ways your migrated application could benefit from the move to .NET. Listing the pluses associated with migration is fairly easy to do if you understand all the new .NET features, and you should be pretty excited about the migration after you have envisioned all the benefits your software will reap. The following list points out some of the biggest benefits of migrating your code to .NET:

- Develop your application using a truly object-oriented version of Visual Basic

- Take advantage of inheritance in your application

- Use free threading to spawn processes off onto their own threads

- Use the new Web Forms as interfaces to your application

- Add shared members to your application to share variables globally

- Enjoy the new features of the improved Windows forms

- Turn your unmanaged code into managed code and use the Common Language Runtime (CLR), which can make your code more efficient

- Improve your development team's ability to code and test an application using multiple programming languages in a single environment

You likely can think of a dozen more good features of .NET that you can take advantage of. Creating a list of reasons why you should migrate will not be too hard, but prepare yourself for the next question, which is intended to bring you back to reality.

When Should You Not Migrate?

A wise man once said: "If it's not broke, don't fix it." For software developers looking at .NET, this bit of advice means that if you wrote an application in Visual Basic 6 that is working well for you, or you have already delivered that application to the customer (and if you have delivered something that works well, good for you!), then instead of looking back on what you have done and wondering how you can accomplish all of that hard work again, you should instead think about how you can build on it and incorporate your completed COM components into your new .NET Projects. In most cases, your customers do not want to be told that the software you delivered to them, or the project that they have been paying for, could be done differently or better. News like this is liable to shake up a customer's confidence in your abilities.

When it comes to completed software projects, ultimately it will be up to the customer to decide whether they want to pay for even more development time based on the benefits of .NET that you describe to them. If your coding team is still in the early stages of a development project, then you will have a lot more freedom to introduce a radically different design approach to the customer. Do not migrate your projects just for the sake of using .NET. A great deal of work is involved in going back and changing your code to work in .NET, and unless you scrap the entire development project and start over at the design stage, your application will never fully take advantage of all that .NET has to offer. Ask yourself the following questions if you are not sure whether you should migrate a development project to .NET:

- Will my customer agree to pay more to cover the time my developers will need to properly migrate their code?

- Is the project's schedule flexible enough to allow for the added migration time?

- Do the benefits of migration outweigh the added development costs?

- Can I forego the migration and use my already completed COM components from within .NET?

- Is my current development project too far along in its schedule to consider a complete redesign and migration to .NET?

- Do I have developers on staff who are familiar enough with the .NET principles to make my project's migration as painless as possible?

If the obvious answer to the question "Should I migrate this application?" is no, don't panic: this is the software industry! Redesign it for version 2 and blow the customers away with the .NET features you have added to your application. Use that old code in your new software projects. COM is not going away any time soon, and years from now you probably will still be encountering COM components when you are addressing your future application integration issues.

A lot of development shops will draw a proverbial line in the sand separating past projects created in Visual Basic 6 from the future projects they will create in Visual Studio.NET. They will continue to maintain and patch their older code using Visual Basic 6, while moving their new projects to .NET to take advantage of the latest and greatest developments. This is an acceptable approach, though it will require that development shops be proficient in two different versions of Visual Basic.

Visual Basic Pack Rats

In my closet, I still have the three floppy disks for Visual Basic for DOS version 3 that I purchased in 1994. I also have a disk in there with a copy of QuickBasic on it. When I upgraded to later versions of these products, those disks were packed away into my closest, never to be used again. I suspect that I keep those disks for sentimental reasons, or maybe I'm just too busy to clean my closets. When you buy the latest version of something, it's traditional to first uninstall the older version, abandoning the past and plunging headlong into the future. Should you take this same approach with .NET? Don't even think about it!

Warning
Do not uninstall all of your company's copies of Visual Basic 6.

Until the day arrives when your company can safely say that it no longer supports applications written in Visual Basic versions prior to .NET, you need at least a few copies of Visual Basic 6 installed around the office to do your job. Visual Basic.NET cannot open your older source-code files without first migrating them to .NET. Once your code has been migrated, you will be unable to create unmanaged COM components from Visual Basic.NET. Because software companies typically support applications for many years after their release, it is safe to say that you will still encounter Visual Basic 6 installations for years to come. Although this outdated version of Visual Studio will no longer be considered on the cutting edge of the development scenes, it will be a necessary tool to maintain and fix your unmanaged components. Do not uninstall Visual Basic 6, and do not throw those version 6 books into the closet just yet.

The good news is that Visual Studio.NET was developed to run side by side with Visual Studio 6 on the same machine. This means that an installation of Visual Studio.NET will not be seen as a traditional software upgrade in which the older version is removed and the newer version completely takes over. Instead, Visual Studio.NET installs as its own separate program, and because all the file extension names have changed, you will still be able to open your VBP Project files and VBG Project Group files in Visual Basic 6, and simultaneously open your .NET Projects and Solutions into their associated development tools. You can even have a copy of Visual Studio 6 and a copy of .NET open simultaneously if need be. This coexistence enables your developers to work on their version 6 code prior to migration, and then migrate the code to .NET all on the same machine.

Managing the Migration

If you have reached the decision that you do, indeed, need to migrate your project to .NET, you need to carefully plan and execute a migration process to ensure that the resulting .NET code is correct and operational. Visual Studio.NET ships with a wizard to help developers accomplish the migration of their code. The Upgrade Wizard is a tool to assist you in updating the code, but it is not the answer to all of your problems. When the wizard is finished migrating the code, many holes will be left in your code to fill in, and a thorough review of your code will be required to ensure that the Upgrade Wizard has correctly translated your project's code. Just as when developing software from scratch, you should implement and follow a process to achieve the best migration possible in the shortest time. The following steps outline the proper process involved with migrating a Visual Basic 6 Project to Visual Studio.NET:

1. Design review. Examine the architecture of the VB6 Project and decide whether a redesign is required. Can your VB6 code take advantage of new features in .NET such as free threading and inheritance?

2. Code upgrade. The developers familiar with the code need to examine every line of code and make the necessary changes to make the transition to .NET as smooth as possible. These changes are covered in the next section.

3. Code migration. Here is where the Upgrade Wizard finally steps in and transforms your VB6 Project into a Visual Basic.NET Project. A team leader or senior developer should monitor this step and save all outputs for the next stage.

4. Code review and gap filling. When the Upgrade Wizard is finished, review the upgrade report. The developers again have to walk through their code to ensure that the migration was a success. Many gaps may be left by the Upgrade Wizard that your developers need to fix or create code for.

5. Testing. Even if your VB6 Project was perfect, thoroughly test your new .NET version, because the level of changes made is extreme. Perform your testing at the component level first, and then at a system-wide level. Finally, perform a miniacceptance test to ensure the application still meets the customer's requirements.

After looking at the preceding steps necessary to migrate your projects, you may want to rethink your decision and re-estimate the developer costs associated with this move. Management will play a large role in a successful migration process. An unmanaged migration team might jump straight to the Upgrade Wizard step, perform a few spot fixes from the code review step, and then perform a few basic tests to prove that the system at least starts and appears to run. Trying to breeze through the migration would be a huge mistake that almost certainly would result in major bugs being discovered at some embarrassing moments. Probably the most important step is the design review phase, in which you analyze your older project and plan out the rest of the migration process. Thinking before doing can save you hours of time. The process of migrating to .NET should not be taken lightly, and it is not going to be as easy as opening your Word 97 document in Word 2000. The flowchart in Figure 15.1 shows how each step flows into the next, and how some steps may need to be revisited during the migration process if problems are encountered. Now that you know the dangers of migration, you are ready to find out how you can overcome this hurdle and succeed with your migration.

Design Review

The first step of the migration process can be a crucial step, and may cause you to change your decision to migrate your application to .NET. It is imperative that the developers reviewing the overall architectural design of your VB6 application be well versed in the intricacies and features available in .NET. The main purpose of the design review is to decide whether the application you are planning to migrate could benefit from a redesign to take advantage of the new features in .NET. Your software architects will examine the application at a high level, which means they will look at the object models and deployment layouts and not at the actual code of the application. The reviewing architects should ask themselves the following questions when they are reviewing the application:

♦ Could this project benefit from inheritance?

♦ Could any processor-intensive functions be free threaded?

♦ Does this application properly separate presentation, business, and data logic?

♦ Is the code properly object-oriented?

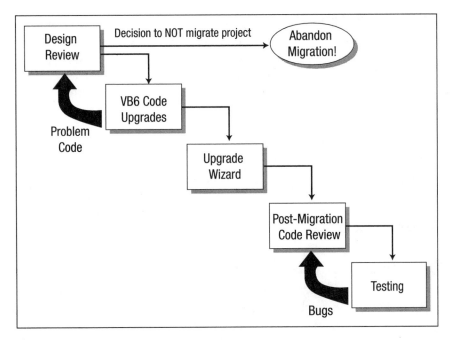

Figure 15.1
Flowchart of the migration process.

- Can object loading and initializing code be moved over to the **New** constructor event?

- Where is the object cleanup being performed in this project, and how can I update this code to take advantage of the Garbage Collector?

- Which User Defined Types (UDTs) will need to become Structures?

- Can I use Shared Members to allow multiple instances of the same block of code access to globally shared values?

- After migration, should I continue to use the unstructured exception-handling routines from VB6, or update some or all of this code to the **Try**, **Catch**, and **Finally** exception-handling model?

- Does the project use outdated commands such as the **GoTo** or **GoSub** command, which will require a great deal of time and effort to bring up to date?

- Does the project use ADO to work with the database using server-side cursors? If not, should I migrate all of my database calls to ADO.NET, or use an older version of ADO to connect to the data?

Some of these questions may seem simple and obvious, but a lot of applications do not meet these criteria. If your application was not designed in an object-oriented fashion, and does not properly separate the different logic tiers, then it is almost certainly a poor candidate for migration into the highly object-oriented .NET environment. It is better to acknowledge the application's weaknesses at this stage and accept that a complete redesign of this application will be required to drag it into the twenty-first century. If a redesign is in order, then you can abandon your plans for migration and prepare to redevelop this application.

Visual Basic 6 Code Changes

Although it is possible to simply point the Upgrade Wizard at a VB6 Project and speed through the migration process, it is highly recommended that you first examine your VB6 code and make certain changes that will prevent the Upgrade Wizard from making mistakes. This section discusses the parts of your code that you will want to pay particular attention to when performing a premigration code review.

Premigration Preparations

The first step in preparing your code to migrate to Visual Basic.NET is to make a complete copy of your VB6 Project. Make all of your premigration preparations to a copy of your code and not to the original. This will enable you to go back to your older, working version of your project if you run into any problems during the migration. Some of the changes you will make during the migration process will either cause the code to be unusable in version 6 or cause your project to not run properly. Migration to .NET is a one-way street, and you will not be able to "unmigrate" your work back to version 6. Maintaining a version 6–specific copy of your source code is like packing a spare parachute; you'll have something to fall back on should bad things happen.

Warning

The Upgrade Wizard only upgrades VB6 Projects to .NET. If you would like to migrate code from any version of Visual Basic prior to 6, you must first migrate your code to VB6 and then use the Upgrade Wizard to bring it into .NET.

You will perform three types of actions on your VB6 code to prepare it for migration: change something, delete something, and ignore a problem. You will change items in your code that will not be compatible with the .NET specifications. Changes to your older code will help the migration tool to better understand what the code is doing and will prevent unnecessary mistakes from happening during migration. The second action, deleting, removes code that no longer is needed in the migrated project. Lines of code such as those that set object references equal to **Nothing** for cleanup no longer are needed because of .NET features such as the Garbage Collector. The last action is to ignore an item that will need to be changed. This action passes the buck to the .NET migration tool, letting it make all the appropriate changes for you.

ByRef and ByVal

In .NET, all parameters are declared as either **ByRef** or **ByVal**. Even if you do not specifically declare one or the other when you are typing the parameters, the .NET IDE will choose the best one for you. If the code you are migrating to .NET does not specifically declare the parameters to be **ByRef** or **ByVal**, then, once again, .NET makes this decision for you. Generally, .NET makes the best choice possible when deciding how to declare parameters, but you will encounter situations in which you will want to avoid allowing .NET to decide and instead specifically declare which level of protection your parameter needs. They're your parameters, and you know better than the wizard whether something should be **ByRef** or **ByVal**. Review all the parameters being passed into your properties and methods in your VB6 code, and add **ByRef** or **ByVal** as appropriate.

Default Properties

Visual Basic 6 understands default properties and methods. The default property for the textbox is **Text**, and the default method for the CommandButton is **Click**. Because Visual Basic.NET no longer uses default properties and methods, you need to specifically state which property or method your code is referring to. Review your code from top to bottom, and be on the lookout for objects referenced in code without specific references to a property or method, and update these to remove this ambiguity. Take a look at the following two lines of code:

```
Textbox1 = "My Text"
Command1
```

The first line of code is making an implied reference to the **Text** property of **TextBox1**, and the second line of code is calling the **Click** method of the **Command1** button. To upgrade these two lines for migration to .NET, you would change them to look like this:

```
TextBox1.Text = "My Text"
Command1.Click
```

Once again, these changes will avoid putting the .NET migration tool in a position where it will have to guess which property or method your code intended to use. The majority of your version 6 default references will be connected to the controls on your forms.

Variable Declarations

Variables declared as **Variants** and **Currency** in VB6 Projects need to be converted to a different data type when migrating your code to .NET. You can allow the Upgrade Wizard to make these changes for you, and your **Variants** will become **Object** data types, and your **Currency** variables will become **Decimal** data types. If this is not acceptable based on the usage your variable sees, you must locate your variables in your VB6 code and assign these to another data type. Any variables that are not specifically assigned a data type should be given a specific data type before the Upgrade Wizard migrates your code and turns them all into an **Object**. The Upgrade Wizard will convert any untyped variables in your code into **Object** data types.

Not only have the data types changed in .NET, but the way that you declare your data types also is significantly different. The effect of declaring more than one variable on a single line of code has changed significantly from version 6 to .NET. Take a look at the following line of code:

```
Dim FirstName, LastName As String
```

In version 6, the **FirstName** variable would be a **Variant**, while the **LastName** variable would be a **String**. If this line of code is migrated to .NET, the migration tool will separate these two variables, and set the **FirstName** to be an **Object**, and the **LastName** to be a **String**. In many cases, this change will not be exactly what the developer intended in the first place, and problems can occur with lines of code that were written to deal with the **FirstName** variable as a **Variant** and not an **Object**. Also, ensure that all of the dates your code works with are stored in a **Date** data type. Visual Basic 6 allows you to work with dates using a **Double** data type, which will not work in .NET.

If your VB6 code declares multiple variables on a single line of code, you should first separate these declarations so that each one has its own line of code. Then, after the migration has been completed, you need to thoroughly test your code to ensure that a variable has not unexpectedly changed data types because of a misunderstood declaration line in the older version of your code. VB6 enables you to declare multiple variables simultaneously using commands such as **DefInt**, **DefLng**, and **DefBool**. These are not compatible with .NET, so you need to replace these with specific declarations for each variable you intend to use.

Fixed-Length Strings

Visual Basic.NET does not natively support fixed-length **String** data types. You have two options for migrating your fixed-length **String** data types to .NET: change your code before migration and remove the fixed-length declarations, or allow the Upgrade Wizard to migrate the **String** and translate your fixed-length definition using the backward-compatible **FixedLengthString** function in the VB6 Namespace. In your VB6 code, fixed-length **String** declarations look something like this:

```
Dim MyFixedString As String * 50
```

Although you can use the compatibility function to replicate your fixed-length **String** data types in .NET, you cannot use this function within a Structure created in .NET. You must change your fixed-length **String** data types in UDTs to normal **String** data types before migration so that when the UDT is converted to a Structure in .NET, the **String** will properly convert as well.

LSet

The **LSet** command is also not supported in .NET. **LSet** commands were used with UDTs to assign values from one UDT to another. UDTs have been changed to Structures in .NET, leaving the **LSet** command obsolete. You need to replace your **LSet** commands with specific code to handle the assigning of data from one Structure to another.

Constants

For years, it has been considered a bad practice to use actual numbers in your logic statements. The preferred way to write a logic statement is to replace all of your numbers with variables or constants. This makes the code more readable because a user will understand your code if you are multiplying the **NumDependants** by the **TaxRate**, but it may not be obvious what a line of code is doing if it multiplies the number 3 by .35. When planning to migrate your code to .NET, using constants in place of raw numbers not only improves your code's readability, but may also prevent a mistake from happening when the Upgrade Wizard translates your code, because some constants in .NET have a different numerical value than they had in VB6. Take a look at the following line of code from VB6:

```
Form1.WindowState = 2
```

For starters, unless you know that a 2 translates into a maximized **WindowState**, someone reading this line of code may not understand what this line is meant to do. For your .NET migration, a problem can arise if the value of the Maximized constant is no longer equal to 2. If you migrated the preceding line of code to .NET, the resulting line would look like this:

```
Form1.DefInstance.WindowState = System.Windows.Forms.FormWindowState._
  Maximized
```

Notice that the 2 in the VB6 code was correctly translated into a **Maximized** value for the **FormWindowState** property. To be on the safe side, you should review all of your VB6 code and replace all references to the numerical values of a constant with that actual constant's name. These changes should also include any **Boolean** variables being checked for a 0 or −1 value. If you upgraded the preceding VB6 line of code with the constant name for the value 2, it would look like this:

```
Form1.WindowState = vbMaximized
```

By using the constant names instead of numerical values, you can be assured that the Upgrade Wizard will translate these references correctly. Some of the most common locations where you will find numerical values that should be replaced with constants will be in control property settings and message box parameters. Find these numbers and replace them before you migrate your code.

GoTo and GoSub

The **GoTo** and **GoSub** commands are not supported in .NET. You should review the code you are planning to migrate and replace any code using these two commands with proper procedural redirects and method calls. If your code uses these outdated commands, more than likely your code is not very object-oriented in its design or your code jumps around in a confusing and inefficient manner. This may be an indicator that your project is a poor candidate for migration to .NET. The exception to this rule is the **On Error GoTo** command. You can still use the **GoTo** command within the **On Error** line for unstructured exception handling. All other uses of **GoTo** and **GoSub** must be replaced.

Arrays

All arrays in .NET are zero-based, meaning that the lower bound's default value of your arrays will be always zero. In VB6, you can place an **Option Base** statement in the General Declarations area that states whether you will be using zero or one as the bottom element during programming. Without an **Option Base** statement, zero becomes the lower bound's default value. The Upgrade Wizard will remove your **Option Base** statements when migrating your code to .NET because everything is zero-based in .NET. This means that you should redesign any arrays in your VB6 code that do not have a lower bound of zero. Take a look at the following two array declarations:

```
Dim FirstArray(10)
Dim SecondArray(5 to 15)
```

The **FirstArray** is dimmed to 10, with a lower bound set to the default of zero. The **SecondArray** defines the range of the array, with a lower bound of 5 and an upper bound of 15. The **FirstArray** will migrate to .NET without having its bounds changed, but the **SecondArray** will loose its lower bound's definition and will look like this after migration:

```
Dim SecondArray(15) As Object
```

Instead of having 11 elements ranging from 5 to 15, your array now has 16 elements ranging from 0 to 15. Note that the upper bound value is still the same. If you migrate an array that defines a lower bound to be something other than zero, the Upgrade Wizard will remove your lower bound's definition and leave a comment above the array declaration line to let you know the lower bound is now zero. To avoid confusion stemming from changed lower bounds in your arrays, you should locate these arrays in your VB6 code and adjust your code so that your arrays do not define a lower bound, but instead use the default zero.

If your VB6 code creates UDTs that have arrays in them, you need to remove or replace these arrays with a different data type. Structures in .NET do not support arrays or fixed-length **String** data types. If you migrate a UDT with an array in it to .NET, the array will be removed for you.

VB6 Forms

Up until now, the new .NET Windows forms probably looked and felt a great deal like the old forms you are used to using in VB6. Although they look extremely similar on the surface, behind the scenes, these two forms are based on two entirely different models. The good news is that the new .NET Windows forms are more powerful than ever, and you probably have already found plenty of things you like about them. The bad news is that the migration of your older version 6 forms to the new Windows form model will not be a smooth one for some developers. The differences between the two form models is too great to migrate some of the features that Visual Basic developers have used with their forms.

Many of the problem areas for form migration center on the graphical display of your form. The new Windows form uses GDI+ to handle all of its drawing and display functions, and many of the version 6 controls that you may have used to draw on your form have now been replaced with code-based drawing tools that use GDI+. This means that the shape and line controls will not migrate to .NET. Also affected are the code-based drawing functions you may have used in version 6, including the **PSet**, **CLS**, and **Circle** commands. In preparation for the migration, you should remove these controls and their associated lines of code. The Windows form only supports TrueType fonts, so if you have opted to use a non-TrueType font to display text on the surface of your forms, you can either change these to use a TrueType font such as Arial, or allow the Upgrade Wizard to reset any nonsupported fonts to the Visual Studio.NET default font. Any fonts that are reset by the Upgrade Wizard will also loose their style features, such as bolding, sizing, and underlining.

You need to be aware of some other control changes as well. Because Visual Studio.NET is not based on OLE (object linking and embedding), the OLE Container control will not migrate over. The Timer control will migrate, but will operate differently for some developers. In version 6, you could set the Timer's **Interval** property to zero to disable the Timer. This will no longer work in .NET, in which you instead need to set the **Enabled** property to either **True** or **False** to control your Timers. Here is some good news for you: If your application uses a resizer control to resize the controls on its surface, you can ditch this third-party control and use the built-in **Anchor** property every control has to handle resizing automatically. Many applications will be able to remove a lot of code that has been placed behind the form to handle exactly what the **Anchor** control now handles for you.

Finally, version 6 forms that use the form's drag-and-drop features or access the Clipboard will not be able to migrate these features over to .NET Windows forms because of the extreme differences between the old and new drag-and-drop and Clipboard features. This list of migration issues will make some developers groan in pain, whereas others will not be worried at all by these problems. If your Visual Basic forms are simple, then the migration will be simple as well. If you find that many of these changes affect your application's migration, you may consider either redoing these features after the migration is finished or going back to the design review phase and reassessing whether or not migration is the best route to take.

Form Controls

Some controls will not be support by the Windows forms in .NET. If the form you are migrating uses only VB6 ActiveX controls, then you should not run into any troubles, but VB6 allows you to place controls on your forms that came with earlier versions of Visual Basic, such as version 5. Any controls from a version of Visual Basic prior to 6 will not be migrated to your new Windows form. You should try to acquire the latest VB6 version of the control prior to migrating your project to .NET or replace this control with a native .NET control after migration.

Data Access Migration

If your application accesses a database, then you also have to decide whether you are going to migrate your data access methods to the new ADO.NET. Once again, the syntax that ADO.NET uses is so different from previous versions of ADO that you will be required to almost completely rewrite all of your data access code if you choose to go with ADO.NET. Hopefully, all of your data calls are centralized in one easily updated data-aware class, and not spread out all over the application. Such neatness is a sure sign of proper n-tier design.

If your database calls are designed to work with server-side cursors that keep your application connected to the database during operation, then you need to migrate your data access code as-is and continue to use a prior version of ADO, such as version 2.6. ADO.NET does not support connected communications with databases. If the application you are migrating uses DAO (Data Access Objects) or RDS (Remote Data Services), you will not be able to migrate your application to .NET because of the lack of support in .NET for these older data access techniques. Data binding controls can be migrated to .NET provided that they use ADO to bind with the data, and not an older data access technique.

Good Habits for the Future

Early in the Visual Studio.NET beta testing phase, some additional changes were made to Visual Basic that ruffled a few feathers among the developer population. To ease the transition from version 6 to .NET, Microsoft reversed its position on a few of these suggested changes. Two of the removed changes are significant, and developers should be aware of these suggestions because, in all likelihood, you will see these changes happen in the next version of Visual Studio. While these suggestions do represent a big change for Visual Basic developers, in reality, these changes would have brought Visual Basic more in line with the other programming languages in use today, and would have made it easier to integrate your Visual Basic code with items written in other languages such as Visual C++.

The first big change is one that you should adopt right away, and when the change is finally made official in the next few years, it will come as no shock to you. To adopt this change, you merely need to stop using the numeric values for the **Boolean** data type and start using the keywords **True** and **False**. The change that almost happened was that the value of **True** would have been made 1 instead of –1. Any code that checked for the –1 would not be compatible in .NET. Every other programming language understands that **True** is equal to 1, and **False** is equal to zero, just as binary uses 1 and 0 to communicate an off and on state. While you can still use the –1 in Visual Basic.NET, it is highly recommended that you cease checking **Boolean** data types for numeric values and instead check for the constant values **True** or **False**.

The second change you should be aware of has to do with arrays. In Visual Basic, you can **Dim** an array to be 10, which gives your array 11 elements ranging from 0 to 10. In any other language, this same array would have 10 elements, ranging from 0 to 9. This change could have broken a lot of legacy code that checked all 11 elements, causing an **Array out of Bounds** exception. Thus, you should only use the number of elements you declare your array to have, and avoid using and checking that last extra element. This good habit could save you a lot of trouble when the time comes to migrate your code to the next version of Visual Studio; hopefully this change will someday be made official so that the Visual Basic language can finally stand toe to toe with all the other development languages in use today.

The Upgrade Wizard

After you are confident that your code is ready to make the leap into .NET, you can fire up Visual Studio.NET and use the Upgrade Wizard. This is a very powerful tool that will make a great many changes to your code as it is moved from the VB6 environment to .NET. The purpose of your premigration code changes was to ease this transition and avoid as many problems as possible with your migration. The Upgrade Wizard itself is quite easy to use, but it may require some time to convert your code to .NET, depending on the size of the project you are migrating. Before you learn how to use the Upgrade Wizard, you will create a test project in Visual Basic 6 that will highlight many of the changes that the Upgrade Wizard will make when you migrate this project to .NET.

The MigrateMe Visual Basic 6 Project

Exercise 15.1 describes how to create a very simple project in Visual Basic 6 that highlights a lot of older version 6 features that the .NET Upgrade Wizard will change during the migration process. This is a terrific project to use as your first migration project because you will see how radically different your code will be after the Upgrade Wizard is through migrating it.

If you do not have Visual Basic 6 installed locally, skip over Exercise 15.1 and locate another VB6 Project to use in Exercise 15.2 so that you can learn how to use the Upgrade Wizard and see some of the changes that are made. You will be able to download VB6 Projects from the Internet by visiting Web sites that offer source code for developers to download.

Exercise 15.1: The Visual Basic 6 MigrateMe Project

1. Start Visual Basic 6.

2. Create a new Standard EXE Project. When the new project loads, select Project | Properties and set this project's name to MigrateMe. Click the OK button to accept this new name.

3. Add one command button, one label, and one textbox to the surface of **Form1**.

4. Double-click the button **Command1**. Add the following code in the General Declarations area and to the **Click** event for **Command1**:

```
'NOTE: This code is for the MigrateMe VB6 Project
'Option Base is out
Option Base 0
Option Explicit

'Here is a UDT
Private Type Customer
    CustName As String
    CustID As Integer
End Type

Private Sub Command1_Click()
    'Multiple variables dimmed on one line
    Dim FirstName, LastName As String

    'Variant and Currency variables
    Dim MyVariant As Variant
    Dim MyMoney As Currency

    'The Caption property becomes Text in .NET
    Label1.Caption = "My Label"

    'The old Integer and Long variables
    Dim MyInt As Integer
    Dim MyLong As Long
```

```
'Set length string
Dim MySetString As String * 25

'Outdated Date and time functions
Dim MyDay As String
MyDay = Date
MyDay = Time

Dim MyObject As Object
'The following is a usage of the Set command and Nothing to cleanup
Set MyObject = Nothing

While MyInt > 5
    'while loop here / wend is outdated
Wend

'Default property being used here (Text1.Text implied)
Text1 = "Set my default text"
End Sub
```

5. In the Project Explorer window, right-click the MigrateMe Project name and select Add | Class Module. In the Add Class Module window, select the Class Module icon and click the Open button. Now your project has a file named Class1 in it.

6. Add the following code to Class1:

```
Public Property Get MyName() As String
    'Get MyName property
    MyName = "Dave"
End Property

Public Property Let MyName(sName As String)
    'Let MyName
    sFirstName = sName
End Property

Public Function DoCalcFee(HourlyRate As Double, Optional EmpID As _
  Integer) As Double
    'Here is an old unstructured exception handler
    On Error GoTo DoCalcFeeErr

    'EmpID is an optional param, no default
    If IsMissing(EmpID) Then MsgBox "No EmpID given!"
    Exit Function
```

```
DoCalcFeeErr:
    MsgBox "ERROR HAPPENED!"
End Function

Private Sub Class_Initialize()
    'Some code in the class initialize area
    Dim TestMe As Integer
    TestMe = 55
End Sub

Private Sub Class_Terminate()
    'Some code in the class terminate area
    Dim TestMe2 As Integer
    TestMe2 = 1
End Sub
```

7. Click the Save icon on your toolbar. When asked where Visual Basic should save this project, create a new directory named MigrateMe and then save all the project files in that directory.

8. Run the MigrateMe Project once and click the **Command1** button to ensure that your code has no errors.

Using the Upgrade Wizard

Now that you have a Visual Basic 6 Project stored on your hard drive, it is time to fire up Visual Studio.NET and migrate your code. The Upgrade Wizard is a very simple tool to use, and requires that you only make a few decisions to start the migration process. Depending on what type of VB6 Project you are migrating, you will be asked to decide whether you are creating an EXE Project or a DLL Project in .NET based on your old code. You will also be asked where you wish to create this new project. Other than those two simple questions, the Upgrade Wizard handles all the hard work for you. This is not a simple copy-and-paste migration tool. You will see a stunning number of changes occur to your source code when the migration is completed. Try out Exercise 15.2 to see how easy it is to use the Upgrade Wizard, and then compare your VB6 Project to your new .NET Project to see all the changes that have occurred along the way.

Exercise 15.2: Using the Upgrade Wizard Tool

1. Start Visual Studio.NET.

2. Select File | Open | Project.

3. Browse for the VBP Project file for the VB6 Project you plan to migrate (use the MigrateMe Project you created in Exercise 15.1). Remember that your VB6 Projects will be located under the \Program Files\Microsoft Visual Studio\VB98 directory,

and not in the My Documents folder with your .NET Projects. Highlight the project file when you locate it and click the Open button.

4. The Upgrade Wizard will automatically start on the introduction page. Click the Next button to continue.

5. Because the MigrateMe Project is a simple Standard EXE Project, your only option is to upgrade this to an EXE Project. If you were upgrading a Class Library Project or an ActiveX control, you would have the option to create a DLL Project. Page 2 of the Upgrade Wizard is shown in Figure 15.2. Click Next to accept the EXE Project setting.

6. Page 3 of the Upgrade Wizard asks you where you wish to create the .NET files. Change the path to read C:\MigratedProjects\MigrateMe. Click Next, and when a pop-up message asks you if you wish to create this file, click the Yes button.

7. The Upgrade Wizard now reports it has enough information to complete the migration. Click Next to start the migration process. When the migration is completed, your new .NET Project will be loaded in Visual Studio for you to view.

Notice that your .NET Project has one file named Class1.vb, and one form named Form1.vb. These two files match the Class and form you created in your original MigrateMe Project. The next section describes the changes that have occurred to the MigrateMe Project during migration.

Examining the Changes to MigrateMe

Even though the MigrateMe Project is not a usable application, many features of VB6 are illustrated in the code that you will want to make a note of. In fact, every item in MigrateMe is there for one purpose only, which is to show how the Upgrade Wizard examines these

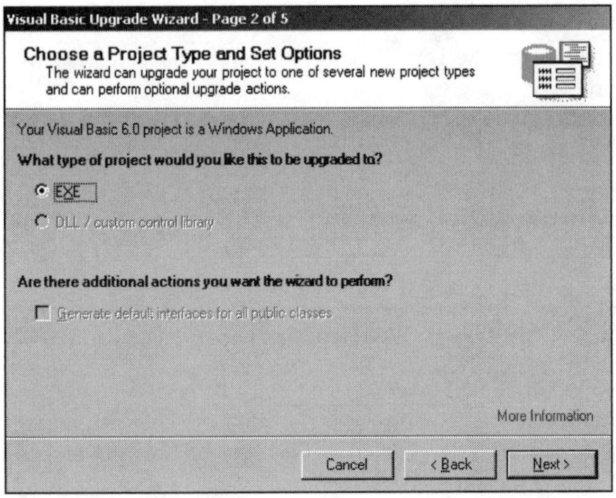

Figure 15.2
Page 2 of the Upgrade Wizard.

pieces of VB6 code and changes them around to fit into the .NET Framework. Table 15.1 lists all the key features of the MigrateMe Project that you will notice a distinct change in when the migration process is finished.

Having reviewed the changes made to your code during the migration process, you should have a firm understanding of how the Upgrade Wizard handles the differences between

Table 15.1   Features of the MigrateMe code.

VB6 Feature	Changes During Migration
Option Base 0	No longer applicable in .NET; line removed.
Code-behind	You now see the code behind your Windows form that lays out and draws your interfaces for the users.
UDT	The **Customer** UDT (in the Private Type block) in **Form1** became a Structure.
FirstName, LastName	Two variables declared on the same line were separated in .NET, with the **FirstName** being assigned as an **Object** data type, and the **LastName** as a **String**.
MyVariant	This **Variant** data type is now an **Object**.
MyMoney	The **Currency** data type is now a **Decimal**.
Label1	The **Caption** property was converted to the **Text** property to fit in with .NET.
MyInt	This **Integer** data type has been made a **Short**.
MyLong	This **Long** data type is now an **Integer**.
MySetString	To create a fixed-length **String** in .NET, you must use the backward-compatible **FixedLengthString** in the VB6 Namespace.
MyDay	The **Date** and **Time** functions have been replaced by **Today** and **TimeofDay**.
MyObject	The **Set** command is no longer needed; a note has been left that the **Nothing** reference will not affect the Garbage Collector's cleanup decision. While the **Nothing** reference remains, it can be removed.
Wend	The **Wend** line to end the **While** loop is now an **End While** line.
Text1	The line referencing the **Text1.Text** property now specifically names the **Text** property.
MyName	The two separate **Get** and **Let** properties have been merged into a single **Property** block of code.
HourlyRate	This parameter was declared as **ByRef** or **ByVal**, so the Upgrade Wizard made it **ByRef**.
EmpID	The **EmpID** optional parameter now has a default value of zero.
IsMissing	The **IsMissing** keyword has been changed to **IsNothing**.
On Error GoTo	Nothing at all has changed about the unstructured VB6 exception-handling code.
Initialize and Terminate	The Class1 **Initialize** and **Terminate** methods have been renamed to **Class_Initialize_Renamed** and **Class_Terminate_Renamed**. The new .NET Class's **New** method references the **Class_Initialize_Renamed** method, and the **Finalize** method references the **Class_Terminate_Renamed** method.

VB6 and .NET. Unneeded lines are removed or left with a comment to draw your attention. Items such as outdated data types are upgraded to newer .NET data types. Code structures are changed, such as the merging of the **MyName** property's **Get** and **Let** statements into one single property structure. With this knowledge, you are better prepared to look at your VB6 code prior to migration and be able to spot what changes need to be made before the Upgrade Wizard steps in and makes its own decisions. You will also be able to spot some trouble areas that will require extra attention in the post-migration phase, to include code changes and additional code testing.

Post-Migration Review

When the migration tool is finished moving all of your code to .NET, your work is far from over. Much of the migrated code will not be optimized, or will not take advantage of new .NET features and syntax that could make your project even better. Once again, you should review your code from top to bottom and look for areas where you can improve your code and make it fit better into the .NET system.

The Upgrade Report

When the Upgrade Wizard is finished migrating your VB6 Project to .NET, all of your migrated modules will be listed in the Visual Studio.NET Solution Explorer window along with a file named _UpgradeReport.htm. This report was generated by the Upgrade Wizard to provide you with a summary of any issues encountered during the migration process. This report is the first thing you should look at when the Upgrade Wizard is finished, to get a quick overview of the problems the wizard encountered. This report provides you with a preview of the pieces of your code that require additional attention. Take a look at Figure 15.3, which shows the _UpgradeReport.htm file for the MigrateMe Project.

Looking at Figure 15.3, notice that the Upgrade Wizard reports that no warnings or errors were raised during the migration process. But you know from looking at Table 15.1 that quite a few things have been changed in your project. What the upgrade report is trying to tell you is that it did not encounter any problems when making these changes to your code. A project that migrates to .NET without any errors or warnings should, theoretically, be able to execute right away without any further attention. Of course, you should still perform your post-migration review to ensure that everything still works as you intended it to. Figure 15.4 shows an upgrade report that indicates some issues were encountered during the migration process.

The project migrated in Figure 15.4 included an array that defined its lower bound as 11, and a mathematical operation involving two **Variant** data types, **X** and **Y**, which .NET converted to **Object** data types. The changes made to these **Variant** data types and the array resulted in warning messages from the Upgrade Wizard, which indicates that the migration was successful, but the developer should review these changes to ensure that the code will

Upgrade Report for MigrateMe.vbp

Time of Upgrade: 6/2/2001 1:40 PM

List of Project Files

New Filename	Original Filename	File Type	Status	Errors	Warnings	Total Issues
⊞ (Global Issues)				0	0	0
⊞ Class1.vb	Class1.cls	Class Module	Upgraded	0	0	0
⊟ Form1.vb	Form1.frm	Form	Upgraded	0	0	0
Upgrade Issues for Form1.frm: None						
2 File(s)		Class Modules: 1 Forms: 1	Upgraded: 2 Not upgraded: 0	0	0	0

Click here for help with troubleshooting upgraded projects

Upgrade Settings

GenerateInterfacesForClasses: 0
LogFile: MigrateMe.log
MigrateProjectTo: WinExe
OutputDir: C:\Program Files\Microsoft Visual Studio\VB98\MigrateMe\MigrateMe.NET
OutputName: MigrateMe.vbproj
ProjectName: MigrateMe
ProjectPath: C:\Program Files\Microsoft Visual Studio\VB98\MigrateMe\MigrateMe.vbp

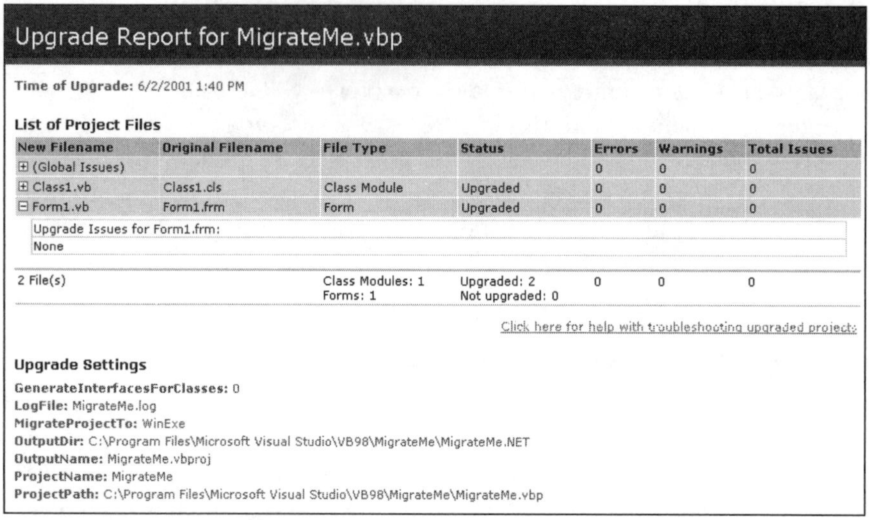

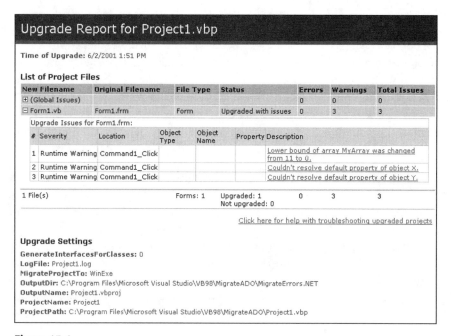

Figure 15.3
The successful upgrade report.

Upgrade Report for Project1.vbp

Time of Upgrade: 6/2/2001 1:51 PM

List of Project Files

New Filename	Original Filename	File Type	Status	Errors	Warnings	Total Issues
⊞ (Global Issues)				0	0	0
⊟ Form1.vb	Form1.frm	Form	Upgraded with issues	0	3	3

Upgrade Issues for Form1.frm:

#	Severity	Location	Object Type	Object Name	Property	Description
1	Runtime Warning	Command1_Click				Lower bound of array MyArray was changed from 11 to 0.
2	Runtime Warning	Command1_Click				Couldn't resolve default property of object X.
3	Runtime Warning	Command1_Click				Couldn't resolve default property of object Y.

1 File(s)	Forms: 1	Upgraded: 1 Not upgraded: 0	0	3	3

Click here for help with troubleshooting upgraded projects

Upgrade Settings

GenerateInterfacesForClasses: 0
LogFile: Project1.log
MigrateProjectTo: WinExe
OutputDir: C:\Program Files\Microsoft Visual Studio\VB98\MigrateADO\MigrateErrors.NET
OutputName: Project1.vbproj
ProjectName: Project1
ProjectPath: C:\Program Files\Microsoft Visual Studio\VB98\MigrateADO\Project1.vbp

Figure 15.4
An upgrade report with issues.

still work properly. The red-underlined pieces of text in the upgrade report are hyperlinks to the MSDN help file where you can look up more information on the reported issue.

Upgrade Issues

Your upgrade report has many columns in it. The first column you will look at for each file name listed in the report is the Status column. You should see an "Upgraded" entry here if the migration of this file was completed. The next two columns are Errors and Warnings. An error is a problem with the migrated code that will prevent your application from compiling and running in .NET. Obviously, these problems require your immediate attention to get your application working again. Comment tags will be placed in your code above the line containing the error.

Warnings are given to items noted by the Upgrade Wizard that will not prevent your application from running but could result in erroneous results or crashes. A comment starting with the tag **UPGRADE_WARNING** will be placed above the line of code that generated the warning. You should review each Warning column item to see what effect it will have on your application. Each line of the upgrade report is expandable to give you more details on the problems the Upgrade Wizard encountered with your code.

The Task List

The second thing you should review when the Upgrade Wizard has finished migrating your code is the Task List window. Any problems the Upgrade Wizard encountered during migration will be noted in the Task List. This window acts as your to-do list to help you iron out any wrinkles caused by the migration. Remember, you can double-click a line in the Task List to quickly jump to the line of code that message is referencing. Work down the Task List item by item until you have all the problems resolved, and then you can move on to the next part of the post-migration review phase, which is optimizing and upgrading your code to take advantage of the latest .NET features. By default, the **UPGRADE_WARNING** comments do not appear in the Task List for you to see. You can add these comments to your Task List window by editing the Token List tags found in the Tools | Options window.

Variable Initializers

Because .NET enables you to define the initial value for your variables as soon as they are declared, it is a good idea to assign each variable an initial value. Even if this means assigning a zero to an **Integer** data type, it is still a good idea to initialize each and every variable. Search through your code and stop at each variable declaration line and ask yourself whether this variable could be initialized at this point. Often, variables in VB6 are initialized in locations other than where they are declared, so if you do initialize a variable in the .NET version of your code, you will want to remove any initializing code that appears later on in your project.

Object Cleanup

The Garbage Collector now handles all the object disposal chores, so you can remove any lines of code that were meant to destroy the objects you created. Any code that wants to set an object to be equal to **Nothing** can be removed from your .NET Project. Any specialized functions that need to be executed when your object is destroyed should be relocated to the **Finalize** method for that object. This is the code that the Garbage Collector will execute when it comes along and decides that your object is no longer needed and can be safely destroyed. Any additional code you have added to your project to check for circular references can also be removed because the Garbage Collector is capable of detecting these references for you.

Note

*Remove any code setting an object equal to **Nothing** in your migrated project.*

Constructors

If any of your objects require special initialization or loading, such as filling in an object's properties with information from a database, you can move these object initialization features to the object's **New** event in .NET. Placing your object construction code here will remove the need for calling code to execute a specialized **Load** method to initialize your object with data. You can also make the **New** constructor parameterized to accept information that the constructor code can use to customize the loading process, such as an employee's ID number that can be used to query that database for all of the employee's information.

Optional Parameters

Because .NET no longer supports the **IsMissing** keyword that VB6 uses to check whether an optional parameter was supplied, you need to provide all of your optional parameters with default values. This way, if the caller does not supply an optional parameter, your code will still have some data to work with. Locate all of your routines that allow optional parameters and add a default value after each parameter. The following line of code illustrates Visual Basic 6's version of an optional parameter:

```
Public Function DoCalcFee(BillHours As Double, Optional HourlyRate As _
  Double) As Double
```

The Upgrade Wizard will automatically give your optional parameters a value during migration, but often these default values will not be the value you wish to use. To update your optional parameters to .NET standards, you would add a default value to the optional parameter like this:

```
Public Function DoCalcFee(ByRef BillHours As Double, Optional ByRef _
  HourlyRate As Double = 60.50) As Double
```

The ability to add a default value to your parameters may enable you to remove redundant code within the procedure that checks whether or not a value has been passed into the procedure and assigns that parameter a value if no value is found. Because the **IsMissing** keyword is no longer available in .NET, the Upgrade Wizard replaces all instances of **IsMissing** with the **IsNothing** keyword. Search your code for any uses of the **IsNothing** keyword and check to be sure that this code is still needed. Because the optional parameter now always has a value, even if it is just the default value, you may wish to remove the **IsNothing** check. If you used the **IsMissing** keyword in version 6 to decide between multiple execution paths, you can instead check whether the parameter is equal to its default value, which it will be if no parameter has been supplied.

Shared Members

The ability to use shared members did not exist in VB6, so shared members are not a concern for the developer during migration. After your application has been successfully migrated to .NET, you can then ask yourself whether your code has any places that can take advantage of the new shared members feature. Some applications may write data to either a file or a database to share that information among multiple copies of the same application. You greatly simplify your code and free up some precious resources by moving these data-sharing functions over to share members. For a review on how to use shared members, refer to Chapter 4.

Exception Handling

All of your **On Error** unstructured exception-handling code will be migrated to Visual Basic.NET virtually unchanged, except in cases where other changes affect your code, such as data type upgrades. If you leave your exception-handling routines untouched, they should work just as they did in version 6. But could these exception handlers be done better? Hopefully this question was addressed during the premigration design review phase, and routines that can benefit from the new structured exception-handling format have already been identified. If this has not been addressed, ask yourself where you should update your exception-handling code.

While the new **Try, Catch, Finally** model is a wonderful way to deal with exceptions, it's not always necessary. A great deal of your code can keep the old **On Error** model and will require no changes. One key thing to look at when deciding whether or not to upgrade the exception-handling code is the amount of decision-making code within the exception-handling section at the bottom of your function. Does your exception handler spend a lot of time checking for the value of **Err.Number**, or if your function is really long, does your code have to figure out exactly what state all of your resources were in when the exception occurred? If you migrated this exception handler to the **Try, Catch, Finally** model, you could eliminate a lot of the **If** statements in your exception-handling code because the structured exception-handling model allows you to catch your exceptions closer to the source and then intelligently close your resources based on where the exception occurred.

Use multiple **Try, Catch, Finally** blocks to segment different operations so that you can better trap and handle your exceptions. The ability to create more than one exception trap is one of the greatest advantages the newer structured exception-handling model has over the **On Error** approach. Any routines your code uses to access databases and files on the hard drive can almost certainly benefit from the **Try, Catch,** and **Finally** Structure. These resources require that the code first open a connection to them before the application can read or write to the resource. When an exception occurs during the data access steps, your resource can be left open, possibly causing further troubles during later calls. Be sure to place all of your resource closing code in the **Finally** block to ensure that the connections are closed regardless of whether an exception was raised.

Update Your Object Models

If your development team originally modeled your application's objects using Unified Modeling Language (UML) modeling software such as Visual Modeler or Rational Rose, then you will want to regenerate your models from your newly migrated code. More than likely, the interfaces for your objects have changed during the course of the migration. Changes such as parameters now having default values and **Variants** having changed data types need to be properly reflected in the models for future reference and updating. If your modeling software is .NET-aware, you can reverse-engineer your new Assembly and generate an updated model of your objects. Models are a terrific way to understand how a system works, just as a map can show you the layout of a city and help you get where you are going. If your maps (and models) are badly out of date, odds are you'll get lost if you try to use them, so be sure to keep them up to date.

Testing

If the application you are migrating to .NET is one that has already been completed and subjected to a rigorous testing cycle, then you are probably not too thrilled to find out that your application must once again undergo even more rigorous testing. Face it, the migration process makes so many changes to your code that you just cannot be sure that your application is going to work the same as it did before migration. The first indications of life you will see for your application will come from the Task List window. If you do not see any tasks added here by Visual Studio warning you of a syntax error somewhere in your code, then you are indeed ready to enter the testing phase. But if you do still find items that need attention in the Task List window, then you should again revisit your code for some more post-migration tweaks.

Like any good testing plan, your tests should start at the lowest level, the unit. Test each module that has been migrated to .NET to ensure it starts and appears to perform as expected. After all the individual units have been tested, you can put all of these pieces together and perform some system tests to ensure they still work together properly. After you are satisfied that the application is working again, it's time for some user testing—and lots of it. My experience has been that no matter how thoroughly developers think they have tested their application during unit and systems testing, when you put that application in front of a user, all hell tends to break loose. The more accident prone and clueless the user, the better the tester. Finally, if your application has already been delivered to the customer in its VB6 form, you probably need to go through another round of acceptance testing with the customer. When testing your application, pay particular attention to how your variables appear in your application. Due to the significant changes in data types and structures made in .NET, variables are a great area to focus on when verifying that your application is once again operational.

Web Application Migration

In Visual Studio 6, your Web application can take on many different forms, from plain HTML pages to the VB6 ITS Application Project that features both ASP pages and Web Classes. Some types of Web applications will be upgradeable to .NET, while others will not be. Internet technologies are still rapidly changing, and some Web application types and features that looked great when they first came out may not look so hot today. The Internet is in many ways still a testing ground, where developers and companies are trying to figure out what works well and what does not. This section covers some of the Web application types you may have encountered as a Visual Basic developer, and discusses how you can upgrade ASP pages to .NET.

DHTML

A DHTML (dynamic HTML) page is either an HTML page with client-side VBScript embedded in it or a HTML page that uses ActiveX controls in the client's browser. Support for DHTML pages is limited to the Internet Explorer browser only, so any developers looking to support multiple browsers cannot take advantage of the advanced functionality offered by DHTML. Visual Studio.NET realizes that providing features that work in only one type of browser is not the answer developers are looking for, so .NET has shifted away from a browser-specialized approach to a more general all-browser approach, which is supported by the new server controls in ASP.NET. What this means is that DHTML pages do not fit in with the .NET vision, and cannot be migrated or upgraded to ASP.NET pages. If you have a project that uses DHTML pages, your options are to leave it as DHTML and maintain it with an older development tool, or redesign the pages from scratch to take advantage of ASP.NET's features.

ActiveX Documents

Visual Studio 6 introduced ActiveX Documents as a form of Web-based applications. An ActiveX Document application can only be executed inside of a special container that knows how to run it. This means that only Internet Explorer and the Microsoft Office Binder application can run ActiveX Document applications. The concept behind these specialized applications closely resembles an ActiveX control, except instead of a simple form control, an entire application is downloaded and run within the user's browser. Using ActiveX Documents to make applications available over the Internet never really caught on with developers, which is lucky, because these projects cannot be migrated to .NET. ActiveX Documents are similar to the DHTML applications that rely heavily on client-side processing to do their job, and both application types only work with Microsoft browsers. Because ActiveX Document applications cannot be upgraded to .NET, you will need to maintain these using Visual Basic 6.

Web Classes

Visual Basic 6 enables you to create special Web Classes for use with Web-based applications. A Web Class is capable of reading in request data posted to a Web server and responding back with HTML to the browser-based client, two features that were not available to regular Visual Basic Classes. Visual Basic.NET now uses ASP.NET to handle Web-based interfaces to your application, and .NET does not have a specialized Web Class such as the one in VB6. You can migrate your Web Classes to .NET, and the Upgrade Wizard will convert them to normal Classes. Many of the special features of the Web Class are no longer supported in .NET, so you will have to make some changes to your Class after the migration is completed.

ASP and ASP.NET Interoperability

Both ASP and ASP.NET Web applications can be run by the same Web server at the same time. The Web server will know by the file name extensions (.asp for older ASP pages, and .aspx for the newer ASP.NET pages) whether a page contains script that needs to be interpreted or is a newer compiled ASP.NET Web page.

The one limitation you will be faced with when mixing ASP and ASP.NET on the same Web server is that these two different application types cannot share the same session and application state. This means that when an ASP page links a user to an ASP.NET page, the session and application variables will not follow that user to the new application. The user will have two separate sessions active on the Web server, one for the ASP application and a second one for the ASP.NET application. Any data stored within the session cannot be passed back and forth between ASP and ASP.NET pages. You can use both ASP and ASP.NET pages in a single Web application, but these two different page types will run in separate sessions and will not be able to directly share session variables.

Moving ASP to ASP.NET

Because of the extreme differences between script-based ASP pages and the newer compiled ASP.NET Web pages, you need to rewrite your Web application if you wish to move it to .NET. This can be a great deal of work depending on the size of your application. If your ASP Web application relies on compiled DLLs for much of its processing functions, then your migration path will be a lot easier because you can migrate those DLLs to .NET

Assemblies, and then simply rework your ASP pages into Web Forms that use your newly migrated Assemblies. You also have the option of leaving some pages in your Web application as script-based ASP pages, while migrating other pages that could definitely benefit from ASP.NET. Once again, when mixing and matching ASP and ASP.NET pages, you need to remember that these two page types cannot share session and application states on the Web server.

If you have Web pages that perform a lot of processing, then they can certainly benefit from the newer compiled Web Forms in ASP.NET. You can also use the new server controls to replace a lot of interface customization code in your ASP pages. One such control is the new DataGrid control for displaying data on a Web page. The ability to use any programming language available in Visual Studio.NET to create your ASP.NET pages will appeal to many developers, and Visual Basic developers' Web pages will benefit from the full range of the Visual Basic programming language, as opposed to the somewhat limited subset available with VBScript.

At the time of this writing, Visual Studio.NET beta 2 does not have an ASP-to-ASP.NET migration tool included, and one may not be made available in the final release. You can rename your ASP files by changing the .asp extension to .aspx and then add these to a Web Application Project as a manual way of migrating your pages. VBScript is still supported in .NET, though this is not the preferred language for creating ASP.NET pages. If you rename your ASP page to give it the .aspx extension, more than likely, you will have a lot of problems reported to you in the Task List that you will need to deal with to get this page to run. Here is a list of a few of the changes you will need to make to your migrated ASP pages:

♦ All of code within the **<%** and **%>** tags needs to be converted to functions to better fit in with the Visual Basic language

♦ Add data types to your variable references to make your page strongly typed

♦ Remove all references to default properties and methods

♦ Change all of your late binding references to use early binding

♦ Add a **RUNAT="Server"** parameter to your **<SCRIPT>** tag

♦ Remove any script not written in VBScript

♦ Add **Option Explicit** to the top of your page to enforce strict data typing

♦ Place parameters for subroutines inside parentheses

If you created a Web Application in Visual Studio 6 using Visual InterDev, then you will be able to migrate this project using the same process you used to migrate a VB6 Project. Simply select File | Open | Project and then browse for your Visual InterDev Project file. Although loading a Visual InterDev Project promises to be easier than renaming all of your ASP files to give them an .aspx extension, you still have numerous problems to attend to after the migration is finished. Generally, the best advice for Web developers looking to migrate older projects to the .NET Framework is to redesign and recode each ASP page using the latest features in ASP.NET. In the long run, the "from scratch" approach may actually take less time than trying to migrate and then fix your older ASP pages, and your pages will be far more efficient and easier to maintain if they are built from the ground up using .NET technologies.

Summary

The decision to migrate your code to .NET is not a choice you should take lightly. You can probably safely migrate small, simple applications to .NET with very little trouble, but the larger the application, the tougher your decision will be. You should not feel that you must migrate all of your code to .NET, because you can still use your COM components from within your .NET Assemblies, and your COM components can even use your new Assemblies. Weigh the advantages and reasons for moving your code to .NET against the estimated time and effort such a move will require. .NET has some terrific new features, and all software projects from now on should be developed in Visual Studio.NET, but not all of your code written in VB6 will need to be brought into the .NET world.

Chapter 16
.NET Development Best Practices

This final chapter of the book takes all the pieces of the .NET puzzle covered individually up until this point and snaps them together to form the big picture of .NET software development. If the term "process" is a foreign word in your organization, then this chapter will help you to understand why a proven organized approach to software development has far better odds of succeeding than a random and unmanaged project. Even having a development guru or coding superhero on staff is no substitute for proper planning and organization. This chapter begins by discussing the finer points of the iterative development process, to give you a general understanding of how the overall process fits together. Next, each stage of the process is broken down, with an explanation of the easiest ways to implement these stages in your development projects.

Iterative Development

The two general approaches to organizing software development projects are the waterfall approach and the iterative development approach. More than likely, you have had your first development experiences in a waterfall project. You can identify a developer who has been put through a waterfall project by their endless comments about how things could have been done differently to make the project a success. A better way to develop software exists, one that enables you to learn early in the project the difficulties your project may pose, and adjust your process to compensate for any setbacks that you may encounter.

The Waterfall Approach

A development project that follows the waterfall approach has distinct stages, such as the gathering of requirements, planning, coding, testing, and deployment, but what you normally will not see in a waterfall project is a revisiting of an earlier stage. After the planning is finished, all the coders will press forward with their development until the project is ready for testing. One large-scale testing cycle encompasses the entire application, followed by a final single-deployment phase to get the product out to the customer. Figure 16.1 illustrates the waterfall approach to software development.

On the surface, this approach seems acceptable. You plan, you develop, and then you release. In fact, the waterfall approach is fairly easy to manage and coordinate, and this approach will seem natural to anyone who has not ever experienced an iterative development project. Your customers will understand this approach because it closely resembles the approach humans take to almost any type of project they take on. If you want to build a deck to add on to the back of your house, you plan it, build it, jump up and down on it a few times, and declare the job finished. So why is the waterfall approach not the best way to develop software? I am a big supporter of "keeping it simple and straightforward," but after you have experienced both the waterfall approach and the iterative approach, you will see why the straightforward approach is not the best approach for software development.

The waterfall approach is aptly named, because essentially your development team just jumps in the river and floats along with the process, straight ahead, and then ultimately straight down. Floating along feels natural and takes little planning, because you know that eventually you will reach the end of the river on this course, but when you go over a waterfall, those final moments may hurt. But when you are floating downstream, you don't think

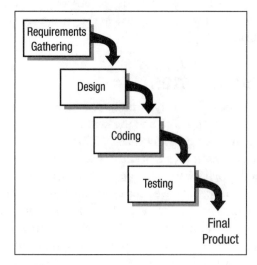

Figure 16.1
Waterfall software development.

too much about that ending. What if the river isn't flowing as quickly as you originally thought it would be? Halfway down the river, your ability to judge distances is hampered, so the date you set to reach the end is really just a wild guess. When you reach the end of that waterfall and realize that your designs did not fully satisfy the requirements, how are you going to fix it? More than likely, it requires going back up to the top of that waterfall for another ride.

Iterative Development

The word *iterate* means repetitive. In contrast to the straight-ahead waterfall approach, an iterative development loops through the development steps repeatedly, so you have multiple design stages and multiple testing stages in your development project. This does not mean that you will be coding the same pieces over and over. Instead, the project requirements are broken up into iterations, so that the application is attacked in stages. At the end of each iteration is a testing and release stage, which should result in a polished product that the customer will be able to examine. Mind you, the products of your early iterations will not even be close to the final application that you are developing, but each release will have enough functionality for someone to test out.

Iterative development encompasses many different phases, and each development team has its own unique set of phases to follow. The following plan is my own customized iteration map, which I feel keeps things simple and efficient. Your team can add or change phases as they wish so that the process suits your own needs. Invariably, all development processes begin with a requirements-gathering stage. My plan follows up this stage with a high-level design phase, which helps managers plan how the rest of the stages will be executed. After the high-level design phase, your development team will begin iterating or looping through the remaining phases. Each set of milestones has planning, development, and testing phases to go through. After an iteration is completed, the team will release its completed work, review its process and update its plans, and then head back to the planning stage for the next set of milestones. Figure 16.2 shows the stages of my iterative development plan.

Figure 16.2 shows a simplified iteration process. It has two lead-in phases that occur only once: the requirements-gathering phase and the high-level design phase. After these initial knowledge-gathering phases, your project enters into a loop in which your team designs the application further, creates the actual code, and finally tests and releases its work. After an iteration is finished, your team will return to the detailed design phase to complete another portion of the application. The next few sections provide a brief summary of each phase. Then, each phase is described in depth, and you will see how each phase is addressed in a .NET application development project.

Requirements-Gathering Phase

The first phase of any well-planned development project is the requirements-gathering phase. Typically, the inch-thick document of requirements that the customer hands you will not be enough to fully understand what the customer's needs are. It takes a team of experienced

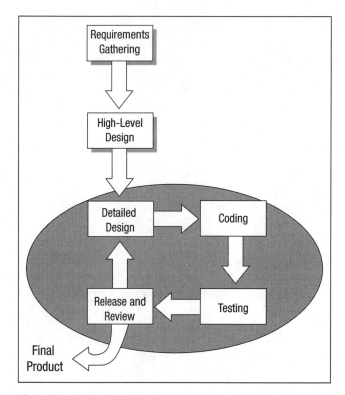

Figure 16.2
Iterative development phases.

business analysts visiting with the customer to learn all they can about the customer's job so that the best possible system can be designed. Do not be surprised if your requirements team uncovers processes that even the customer cannot explain, or if the analysis team finds better ways to get a job done. That's why the customer came to you in the first place—to have you write an application that makes their job easier. Before any planning and designing can take place, however, your team must have a good understanding of the problems it is expected to tackle.

Requirements are rarely perfect at the end of the gathering phase, but they should feel perfect to the designers. If a designer asks what a particular feature does, but can't get a clear answer from the business analysts, the requirements gathering is not complete. After the developers take over, they will encounter instances in which they will need the business analysts to seek clarification from the customer on some items; this process is known as *requirements refinement*. Do not confuse requirements refinement with *requirements creep*, which will be discussed in conjunction with requirements management later in the chapter.

High-Level Design Phase

After you understand the system well enough to start developing it, you enter the first design phase, the high-level architecture phase. In this phase, your software architects map the requirements to components and create a high-level blueprint of what the system will look like. The two main views your architects should focus on are the components diagram and the deployment diagram, which map out where the individual pieces will physically be located. Absolutely no coding is done during the high-level design phase. Most of your objects will not be designed during this phase, although some analysis should be performed on the envisioned components to identify common objects that will be shared throughout the system. This phase may require some object modeling to accomplish this analysis.

When the components and deployment diagrams are completed, it is time to bring in the project manager and discuss what the major features of the system are and how you are going to break up these features into iterations. Those individual features that your developers will create are known as *milestones*. At the end of the high-level design phase, you should have a clear vision of the path your development team will take and a rough schedule to provide your customer with. The high-level design phase is not a recurring phase, unless of course your customers report back to you at the end of an iteration that the design is all wrong. Hopefully that will never happen, but it has been known to happen.

Detailed Design Phase

Every iteration starts with a detailed design phase, which takes the designs created in the high-level design phase and fleshes them out into a more detailed form that the coders can then use to generate code and begin the actual coding of the application. This is where your designers will perform their object analysis based on the high-level designs and requirements, the product of which should be object models created in Unified Modeling Language (UML) that describe the subsystems that the current iteration addresses. Often, business analysts take part in the detailed design phase to assist the software architects in creating use cases that map out and role-play the user's responsibilities and actions within the envisioned system. After the process is thoroughly understood and drawn out, the developers can identify the objects they need to create in their code and model these objects as well as the relationships between the objects.

Each detailed design phase is dedicated solely to the iteration it is associated with, and the designers address only the milestones associated with the current phase. It might seem somewhat nearsighted to address only a limited set of milestones and to purposely avoid designing later pieces, but designers are strongly encouraged not to get ahead of themselves here. If you design a piece of your application that is not going to be created until a later iteration, you may discover that when the time comes to actually code that piece, your understanding of the system will have changed and you will need to redesign that piece. What about objects that are shared among many different iterations? These objects should be identified in the high-level design phase and then addressed in the detailed design phase of the first iteration. By getting the common pieces done first, you are creating a foundation of code to work with throughout your project.

Coding Phase

This is the phase in which all the "real" work gets done. This is where your developers finally get to sit down at their desks and pound out thousands of lines of source code. Any adjustments made to the designs during the coding phase should be communicated to the lead architect for approval, in case such changes will conflict with the overall architecture. If you are using software modeling software, you should regularly reverse-engineer your code into the UML models to keep the models up to date for other developers to reference. A small amount of testing will occur in the coding phase in the form of unit testing. This is where a developer tests for proper operation and results the small pieces he or she is working on. In the next phase, all the work accomplished in the coding phase is brought together and tested as a whole.

For managers, the coding phase is the hardest one to provide a time estimate for. What seems like a reasonable time estimate during the iteration design phase can very easily turn into a wild guess after the coding begins. The coding phase is where all of those issues you missed in the design phase materialize, adding days or even weeks to your estimates. Because coding is a solitary activity (unless you prefer to pair up with another programmer), keeping abreast of problems and issues can be difficult for a manager. Regular team meetings, peer reviews (which you will learn about later in this chapter), and tracking of completed milestones will help you to get a feel for how well the team is meeting the schedule. In most cases, if the schedule slips, it likely was a poorly conceived schedule and the slippage is not the fault of the developers. The timeframe for the early iterations will tend to be more ambitious than the timeframe for the final iteration schedules, because the project manager by then will have a good feel for how long certain development tasks take to complete.

Testing Phase

The testing phase is crucial to iterative development, because this is where you verify that you have met your milestones and that the code you have completed is bug-free. One major hazard associated with the waterfall approach is that bugs and incorrect requirements often are not discovered until the very end of the project, resulting in either a greatly extended schedule or the possibility of your project being canceled. Formal test cases should be constructed based on the requirements and any use cases your designers built. Testers should be using testing software to record their tests if possible, so that they can be replayed at a later date when your code is regression-tested. Each iteration's testing phase should test all the work completed up to that point, to include work done in previous iterations. This will identify new bugs introduced to already-completed code by your new pieces. Only after all tests are completed successfully can your iteration come to an end in the review phase.

Release and Review Phase

One of the most important concepts in iterative development is the release phase. Instead of making one final all-inclusive release at the end of your project, as you would in the waterfall approach, you instead make incremental software releases at the end of each iteration. Releasing software does not always mean that you will deliver this product to your customer, but the concept of release does force your developers to bring the project to a completed and stabilized state that could be released to the client if such a request were made. If you get to the end of an iteration and your completed work is not worthy of the customer's scrutiny, then you need to revisit the testing phase and fix what's wrong with your code. You should strongly encourage team leaders to bring in the customer at the end of an iteration and show them the released product of your work. This will give the customer the opportunity to provide feedback on what they see, and it will give the customers confidence in your team's progress.

Iterative development enables you to learn and adapt as you go along. If the first iteration did not go smoothly, then change it and do it better the second time around. The review at the end of each iteration is where you review the work you did to ensure you delivered what you planned. This phase also provides a review of your process, much like a child's yearly physical. If something is wrong, fix it now, or else the problem is bound to get worse. Update your project schedule in this phase to reflect any schedule changes or improved timeframe estimates. This is a good phase to include the customers in, because you will have some completed software to show them and an up-to-date schedule to share. It is generally a good idea to start letting the customer know about schedule slippages early on in the project, instead of telling them on the final due date that you need three more months. Smaller pieces of bad news are much easier to swallow that one big chunk.

Implementing Iterative Development

Never allow yourself to believe that a software development process must be followed to the letter, exactly as the book told you to do. What works for an organization with dozens of developers may not be the best path for a team of three developers working on a small-scale project. Staffing will have a large effect on how you implement your development plan, as will the types of tools you will use to manage your development. Having experienced developers and business analysts is a huge plus, but they may not always be available. Iterative development training is a must so that all participants understand and buy in to the process. If your organization cannot afford formal training, train one expert in your group and then have that person share the knowledge.

To manage the process, your company could either invest in a large development suite, such as that distributed by Rational Software, or develop your own in-house tools using readily available products such as Microsoft Word, Excel, and Access. The point is, whatever works for your team, use it and keep it simple. Try out the sophisticated tools and techniques, and then throw out anything you feel did not save you time or money on your project. The whole point of iterative development is to develop software faster and cheaper.

Advantages of the Iterative Approach

The waterfall approach saves the big hurrah for the very end, which can make a project seem long and unexciting. Workers crave feedback, even if they claim they don't want to hear it. Your team will be a lot more productive it it's receiving feedback at regular intervals through the repeated testing and re-evaluation stages. Iterative development projects mark their progress by establishing milestones to be accomplished. A single iteration may accomplish one or more milestones, such as completing the user interface or adding a reservation function to the system. Completing a milestone gives the developers a little morale boost because they have accomplished a goal. Give developers a lot of milestones, and they will continually feel that rush of accomplishment throughout the project. Plus, completed milestones are something that you can report back to your customer as evidence of your progress. Tracking the progress of large-scale waterfall projects and making adjustments to their delivery dates is difficult because of the lack of milestones and customer feedback.

At the end of each iteration, you will have a working piece of the application to show to your customers. This gives the customers a chance to look at the individual pieces of their application and determine whether or not each piece is what they wanted. Wouldn't you prefer to hear that bit of bad news a few weeks into the project rather than at the bottom of the waterfall? It's never fun to hear a customer tell you that you misunderstood a requirement and that what you spent a great deal of time creating does not meet their needs, but it is always better to hear the bad news early in the project than at the final acceptance testing meeting. Getting the bad news early gives you the chance to revisit your requirements and replan your application to make the necessary changes. Hopefully, after the first iteration or two, your application will be on the right path to success, and the customer's feedback will involve only minor changes and tweaks.

Note

.NET Development Best Practice #1: Develop software iteratively!

Testing is a critical part of each development iteration. Instead of saving your system-wide tests for the very end of the project, iterative development forces you to test your applications early and often. An iteration stage should not be considered complete until all the accomplished work has been thoroughly tested for bugs. These tests should also include all the work completed for earlier iterations. Running tests on pieces that were finished in previous iterations is known as *regression testing*. Because running these tests over and over can be awfully repetitive, you should consider using a professional software testing suite that enables you to record your tests for later playback so that you can run your recorded regression tests unattended overnight instead of manually. The point of regression testing is to check whether any of the newly completed work has caused any new problems with the pieces you had previously declared bug-free.

When deciding between an iterative and waterfall approach to developing your project, consider the following list of iterative development advantages:

- Creates a set of milestones to measure your project's progress against

- Enables you to continually update your project schedule based on measurable progress

- Gives your team a morale boost, and provides you with solid evidence to point to in your progress reports, when milestones are achieved

- Enables you to show customers the completed pieces at the end of each interval, thus enabling customers to provide feedback to you early in the development process

- Enables you to identify misunderstood requirements and development glitches early in the project, giving you the chance to adjust or change your development plans

- Enables you to identify through iteration testing any catastrophic bugs long before the application is due, giving you more time to fix or redesign troublesome pieces

Requirements

Before you can begin coding an application, you must understand what that application is supposed to do. When your development project begins, the customer may give you a thick document full of requirements that you are expected to meet. If you encounter a customer that has not put their requirements on paper, you have even more work cut out for you, because you must help them to understand their own software needs. Nobody fully understands the customer's needs on the first day of the project. Even the most detailed requirements document cannot make you fully understand the problems and concerns that your application will be addressing.

One of the most enjoyable aspects of software development is learning about other people's jobs and responsibilities. To develop a piece of software that will help a bank manage their loan process, you must first understand all of the concepts and issues surrounding loans and banking. A professionally developed application is not about calculations and databases. It is about process improvement and making people's jobs easier. Doing calculations is easy, but writing an application that shaves hours off of a person's day and saves a company millions of dollars is the true challenge. The funny thing is, many customers do not realize that this is their main goal. Your job during the requirements phase is to gain a complete and robust understanding of the user's job. You will use this knowledge to either develop or improve upon the requirements already in hand so that the design team can design the best possible application.

Developing Requirements

The first item your business analysts need is a requirements document. Often, the customer will have one ready to hand to you, but sometimes your team will need to help the customer develop this document. To develop a usable set of requirements, you must ask a lot of questions of the customer, such as what it is they want their application to do, and how they want it done. Each of the requirements you develop can be categorized into one of four categories: goals, functions, performance, and usability. Table 16.1 describes these four categories.

Table 16.1	Requirements categories.
Category	**Description**
Goals	High-level aspirations for the application, such as to improve efficiency by 80 percent or reduce response time to one hour
Functions	What the system will do; for example, performing a calculation, such as figuring out the sales tax on an order
Performance	Requirements for availability or maximum workload your system can handle
Usability	Such things as the ability to locate data quickly, context-sensitive help, easy-to-understand controls, and proper user-interface design

Typically, your business analysts will work closely with a few representatives of the organization needing the new application. The users will explain their processes, which the analysts should capture by creating workflow diagrams or scenario narratives. The requirements document should map directly to your workflow diagrams. Where a requirement might say "The system must produce weekly reports," the workflow diagram will further explain the process of creating such a report and the types of data this report will contain.

Your analysts may identify ways to improve the user's process, which may modify requirements during this phase. These changes need to be addressed with the customer and made a permanent part of the requirements document. It is important that the requirements your team develops are realistic and agreed upon by both the customer and the developers, because at the end of the project, your application will be compared to this document to decide whether your team has contractually met the customer's expectations. The requirements document is an agreement between the customer and the developers that states the customer's needs. If the customer fails to state a need, your company cannot be held at fault, but if the customer does state a need and your application does not meet that need, the customer will not be satisfied. Check your requirements document frequently during development to ensure that your plans address all the stated requirements.

Business Rules

Business rules provide boundaries for your application's logic. If you do not fully understand a customer's business rules, the results your application produces will be incorrect. For example, you may have a requirement to track all orders within a purchasing system. A business rule may state that no orders can be closed out until all items in that order have been shipped. You might also have a business rule stating that certain customers of your system receive a 10 percent discount on their orders. All business rules your customer identifies need to be recorded along with the requirements and designed into your system.

The Process Improvement Approach

A new piece of software introduces a change into the user's working environment. You likely were a bit apprehensive about migrating to Visual Studio.NET when you picked up this book, because change causes stress. My experience has been that no matter how great your application is or how much time you save the users, some of the users will hate it. The application is new, it's not the same thing they used before, and it scares them. You can minimize the negative reaction your application receives when it is delivered to the customer in two ways:

♦ *Involve as many users as you can in the requirements and development phases.* This helps you slowly introduce new concepts to the users, and helps them work out their anxieties about the change. Plus, if they feel partly responsible for the development of their new software, they will be less likely to complain after it is delivered to them. However, involving everyone in the customer's company with the development project is not always feasible.

♦ *Present all of your changes in the form of a process improvement.* The difference may sound extremely subtle, but think of it this way: What would cause you less stress, being told that you were going about your job the wrong way and that an entirely new process was needed, or being told that with a few minor improvements to your process, you could be twice as efficient? How you package these adjustments will have a large effect on how it is accepted. Also take the improvement approach when gathering requirements and designing the system. Do not throw out a process that is not working if it can be improved upon and made better. The truest measure of an application's success is how happy the end users are after the software has been delivered.

Note

Do not change the users' processes. Instead, seek to improve the process they have already come to accept.

Prototypes

Trying to describe a system in words is very difficult. The users will try to describe the system they envision to you, and you may try to describe the application you are envisioning to them to get their approval. Users will greatly appreciate it if they can see pictures and screens that represent your understanding of their descriptions, so that they can say "Yes, that's it" or "No, that's not what I meant." Your business analysis team can create some mock-up screens based on their understanding of the requirements, to get even more feedback from the users. You can also involve some developers at this stage to create a prototype that the users can actually sit in front of and play with. A prototype should offer little or no functionality, but should instead illustrate a suggested user interface approach and layout for the users to review. Pop-up windows and screen-to-screen navigation can be shown in a prototype to help the users see the same vision that your developers are seeing. A well-done prototype will boost the customer's excitement for the project because they will finally have something they can touch that represents the requirements they have stated. One of the benefits of using Visual Basic.NET to develop your prototype is that you can quickly modify your prototype during the demonstration based on your customer's feedback.

Artifacts

Museums are full of artifacts from ancient times. Everything that an ancient civilization used is considered an artifact. A crusty and cracked wooden spoon in a display case is an artifact. Everything you create during the development of your application is an artifact as well, and should be protected and tracked. The requirements document is one of the first and most valuable artifacts in the entire project. The workflow diagrams and scenarios your team creates during the requirements-gathering phase are also artifacts. Every model, development plan, and business proposal created for your project will become another artifact in your application's museum. By preserving your project's development artifacts, you are creating a historical record of your project that other developers can use to learn about how that application was designed, just as that old wooden spoon in the museum tells a lot about an ancient civilization.

To protect your artifacts, you should include all of them in your version-control system. Microsoft Visual SourceSafe and Rational ClearCase are two examples of versioning systems. The main use for version-control systems is to track and maintain different versions of your code, but you can just as easily track your artifacts with these very same systems. When an item is version-controlled, every change made to that item is tracked and past versions of that item are maintained in a database so that the item can be rolled back to a previous state. For example, suppose that you read through your requirements document and discover a requirement that you swear was not there a week ago. If this document is under version control, you can track down everyone who checked it out and use the version-control software to compare the current version of your document with prior versions to help you spot the changes.

Requirements Management

The biggest problem software developers are faced with today is shifting requirements. When you enter into the high-level design phase, you are assuming that your understanding of the proposed system is complete and correct, because that is what you are basing your plans on. From a manager's point of view, the set of requirements that you have approved for development is also used to base the project's schedule and development costs on. What happens when halfway through the project a new feature is requested by the customer? Your schedule changes, your cost estimates change, and the high-level design you created at the beginning of the project is now looking inadequate. The next thing you know, the schedule has slipped, your developers are grumbling, and the customer blames you for being late. Sound familiar?

Managing your requirements can help control or even prevent these unwanted changes to your plans. During the requirements-gathering phase, your requirements will be somewhat fluid as the business analysts seek clarification from the customer. If an estimate for the entire project has been delivered to the customer prior to the requirements-gathering phase, you should start controlling proposed changes to your requirements from day one. For certain, you should strictly control any requirement changes from the moment your software architects start designing the system, because after those designs are made, any changes to them will have a negative effect on your schedule and budget.

What requirements management really entails is customer management. When the customer comes to you and says they need a new feature added, or the definition of an agreed upon feature has changed, you should record their request but not immediately add it to the requirements. It is also a good idea to not allow customers to submit suggestions to your developers, because they may try to incorporate the new suggestion in the current iteration immediately. All proposed requirement changes should be pooled and discussed with the customer at a later time. Introducing changes to your developers while in the middle of an iteration can be disastrous, so the best time to discus these changes is in the final review phase of an iteration. Slipping a new requirement into the project is known as *requirements creep.*

You can hold a meeting with the developers and customers to assess what the impact of these changes will be—on both the schedule and the development costs. Prepare solid cost and schedule estimates to show the customer what effect their changes will have. This places the responsibility of accepting the cost of such changes solely on the customer. Changes introduced to the requirements will always have an impact on your schedule, and if you do not communicate the effects of these changes to the customer, the responsibility for a late or over-budget project will land on your head instead of the customer's.

Requirements Best Practices

Follow these requirements management best practices:

- Work one-on-one with the users to understand their processes

- Record nonfunctional requirements, such as performance and usability requirements

- Ensure that your requirements address all of the customer's business rules

- Develop a prototype or mock-up screens to illustrate the user interfaces for customer approval

- Use requirements management software, such as Rational RequisitePro

- Seek to improve a faulty process, not change it

- Place your requirements and all other artifacts under version control

- Use requirements management to prevent requirement changes and new requirements from affecting your schedule and budget

High-Level Design

Turning the needs and desires of the customer into software starts in the high-level design phase. It is here that the development team's software architects create the plans and diagrams that the team follows like a roadmap throughout the rest of the project. Your high-level designs can either make or break your project. If the architects fail to design an application that fulfills the customer's needs, your project is doomed to fail. If the designs are not realistic, the schedules and budget estimates that are derived from these plans will also be unrealistic, causing even more troubles for your project. The requirements and the high-level designs are the foundation on which the entire development effort is built, so every effort should be made in these stages to get it right the first time. This section discusses high-level design from a manager's point of view.

Note

For more details on designing an application for Visual Basic.NET, refer to Chapter 2.

Architecture

The first designs of your application that you create will lay out the overall architecture of the project. The first issue you need to address is the type of application you are creating. In .NET, the following are the application types you will be working with:

♦ Windows interfaces

♦ Web interfaces

♦ Windows Services

♦ Web Services

Your application can actually use a combination of these application types, such as an application that provides both a Web-based and a Windows interface to its users and also uses Web Services hosted on remote servers to get the latest airline flight times. After you know the type of application, you begin to develop a deployment diagram that displays the different physical locations that your application will touch. This diagram should include servers, client machines, browsers, mobile platforms (such as phones), and remote machines (such as those hosting Web Services). Any interactions your application has with outside systems, such as another company's database or a Web Service on the Internet, should also be shown in the deployment diagram.

Along with the deployment diagram, you can map out the major components that will make up your system. The component diagram shows a code-level view of your system, with no reference to the physical location of these pieces. For example, the Oceanside Resort application will have a reservations component, which may include many classes located on one or more machines. Remember that the Assembly is the major building block of

.NET, and the pieces that make up an Assembly can be dispersed among many locations yet still appear as one solid component to a client.

N-Tier Design

After you have identified your major components, identify which tier of your application each component is associated with. The basic three tiers are presentation, business logic, and data access, although each of those three tiers can be further divided into other tiers to suit your needs. If you discover that a component is performing functions that span multiple tiers, you may need to break it up into separate components. An example of this is a Windows form that contains some business logic, such as a sales tax computation. The Windows form should be focused only on the user interface, and the Windows form fits into the presentation tier nicely. The sales tax calculation is a piece of business logic that belongs on the business tier. Map your components into tiers to help you spot any components that need to be broken up into separate presentation, business, and data access logic.

Design Issues

While designing your application's overall architecture, you need to consider many important design issues. If you do not include these issues in the design of your application at this stage of the project, you will have a very hard time working these issues into your application later during the development cycles. Table 16.2 lists the major issues you should consider when creating your high-level application design.

Table 16.2   Application design issues.

Issue	Description
Security	Determine whether your application requires special security mechanisms that you need to plan for.
Maintainability	Locate the bulk of your code on a centralized server to improve your application's maintainability.
Scalability	Develop your application using multiple components to allow for future application scaling and farming out.
Extensibility	Customers often want to add functionality to an application after delivery. Design your application so that it can be upgraded or improved upon at a later date.
Durability	Design applications to avoid crashes and preserve users' data when things go wrong. Use extra exception handling around delicate functions to handle the unexpected and to protect data. Consider whether your customer has reliability criteria that your application needs to meet.
Performance	Ask yourself how you can design this application to limit processing and network delays. Consider whether your application can use free-threading to offload a processor-intensive operation to a new thread while continuing to process the main application on the original thread.
Reuse	Identify areas where your developers can reuse code. Deriving objects from superclasses through inheritance is a terrific new feature in Visual Basic.NET that promotes code reuse.

Integration

Over the years, applications have evolved from standalone systems up to the modern-day business-to-business applications that customers are now asking for. The warehouses want to talk to the shippers, and the shippers want to talk to the packing material companies. During the high-level design phase, you must identify all the systems your application needs to interface with. Maybe your application will share data in XML format with another company's system, using the Internet as the communications medium. You may also be designing an application that integrates with another application on the same platform. For example, your software might use Microsoft Excel for a part of its spreadsheet functionality.

As projects move from the COM world to the .NET world, plenty of integration issues will relate to .NET Assemblies talking to COM components and vice versa. Recall from Chapter 15 that not all of your COM components need to be migrated to .NET. You can instead continue to use your older COM components from within your .NET application, saving you both time and money. When you are considering using COM components that you have the source code for, spend a little time analyzing that component to decide whether it should remain COM-based or should be migrated to .NET.

Planning the Iterations

The final step of the high-level design phase is to take the designs you have created and break them into logical pieces that you can then map to your development iterations. Typically, your iterations will be feature-oriented, with the most critical features being scheduled first. Any features you consider extraneous or "nice to have" can be scheduled for the last few iterations. This way, if the project schedule slips and the customer wants to discuss ways to still deliver the project by the original delivery date, you can simply lop off later iterations, thereby sacrificing expendable features to meet a deadline. All too often, software projects come under schedule pressure late in the development cycle. If all the critical features for your application have already been completed, the decision to drop features from the development plan should be relatively painless.

Based on your high-level designs, identify all the major features and components for your application. Each feature or piece can be directly translated to a milestone for your team to shoot for. Take your identified milestones and prioritize them, with the most critical pieces receiving the highest priority. For example, a User object that identifies and tracks users within your system will be used by almost every feature in your system, and therefore developing the User object should be considered a top-priority milestone. Obviously, you will design your highest-priority pieces first, working your way down the milestone list in priority order.

Finally, after you have your milestones listed in order, you can break them into the iterations that the rest of your project will revolve around. An iteration can be as long or as short as you like, although iterations generally should be no shorter than a week and probably no longer than a month. For my projects, one to two weeks is my ideal iteration length. This allows for more frequent process reviews and adjustments at the end of each iteration. You do not want to tackle too many milestones in a single iteration, and you will want all the milestones you have grouped together to be related in some way.

After you have a complete list of project milestones, you can then begin thinking about the schedule you will use for the remainder of the project. Figure 16.3 shows an example of an iteration schedule. Notice that no overlap exists anywhere in this schedule. One iteration starts only after the previous one has ended. The same thing applies to the individual phases within each iteration.

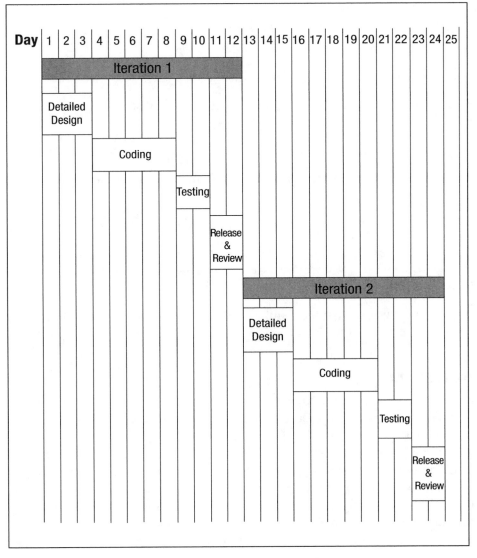

Figure 16.3
An iterative project schedule.

When you have a final milestone list and an iteration schedule, it may be time to hold another meeting with the customer so that you can share your plans with them. The requirements-gathering and high-level design phases are really precursors to the true development effort, which is accomplished in the iterations you have planned. Prior to this point in the project, it will be really hard to give the customer an honest estimate on the expected delivery date for their application. Until you have a firm grip on the requirements, and your software architects have mapped out the work that needs to be accomplished, any delivery estimates you provide will be wild guesses that may prove to be impossible to live up to. Avoid promising the customer delivery dates until your team has come up with an iteration schedule on which to base your estimate.

High-Level Design Phase Best Practices

Follow these best practices during the high-level design phase:

♦ Create deployment and component diagrams to get a high-level view of your system

♦ Organize your components by tiers to identify components that are expected to do too much

♦ Consider important issues, such as security, scalability, maintainability, performance, durability, and code reuse, during the early stages of your application's design

♦ Identify outside organizations and commercially available off-the-shelf (COTS) software your application will need to integrate with

♦ Group related milestones together, and schedule the most critical pieces first

♦ Schedule unnecessary or advanced features that the customer can live without for the final iterations so that if you need to drop some features to meet a scheduled delivery date, your iteration plan will support this

♦ Do not promise a delivery date until your team has produced an iteration schedule based on the requirements and identified milestones

Detailed Design

Each iteration has its own design phase in which the plans created in the high-level design phase are elaborated on and fleshed out into actual object models that can then be used to generate code. Teams should use the detailed design phase as an opportunity to sit down as a group and discuss the milestones ahead. The entire team should be a part of the detailed design phase so that everyone develops the same understanding of the work that will be accomplished. Because your team will be developing use cases or scenarios during this stage that describe the customer's process, you should also include the requirements-gathering team in the detailed design phase. At the end of the detailed design phase, you should have a solid understanding of all the milestones your team will be shooting for in this iteration, and all the plans should be in place to allow your developers to start the long and hard coding process.

Use Cases and Scenarios

Developers new to object-oriented programming invariably ask the question "How do I identify the objects that I will create in my system?" You learned in Chapter 2 that you can discover the objects in your system, along with their properties and methods, by analyzing the customer's processes via either use cases or scenarios. Whether you use scenarios or use cases to analyze a process is a matter of preference. Scenarios generally are text-based descriptions of a process, whereas use cases are graphically oriented. The use case explains step by step how the process is completed. Use cases are not technical in nature and are often created by the requirements team, because of its intimate knowledge of the customer's processes. It is a good idea to share your use cases with the customer to ensure you understand their process before the coding begins.

Business analysts can also create sequence diagrams and interaction diagrams to further help developers understand the customer's process. A *sequence* diagram illustrates the order in which the steps occur in a process from left to right in a timeline layout. An *interaction* diagram lists the customer's business interactions, and can describe an interaction between two departments in the company, or an interaction between the company and an outside business. A great deal of time and effort can go into your business analysis diagrams, but you should concentrate only on those processes that relate to the milestones the team is committed to develop for the current iteration.

Object Modeling

Drawing from the use cases, scenarios, interaction diagrams, and sequence diagrams, the team's developers can now identify the objects within the system that they need to create. If you have a decent set of diagrams outlining the customer's process, identifying the objects will be a snap. Typically, the nouns used to describe the process will translate directly into objects. If a step in the process you are examining says "The customer presents their reservation number," you can identify the noun "customer" in this sentence, which becomes an object in your system. The reservation number is something that belongs to that customer, so you might design this to be a property of the Customer object. If the check-in process also requires that the customer provide their name, address, and phone number, you could associate this information with your Customer object by making these items properties of the Customer object as well.

Modeling the objects in your system is critical for large-scale development projects. If another developer does not know that you have developed a Customer object, they might be inclined to create their own object, duplicating your effort and wasting valuable time. Widely used mathematical functions can be assigned to an object within your system to allow all the developers to reuse that code. Without a common object model, developers will have a hard time discovering other developer's code that they can reuse. Most popular software modeling utilities will generate an empty skeleton of your Visual Basic routines for you and will even include debugging code for you if you wish. Generating code from your models helps to enforce neat programming habits.

Usability

As your development team creeps closer to the coding stage, in which the application will actually come to life, your team should spend a great deal of time in the detailed design phase thinking about the interface. To design a usable interface, you need to think like a user and not like a developer. What menu items will the users expect to see, and where will they expect the buttons to be located? What labels and captions will the users understand? Use the scenarios and use cases you have developed to figure out the steps the user will take to complete a task. If step one is to enter the customer's name in a textbox, then this textbox should be in the top-left section of the screen, which is where a user will visually start to process a screen. I often like to label these steps on my interface to let users know that a particular textbox is for step one, and a particular button is for step two, and so on.

Developers tend to be more at ease around computers and are sometimes offended by software that treats them like dummies. More than likely, your users are not as computer-literate as you are, and thus your interfaces need to hold their hands and walk them through your processes step by step. A perfectly designed application should be intuitively easy to use, even to a brand-new user. If the user understands the task at hand, and your application is properly designed to perform that task, then user manuals and online help should be unnecessary. Of course, you should still provide help to the user in any way possible, including context-sensitive help and online tutorials that explain how to use the application. Because your users will grow more and more comfortable with the application, you should provide them with shortcuts and hot keys to enable them to perform their tasks as quickly as possible. A great application should cater to both the novice and the expert equally well.

Detailed Design Phase Best Practices
Follow these best practices during the detailed design phase:

♦ Analyze the processes associated with the milestones you are developing by creating use cases, scenarios, sequence diagrams, and interaction diagrams

♦ Identify the objects in your application by using the business analysis diagrams, and then model your objects before trying to code them

♦ Create one centrally maintained object model and make it available to all of your developers so that they can understand the pieces of code that other developers are working on

♦ Design your interfaces for maximum usability and understandability

♦ Provide help to your users whenever and wherever possible

Coding

The bulk of this book addresses how the developer can use Visual Basic.NET to create their applications. All of this information on how to create certain projects and how to use the new language features in Visual Basic.NET will be put to work at the developer's desk during the coding phase. No matter how much or how little planning you do for your project, you eventually need to sit down in front of your monitor and turn those plans into source code. Of course, the better your plans are, the easier your job will be to create the code for the individual pieces. This section discusses what the best way is to manage the coding phase, and what a project manager can do while the developers are hard at work coding their creations.

Coding Phase Management Approaches

The management approach has two extremes that can be used during the coding phase of your project. The first approach is simply to hand out the coding assignments and then sit back and wait for the programmers to finish. This approach is purely results-oriented, meaning that you do not really care how the developers create their individual pieces, only that the pieces work after they are completed. If your developers are experienced and self-motivated, then this approach may work for your project. One of the drawbacks of a hands-off results-oriented approach is that it provides a poor learning environment for junior developers. Some junior developers may seek out help if they encounter problems, but all too often, they will instead spend days or even weeks spinning their wheels and getting nowhere on their own. Senior developers can also benefit from other developers' insights and experiences, which may not be shared if the developers are encouraged to operate in solitary mode.

The opposite of the hands-off approach is often referred to as *micromanagement*. This is when managers hover over the developers and constantly ask for progress reports and statistics, such as the number of lines of code completed. The one good point of the micromanagement approach is that it enforces good programming habits. If you know that someone is going to be peeking over your shoulder at your code, then odds are you will spend a little extra time making it neat and readable. But aside from this one benefit, developers do not like to be pushed and monitored, and being bothered with constant inquiries and mandatory progress meetings is a sure-fire way to irritate and alienate your team. A funny thing happens when you watch developers closely to monitor their progress. When you stop watching them, they stop progressing. Why put forth a good effort if no one is around to see it? In the long run, the result of micromanagement are reduced team productivity and an increase in online want-ad searches.

So, what is the happy medium that will enforce both a quality-oriented approach to coding and encourage developers to share ideas and work together like a well-oiled machine? Most developers work best when left alone, but when left alone, those same developers often ignore development best practices, resulting in sloppy and inefficient code. The way to have the best of both worlds is to firmly let the team members know what you expect out of them and their code. A set of coding guidelines will help spell out your expectations for everyone to see. The next management step is to encourage the team to work together and to check each other's work to ensure that your expectations are being met. You can do this by requiring peer reviews of completed code (covered next). You can task your programming leads to enforce the reviews and encourage team interaction, which will help the team manage itself, and allow you to monitor its progress using a hands-off approach.

Peer Reviews

Using peer reviews can be a touchy subject, because some developers will be sensitive to the opinions of others. The purpose of a peer review is to check that each programmer's code meets the manager's expectations, as well as to encourage the sharing of ideas and knowledge among team members. Your junior developers will learn a lot from having a senior developer review their code and make suggestions, greatly accelerating their learning and professional growth in the process. Reviews should always be positive and helpful, not competitive and hurtful. If a developer thinks that someone is picking on them, then the peer review will only succeed in tearing the team apart.

Like the testing phase, many development teams intend to use peer reviews but quickly abandon their plans in the interest of speeding up their process. If the project's management does not continually push peer reviews, the team will see this step as a unnecessary bother that it can ignore. Make each component's peer review a milestone that needs to be achieved before the team can move on to the next phase. Do not use grades or scoring during the peer review. If a peer review reveals that a developer's work could use a lot of improvement, simply hearing this from the reviewer should be enough to positively motivate that developer. Having the stigma of a grade or score permanently recorded will only serve to embarrass that worker and alienate them from the rest of the team. Reviews should encourage learning among team members, while encouraging them to develop quality software.

Round-Trip Engineering

Often, the components you deliver at the end of the coding phase will not exactly match the component model you developed before the coding phase. This could be because your understanding of a function changed during coding, or you figured out that another interface was needed for your object. It is vitally important to the rest of your team that the component model for your piece be as up-to-date as possible. When one developer wants to work with another developer's piece, they will do so by using that piece's interfaces, which is why it is so important to constantly update your models that map out those interfaces. The larger your development team, the larger the role your model will play in sharing your component structure and interfaces with other team members. As you already know, component models promote an understanding of the work someone else is doing. A good model will also encourage code reuse. If you need a function to calculate sales tax, and you see from the model that Steve's object has a CalcSalesTax interface, you can save time and effort by simply referencing Steve's code from your component and using his function to do the work.

If you are using a modeling software package, you should be able to have Visual Studio.NET communicate directly with the modeling software and push your changes back into the model with little effort. Updating or creating a model based on source code is known as reverse engineering, because your model is updated from the code, instead of your code originating from a model. If you are not using a modeling package that integrates with Visual Studio.NET, you have to spend a little extra time manually updating your models. The process of modeling a component, coding that component, and then updating the model from the code you have written is known as *round-trip engineering*, because it is a continual cycle of modeling, coding, and more modeling. Figure 16.4 illustrates the round-trip engineering cycle.

Coding Phase Best Practices
Following these best practices during the coding phase of a project:

♦ Require individual developers to review all the Visual Basic best practices discussed in Chapter 5

♦ Allow developers to work alone and unhindered, but encourage the team to consult one another and share ideas to promote learning

♦ Develop a set of coding guidelines and present them to the team as your expectations

♦ Require the team to conduct peer reviews amongst themselves to verify that team members are following the coding guidelines

♦ Develop a chart of the components being developed and ask developers to check off completed pieces after a peer review has been accomplished

♦ Use round-trip engineering to continually update your models

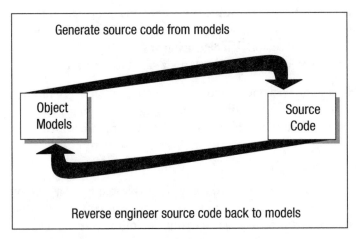

Figure 16.4
Round-trip engineering.

Testing

Software can be tested on many different levels using many different techniques. Yet, despite the numerous methods you can use to test your software, the testing phase is sometimes the most overlooked and ignored phase in the entire development cycle. This is truly bad news, because failure to test your software will always lead to software failure. The customers will quickly lose faith in your application if it is bug-ridden and fails to fulfill their needs. Your developers will feel the sting of the bugs as well when they are flooded with trouble reports and forced to revisit their code time and again. No developer likes to receive a bug report, because it not only is a blot on his or her reputation, but also requires reviewing a component he or she may have hoped never to see again.

Why is the testing phase so underemphasized? The majority of the time, the project schedule dictates how much effort will be put into testing. If the project is well ahead of schedule, the team has plenty of time to test its work and do it right. But how many times have you seen a project ahead of schedule? When the project is behind schedule, where can managers cut corners to make up that time? The only phase you can cut back on and still have a product to deliver is the testing phase. While this management decision will get your product out the door on schedule, in the long run, your application will cause even more work for your developers and most likely damage your company's reputation. This section discusses what a proper testing phase entails and how you can ensure your application is of the highest quality possible.

Types of Testing

The following are the four main types of testing and a description of each type: unit, integration, system, and acceptance.

♦ *Unit testing*—Performed by developers at their desks to check the operation of their individual code components line by line to ensure that they work properly on their own. Unit testing occurs during the coding phase, and is the responsibility of the developer. Chapter 9 discusses the Visual Studio.NET debugging and testing tools the developer can use to step through their code and spot-check their variables and equations.

♦ *Integration testing*—Checks how well one component integrates into the system, and verifies that it works properly with the other components. Integration testing is the first type of testing that you perform in the testing phase. Integration testing can also occur in the coding phase if the developer needs to test the interaction between his or her component and somebody else's.

♦ *System testing*—Using test cases, the compiled application is tested for bugs and proper operation. This is the main focus of the testing phase, and is used to verify that the application works and does what it was designed to do. Compiling your application and running it as a complete system to verify that it starts without error is often referred to as "smoke testing." If you have ever replaced a part on your car's engine, then you probably understand this term. You turn the key and pray that you don't see smoke. If everything appears to be running properly, it's time to perform some tests. Organized testing groups use test cases to provide a script for their testing that ensures every operation is checked. Test cases are developed before the testing phase begins, and are based on your use cases, scenarios, and requirements. Every requirement and function slated for the current iteration needs to be tested and verified before the iteration can be declared a success.

♦ *Acceptance testing*—Performed by your customers at the time of delivery to verify that the delivered product meets their needs. Normally, your customers will have their own tests and criteria that they will use to determine whether your application meets their requirements.

Testing Plans

One mistake that many development teams make is to assume that software testing is random and unorganized. The truth is, if you want your application to be a success, you must plan your testing phase as thoroughly as you plan the rest of the project. You should create an artifact known as a testing plan that describes in plain English how you plan to test your software and what criteria you will use during your testing. Create this plan early in the project, preferably before the first iteration begins. You can even use testing plans from other projects and modify them to adapt to your software's unique architecture. After your plan is finished, stick with it. Do not allow management to persuade you to deviate from your plan. If you get both the customers and your management to sign off on a robust testing plan, they will be reluctant to ask you to rush your testing phase later in the project.

To prevent random and unreliable testing, you need to develop scripts for your testers to follow. These scripts are known as *test cases*. A single test case will verify that one single requirement has been met using the steps defined in that requirement's use case or scenario. Take a look at the following example requirement:

♦ Requirement 2.1: the reservation system will assign each new customer a unique customer ID.

You could develop a use case that describes the steps required to complete this action during your detailed design phase. Using that use case, you could then easily create a testing script that can later be used to verify that the completed function works as designed. Here is an example of a test case that verifies requirement 2.1:

1. Log in to the reservation system.

2. Click the Create New Customer button.

3. Enter the customer's information in the form.

4. Click the Save button.

5. Verify that the CustomerID box now displays an alphanumeric ID.

If you have not used test cases before, this example test case may seem overly detailed. A good reason exists for this level of detail. If you were a scientist performing an experiment, you would want to write down every step and every detail of your experiment so that you could duplicate your work at a later date. With testing, if you simply give the tester a goal without defining the steps, you will have no control over how the tester achieves that goal and you will be unable to duplicate the exact test during regression testing. Using test cases is a very ridged and structured form of testing that is used to verify functionality and that checks whether the requirements have been met. The results of a test case should be expressed with a pass or fail grade.

Free-Form Testing

Your test cases will verify that your application has met the requirements, but how do you shake out those annoying bugs buried deep within your code? Following the same test case script over and over is like following the same path through the woods over and over. You miss a large portion of those woods, and the opportunity to squish a lot of bugs. Sometimes you just have to run free to find the really juicy bugs that are out there. Free-form testing does not follow a script. This form of testing is actually more enjoyable than scripted testing because the goal is to break things. Encourage your testers to be creatively destructive with their free-form tests. The more defects they discover now, the less your customers will be complaining about later.

The best way to break something is to do everything that is not in the test cases. If the test case says to type your name in a textbox, then you could try to cut and paste three pages of text into that textbox to see what happens. If the test case says click button A, then you could try clicking button Z to see what happens. Here are some destructive tips to help shake out your code during free-form testing:

◆ Entering bad data is the best test. Put numbers where text is requested and text where numbers are requested.

◆ Do things out of order. If the proper order is button A, B, C, then try this sequence backward.

◆ Give a nondeveloper a task to perform using your system without providing an explanation and see whether your interface is understandable. A poorly designed interface is a defect.

◆ Test the application with other applications running, or start multiple copies of your application and check for conflicts.

◆ Find out how the application reacts when remote resources such as databases and Web Services are unavailable.

The free-form style of testing has one catch: You must document the steps you take. Finding a bug during free-form testing is terrific, and a real victory for the tester, but if you cannot tell the developer the steps you took to cause this bug, then your bug may not be duplicated and could go unfixed. Often bugs are a result of a specific piece of data being entered, and if you do not know what piece of data caused the error, you cannot duplicate the error.

Regression Testing

When you are using an iterative development process, it is very important that you test not only the work completed in the current development cycle, but all work completed before that cycle as well. Often, components added to an application in a later cycle can affect or even break a component finished in an earlier cycle. Your test cases will provide you with the ability to exactly duplicate your tests cycle after cycle. For example, any test cases developed for the first iteration cycle should be retested at the end of every iteration cycle until the final product is delivered. Testing items that you have already tested is known as *regression testing*, because you repeat tests that you have already run. The testing phase for each iteration will be longer and more involved than the last cycle's testing phase.

To simplify regression testing, you can use a third-party software testing suite to record for later playback your testers walking through the test cases. These test recordings allow for automated testing to occur overnight while your team is at home in bed. Software development is a very incremental process, and developers often assume that if a button worked last week, then surely it will work this week. But as each iteration adds more and more components and functionality to your system, the chances of a problem occurring in an older component increase dramatically.

Defect Tracking

Development teams should create a formal means of logging and tracking any and all defects discovered in their application. While some developers may not appreciate their bugs being permanently listed for the world to see, a defect tracking system can be both a great management tool and a handy reference tool for troubleshooting. Project managers can use a defect tracking system to get a feel for how stable and bug-free an application is and report on these statistics to the customer. Developers facing new bugs can use the defect tracking system to find out whether a similar bug has been reported and find out what the last developer did to resolve it. The defect list can also act as a "to do" list for the team by allowing developers to sort the list by the defect's status, to remind them of open trouble reports.

At a minimum, your defect tracking system should track the following:

- The date the bug was reported
- Who reported the bug

♦ A lengthy description of the bug and the steps to reproduce it

♦ The current status of the defect (resolved or open)

♦ The defect's priority level

♦ A lengthy description of how the defect was resolved so that future occurrences can be quickly fixed as well

You could create your defect tracking system using a simple spreadsheet tool, or you could invest in a third-party defect tracking system such as Rational ClearQuest. After your application is fielded, any defects or suggestions submitted by the users can also be added to your tracking system. By prioritizing these defects, you can easily decide which defect reports require immediate attention, and which can be considered "acceptable" defects or unnecessary feature requests. You could assign simple priority levels, such as high, medium, or low, or you could categorize your defects more descriptively by using terms such as "causes a fatal crash" or "confusing interface issue." Whatever terms and data elements you decide to use, be sure to record every single defect found in your application, whether it is discovered by a tester or reported by a user in the field. You will appreciate this system the first time you think to yourself "Haven't I seen this problem before?"

Testing Phase Best Practices
Follow these best practices during the testing phase:

♦ Never shorten or skip your testing phase because of scheduling constraints

♦ Develop test cases based on your use cases, scenarios, and requirements

♦ Use free-form testing to shake out bugs not detected by the test cases

♦ Use regression testing by re-running all of your test cases from all previous iterations

♦ Develop a system to track all uncovered defects from all sources

♦ Prioritize your defects so that you can attack and resolve the most critical defects first

Release and Review

When all the test cases for the current iteration and all prior iterations have been marked as passes, then you can begin your iteration wrap-up. At this point in the process, all of your completed work should be in a releasable state, meaning that your application is ready to be seen by the customer. This does not mean that your iteration releases must be given to the customer, but you could safely provide them if you had to. The main purpose of this phase is to review your team's progress and make any changes necessary to make your future iterations go as smoothly as possible.

Release vs. Deployment

A releasable application is one that meets all the requirements defined for that iteration. Until the end of the last iteration, your application will not be complete, but the features you created up to this point should be functional. If your source code is under version control, this is a good point in the process to increment your build number and archive your completed work. During the review phase, it might be useful to invite the customer in to the development shop to sit down in front of your application and take it for a test drive. Testing applications in the development environment removes the difficulties associated with deploying your application. A *deployment* is when you package your application and deliver it to the customer's site. If you only wish to solicit some feedback from your customers, you should invite them to your development shop. Deploying a solution requires additional testing and effort to be sure the newly installed version works as well as your development version does.

Deployment Testing

When you are finally ready to deploy your application to the customer's machines, you should first test your deployment plans back at the office. It's interesting how an application can work well on a development machine that has every developer tool installed, all the service packs and patches, and the most up-to-date version of every driver available, yet not work the same after you move it to a customer's machine.

To perform a proper deployment test, the first thing you need is an exact duplicate of the customer's system configuration. You should start your machine's build from scratch using the exact same operating system and all the patches and service packs the customer uses. You should also install any utilities the customer uses, such as word processors and spreadsheets. After you have your test machine built, back up your installation using a utility such as Norton Ghost so that you can quickly restore your testing machine to a clean install without having to start from scratch. After you have your test machine built, you can create your deployment package in Visual Studio.NET and copy it to your selected installation media type.

As you install your deployment package on the test machine, document each installation step so that you can create an installation guide that the customer can use onsite to perform the installation without your assistance. Any problems encountered during installation should be noted as defects and immediately checked out. If your application installs successfully, run all of your test cases on the test machine to verify that the application still runs properly. Often, your deployment testing will involve many different machines, such as user desktop systems, application servers, and Web servers. Always be sure to start with a clean installation of the operating system and standard applications so that you can detect any application conflicts or missing component problems.

Deliverables

Anything you are required by contract to give to your customer is known as a *deliverable*. If you are required to deliver anything at the end of the current iteration, or if you have just completed the last iteration of your project, then you will need some time at this point to work on your deliverables. Installation guides and user guides are common types of deliverables the customers will expect, along with the installation media containing their completed application. Writing install guides and user manuals requires a different set of skills than developing code, and you may wish to assign your requirements team with the task of writing these products. Developers tend to write like developers, and the customers may not understand all the technical jargon they use, and things that are obvious to a programmer may not be obvious to a computer novice. For the user's guide, your writers can reuse the test cases and use cases to clearly describe how users can perform functions within the application.

Process Review

The real beauty of a well-run iterative process is that it allows you to learn from your mistakes and easily make changes to your process as you go along. If a part of your process is not working correctly or does not feel natural to the team, then replace it or drop it all together. The very first iterative development process that you attempt very likely will go through some changes before you find a process that suits your team's needs. A process that works for a team of 100 developers probably will not be suitable for a team of 3 developers, and vice versa. Don't be afraid to change things around, but be sure to include the entire team in the decision process and solicit input as to what worked and what didn't.

Note

If your development process is not perfect, fix it.

Now is the time to update your project's schedule. A schedule is really just a guess—sometimes a wild guess and sometimes an educated guess. If you create a schedule at the very beginning of the project and hope to meet your final delivery date as planned, you are setting yourself (and the customer) up for a huge disappointment. Software development is all about tackling the unknown and dealing with unexpected problems. One iteration will not take the exact same number of days that the next iteration will take. But you can learn from one iteration and apply those lessons to your schedule to make your delivery date more realistic as the project progresses. For example, if you originally guessed that an iteration would take two weeks, but the first iteration takes three weeks, you should adjust your schedule based on three-week iterations. Letting the customer see the schedule at the end of each iteration will allow them to gradually accept a slipping delivery date. This is a much better approach than announcing on the day the project is due that your team needs three more months to complete the work. That is how projects get canceled.

Metrics

A *metric* is piece of data that enables you to measure progress. During the review phase of each iteration, you should collect all the metrics you can on the team's progress. You can use this information to provide the customer solid proof that their project is in fact progressing, and you can also use this data to find out which parts of your process are working and which are not. You can track metrics such as the total lines of code in the application, the number of classes created, the hours spent on each phase (design, coding, and testing), and the number of defects reported. This data can be compared with metrics from past iterations, and even for past projects, to enable the project manager to get a feel for how well or how poorly the team is progressing.

If you collect metrics separately for each developer, you can get a better feel for which of your workers are your fastest producers and which may need mentoring and support from your senior developers. Remember that not everybody can write 1,000 lines of code an hour, and that a faster developer may be creating twice as many bugs as a slower developer. Metrics should be used for planning and reporting purposes only, and not as a means of singling out developers. If you can identify a developer on the team that is both fast and has a low occurrence of defects, then you will know who your go-to person is when the project needs a new feature added the Friday before delivery. You can also use this data to pair up developers to provide your junior developers with an optimum learning environment.

Release and Review Best Practices

Follow these best practices during release and review:

♦ Wrap up an iteration cycle only if the completed work passes all the selected test cases

♦ Invite the customer in to let them see your work so they can provide you feedback on it

♦ If you must deploy your application to the customer's site, first test your deployment package using clean testing machines

♦ Back up your clean testing machine's configuration so that you can quickly wipe out and restore your machine to a clean state for additional tests

♦ Use nontechnical personnel to develop your user guides and other paper-copy deliverables

♦ Review your process at the end of every iteration and make adjustments as necessary

♦ Update your schedule at the end of each iteration using the lessons you have learned during the course of the project

♦ Communicate any delays and schedule slippages to the customer to help them adjust to the idea of a delayed delivery date

♦ Collect metrics on your development project and compare them to prior iterations to measure efficiency and progress

Summary

Throughout this book, you have read about all the changes made to the Visual Basic programming language, and the terrific selection of new features and project types creatable in Visual Studio.NET. From Windows forms to Web Forms, and from inheritance to free-threading, Visual Studio.NET offers Visual Basic developers more freedom and power than they have ever had. If you are a coder ready to write your first .NET application, you now have the background you need to create the best software possible. Project managers and team leaders should understand all the .NET concepts and how they affect the software your teams will be developing for the next few years. You should also have a clear understanding of iterative development principles as applied to .NET development projects. Using the best practices defined within this book will help you develop software faster and with less defects. The .NET world awaits you. Go forth and conquer!

Appendix A
Visual Basic.NET Best Practices

Readability Best Practices

- Use the .NET IDE's code indenting feature, and indent more if it helps.

- Use the carriage return generously to help separate procedures and ideas.

- Do not use the underscore (_) to break up long lines of code.

- Use the Namespace to group like Classes logically in your source code.

- Place frequently used Classes at the top of their Namespace.

- Place frequently used procedures at the top of their Classes.

- Give data types descriptive names using Hungarian notation.

- Give your procedures descriptive names that tell what they do, and to what.

- Create comment outlines of your procedures before you begin coding them.

- Create comments that tell what the purpose of a section is, and do not explain the code itself.

- Add a header to each module with your name, date, project name, and module summary.

- Use comments starting with keywords that show up on the Task List to point out problem areas or special sections of code.

Variable Best Practices

♦ Choose the best data type for your variable—avoid the **String** if you can use a **Boolean, Date,** or **Char** instead.

♦ Give your data types the proper scope (**Public, Private, Friend, Protected**).

♦ Declare all variables at the very beginning of the procedure.

♦ Use the **Short** data type for counters and **For** loops using numbers under 32,767.

♦ If you know the starting value of a variable at declaration time, initialize it.

♦ Centralize your constants in one section of your project, giving them **Public** scope.

♦ Never use numbers in your **If** statements; replace these with constants.

♦ Use a **Structure** to group variables, constants, and simple functions under one title.

♦ Use a **Structure** as a single parameter for your procedure to serialize a large amount of data.

♦ Do not use a **Structure** to present data outside your Class.

Planning Procedures Best Practices

♦ Separate your procedures in to smaller reusable parts.

♦ Centralize your database connections in one **Data** Class to be used by all.

♦ Use overloading to make reusable components more flexible.

♦ Use constructors to initialize your Class properties, and allow the user to pass in a parameter so you can build your object intelligently.

♦ Validate all parameters passed in to your procedures.

♦ Validate the output of all procedures before using them.

♦ Test all procedures to verify whether they can handle bad parameters.

♦ Design you methods to share functions like **Delete** and **Add** through overloading.

♦ Plan your procedures to recover from expected exceptions.

♦ Raise meaningful exception messages to callers.

♦ Rollback transactions, save files, and crash gracefully to avoid data loss.

♦ Write exception information to a log file for later troubleshooting.

Logic Functions Best Practices

♦ Use a **Case** statement in place of an **If-Then-Else** pattern if you can.

♦ Place the most common matching values at the beginning of your **case** statement.

♦ Start your Array loops at zero, and do not exceed the top position (subtract 1 from the value you **Dim**med the Array to).

♦ Do not perform calculations in your **If** statements, precompute the values.

♦ Do not call functions from inside your **If** statements—call them beforehand.

♦ Use the new **BITAND**, **BITOR**, and **BITXOR** bit-wise operators for comparing numbers position by position.

Threading Best Practices

♦ Give your Classes callback events if they will be launched on to their own threads.

♦ Create event handlers in Classes that create and spawn new threads.

♦ Use thread events to communicate the results of a threads processing or to relay the threads status back to the caller.

♦ Use the thread controlling commands carefully.

♦ Never **Sleep** or **Suspend** a thread that manipulates a database, form, or control.

Delegates Best Practices

♦ Use delegates for Events and multicasting.

♦ Use the **Delegate** to point a delegated object to any subroutine that has a matching input parameter.

♦ Group **Delegate** objects together using the **System.Delegate.Combine** method.

♦ Use more than one **Combine** statement to add more Delegates to a grouping.

♦ Use the **AddressOf** statement to change the function pointer of an object dynamically in your code.

Inheritance Best Practices

♦ Examine your objects for parent-child relationships to identify possible superclasses from which to derive your subclasses.

♦ Look for multiple levels of parent-child relationships to build an Inheritance Tree.

♦ Write superclasses in other languages such as Visual C++ and C# and derive new Classes from these in Visual Basic, if you wish.

♦ Override attributes in the derived Class when the inherited functionality does not fit your needs. (If you are overriding most of the inherited functions, then this probably is not a good candidate for inheritance.)

♦ When modeling, decide which superclass functions *can* be overridden and which *must* be overridden, and declare these as **Overridable** or **Must Override**.

Appendix B
.NET Development Best Practices

Requirements Best Practices

- Work one-on-one with the users to understand their processes.

- Record nonfunctional requirements, such as performance and usability requirements.

- Ensure that your requirements address all the customer's business rules.

- Develop a prototype or mock-up screens to illustrate the user interfaces for customer approval.

- Use requirements management software such as Rational's Requisite Pro.

- Seek to improve a faulty process, not change it.

- Place your requirements and all other artifacts under version control.

- Use requirements management to prevent requirement changes and new requirements from affecting your schedule and budget.

High-Level Design Phase Best Practices

- Create deployment and component diagrams to get a high-level view of your system.

- Organize your components by tiers to identify components that are trying to do too much.

- Consider important issues such as security, scalability, maintainability, performance, durability, and code reuse during the early stages of your applications design.

- Identify outside organizations and commercially available off-the-shelf (COTS) software your application will need to integrate with.

- Group related milestones together, and schedule the most critical pieces first.

- Schedule unnecessary or advanced features that the customer can live without for the final iterations so that if you need to drop some features to meet a scheduled delivery date, your iteration plan will support this.

- Do not promise a delivery date until your team has produced an iteration schedule based on the requirements and identified milestones.

Detailed Design Phase Best Practices

- Analyze the processes associated with the milestones you are developing by creating use cases, scenarios, sequence diagrams, and interaction diagrams.

- Identify the objects in your application using the business analysis diagrams and then model your objects before trying to code them.

- Create one centrally maintained object model and make it available to all of your developers so they can understand the pieces of code that other developers are working on.

- Design your interfaces for maximum usability and understandability.

- Provide help to your users whenever and wherever possible.

Coding Phase Best Practices

- Individual developers should review all the Visual Basic Best Practices listed in Appendix A and discussed in Chapter 5.

- Allow developers to work alone and unhindered, but encourage the team to consult one another and share ideas to promote learning.

- Develop a set of coding guidelines and present them to the team as your expectations.

- Require the team to conduct peer reviews amongst themselves to verify that team members are following the coding guidelines.

- Develop a chart of the components being developed and ask developers to check off completed pieces after a peer review has been accomplished.

- Use round-trip engineering to continually update your models.

Testing Phase Best Practices

- Never shorten or skip your testing phase due to scheduling constraints.

- Develop test cases based on your use cases, scenarios, and requirements.

- Use free-form testing to shake out bugs not detected by the test cases.

- Use regression testing by re-running all your test cases from all the previous iterations.

- Develop a system to track all uncovered defects from all sources.

- Prioritize your defects so you can attack and resolve the most critical defects first.

Release and Review Best Practices

- Wrap up an iteration cycle only if the completed work passes all of the selected test cases.

- Invite the customer in to let them see your work so they can provide you feedback on it.

- If you must deploy your application to the customer's site, first test out your deployment package using clean testing machines.

- Back up your clean testing machine's configuration so you can quickly wipe out and restore your machine to a clean state for additional tests.

- Use nontechnical personnel to develop your user guides and other paper-copy deliverables.

- Review your process at the end of every iteration and make adjustments as necessary.

- Update your schedule at the end of each iteration using the lessons you have learned during the course of the project.

- Communicate any delays and schedule slippages to the customer to help them adjust to the idea of a delayed delivery date.

- Collect metrics on your development project and compare to prior iterations to measure efficiency and progress.

VB6 Migration Checklist

✓ **Design Review**

_____ Could this project benefit from inheritance?

_____ Are there any processor-intensive functions that could be free threaded?

_____ Does this application properly separate presentation, business, and data logic?

_____ Is the code properly object-oriented?

_____ Can you move object loading and initializing code over to the **New** constructor event?

_____ Where is the object cleanup being performed in this project, and how can I update this code to take advantage of the Garbage Collector?

_____ Which User Defined Types (UDTs) will need to become Structures?

_____ Can I use Shared Members to allow multiple instances of the same block of code access to globally shared values?

_____ After migration, should I continue to use the unstructured exception-handling routines from Visual Basic 6, or update some or all of this code to the **Try**, **Catch**, and **Finally** exception-handling model?

_____ Does the project make use of outdated commands such as the **GoTo** or **GoSub** command, which will require a great deal of time and effort to bring up to date?

_____ Does my project use ADO to work with the database using server-side cursors? If not, should I migrate all my database calls to ADO.NET, or use an older version of ADO to connect to the data?

✓ Code Upgrades

_____ Upgrade projects created in versions prior to Visual Basic 6 to VB6.

_____ Add **ByVal** or **ByRef** to all parameters being passed into your functions.

_____ Locate code that references default properties and methods and explicitly name the property or method your code is referencing.

_____ Separate each variable declaration to its own separate line of code and define a data type for every variable.

_____ Remove fixed-length **Strings** from your code.

_____ Remove any usage of the **LSet** command.

_____ Change any references to the numerical value of a constant to the constant's actual name.

_____ Remove all **GoTo** or **GoSub** commands, except in the **On Error** lines.

_____ Change all arrays to be zero-based.

_____ Remove arrays from your User Defined Types (UDTs).

_____ Remove the OLE Container control from your forms.

_____ Remove form drawing commands such as **PSet**, **CLS**, and **Circle** from your forms.

_____ Disable the Timer control using the Enabled property, not by setting its Interval property to zero.

_____ Upgrade all form controls to Visual Basic 6.

_____ Change all Boolean value checks to check for the constants True and False.

✓ Post-Migration Review

_____ Review the Upgrade Report located in the Solution Explorer.

_____ Resolve any upgrade issues noted in the Upgrade Report and in the Task List window.

_____ Add initializer values to your variable declarations.

_____ Remove all object cleanup code that sets objects equal to Nothing.

_____ Relocate all constructor code to the class's **New** event.

_____ Relocate all cleanup code to the class's **Finalize** event.

_____ Give all Optional parameters being passed into your functions default values.

_____ Check to see if any lines of code that migrated from the **IsMissing** to **IsNothing** are still needed.

_____ Look for uses of shared members in your Solution.

_____ Implement structured exception handling in functions that access outside resources.

_____ Update your object models with your newly migrated code.

_____ Perform rigorous testing on your migrated Solution.

Appendix D
.NET Deployment Checklist

✓ Creating the Deployment Package

_____ Identify the type of deployment you will be creating (standalone, client/server, distributed deployment, farmed-out servers).

_____ Identify the media you plan to use to deploy your Solution (diskette, CD-ROM, network, Internet).

_____ Add one or more deployment Projects to your Solution depending on the number of locations you are planning to deploy the individual pieces to.

_____ Configure each deployment Project (refer to Chapter 14 for configuration details).

_____ Create a "release" build of all of your Assemblies to verify the build process completes successfully.

_____ Deploy your Solution by right-clicking on the Solution's name in the Solution Explorer window and selecting the Deploy menu item.

_____ Locate the MSI file created for your Solution and move the file to your selected distribution media.

_____ Test your package's installation before delivering the media to the customer.

✓ Testing the Deployment Package

_____ Identify the target deployment machine (operating system, service packs, patches, typical software load-outs).

_____ Build a deployment testing machine from scratch to mirror the customer's target machine.

_____ Back up your deployment testing machine so you can quickly restore it to a clean state.

_____ Using the media created in the deployment phase, install your application on the test machine.

_____ Perform system testing on the newly installed application to ensure everything is working properly.

Object Models

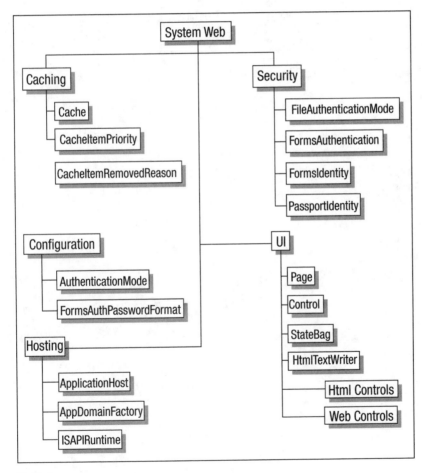

Fig E.1
ASP.NET object model.

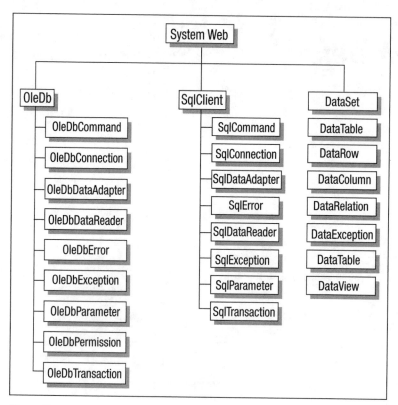

Figure E2
The ADO.NET object model.

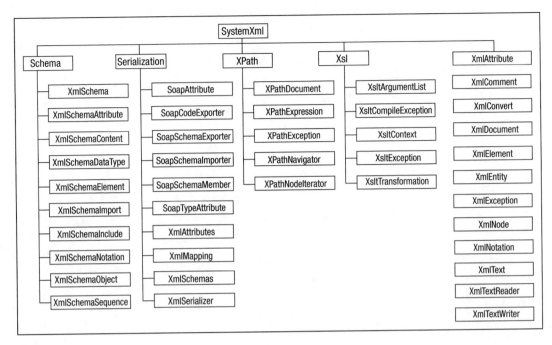

Figure E3
XML and SOAP object model.

Index

X